EVERYDAY ARGUMENTS

EVERYDAY ARGUMENTS

A Guide to Writing and Reading

Effective Arguments

THIRD EDITION

KATHERINE J. MAYBERRY
Rochester Institute of Technology

HOUGHTON MIFFLIN COMPANY
Boston   New York

Publisher: Patricia Coryell
Editor-in-Chief: Carrie Brandon
Sponsoring Editor: Lisa Kimball
Marketing Manager: Tom Ziolkowski
Senior Development Editor: Kathy Sands Boehmer
Senior Project Editor: Rosemary Winfield
Art and Design Manager: Jill Haber
Cover Design Manager: Anne Katzeff
Photo Editor: Jennifer Meyer Dare
Composition Buyer: Chuck Dutton
New Title Project Manager: Priscilla Manchester
Associate Editor: Sarah Truax
Marketing Associate: Bettina Chiu

Cover Image: *Blue Rhapsody* © Diana Ong / Superstock

Credits continue on page 427, which constitutes an extension of the copyright page.

Printed in the U.S.A.

Library of Congress Catalog Card Number 2007932698
1 2 3 4 5 6 7 8 9 – EB – 11 10 09 08 07
ISBN 10: 0-618-98675-8
ISBN 13: 978-0-618-98675-0

Brief Contents

v

Contents

Part II   Reading Arguments   233

Preface

Everyday Arguments combines a straightforward, commonsense rhetoric with a comprehensive collection of readings.

The rhetoric section (Part I, Chapters 1–13) is based on the principle that virtually all writing is some form of argument. Updates in Part I include an entirely new Chapter 5 on research and plagiarism—"Supporting Your Arguments Honestly and Effectively"—as well as a number of updated illustrative arguments.

The readings section (Part II, Chapters 14–19), which contains a wide variety of largely contemporary texts, illustrates the principles and practices contained in the rhetoric, as well as the critical link between writing and *reading* arguments. Part II contains over 35 examples of written arguments. This anthology is gathered from the kinds of writing that most of us read every day. The arguments are contemporary and varied, with each one illustrating practices and principles taught in Part I. From a Web site for men with eating disorders to a prize-winning article in *Sports Illustrated*, these writing samples demonstrate the central premise of the rhetoric—that most of the writing and reading we do in our daily lives falls under the heading of argument. By helping students become critical readers of argument, these sample arguments likewise contribute to their becoming effective argument writers.

PART I, WRITING ARGUMENTS

Organization of Part I

Part I of *Everyday Arguments* is organized around the three major phases of argument writing—focusing, supporting, and reviewing:

- Chapters 1 through 6 discuss how to bring a developing argument into focus—including finding and focusing a claim, identifying and accommodating the audience, and understanding the relationship between claim and support.

- Chapters 7 through 10 show students how to support the four different classes of argument—arguments of fact, cause, evaluation, and recommendation.
- Chapters 11 through 13 present the reviewing activities necessary to refine and polish an argument—considering image and style, composing openings and closings, and revising and editing the argument draft.

These three writing phases are presented in the order students typically follow when composing arguments, but there are perfectly acceptable and effective exceptions to the typical. The order presented is meant to guide, not prescribe. Further, the sequential presentation of these writing phases is not meant to contradict the received wisdom about the recursive nature of good writing. In the real practice of writing, changes made in one phase lead to changes in others.

Special Features of Part I

The discussion of dissonance in Chapter 2 is unique to argument texts. The question of what moves people to write arguments is a critical one for students that can lead them to make a greater personal investment in their own writing.

Chapter 5, "Supporting Your Arguments Honestly and Effectively," discusses plagiarism within both traditional and digital environments, offering clear guidelines for avoiding plagiarism and examples of acceptable and unacceptable use of the texts and ideas of others. The second part of this chapter presents helpful principles for distinguishing between reliable and unreliable research sources.

Formal and informal logic are treated uniquely in this text. They are introduced at the point in the argument process where they are most useful—the development and evaluation of the argument's support. Too often, argument texts include the theory of logic and examples of informal fallacies without addressing how they are useful in the actual writing process. Chapter 6 presents both formal and informal logic as practical tools for creating reasonable arguments.

The inclusion of an entire chapter on style and image (Chapter 11) enriches the traditional view of argument, which sometimes seems to suggest that effective arguments have more to do with formulas and principles than with using language fairly and effectively. Here, a writer's style—the image that he or she projects through the writing—is a fundamental component of argument, not just a lucky accident of talent.

Everyday Arguments contains many examples that today's college students can relate to, plus examples from diverse academic and career areas. This range of application helps students see the importance of writing effective arguments in their college courses and also in their postcollege careers.

Because improvement in writing comes only with practice, the emphasis in all the activities in Part I is on *writing*. Each chapter gives students many opportunities to practice what they are learning by writing (and rewriting) full and partial arguments.

PART II, READING ARGUMENTS
Organization of Part II

The readings in Part II of *Everyday Arguments* are divided into six topic areas—"Today's College Student," "The Internet," "Sports," "Earning Your Living," "Diet," and "Reading Popular Culture." By design, these are not the typical subjects of traditional argument anthologies, which tend to focus on abstract issues—such as capital punishment or euthanasia—and the classical canon of arguments addressing them. These six topics were selected to engage students' attention and demonstrate the importance of regular critical reading and critical writing.

Each topic area begins with an introduction, including a discussion of the importance of critical reading on that topic. The first argument in each section is accompanied by a detailed commentary that serves as a model for the attentive, critical reading of argument. Following each reading are a set of discussion questions and suggestions for writing.

Special Features of Part II

The arguments contained in Part II of *Everyday Arguments* are representative of the reading we do on a daily basis, so students can see the immediate usefulness of the writing and reading skills they are learning. The arguments are also drawn from a wide range of contexts—newspapers, Websites, magazines (from the *New Yorker* to *Wired*), and books. The variety of sources gives students many opportunities to study the effect of context and audience on written argument.

The discussion questions following each argument encourage collaboration among students and are closely tied to the contents of Part I. The suggestions for writing following the discussion questions are directed toward students of all ages, backgrounds, and majors, with an emphasis on the stages of composition. Part II is in continuing conversation with Part I, repeatedly demonstrating the connection between principle and practice. Part II of *Everyday Arguments* maintains the same highly practical, student-friendly, writing-intensive approach to learning how to compose an argument.

SUPPLEMENTS

Instructor's Manual An Instructor's Manual is available online at college.hmco.com/pic/mayberryEA3e.

Companion Website A companion Website includes information for students including chapter summaries, critical reading tools and writing tasks and writing assignments and Web resources. It also is available at college.hmco.com/pic/mayberryEA3e.

ACKNOWLEDGMENTS

Everyday Arguments remains closely tied to the vision I shared with Robert E. Golden when we began the first edition of *For Argument's Sake* more than 25 years ago. Joe Opiela, then at Little, Brown, understood this vision and published the book. I am grateful to Anne Smith and her staff at HarperCollins for supporting my desire to expand *For Argument's Sake* into a combination rhetoric and reader—what became *Everyday Arguments*. Since then, dedicated editors from HarperCollins, Addison Wesley Longman, Longman (where I reencountered Joe Opiela), and Houghton Mifflin have contributed to the evolution and longevity of this text.

Readers are critical to each new edition of a book, and I have been fortunate to have benefited from the keen minds of such colleagues as Steven L. Climer, Baker College of Allen Park, MI; Anthony Gargano, Long Beach City College; Daniel Gribbin, University of Central Florida; Janet LaBrie, University of Wisconsin at Waukesha; and Bernard W. Quetchenbach, Florida Southern College.

Finally, I am grateful to Stanley McKenzie, provost at the Rochester Institute of Technology, for giving me time and occasionally resources to continue my commitment to *Everyday Arguments*.

EVERYDAY ARGUMENTS

PART I

WRITING ARGUMENTS

1

An Introduction to Argument

AN EXTENDED DEFINITION

Let's be clear from the start what the term *argument* will mean in this book. If you're like a lot of people, when you hear the word you think of verbal disagreements—the fights you've had with your parents or siblings about curfews or allowance or borrowing clothes, for example. You've probably had lots of practice at this kind of communication and may feel there's not much a book can teach you about it. And you would be right, if by *argument*, you meant a verbal battle where reason is absent and agreement rarely reached. Here's how a daughter might "argue" with her parents in an e-mail about changing her college major.

I don't believe you 2! Finally I've found a major I'm really interested in and all you can talk about is money and being respectable! I'd rather live on frozen peas than do a job I hate and I know I'll just love photography—you can't believe how cool it is! This teacher we had in the intro. class is young and hip and really gets me. How come you always object to the things I love? You wouldn't let me go out with Eric, you took away my cell phone, and now you say you're not paying for me to learn how to take pictures. You guys are just impossible! Well, I don't care what you think, I'm going to become a photographer whether you pay for it or not!

The unpleasant and usually unproductive practice illustrated in this fictitious e-mail is *not* the subject of this book. In fact, this example is the exact opposite of the kind of writing this book is about. *Everyday Arguments* will teach you about

3

formal, traditional argument: the process of establishing, through the presentation of appropriate evidence, the certainty or likelihood of a particular point or position.

Our aspiring photographer above would have a much better chance of convincing her parents to support her choice if she were to use the principles of traditional argument. A more productive e-mail might read as follows:

```
You must have been really surprised when I told you I was
changing majors to photography. I mean, I've been talking
about being an engineer since my first set of Legos. I know
that I don't know a lot about photography yet, or whether I
could be any good at it. But this course made me excited about
learning for the first time in my life, and I don't want to
ignore anything that makes me feel that way. I've thought a
lot about this, and I'd like to suggest a compromise: why don't
I take 2 more photography courses next term, as well as the
math and chemistry courses I'll need for engineering, and use
that time to get more information about careers in photography
and my own potential in the field? We can talk about this again
at the end of the term. I know you're making sacrifices to send
me to college, and I understand why you'd be concerned by my
making a quick decision.
```

While there's no guarantee that the second e-mail would succeed, it *is* a reasonable argument. The writer is understanding of her parents' reaction ("You must have been really surprised"), she acknowledges the legitimacy of her parents' concern that the decision is impulsive ("I know that I don't know a lot about photography yet"), and she has come up with a compromise plan that will keep her from burning bridges. Further, her overall tone is much more pleasant and conciliatory in the second e-mail, which will likely take her parents off the defensive.

Much of the writing you will do in college and in your careers following college falls within this second definition of argument: writing that seeks agreement about a point through the use of reasonable evidence. Research papers, lab reports, literary interpretations, case studies—all these forms of writing aim to convince an audience (usually a professor) of the reasonableness of certain conclusions. All these forms of writing, as well as application letters, instructional manuals, and corporate annual reports, are built around the simple objective of making a reasonable point.

An argument, whether written or oral, is different from an opinion. An *opinion* is based not so much on evidence as on belief, intuition, or emotion. Argument, on the other hand, is a position supported by clear thinking and reasonable evidence, with a secure connection to solid facts. While arguments rarely prove a conclusion to be absolutely true, they do demonstrate the probability of that conclusion. Opinions tend to be expressions of personal taste that have not been tested by the application of reasonable principles. Your opinion may be that history is a more interesting subject than literature, or that yellow is prettier than red, but these remain only opinions until they are thoughtfully and fully justified.

Effective arguments are ethical as well as reasonable. They make their points openly and honestly, avoiding underhanded methods and false promises, and seeking to remove ambiguity rather than exploit it. We make arguments in order to advance a reasonable position, not to trick a reader into serving our self-interest. As writers of ethical arguments, we recognize the influence that skilled writing can exert over credulous or ignorant readers, and we are committed to exercising that influence reasonably and responsibly.

Of course, what constitutes a reasonable and responsible argument is sometimes up for grabs. When they argue, people disagree about basic assumptions, beliefs, and values, and those disagreements affect their understanding of what is reasonable. The second e-mail in the previous example is working from the assumption that a student should be interested in her college major. This seemingly inarguable assumption leads this student to the conclusion that she should be allowed at least to explore photography. But perhaps her parents believe it is their parental responsibility to protect their daughter from the consequences of an impulsive decision—an assumption that reasonably supports their opposition to her proposal. Both daughter and parents are being reasonable, but their values and assumptions could lead them to different conclusions.

So this book will not be able to define what constitutes a reasonable argument for every writer, every audience, and every occasion. But it will introduce you to some concepts, processes, and tools that will help you make informed and effective decisions about how to construct your own arguments. And the many writing samples included at the end of most chapters and in Part II will demonstrate how the principles and practices of formal argument carry over into a wide variety of writing contexts.

THE CLASSES OF ARGUMENT

Once you begin paying attention to the writing you do for school and work, you will notice how frequently your assignments fit within the definition of argument. You may also notice that the claims, or propositions, of these arguments tend to fall into certain patterns. Papers in economics or history courses may tend to concentrate on identifying the causes of certain events, whereas lab reports in biology or physics focus on describing a particular process and interpreting its results. In fact, argument can be divided into four classes: (1) factual arguments, (2) causal arguments, (3) evaluations, and (4) recommendations. These classes are distinguished both by the type of claim being argued and the degree of agreement expected from the reader.

Factual arguments try to convince an audience that a certain condition or event actually exists or has existed. Factual arguments, though they sound quite simple, are the most ambitious type of argument, for they try to convince readers of the truth or factuality of a claim. Those laboratory reports from biology or physics are examples of factual arguments, and their purpose is to convince their reader (usually a professor) that certain steps were taken and certain things actually happened.

Causal arguments—often found within those economics or history papers— try to convince readers that one event or condition caused another or is likely to cause another in the future. A paper identifying the complex economic reasons for the 1987 stock market crash would be a causal argument. Causal arguments can only rarely claim truth or certainty; most are judged successful if they establish a certain cause or future effect as *probable.*

Evaluations, or **evaluative** arguments, make value judgments. The film critics Roger Ebert and Richard Roeper are in the business of oral evaluations as they share their judgments about the quality of recent films with their television audience. Because evaluations are often tied up in personal tastes and opinions, they are the hardest of all arguments to make successfully; nevertheless, they *can* be reasonable and effective.

Finally, **recommendations,** as their name suggests, try to get readers to *do* something, to follow a suggested course of action. While the other three classes of arguments aim for armchair agreement, most recommendations want the reader's agreement to be translated into action.

This book will take up the principles and practices of each argument class in isolation from the others, but you should realize from the outset that many of the writing assignments you will do for this course, for other courses, and on the job will *combine* these classes. In fact, the most common type of argument is the combined, or *hybrid,* argument.

ARGUMENT THROUGH IMAGE

An argument's success depends on many things: the clarity and exactness of its claim, the appropriateness and adequacy of its supporting evidence, and the particular *image* it projects. Image is the total impression a reader gets by reading your writing, and it is composed of a number of elements. Among these is the writing *style,* which consists of word choice, sentence length and structure, and the writer's tone of voice. Other elements of image include grammar, punctuation, neatness of the page, and quality of graphics. Together, these elements compose an overall impression of the writer and the work that will influence the reader's final acceptance or rejection of the argument. A positive image will help to secure the reader's confidence, respect, and attention; a negative image inevitably gets in the way of the agreement that all arguments seek from their readers.

Consider the example of an application letter for a job. Let's say that you are the head of the work-study program at your college, the person responsible for placing students in campus jobs. You have whittled the pool of applicants for the desirable job of dean's assistant down to two applicants: Jon Marshall and Becky

Quinn. Both students have comparable academic qualifications, and both have been highly recommended by faculty and former employers. Becky's application letter is a well-organized, neatly typed business letter that carefully lists and develops Becky's qualifications for the job. Jon's letter also contains his qualifications, but it is filled with misspellings and faulty punctuation, it addresses you by your first name, and it has a grease spot on the upper-right corner. All other things being equal, which candidate is likely to have the edge? Which image better argues the writer's suitability for the job?

THE ARGUMENT PROCESS

It is one thing to recognize the prevalence of argument in the writing you do but quite another actually to create effective written arguments. While this book contains no single blueprint or recipe for writing effective arguments, it will suggest a practical process, as well as theoretical principles, that will help you reach the desired product of an effective written argument. Unless you are extraordinarily gifted—one of those rare students who can produce a perfectly acceptable essay in a single sitting—your writing process will consist of at least three broad stages: forming the argument, supporting the argument, and reviewing the argument.

In order to explain and illustrate these stages, we have created the hypothetical case of Rob Wade, a journalism major with the ambition of becoming a radio sports announcer. In this age of high-tech video, you may find Rob's ambition a bit old-fashioned, but it is based on his belief that television is ruining sports for the American public. After watching the television coverage of the 2008 NCAA basketball playoffs, Rob's convictions have grown so powerful that he feels compelled to communicate them to a large audience. He decides to kill two birds with one stone: his professor has assigned a "Letter to the Editor" as part of his journalism portfolio, and Rob plans to use this requirement to communicate his strong disapproval of television sports coverage. Let's watch how Rob moves through the three stages of argument composition as he creates his letter.

Forming the Argument

Forming your argument consists of discovering a motive for writing, identifying an audience to address, and discovering and sharpening the point or points to be argued.

Most successful arguments originate in the writer's strong personal interest, which often includes a desire to change the status quo. The origin of Rob's letter to the editor, his *motive* for writing it, is his long and growing discomfort with television sports coverage. He is disappointed in this coverage, angry at how it packages sports for the public; the desire to communicate these feelings and to remedy the harm he sees being done are powerful motives that will energize his writing.

Once Rob has decided to act on these motives, he needs to think seriously about where he would like his letter to be published—in the school newspaper, the city newspaper, the *New York Times,* or *Sports Illustrated*? This decision must be made before he begins writing; otherwise he will lack the necessary sense of audience. *Audience* is an inescapable consideration in writing, yet writers often underestimate its importance, forgetting that argument always consists of one person addressing another person, or a group of people. In Rob's case, a letter to the editor of the school newspaper, whose readers consist largely of young men and women in their late teens and early twenties, would be very different from a letter to the editor of *Sports Illustrated,* whose readers are typically educated males of all ages. Also, *Sports Illustrated* will be more selective in choosing which letters to publish than the school paper is likely to be. Regardless of where Rob decides to send his letter, his argument will gain focus and immediacy if he has a clear sense that he is writing to a particular audience, with particular backgrounds, expectations, values, and beliefs.

Rob also must be clear from the outset about the exact point or points he plans to argue. Sure, he knows he wants to attack television sports coverage, but he will soon find that such a goal is too vague and too emotional to inform what must be a clear and reasonable argument. Before he starts writing, he'll need to compose a clearly focused statement of the point or points he wants his readers to agree with. In most arguments, such a statement is a one- to three-sentence summary of the argument's conclusion—called the *claim.* Some claims come to writers early and easily in the writing process, whereas others are the result of considerable reading, thinking, and narrowing. Though Rob knows generally what he wants to write about, it will take him some time to develop a claim that will interest his readers, that will be clear, and that he can reasonably support.

After more thinking than he had anticipated, Rob finally comes up with the following as his working claim: "While television coverage of sporting events allows us to be armchair spectators of exciting athletic contests that we would otherwise never see, we are paying a price for the convenience of this coverage. For what we are watching from our comfortable vantage point is glossy, high-tech artifice, not *real* sports."

Supporting the Claim

Having identified his claim and his audience, Rob now must decide how to support that claim. An argument's *support* is all the material that turns a tentative claim into a justified conclusion. Support is the most important component of argument. Without adequate and suitable support, a claim remains merely a hunch or an opinion; with appropriate support, it becomes a sound and credible conclusion.

At the very least, Rob can support his claim through his own viewing experience, which is, after all, what led him to the claim. But he's pretty sure that one person's experience is not enough to support an argument, so he knows he has some work to do. Identifying the class of his argument will help Rob select appropriate support, because certain kinds of support tend to apply to certain classes of argument. After careful consideration of his claim, and a thorough review of the four classes to which it might belong, he decides that his claim introduces an evaluative argument: it is making a negative judgment about the quality of television sports coverage.

This identification will help him, but there is more to selecting support than matching it to the class of the argument he is making. Rob will also need to ensure that the relationship between his claim and its support will be *reasonable,* that it will accord with the principles of formal and informal logic. So he will review carefully the material in Chapter 5 of this book, which presents these principles.

Reviewing the Argument

The product of these three steps—identifying an audience, composing a claim, and selecting appropriate support—will be a first version, or *draft*, of Rob's argument. As a journalism major, Rob has a fair amount of writing experience; he knows how difficult it is to evaluate your own writing, particularly when you have no distance from it. So, as he always tries to do, he puts his first draft away for a couple of days, so that when he returns to it, he has a fresh perspective that allows him to see problems in style and organization and reasoning that he hadn't noticed two days ago.

While getting distance from his argument will help to freshen his perspective, there is no fresher perspective than that of a second party who is unfamiliar with the work. In his writing classes, Rob has learned how well the process of "peer reviewing" works. As the name suggests, peer review is getting a friend or classmate or coworker to read your writing before you submit it to your professor, or, in Rob's case, for publication review. Peer review works best when you ask your reviewers to consider certain questions as they read. In the case of Rob's argument, these questions might be listed as follows: Does the argument effectively address its intended audience? Is its claim completely clear, and does it stick to that claim throughout? Is the supporting material reasonable and relevant to the claim? Does the argument project a positive image of its writer? Does the argument convince its audience? Friendly readers of your writing can identify problems and suggest solutions that you yourself are too close to the writing to see. Peer review is not cheating; it is not the same thing as getting someone else's answers to a calculus test. Peer review is a perfectly acceptable form of collaboration, providing an invaluable supplement to the writing process that the writer alone simply cannot supply: a *reader's* perspective. As a college student, Rob is lucky to have plenty of reader perspectives to call on. And his experience tells him that he would be foolish to ignore them, that without this collaboration, the revision process might become nothing more than superficial editing for spelling, punctuation, and grammatical errors. While editing is a necessary part of the review process, it is the final "spit-and-polish" step; revising often entails significant changes.

One addition that Rob will make to the first draft during the revision process is composing an introduction and conclusion. Like many writers, he finds it difficult to write interesting and representative introductions right out of the gate; the problem is partly psychological (first paragraphs are always the hardest) and partly practical (he won't know the exact content of the argument until he has finished a first draft). Likewise, it makes little sense to labor over a conclusion if the content of the first draft is going to be changed substantially during the revision process.

READING ARGUMENTS

There are many reasons why you should become an effective *reader* of arguments as well as an effective writer. For one thing, reading carefully and critically will prevent you from being "taken in" by an argument that does not proceed reasonably. For another, the more careful reading of arguments you do, the better writer you will become. All successful writers—whether novelists, poets, or journalists—are avid readers. Interviews of famous writers inevitably include the question, "What do you read?" Writers learn from other writers—both unconsciously, by a kind of osmosis, and intentionally, through critical observation and imitation.

And finally, there is no better way to become effective at revising the early drafts of the arguments you write than by learning to read critically the writing of others. If you can understand and evaluate the writing of others—that is, read actively and critically—you can judge and thus improve your own writing. You'll find that the critical objectivity so difficult to summon when reading your own writing is much easier to apply to someone else's.

While you may think of reading as a passive and reactive process, *critical* reading is actually creative and active, employing many of the skills used in effective writing. In this section, we offer some guidelines for critical reading that will help you learn from the writing of others and sharpen your revising skills.

Reading as Evaluation

One good technique for reading critically is to approach the text you're reading as if it were the subject of an evaluative argument. While you won't actually write an evaluation, you can mentally follow steps very similar to those that will be presented in Chapter 9. First, and obviously, you need to read the text all the way through to get a sense of the class of writing to which it belongs and its major claims and conclusions.

Your subject will be the text you're reading—let's say it's an editorial identifying the reasons your mayor was not reelected (a short causal argument). Your evaluative term will be something like "effective," "well reasoned," or "convincing." You will then stipulate mentally the defining elements of your evaluative term. In this example, you might actually work from two related sets of standards: those that characterize effective arguments in general and those that characterize effective causal arguments. A book reviewer does much the same thing, evaluating a book in terms of the overall writing quality and also in terms of the standards applicable to the genre of the book—a mystery novel, for example, or a biography.

The defining qualities of "effective" argument might be as follows:

- Clear central claim
- Reasonable, relevant, and concrete support
- Acknowledgment of opposing point of view

And elements constituting an "effective" causal argument could be:

- Proposed causes are sufficient
- Argument passes appropriate causal tests
- Factuality of cause and effect are established

As you read the argument through a second time, you will look for all these elements. Not only will this process allow you to judge the reading fairly, it will also make you a very attentive reader.

Of course, in much of the reading you will do, you won't go through this process step by step. But you should always identify to yourself what class of argument you're reading and be alert to those elements within it that characterize effective arguments of that class. When you're rereading drafts of your own arguments as the first step in revision, you can't go wrong by actually defining the evaluative term through a list like the one above and checking for those elements as you reread.

Additional Hints for Reading Critically

As we mentioned earlier, critical reading is active reading. If you find yourself getting too passive, accepting what you read without questioning it, you may find the following suggestions useful.

1. Accept that critical reading always entails multiple readings of a text. No matter how carefully you read, one time through is never enough to follow the writer's meaning and logic.
2. Use a pencil as you read, not a highlighter. The practice of highlighting or underlining text is an easy way to fool yourself into thinking you're being an active reader, when all you're really doing is guessing about what may turn out to be important. When you review the material, you'll tend to ignore completely those parts you did not highlight, thus ending up with a very incomplete understanding of the writing.
3. Try making notes instead of highlighting. Reading critically involves a running conversation with the writer of the text—questioning, commenting, admiring. The writer's side of the conversation is the text itself; yours is the comments you write in the margins (assuming that you own the document) or on a separate piece of paper. The process is slower than highlighting or underlining, but you'll get much more out of it.
4. After you've read through the document once, go back and make an outline of its structure. If you can do this, you'll understand a lot about the structure and reasoning of the reading.

CONCLUSION

Having provided an extended definition of argument and a brief overview of the writing and critical reading processes, let's proceed to a detailed description of the steps involved in creating effective written argument, the reasoning principles that inform effective argument, and the special elements and requirements of each of the four classes of argument.

SUMMARY

An Introduction to Argument

- Written argument attempts to convince the reader of the writer's point of view, using reasonable and ethical methods. Most effective writing contains some form of argument.

- The *image* projected by the argument is the overall impression the writer makes on the reader. Image is created through writing style; correct spelling, punctuation, and grammar; and the physical appearance of the document.

- Argument can be divided into four classes: arguments of fact, cause, evaluation, and recommendation.

- While the process of argument composition varies from writer to writer, most writers follow these three stages: (1) forming an argument, which can consist of discovering a motive for writing and identifying an audience to address, discovering and sharpening a position, and developing an appropriate style; (2) supporting the argument; and (3) reviewing the argument, which can include considering the image projected by your argument, making substantial additions or deletions to a first draft, and adding an introduction and conclusion.

- Critical reading of other people's arguments will make you a better writer of your own arguments.

- Approaching what you read as if it were the subject of an evaluative argument is an excellent way to ensure attentive reading and revising.

SUGGESTIONS FOR WRITING (1.1)

1. If you are planning on finding a summer job or a part-time job while in school, you will probably need to write a letter of application to your prospective employer. Give yourself some practice by writing a one-page letter of application for a real or made-up job. Try following a sequence like the following:

   Paragraph 1: State the position desired and your primary qualification for it.

   Paragraph 2: Expand on the primary qualification.

   Paragraph 3 and following: Develop other qualifications for the job.

   Concluding paragraph: State your willingness to answer questions and be available for an interview.

   Before writing, be sure to identify to yourself the needs and expectations of your reader—that is, your prospective employer. Then be sure your letter addresses these needs and expectations through such elements as the content of the letter, its level of formality, and the overall image projected by the letter.

2. Find an editorial in your local newspaper or online. With two or three class-mates, analyze your responses to the editorial. Do all members of the group find the argument convincing? Why or why not? Do your disagreements reveal anything about your different concerns and values as readers? What image is projected by the editorial? Does the image appeal to all members of your group? Why or why not? Are there ways that the editorial could be changed to be effective for all members of your group?

3. With a small group of your classmates, review an essay examination that one of you has written recently. As a group, identify the expectations of the professor giving the exam. To what extent does the claim, the support, and the overall image of this one essay meet these expectations? As a group, rewrite the essay so that all of these considerations are met.

2

Where Writing Begins: Motives and Audience

Most of us write because we have to, not because we want to. As a college student, you write a research paper because your political science professor has assigned it; a sales rep writes a monthly report because her boss requires it; a mother writes a note explaining her son's absence from school because school policy insists on it. Yet the best writing, the kind we read voluntarily and the kind that endures over centuries, springs from some source other than mere necessity. And even when necessity drives great writing, other motives are also at work. Shakespeare wrote *Hamlet* to make a living, Dickens wrote *David Copperfield* to feed his many children, but these writers were surely inspired by some motive beyond making money.

MOTIVES FOR WRITING

What are these other motives for writing? They are powerful intellectual and emotional drives of enormous variety—from the desire to create a lasting record of some important experience (think of Anne Frank's *Diary of a Young Girl*), to the yearning to express love or joy (a common motive for music through the ages from Renaissance musicians to Norah Jones), to the need to disagree strongly or even complain (Harriet Beecher Stowe's *Uncle Tom's Cabin* was written from a deep disagreement with the institution of American slavery). One common motive for writing, especially for writing arguments, is our drive to resolve personal dissonance. *Dissonance* is actually a musical term meaning an inharmonious arrangement of tones that the listener wants resolved into harmony.

On a more general level, the term *dissonance* suggests tension or uneasiness. It is a good word for describing the mismatch between the way we want life to be and the way it is. Dissonance drove the angry voice of the prophets in the Old Testament, the determined defiance of the Declaration of Independence, and the heartfelt challenges in the *Communist Manifesto*. Driven by intense dissatisfaction with the way things were, the writers sought a resolution of this tension by expressing it in writing.

The Value of Dissonance

The principle of dissonance is a useful starting point whenever you are at a loss to discover an argument worth making. If you find yourself doing nothing but staring at a blank page when you are supposed to be writing a ten-page paper for an English composition class, try asking yourself the following questions: "What really bothers me? What do I wish were different? What could be done to improve the situation?" The cause of the dissonance may be anything from parking problems on campus, to the status of women in large corporations, to the chemistry professor you don't understand.

If you begin the process of forming your argument by identifying a cause of dissonance, you will find both a subject to write about and a position to take on that subject (i.e., a claim). Because this position comes from your own interests and experience, developing it into an argument will be interesting to you, and if it's interesting to you, it's likely to be lively and interesting to your reader.

Let's assume that in an English composition class, you are asked to write about the impact of technology on education. An obvious position to take would be that the computer and associated technologies like educational DVDs and the World Wide Web enhance the learning process for children and young adults. A solid position, certainly, but a bit predictable: probably 90 percent of your class will take this or a similar position. Plus, though you know it's a defensible position, it's not one that you find particularly exciting. So put that tentative claim on a back burner, and take some time to probe the general topic for personal dissonance. What discomforts, uneasiness, or inconveniences have you experienced from the new educational technology? Perhaps you were an avid reader as a child, someone who treasured the physical properties of books—the texture of the pages, the shape and heft of the volumes, the warm look of a filled book shelf. As you think about it, you realize that as amazing as educational technology is, it threatens the reader's important physical relationship to books, to tangible texts. Reading about the Byzantine Empire or cell mitosis from a computer screen just isn't the same as learning about them from a volume taken down from your living-room shelf. This could be the beginning of an interesting argument about the losses incurred when screens replace pages, when electronic texts make the comforting tangibility of books obsolete.

This approach has a number of advantages. First, it promises to be different, unusual. In writing, an unusual approach, as long as it is intelligent and not merely eccentric, is often effective: it gets people's attention. Second, working from dissonance lets you get to the core of your discomfort by discovering reasons for it. Turning an opinion into an argument is a great way to challenge and define your unexamined views. And finally, focusing on problems is more useful and productive than ignoring them; neither you nor your readers can improve a situation until you have identified and accounted for its problems.

Don't take this advice to mean that you should turn every writing assignment into an occasion for complaining. Searching for dissonance should help you learn to be a critical and discerning thinker, not a cynic or whiner. And one of the hallmarks of a discerning thinker is the ability to recognize value where it exists: a student writing on the disadvantages of educational technology should acknowledge its obvious positive impacts. To pretend that they don't exist will only make the argument seem nearsighted and unfair. Of course, sometimes balance and fairness are not appropriate; the Declaration of Independence would be much less effective if it presented a balanced view of the British government. But extreme situations calling for one-sided appeals are relatively rare.

Writing Arguments That Are Meaningful to You

Of course, not every writing assignment will allow you to call on your own feelings and opinions; sometimes you are required to write about topics that simply don't interest you. Yet there are ways to make even those assignments more relevant to your interests and experience. The next time you find yourself working with an uninspiring assignment, try these three suggestions for making that assignment more meaningful to you:

1. *Search for the most interesting facets of the assignment.* If you must write on the American Civil War—a topic that holds little interest for you—try to find one aspect of the war that is at least potentially more meaningful to you than any other. You may need to do some research, but your time is well spent if you get excited about the topic. If you are interested in medicine, for example, why not write about the medical treatment of the wounded during the war?

2. *Don't lie.* Express only those opinions you honestly believe in. If you are unsure of your claim despite your best efforts to become comfortable with it, don't hesitate to use qualifiers such as *perhaps, probably, usually,* or *likely.* Never be lukewarm when you can be hot or cold, but don't take a position simply for the sake of taking it. A qualified claim, such as "Athletes who train with professional coaches usually perform better than athletes who do not," is preferable to the unqualified statement "Athletes who train with professional coaches perform better than athletes who do not" because there are bound to be some exceptions to this rule.

3. *Don't be pompous.* You don't want your writing to be too informal and colloquial, but you also don't want to sound like someone you're not—like your professor or boss, for instance, or the Rhodes scholar teaching assistant. Good writing is always genuine writing.

These suggestions apply to any assigned writing, from a monthly sales report to a memo on improvements in office procedures, to a lab report, to an anthropology research paper. You may not have chosen to do the writing in the first place, but energy spent making the project your own will result in a more lively and credible argument.

ACTIVITIES (2.1)

1. Look at the last four things you have written: letters, e-mail, reports, essays, memos, and so on. What were your reasons for writing them? How many of them were not written out of choice? Would these have been better if you had tried to write about what is important to you? Adjust the topic of one of these to make it more meaningful to you, and then rewrite it following the suggestions presented in the preceding part of the chapter.

2. List four aspects of your life or of the world around you that you wish were different. From these four aspects, derive tentative topics for essays.

THE IMPORTANCE OF AUDIENCE

When you prepare writing assignments for a college professor, you are usually writing for an audience of one: a professor who is a specialist in the subject of the paper, who has certain expectations of the paper, and who is obliged to read it carefully. Having such a predictable audience is actually a luxury to students, freeing them from one of the most important steps in argument formation: identifying the audience. But in most of the writing you will do outside an academic setting, you won't be able to ignore this step. Written argument assumes a relationship between a writer and a reader: the writer speaks and the reader listens and reacts. As a writer, your first and most basic goal is simply to engage your audience—to get their attention. Taking the time before you write to consider your audience will help you avoid boring or offending or confusing them. Considering your audience will also add focus and purpose to your writing: you will write with an imaginary "reader over your shoulder," as poet Robert Graves put it, which is vastly preferable to writing into a void.

Audience consideration is important to all writing, but particularly to arguments. Since the purpose of all arguments is to convince someone of something, knowing who that "someone" is is crucial. An argument seeking to convince college students of the need for a tuition hike would proceed very differently from an argument seeking to convince the school's board of trustees of the same claim.

Developing an accurate sense of audience depends in part on experience, but you can sharpen this sensitivity by considering the following questions each time you prepare to write: *Who* is the audience? *Why* will the audience read your argument? *What* should the audience be able to do after reading your argument? You should try to keep the answers to these questions in mind not only as you form the argument, but also as you write it.

Who Is the Audience?

Sometimes this question will be answered in terms of specific individuals (my supervisor, my prospective employer). More frequently, it is answered in terms of categories or groups of readers (readers of a certain magazine, users of a certain product, students in a particular class).

Having identified your audience, you will want to consider how familiar they are with the subject matter. Readers usually know much less than writers about the topic at hand; even readers in the same organization with similar education and experience may be unfamiliar with the subject matter of your report. With this in mind, consider where you might provide background information, what terminology you might define, what difficult concepts you might explain or illustrate. No matter how convincing your argument is, if it baffles its readers it's not going to succeed. Most readers, if they have any choice in the matter, will stop reading a difficult argument before they will struggle through its unfamiliar language and concepts. If you don't know how much your audience is likely to know, or if they have different levels of knowledge, you are better off providing too much explanation than too little. Most people prefer feeling superior to feeling ignorant.

Finally, audience identification also includes considering your readers' probable disposition to your claim. Are they likely to be friendly or hostile to your position? The answer to this question will influence a number of your argument strategies. For example, if you expect your audience to be hostile to your claim, you might give them credit for their views at the outset. In recommending an expensive federal crime prevention program to an audience already frustrated by the cost of crime to taxpayers, acknowledging and legitimizing that frustration may help to neutralize their hostility: "There is something wildly unjust about living in fear of crime *and* having to pay for that crime as well." Once you have conceded that your audience probably won't want to pay more to prevent crime, you could proceed to argue for a new crime bill that, while temporarily costly, offers an excellent chance of reducing crime and its costs to the taxpayer. Telling the audience that they are selfish or pigheaded or shortsighted will not gain you much agreement, but expressing a genuine understanding of their frustration may convince them that your motives and theirs are essentially the same.

When you know that someone in your audience holds a view completely different from your claim, or even when you know that there is a good counterargument to your position, you may need to include a *refutation* of that opposing argument. (Refutations are discussed in Chapter 4, under "Addressing the Counterargument.") Even if you don't refute such a counterargument directly, acknowledging that you are aware of its existence can convince your audience that you have taken time to learn about the issue.

If you are confident that your audience shares your views, your work will be easier, but don't let yourself become sloppy, or you may lose the agreement you started with. To guard against triteness and predictability, try playing devil's advocate (appearing to support the opposing view), or expressing your central claim outrageously, or reminding your audience of the dangers of knee-jerk responses.

If you have no idea how your audience might respond to your claim, perhaps you can get some information about their general beliefs and values, which you can then appeal to in the course of your argument. Some arguments—particularly evaluations and recommendations—depend on successful appeals to readers' values and beliefs. An argument written for the *New Left Journal* recommending the recitation of the Pledge of Allegiance in public schools will succeed only if it appeals to a value held by the *Journal's* politically liberal readers. These readers will not be moved by a "Your country: love it or leave it" approach. But if your claim rests on the principle of free choice, arguing that every student should have the choice of saying the pledge, your argument may succeed with this difficult audience.

In considering these questions about your audience—who they are and what they know, think, and believe—you are considering audience psychology. But it is important that you understand your reasons for doing so. You are not going to the trouble to understand your audience so that you can manipulate them through underhanded, unreasonable, unethical methods. Rather, you are giving your good argument the best chance at success by trying to ensure that the audience will approach it fairly and reasonably.

ACTIVITIES (2.2)

1. Examine a copy of *four* of the following and try to identify the probable audience for each. Estimate the level of education and the kinds of occupations each audience would probably have.

   Example: *Publications of the Modern Language Association* (PMLA). Level of education: usually at least some graduate education. Occupations: primarily graduate students in English or foreign language and literature and college-level instructors in these subjects.
   a. The *Wall Street Journal*
   b. *Time* magazine
   c. *Cosmopolitan*
   d. *People* magazine
   e. The *New England Journal of Medicine*
   f. *Popular Mechanics*
   g. *Soldier of Fortune* magazine
   h. The "help" feature of a software program like PowerPoint or Excel.
   i. *Mad* magazine
   j. The *New York Times*

2. The following passage is from a brochure on how employees can use statistics to improve the quality of their organization's products. The intended audience for this brochure is company employees with a high school diploma and little previous knowledge of statistics. How well does this passage communicate with its intended audience? If you believe the passage would be difficult for its intended audience, rewrite it so that it addresses its audience more appropriately.

   Quality can be best maintained by preventive action in advance of complete tool wear or predictable machine maintenance. If we check characteristics of parts on a sampling basis as they are produced, it is better than sorting through a bin of hundreds of parts looking for the defective parts and then trying to determine which parts can be salvaged.

   Collecting and analyzing data on current operations is essential in supplier and company plants. By studying the data, the causes of defects for each main quality characteristic can be investigated and determined. Appropriate solutions, including redesign or reprocessing, can be developed. Once problems are identified, a decision can be made whether to analyze past data, to collect new information, or a combination of both.

Why Will the Audience Read the Argument?

Readers can be divided into two broad groups: those who *have* to read the argument (a professor, a supervisor, etc.) and those who are free to read or not read, depending on the argument's appeal (think of the fickle magazine browsing you do in waiting rooms). As part of your preliminary consideration of audience, it pays to determine why your audience will read your argument—because they have to or because they want to?

If your readers are a captive audience—if they have no choice about reading your argument—you are not freed from making your writing interesting and engaging. In fact, the captive audience puts considerable pressure on the writer to be engaging. The professor with piles of student compositions to read, or admissions committee members with hundreds of application essays to evaluate, are likely to be bored and irritable by the time they come to your composition or essay. Knowing this, you should put more, not less, effort into getting and keeping their attention. In some cases, this may mean getting to the critical issues quickly and directly, or it may mean taking care to follow directions exactly, or putting a unique spin on your argument that will distinguish it from all the others your audience has to read.

When your audience is a purely voluntary one—readers of popular magazines, for example—they may not approach your work bored and irritable, but they are under no obligation to read further than your title if they don't find your argument interesting. Writers who write for daily or weekly periodicals are continually looking for "hooks" that will attract their readers to subjects that are already quite familiar. For example, the disarray of the airline industry has become an all-too-familiar subject for journalists in the past few years. Articles on the subject appear regularly in all varieties of magazines, newspapers, and blogs. For the topic to continue to be front-page news for a public tired of reading about—much less experiencing—the difficulties of air travel, it must be engagingly and compellingly introduced. The Sunday *New York Times* did just this in a front-page article whose opening sentence read, "Airlines are getting serious about saying they're sorry." Since there is likely a high correlation between *New York Times* readers and disgruntled air travelers, we can guess that such an opening is well-designed to capture the attention of readers.

ACTIVITIES (2.3)

The following audiences are likely either to be uninterested in or hostile to the following claims. Working with two or three students in your class, rewrite the claims, and add whatever additional sentences would help to engage audience attention. Be prepared to justify your changes to the rest of the class.

1. Parents of a college student: Tuition must be increased.
2. A social worker: Because of budget cuts, your caseload will increase.
3. An African-American woman: Affirmative action results in reverse discrimination.
4. An inner-city high school principal: Metal detectors are unconstitutional.
5. A software specialist: Our society looks at too many screens.

What Should the Audience Be Able to Do After Reading the Argument?

All arguments want something from their readers. At the very least, they want to convince their readers that the claim and its supporting material constitute a reasonable position, even though readers may not agree with it completely. Many arguments are more ambitious, looking for their readers' full agreement, which may mean changing readers' minds. The most ambitious arguments want not only full agreement from their readers, but also action taken on the basis of this full agreement. What you expect from your audience will influence the nature and extent of your supporting material as well as the overall tone of your argument.

For example, if you were trying to convince an audience that fraternity term paper files on your campus are a problem, you would argue why and to what extent they are a problem. But if you wanted your audience to take action to solve this problem, your argument would need to include specific steps to be taken, such as applying pressure on fraternity councils, setting up a more rigorous honor code for students, and encouraging faculty to change term paper assignments yearly. Including these steps means convincing your audience that they are likely to be effective: fraternity councils will monitor the problem more carefully if they are in danger of losing campus support; term paper files will be useless if assignments are not repeated from year to year; and so on. Arguments that seek to inspire the reader to action should be specific about the action proposed, show the connection between the claim and the proposed action, and convince the reader that the action will lead, or at least will probably lead, to the desired changes.

The expectations you have of your readers should also influence your argument's tone. If you want to convince gently, the tone can be mild: "Members of the International Students Club need to consider an alternative to their international banquet for raising money for travel." If you intend to exhort, the tone should be more forceful, as in Winston Churchill's famous address to the British people in their darkest days of World War II: "We shall fight on the beaches, we shall fight on the landing grounds, we shall fight in the fields and in the streets, we shall fight in the hills." If you want to command (in which case, you are no longer seeking reader agreement), you can afford to be very blunt: "No smoking is allowed in this computer room."

ACTIVITIES (2.4)

For which of the following occasions should the argument spell out the actions it wishes its readers to take? Why?

1. **Claim:** The flood of no-fat and low-fat packaged foods is turning a generation of kids into low-fat anorexics.

   Audience: High school dietitian.

2. **Claim:** Our college needs wireless computer capability.

   Audience: President or "Information" Administrator of your college.

3. **Claim:** The new mandatory bicycle helmet law is an infringement of personal liberty, depriving the citizen of his or her right of self-determination.

   Audience: Listeners of a local call-in talk show.

4. **Claim:** Bicycle helmets should be made mandatory in this state, just like motorcycle helmets.

   Audience: Your state legislature representative.

5. **Claim:** While I have had some academic difficulties over the past year, my commitment to receiving a college degree and my newfound understanding of study strategies will contribute to my eventual academic success, if only you will agree to waive my suspension.

   Audience: Dean of your college.

SUMMARY

Where Writing Begins

- Dissonance—the mismatch between the way we want life to be and the way it is—is a motive for effective arguments.

- When you write, try to write about what is important to you, expressing only those opinions you honestly believe in and avoiding pomposity.

- Before you write, consider these three questions:

  –*Who* is the audience?

  –*Why* will the audience read the argument?

  –*What* should the audience be able to do after reading the argument?

SUGGESTIONS FOR WRITING (2.5)

1. From your list of topics from the second activity in Activity (2.1) at the end of the first section of this chapter, "Motives for Writing," select one of the topics and write a two- to three-page essay proposing a solution to the problem that bothers you.

2. Write an e-mail to your parents asking them for something you know they won't want to give you—for example, a car, a charge card, or a round-trip ticket to Europe. What steps can you take to neutralize the objections you know they are going to have?

3. Examine the last report or essay you wrote, and answer the following questions: Who was your audience? Why would they read what you wrote? What did you expect them to do after they finished reading? How well does that report or essay, when viewed in light of these questions, communicate with its intended audience? What changes would you make?

4. To recognize how audience affects the tone and content of an argument, write an informal evaluation of one of your current professors for your student e-mail conference system; then write a one-page evaluation of that instructor for the instructor himself or herself.

5. Attend a lecture or speech sponsored by your college or university. Then write a letter to the speaker evaluating her or his sensitivity to the audience.

ILLUSTRATIVE ARGUMENTS IN PART II: WHERE WRITING BEGINS

3

The Claim

You've discovered a subject and motive for your argument, and you've considered some key questions about your audience. Now you are ready to begin focusing your argument. Focusing—clearly defining the center and extent of your argument—occurs throughout the writing process, from discovering a motive to revising a final draft. This chapter concerns an early and critical stage in the focusing process: formulating, modifying, and positioning your argument's claim.

While some writers compose their claims before they begin writing, others let their claims evolve during an exploratory first draft, clarifying and modifying as they write. You can experiment with the sequence that works best for you, but regardless of how and when you reach your claim, your argument is not focused until you can summarize its principal point within a few sentences.

HOW CLAIMS WORK

An argument's claim is a short summary of its central point or points. All arguments have at least one claim; some longer arguments have more than one. Usually, the claim is stated directly, but sometimes, it is only implied by its supporting material. Regardless of where and whether it appears in an argument, the claim shapes and moves the argument, giving it structure and energy.

Claims can be short and tightly packed, as in the statement "America's youth are entirely apolitical," or they can be long and intricate, reflecting the argument's structure as well as its main points: "Because a capitalist system rewards aggressiveness, competitiveness, and intelligence, it is an almost perfect economic extension of Darwinism. In a capitalist society, the 'fittest' get rich; the unfit stay poor."

Crystal-clear claims are extremely useful to readers. All readers, whatever their levels of interest, knowledge, and intelligence, approach an unfamiliar manuscript clueless about its content and direction. An unequivocal, succinct statement of an argument's chief point or points alerts them to the argument's goal and prepares them to understand the relationship between the parts and the whole.

Good claims also help readers evaluate an argument. Knowing the proposition to be argued, they are equipped to judge how successfully it has been made. In the last two sentences of the introductory chapter of *Bowling Alone,* Robert Putnam succinctly announces the claim of his 513-page book: ". . . we Americans need to reconnect with one another. That is the simple argument of this book."[1] Not only is this explicit claim statement reassuringly clear and simple at the introduction of a long and scholarly book, it also provides a benchmark against which readers can judge the supporting argument.

While claims can be discovered or changed at virtually any point in the writing process, you will probably find that formulating a tentative working claim early in the process is quite helpful. Such a preliminary claim will help you to determine the kinds of supporting evidence you will need, will guide your argument's organization and direction, and will keep you from darting off on tangents.

Finding a Claim

Many student writers are insecure about their ability to come up with a position worth arguing. But even experienced, mature writers with a wealth of experience and opinions often have to work to find a claim. For inexperienced and experienced writers alike, claims tend to evolve gradually from reading and thinking (at both the conscious and the unconscious levels) about the subject or from personal discomfort with a particular situation or issue.

On occasion, however, the process of developing a claim can be short-circuited. In many college classes, particularly introductory ones, claims are actually assigned. Students in English composition courses, for example, are often assigned a particular thesis (claim) to develop ("Write a two-page essay supporting your view of the effectiveness of student orientation at this college"). And essay exams offer students at least the foundation of a claim. For example, the question "Was dropping the atom bomb in 1945 on Hiroshima and Nagasaki necessary to achieve Japan's surrender? Support your answer with specific reasons" dictates the form, though not the content, of the claim that will begin the essay: "Dropping the bomb was/was not necessary, for the following reasons."

And some writers do come to their work with their main point firmly in mind. But what usually happens to these seemingly lucky folks is that this main point gets modified, changed, and sometimes even reversed as they go about the business of developing and supporting it. And this is as it should be; clinging to a claim that clearly needs modifying can doom an argument at the outset. So if you find yourself passionately attached to a particular position at the beginning of the writing process, try to treat that position as a starting point, a tentative claim that will guide your research and thinking, not a commandment set in stone.

[1]Robert D. Putnam, *Bowling Alone: The Collapse and Revival of American Community.* New York: Simon and Schuster, 2000, p. 28.

Some assignment topics cause problems because they are too vague. A literature student assigned a fifteen-page analysis of the early poetry of William Wordsworth will set out with little focus or sense of direction. A new employee asked to evaluate the product quality and cost-effectiveness of a particular supplier would probably be equally adrift.

How do such writers move from vague assignments like these to working claims that will give the developing argument some direction and discipline? There are many answers to this question, because coming up with a claim— indeed, the entire writing process—is a highly idiosyncratic business. Some writers logically deduce claims from the evidence, in Sherlock Holmes fashion, whereas others discover them unexpectedly while daydreaming or jogging or listening to music. Claims can be slowly and painfully dredged from the earth, or they can come like lightning from the sky.

When you find yourself doing more dredging than you'd like, consider the following suggestions:

1. Don't press to arrive at a claim prematurely. More time is wasted following up a forced, dead-end claim that eventually has to be scrapped than in thinking, reading, and taking notes as preparation for deciding exactly what your position is going to be.

2. Instead of rushing the claim during the preliminary research phase (and research can mean nothing more than tapping the contents of your own brain without ever opening a book), concentrate on gradually narrowing your topic. For example, if you're preparing to write a paper on the poetry of Wordsworth, your reading and thinking might lead you originally (and accidentally) in the direction of thematic content, then to the narrower concern of images of nature, then still more narrowly to the recollection of nature as an inspiration to poetry. By the time you have gathered material on this focused subject, you will not be far from imposing a particular point of view on the subject. This point of view on a focused topic will be your claim, which might be something like "Wordsworth as a poet was inspired by nature, but nature sifted through memory, not nature as it is immediately perceived." While you may have accumulated a lot of seemingly useless notes along the way, you should be saved the agony of distorting your paper to fit an unworkable claim you have discovered with too little consideration. As you are closing in on a claim, keep in mind that good claims are rarely too narrow, and that poor ones are often too broad.

3. In the early stages of writing, don't spend too much time polishing and refining your claim. At this stage, a claim needs a narrow topic and the expression of a definite attitude toward that topic. A good working claim could be no more than "Smoking in public places is harmful to everyone." Later, after the first draft, you can refine and shine, adding a summary of supporting reasons if necessary.

4. Today's computer technology offers valuable tools for narrowing a broad topic to a focused position. Most libraries have moved their card catalogs to computer databases and are now adding electronic catalogs and major bibliographic indexes stored in electronic format. You will probably also have access to the

Internet, which contains not only databases, but huge volumes of information in various forms. (Chapter 5 will discuss resource materials and steps to help evaluate credible sources.) Whether we are looking for books or articles, we get at the information we want through *keywords* or *descriptors*—words or brief phrases that describe our subject. Searching for information by keyword can give you good ideas for narrowing your topic.

Say you're planning to write an evaluative essay on the films based on Stephen King's books, and you search several film indexes (e.g., *Film Research: A Critical Bibliography* or *Film Review Annual*), using *King, Stephen* as your descriptor. You get close to a hundred "hits" through this search, and you notice that many of the sources have to do with King's novels as well as his films. You become interested in the whole question of adaptation, so you search other film indexes using narrower descriptors like *King, Stephen, and adaptations* or, even more narrowly, *The Shining*. Through this early search for sources, you have imposed considerably more focus on your initial, broad topic—a focus that would soon lead to a working claim like "The true genius of Stephen King is in his ability to adapt the printed page to the medium of film."

Keeping Your Working Claim Flexible

As you proceed with a rough draft that works from a tentative claim, you may discover that the preliminary claim needs modification. Perhaps the thinking and research you have done on the subject have made you realize that your claim does not apply as widely as you thought, and that there are significant exceptions to your position. Be flexible enough to accept these discoveries and change your claim accordingly. Writing is not simply the recording of previously established thoughts but also a way of clarifying your thoughts, of discovering if what you meant to say can be said in a coherent and defensible way. If possible, take advantage of the guidance offered by a thoughtful claim, while remaining open to those discoveries to which writing and thinking can lead you.

Let's say you begin the composition process with a claim that arises fairly easily out of your own strong opinions about the issue of affirmative action. Your preliminary or working claim is "Jobs should be given to the most qualified applicant, not to the most qualified minority applicant. To reject the best candidate on the grounds of his or her majority status is unjust and inequitable." This claim statement not only summarizes your position toward affirmative action but also points to the main support for that position—that affirmative action is unjust and inequitable. In order to argue this evaluative claim convincingly, to convince your audience that one's minority or majority status is irrelevant to considerations of merit, you will need to demonstrate the injustices of affirmative action.

So far, so good. Even though you aren't personally aware of a wide range of cases, it should be easy to come up with examples of the basic unfairness of affirmative action. In the course of your reading, however, you keep coming up against the stubborn argument that majority candidates are often more qualified for jobs and educational opportunities because they are more educationally and economically privileged than members of minority groups. To reward the most qualified, this argument continues, is to perpetuate this tradition of unequal opportunity. You find this position persuasive and reasonable, though it doesn't change your central view that qualifications, not race, should determine one's success in the job market. Gradually, you realize that this is a more complicated issue than you had recognized; a hard-line position is not completely defensible.

You consider ignoring the counterargument and sticking to your original claim, but you conclude that your argument will actually be stronger if it reflects the ethical complexity of the issue and your awareness of the unfair advantage long given to the majority group. So you rewrite your working claim to read:

> In the United States, all men (and women) may be *created* equal, but for many, that birthright of equality is fleeting at best. Few would argue that, where women and minorities are concerned, inequality in economic and educational opportunity has been our national tradition. The affirmative action legislation of the 1960s was designed to redress the harms resulting from this indefensible tradition. Impeccable in its intent, affirmative action has been problematic in application: hiring on the basis of race and gender with secondary consideration to qualifications does not solve the problem of inequity; it merely changes the victims.

This new working claim is richer and more balanced than the first, reflecting your new understanding of the issue as well as your continuing disagreement with affirmative action laws.

The primary lesson to be learned from this example is that working claims should be seen as starting points, not as immutable conclusions; the thinking and writing processes will inevitably influence the starting point of an argument, shaping and modifying and in some cases even reversing the original position. Your final argument will benefit if you remain flexible about the original claim; always be prepared to alter it in the face of contrary evidence or new ideas.

ACTIVITIES (3.1)

1. With a small group of your classmates, select three of the following topics to work with. For each selected topic, work together to narrow the topic to one that could be written about in a seven- to ten-page essay. From this narrower topic, derive a working claim for this paper. Remember that the working claim is the claim with which you would begin to write the essay, though it might be refined or changed as you write.

   Example topic: The risks of cigarette smoking.
   Narrower topic: The health effects of cigarette smoking in public places.
   Working claim: Cigarette smoking in public places is harmful to everyone.
   a. Japanese automobiles
   b. Social security
   c. Women's rights
   d. College education
   e. Television
   f. Unemployment

g. Presidential elections
h. New York City
i. Careers
j. Popular music

2. With one of your classmates, agree on a very broad topic of interest to you both, for example, professional basketball, computer games, or a certain actor. Then conduct independent computer searches on the subject, progressively focusing it (and focusing your keywords) as you get a sense of the information available. When you have reached a focused topic that could be argued about in a five-page paper, compare that topic with your classmate's. How similar or different are the two? Retrace the evolution of your keywords for each other.

Positioning the Claim

Another important decision you'll have to make about your claim is where to place it in your argument. You can make this decision before, during, or even after your first draft, but whenever you make it, it's one that requires careful thought. Different placements will have different effects on your audience, in some cases influencing their ultimate acceptance of your argument. As long as you base your decision on audience consideration and the intended function of the claim, you can put the claim almost anywhere. There are two main points to consider in positioning your claim: first, what is the function of your claim? second, what is your audience's probable disposition toward your argument?

Claim Stated Up Front

Stating your claim within the first couple of paragraphs makes sense

- if your argument is complicated or the subject matter is unfamiliar to readers (an up-front claim will let your readers know what's coming)
- if your audience is likely to be comfortable with your argument (so that its claim will not alienate them at the outset)
- if your claim is particularly engaging, curious, or intriguing (an up-front claim will lure readers into your argument)

The following excerpt from an article on fund-raising in higher education, where the claim (in italics) appears after a brief introduction, illustrates the second and third of these conditions. Readers of the *New York Times* (where this article appeared) are not likely to object to the article's claim, though they may be intrigued by the argument's redefinition of the traditional practice of fund-raising.

As the last mortarboards are flung like Frisbees into the air and the last speaker winds up a peroration on endings and beginnings, at least one campus office marches on into summer on an unending mission: raising money.

The task is ancient but the tools get more modern all the time. Colleges and universities, long seen as aloof from the commercial crush of life, are increasingly willing to pull out all the stops in getting alumni to give.

It's still called fund-raising—or development or even institutional advancement. But it's getting to look a lot like marketing. ("Some Schools Won't Take No for an Answer," Janny Scott, the *New York Times,* June 19, 1994, section E, p. 3; emphasis added)

Claim Stated at the End of the Argument

Delaying your claim until the end of the argument can be effective

- when your audience may find the claim objectionable (readers who accept a claim's support as reasonable before they know precisely what the claim is may be less hostile to that claim once it is stated)
- when your evidence builds directly and inevitably toward your claim, which can then serve as your argument's conclusion

Let's say you write for your school newspaper. An example of the first instance would be your editorial recommending stricter enforcement of quiet hours in the dorm—a position that may not be welcome to all student readers. In this case, you can first present all the problems associated with the nightly bedlam in the dorms. Once you have established the seriousness of the problem, you can conclude the argument with your recommendation for stricter quiet hours. Having been convinced of the seriousness of the problems, your readers will be more likely to accept the final claim as necessary and logical.

Or to exemplify the second case, if you were reviewing a film for your newspaper, you might choose to describe various elements of the film first—acting, plot, cinematography—before summarizing these remarks with the inevitable statement of the central claim: "Find the time to see this film."

Unstated Claim in an Argument

You may choose to omit an explicit statement of your claim in situations like the following:

- when your readers will see red at your claim (because it is so bold or so objectionable) regardless of where you place it
- when the claim is very, very obvious
- when stating your claim will oversimplify your argument
- when stating your claim will break the momentum or shape of your argument

A wise mother might use this strategy in a letter counseling her college-age son to hit the books. She knows that outright directions won't work, but she might tell a story that implicitly makes her point—a story about an uncle who frittered away his college opportunities and always regretted it. She does not end her letter with the point "Don't be like Uncle Jake"; that would be too obvious, too heavy-handed. Instead, she lets her narrative speak for itself.

A word of caution, however, about omitting claims: make sure that you have a very good reason for using this tactic, and that the point or points of your argument are absolutely clear without being stated.

ACTIVITIES (3.2)

1. Read the following essays included at the end of Chapters 8 and 10: "I, Too, Am a Good Parent" (8); and "The Side Effects of Affirmative Action" (10). In a discussion with three or four classmates, identify the central claims and consider the reasons for their placement in each essay.

CLASSIFYING YOUR CLAIM

Once you have come up with a claim—even a tentative one—you'll need to identify the class it belongs to. Knowing at the outset of a first draft that you are working with a factual, causal, or evaluative claim or with a recommendation will simplify the gathering and presentation of support, since each class uses different kinds and arrangements of support. Recognizing your claim's class requires familiarity with the characteristics and functions of each class. The following section offers a full discussion of the different categories and examples of claims from each.

Factual Claims

The purpose of *factual claims* is to convince an audience that a certain statement is factual—that a given condition or phenomenon exists or has existed. The fact can be as basic as "Despite appearances, the sun is the center of our solar system, not the earth," or as unfamiliar as "In 2006, 32,533,974 people flew in and out of Miami International Airport." Writers of arguments introduced by factual claims attempt to convince their readers that their claims are true, although perhaps not true forever and under all circumstances (in the Middle Ages it was a "fact" that the earth was the center of the solar system).

Perhaps you find the idea of arguing facts a contradiction in terms; to you, facts are unchanging statements about reality, not provisional statements requiring support and verification. If it's a fact, why argue it? But a statement becomes factual only if it is accompanied by evidence that makes it extremely probable to its particular audience. Because facts become the cornerstones of so much of what we know and expect of the world, we cannot afford to accept them on faith. In short, factual claims must be supported carefully.

Facts are crucial to argument; indeed, it is hard to imagine an argument succeeding if it doesn't include some facts. In the arguments you write in college and beyond, facts will play three roles:

1. They will sometimes appear as an argument's central claim, as in a laboratory report claiming that "The addition of sulfur to the compound created sulfuric acid."
2. They will function as support for other claims. A general claim such as "All the teachers in the Child's Play Day Care Center have experience working with preschool children" would be supported by facts about the specific experience of each teacher.

3. They will serve as examples or illustrations of difficult, unfamiliar, or abstract ideas. Suppose you're writing an essay on photosynthesis for an audience unfamiliar with the process. You might follow the scientific definition of the term ("the formation of carbohydrates in living plants from water and carbon dioxide, by the action of sunlight on the chlorophyll"—*Webster's New World Dictionary*) by the more familiar description of the yearly cycle of a cherry tree.

The four types of facts that will figure most commonly in your arguments are (1) common knowledge facts, (2) personally experienced facts, (3) facts reported by others, and (4) factual generalizations.

1. **Common knowledge facts** are so widely acknowledged as true that they require no support or proof beyond mere statement.

   Examples: Men cannot bear children.

   Opposite poles attract.

2. **Personally experienced facts** are the events, observations, and conditions that you have personally experienced.

   Example: I have taken countless history courses in my life, and I have never had a teacher who excited me about the subject.

3. **Facts reported by others** are those that you have learned from second-or third-party sources. A second-party source is the person who ascertained the fact. A third-party source is the person or document reporting facts ascertained by someone else.

   Examples: "The 'man shortage' and the 'infertility epidemic' are not the price of [women's] liberation; in fact, they do not even exist" (Susan Faludi, *Backlash,* xviii; second-party source).

   "The mental health data . . . are consistent and overwhelming: The suicide rate of single men is twice as high as that of married men" (Faludi, 17; third-party source).

4. **Factual generalizations** claim that an assertion is true for a large number of subjects or over a long period of time. Factual generalizations can be common knowledge facts, personally experienced facts, or facts reported by others.

   Examples: Most of my friends are interested in sports.

   In 2005, 42% of those Americans who lived alone were male, (Infoplease, http://www.infoplease.com/ipa/A0005050.html. Consulted March 18, 2007.)

All factual claims are stated as definite and unequivocal assertions, as in the following examples:

- New York City is the banking center of the United States. (The claim makes a quantifiable assertion that can be verified by a survey of the number of banks and banking transactions in major American cities.)

- Our solar system is approximately five billion years old. (While no individual can verify this claim through firsthand experience or knowledge, it represents the consensus of experts on the subject and can be documented in this way.)
- Steel radial tires last longer than tires made with nylon. (Again, this claim can be verified, though the process may be tedious and time-consuming.)
- Most of my friends are involved in intramural sports. (A statement of fact that can be supported, if necessary, by a listing of the number of friends who are involved and not involved in intramural sports.)

ACTIVITIES (3.3)

1. For each of the factual propositions in the following list, identify the category or categories of fact (common knowledge, personal experience, second- or third-party, generalization) in which the proposition belongs.

   Example: The Cuban Missile Crisis occurred in October of 1962. Second- or third-party for most students; personal experience for older people.
   a. The disappearance of former Teamsters Union leader Jimmy Hoffa is still unexplained.
   b. The risk of getting cancer is decreased by a high-fiber diet.
   c. My communications professor routinely missed her 8:00 class.
   d. Alaska is the largest state in the United States.
   e. An apple a day keeps the doctor away.
   f. I get better grades on the papers I take the time to revise.
   g. Severe air pollution is dangerous for people suffering from lung disease.
   h. Women under age 30 have better driving records than men under age 30.
   i. In Italy, people take more time to enjoy life than we do in the United States.

Causal Claims

Causal claims propose a causal connection between two events or conditions. They can argue that A caused B or, more speculatively, that A may cause B at some future time. Statements such as "The violence represented in movies and television has numbed us to the horrors of violence in the real world" or "High consumer spending will lead to greater inflation" are examples of causal claims.

It is human nature to be curious about cause. We watch the careers of prominent public figures and wonder about the reasons for their spectacular successes and failures. We reflect on a tragedy like the Holocaust and demand to know how such a thing could happen. We look for the reasons behind events to assure ourselves that the world is governed by certain rules, not merely by random chance. We also learn by discovering cause. Knowing what causes higher automobile accidents involving specific vehicles gives us a reasonable chance of preventing similar events in the future. And you can be sure that business entrepreneurs will do whatever they can to reproduce those factors that led to Bill Gates's phenomenal financial success.

Just as we are given to discovering cause, we are also fascinated by predicting *effects*. Stockbrokers must be skilled in this form of causal argument, as they try to enhance the interests of their clients by predicting market activity. Doctors practicing *preventive* medicine are also in the business of predicting probable effects: they tell their patients to reduce dietary fat in order to prevent a future heart attack, or to exercise regularly to maintain bone density. And in business and industry, the long-term health of a corporation often depends on the accurate prediction of future trends. Eastman Kodak, for example, with its enormously successful business of traditional photographic products, had to determine the probable future of those products in the face of electronic imaging.

Under carefully controlled scientific conditions, it is possible to identify cause and even to predict effect with so much certainty that the causality can be established as *factual*. Researchers have determined that smoking increases the risk of lung cancer and that lobar pneumonia is caused by pneumococcus bacteria. But in the causal arguments that most of us make, arguments concerning human behavior—our actions, our successes and failures, our relations with others—certainty is impossible to reach. In these more speculative arguments, the best we can hope for is to establish *probable* cause or effect convincingly.

But because a claim cannot be proven with certainty doesn't mean it isn't worth arguing; if we always waited for certainty before acting, our progress would be slow. An argument that establishes probable cause or effect *can* be a reasonable basis for decisions or actions. In fact, probability is the goal of most of the arguments we write. But even probability isn't easy to achieve; in many cases, it calls for more skill than establishing certainty in factual arguments.

Causal claims are easy to spot because they (1) often contain words indicating causality—*cause, produce, effect, consequence*—and/or (2) involve the relationship between two phenomena occurring at different points in time. The following are examples of causal claims:

- According to social critic Neil Postman, technology is causing the surrender of American culture. (The word *caused* is a dead giveaway of a causal argument.)
- If Sally had written a better résumé, she might have landed that job. (An early event—Sally's poor résumé—caused a later one, her failure to land the job.)
- A balanced budget promises a stable government. (The claim proposes a close causal relationship between a balanced budget and a stable government. The verb *promises* indicates cause.)
- Increasing numbers of two-career families have contributed to the rising divorce rate. (*Contributed to* suggests a causal relationship between the two facts.)

ACTIVITIES (3.4)

1. Look back at the distinction between factual and probable causes. For which of the following causal claims could you establish a factual cause—one that

few people would dispute? For which could you establish only a probable cause—one for which you would have to argue?

a. If Abraham Lincoln had not been assassinated, he could have lessened the bitterness between the North and the South after the war.

b. The widespread use of computers in business and industry will increase total employment, not decrease it.

c. If it had not snowed, Ohio State could have defeated Michigan in that football game.

d. In most automobiles, failure to change the oil at regular intervals will damage the engine.

e. The decline in the percentage of the population attending organized religious activities has caused the rise in the crime rate in the past forty years.

f. The use of seat belts decreases the number of fatalities in automobile accidents.

g. If newlyweds had more realistic expectations about marriage, there would be a decline in the divorce rate.

h. The children of the affluent would be happier if they had to do more for themselves.

i. Some cold medicines cause drowsiness.

j. The existence of nuclear weapons has prevented the outbreak of World War III.

2. Write a claim for a causal argument for one of the following; then make a list of all the reasons you can think of that would convince a reader of the cause or effect you identify. Describe these reasons in a paragraph.

a. The cause of a particular war

b. A team's victory or loss in a certain game

c. A change in some aspect of the government's social or economic policy

d. A change in exercise or dietary behavior

e. The cause of a person's career success or failure

Example of (c): "There would be fewer homeless people if the federal government increased its aid to cities."

Reasons: Money could be used for low-income housing. Money could be used for training programs that would give the poor a means of self-support. Other countries that give substantial aid to cities do not have the problem with the homeless that we do.

Evaluations

When we argue an evaluation, we are proposing our personal judgment of the value of a work of art, a policy, a person, an action, even another evaluation. No doubt you often find yourself making informal pronouncements of personal taste: "Your tie is ugly," "That restaurant serves the best chicken wings in town," "I enjoy playing basketball more than playing tennis." These pronouncements are so purely subjective, so clearly a matter of personal preference, that there is little point in trying to argue them reasonably. We are all inclined to pass judgment on what we observe, and frequently we don't much care whether these judgments are taken seriously.

But sometimes we do care about the impact of these judgments; sometimes we want our opinions to influence others. In these cases, we must understand how to argue judgments of value. And many value judgments, even those originating as unconsidered personal opinion, *can* be convincingly argued. Claims such as "Pornography is an offense to all women" or "The government was mistaken in trading weapons for hostages," if they are serious, carefully considered judgments, can be developed into meaningful arguments.

Evaluations are probably the hardest of all arguments to argue successfully. Not only do they originate in the writer's personal value system, they also speak to his or her readers' equally personal, passionately held, and often unexamined values. Changing someone's mind about an opinion or judgment is an uphill struggle, so your goals in arguing evaluations should be rather modest: to gain your audience's sympathy toward a conclusion that you have reached through responsible and reasonable evidence rather than to change the mind of everyone who reads your argument.

An important variant of the evaluative claim is the *interpretive* claim. Interpretations are *explanatory* evaluations of a person, event, or object: "Dreams of beautiful gardens often suggest a state of profound satisfaction in the dreamer" or "Will's domineering and self-centered style is an expression of his profound insecurity." Neither of these examples is simply factual or descriptive; each reveals something unexpected beneath the visible surface of behavior. Interpretive claims surpass mere opinion only when they are supported by facts and reasoned argument. Reasonable, intelligent people may differ in their interpretation of a person or a situation, but not all interpretations are equally plausible or illuminating. To argue, for example, that Hamlet's actions are the symptoms of gout, when there is no evidence to support that view, is an example of poor interpretation.

The following statements are examples of claims introducing evaluative arguments:

- Many people do not realize that Herman Melville, the author of *Moby Dick,* was also an accomplished poet. (Evaluative claims often contain descriptive modifiers, like *accomplished* in this example.)
- Former president Jimmy Carter may not have been a great president, but he was an honorable one.
- Mary's constant chatter is an attempt to keep people from abandoning her. (An interpretive claim, in that it offers a beneath-the-surface explanation of Mary's behavior. Like many interpretive claims, this one contains causal elements, but what distinguishes it as primarily interpretive is the identification of a *coincidence* between visible and hidden phenomena.)
- For my money, soccer players are the most gifted of all athletes. (*Gifted* is a subjective term: it not only means different things to different people, but it also cannot be conclusively verified. Claims including superlative or comparative adjectives are likely to be evaluative claims.)
- "Human memory is a marvelous but fallacious instrument." (Primo Levi, *The Drowned and the Saved.*) (This claim makes two judgments about memory.)

ACTIVITIES (3.5)

1. Write claims for evaluative arguments for the following subjects.

   Example subject: Theft of library books
   Example claim: Stealing library books is not only a criminal act; it is a serious trespass against the ideals of community.
   a. Political campaign spending
   b. Computer games
   c. Pass-fail grading
   d. A particular television show
   e. Distance Learning courses
   f. Your composition instructor
   g. Rap music
   h. Television sports coverage

2. Give an example of an interpretive claim for the following topics.

   Example of topic (a): The cinematic revival of Shakespeare is an expression of *fin de siècle* anxiety.
   a. The significance of a play, movie, or short story
   b. The importance of a contemporary political figure
   c. The meaning of a current trend in fashion
   d. The attitude of students at your college toward their future careers
   e. The attitude of young Americans toward religion

Recommendations

A common goal of argument is to convince an audience that existing circumstances need to be changed. Some *recommendations* seek only to gain an audience's agreement with an idea or a decision, but others have a more practical (and ambitious) purpose: they try to convince their audience to take a particular action or, more modestly, to convince an audience that a particular action should be taken by others. As a student in English composition, you might write a paper for your instructor arguing that the legal drinking age should be lowered, or you might make that same argument in a letter to your congressional representative with the hope of getting him or her to take action. A lab technician might write a memo to her supervisor suggesting the purchase of new equipment. Or the chairperson of the history department might write to the dean requesting an adjustment in faculty salaries. All of these arguments would be recommendations.

All recommendations are concerned with the future, with what should be done at a later time, but they also imply a judgment about present conditions. Writers propose change because of dissatisfaction with an existing situation. Early in arguing a recommendation, you'll need to determine whether you want to concentrate on the current problem or on the improvements resulting from your recommendation; in some recommendations, you'll emphasize both.

- The main goal of recommendations emphasizing *present* conditions is to demonstrate the problems in the current situation. Because these recommendations argue *that* something needs to be done rather than *what* exactly that something is, they usually don't discuss a proposed change in any detail.

- The main goal of recommendations emphasizing the *future* is to present a plan for change and to demonstrate that it is feasible and likely to produce the desired effects.
- Recommendations with *equal* emphasis on present and future argue the problems of the current situation *and* the likely effects of the proposed change.

You may have noticed that recommendations are hybrid, or combination, claims with elements of both causal and evaluative arguments. That is exactly right. When proposing that an existing situation be changed, you are at least implying a negative judgment of that situation. And implied in the changes you recommend is a positive evaluation of those changes. Furthermore, you will support the recommendation itself through an argument of effect—demonstrating the positive future effects of the change.

Because arguments of recommendation argue for an action not currently in effect, words such as *should, would, must, ought, needs to be, will* or *might* typically introduce these arguments. The following are some sample claims for arguments of recommendation:

- We need more emphasis on science and math in our schools to prepare the next generation for a world of international economic competition. (The claim proposes a *change* in the current curriculum.)
- In order to attract more nontraditional students, this university must review and revise its course offerings. (Again, this claim calls for a change in an existing situation—a change that will have positive effects in the future.)
- If this company is to regain financial health, it must divest itself of all divisions not directly connected to its traditional core business. (The words *must divest* identify this claim as a recommendation—a suggestion for a particular action is being made.)
- Take back the night. (A trenchant recommendation expressed in the imperative mode. In the word *back*, the command implies making a change in an existing situation.)

ACTIVITIES (3.6)

1. For the following situations, write two claims of recommendation, one focusing on current conditions and one on the results of recommended improvements.

   Example: Taking a keyboarding course
   Claim with a focus on current conditions: I need to take a keyboarding course because I can't use the word processor required in my English composition course.

Claim with a focus on future improvements: I need to take a keyboarding course so that I will be ready for the day when every office has its own computer.
   a. Replacing a television
   b. Requesting a new strict policy on noise in a dormitory
   c. Advocating a freeze on the research for and manufacturing of nuclear weapons
   d. Purchasing a new car to replace your or your family's current one
   e. Increasing the number of police in the most dangerous sections of a city

2. Read the two recommendations at the end of Chapter 10. As you read, consider whether these recommendations emphasize the present, the future, or both. See how well your ideas match up with those of a group of your classmates.

Combination Claims

A brief look at any essay anthology may persuade you that "real" claims in "real" arguments don't always fit neatly into the four categories presented in this chapter. But your experience of writing *and* reading arguments will persuade you that all arguments contain claims that fulfill one or more of these four functions.

In some cases, you will need to recast claims mentally to decide what kinds of arguments they are. For example, the famous claim "The only thing we have to fear is fear itself," which is a forceful, lively claim needing no revision, can be translated to mean "We should beware of the dangers of fear"—a recommendation based on an argument of effect identifying the negative consequences of fear. The claim itself need not be rewritten; having identified the category of the recast version of the claim, you can proceed to support the original claim.

Often, as the preceding example demonstrates, the context of a claim will help you categorize it. This quotation about fear is taken from President Franklin Delano Roosevelt's first inaugural address in 1933, during the heart of the Great Depression, when fear about the future pervaded America. In this context, Roosevelt's remark is part of a broad recommendation to the American people to regain their confidence and to begin to plan for the future with new hope. In a less urgent context, "The only thing we have to fear is fear itself" might be a causal claim meaning "The experience of fear is dangerous because it builds on itself."

If you are arguing a claim that doesn't seem to fit into any of the categories discussed here, and you can't seem to recast it mentally, ask yourself some questions about the function of the argument that will support the claim. For example, is the claim verifiable? If not, it is not factual. Does it make an unverifiable judgment about something or someone? If so, it is probably evaluative. Does it propose a course of action? If so, it is a recommendation. Does it account for or predict a particular phenomenon? Then it is a causal argument.

Some claims actually contain two propositions to be argued, as in the sentence "Acts of terrorism are serious offenses against human freedom and should meet with deadly retaliation." The first claim is the *evaluation* that acts of terrorism are serious offenses, and the second is the *recommendation* that they should meet with deadly retaliation. In supporting this double claim, you would have to defend the value judgment about terrorism before moving on to the second assertion, the recommendation. Ideally, both claims should be defended, though writers frequently assume that their audience agrees with them on the most basic points—that terrorism is abhorrent, for example—and concentrate on one or two more arguable points, such as the need for deadly retaliation.

While space constraints may require this kind of corner cutting, be careful not to assume too much about your audience's position. A writer dealing with the controversial topic of terrorism should at least *consider* whether terrorism is always completely unjustified, even if she doesn't address this question in her essay.

Often, a factual claim is combined with one of the other three kinds of claims. When this is the case, as in the statement "The rise in the divorce rate in the last 30 years may increase the divorce rate in the next generation," you must establish the accuracy of your facts (the rise in the divorce rate) before you go on to speculate about the possible effects of this fact. So, too, with the statement "The flight of business and industry from the Northeast to the Sun Belt will eventually have a damaging effect on the quality of public education in the Northeast." First, the flight of business and industry must be established as a fact, probably through outside research; then the long-term causal argument can be made.

The following are examples of combination claims:

- The recent rise in interest rates may contribute to higher inflation. (This statement combines a factual assertion about rising interest rates, which can very quickly be supported, with a causal argument predicting the effect of the higher rates. This second claim would be the focus of your argument.)
- No nation is truly free that does not offer its citizens equal opportunity in education and employment. (This statement combines a causal argument—lack of equal opportunity results in an unfree nation—with an evaluation judging the degree of a nation's freedom.)
- If the candidate wants to win votes, he must convince constituents that his reputation for moral laxness is undeserved. (This statement combines a recommendation that the candidate make his case to his constituents and a causal argument that making this case will win him their votes.)
- While men seem to be driven to success by a fear of failure, women are made comfortable with failure by their fear of success. (This breathtaking generalization combines interpretation—identifying hidden motives for behavior—with elements of a factual argument. The writer will have to present *many* instances of these gender-linked phenomena in order to warrant the generality of the claim.)

ACTIVITIES (3.7)

Into which of the four main argument types or combination of types do the following belong? Be prepared to support your answer.

Example: Automobiles should be designed so that they get a minimum of 30 miles per gallon of gasoline.

Type of argument: Recommendation
1. Excessive consumption of alcohol can lead to many illnesses.
2. Honesty is the best policy.
3. Cutting defense spending will create a safer world.
4. Tariffs on imports merely raise prices for domestic consumers.
5. Alley cats are a public nuisance in this neighborhood.
6. Politics is the art of the possible.
7. An improved sewer system would solve these flood drainage problems.
8. America should protect its domestic industries with tariffs and quotas.
9. Without a belief in God, life has no meaning.
10. Obesity can help cause heart disease.

SUMMARY

The Claim

- Claims help readers to understand and evaluate arguments, and they help you, the writer, to generate the direction and content of your arguments.

- If you have difficulty coming up with a working claim, you probably need to do more thinking and reading about your topic. When you are knowledgeable enough, a claim should come to you.

- Always be prepared to modify a working claim to fit with new ideas and information.

- Claims can be placed virtually anywhere in an argument. The most effective placement depends on the nature of your argument and its probable reception by your readers.

- *Factual claims* seek to convince an audience that a given object or condition exists or has existed. The four kinds of facts are common knowledge facts, facts experienced by you, facts reported by others, and factual generalizations.

- *Causal claims* assert that one event or condition produces or helps to produce another event or condition. In claiming *cause,* we look for what produced a past or current event or condition. In claiming *effect,* we predict a future occurrence on the basis of certain current or intended circumstances.

- *Evaluations* make a value judgment of a person, activity, or object.

- *Recommendations* argue for a particular course of action in order to change existing circumstances. Recommendations can focus on present conditions, future effects, or a combination of both.

- Some arguments work from claims that combine elements of the four classes.

SUGGESTIONS FOR WRITING (3.8)

1. Read an argumentative essay (hardcopy or online) in a magazine like the *Atlantic Monthly* or the *New York Times Magazine*, and write a one- to two-page essay on what kind of argument it is and why. Be sure to give your instructor a copy of the argumentative essay you are analyzing.

2. Select a familiar document, such as Martin Luther King, Jr.'s "I Have a Dream" speech, Lincoln's Gettysburg Address, the Declaration of Independence, or a famous Shakespearean soliloquy, and identify the class or classes of argument it represents. In a one- to two-page letter to your instructor, support your identification. (Texts of each of the suggested sample documents are available online.) Be sure to give your instructor a copy of the document you are analyzing.

3. Find the lyrics to your favorite song, probably available online, and determine whether or not an argument exists. Support your reasoning in an e-mail message to one of your classmates. Be sure to provide your instructor with both a copy of the lyrics and your response.

ILLUSTRATIVE ARGUMENTS IN PART II: THE CLAIM

4

An Argument's Support

Now that you have a working claim and a good idea about the kind of argument it summarizes, you are ready to begin supporting that claim. The body of your argument, the material that will convert your claim into a conclusion, is your presentation of support. Broadly defined, an argument's support is all the material you insert into your argument to strengthen the probability (and in some cases, truth) of your claim. To argue your claim successfully, you must know how to select appropriate support for your particular claim, how to determine how much support is necessary, and how to arrange that support in the most convincing way.

Once you have a working claim, you will probably find that you have some ideas for supporting it. The more your claim emerges from your experience of dissonance and from your own interests, the more likely you are to have solid support ready at hand, though you will have to do *some* research on even the most familiar topics. On the other hand, regardless of how much research goes into them, claims having no connection with your own experiences, interest, or knowledge will be more difficult to support.

Let's say that you are worried about your grandmother, who, although healthy, is growing increasingly depressed and withdrawn. You know from talking with her that she feels useless, ignored, and aimless. Your concern makes you angry about the way our society treats its older citizens, and you decide to let this concern and anger fuel an argument about age discrimination. Your grandmother's experience has given you a number of specific examples of age discrimination and its effects. Some of these examples will help to support the claim "American society, for all its public attention to human rights, is guilty of systematically depriving its senior citizens of countless 'inalienable' rights." But you know that in order to argue such a far-reaching claim convincingly, you will need to find support beyond your personal observations.

Since different classes of arguments often require different kinds of support, knowing the class of argument that your claim belongs to will help you know what kinds of additional support to look for. Chapters 7 through 10 discuss these specific requirements. There are also more general types of support, not specifically associated with a particular class, that you will want to be familiar with. And you will need to determine how much support will be enough and how to arrange that support strategically. These generic supporting tactics are treated in this chapter.

SOME VARIETIES OF SUPPORT

It is useful to think of supporting material as separate units or building blocks that strengthen a claim in different ways and to different degrees. What follows is a discussion of some of the generic varieties of support commonly used to strengthen arguments.

Secondary Claims

All claims, regardless of their class, are supported by further claims, which will require their own support. Sometimes these *secondary* claims will belong to the same class as the main claim, sometimes to a different class. If you were arguing the factual claim "Students in my major are more interested in learning marketable skills than in truly educating themselves," you would need to support your fairly general claim with individual examples of this phenomenon. You probably would cite conversations in which individual students had expressed this preference to you and/or perhaps a survey asking students in your major to rank their educational priorities. In both cases, you are supporting your main claim with a secondary factual claim, which will itself need to be verified.

A recommendation claiming "This university should offer a pass-fail grading option to its students" may include as support the secondary *causal* argument "Removing the traditional evaluative system of letter grades will facilitate learning by reducing pressure." While not the chief point of this argument, this secondary causal claim still needs to be supported. One way to support it is through a third, *factual* claim. Perhaps the writer has access to a survey taken at another university that offers the pass-fail option, and this survey demonstrates a positive student response to the option. Or maybe the writer has friends at other schools who have spoken favorably about their pass-fail grading policy. Whether these responses are gathered through a large survey or individual conversations, they are facts that will strengthen the secondary claim (provided they are responsibly obtained and accurately reported).

As these examples illustrate, eventually all main claims will come to rest on factual claims that are supported by observations, examples, statistics, studies, and so forth. While some arguments depend more heavily on facts than others, no argument is likely to be convincing if it doesn't at some point refer to verified factual claims. In the previous example, the factual generalization about learning goals is supported by secondary factual claims: the expressed preferences of other students in your major and/or a survey of student learning goals. In the second example, a recommendation ultimately comes to rest on a secondary factual claim: positive student response to the pass-fail option. As you will see in Chapter 7, these fundamental factual claims would be supported by the writer's assurance that they have been gathered, interpreted, and reported responsibly.

ACTIVITIES (4.1)

Supply secondary claims that would support the following main claims of arguments. In each case, identify the class of the secondary and primary claims.

1. The *Boles GRE Study Guide* is an excellent tutorial for students preparing to take the GRE.
2. Television newscasting influences how Americans think about social and political issues.
3. In my high school, food abuse was a far bigger problem than alcohol or drug abuse.
4. Dostoyevsky's *Crime and Punishment* is a ponderous novel of sin and redemption.
5. If we really want to eradicate racism, we must institute within the primary grades curricula that honor diversity.

Comparisons

You can support some claims by citing a comparable claim that has already gained wide acceptance. Note, however, that this supporting strategy will work only if the two claims are truly comparable, not just vaguely similar. In an argument predicting financial difficulties for a new snowboard store in your town mall, you might cite the failure of the three other stores that have rented the same space. Or if you are arguing against proposed cuts in state money for scholarships, you may cite what another state has done to avoid reducing its education budget. This comparison will work only if the fiscal situation of the state you refer to is truly comparable to that of your state. In order to know this, you will have to get considerable information on each and probably present that information in the argument itself.

Appeals to Authority

You can support any claim by referring to a similar view held by a recognized authority in the field. You could support an evaluative argument claiming that Carmello Anthony is the most talented professional basketball player in the game today by quoting Michael Jordan pronouncing the same judgment (of course, Jordan has to have made this pronouncement—you can't make it up). Just be sure that the person whose judgment you cite *is* an established expert in the subject of your argument. Even though Jordan is a sports celebrity, his fame does not make him an expert on investment strategies or health care.

Appeals to Audience Needs and Values

Remember the emphasis of Chapter 2 on audience consideration, including an identification of audience needs and values? You can convert this preliminary identification into explicit support for your argument. Obviously, audiences will be more accepting of arguments that they see as likely to satisfy their needs or affirm their values. Many arguments presume these needs and values without referring to them explicitly. But you can strengthen some arguments by directly addressing these considerations, particularly when the match between claim and audience needs or values is not obvious. For example, a recommendation addressed to the administration of your college proposing a change from a trimester to a semester calendar should identify precisely how the change would benefit the administration—perhaps in the form of increased enrollment, higher student satisfaction, or long-term savings.

ACTIVITIES (4.2)

Get together with a small group of your classmates and discuss which methods of support (comparison, appeal to authority, appeal to audience needs and values) could be effectively applied to the following claims:

1. The costs of statewide and national political campaigns will discourage all but the rich from running for office.
2. The study of homosexuality is (is not) appropriate in a college course.
3. Using e-mail to keep in touch with friends who have gone off to other colleges is better than making telephone calls.
4. Parents should recognize how they risk their children's intellectual development by parking them in front of a television.
5. The widespread use of antidepressant drugs has revolutionized the psychotherapeutic community.

Addressing the Counterargument

A defining feature of argument is that its claim or claims are subject to disagreement: they are arguable. Thus, any claim you argue should be capable of evoking a *counterargument*—a position different from and often directly opposed to your claim. Just as you must carefully consider certain questions about your audience before you begin arguing, you must also identify the probable counterargument or arguments. Though this statement may seem counterintuitive, your arguments will be strengthened by your acknowledgment of their most powerful counterarguments. Why? For one thing, it is entirely possible that your readers are aware of the counterargument and even convinced by it. In stating and rebutting this position, you are dealing head on with the opposing view. Second, even if your readers aren't familiar with the alternative view, identifying it in your own argument will contribute to your image as a responsible and well-informed thinker.

The following are approaches to dealing with your argument's counterargument:

- You can omit direct reference to the counterargument when it is a weak position or likely to be unfamiliar to your audience. But note that omission does not mean ignorance: you should keep even the weakest counterargument in mind while you are writing, if for no other reason than that a reader may raise it.
- You can acknowledge or identify the counterargument without directly refuting it. This technique shows your readers that you are aware of the complexity of the issue and the legitimacy of other positions; it gives the impression that you are reasonable and broad-minded. In the following example, Margaret Whitney includes a brief acknowledgment of some predictable objections to her claim that competitive athletics are good for girls:

> I am not suggesting that participation in sports is the answer for all young women. It is not easy—the losing, jealousy, raw competition, and intense personal criticism of performance.
>
>   And I don't wish to imply that the sports scene is a morality play either. Girls' sports can be funny. You can't forget that out on that field are a bunch of people who know the meaning of the word cute. During one game, I noticed that Ann had a blue ribbon tied on her ponytail, and it dawned on me that every girl on the team had an identical bow. Somehow I can't picture the Celtics gathered in the locker room agreeing to wear the same color sweatbands.

Whitney has chosen not to refute these objections, probably because of the relative brevity of her argument, but her identification of the objections does suggest that she is reasonable and flexible.

- You should identify and directly refute an opposing position in the following situations:
  –When you know your audience holds that position.
  –When you know a credible, often-cited countercase exists, regardless of whether your audience subscribes to that position.
  –If it is vital to your argument to project a broad-minded, well-balanced image.

The full text of Martin Luther King, Jr.'s 1963 "Letter from Birmingham Jail" appears on multiple websites, including "The Martin Luther King, Jr. Research and Education Institute at Stanford University." Some of the links reveal the various rhetorical strategies that King uses to develop his response to criticism by Alabama clergy of his program of nonviolent resistance to racial segregation. The following excerpt from paragraph eight of his letter is an example of direct refutation:

> You may well ask, "Why direct action? Why sit-ins, marches, and so forth? Isn't negotiation a better path?" You are quite right in calling for negotiation. Indeed, this is the very purpose of direct action. Nonviolent

direct action seeks to create such a crisis and foster such a tension that a community which has constantly refused to negotiate is forced to confront the issue. It seeks so to dramatize the issue that it can no longer be ignored. My citing the creation of tension as part of the work of the non-violent resister may sound rather shocking. But I must confess I am not afraid of the word "tension." I have earnestly opposed violent tension, but there is a type of constructive, nonviolent tension which is necessary for growth. Just as Socrates felt that it was necessary to create a tension in the mind so that individuals could rise from the bondage of myths and half truths to the unfettered realm of creative analysis and objective appraisal, so must we see the need for nonviolent gadflies to create the kind of tension in society that will help men rise from the dark depths of prejudice and racism to the majestic heights of understanding and brotherhood.

Notice how King identifies the opposition's position and even concedes them a point (they're correct in calling for negotiations) before he refutes their position and moves to an idealistic statement of his own. This pattern of statement-concession-refutation is typical of effective refutations, though you have to be careful not to give away too much in the concession.

Direct refutations should be thoughtfully placed in your argument. If your audience appears to be firmly committed to an opposing position, you're not likely to convince them of the error of their views at the outset. On the other hand, readers without strongly held views are less likely to be swayed by a counterargument if it follows an impressive array of support for your claim. But if you include your refutation as the final piece of support, remember that it may linger in your reader's mind for some time, so make it as strong and convincing as possible. And finally, some very powerful arguments are exclusively refutations of opposing positions; these arguments gain form, precision, and intensity from the position they are opposing.

SUPPORTING YOUR ARGUMENT VISUALLY

You might find it curious that a book on *written* argument should include a discussion of *visual* support. Fifteen years ago, when the first edition of this book was published, including a section on visual images was not even discussed. Written arguments might invoke a chart or graph to summarize data, but the vast majority of the arguments students would be writing—both in college and beyond—would be predominantly textual. A good part of the reason for this was that it was difficult to create and/or reproduce accurately drawn graphics (the term we'll use for visual images). But digital technology has changed all this. Now, thanks to computers, scanners, and presentation software, virtually any writer can easily create, duplicate, and distribute images. Today, it is hard to find any text that doesn't supplement its message with some form of visual representation, whether it be a chart, a table, or a photograph.

You should never include graphic material for its own sake—simply because you can; exclusively verbal arguments can still be highly effective (think of

Supreme Court decisions). When a visual image will strengthen your argument, by all means use it, but use it responsibly.

It is useful to think of graphics as a class of support for your argument's claim or claims. However easy graphics may be to create and manipulate, like all forms of support, they are subject to certain standards and principles. The graphics we will concentrate on in this section—charts and tables—will typically support *factual* claims drawn from statistical evidence. (Chapter 7, "Arguing Facts," will cover the use of statistics in written arguments.) Photographs and drawings can also be used as support, but their rich and often emotive content makes them less useful for factual claims and arguments.

An argument can be exclusively visual, relying on nothing but an image itself to make its point. Think of political cartoons, where claims are represented not by language but by drawing skill, caricature, spatial relationships, and perspective.

The visuals that you are most likely to use in your written arguments are charts, tables, and diagrams. All of these graphics are visual representations of numerical data. What makes them so useful is their efficiency: they can summarize relationships between and among data over time much more economically and clearly than text alone.

Charts

You are probably familiar with the most commonly used charts, so we offer here just a brief refresher on their types and capabilities.

Pie Chart

Perhaps the simplest chart is the pie chart. Pie charts, so called because of the slices that make up a round circle, are best used to depict approximate proportional relationships among common categories at a single point in time. The following pie chart shows the relative percentages of different ethnic groups participating in a diversity workshop.

Percentage of Ethnic Group Participation

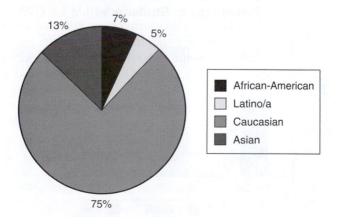

Pie charts almost always represent approximations of quantifiable values; if you need to be precise about relative proportions, bar graphs are a better choice. A single pie chart cannot represent changes over time. What pie charts are best at is giving a viewer a sense of the relative size of those categories making up the whole.

Bar/Column Chart

Unlike pie charts, bar and column charts can represent changes in data values over time. Data values on the *bar* variant are drawn as horizontal bars; on the *column*, as vertical bars. Because they are based upon a double axis (a value axis and a category axis), these charts can represent considerably more data than pie charts. A simple version of a column chart might depict the variations in the size or amount of a single category over time, as in the following example.

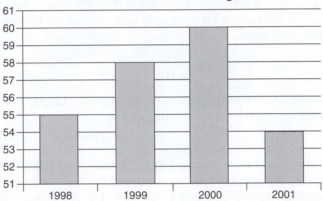

Percentage of Freshmen Engineering Students with a GPA of 3.0 or Higher

The same scheme could include more data. We could also use the column chart to indicate the gender breakdown of students with 3.0 grade-point average (GPA) or better.

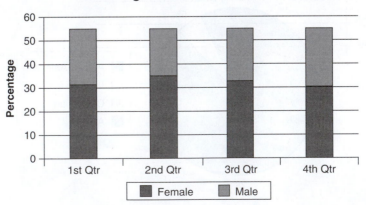

Percentage of Students with a 3.0 GPA

Column and bar charts can get still more complex, with breakdowns of three or four subgroups within a single category and multiple bars or columns side by side, representing comparative size of different categories. For example, we could show the same data for students at three other institutions by placing different colored columns adjacent to the existing columns for each year.

Percentage of 3.0 Students at Three Universities

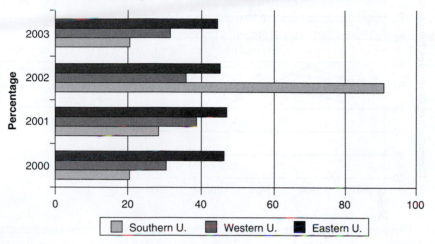

Line Graphs

Line graphs have the potential to show more data in one place than any other chart. Like bar/column charts, they use two axes—one of which often represents consecutive units of time. Thus they are useful in showing trends over time.

The simple line graph that follows represents employment history for communications students at Cardinal University one year after graduation.

Employment of Communications Students

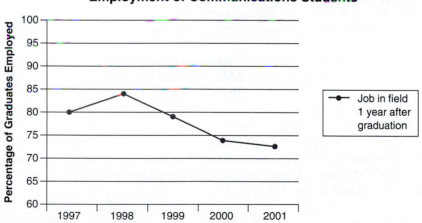

But line graphs have the capacity to contain far greater amounts of data than represented in this simple example. Using exactly the same units as in the second graph on page 51, we could depict employment data on graduates in a number of majors at Cardinal University.

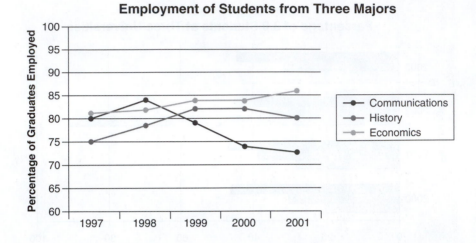

Employment of Students from Three Majors

There are other variants of these three major types: area charts, Gantt charts, histograms, scatter plots, and more. If you're interested in reading in more detail about charts and graphs, we suggest two classic volumes: *Graphs and their Uses* by Oystein Ore, and *The Visual Display of Quantitative Information* by Edward Tufte.

When Is a Chart Appropriate?

Thanks to computers and presentation software, including accurately drawn charts in your arguments is easy and even fun. Nevertheless, you need to exercise good judgment in deciding whether to include charts and, if so, what kinds to use. An overreliance on visuals can distract your readers from the flow of your argument, and even insult them if charts are used to represent very simple data.

A good question to ask yourself when you're considering the use of graphics is, "Would a chart or diagram or table clarify the data under discussion?" If the answer is "not really," then have faith in the ability of your writing to express the data. As Edward Tufte, a premier expert on visual information, says: "Excellence in statistical graphics consists of complex ideas communicated with clarity, precision, and efficiency." Another rule of thumb is, never use any visual support for its own sake—simply because it's attractive, or it looks authoritative, or it takes up otherwise blank space. If you can't think of a good reason for including a visual, then don't include it.

What Is the Best Type of Chart to Use?

Different types of charts can represent the same data with different effects, so you should take some time to consider what effect will best support or illustrate your claim. Let's take the line graph example used on the previous page. Precisely the same data could be depicted in a column chart, as follows.

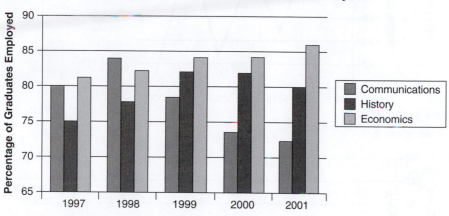

If you wish to emphasize the differences in employment within each year, the columns above serve that purpose well. But if your emphasis is continuing trends over time, you'd probably be better off using a line graph, which more graphically suggests continuity than a bar chart.

There won't always be a clear answer to the question, "What kind of chart would best represent this data?" but if you consider carefully the point you wish to make or emphasize by including a chart, you're not likely to go too far wrong.

Using Charts Responsibly

Like any other form of support, graphics can misrepresent and mislead. As support for factual claims, they are subject to the same principles of reliability as written support. The shape, color, and scale of your graphics are its visual vocabulary, which can be as irresponsible, loaded, or misrepresentative as emotional or duplicitous language.

Consider the very different effects of the following two versions of a line graph representing snowfall trends during the past six winters in your region.

The data are the same in both graphs, but by increasing the range of the scale on the vertical axis and the length of the horizontal axis, and the color of the line, we have created a very different impression. Version 1 could support a claim such as, "We have seen significant variations in snowfall over the past seven years." Version 2 might support the claim, "Snowfall amounts over the past seven years have been remarkably steady."

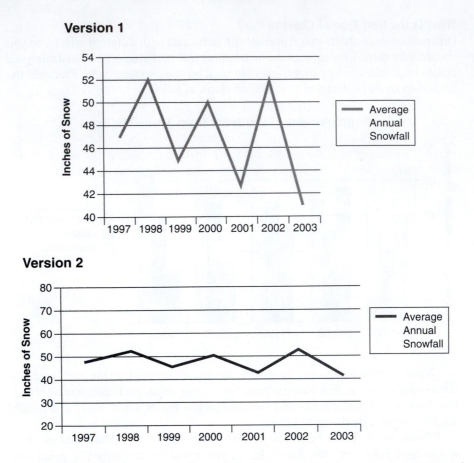

Which version is correct? The standards you apply to your representation of data are essentially the same as those you apply to your choice of language. In both cases, your goal is to be reasonable and objective. Just as you would avoid slanted or loaded words in stating a claim, you will avoid skewing graphic elements to suggest a situation that does not conform with objective standards. In the snowfall example, your decision about how to draw the data should be guided by expert consensus and comparative data. Is an eleven-inch variation of accumulation significant or negligible or somewhere in between? Perhaps when compared to national averages, or the average snowfall for your state, an eleven-inch variation is comparatively insignificant. In this case, Version 2 would more reasonably illustrate the data.

Tables

Tables are another shorthand way to represent data. While charts consist of shapes, tables arrange texts (verbal and numerical) into rows and columns. Like charts, they should be used for purposes of efficiency. Tables are less likely than charts to leave a subjective impression with the viewer, but they do carry with them an aura of objectivity and authority.

While tables are generally more limited in what they can represent than are charts, tables do have their own kind of versatility: a single table can satisfy multiple information needs. In the following simple nutritional table, one viewer on a low-fat diet might be interested in identifying the meat or fish with the lowest fat content; he would read down the "Fat" column. Another might want to check the overall nutritional damage of that bacon cheeseburger she's craving. She would read the first row straight across. Still another limiting himself to 1300 calories per day would focus on the "Calories" column.

Tables are useful only if the items about which the data are given belong to the same category. In this example, while the foods are presented in different units (ounces, pieces, cups), each is a single serving of a main course—meat and fish.

Food	Serving	Calories	Cholesterol (mg)	Fat (g)
Bacon cheeseburger	1	561.8	91.8	32.6
Beef and rice with gravy	1 cup	319.1	59.4	13.1
Chicken, boneless, skinless, cooked	4 oz.	181.3	84.9	7.1
Duck cooked, skinless, boneless	4 oz.	103.9	46	5.8
Fish, baked/broiled	4 oz.	149.5	62.8	4.9
Fish battered/fried	4 oz.	221.3	61.5	12.5
Lamb chop, cooked, lean	1 chop	182.2	70.6	10
Pork chop, cooked, lean	1 chop	143.5	55.5	6.5
Sardines, cooked	1 fish	10.4	7.1	0.6
Tuna, canned in oil, drained	1 cup	316.8	28.8	13.1

Spreadsheets are more extensive, more tightly packed data charts that you can create electronically by software programs such as Excel. Complex budgets are often represented in spreadsheets, which can make calculations about data in single rows and columns. You are not likely to use spreadsheets as visual support for an argument, as more often than not, they do speak for themselves.

Pictorial Images

Pictorial images—diagrams, cartoons, photographs—usually do not represent statistical data, but support an argument through explanation or illustration.

Diagrams

Perhaps most simple is the diagram, whose purpose is to explain, clarify, and/or simplify. The diagram below makes mitochondria—microscopic cellular structures—visible through enlargement and simplification.

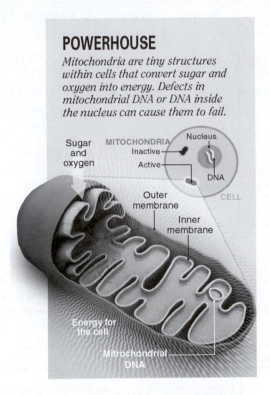

Like charts, diagrams are a form of support for factual claims. As such, they must be clearly drawn, dimensionally representative, and visually neutral. Imagine an article identifying AIDS as the devil's scourge that represented the virus in steaming reds and blacks.

Cartoons and Drawings

Cartoons and simple drawings are ubiquitous in contemporary publications. Sometimes these images are used merely for eye relief. In *The New Yorker* magazine, for example, long stretches of text are regularly punctuated by cartoons and sketches that are often unrelated to the text into which they're inserted. Often cartoons and sketches can also be used to summarize or emphasize an argument's major point. The short essay below, "The Future of the Past," includes a cartoon that pictorially represents the essay's claim that information can impede the attainment of wisdom.

THE FUTURE OF THE PAST

Literacy has been a mixed blessing to scholars, generating more information than they could digest. While decay and destruction erased historical records, the antlike labor of studious generations rebuilt, multiplied, and restocked knowledge repositories until they overflowed unmanageably.

In ancient Greece, the oral recital of poems, plays, and histories was accompanied by a trade in scrolls and the growth of private and public libraries. "Aristotle . . . could have scarcely compiled his works without a considerable reference library," book historian Norma Levarie observes. The great library in Alexandria may have housed a million papyrus scrolls hand-copied by legions of scribes. The need to visit a distant library, to make its holdings accessible by a catalog, and to acquire a personal working collection—all the problems of modern scholars—were already evident.

Gutenberg reduced and magnified these problems. Identical, widely distributed texts gave students a common frame of reference and protected their work from extinction. But the multiplication of copies and libraries, coupled with the growth of literacy, population, schools, and enters of learning, vastly increased the information dispersed in households and repositories. Scholars could examine only a fraction; the rest was discarded or slowly decayed in attics, storerooms, and archives.

The spread of literacy and ever more advanced technology has eased and exacerbated our battle with historical records. Living sounds and sights can now be captured on tape, film, and digitized media and instantly transmitted anywhere. Literate populations have prodigiously enlarged the volume of information recorded in new and traditional forms. The taped conversations of Presidents Johnson and Nixon can be augmented by a visual record of every motion and gesture in the Oval Office—and the offices and homes of congressmen and citizens. Will historians and biographers, humanists and social scientists be better or worse off, will their understanding or their uncertainty be more enhanced by all this information? How much information does the nation need?

Borges [20th century Argentinian writer] imagines a map the size of the territory it maps. In some spheres, we are approaching a condition where the record of the past is as inordinate as the living world, too compendious and complex to be comprehended by any discipline or multitude of scholars.

Great data collections are needed, some say, so that each expert can master a part and the community of experts, the whole. Conversely, it is said, only an individual, not a community, gains understanding; each expert now learns more and more about less and less; and each generalist, less and less about more and more.

It takes time to sift vital information from the mountainous dross in which it lies and we must often act without it. Observable conduct can be recorded, but not its meaning to, or the motives of, each actor. Did the Warren Commission report and the Zapruder film give us a better understanding of President Kennedy's assassination than Plutarch and Shakespeare gave us of Caesar's? Could either assassination have been prevented?

Source: "The Future of the Past," *Change: The Magazine of Higher Learning.* January/February 2004. p. 8.

Photographs

Photographs, too, can lend strong support to an argument, as is the case with the two examples of high school senior portraits used by Joan Jacobs Brumberg in her book, *The Body Project: An Intimate History of American Girls*. Brumberg uses these photographs to support her claim of the increasing centrality of the female adolescent body. Here is a summary of the claim these photographs are meant to support:

> Yearbook pictures reflect the shift in emphasis from a girl's face to her entire body. This 1963 senior photograph from Traverse City, Michigan, is typical of an older era when senior photographs showed only the head and shoulders, and every young woman wore the same blouse or sweater with a similar locket, pendant, or pearls. Many girls in the 1990s have made their bodies into projects, and recent yearbook pictures, such as this 1995 senior picture from a Connecticut high school, often imitate contemporary fashion shots.

It is difficult to conceive of a photograph that doesn't tell a story or make a point. The beauty of the medium is that it can communicate so richly in the complete absence of text. While you need not avoid using photographs to support a claim, you will need to be exceedingly aware that your supporting photograph can be "read" in ways that could contradict or unfairly support your claim(s).

Commercial advertising overwhelms us with images that are both artificial and visually persuasive. Not only are the attractive models with impossibly perfect faces and bodies figments of digital manipulation, airbrushing, and sophisticated graphic design, but they also prey upon female feelings of physical inadequacy. If we buy that perfume or those blue jeans, perhaps we'll end up looking like those models.

ACTIVITIES (4.3)

1. Which (if any) kind(s) of chart would be most suitable to support each of the following claims, and why? (Assume that data are available for all claims.)
   a. Tuition at public and private universities increased by 6% between 2005 and 2006. (U.S. News.com, October 29, 2006, "College Costs Climb," Kim Clark)
   b. The recent five-year decline in mortgage interest rates has been matched by sharp increases in home refinancing.
   c. Of the twenty introductory courses offered by the College of Liberal Arts, only five were fully enrolled this past semester: History 101, Economics 100, Introduction to Political Theory, Calculus I, and Computer Programming I.
   d. Increases in gas prices have been directly contemporaneous with the Iraqi war.

ARRANGING YOUR ARGUMENT'S SUPPORT

Having accumulated support for your claim, you now have to consider the best way to arrange it in your argument. You can make strong support even stronger by arranging it to have the most powerful impact on your readers. Once again, audience consideration is key: your decisions about the organization of your argument's support should be based on your readers' familiarity with the subject, their ability to follow the path of your argument, and their probable disposition toward your claim.

It helps to think of your support as separate units that can be moved around within your argument. In an essay claiming that "The Student Activities Board should bring Matchbox 20 to campus," the units of support could be listed as follows:

1. A survey shows that Matchbox 20 is the most popular performing group with students at your college.
2. The college would increase student satisfaction by showing their willingness to please students.
3. Ticket sales would be brisk and therefore would substantially offset the cost of bringing the band to campus.

4. In a letter to the *Chronicle of Higher Education,* the vice president of student affairs at a college in the adjoining state praised Matchbox 20 for their entertainment ability. "This is a band that any school should be proud to host," the letter concluded.
5. The band has a solid reputation for being professional and audience-appropriate.
6. Bringing such a popular band to campus would increase the college's community visibility.
7. Student enrollment would increase as a result of bringing Matchbox 20 to campus.

A good general principle is that the *strongest* support should be presented first, so that you gain some early agreement from your readers. If possible, you should also save an effective supporting point for the end of your argument; it will leave your readers with a positive final impression. In the preceding list, the strongest argument may be Argument 2, particularly if the college in question is, like most schools in today's competitive higher-education environment, extremely concerned about student satisfaction. Argument 6, a secondary causal claim, is likely to be persuasive to the Student Activities Board as well, since community visibility is always a plus to college administrators.

What constitutes strong support? To some extent, this will depend on your audience. A credulous, inexperienced group and a cynical or expert audience will be convinced by different points. However, relevant factual support (figures, examples, and statistics, as in Argument 1) is usually very strong, whereas highly speculative arguments (predicted effects with a remote chance of being realized) are weaker; for example, Argument 7 would be extremely difficult to predict convincingly and probably should be omitted altogether. Citing expert opinion, as in Argument 4, is usually effective, provided your expert is credible and his or her support is documented. In Argument 4, does the opinion of a vice president for student affairs qualify as expert in this context? Does she have an obvious bias that might weaken her statement? How respectable a publication is the *Chronicle of Higher Education?* Are your school and hers comparable?

Sometimes you have little choice about the arrangement of your support. Scientific experiments dictate a certain organization, as do causal chains, where Cause A must be discussed before Cause B, Cause B before Cause C, and so on. In these cases, you'll need to make sure that all supporting arguments are strong and that they fit tightly together, because one weak link can destroy the entire argument.

ACTIVITIES (4.4)

1. The following argument, written by student Sharon Bidwell, contains a number of varieties of supporting material. Pretend that you are the editor of your school newspaper and have decided to print Sharon's letter. In a two-page letter to Sharon, comment on the effectiveness of her choice and arrangement of support.

The administration's decision not to allow Dr. Fasciano and his white supremacist group to participate in a roundtable discussion with the students on our campus is clearly an act of censorship and should not be tolerated in a country that prides itself on free thought and expression. Censorship, as defined by the *Encyclopaedia Britannica,* is "the suppression or prohibition of speech or writing that is condemned as subversive to the common good." It is obvious that the administration is making a selective decision of what the "common good" is for the students of this campus.

There is no doubt that the administration has legitimate concerns that need to be addressed. First of all, Mr. Fasciano's visit will raise some eyebrows among those who make regular contributions to the university. Second, Mr. Fasciano's visit is likely to set off active protests which have the capacity to seriously disrupt the campus and even threaten the safety and security of the students.

Despite these very real risks, the administration must make it known that this university supports the Constitution of the United States—namely, the First Amendment—and does not bow to pressure when it comes to suppressing free speech. To paraphrase John Milton in his *Areopagitica* of 1644, we must allow that free and open encounter in which truth may indeed prevail over error.

The argument against censorship has been made by many who fought hard against it—against anything, in fact, that interferes with self-development and self-fulfillment. For example, in his first inaugural address, Thomas Jefferson addressed the necessity of free dissent: "If there be any among us who would wish to dissolve this Union or to change its republican form, let them stand undisturbed as monuments of the safety with which error of opinion may be tolerated where reason is left free to combat it."

The administration must give the students the freedom to be the best guarantors of quality and fairness. We rely on these institutions of higher learning to *teach* future generations by allowing them to choose *freely* and make difficult decisions. For those who oppose Mr. Fasciano and his views, let there be an open forum with a free exchange of ideas. Our forefathers fought for this privilege. Let's not let them down.

DEFINITIONS

Obviously, readers can't agree (or reasonably disagree) with what they don't understand. Clarity is the result of many different elements in written argument: precision of ideas in the writer's mind, an understanding of the relationship among these ideas, careful organization of claim and supporting material, clear transitions among parts of the argument, reliance on the conventions of grammar and punctuation, and comprehensible, unambiguous language. It is this final element—the clarity of your language—that concerns us here. Ideally, writers of argument would use only those words that they knew their readers would understand. But arguments can't always rely on simple language, and even the simplest words mean different things to different people. This is where *definition* comes in: the careful delineation of the intended meaning of a potentially troublesome word or term.

Knowing when and how to define terms is critical to successful argument. Because effective and strategic definition strengthen any argument by making it more accessible to readers, it can be viewed as a form of support. In some cases, definition moves from its clarifying supporting function to that of a secondary claim, where the writer must convince the reader to understand a term in a particular way before the central claim can be argued. Sometimes definition of a key term is so crucial and controversial that it becomes a central claim in itself.

When to Define

You should plan on defining the following types of language in your arguments:

- *Unfamiliar terminology.* Any specialized or unusual terms that may be unfamiliar to your readers must be explained. If, for example, you aren't sure whether your readers will have heard of "Maxwell's Demon," or a "net revenue model," or "dysthymic disorder," provide a clear definition.

  Unfamiliar terminology includes *jargon* (specialized vocabulary and idioms). Generally speaking, jargon should be avoided, but there are times when it is the best language for the job. If you must use phrases like "the dialogic principle of feminist discourse," don't assume that everyone in your audience will know precisely what you mean; provide a definition.

- *Nonspecific language.* In general, avoid vague, fuzzy terms, particularly in statements of evaluation and measurement. If you claim, "U2 is the most popular band in contemporary music," consider how little this statement tells the reader about the nature and extent of that popularity. Popularity based on CD sales? Popularity based on money earned? On concert attendance? And popularity with whom? Certainly they are not the most popular band with people over 65. A more specific statement, such as "U2 has sold more CDs in the last year than any other contemporary band" is far more useful to the reader.

  And when you use nonspecific words like *poor, excellent, large, grand,* or *considerable,* make sure you explain the meaning of your modifier as precisely as possible.

- *Abstract terms.* While you should try to make your writing as concrete as possible, sometimes you can't avoid using abstract terms in argument, especially in evaluations. The problem with abstractions is that they can be understood in different ways; that is, they can be *ambiguous.* If you must use a term like *popular,* or *talented,* or *conservative,* be sure to pin down explicitly your understanding of the term. While your readers may not agree with your definition, at least they will understand how you intend to use the word and will judge the success of your argument within those parameters.

- *Controversial terms.* Some terms have been at the center of heated public debate for so long that they are emotionally and politically loaded. Their meaning is ambiguous—that is, it can be interpreted in more than one way—and people tend to argue over which interpretation is correct. *Euthanasia* and *gay marriage* are examples of such controversial terms; how one defines them often determines one's position toward them. When you use such terms in your arguments, you will almost certainly need to clarify what you mean by them.

Sometimes such terms are so controversial that your definition, because it implies a position on the subject, becomes the point of the argument. Consider, for example, an essay on doctor-assisted suicide: a carefully delineated definition of what the practice *is* (or is not)—the prescription of lethal amounts of medication to a dying patient at the patient's request, for example—would take you a long way in an argument supporting the practice.

Types of Definitions

Terms requiring clarification can be defined briefly or extensively, depending on the needs of your audience and the importance of the term to your argument. The four types of definition you will most commonly use as support for your argument are the shorthand definition, the sentence definition, the extended definition, and the stipulative definition.

Writers often resort to *shorthand* definitions when the term in question requires only a quick explanation. A shorthand definition substitutes a familiar term for an unfamiliar one, as in the following example: "Acetylsalicylic acid (aspirin) is an effective medicine for most headaches."

A *sentence* definition, similar to a dictionary definition but written as a grammatical sentence, consists of the term to be defined (the *species*), the general category to which it belongs (the *genus*), and those characteristics that distinguish it from all other members of that general category (the *differentiae*). A sentence definition has the following structure:

SPECIES = GENUS + DIFFERENTIAE

An example of this form of definition is "A heifer [species] is a young cow [genus] that has not borne a calf [differentiae]."

An *extended* definition includes this basic sentence definition *and* any additional material that would help a reader understand the term being defined. The following are strategies for extending a sentence definition.

- **Evolution of Definition.** Sometimes an understanding of the historical development of a word's usage will illuminate its richness for readers. The word *queer,* for example, means strange or out of the ordinary. Thus it was eventually coined as a derogatory term for a male homosexual. Recently homosexuals have embraced the term, converting it from a slur to a compliment. There is now an academic field called Queer Studies.

- **Comparison.** Readers can gain a better understanding of a term if it is compared to something with which they are familiar. An argument that needs to define the term *docudrama* might explain that a docudrama is similar to a movie, except the events depicted are based in fact.
- **Example.** Offering specific examples of unfamiliar terms is an excellent way to explain them. To define what a *haiku* is, for example, you would almost certainly present an example or two.
- **Definition by Negation.** Sometimes you can explain a term by telling your reader what it is not, what it should not be confused with. For example, at the beginning of this textbook, we defined the term *argument* by distinguishing it from *opinion,* a term often mistaken as being synonymous with argument.
- **Etymological Definition.** Providing the etymology of a word—the meanings of its original roots—can also help to explain its meaning. The word *misogynist,* for example, derives from the Greek *miso,* meaning "hate," and *gyne,* meaning "woman."
- **Definition by Description.** Unfamiliar or abstract terms can often be explained or introduced by a physical or figurative description. If you were defining a Phillips screw, you might explain what the screw looks like. Or in defining contrapuntal music, you could describe the sound: the listener hears two distinct melodies going on at exactly the same time.
- **Functional Definition.** You can explain some unfamiliar terms by telling readers what the object or person does or how it operates. It would be helpful for a reader unfamiliar with the meaning of *provost* to learn what duties that academic officer performs. Functional definitions are particularly helpful in explaining unfamiliar *objects* such as tools. After describing the appearance of a particular drill bit, for example, you could explain what that particular bit is used for or how it is used.

The following extended definition of "poetry," from Laurence Perrine's *Sound and Sense,* contains many of these strategies of extended definition:

Between poetry and other forms of imaginative literature there is no sharp distinction. You may have been taught to believe that poetry can be recognized by the arrangement of its lines on the page or by its use of rime [*sic*] and meter. Such superficial tests are almost worthless. The Book of Job in the Bible and Melville's *Moby Dick* are highly poetical, but the familiar verse that begins: "Thirty days hath September, April, June, and November . . ." is not. The difference between poetry and other literature is one only of degree. Poetry is the most condensed and concentrated form of literature, saying most in the fewest number of words. It is language whose individual lines, either because of their own brilliance or because they focus so powerfully on what has gone before, have a higher voltage than most language has. It is language that grows frequently incandescent, giving off both light and heat.

This definition uses a sentence definition ("Poetry is the most condensed and con-centrated form of literature"), a definition by negation (indicating what poetry is *not*: poetry has little to do with line arrangement or rhyme or meter), comparison ("Between poetry and other forms of imaginative literature there is no sharp distinction"), and figurative description ("It is language that grows frequently incandescent, giving off both light and heat").

Stipulative definitions *argue* that a particular definition should be assigned to a term. In other words, a stipulative definition argues a claim about meaning. While all definitions can be seen as claims, in that they propose meaning, and meaning is never fixed, the types of explanatory definitions discussed so far record meanings that most audiences would agree on. Stipulative definitions, on the other hand, argue for a par-ticular meaning rather than record a consensual one. Sometimes stipulative defini-tions are made for convenience and clarity: "When we use the term *argument,* we are referring only to its primary meaning of demonstrating the reasonableness of a proposition." In this example, the writer is clarifying, not arguing.

But extended stipulative definitions are often fully developed arguments sup-porting an arguable, often controversial, claim about meaning. Think of the often-repeated argument "Abortion is murder." This short sentence definition opens a Pandora's box of controversies about meaning. First, there is likely to be disagree-ment over the meaning of the term *murder* in this context. The dictionary tells us that murder is the "unlawful killing of one human by another", especially with premeditated malice (*The American Heritage Dictionary of the English Language*). But abortion is not illegal, so an antiabortion argument would have to reject this definition and stipulate its own. Or to open another controversy: is the fetus a "human being?" Is there consensus about the meaning of this term? Clearly not: a prochoice advocate would want to restrict or stipulate the meaning of *human being.* Through your stipulated definitions of *abortion, murder,* and *human being,* you are actually arguing your position on the issue of abortion.

Extended stipulative definitions are essentially interpretive arguments: in proposing a restricted, possibly unusual, definition of a concept, you are arguing a particular interpretation or understanding that is suggested and supported by the context of the argument. Stipulative definitions can be supported through a variety of supporting methods. One of the most useful is an argument of effect—that is, demonstrating the positive effects of adopting your particular definition of the term. For example, if you were proposing a new definition of the word *minor* as a way of making a case for lowering the legal drinking age ("The traditional definition of *minor* as someone under the age of 21 leaves out those 18–20 year olds who are considered old enough to die for their country, to get married, and to terminate their education"), you might introduce a supporting argument of effect that money could be saved if police didn't have to enforce the current drinking age. Or if you were arguing that education is a lifelong process, you might base your argument on a stipulative definition of *education,* supporting that definition through the secondary causal argument of the positive consequences that educa-tion, so defined, can lead to.

Chapter 11 of this book, "Writing and Image," begins with a stipulative definition of the word *image* as applied to written argument. This definition serves
more of a clarifying than an argumentative purpose, but it does make the claim
that despite the largely negative popular understanding of the term, a writer's "image" is positive and important.

ACTIVITIES (4.5)

1. Examine an extended definition in an online encyclopedia, reference guide,
   or textbook, and write a one- to two-page essay that describes what elements
   (sentence definition, examples, history of the object or concept being defined,
   comparison or contrast, and so on) have been included in the definition, and
   speculate on why they have been included. Are there other elements you
   believe should have been included to help the definition? Are there any
   elements that could have been omitted?

2. Write your own stipulative definition of *beauty, murder,* or *friendship.*
   Compare your definition with those of your classmates who define the
   same term.

SUMMARY

An Argument's Support

- An argument's support is all the material that transforms your working
  claim into a reasonable conclusion. Knowing the class of the argument
  you are making will help you determine the appropriate support, but
  there are some generic varieties of support that can be used to
  strengthen any class of argument. These are

  – secondary claims

  – comparisons

  – appeals to authority

  – appeals to audience needs and values

  – addressing the counterargument

  – defining key terms

  – graphics

- Visual images (charts, diagrams, graphs) can clarify factual claims or support, but should never be included without a good reason for doing so.

- When possible, arrange your support to have the greatest impact on your
  readers, with strong support placed at the beginning and end of your
  argument.

- Any terms in your claim or the body of your argument likely to be unfamiliar to your readers should be defined by a sentence definition, an extended definition, or a shorthand definition.

- Stipulative definitions, which restrict the meaning of a term to one of the term's possible meanings, can be used to clarify an argument or to make an interpretive argument.

SUGGESTIONS FOR WRITING (4.6)

1. Write a claim that comes out of a position or belief you hold strongly (about a political issue, a policy at your university, or your relationship to your family, for example). Identify the category of your claim, and make a list of all the points you can think of to support your claim. Give your list to a classmate and see if he or she can add any supporting reasons you haven't thought of.

2. Create graphic support for one of the claims in Activities 4.3. You may create your own data as necessary.

ILLUSTRATIVE ARGUMENTS IN PART II: AN ARGUMENT'S SUPPORT

5

Supporting Your Arguments Honestly and Effectively

As the previous chapter suggests, much of the material you will use to support your argument will not be original with you. If you're supporting a claim through inclusion of an expert's views on the topic, you will have had to search for those views in external sources—websites, library books, textbooks, reference materials. Likewise, if you're addressing the counterargument, you'll likely have discovered that position through reading and research. And many of those verified factual claims that ultimately support all arguments will be data, research studies, and professional surveys that you found in your reading and research.

The fact is that readers are more likely to agree with an argument if it refers to external information, ideas, and arguments. True, some of the most classic and incontrovertible arguments ever composed are completely independent of references to external authority—the Declaration of Independence and the Gettysburg Address, for example. But many of the arguments and all of the research papers you will write for college courses will include expert opinion, alternative viewpoints, and unfamiliar data, as well as your own ideas and reasoning about the topic.

The first part of this chapter will concentrate on the importance of scrupulously identifying the sources of supporting material that *is not your own*. The cardinal offense in any form of creativity—and writing arguments is as much a creative act as painting or composing music—is taking credit for work that is not original with you. When you include phrases, ideas, facts, or opinions in your argument that you read or heard elsewhere, and you fail to indicate clearly where you read or heard them, you are committing *plagiarism*.

The second part of the chapter will provide guidelines for conducting research and incorporating it into your arguments.

PLAGIARISM AND WRITTEN ARGUMENTS

You can't have progressed this far in your education and not be familiar with plagiarism. Simply put, plagiarism is including the work or ideas of others in your argument without giving credit. Plagiarism—which can be intentional or unintentional—comes in many forms:

- copying entire documents and presenting them as your own;
- cutting and pasting from the work of others without properly citing the author;
- stringing together the quotes and ideas of others without distinguishing between their work and yours;
- asserting ideas without acknowledging their sources;
- reproducing sentences written *verbatim* by others without properly quoting and attributing the work to them.[1]

Clear enough, right? But in the current climate of blogs, wikis, file "sharing," and online term-papers-for-sale sites, the lines between originality, collaboration, editing, plagiarism, and cheating have blurred. Many professors now favor group projects and team assignments, which can further confuse the principles of attribution. How do you identify authorship in a group paper? Further, some international students bring with them to U.S. colleges very different understandings of proper attribution. In parts of Asia and the Middle East, to identify a source with which the professor is familiar can be a grave insult.[2]

As the distinctions blur, the incidences of plagiarism increase: in 1999, 10% of college students surveyed had committed "cut and paste" plagiarism; in 2001, that number had risen to 41%.[3] But at the same time, faculty vigilance and intolerance have sharpened. Your school's website may well have a page that hones your professors' plagiarism-detecting skills. And web services like "turnitin.com" make the submission of purchased papers increasingly risky for students.

Plagiarism is probably more frequently born of insecurity than of laziness or intentional dishonesty. A first-year college student can become paralyzed by an assignment asking him to express his own ideas on a topic, or even to summarize the ideas of others. Not only may he feel that he has no ideas worth expressing, but he will also quickly recognize how much better others express themselves. Surely, this student might argue, I'm better off "borrowing" these ideas than handing in a paper with a bunch of stupid ideas or a blank page.

Many students don't realize that professors assign papers so that students will develop their own ideas; your professors know that the processes of writing and thinking are closely aligned. The combination of reading, taking notes, thinking, and writing early drafts is guaranteed to generate original ideas. Understand that the panicked feeling you may have when you first address a writing assignment is

---

[1] <http://www.wsulibs.wsu.edu/plagiarism/what.html>.
[2] "Cultural Perspectives on Plagiarism" (2004), <http://www.wsulibs.wsu.edu/plagiarism/culture.html>.
[3] Center for Academic Integrity (2003), <http://www.coastal.edu/library/papermil.htm>.

very common; no one begins a writing assignment with a clear sense of what the content and direction of the paper will be. The going may be slow at first, but before long, your brain will be fully firing with reactions, comparisons, and ideas.

You may be interested to know that it's not just *student* writing that is under the microscope. In the recent past, a number of college presidents have been publicly exposed for "borrowing" speeches from others. Publications like the *New York Times* have censured respected historians for their failure to document their sources. One noted writer recently exposed for plagiarism cited technology as his excuse. Here's how the *Times* reacted: "The excuses were speedy compilations, editing oversights, the ability of computers to cut and paste. It was as if the modern techniques of composition were alive and had run amok, and the author had no control."[4]

For college students, the punishment for plagiarism ranges from automatic failure of the assignment to failure of the course to suspension to expulsion. Recently, forty-five students were expelled from the University of Virginia for plagiarism and three students had their graduate degrees revoked.[5] In other words, the stakes are high.

In the midst of the confusion and the vigilance, we'll provide some clear and useful guidelines about when and how to document your sources in your written arguments. Much of this will be familiar to you, but it always bears repeating.

Guidelines for Avoiding Plagiarism

We'll anticipate the guidelines with this simple dictum: *when in doubt, identify your sources.* As you'll see in the next section, how you identify your sources will depend upon the subject matter you're writing about and the formality of the assignment. But regardless of the method used—footnotes, endnotes, textual citations, or a final bibliography—too many citations is far better than too few.

Below are the kinds of materials whose sources must be explicitly identified.

Quotations

Any time that you include in your argument someone else's exact words—whether written, spoken, published, or unpublished—you must (1) place double quotation marks around the passage and (2) provide the source of the passage. The quotation can be as short as one word or as long as multiple paragraphs (though you should avoid very long quotations).

Paraphrases

A paraphrase is like a translation of someone else's language into your own words. But if the "translated" idea is not original with you, you must acknowledge its source. Journalist Joan Ryan writes "Yet while gymnastics and figure skating are among the most-watched sports in the country, the least is known about the lives

[4] Martin Arnold, "History Is an Art, Not a Toaster," *New York Times*, February 28, 2002, p. E1.
[5] Margaret Fain and Peggy Bates, "Cheating 101: Combating Internet Plagiarism" (2003), <http://www.coastl.edu/library/papermil.htm>.

of their athletes."[6] A student may paraphrase this assertion as follows: "Even though gymnastics and ice skating are very popular in the U.S., we don't know as much about these competitors as we do about those in other sports." The student has avoided the language of the original, but has borrowed the observation. Thus, the paraphrased statement must be attributed to a source.

In general, paraphrases are preferable to direct quotations. If the original quotation is particularly memorable or nuanced, then by all means include it. But don't be a lazy writer, including multiple quotations because it's easier to use someone else's words than to digest thoroughly the original meaning by putting it in your own language.

Summaries

Summaries are looser paraphrases in which the intent is to summarize briefly the original source while avoiding the original's level of detail. Summaries can be particularly useful in research papers that require overviews of a topic as background material. A paper focusing on the theory of behavioral psychotherapy might summarize alternative therapeutic methods. Even though summaries condense material from multiple sources, identification of the sources is still required.

Primary or Secondary Sources?

Let's say that in your research on behavioral psychotherapy, you come across someone else's published summary of alternative therapies, and that this summary appropriately cites multiple sources. If you use this summary in your own work, do you cite the summary (the secondary source) or do you cite the summarizer's sources? Do you cite the psychology textbook (secondary source) that summarizes an idea of Freud's (primary source), or do you cite the original passage from *An Interpretation of Dreams* that the textbook cites? It's tempting to do the latter: it makes you look more widely read, and you're not, after all, taking credit for Freud's idea. But resist the temptation and cite the textbook, not the original source.

Facts

Determining when to give credit for facts—whether complex data or unfamiliar information—requires good judgment. The standard criterion for the determination is how widely the fact is known. Even if you read in multiple sources that Hurricane Katrina made landfall in August 2005, the fact is so commonly known that it does not require citation. But if you read that Hurricane Katrina had winds in excess of 140 miles per hour, a minimum central pressure of 902 mb, and dropped eight to ten inches of rain in southeastern Louisiana, these facts would require citation;[7] few people except professional meteorologists would have these details at their command.

---

[6] Joan Ryan, *Little Girls in Pretty Boxes: The Making and Breaking of Elite Gymnasts and Figure Skaters* (New York: Time Warner Books, 2000).
[7] NOAA Satellite and Information Service, <http://lwf.ncdc.noaa.gov/oa/climate/research/2005/Katrina.html>, accessed October 30, 2006.

Data tables, charts, and graphs that you import exactly into your text will also need their sources identified. If you create your own table or graph to illustrate unfamiliar data that you have found elsewhere, you'll need to credit the source of the data while making it clear that the graphic is yours.

Internet Material

Keep in mind that the ease with which you can locate supporting material on the Internet does not exempt you from documenting that material as carefully as you document printed material. The principles and guidelines presented above apply equally to digital material.

Plagiarism Illustrated

Let's take a look at what some instances of plagiarism really look like. The first passage below is the *verbatim* transcription of our original source: a paragraph from an essay titled "The Effects of Computers on Traditional Writing."[8] Each succeeding box illustrates a plagiarized variant of the original.

> Written expression differs from oral expression in that it is dependent entirely on the alphabetic word—and not on the visual and vocal elements that help people communicate in face-to-face speech. Writing requires a codifiable medium to convey meaning. Also, it uses a vocabulary, based on known conventions and rules of usage, to create new ideas. In written expression, discrete elements (the alphabet) are combined and recombined to help convey new ideas, often using new words created to meet the needs of conveying those new ideas. Finally, written language must have a fixed relationship with spoken language, so that people can communicate the same thought in two different media simultaneously—as in reading to one another. These elements give writing its characteristics of permanence and completeness.

Plagiarism 1

```
Writing is different from speaking because it uses the alphabet.
Writing must have a codifiable medium to convey meaning. It
also uses a vocabulary based on known conventions and rules
of use to create new ideas. In writing, discrete elements
are combined and recombined to help convey new ideas.
Finally, writing has to have a fixed relationship with
speaking so that people can communicate the same thought in
two different media simultaneously — as in reading to one
another.
```

[8] Sharmila Pixy Ferris, "The Effects of Computers on Traditional Writing," *JED: The Journal of Electronic Publishing* 8, no. 1 (August 2002), <http://www.press.umich.edu/jep/08-01/ferris.html>.

The author of this example has lifted *verbatim* the majority of the original text, making only token efforts to disguise the original. Parts of the original are omitted, "writing" is substituted for the original's "written expression," and "speaking" is substituted for "spoken language." Because no quotation marks are used and no source is cited, this first example blatantly plagiarizes the original.

Plagiarism 2

> Writing is different form speaking for a number of reasons. It depends **on the alphabetic word**, and it requires **a codifiable medium to convey meaning**. Writing also uses language, which has **conventions and rules**, to express original thoughts. Lastly, writing and speaking stand in a **fixed relationship** with each other. This way you can use writing and speaking at the same time, as in reading a book to someone. It is these characteristics that make writing lasting and **complete**.

This writer has made more effort to paraphrase the original, but exact phrases have slipped in. The structure and ideas of example 2 are also extremely close to the original. Note that if the writer had paraphrased *all* of the text in bold type, then the passage would still be plagiarized if it lacked a citation.

Plagiarism 3

> Writing is a more lasting and inclusive medium than speaking because it relies on an alphabet and the set customs of grammar and **vocabulary**.

This sentence is a paraphrased and highly condensed summary of the original, but since the assertions are not original with the writer, the source of the idea must be provided. To be on the safe side, the word "vocabulary," which appears in the original passage, should be enclosed by quotation marks.

FINDING REPUTABLE SUPPORT

Your professors are going to look for more than scrupulously documented sources; they will also insist that the sources you incorporate into your argument are authoritative, or at least reliable. The principles for conducting research "the old-fashioned way"—through books or articles found through library catalogues—remain relatively straightforward. Let's take a look at these before considering the Internet as a research tool.

Traditional Research

When your sources are printed texts (e.g., books, journals, newspapers), you have some assurance that the material has been reviewed by someone, though this assurance does not relieve you of responsibility for further evaluating their reliability.

The first thing to look at when evaluating print sources is the identity of the author. Books and journal articles are almost always published under the author's name. If you are familiar with the author and know he or she is an acknowledged expert with a proven track record in the field, you can have some confidence that the contents are reliable. You are probably safe trusting the ideas of the editor of a professional journal or the economist Milton Friedman, because both have established professional reputations. But be wary of predictions about stock market performance obtained from an astrologer.

If you're not familiar with the author of a source you'd like to use, do some investigating. Your library has a number of professional biographical dictionaries either in its reference section or online, and of course you can find loads of unreviewed information about the author on the Internet. You want to obtain enough information to assure you that the author knows the subject and is likely to be objective about it. Tiger Woods is a great golfer, but would you accept his assertion that Nike makes the best running shoe in the world?

If you can't discover anything about the reliability of the author, or if the author isn't identified (as often happens in reference books, magazines, and editorials), consider the reputation of the publisher. Most university presses, for example, have their books reviewed by multiple experts before publication, as do most academic journals. The publisher's good reputation will not ensure that the material in question is reliable, but it does increase the odds substantially. Certainly a report found in the *New England Journal of Medicine* is more credible than one found in the *National Enquirer*. If you don't know anything about the publisher of the source, check with a librarian or a professor in the field.

You also want to be sure to check the date of your source's publication. While a book on Abraham Lincoln dated 1966 might not be considered outdated, a 1966 book on medical imaging technology would be barely worth reading, unless you were doing a historical survey of the field.

Electronic Research

The huge growth in Internet-based information is both a blessing and a curse to writers who seek reliable sources. On the one hand, finding information has never been easier. Millions of sources on a given topic are available within an instant. A student writing a paper on the origins of the tar baby story will be greeted with over seven million "hits" after "googling" the term "tar baby." But the sheer volume of information available through Web searches can make us less discriminating researchers. And because anyone with a computer and Internet connection can post information on the Web, there is more unreliable material online than between the pages of a book or journal that has gone through some kind of review process. (The article " 'Vonnegut Speech' Circulates on Net" at the end of Chapter 7 shows how quickly misinformation can circulate on the Internet.)

For the most part, evaluating electronic sources isn't all that different from evaluating print sources. Begin by trying to determine the author's reliability—again, through biographical dictionaries or perhaps the *National Dictionary of Addresses and Telephone Numbers.* While you're on the Internet, try a search through the World Wide Web using the author's name as your keyword; you may find some useful information on his or her reputation.

Checking the electronic address of your sources gives you some generic information about its origin and thus at least a hint of its reliability: *edu* means it comes from an educational institution; *gov* is a governmental organization; *org* is a nonprofit organization; and *com* is a commercial organization.

Make sure to check the date of the material if it's available. Much of the material on the Internet has the virtue of being very current, but in quickly moving fields, information may become out of date in a matter of days.

If you find useful information on a listserv, try communicating with the author (whose name and e-mail address are included on the listserv posting) to get information about the sources of his or her information. Or if you find unattributed information on a website, try following up some of the related links on the site; these may lead you to the background you need on the sources of the website material.

If you're doing ongoing research on a topic and find some particularly valuable websites, you can use an RSS service (Really Simple Syndication) like "Pluck" or "Onfolio" to track and record relevant entries to that site. This will save you the trouble of visiting the actual sites to check for recent additions about your topic.

Here are some additional guidelines for locating reliable information on the Web:

- *Google* is a mammothly powerful search engine, and can be a good place to start an electronic search, but it should never be the only place you look for supporting material. College student Tony Yarusso, contributing to the *Chronicle for Higher Education* blog, writes, "some students just list the first 10 Google hits regardless of where their info comes from."[9]
- *Blogs* (short for "web logs") are websites on which anyone can post comments. Blogs are interesting to read and to participate in, but they contain much unauthoritative, opinionated material. Blogs are very interesting barometers of opinion and trends of thought, but you don't have to be an expert to participate. Since blogs operate a bit like online clubs that attract participants of similar perspectives, you're likely to get a set of slanted viewpoints on a given topic.

---

[9] "Wikipedia Founder Discourages Academic Use of His Creation," *Chronicle of Higher Education*, June 12, 2006, <http://chronicle.com/wiredcampus/article/1327/wikipedia -founder-discourages-academic-use-of-his-creation>.

- *Wikis* (*wiki* is Hawaiian for "quick") are fascinating collaborative websites in which any visitor can edit or add to posted text. A highly reliable authority on global warming could post a comment on Tuesday that by Thursday of the same week could contain highly unreliable edits and additions. Though most wikis allow you to follow the editing history of a particular thread, the whole concept of "authorship" is highly blurred. Wikis offer tremendous creative opportunities to their users, but they can be a risky source of effective support for your arguments. In your Web searches, you will often come upon the Wikipedia as the source of extended definitions of terms. Wikipedia is an online encyclopedia authored by a corps of volunteers. While useful in its way, like blogs and wikis, it is not authoritative. Even founder Jimmy Wales cautions students against taking his creation too seriously. He receives frequent e-mails from students saying, "'Please help me. I got an F on my paper because I cited Wikipedia.'" Mr. Wales's response: "'For God's sake, you're in college; don't cite the encyclopedia.'"[10]

Most colleges and universities have excellent websites about how to use electronic resources for class assignments. These websites—usually created by your school librarians—can tell you how to search effectively, which databases to use, and how to narrow the results of a search. If your school doesn't have this kind of information, some of the best such sites can be found on the main websites of Northwestern University, Purdue University, Rochester Institute of Technology, and the University of Maryland.

CITATION FORM

In most cases, your citation of a source will take the form of a footnote, an endnote, or inclusion of the work in a "Works Cited" list at the end of your argument. The subject matter of your argument and the course you are writing for will determine which citation form you should follow. For example, many education programs require students to follow the *Chicago Manual of Style* footnote format, whereas sociology will probably rely on *The Publication of the American Psychological Association*, more commonly known as APA. Most English professors insist on MLA, the Modern Language Association's format, but some may require APA. Scientific notation and documentation procedures can vary widely, so you should ask your instructor which format he or she wants you to follow if it is not specified in the assignment.

You can find models of these forms in most college writing handbooks and online through your library and many college writing lab pages. Purdue, Washington State, North Carolina University, and Dakota State are only a few of the universities that have published their OWLs (Online Writing Labs) and made them available to the public through the Internet.

---

[10] Ibid.

Electronic sources are copyrighted, so they also need to be cited. If you are using the APA style in your paper, apply it to electronic sources as well. When available, the citation should include the author or editor, the title of the text, the name of the site, the sponsoring organization, the date you visited the site (remember, websites are dynamic), the page number, and the URL.

SUMMARY

Supporting Your Arguments Honestly and Effectively

- The most common instances of plagiarism in written argument involve falsely taking credit for supporting material that is not original with you.

- Whether intentional or accidental, plagiarism—taking credit for someone else's ideas and/or writing—is a serious form of academic dishonesty that meets with grave consequences.

- It is always better to include too many citations of external sources than too few.

- You need to be discerning about the outside sources you use in your arguments—particularly about the reliability of Internet material.

- Use a citation format that is appropriate to the subject matter of your argument and acceptable to your instructor.

The following argument was written by a graduate student in education at the University of Florida. In addition to offering an interesting perspective on the pertinent subjects of plagiarism and cheating among college students, the article illustrates responsible use of paraphrase and summary as well as the APA documentation style. The article appeared in the June 2006 issue of the *Journal of College & Character*.

THE DOWNSIDE OF THE INTERNET:

CHEATING AND TECHNOLOGY IN HIGHER EDUCATION

Adam Gismondi

Theorists, led by Lawrence Kohlberg, have discussed moral and ethical issues in higher education at length (Evans, Forney, & Guido-DiBrito, 1998). Various ethical pitfalls have long

Source: Adam Gismondi, "The Downside of the Internet: Cheating and Technology in Higher Education," *Journal of College and Character* 7(5) (June 2006).

existed for students on college campuses across the country. However, in a rapidly changing world, new technology creates the need to take another look at academic cheating in college within the modern context. In the case of higher education, both professionals and students are faced with new and complex ethical problems because of new forms of technology each and every day. In particular, technological changes have brought about new issues in terms of cheating and plagiarism.

The Internet poses a new threat to the moral behavior of college students, as its increased usage represents a unique facet of the problem of cheating in college. Although the Internet has helped to expedite the research process for many academics, it has also created easy access to methods of cheating and plagiarism for students (Tichenor, 2001). This article aims to look at the role of the Internet in student cheating and plagiarism and the insights offered by Kohlberg's theory of moral development.

Kohlberg's View on Development

The work of Kohlberg is largely influenced by Piaget's past studies, which included research in the area of moral development in children (Evans et al.,1998). Piaget's theory introduced the idea that young children went through stages in their moral development. Kohlberg advanced this theory by adding on stages that apply to development later in life. This expanded model of moral development allows us to study college students, and not just younger children.

The theory put forth by Kohlberg is focused on the notion of "justice" (Evans et al., 1998). A core theme of Kohlberg's work is that as people develop morally, they begin to make decisions that focus on universal rights, looking to achieve equality across all boundaries. The term "justice" represents the goal of moral development in Kohlberg's theory, and it allows us to have a helpful guideline for how we view development.

According to Kohlberg, there is a sequence to the levels and stages that individuals must follow towards moral and ethical

development (Evans et al., 1998). The theorist's model consists
of three distinct levels and six sub stages. The journey goes
from level I, in which a person follows rules because he or she
fears punishment, through level II, in which the person develops
a concept of a greater social system, to level III, where the
person shifts his or her thinking towards a justice-based concept
of right and wrong. Individuals move through the stages through
experiences of cognitive dissonance. When a situation is
presented in which a person's rationale of a moral or ethical
solution is questioned, development can occur. Movement through
this developmental process represents a shift in thinking; the
person is actually changing the way in which he or she frames
moral questions and understands the world.

Application

   Despite theoretical advancements in understanding moral
development, it has been documented that cheating remains
a persistent problem on college campuses (Tichenor, 2001).
How can this unrelenting issue of cheating be explained? One
possible rationale, offers Tichenor, is that the new environment
at schools makes cheating both rational and accessible. Academic
study in college has moved away from the classroom and onto the
Web in recent years. Many professors have not only shifted to a
greater use of technology in their lectures, but they also make
their lectures available for online access. Students today can
complete academic courses without ever setting foot in an
actual classroom because of these advancements.

   Wider implications can be seen when the newly integrated
technology is extensively considered. Along with the movement
towards Web-based lectures, an increased reliance on the
Internet for research projects can be seen (Tichenor, 2001).
While the integration of Internet technology adds to the
convenience of information gathering, it also can create
problems related to student cheating. Numerous websites exist
that make plagiarism a mere click away for users. These sites
are targeted at college students as they research online and

offer a wide variety of papers at minimal prices. Students who are looking to get the best grades possible with the least amount of time invested can often use these resources with little fear of negative consequence.

Moral development theory helps to provide a context for explaining why students are able to justify these cheating behaviors. For example, stage three of level II in Kohlberg's model of moral development describes the morality of individuals who are looking to gain acceptance of others (Evans et al., 1998). At this stage, individuals may not yet understand their role within the realm of larger societal guidelines. As such, upholding the moral values of the college community may not yet be a priority for these students. Instead, an individual still at this level of moral development will most likely be looking to gain personal advantage above all else. This situation becomes increasingly complex when viewed within the context of student life on campus today.

The conveniences of technology, however, have done little to reduce the pressures facing students today. Institutions are becoming increasingly competitive, and students are being forced to do more with less time (Larkham & Manns, 2002). Those enrolled in college are often faced with rising tuition rates, and many students have taken on jobs to help offset costs. As a result, these students have less time to involve themselves in their schoolwork. While it is difficult to say that the rise in cheating and plagiarism are [sic.] caused by inappropriate uses of the Internet (some universities are reluctant to release this sort of information), Larkham and Manns posit that there is a connection.

Plagiarism works as a way for students to satiate their psychological need to be successful in college and accepted socially, even if they do not have the innate skill to meet the demands of college life. In conjunction with the increased financial pressures and access to new cheating methods, students may also be coming into college with less academic skills than in past years. Kathleen Klompien (2001) argues that high school students simply aren't facing the same demands as their predecessors. Unprepared students enter the college environment, and as a result, many modern undergraduates don't know how to research and write a research paper. For a student who is in Kohlberg's stage three of moral conformity, social acceptance is the imperative outcome. Therefore, cheating through plagiarism is seen as a way to compensate for lack of academic preparedness.

Some students simply ignore the ethical questions related to their actions. Some websites allow students to "outsource" assignments, and these are placed in a bidding format, to ensure the best prices. To some users of these sites, homework is seen as nothing more than an inconvenience; hiring others to complete their academic work allows them to continue with their busy lives unrestrained by the demands of college. Moral implications of these actions are simply overlooked (Gomes, 2006).

Ethical Decision Making: Providing Guidance for Students

Internet technology has opened up a wide range of ethical dilemmas for students. This situation also affects faculty and student affairs practitioners who seek to guide the educational and ethical development of students. What role can they play in guiding the development of college students? Certainly educators can establish credibility by being role models for students and serving as a resource for students when they face tough ethical decisions.

On college campuses, students are daily witnesses to ethical decision making by all members of the surrounding community. Due to their close proximity to students, faculty members and student affairs practitioners are often in the best positions to set an example for students. Professionals must be better informed themselves about technology developments and how college students are using such technology to cheat on academic work.

By being more ignorant of new technology than the students they teach and serve, campus leaders make themselves irrelevant allies in the battle against technology-based cheating. Through his work, Kohlberg (Evans, et al., 1998) demonstrates that mentors can be very valuable when they guide students towards cognitive dissonance and help them to resolve the inherent ethical conflicts that come in college life. If higher education professionals remove themselves from the dialogue, students may languish and never confront the most meaningful situations that help to challenge lower-stage methods of rationalization.

Proposed Solutions and Further Implications for College Professionals

In addressing this issue of cheating, both long-term and short-term solutions must be considered. In the short term, there are a number of resources that presently exist to help curb cheating. Several websites offer programs that can search articles and compare them with thousands of others to look for evidence of plagiarism (Jenson & De Castell, 2004). Instructors can also employ the practice of checking assignments at random against cited sources to look for proper writing practices. These solutions are not flawless, however. As comprehensive as they may be, websites are not capable of accounting for every piece of literature ever written. Further, it is unreasonable to expect educators to personally check sources for all assignments.

Long-term solutions include the need for a campus culture that strongly affirms ethical behavior and discourages academic cheating. This environmental shift requires campus educators and staff not only to discourage cheating through threats and punishments but to help to create a learning environment that honors integrity and fosters ethical behavior throughout the institution.

College professionals must also stay current on technological developments in order to be aware of issues that may arise. Finally, campus professionals must understand the nature of student moral development, and they must adjust their practice accordingly.

Many studies that look at contemporary problems in American higher education conclude that both faculty and student affairs practitioners must work together to solve difficult issues (Tichenor, 2001). In the case of cheating and technology, these two constituencies of college campuses must be united once again. The modern rigors of academia are not reason enough to justify student cheating. In approaching these issues with care, college professionals can set the example for students. This is part of a developmental culture shift in which those within the college environment can all take part. This all begins with setting up a safe environment for students where moral and ethical growth can be promoted.

In his research, Kohlberg emphasized the need to challenge students in such a way that they question their personal beliefs (Evans et al., 1998). Through this process of cognitive dissonance, personal ideas regarding morality shift away from a focus on oneself, and move towards justice for all. Most college students are at a formative level, and many have had little experience away from their home community previous to these years. Therefore, it is vital that professionals on campus are aware of these factors when helping to guide development.

Although Kohlberg claims that individuals follow a sequential path in their moral development, it is also important to note that there is no set timeline for every person. Students develop at varying rates; campus professionals should recognize this fact and adapt their interactions accordingly. Much work has been done since Kohlberg's model was brought to the academic world, but it is still relevant to achieving certain outcomes. We can use this model to help us understand the development of our students. College professionals can challenge students in ways that encourage moral development and help students to face the practical challenges they confront with cheating in college. Situations involving ethical development can be addressed in college that help students for years to come.

REFERENCES

Evans, N. J., Forney, D. S., & Guido-DiBrito, F. (1998).
    Student development in college. San Francisco:
    Jossey-Bass Publishers.

Fernandez, L. (2005). The politics of technology.
    Chronicle of Higher Education, 51(42). Retrieved May 20,
    2006, from Academic Search Premier database.

Gomes, L. (2006, January 18). Some Students Hire Experts to Do
    Their School Work. *Wall Street Journal*, p. B1.

Jenson, J., & De Castell, S. (1004). "Turn it in":
    Technological challenges to academic ethics. *Education,
    Communication, & Information, 4*(2). Retrieved May 20,
    2006, from Academic Search Premier database.

Klompien, K. (2001, March). The writer and the text: Basic
    writers, research papers and plagiarism. Paper presented
    at the annual meeting of the Conference on College
    Composition and Communication, Denver, Colorado.

Larkham, P. J., & Manns, S. (2002). Plagiarism and its treatment
    in higher education. *Journal of Further and Higher
    Education, 26*(4). Retrieved November 11, 2005, from
    Tayler & Francis database.

Tichenor, S. (2001, May). Cutting edge technology: Inspiration
    or irritation? Paper presented at the annual meeting of
    the National Institute for Staff and Organizational
    Development, Austin, Texas.

SUGGESTIONS FOR WRITING (5.1)

1. Using a paragraph from this book as the original text, write the following:
   1) a paraphrase of the paragraph incorporating some direct quotation;
   2) a paraphrase with no quotations; and 3) a brief summary. Be sure your
   instructor approves the original paragraph.

2. Using two different databases and one popular search engine, find three
   different websites containing biographical material on one of the following
   individuals: Jonas Salk; Daniel Pink; Hillary Clinton. Then write a one-
   paragraph evaluation of the reliability of each of the websites, based upon
   their sponsoring organizations, their domain name, and the reputations of
   the websites' contributors. Finally, create bibliographical citations for
   each of the websites.

ILLUSTRATIVE ARGUMENTS IN PART II: SUPPORTING YOUR ARGUMENTS HONESTLY AND EFFECTIVELY

6

Making Reasonable Arguments: Formal and Informal Logic

In Chapters 7 through 10, you will learn the most appropriate supporting methods for each class of claim. But before you begin working at the specific levels of claim and support, you should have some understanding of the principles of logic. The primary definition of the term *logic* is "the science of correct reasoning." The many and complicated rules of formal logic do, in fact, make up an intricate mathematical system that yields absolutely right and absolutely wrong answers. But this system does not dominate the fuzzier province of written argument, where variations in context, occasion, audience, and purpose make absolute conclusions exceedingly rare. Nevertheless, the fundamental principles of formal logic and their less formal derivatives do have their use in written argument: they are excellent tools for testing the reasonableness of the relationship between claim and support, for measuring the probability of an argument's conclusion. Think of it this way: you can't write successful arguments without some familiarity with logic, but this familiarity will not ensure that your arguments will be successful.

FORMAL LOGIC

The principles of formal logic were identified by the Greek philosopher Aristotle (384–322 B.C.). Today, almost 2,500 years later, these principles continue to influence what we mean by *reasonable* thinking. Just as children learn to speak their native language unaware of its underlying linguistic and grammatical principles, so we learn to think reasonably with little understanding of those complex principles informing reasonable thought. At some point in their education, children must learn the rules of grammar in order to refine their language skills; similarly, as educated adults and certainly as writers of argument, we must become familiar with the principles of logic to refine our reasoning skills.

Formal logic comes in two broad varieties: induction and deduction. *Induction,* or inductive reasoning, involves reasoning from observed evidence (the support) to a general statement (the claim or conclusion). *Deduction,* or deductive reasoning, involves reasoning from premises (assertions accepted as true or probable) to a conclusion or claim.

Induction:

> **Observed evidence:** In the 20 years I've lived in New York State, warm weather has begun every year between March and May.
> **General statement:** In New York State, warm weather begins between March and May.

Deduction:

> **Premise:** All human beings are mortal.
> **Premise:** Jane is a human being.
> **Conclusion:** Jane is mortal.

In the first example, notice the movement from specific examples (every spring for 20 years) to a very general assertion. But notice also that the specific examples suggest only that the general assertion is likely or probable, not necessarily true. The move from specific examples to a general conclusion is often referred to as the *inductive leap,* a term which underlines the large gap between the truth of the individual instances and the truth of the generalized conclusion.

In the deductive example, on the other hand, the statement that Jane is mortal is *necessarily true* if the premises preceding it are true. If certain conditions are met, deductive arguments *can* lead to necessary, or absolute, conclusions. But the "if" is a big one; in reality, the principles of deduction will enhance the reasonableness of your argument, but they will rarely ensure its absolute truth.

As you'll see in the next four chapters, some logical principles are more useful with one kind of argument than with another. The remainder of this chapter offers a general introduction to the principles themselves.

Induction

In inductive reasoning, we make generalizations on the basis of individual instances. For example, if you observed repeated instances of male students dominating class discussion, you might conclude that at your school, male students participate in class more than female students. Your conclusion is useful not because it represents the absolute truth, which of course it doesn't (there are exceptions to any generalization), but because it summarizes a set of similar events that you have observed. Inductive reasoning comes naturally to all of us, whether we're highly trained in Aristotelian logic or don't know the difference between a reasoned argument and a shouting match.

But the process does carry risks. For one thing, irresponsible induction can lead to harmful misconceptions. There is a world of difference between the conclusion

"Male political science majors at Miller College tend to dominate class discussion" and one claiming "Men are more skillful speakers than women." You can avoid making irresponsible conclusions if you heed the following three cautions: (1) be sure you have *enough* individual examples to warrant the conclusion (your experience in one political science class is not enough to warrant even the preceding first conclusion); (2) provide the context of your examples and conclusion—in this case, your observations of students in a particular major at a particular college; and (3) always qualify your conclusion by using verbs or modifiers that limit the degree of certainty you're insisting on ("Male students often dominate class discussion").

A second risk of inductive reasoning concerns the use to which we put its conclusions. Inductive conclusions are safest if they are used *descriptively,* as a way of summarizing a set of observations or facts ("Male political science majors at Miller tend to dominate class discussion"). But induction is more commonly used to *predict* events or behavior. Many of the predictions we make on the basis of induction are perfectly harmless. If you know that the shopping mall is usually crowded on Saturday afternoons, your decision to shop Saturday morning is a harmless and quite useful prediction based on inductive reasoning. But predictive inductive reasoning can lead to harmful stereotypes. It may be true that women in your major do not participate in class discussion, but if you assume, on the basis of these limited observations, that all the women you associate with will be quiet and unassertive, your false conclusion may put you in personal and political hot water.

Responsible inductive reasoning depends in large measure on recognizing and arguing factual claims, since induction involves supporting a general claim by individual factual instances. For this reason, a full discussion of induction is reserved for Chapter 7, "Arguing Facts."

Deduction

The basic form of the deductive argument is the *syllogism:* a three-part argument consisting of a *major premise* (a premise is an assertion or proposition), a *minor premise,* and a *conclusion.* The earlier sample of deductive reasoning is a classic example of a syllogism:

> **Major premise:** All human beings are mortal.
> **Minor premise:** Jane is a human being.
> **Conclusion:** Jane is mortal.

This syllogism is an example of thinking in terms of classes. The major premise establishes two classes—a larger one of mortal beings and a smaller one of human beings—and it asserts that the smaller class belongs in the larger. The minor premise establishes that a still smaller class—in this case, one individual (Jane)—belongs in the smaller class of the major premise. From there it necessarily follows that Jane will also be a member of the largest class, mortal beings. The syllogism can also be displayed visually.

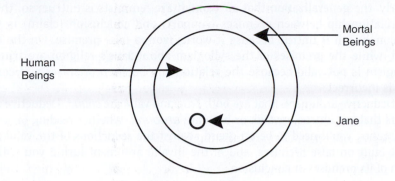

Thinking in terms of classes can be misleading if the process is done incorrectly. Examine the following syllogism:

Major premise: All Catholics believe in the sanctity of human life.
Minor premise: Jane believes in the sanctity of human life.
Conclusion: Jane is a Catholic.

At first glance this argument may seem plausible, but as the diagram below shows, the argument is seriously flawed because the minor premise puts Jane in the larger group of those who believe in the sanctity of life but not in the smaller group of those who are Catholics. All the argument can really tell us is that Jane and Catholics share this one trait. They may differ in everything else.

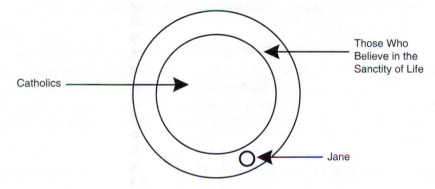

This sample syllogism leads us to an important distinction in deductive reasoning: the distinction between validity and truth. A syllogism is *valid* when it's set up correctly, according to the rules of formal logic. You can look these rules up in a logic textbook, but in many cases, you can tell when a syllogism doesn't follow them correctly because, as in the case of Jane's religious persuasion, you recognize instinctively that the conclusion doesn't make sense. On the other hand, a syllogism is *true* only if its premises are true. The syllogism about Jane's mortality is both valid and true. But consider the following syllogism:

All women are feminists.
Jane is a woman.
Jane is a feminist.

Clearly, the generalization that *all* women are feminists is untrue; so, though the relationship between premises (support) and conclusion (claim) is valid, the conclusion is untrue because it works from a false premise. On the other hand, while the premises of the syllogism about Jane's religion are true, the syllogism is not valid because the relationship between premises and conclusion is incorrect.

Deductive arguments that are both true and valid are *sound.* Deductive arguments that are untrue, invalid, or both are *unsound.* Whether reading or writing arguments, you'll need to be on guard against the seductions of the valid argument built on false premises, and of the invalid argument luring you with the truth of its premises or conclusion.

Conditional Syllogism.   The conditional syllogism, sometimes referred to as the *if-then syllogism,* takes the following form:

> If John drops the glass on the sidewalk, then the glass breaks.
>
> John drops the glass on the sidewalk.
>
> The glass breaks.

This syllogism is valid, and if its premises are true, it is also sound.

With conditional syllogisms, however, you need to watch out for a very common error, usually called *affirming the consequent,* where the "then" clause of the major premise is turned into an affirmative statement in the minor premise:

> If John drops the glass on the sidewalk, then the glass breaks.
>
> The glass breaks.
>
> John drops the glass on the sidewalk.

The argument is invalid because the major premise merely claims that John's dropping the glass causes it to break; it does not exclude other ways of breaking the glass, such as hitting it with a hammer. Given this major premise, we cannot conclude that John has dropped the glass simply because the glass is broken.

Disjunctive Syllogism.   The disjunctive, or "either-or," syllogism takes the following form:

> Either the doctor gave the patient oxygen or the patient died.
>
> The patient did not die.
>
> The doctor gave the patient oxygen.

Note that this argument is invalid if the alternative is affirmed—that is, if it turns out to be true—rather than denied, or declared untrue, as in the preceding example:

> Either the doctor gave the patient oxygen or the patient died.
>
> The patient died.
>
> The doctor did not give the patient oxygen.

The major premise merely asserts that we can assume that the first alternative occurred because the second one didn't. (In other words, if the doctor hadn't given the patient oxygen, the patient would surely have died.) But if the second one, the patient's dying, did occur, we can't turn around and assume that the doctor failed to give the patient oxygen. Again, the patient could have died from a number of other causes even if the doctor did his "duty."

Making Use of Deduction in Written Arguments.   For writers of argument, classical logic offers a good way of "checking your work." Familiarity with the basic principles of deductive reasoning will probably not help you *create* arguments, but it will help you test the reasonableness of your claim and support once they are composed. Of course, the writing and thinking we do every day do not come packaged in classical syllogistic form, so that detecting sound and unsound reasoning is a little more difficult than in the preceding examples. But with a little practice, you can become adept at recasting your claim and support into the syllogistic model.

Let's say you are writing an argument claiming, "Your name does not determine your destiny." You plan to offer the following support for your claim: (1) students with common names receive higher grades than students with unusual names, but there could be other issues operating here; (2) studies of prisoners reveal half of the inmates in prisons undergoing psychiatric evaluations have uncommon names; and (3) many successful people have unusual names. To determine whether your claim and support are logical, you'll need to work with each supporting claim separately, finding the place it would occupy in a formal syllogism that concludes, "Your name does not determine your destiny."

So where would your first supporting claim be placed? Because it's fairly specific, it is likely to be a minor premise, since minor premises of syllogisms are almost always more specific than major premises. You now have an incomplete syllogism that looks like this:

> Major premise: ?
> Minor premise: Students with common names receive higher grades than students with uncommon names, but there could be other reasons involved.
> Conclusion: Therefore, your name does not determine your destiny.

The syllogistic formula requires that the major premise establish a larger class of which the class in the minor premise is a subset. Here, the major premise would read something like "Your name does not determine your destiny." Now the syllogism looks like this:

> Major premise: Your name does not determine your destiny.
> Minor premise: A study showed teachers gave students with common names higher grades than students with uncommon names, but there could be other reasons involved.
> Conclusion: Therefore, your name does not determine your destiny.

You don't have to state the major premise in your argument, but it is extremely helpful to know what it is so that you can determine whether that assumption—and its relationship to the rest of the argument—is reasonable.

To determine its reasonableness, you test the validity and soundness of the syllogism. The syllogism is valid: the internal relationship among premises and conclusion is deductively proper. But its soundness (the truth of the premises) is another question. Let's take the minor premise first. You would need considerable evidence of incidences where names have been studied to support this premise. One or two examples of names and their co-relations do not justify the premise. But if you can find examples where names do or do not consistently lead to success, and illustrate this through factual support and perhaps a comparison based on character names in a novel, the premise could be accepted as true. (Chapter 7 will discuss the principles of support for factual claims like this one.)

The major premise is much more problematic. At the very least, it is debatable. Some might say that it is indefensible, since it asks readers to accept as universally applicable a single notion related to a complex problem. Even if the premise is true, its truth is too controversial to be assumed; it must be justified through a careful secondary argument.

The incomplete syllogism discussed above (the one lacking a major premise) is an *enthymeme*—a form of syllogism common to spoken and written arguments, where presenting all components of the syllogism may be tedious for the audience. An enthymeme is a rhetorical syllogism that implicitly relies on an audience's existing beliefs to support the conclusion. Enthymemes are not inferior syllogisms; their very incompleteness helps to convince. An audience that helps to complete the argument will have a stake in it and thus will be more likely to accept it. But as in the case above, the writer must have good reason to believe that the audience will accept the premise provided. As you will see in Chapters 9 and 10, this process of uncovering the syllogism or enthymeme of an argument can be particularly useful when arguing evaluations and recommendations.

ACTIVITIES (6.1)

1. Identify the major premise of the following incomplete syllogisms, as in the following example.

   Conclusion: My physics professor is a skilled teacher.
   Minor premise: My physics professor knows her physics thoroughly, uses imaginative examples, is concerned that her students learn, and is an excellent speaker.
   Major premise: A skilled teacher knows his or her subject matter thoroughly and can present it imaginatively, is concerned that students learn, and speaks clearly and compellingly.

   a. **Minor premise:** Mack's résumé was poorly written.
      Conclusion: Mack did not get the job because his résumé was poorly written.

    b. **Minor premise:** Jessie made faces at the refs behind their backs, cursed members of the other team, and refused to congratulate them on their victory.
    Conclusion: Jessie is a poor sport.
    c. **Minor premise:** Professor Callahan constantly interrupts his students.
    Conclusion: Professor Callahan does not respect his students.
    d. **Minor premise:** Young people of today do not value family or community.
    Conclusion: Our young people will not grow up to be good citizens.
    e. **Minor premise:** Henry Clay was a master of the art of compromise.
    Conclusion: Henry Clay was a fine statesman.
    f. **Minor premise:** There is no way I can write my final research paper for this class.
    Conclusion: I will not pass this class.

2. With a small group of your classmates, discuss the extent to which the major and minor premises of three of the preceding syllogisms would need to be argued.

3. Examine an essay you wrote recently and present its major argument as a syllogism. What are the argument's major premise, minor premise, and conclusion? Are any of these components implicit rather than explicit in your essay? Is the syllogism sound and valid?

THE TOULMIN MODEL:
A MODERN VARIANT OF FORMAL LOGIC

Formal deductive reasoning yields necessary or certain conclusions, yet written arguments about our complex, provisional, and messy world rarely presume to discover absolute truth. It is in this mismatch between the goals of formal reasoning and those of written argument that the limitations of deduction are exposed. The fact is that most of the arguments we judge to be worth making are worth making *because* they are arguable, because they admit the possibility of more than one reasonable position. Few people waste time, for example, arguing about whether the sun will come up tomorrow, but they do argue about whether the problem of ozone depletion in the atmosphere warrants strict regulation of pollutants.

Recognizing the limitations of Aristotelian logic for practical rhetoric, the twentieth-century philosopher Stephen Toulmin identified and formalized a slightly different relationship between an argument's claim and its support. Toulmin's model is a useful way to judge the reasonableness of many of the arguments you construct.

According to the Toulmin model, a claim is linked to its support through what is called a *warrant*. A claim's warrant indicates how one gets from factual support (which Toulmin calls *data*) to the claim. It is the general belief, convention, or principle that permits the data to support the claim.

Suppose you were proposing that your college major institute a junior-year-abroad program. You have a number of supporting reasons for this claim: the program will attract students to the major; it will be an invaluable educational experience for students; it will allow the department to establish important international connections. The Toulmin model requires that each supporting reason be linked to the claim through some assumption or principle acceptable to the audience. Using the last support cited, a diagram of this argument would look like this:

Data		**Claim**
A junior-year-abroad program will help the department establish international connections.		My college major should start a junior-year-abroad program.

Warrant
International connections would
be valuable to my college.

We can identify an argument's warrant (which is not always stated explicitly in the argument itself) by asking, "What is it about the data that allows me to reach the claim?" In this case, it is the *value* of international connections that makes the claim desirable. Just as major premises are sometimes left unstated in real arguments, warrants are sometimes only implied. If you have any reason to suspect that your audience will not accept the warrant as generally true or at least reasonable, you will have to support it with what Toulmin calls *backing.* In this case, one backing for the warrant might be identification of the benefits of international connections in a world where more and more college graduates will be working for international organizations.

A fifth element of the Toulmin model, which makes the concept particularly useful to written argument, is the *qualifier.* The qualifier is a word or words that modify or qualify the claim. In our example, that qualifier is the word *should,* a word that makes the recommendation less strong than *must,* but more strong than *might want to consider.* Unlike the syllogism, the Toulmin paradigm gives the writer room to entertain claims that are less than necessary or certain. Adding the backing and the qualifier to our example, we come up with the diagram on page 95.

Applying Toulmin's model to your own arguments can help you flush out the assumptions that generate your claim and evaluate their reasonableness. You may find that this model is most useful in making recommendations (as in the preceding example) and causal arguments. The most useful point in the composition process at which to apply both the Toulmin and the Aristotelian models is after you have formulated a claim and collected some support. Fitting these elements into one or the other paradigm will help tell you what is missing, what needs further support, and what is patently unreasonable. Don't *begin* the argument process by trying to fit ideas into the models; this will only frustrate your thinking and limit your inventiveness.

Data
A junior-year-abroad program
will help the department establish
international connections.

Claim
My college major should
start a junior-year-
abroad program.

Qualifier

Warrant
International connections would
be valuable to my college.

Backing
In our increasingly global economy,
college graduates will be working
for international organizations.

ACTIVITIES (6.2)

1. Identify the unstated warrants for each of the following pairs of claim and
   support.
   a. **Claim:** Secondary smoke is harmful.
      Support (or data): The Surgeon General's report on smoking establishes
      this.
   b. **Claim:** Celebrities who stand trial for capital crimes are not likely to get
      fair trials.
      Support (or data): The media focus unrelentingly on celebrity suspects.
   c. **Claim:** If you have the flu, you should stay at home.
      Support (or data): This year's strain of the flu is highly contagious.
   d. **Claim:** Writing is a dying art.
      Support (or data): My freshman students don't know the difference
      between an independent clause and Santa Claus.
   e. **Claim:** Mick is an unorthodox runner.
      Support (or data): Mick holds his arms high when he runs, and his heels
      never touch the ground.
2. Which of the previously supplied warrants would require some backing in
   order to be acceptable to readers? What kind of backing might you supply?

INFORMAL FALLACIES

Unfortunately, even when we pay careful attention to the logical principles discussed in this chapter, our reasoning can still go awry through any of a number of
informal fallacies. Like the principles of formal logic, informal fallacies usually involve a faulty relationship between an argument's claim and its support.
Familiarity with these flaws in reasoning is especially useful during the revision
stage, when, with these fallacies in mind, you examine the relationship between
your claim and its support. Since an inclusive list of these fallacies is a very long

one—as inexhaustible as human inventiveness—included here are only those fallacies that frequently turn up in student writing. For each fallacy, the category or categories of argument in which it is most likely to occur are also indicated.

Ad Hominem Argument

An *ad hominem* argument is against the arguer (in Latin *ad hominem* means "to the man") rather than against the argument: "Smith's argument against increasing taxes on the rich is worthless because he himself is rich." This fallacy, which substitutes irrelevant judgments of an individual for reasonable evaluations of an issue, is most likely to occur in evaluative arguments.

Ad Populum Argument

Ad populum is Latin for "to the people." One commits the *ad populum* fallacy when supporting a claim by referring to popular opinion or behavior to justify it. A teenager trying to convince her parents to remove her curfew because "everybody else's parents have done it" is attempting to convince her parents through an appeal to popular behavior rather than to reason. This fallacy is a corruption of the legitimate tactic of appealing to established authorities to strengthen a claim.

Circular Argument

A circular argument (also known as *begging the question*) is one in which the claim is already contained in the support: "John did not succeed on the track team [the claim] because he did not do well in track events [the support]." In this example, "did not do well in track events" really only restates "did not succeed on the track team"; it adds no new information about *why* John didn't succeed. Another common version of circular argument, or begging the question, assumes what has to be proven, as in the statement "This film should be banned because it contains immoral scenes." This claim requires a definition of *immoral* and evidence that the film meets this definition. Lacking such material, the claim begs the question of the immorality of the film. Evaluative, interpretive, and causal arguments seem to be particularly subject to this fallacy. One giveaway that your argument is circular is that your supporting statements repeat a key term from your claim.

Distraction

Distraction is bringing in irrelevant points to distract attention from the issue being argued: "Sure I cheated on my income taxes, but I've never broken any other laws." It is also known as the *red herring,* from the practice of dragging a dead herring across a trail to distract hunting dogs from the scent of their prey. Distraction is frequently used to deflect unfavorable evaluations.

Either-Or Argument

The either-or argument is setting up two extreme positions as the only alternatives and denying any possible middle ground: "The painting is either a masterpiece or trash." The painting could be something in between. Also known as *bifurcation* or the *fallacy of the excluded middle,* this fallacy can occur in any category of argument, though it is probably most frequent in evaluations (as in the claim about the painting) or in recommendations, where extreme solutions are sometimes seen as the only options: "Either we build a new computer facility or we give up on using computers at this school."

Emotive Language

The fallacy of emotive language involves making a case through slanted, value-laden language rather than through reasonable support, as in the statement "Smelling blood, the media will attack and destroy any candidate with a newsworthy weak spot." This claim, in its implicit identification of the media with carnivorous beasts, presumes a value judgment about the media that the claim does not justify. Writers of argument should try to refrain from using prejudicial language, at least until their claims have been reasonably made. Emotive or slanted language can be used in any kind of argument, but it is most common in evaluative arguments.

False Analogy

The false analogy supports a claim by comparing its subject to something not *essentially* similar: "Offering courses in gay and lesbian theory is no more defensible than teaching pedophilia or necrophilia." While both sides of the comparison refer to noncustomary sexual preference, there are more *differences* between gay theory and pedophilia than there are similarities, and comparing them attempts to prejudice the reader against gay and lesbian theory. As pointed out in Chapter 11, analogies can be useful in generating and illuminating arguments, but they can never prove a point. Just as legitimate comparison can be used to support any kind of argument (see Chapter 4), analogies can be misused in all of the four classes of argument. If you find that you have introduced an analogy to *support* rather than explain or illuminate a claim, you have probably committed this fallacy.

Hasty Generalization

Basically a misuse of the inductive method, hasty generalization consists of a general claim based on an insufficient sample: "Young professional people tend to be self-centered and materialistic. My friends Eric and Melanie certainly are." This fallacy typically occurs in factual arguments and in the supposedly factual support for evaluative statements about entire groups of people: "Women are sentimental"; "Asian-American students are good in mathematics."

Non Sequitur

A *non sequitur* claims a logical relationship between a conclusion and a premise where none exists: "Henry should make a good governor because he is tall and handsome." *Non sequitur* in Latin means "it does not follow"; *non sequitur* reasoning is behind almost all fallacies. The term is really a generic one that has been specifically applied to cases where the relationship between a premise and a conclusion is seriously askew. The term is also used to cover some fallacies in causal analysis: "I performed poorly on that speech because I wore my green tie rather than my red one." This is an example of our next fallacy—*post hoc, ergo propter hoc*. *Non sequitur* reasoning can occur in any category of argument.

Post Hoc, Ergo Propter Hoc

Post hoc, ergo propter hoc is Latin, meaning "after this, therefore because of this." It means claiming that because one event preceded another, it must have caused the subsequent event to occur: "I performed poorly on that speech because I wore my green tie rather than my red one." This fallacy is at the root of much superstition, as in the case of a pitcher who carries a red handkerchief with him whenever he pitches because he had one with him the day of his no-hitter. It is a serious risk in any causal analysis, and a writer can guard against it by following the principles of causal reasoning presented in Chapter 8.

Slippery Slope

Designating a first and a last step in a causal chain, when the intervening steps have not occurred, constitutes the slippery slope fallacy: "I didn't get the first job I interviewed for, so I guess I'd better forget about a career as an engineer." In this simple example, the speaker creates a worst-case scenario (forgetting about engineering) based on a series of events that has not yet occurred and will not necessarily occur, that is, repeated failure to be hired in engineering jobs. This fallacy appears most commonly in arguments of effect, usually when the writer wishes to prove that the consequences of a particular action are likely to be negative.

Strawperson Argument

A strawperson argument involves attacking a view similar to but not identical with that of an opponent: "How long will America tolerate softheaded opponents of gun control who want only criminals to have guns?" Advocates of gun control vary in their views, but they do not want only criminals to have guns. The adjective *softheaded* is an example of emotive language; in this sentence, it is designed to arouse a particular emotional response. Negative loaded terms are frequent in strawperson arguments. This fallacy is a common but misguided tactic of evaluative arguments.

You can improve your ability to analyze your own and others' arguments by familiarizing yourself with the kinds of fallacies previously defined, but you need to remember that what is considered "correct" thinking depends on your context.

What may be incorrect in one context may be perfectly acceptable in another: *ad hominem* arguments are frowned on in academic writing (though they do occur), but they are perfectly acceptable in a court of law, where questioning and at least implicitly attacking witnesses' backgrounds and motives are frequently practiced. In addition, some of these fallacies are only a slight step off the path of correct reasoning. For example, there is nothing inherently fallacious about either-or reasoning, but this kind of reasoning goes wrong when either-or alternatives lead to excluding other, real possibilities.

ACTIVITIES (6.3)

Identify the informal fallacies committed in the sentences that follow. Select from the following list:

ad hominem argument	false analogy
ad populum argument	hasty generalization
circular argument	*non sequitur*
distraction	*post hoc, ergo propter hoc*
either-or argument	slippery slope
emotive language	strawperson argument

1. Legalized abortion puts us only a step away from legalizing murders of anyone we deem undesirable or inconvenient.
2. If you can't beat them, join them.
3. I strongly disagree with your proposal to allow women to join fraternities. Fraternities are men-only clubs.
4. Those traitorous, draft-dodging youths who preferred deserting their country to serving it should never have been granted amnesty.
5. Discrimination should be fought on every front—whether it's practiced against members of a certain race, a certain sex, or those who bear arms.
6. I spent two weeks at a military academy and realized that private school is just not for me.
7. It is unfair to penalize corporations for harming the environment when they are supporting the global economy.
8. *The Office* had the highest ratings of any television series. Clearly it is a superior series.
9. Tom Hanks is a brilliant comedian; he should leave heavy drama alone.
10. Opponents of the Equal Rights Amendment believe that women should stay barefoot and pregnant.

SUMMARY

Making Reasonable Arguments: Formal and Informal Logic

- Understanding the principles of formal logic will help you link claim and support reasonably.

- The principles of inductive logic—moving from specific instances to general conclusions—are important to all writers of argument and are particularly applicable to factual arguments.

- The syllogistic formula, common to most deductive reasoning, can be applied to an argument's claim and support as a way of determining the reasonableness of their connection.

- The Toulmin model of claim-warrant-backing is particularly useful to writers of argument, as it does not make absolute certainty a requirement of the claim.

- Informal fallacies are any of those errors in reasoning that can undermine the credibility of a claim. The best time to consider the possibility of informal fallacies is during the revision process.

The following article by Leslie Knowlton (*Psychiatric Times,* XII, 9, September 1995) contains a number of claims supported in a variety of ways. One important claim is Knowlton's explanation for the lower incidence of eating disorders in males as compared to females. The reasonableness of this causal claim can be tested by applying the Toulmin method. Placed within the Toulmin structure, the assertion that fewer men than women experience eating disorders would be the claim, and the data would be that men are subjected to less social reinforcement of thinness than women. As is often the case, the warrant—that principle linking claim and data—is unstated, but it would read something like "social reinforcements influence behavior."

EATING DISORDERS IN MALES

LESLIE KNOWLTON

1   About 7 million women across the country suffer from eating disorders including anorexia nervosa and bulimia and, as a result, most research into those two diseases has been conducted on females. However, as many as a million men may also struggle with the diseases.

2   One of the nation's leading researchers on eating disorders is Arnold E. Andersen, M.D., a professor of psychiatry in the University of Iowa College of Medicine. In addition to his academic and clinical work— some of it conducted as director of the Eating and Weight Disorders Clinic at Johns Hopkins—Andersen has edited a book of studies, *Males with Eating Disorders* (Brunner/Mazel 1990), and is writing another for families faced with the problem. His most current research project involves tracing and comparing the development of attitudes about body shape and weight among fifth- and sixth-grade males and females in the United States and India.

3   Speaking by telephone, Andersen said that despite being mentioned among the first case presentations in the English language three centuries ago, males with eating disorders have been "relatively ignored,

neglected, dismissed because of statistical infrequency or legislated out of existence by theoretical dogma."

4 "There's a need to improve our recognition of eating disorders in males and to provide more adequate treatment," he said. "In addition, the category of males with eating disorders presents intellectual challenges regarding the etiology and mechanism for this gender-divergent abnormality of human-motivated behavior."

5 Andersen said that although the disorders look the same for men and women, the paths for getting there are quite different.

6 "The twin spotlights of empirical scientific studies and broad clinical experience can be brought to focus on either the similarities or the dissimilarities between males and females with eating disorders," said Andersen. "When individuals are very ill, suffering from emaciation or abnormal electrolytes and other medical complications, they appear very similar and require similar treatment."

7 But as patients become medically more healthy and the symptoms are "deconstructed," the individual life story behind each patient unfolds to reveal differences between the sexes in predisposition, course and onset, Andersen explained.

8 "We have to go back to where the roots are formed and look at gender diversity," he said.

For example, while women who develop eating disorders *feel* fat before they begin dieting, they typically are near average weight, whereas the majority of men who develop the diseases actually *are* medically overweight. Males with eating disorders are also more likely than women to have alcohol-related conditions and obsessional features.

9 Also, whereas women are concerned predominately with weight, men are concerned with shape and muscle definition. Additionally, more males than females diet in relationship to athletic achievement or slimming to please a homosexual lover.

10 "More men who develop anorexia or bulimia were seriously teased as overweight children," Andersen said, adding that about 21 percent of males with eating disorders are gay.

11 Finally, more men diet to prevent medical consequences of being overweight than do females, said Andersen.

12 So why do fewer males than females develop full-blown eating disorders?

13 Andersen said definitive answers are not available, but sociocultural influences have a lot to do with it.

14 "There's clearly less general reinforcement for slimness and dieting for males than for females, with only 10 percent as many articles and advertisements promoting dieting in magazines read by young males as compared to those read by young females," he said, referring to a study he conducted. "But when subgroups of males are exposed to situations requiring weight loss—such as occurs with wrestlers, swimmers, runners and jockeys—then a substantial increase in the behaviors of self-starvation and/or bulimic symptomatology follows, suggesting that behavioral reinforcement, not gender, is the crucial element."

15 Therefore, he continued, there's an apparent "dose-response" relationship between the amount of sociocultural reinforcement for thinness and the probability of developing an eating disorder, with the intermediate variable being dieting behavior.

16 "The process of transition from a normal behavior such as dieting, which is not in itself abnormal, into a fixed illness meeting *DSM-IV* criteria for an eating disorder has not yet been well-defined," he said. "But it probably involves a transition from psychosocial to biomedical mechanisms."

17 Andersen said men who develop eating disorders can generally be divided into three groups: those in whom the onset was preadolescent, those in whom it was adolescent or young adult and those in whom it was adult. As in females, most male onset is adolescent.

18 While diagnostic criteria for anorexia and bulimia in men are similar to that in women, doctors often are less likely to think of making a diagnosis of eating disorders in males than in females. Likewise, the patient and his family and friends may not recognize it.

19 One reason anorexia may elude diagnosis in men more than in women is that men

don't experience the on-off phenomenon of loss of menstrual periods, which can alert professionals and others to the problem, Andersen said. Rather, testosterone is gradually reduced, with an accompanying decline in libido and sexual performance.

20   Binge eating disorder may go unrecognized in males because an overeating male is less likely to provoke attention than an overeating female.

"And men are hesitant to seek medical   21 attention for a disorder they fear will be seen as a girl's disorder or a gay guy's disease," Andersen said.

Source: *Psychiatric Times*, XII, 9 September 1995

SUGGESTIONS FOR WRITING (6.4)

1. Pay attention to the informal conversations and discussions of your friends. Start a list of all the generalizations you hear them make. Then write a one- to two-page letter to your friends telling them what information and evidence they would need to support their generalizations reasonably.

2. Focus on three advertisements you see repeatedly on television or in print. Write a one-page essay on each advertisement, discussing your application of the syllogistic and Toulmin models. How would the advertisement look within the format of each model? What premises or warrants are only implied? Are those claims true? What would have to be argued in order to make the advertisement more reasonable? Finally, rewrite the ad so that it conforms to the principles of deduction and the Toulmin model.

ILLUSTRATIVE ARGUMENTS IN PART II: MAKING REASONABLE ARGUMENTS

7

Arguing Facts

You now know that all arguments are ultimately supported by factual claims. An argument claiming that "First-time DWI offenders should have their driver's licenses revoked" (a claim of recommendation), might be supported by the secondary claim "The threat of license revocation would deter many from driving while intoxicated." This secondary causal claim (predicting the *effect* of the change) might in turn be supported by data you have located citing the effectiveness of such a law in other states: these data are a form of factual claim.

But a fact can also be the primary claim of an argument. This is the case with most articles in medical and scientific research journals, which argue the validity of newly discovered facts. Laboratory reports that you might have to write for biology or chemistry or computer science classes are essentially factual arguments that summarize a set of activities. The first sample factual argument at the end of this chapter, "Advantages of Matlab," is a lab report written for an introductory engineering course.

Whether your primary claim or secondary support, any fact you invoke in your argument must itself be successfully argued. While it may seem unnecessary to "argue" something that is supposed to be a fact, the landscape of factual assertions is a treacherous one that you must know how to navigate in order to write effective arguments.

WHAT IS A FACT?

The New College Edition of *The American Heritage Dictionary* defines a fact as "Something known with certainty." According to this definition, a fact is a statement that is known to be true and about which there can be no debate or doubt. Assertions like "My physics teacher is a woman," "George Washington was the first president of the United States," and "Human beings are mortal" would fall under this definition; they are inarguable, unambiguous, proven facts that in most arguments would require no support beyond their simple assertion. Facts like these often come from your own experience or have been confirmed by your experience; sometimes they fall under the heading of "common knowledge." In any event, they can be accepted as indisputable.

But what about statements like "Beta-carotene is a carcinogen," "Secondary smoke is not harmful," or "The FDA-established minimum daily nutritional requirements are inadequate"? While these claims are stated as if they are known with certainty, careful readers might hesitate to call them indisputable. For one thing, they come from fields in which most of us are comparatively ignorant; we lack the expertise to judge their accuracy. Second, anyone who reads the newspaper regularly knows that these are the kinds of "facts" that seem always to be retired or revised when new evidence or new research methods emerge. Indeed, each of these statements is a correction of an earlier assertion that claimed to prove the opposite: beta-carotene was for years thought to be cancer-inhibiting; the known dangers of secondary smoke are now associated with a number of health dangers; and millions of perfectly healthy people have based their diets on the minimum daily requirements suggested by the FDA.

Assertions like these fall more properly under the dictionary's secondary definition of *fact:* "Something asserted as certain." Such statements are made in good faith, based on the best available evidence, and stated with conviction, but they are the findings of incomplete and ongoing research in comparatively dynamic fields and thus are always subject to revision and correction as newer, more inclusive, more reliable evidence is gathered. In other words, such factual assertions are *believed* to be certain, but not *known* with certainty; they are more like state-of-the-art educated guesses.

Readers are constantly faced with assertions that are stated with certainty, dressed up as factual, and credited to seemingly impeccable sources, but that are nonetheless utterly preposterous. Some of these impostor facts are easy to detect; we know never to trust anything we read in the *National Enquirer,* for instance. But in more cases than we'd like to admit—particularly with the rush by the media to be the first on the scene—these preposterous facts can sneak right by you without your even suspecting that they are unreliable. You may find yourself particularly vulnerable to accepting (and circulating) false facts if they will strengthen your own argument.

The more your argument relies on the first and second type of facts, the more solid it will be. Your job in presenting facts supporting your argument's claim will be to convince your readers of their truth or likelihood, to convince them, that is, that your supporting facts are "known with certainty" or "are based on the best available evidence." The principles that follow should help you with this crucial job.

FACTUAL CLAIMS YOU WILL MAKE

Factual claims—both primary and supporting—fall into three categories: 1) those reported by others in primary and secondary sources; 2) those that you arrive at yourself—through a lab experiment or administration of a survey, for example; and 3) those derived through your own personal experience.

Facts Reported by Others.   As you prepare to write your argument, you will inevitably come across factual assertions in primary and secondary sources. To review, a primary source is the individual or group that determined the fact in the first place—for example, a manager reporting that sales declined 5 percent in the last quarter or a research oncologist summarizing the findings of her study on cancer remissions in a medical journal. A secondary source is the person or document reporting facts discovered by someone else—for example, a biology textbook describing some little-known facts about Darwin's work on the HMS *Beagle*, or a member of an electronic listserv summarizing information heard at a professional conference.

Facts Discovered by You.   Some college assignments ask students to establish their own facts. A research project in a Marketing course might require you to conduct original research to determine the market preferences of a set of your peers. Regardless of your research methodology—quantitative survey, qualitative survey, focus groups—the write-up of the project will be essentially a factual argument detailing the data (the facts) you have determined. A lab report for a physics class will include a summary of the steps you followed and the data (results) yielded by that process.

The reliability of this kind of argument will derive largely from 1) your correct use of the appropriate research methodology; and 2) the clarity and accuracy with which you describe the process in your argument. Since you are not relying on externally derived facts, the burden of proof is on your careful implementation and description of the process.

Personally Experienced Facts.   Similar in some ways to facts "discovered" by you are facts experienced or observed by you. Let's say you are writing a report for a psychology class on phobias and you want to demonstrate how extreme phobic behavior can be. As support for this position, you cite your observations of a friend who is terrified to fly: "Traveling with a friend on a short domestic flight, I observed firsthand what phobic panic can look like." Because this statement suggests extreme behavior, it requires as support a careful and accurate description of the panic: the pallor, the tremors, the hysteria you observed in your friend. Your job is to present the fact—in this case the behavior you witnessed—in such a way that your reader will accept that it happened.

SUPPORTING FACTS

Facts reported by others are usually used as support for a primary or secondary claim of your argument. The more reputable, current, and relevant their sources, the more effectively they support the claim. Thus, you must "support" these externally located facts by ensuring and representing that their sources are reliable. In Chapter 5, "Supporting Your Arguments Honestly and Effectively," we presented the principles for locating reliable sources through traditional library searches and electronic searches. You will want to apply these principles to the judgments you make about the reliability and thus the value of your factual support. Understand that whenever you include facts reported by others, you are tacitly saying to your audience, "I believe this to be a trustworthy statement."

Of course, the source of all external material not considered "common knowledge" must be identified within your argument in the form of footnotes, endnotes, and/or a "Works Cited" section. If you suspect the source of a supporting fact might be unfamiliar to your reader—even though you yourself are satisfied about its reliability—it's a good idea to provide credentials briefly in your text. For example, "In his book *The Mismeasure of Man*, Stephen Jay Gould, the noted Harvard paleontologist and popularizer of science, argues that the results of standardized intelligence tests can be misleading and also misused by those in power."

The main way to support facts you have personally discovered or experienced is through establishing your own credibility. This requirement applies to all components of argument, but it is particularly relevant to these two classes of facts. Since you, the writer, are usually the sole support of these kinds of facts, you must give your readers no reason to mistrust your description of the process or experience.

If your readers find your description of a personal experience suspect, your argument will fail. If you refer to your 85-year-old grandmother as support for an argument against mandatory retirement, citing her daily five-mile runs, her ability to bench-press 300 pounds, and her current prize-winning research on recombinant DNA, your readers will be dubious and your credibility as an observer will be undermined.

Jason L. Frand, in an article characterizing your generation of college students, includes the following personal observations:

> The key to winning in Nintendo is constant, persistent trial-and-error to discover the hidden doors. The fastest way to winning is through losing, since each loss is a learning experience. If it (the game environment) breaks, simply reboot! It's no wonder manuals or instruction sets aren't used by today's students—they aren't needed. When handed a digital gadget, these students turn it on, push the buttons, try the knobs. I can always tell if people are from "my" generation or the "Nintendo" generation by how they approach a software package. Do they check out the menus and manual first, or do they begin typing and then search for what they want whenever they need it?[1]

Frand is a computing administrator at UCLA, so his credentials implicitly bolster his observations. But note as well that he resists any temptation to exaggerate the behavior of game players, providing instead a straightforward description of his observation of members of what he calls the "information-age generation."

When you are reporting data that you yourself have established, you can represent your own credibility by providing a clear and careful description of the process by which you obtained the data. If you include graphs or tables to illustrate the data, make sure you select the most appropriate format (see "Supporting Your Argument Visually" in Chapter 4).

[1]Jason L. Frand, "The Information-Age Mindset." *Educause*, September/October 2000, pp. 17–18.

FACTUAL GENERALIZATIONS

Any claim, regardless of the class it falls into, can be stated as a *generalization*. For example, the factual claim "*People* magazine and *USA Today* use much the same format as television news shows" becomes a factual generalization when the communications scholar Neil Postman tells us that "the total information environment begins to mirror television." Similarly, the claim "Frank is a successful sales representative because his father was also a good sales representative" (introducing a limited causal argument with an element of evaluation) can be extended to the following generalization: "Successful salespeople tend to have other good salespeople in their families."

To support any generalization, you need to apply two sets of principles. First, you must convince your readers that your original claims about *People* and *USA Today* or about Frank and his father are plausible—that significant similarities do exist between the television news show *20/20* and *People* magazine, or that there is a demonstrable *causal* connection between a father and a son who are both sales reps. How you support your claim will depend on the category to which it belongs. The first example is a largely factual claim, and the second is a causal claim.

Second, you must show that your generalization is reasonable—that what you've observed about Frank and his father can be plausibly applied to salespeople and their children all over the world. We will use factual generalizations to illustrate this second principle, but it applies to all categories of argument.

Applying the Principles of Induction

All generalizations, even the most informal and sweeping, begin on a specific level. We see something a few times and assume that it happens frequently or even all the time. That is, we move from specific observations to general conclusions; from the particular, we infer the general. In traditional logic, this process by which we assume the widespread existence of particular instances is called *induction*. Conclusions drawn by inductive reasoning are always somewhat risky because they are based on incomplete evidence. You assume that because you have never seen or heard of a flying cat, no such creature exists, yet unless you have seen every cat that ever existed, your claim "There is no such thing as a flying cat" has made a rather staggering leap from the particular to the universal. Yet these leaps are the nature of induction.

Support for a generalization consists of identifying a number of specific, verified instances or examples. If you claim, for example, that American films increasingly show the dangers of casual sexual relationships, you will have to cite individual films to support your claim. Or if you write, "Many young American novelists find universities a supportive and economically secure place to work," you will need to point to specific examples. If the generalization is a factual generalization, the specific examples will be individual facts, which in some cases may need verification. What makes a factual generalization "factual" is not the absolute truth of the generalization, which can never be proven, but its foundation in singular factual instances.

The most credible generalizations are those supported by the most, and best, examples. You cannot reasonably conclude that all algebra teachers are women if your experience is limited to one or two teachers, but you *can* reasonably conclude that many teenagers like rap music if you have known hundreds of teenagers in many different settings who like rap. In supporting generalizations, you need to know how many examples are enough, whether they are representative of all the available evidence, and which examples to include. Unfortunately, no simple formula exists that answers these questions, but the following general rules of thumb are helpful.

How Many Examples Are Enough?   First, the more sweeping your claim, the more examples you will need. You can position a generalization at any point along a continuum of frequency: "*Some* business majors are good in math"; "*Many* business majors are good in math"; "*All* business majors are good in math." Although the word *some* does constitute a generalization, it is a very limited generalization, a safe one to make if you don't have abundant evidence. To support "some," you need only a handful of examples. "Many" requires more than a handful of examples, certainly, but is far easier to prove than "all." In fact, absolute statements using words like *all, everyone, never,* or *always* should be avoided in written argument unless every constituent in the group referred to can be accounted for. Otherwise, the claims these words make are too grandiose to be credible. The following passage supports its factual generalization with carefully chosen examples:

> A number of fraternity members on this campus contradict the broad and usually unflattering stereotypes circulated about "brothers." While I am not a fraternity member myself, I know a number of members well, and none of them fits the popular image of the beer-swilling, women-chasing party boy. For instance, my friend Judd, a dean's list electrical engineering major and obviously a dedicated student, says that fraternity living gives him the supportive environment he needs to excel in a difficult major. Two of my roommates from freshman year who have joined fraternities have become respected student leaders: Brad is vice president of Student Council, and Kelly is the student representative to Faculty Council. Both Brad and Kelly are well-rounded, academically successful students. Finally, I know that the entire pledge class of one campus chapter received the mayor's commendation for public service for their renovation of an inner-city recreation center. Of course, there will always be individuals who confirm the stereotype, but my observations question its widespread applicability.

In this passage, three examples, the last involving a large group of individuals, are presented to support the claim that few fraternity members fit the campus stereotype. In a more formal academic argument, we would probably insist on more rigorous, less personally observed evidence, but we would very likely accept these examples as adequate in a short, informal essay. As a general rule, three is a good number of examples for a short essay, since one or two examples may seem to be merely exceptions, whereas four or more would become tedious.

The less familiar your readers are with your subject matter, the more specific examples you should supply. If your readers are very comfortable and familiar with your topic, they will often accept sensible generalizations that are only minimally supported. If you refer in an internal business report to the "widespread problems with our new computer system," those familiar with the problem will accept the reference and not demand that it be supported. But a reader unfamiliar with this problem may demand evidence that the problem really exists. Of course, some readers unfamiliar with your subject area will accept dubious generalizations simply because they don't know any better. If these readers are misled, however, some of them will probably eventually learn that you were wrong in your generalizations, and they will then suspect your reliability in other situations, even when you are correct in your claims.

Do Your Examples Represent the Evidence Fairly?   In selecting which evidence for your generalization to include in your argument, you should make sure that the examples you choose fairly represent all the available examples, including the ones you omitted. Imagine, for example, that you support the statement "Fraternity hazing is obsolete on our campus" with examples of changes in the rules and practices of the three largest fraternities, but in the course of your research, you discover that there are significant exceptions to this generalization. You are misrepresenting the evidence if you fail to tell your readers about these exceptions. True, you may have provided enough examples to satisfy your readers, but you are misleading them by excluding the contradictory evidence. The best way around this problem is to qualify the claim in such a way that the evidence you omit is not contradictory. If you rewrite the claim as "Instances of fraternity hazing on our campus have decreased significantly in the last ten years," your three examples will perfectly support the claim, and the omitted evidence will no longer be contradictory.

Is Your Conclusion Too Broad for Your Examples?   Inductive reasoning always requires that the breadth of your conclusion match the breadth of your supporting evidence. If your generalized claim is very broad ("Art majors are the most politically liberal of all college students"), it must be based on proportionately broad examples—in this case, instances taken from a number of different colleges in different areas of the country that offer majors in art. If your claim is more limited ("Art majors at my college are the most politically liberal students"), you are justified in citing examples taken only from your college.

But even in this second, narrower case, you still must guard against generalizing on the basis of instances drawn from too narrow a context. If the art students at your school come from all over the country, yet you use as examples only those who come from the New York City area, your support is not broad enough to justify your conclusion. You will either need to limit your claim further ("Art majors from the New York City area are the most politically liberal students at my college") or to collect examples drawn from a broader geographic group.

ACTIVITIES (7.1)

1. The following conclusions are generalizations derived through inductive reasoning. What kinds of examples, and how many, would you need to make each one plausible?

   a. Most librarians are women.

   b. High school librarians tend to be women.

   c. In my experience, librarians have been pretty evenly divided between men and women.

   d. I have attended two major universities and have been struck by the number of librarians who are women.

   e. Library science departments tend to attract more women students than men.

2. Write a generalization that is adequately supported by the examples listed for each of the following cases.

   a. John, Susan, and Jim prefer chocolate ice cream, whereas Jane prefers strawberry, and Henry prefers vanilla.

   b. Last Saturday night I sat alone at a showing of the new film *Anxious Hours*, and I saw no line for the film when I walked by the theater just before show time on Sunday.

   c. It is January 15 here in Minnesota, and so far this winter, we have had two snowfalls that just covered the ground and then disappeared.

   d. There were 25 Mercedes-Benz automobiles parked in the lot the night of my high school reunion, and as I recall, there were only about 70 students in my graduating class.

   e. When I returned from winter break to my classes here in Vermont, I noticed that Jack, Jeff, Mary, Matthew, Carrie, and Megan all had deep tans.

STATISTICS

Statistics are derived from the practice of drawing conclusions about a large number on the basis of a limited number of instances. Statistics are factual information compiled and reported numerically. The following are examples of statistical claims:

- Thirty percent of the American people believe a woman should never be president.
- The unemployment rate is 5%.
- One-quarter of all bridges in this state need repair.

In our world, statistics are an inevitable and integral part of our lives. We judge the quality of our manufactured products and of many of our services through statistics; we constantly encounter statistics on the health of our economy, our educational system, our sex lives, our souls. We tend to suspect claims that lack statistical support, and we use statistics in virtually every field in our society, from weather forecasting to managing baseball teams. But these general conclusions inferred from a limited number of instances are reliable only if the original process of information gathering was conducted according to certain principles. Whether you are conducting your own statistical studies as support for your argument or citing statistics obtained from other sources, you must be sure of the following:

1. The smaller group surveyed (or *sample,* as statisticians refer to it) must be *known.* If you read that eight out of ten women think they are overweight, but no reference is made to the source of the survey or who or how many were surveyed, you should not accept or use the figure. For all you know, only ten women were questioned, and they were picked from a list obtained from a weight reduction clinic. Every cited study should be identified and the sample group defined. Without such information, the figures are suspect.

2. The sample must be *sufficient,* or sufficiently large, in order for you to accept the conclusion drawn from that sample. That both of your roommates prefer classical music to rock does not justify the conclusion that classical music is more popular with college students; you need a much larger sample. Trained statisticians sometimes use small samples, but only under very specific conditions and with very specific mathematical models. Our inability to evaluate the use of these statistical formulas makes it hard for us to judge whether statistics are actually being used correctly. In such cases, it's important to learn as much as you can about the context of the studies and the methods by which the samples were gathered before relying on the figures completely. For example, researchers often critique each other's studies, and their analyses provide valuable information about the reliability of the results.

3. The sample must be *representative.* If a figure is given about the political inclinations of all Californians, the sample surveyed must represent a cross section of the population. If the 2,000 people questioned all have incomes of $40,000 and up, or if they're all over the age of 45, your sample is slanted and not representative of the variety of the population as a whole. Professional polling organizations like Gallup and Harris (groups hired to identify the preferences of large populations based on small samples) choose either a representative or a random sample. A *representative sample* is one that guarantees in advance that the sample will reflect the major characteristics of the population—for example, that the sample will have a percentage of Californians earning over $40,000 that is equal or nearly equal to the percentage of Californians earning over that figure in the total population. In a *random sample* on political attitudes in California, every adult Californian would stand an equal chance of being questioned. When chosen randomly, in 95 out of 100 cases, a sample group of 1,500 people will be within 3 percentage points of duplicating the answers of the entire adult population. In evaluating the usefulness of any poll, you should know the method by which the sample was selected.

When you include in your argument statistics obtained from other sources, not only must you test them for the preceding three principles, you must also be certain they satisfy the requirements of second- or third-party facts. The source should have a reputation for expertise in the field and for objectivity, and the figures themselves should be recent. It is unwise to accept as support for your own argument any statistical data not credited to an authoritative source. If you cannot identify the instrument, individual, or organization through which these facts were obtained, chances are good that those facts are not reliable.

When using statistics in your argument, you also need to be aware of the variety of terms used to report large figures and of the way these terms influence the impact of the figures. A study on high school literacy could report its findings on extracurricular reading habits in a number of ways. It could say that out of 500 high school seniors surveyed, *100* had read at least one unassigned novel in the last year, or the same fact could be reported as *20%* of the students. Of those 100 readers, one could report the *average* number (or *mean*) of novels read (the total number of novels read divided by the 100 readers), the *mode* (the number of novels most frequently read by individual students), or the *median* (the midpoint of the range of frequency of novels read). The mean, mode, and median for this sample of students follow:

	Students	Novels Read	Total Novels
	25	4	100
	10	3	30
	45	2	90
	20	1	20
Total	100		240

Average = 2.4 novels (total number of novels read divided by total number of students)

Mode = 2 novels (the most common number)

Median = 2 novels (the midpoint of the list of number of novels read according to the frequency of the number. Imagine the 100 students standing in a line, starting with all of those who read four novels, then those who read three, then two, and so on. The midpoint of this line of 100 would occur in the group of students who had read two novels.)

Statistics can be powerful tools in argument, but again, it is crucial to realize that they cannot *prove* claims; they can only *support* their likelihood. A recent poll indicating teenage hostility toward adult society is not proof that it was a teenager who attacked your English teacher or even that the students in a particular high school have hostile feelings toward their parents. It merely indicates that out of a sample of so many teenagers a certain percentage indicated feelings of hostility toward the adult generation. Responsibly gathered statistics are not suspect, but the use to which we put these figures may be.

You should also be restrained in your use of statistics; if scattered profusely throughout a written text, they have a deadening effect on the audience. Often, a visual display of statistics in a chart or a table is more valuable to your audience than a verbal summary; graphic representations can clarify the meaning of the statistics and reinforce their significance. With statistics, it is easy to lose track not only of the "big picture" but also of any picture at all, and visual displays can give the reader the necessary perspective.

ACTIVITIES (7.2)

1. For two of the following statements based on statistics, discuss with a small group of your classmates the kind of information necessary to ensure the statement's reliability.
   a. Over 50% of the doctors surveyed in a nationwide study recommend Brand A medicine over any of the leading competitors.
   b. Brand C: the best built truck in America, according to a survey of truck owners.
   c. Over 60% of all New Yorkers favor reductions in state sales taxes.
   d. Despite competition from television and DVDs, moviegoing is still popular in America. When asked how much they enjoyed going to the movies, 88% of moviegoers responded that they enjoyed moviegoing a great deal.
   e. A survey of leading economic forecasters indicates that a mild recession will occur in the next six months.

2. Conduct a survey of some of your classmates or of some friends. Ask them one or two questions that can be summarized in statistics, such as how many hours they studied last week. Compute the mean, mode, and median of these statistics. Write a one-page description of the results of your survey, and also present this information in visual form. Also state how representative you believe this group is of some larger, similar group, such as all students who studied last week.

SUMMARY

Arguing Facts

- All arguments rely on factual claims, either as their primary claim or as a form of support for the primary claim.

- To support facts reported by others, you must be satisfied of their accuracy and identify their sources within your argument (through footnotes, endnotes, and/or a works cited section).

- To support facts founded on your own experience, you must describe the experience accurately and clearly and establish your own credibility through a responsible, objective, and accurate rendering of the experience.

- To support a factual generalization, you must cite a number of the verified facts that have led you to the general conclusion. The more sweeping the generalization, the more examples you will need to cite. If your readers are likely to be unfamiliar with the subject matter, you should provide several examples as evidence. The examples cited must be typical of all the evidence discovered. The breadth of the examples cited must match the breadth of the generalization.

- Statistics can effectively support arguments, provided they are not overused and their significance is made clear.

- When including a statistical generalization, you must be satisfied of its reliability. It is reliable if the sample cited is known, sufficient, and representative.

- You must be aware of the exact meaning of the terms used to report statistical conclusions, particularly *average, median,* and *mode.*

TWO SAMPLE FACTUAL ARGUMENTS

The following analytical report was written by a student in a "Tools for Engineering" course. Unlike most lab reports, it is primarily a factual generalization. The hypothesis in Paragraph 1 is the unsupported claim, which, by the final paragraph, has been converted into a supported conclusion. The writer supports his claim by reporting analytical facts: the procedure he followed and its observed results. Through his attention to detail, his fully developed discussion of the graphics supplied, and adherence to the conventional lab report format, he implicitly demonstrates that he is a reliable reporter.

Advantages of Matlab

Purpose: To discuss the ability to create and run scripts by Matlab. The programmable nature of this application makes it ideal for engineering and many of its repetitively analyzed functions. It combines the power of mathematical software such as Maple or Mathematica with the programming advantages of a language such as C++.

Discussion: An application of this inherent advantage is one working with the function:

$$y = px^2 + qe^{x/5} + r \ln[x]$$

By creating a function that asks for input values of the constants $(p, q,$ and $r)$, one can quickly compare different cases with four plots.

One of the features of such a function that both scientists and engineers would be interested in is that of curve fitting. When scientific data is collected, scientists often try to summarize their results by noticing characteristics such as linearity in their results. Microsoft Excel's charting includes curve fitting options that aid in deciding if a set of data is best fit by a linear, quadratic, logarithmic, or exponential type of curve. This Matlab script gives you a similar advantage.

The supplied constants that best test this and their graphs follow:

Case 1: The values of $p = 1$, $q = 0$, and $r = 0$ yield an equation proportional to the quadratic and produce the graph of:

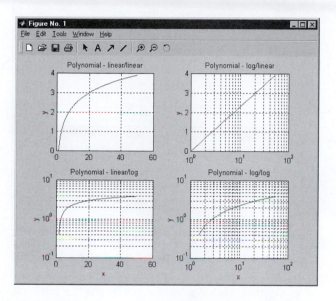

Case 2: The values of $p = 0$, $q = 1$, and $r = 0$ yield an equation proportional to an exponential curve and produce the graph of:

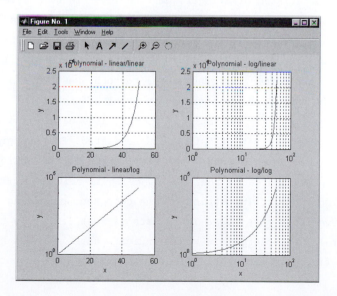

Case 3: The values of $p = 0$, $q = 0$, and $r = 1$ yield an equation proportional to the logarithmic curve and produce the graph of:

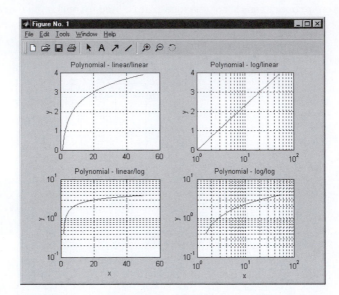

When analyzing these graphs, one needs to note the nature of each of the four subplots. The upper left gives the straightforward linear graphical representation. The upper right offers a graph with an x scale that is exponential. This is characteristic of a logarithm. The lower left is reversed; this time the independent variable remains unaltered while the dependent variable is exponential. This is characteristic of an exponential function. The last plot, the one appearing in the lower-right corner, is exponential on both axes. This plot would be useful to see overall trends of a function.

Applying this information to the three cases allows us to see how each set of data could be fitted. For the graph produced by *Case One* data, the most linear is the third graph. This indicates that the function is neither exponential nor logarithmic. Inspection of the component producing the data verifies this. *Case Two*'s data is most linear in the lower-left subplot. This would indicate that it would be best fit by an exponential function. Once again, inspection verifies this. In regard to the *Case Three* data, the most linear graph is the upper-right graph. This means that the data would be best fit by a logarithmic function, which is again verified.

Conclusion: Matlab has many applications and the ease of creating functions is one of its greatest. Although only three cases need to be considered in this instance, sometimes the best cases are not always apparent. They can only become apparent after trying several different values and inspecting the results. Because of the repetition involved, the ability to create a function to quickly reproduce your results for different values is a highly powerful feature with innumerable applications.

"VONNEGUT SPEECH" CIRCULATES ON NET

DAN MITCHELL

1 A copy of Kurt Vonnegut Jr.'s recent MIT commencement address made heavy email rotation on Friday. The characteristically pithy, funny, thoughtful speech was passed from friend to friend stamped with such comments as "worth a read" and "check this out—it's great."

2 And it *was* great. Trouble is, it wasn't Vonnegut's. "Kurt Vonnegut Jr. had never given a commencement address at MIT," said Robert Sales, associate director of the school's news office.

3 It turns out the "speech" was actually a column penned by the *Chicago Tribune*'s Mary Schmich. The column ran on 1 June— five days before UN Secretary General Kofi Annan delivered the actual commencement address at MIT. That speech "was a lot longer and maybe not as clever" as the purported Vonnegut address, Sales said.

4 Much of Schmich's column—which consists of advice for graduates—sounds like stuff Vonnegut might say: "Don't be reckless with other people's hearts. Don't put up with people who are reckless with yours. . . . Remember compliments you receive. Forget the insults. If you succeed in doing this, tell me how. . . . Keep your old love letters. Throw away your old bank statements. . . . Do one thing every day that scares you."

5 Nobody—least of all Schmich—can figure out why Vonnegut's name was slapped onto her column. "Some prankster apparently decided it would be funny. Why is it funny? If you can figure that out, you're a genius," she said Monday.

6 Perhaps the act itself wasn't funny, but some of the fallout has been. First of all, there's the fact that (ahem) Wired News ran part of the column as its Quote of the Day on Friday. Also, Schmich says she's gotten as much attention from the incident as just about anything she's written. "My email's just flooded with messages," she says. And she says she's actually been accused of plagiarizing Vonnegut—and vice versa. On Friday, she managed to reach Vonnegut, who, Schmich says, said the whole thing is "spooky."

7 In her column on Monday, Schmich writes that she wrote the piece "one Friday afternoon while high on coffee and M&Ms." And, she insisted, "It was not art."

8 In part, Schmich blames the "cyber-swamp" of the Internet for all the trouble.

"At newspapers, things like this have to go through a barrier before they go out to the world," she said. But on the Net "anybody can put anybody's name on anything."

Nonetheless, she added, "No one involved in this did anything bad, except the person who started it."   9

Source: *Wired News*, www.wired.com

SUGGESTIONS FOR WRITING (7.4)

1. Write a two- to three-page essay supporting a fact that runs counter to popular opinion. This fact can come from your own experience, from your studies in college, or from your general knowledge. Examples of such surprising facts are "Despite predictions to the contrary, the increasing use of computers has created more new jobs than it has eliminated existing ones"; "Milk does not always do a body good." This surprising fact can be about yourself, your family, your friends, your hometown, your college, your job, your major, or whatever else comes to mind.

2. Stereotypes are misleading factual generalizations that make the false claim that all members of a group have a certain trait: "The English people have stiff upper lips in times of crisis"; "American men like to watch football." Take a prevalent stereotype and analyze to what degree the stereotype is true and how the stereotype is misleading. Make sure the stereotype is one you can deal with in a three- to four-page essay, such as "Engineering students of my college don't get involved in extracurricular activities." You don't have to do a statistical survey to gather data for this essay, but you should carefully examine and present examples to support your claim.

3. Analyze either a newspaper or a television news show for examples of bias or misleading generalizations (for the television news show, you may have to videotape the show so that you can view it two or three times). How objective is the reporting of the news? Are there any examples of misleading general- izations? What kind of news is *not* included? Write a two- to three-page essay addressing these questions.

ILLUSTRATIVE ARGUMENTS IN PART II: ARGUING FACTS

8

Arguing Cause

The goal of causal argument is to establish a probable cause or effect for a given condition. A claim arguing "Many teenagers abuse alcohol because they are desperately disappointed by their 'real lives' " will establish the *cause* of teen alcohol abuse, whereas the claim "Today's generation of college students will be far more successful in marriage than their parents have been" argues the *effect* of certain conditions. In order to convince your readers that the cause or effect you argue is reasonable, you must have a good understanding of the nature of causality and of the processes used to determine and report causes and effects. Written causal arguments are essentially reports of the process the writer followed to determine causes or effects.

The first part of this chapter concentrates on arguments of *cause*: arguments that identify and support the cause or causes of an existing situation. As you'll see in the last part of the chapter, the principles and processes involved in arguments of cause are identical to those you'll rely on when you write arguments of *effect* (arguments predicting the probable future effects of an existing situation).

DETERMINING CAUSE

Any single effect is the consequence of a number of causes—some powerful and direct, others less influential but still contributing. For this reason, arguing cause usually involves more than isolating *the* single cause of a given effect: most extended causal arguments discover and support those causes most useful to the context, purpose, and audience of your argument. If your goal is to give as full a causal explanation as possible for the effect in question, you will identify and support a number of causes, both direct and indirect. But if the point of your argument is to assign responsibility, you will address only the most immediate causes (such as who did what, regardless of why). If the purpose of your argument is to instruct, or if you want some future action taken or avoided on the basis of the causality you demonstrate in a comparable situation, you are likely to emphasize both the immediate and the more remote causes of the current situation. For example, if you wish to improve your GPA, you might try to reproduce as many of the habits of a successful student friend as you can: careful budgeting of time, keeping up with assignments, regular class attendance, and so on.

Brainstorming for Possible Causes

Whether or not you begin with a particular causal claim in mind, it is a good idea to begin the argument process by listing all the facts and conditions you can think of that seem to be causally linked to the effect you are explaining. Depending on your subject, this list may come from your own thinking and brainstorming and/or from any reading and research you might do. The list should include as many facts or conditions you can think of that seem even remotely connected to the effect. The next step will be to apply your knowledge of causal principles to this working list in order to identify the most influential causes.

Let's assume you are arguing the reasons for the high student dropout rate at your college. Part of your argument will consist of a discussion of individual cases: why particular people you know decided to leave school. You know one student (we'll call her Emma) who explains her plans to drop out of school by saying, "I just don't like college." But you know this is not a satisfactory explanation. Why doesn't she like college? What events and conditions have made her unhappy enough to make this extreme decision? So, in a couple of long conversations, you press Emma further, and you talk with some of the people who know her well. The result of these discussions is a list of more specific possible reasons for her decision.

For one thing, Emma's grades have not been very good. Though her grades were good in high school, Emma can't seem to pull her GPA above a 2.0. It's clear to you from talking to her that she's the kind of person who expects a lot from herself, so her undistinguished grades have to be a blow to her self-esteem. It makes sense that she would want to leave a place where she doesn't feel good about herself. You also learn that Emma is the first person in her family to go to college, and her parents have made many sacrifices to give her every educational advantage. Their ambition for Emma puts a lot of pressure on her, which has probably made it even harder for her to relax and do her best. And Emma's family situation has worked against her in another way: it offers no close role models to emulate, no family tradition of academic success. Add to these factors Emma's crazy roommate and their closet-size room, and you begin to wonder how Emma lasted through the first semester.

Your examination of the situation has identified a number of possible causes for Emma's decisions—all much more specific and useful than her vague claim that she doesn't like college. Some of the possible causes on your list seem directly influential, like her mediocre grades, their blow to her self-esteem, and her crazy roommate; others are more remote, like her parents' lack of a college degree. But you conclude that, one way or another, each of these factors may have influenced Emma's decision.

Only a thorough investigation like the one you have conducted will yield a full explanation of the causes of a particular effect. The next step is to determine more precisely the relative influence of each point in this cluster of causes, and in order to take this step, you must know something about the causal properties of the different points on your list.

ACTIVITIES (8.1)

1. For the following effects, brainstorm a list of possible causes:
   a. The popularity of John Grisham's novels
   b. The success of Japanese products in the American market
   c. The popularity of disaster movies
   d. An increase (or decrease) in the size of the student body at your school
   e. The popularity of a particular major at your school

Necessary and Sufficient Causes

Understanding the concepts *necessary cause* and *sufficient cause* will help you identify which of the causes from your original list are likely to have been most influential in bringing about the effect you are explaining. To qualify as a cause for a given effect, a causal candidate *must* satisfy the conditions of a necessary or sufficient cause, or both. If it does not, it is not a direct cause of the effect, though it may well have contributed to the effect in some way.

A *necessary* cause is a cause without which the effect could not have taken place. One cannot get typhus without the introduction of a rickettsia, or gram-negative microorganism, into the bloodstream. This rickettsia is necessary to the contraction of the disease. Thus you can be certain that anyone who has contracted typhus has been infected by this particular microorganism. But while introduction of the rickettsia is necessary to the contraction of typhus, it doesn't guarantee that the disease will result. People with a vigorous immune system or those who have been inoculated against typhus will be safe from the disease.

Necessary causes are usually easy to identify: if we know the effect, we know that certain causes or conditions had to be operating. To use a nonscientific example, if you had not parked your car next to a construction site, it would not have been hit by falling debris. Parking your car in that spot was necessary to the effect. In the case of Emma, the cause necessary to her withdrawing from college is her unhappiness there. Presumably, if she were happy and liked college, she would stay.

Sometimes identifying the necessary cause will not be particularly helpful in your attempt to explain an effect. Necessary causes can seem like redundant restatements of the effect itself: the necessary cause of a company's filing for bankruptcy is that it ran out of money, but that doesn't tell us very much about the significant factors that led to the bankruptcy filing. In the case of Emma's planned withdrawal from college, the necessary cause—her unhappiness with college—does not shed much light on the question of the student dropout rate. In order to understand her decision, we have to work backward from the necessary cause, identifying those factors that set it up.

Sufficient causes, on the other hand, are always helpful in causal analyses. A sufficient cause is one that by itself is capable of producing a particular effect. A person's decision to join a health club can have a number of sufficient causes: for example, winning a year's membership in a raffle, wanting to meet new people, or wanting to become physically fit. Any one of these motives would be enough to prompt an individual to join a health club, but none of them *has* to exist for that decision to be made; that is, they are all sufficient to the effect, but not necessary. In Emma's case, a number of sufficient causes are operating: her poor self-esteem, her crazy roommate, and her distaste for dormitory life. Any one of these might have been enough to prompt her decision, but none of them was necessary to that decision.

Sometimes a single cause combines the properties of necessity and sufficiency. The example of the rickettsia demonstrates this combination. Not only *must* one be infected with that microorganism to contract typhus (the necessary cause), but this infection is by itself enough to cause the disease (the sufficient cause). For every effect, we can expect at least one necessary cause and any number of sufficient causes.

In determining which factors on your initial list have been most influential, you need to identify those that are necessary and those that are sufficient. Unless you are writing a full causal analysis, you will usually find yourself concentrating on the sufficient causes for the effect in question.

Identifying Sufficient Causes

The ability to identify a factor as causally sufficient depends on your good sense and your personal experience of causality. There is no rule or formula to follow in isolating sufficient causes, yet most of us have little difficulty answering the question "Is this factor by itself sufficient to have caused this effect?"

When your subject involves human behavior as either cause or effect, there is a useful test you should apply to those factors you think are sufficient. Actions performed by an individual or group are linked to their causes by some commonly accepted principle or motivator of human behavior. If you argue, for example, that a sluggish economy is a cause of the increased popularity of taped movie rentals, you are accounting for a particular human behavior: the rental of taped movies. Your claim is a simple claim of cause, with a fact at the causal end and an action (also a fact) at the effect end.

Sluggish economy   Increase in movie rentals

(cause)   (effect)

This causal proposition is plausible only if its two sides are linked by some acceptable motive. Why would people rent more movies for home viewing in a sluggish economy? What motive or need would urge them to react to a particular condition with a particular behavior? In this case, a linking motivation is easy to identify: in tight times, people need to economize, and it is considerably cheaper to watch rented movies at home than to pay high prices in a theater. The cause and the resulting behavior can be linked by a motivation that everyone can understand and identify with:

Sluggish economy.................Increase in movie rentals
{Desire to economize in tight times}

Identifying this motivation doesn't tell you whether this is the only sufficient cause, but it will reassure you that the link between this cause and the effect is plausible. If you can supply no such motivation between cause and effect, your theory is probably not plausible, and it's time to look for another cause.

Applying the Toulmin Model

The Toulmin model discussed in Chapter 6 is particularly useful when you are composing causal arguments. Indeed, the relationship just presented among possible cause, existing effect, and linking principle fits perfectly into Toulmin's data-claim-warrant formula. Here is the example about increased movie rentals translated into the Toulmin model:

In this case, the warrant is that general behavioral principle that connects the cause, which is placed in the data position, and the effect, which is placed under "claim" (even though the actual claim of the argument is the causal relationship between data and claim). When you are trying to identify sufficient causes for a particular effect, you may find it useful to apply the Toulmin model to your cause and effect, making sure that you can provide a warrant that would be widely acceptable to your readers. Remember that in many cases, the warrant will not be acceptable without further support, or what Toulmin calls *backing*. In those cases, the warrant and its backing will need to be provided explicitly in the argument. If the warrant does seem immediately acceptable, it need not be stated outright.

ACTIVITIES (8.2)

1. With three or four other students, study the following effects and possible causes. For each effect, which of the possible causes, if any, do you think are necessary? Which would you class as sufficient? Make sure you can defend your choices.
   a. **Effect:** John's car accident.
      Possible causes: John was driving at night on a poorly lit road; the road was wet from rain; John had taken a very difficult exam that morning; John was driving ten miles per hour over the speed limit.
   b. **Effect:** The dramatic increase in the use of DVD players in the last few years.
      Possible causes: The cost of DVD players is now at an affordable level for most Americans; DVDs of films are increasingly available; viewers can choose what films they will watch with the DVD players; many Americans have a large amount of leisure time available.
   c. **Effect:** The decline in oil and gasoline prices in the mid 1980s.
      Possible causes: On the average, cars were more fuel-efficient than they had been ten years before; there was a growing awareness that petroleum

was a nonrenewable resource; the oil-exporting countries were producing more oil than the world consumed.

d. **Effect:** Louise's winning of an award for the best violin recital at the music festival.
Possible causes: Louise practices the violin three hours each day; Louise's parents found the city's best violin teacher for her when she was five; from a very early age, it was obvious that Louise was talented musically; Louise prefers Mozart to any other composer.

e. **Effect:** Charles's favorite hobby is cross-country skiing.
Possible causes: Charles wants to stay in shape, and cross-country skiing is very good for the cardiovascular system; he likes winter and being out-of-doors; he is on a tight budget and cannot afford downhill skiing this year; he was once injured while downhill skiing; in high school, he won prizes in cross-country ski races.

2. For each following pair below, place the cause and the effect within the Toulmin model and supply a warrant that links the data and the claim acceptably. For which warrants should you also supply backing? What would that backing be?

a. **Cause:** Increased leisure time
Effect: More participation in sports like skiing and windsurfing

b. **Cause:** Fifteen percent increase in tuition
Effect: Decrease in enrollment

c. **Cause:** Special incentives that reduce the price of automobiles
Effect: Higher automobile sales

d. **Cause:** More women receiving professional degrees
Effect: A rise in the average age of women having first children

e. **Cause:** The banning of a book
Effect: Increased demand for the book

DISTINGUISHING AMONG SUFFICIENT CAUSES

Sometimes, in analyzing causes, you will discover a number of possible sufficient causes for an effect and not know which were actually operating. In these cases, you will need other methods for determining probable cause. The following strategies were formulated by the nineteenth-century philosopher John Stuart Mill to determine cause in such situations. While Mill was looking for ways to establish cause with scientific certainty, his methods are also very useful in situations where certainty is unreachable.

Method of Agreement

The method of agreement is useful when you are investigating the cause of *two or more* similar effects. In these instances, you determine what the sets of events preceding each effect have in common; you are looking for a single sufficient cause that operated in all these similar cases.

If you were investigating the reason or reasons for the success of the five best-selling hardbound books of the year, you would list all the factors that might have contributed to the success of each book—that is, the significant characteristics of each. If all the books center on the subject of personal relationships in the 1990s, you could safely identify subject matter as a leading cause of the books' success. Sometimes you will not discover a factor common to all your effects; perhaps the five best-sellers have no single common characteristic, so that a number of sufficient causes are operating in these instances.

Method of Difference

Mill's method of difference can be used to determine why two essentially similar situations turned out very differently. If you want to know why one self-help book succeeded while another failed, why one calculus class with Professor Jones was interesting while another was boring, or why the Confederate army lost the battle of Gettysburg but won the battles of Bull Run, you can apply the difference method by looking for the factor present in one case but absent in the other. If the only difference between your two calculus classes with Professor Jones was that the subject matter of the second class was more advanced, that could well be the reason for your unhappiness in the second class.

This method will work only when you are examining truly similar situations that share a number of common factors. If you were trying to account for the difference between your career choice and that of one of your grandparents, the situations would be too dissimilar for the method of difference to tell you anything; your grandparents faced an entirely different range of career choices than you did.

Method of Proportional Correlation

The method of proportional correlation is useful in determining the cause of an effect that is continuing and varied: the movement of the Dow-Jones industrial average, the increase and occasional decrease in the gross national product, the enrollment of college students in certain kinds of majors. In trying to identify possible causes of such measurable trends, you should look for conditions preceding the trends that vary and persist proportionally. In considering the reasons for the rise in the divorce rate since the 1960s, you might discover that there has been a congruent increase in the number of two-income families over the same time period—that is, that there has been an increase in the number of married women who are economically self-sustaining. This increasing economic independence of women is a plausible explanation of the increased divorce rate if it satisfies the following three conditions: (1) if it is truly independent of the effect (not a result of the same cause); (2) if the two trends, with all their fluctuations, are truly proportional; and (3) if the cause and effect are plausibly linked by an accepted behavioral principle—in this case, the principle or motive of independence or self-reliance. If these three conditions are satisfied, we would accept that the economic independence of wives is a sufficient cause of divorce.

ACTIVITIES (8.3)

1. Take a group of at least three of your classmates or friends who share a common trait, such as their academic major, a hobby, or some other favorite activity, and try to determine what sufficient cause made each member of the group have this trait. Try to find a common sufficient cause for the entire group, but be prepared to end up with different sufficient causes if a common cause does not reveal itself. Write a one- to two-page essay describing the results of your investigation.

2. Compare two classes you have taken sometime in your education, one that you liked and one that you disliked. The two classes should be as similar as possible in subject matter and level of difficulty. What made the one class likable, while the other was not? Write a one- to two-page essay addressing this question.

3. For the next week, compare fluctuations in two phenomena that you believe may be related, such as the weather and attendance at one of your classes. Make a chart comparing the movement of these two phenomena, and then see if any proportional correlation exists between the two. If there is such a correlation, ask yourself if the two are the result of the same cause and if some plausible behavioral principle links the two. Write a one- to two-page analysis of your study. Be sure to give your instructor the chart you have created.

CAUSAL CHAINS

Some effects are best understood in terms of a directly related series of causes, like links in a single chain, or a row of sequentially falling dominoes. In these cases, identifying the entire chain of causes is far more useful than isolating those causes that are closest to the effect, or isolating the more remote cause that originally set the chain in motion.

If someone told you that closed captioning of television shows (where subtitles can be seen on specially equipped televisions) is a result of the rubella epidemic in the United States during the 1960s, you might initially reject the connection as utterly implausible. What you have been given is the first cause and the final effect in a causal chain; if the links in the causal chain are filled in, the connection is reasonable. In the 1960s, there *was* a widespread outbreak of rubella, or German measles (at the time, there was no rubella inoculation). Rubella is a relatively harmless disease except to the fetuses of pregnant women; babies whose mothers contract rubella during pregnancy often suffer birth defects, one of which is deafness. Because of the epidemic, huge numbers of babies were born deaf. In the last 30 years, as these children have grown, we have seen increased sensitivity to the needs of the hearing-impaired, one of the most notable being the media's provision of closed captioning for television. With all the links in the chain identified, the causal connection between a common virus and closed captioning is no longer implausible, though there were other factors at work, including the increasing emphasis on the rights of the handicapped in the last 30 years.

The constellation leading to Emma's planned withdrawal from college contains a causal chain. Beginning with her decision to withdraw, we can move straight back as far as her parents' lack of a college education. The chain works as follows: Emma plans to withdraw from college because she doesn't like it. She doesn't like it because she feels low self-esteem in this setting. This low self-esteem is a result of poor grades, which at least in part have been caused by the enormous pressure she has been under to do well. This pressure comes from her parents, who, because they have never been to college, desperately want Emma to be the first in the family to get a college degree. Not all of the points in the constellation we identified earlier appear in this chain. So while the chain explains much about the evolution of Emma's decision, it does not explain everything, just as the chain linking the rubella epidemic with closed captioning is not the fullest possible explanation of the situation.

CONTRIBUTING FACTORS

In analyzing causes, we occasionally find a circumstance that is neither necessary nor sufficient yet is somehow relevant. This type of circumstance is labeled a *contributing factor*. If Kathy continues to jog even when she is run-down and then catches a virus, her jogging is not a sufficient cause of her illness; the presence of the virus without sufficient antibodies to combat it is the sufficient cause. Nor is the jogging a necessary cause, since she might have gotten the virus even without jogging. Yet her pushing herself while not feeling "100 percent" certainly didn't help and may have made her more susceptible to disease. In this case, we can label the jogging as a probable contributing factor.

Emma's situation contains at least one contributing factor: her lack of a close role model. Clearly, this factor is not necessary to the effect, nor is it sufficiently influential to have caused her decision to withdraw. Yet it has made a bad situation worse, depriving Emma of any positive example from which to take heart. Contributing factors are present in most complicated situations; if your goal is a thorough analysis of cause, you need to take contributing factors into account.

ACTIVITIES (8.4)

1. For two of the following causes and remote effects, find a plausible causal chain that links the cause with the remote effect.
   a. **Cause:** The rise of industrialization
      Effect: The growth of the conservation movement
   b. **Cause:** The invention of gunpowder
      Effect: The decline of knighthood
   c. **Cause:** Jane's high absenteeism in third grade
      Effect: Jane's difficulty with cursive writing
   d. **Cause:** The invention of printing
      Effect: The growth of democracy in Europe and America
   e. **Cause:** Jack's love of parties
      Effect: Jack's becoming the mayor of his city

2. In Activities (8.2), review the clusters of causes presented in Number 1 and identify possible contributing factors for each cluster.

SUMMARY

Determining Cause

- Because causality is always multifaceted, keep your mind open to all possibilities early in your causal investigations.

- The ultimate purpose of your argument (to explain, instruct, or designate responsibility) will determine which causes you will concentrate on in your argument.

- To determine the most influential causes for your effect, you need to be able to identify the necessary and sufficient causes. A *necessary cause* is a cause without which the effect could not have occurred; a *sufficient cause* is one that by itself is capable of producing the effect.

- Where human behavior is concerned, sufficient causes must be linked to their effect through an assumable motive.

- When you have a number of potential sufficient causes for an effect, use the following methods to determine the most probable cause or causes: the method of *agreement,* which will help you determine the cause of similar effects; the method of *difference,* which will help you determine why two similar situations turned out differently; the method of *proportional correlation,* which will help you determine the cause of an effect that varies over time.

- Some effects are best explained by a chain of causes, often originating at a time remote from the effect.

- Thorough causal arguments may also identify *contributing factors* to the effect—circumstances that are neither necessary nor sufficient causes but do play a role in creating an event or condition.

SUPPORTING CAUSAL CLAIMS

You support most causal claims by (1) establishing the factuality of the effect(s) and cause(s) you present; (2) identifying, sometimes only implicitly, an acceptable motive in arguments involving human action; (3) in some cases, describing the process that helped you validate a causal candidate (method of difference, agreement, or proportional correlation); and (4) qualifying the degree of certainty your argument claims.

Establishing Factuality

Facts are the foundations of causal argument. While in most causal arguments you will write, the causal relationship you propose between two events will rarely be certain and verifiable, there can be no room to doubt the certainty of the events you are linking; they *must* be true if your argument is to be meaningful and plausible. If you exaggerate, understate, or misstate the effect, your identification of cause is useless; you are explaining something that didn't actually occur.

If an article in a campus newspaper claims that the firing of a popular hockey coach has resulted in lower student attendance at home hockey games, the reporter needs to be absolutely sure that (1) the coach *was* fired (perhaps this is only a campus rumor and the coach got a job offer elsewhere) and (2) student attendance at home games really has declined since the coach's departure. Both cause and effect need to be presented and, if necessary, supported as individual factual claims before their causal relationship can be explored (see Chapter 7 for supporting factual claims).

Identifying an Acceptable Motivation

When you're dealing with human behavior as either cause or effect, your argument should suggest a common human motive. If a generally acceptable linking motive is obvious, you probably won't need to identify it explicitly. For example, if you are arguing that a decrease in DWI arrests is a consequence of tougher DWI laws, you don't have to point to people's unwillingness to risk the new penalites as the linking motivator between cause and effect; it is so obvious that it can merely be implied.

But let's take a more complicated example: an argument accounting for the increased divorce rate since the 1960s by a proportional rise in two-career families. Here, you would want to state the motive linking the proposed cause and effect, because it may not be immediately obvious to your readers: women who have some degree of financial independence and employment security are more likely to leave unhappy marriages than women who are financially dependent on their spouses. If the motive you identify may not be immediately acceptable to your audience, you will have to provide some backing for it.

There is a tendency among student writers to omit identifying the linking motivation when they should include it; that is, they find obvious what may not be so obvious to their readers. So if you have any doubt about whether or not to include this explanation in your argument, go ahead and provide it. It is usually better to err on the side of too much information than too little.

Describing the Process of Validation

In arguments where John Stuart Mill's processes of determination have been useful to you, you can support your claim by reporting in your argument how the method was applied. You don't need to use the formal terms *method of agreement* and so on, but you should provide a summary, a kind of narrative of your investigation.

If you were to identify the reasons for the failure of four different food concession stands at your school, you would make use of the method of agreement, because you are looking for a single explanation common to the closing of all four operations. Your report of the process might read something like this:

> Between 2002 and 2006, four different concession stands have been opened in the foyer of the Student Union. Not one of these stands was able to draw enough customers to keep operating; each closed within five months of its opening.
>
> The stands had little in common. One was run by students from the hotel program and sold gourmet coffee and pastries; one was a national fast-food franchise; one was a "mom-and-pop" frozen yogurt stand; and the fourth was a minideli operated by campus food services. Prices at the gourmet coffee stand were slightly on the high side, so when it failed, it was replaced by the inexpensive fast-food stand. Frozen yogurt from the yogurt stand was competitively priced, and it was the only frozen yogurt available on campus. Finally, the deli offered the most choice to customers, with food ranging from sandwiches to chips to pasta salads to drinks.
>
> The stands operated at different times of the day: the coffee stand in the mornings between 7 A.M. and 11 A.M.; the fast-food concession between 11 A.M. and 2 P.M.; the yogurt stand in the afternoons from 1 to 5; and the deli between 11 A.M. and 3 P.M.
>
> In short, campus food services tried very hard to learn from its mistakes, trying to eliminate every reason for failure. But the one factor common to all four concerns that they did not address was *location*. All were set up in exactly the same spot in the foyer of the Student Union. The thinking was that since this space saw more daytime student traffic than anywhere else on campus, food sales would be brisk. But the problem with this particular space in the union is that it is very close to the student-faculty cafeteria (on the same floor and open during lunchtime), and to the large student snack bar (in the basement of the union and open for lunch and dinner). It is reasonable to conclude that the food market in this heavily trafficked building was already saturated; if food services wants to make a success of the "portable food" idea, it will have to locate the next food stand in another area of campus.

As indicated in the preceding section on determining cause, some of Mill's methods of determination carry particular risks that you'll want to avoid. The difference method, for example, is reliable only if the effects you examine are truly comparable. And when using the method of proportional correlation, you'll need to be sure that the trends you identify are independent—that is, that they are neither effects of another cause nor mutually contributing (for example, bad tempers causing quarrels and quarrels exacerbating bad tempers).

It's a good idea when supporting your causal argument to point out that your use of a particular method of determination has avoided the associated pitfalls. For example, if you use the difference method to determine why you like golf but your friend with similar athletic ability and experience in golf does not, you should demonstrate that the apparent differences between you and your friend—family background, interest in other sports—are not significant in terms of your argument.

Qualifying Your Argument

Since certainty is rare in causal arguments, you must not mislead your reader and thereby undermine your own credibility by claiming more certainty for your argument than is warranted by its support. You have a wide range of words indicating degrees of causality to choose from, so make sure you use language that accurately reflects your level of certainty. If you are very certain about your causal proposition, you can use such definite words as the following:

necessitated

caused

resulted in

attributable to

produced

created

brought about

was responsible for

But use these words with caution. Without qualifiers like "may have," "probably," "seems to have," and so on, they claim a certainty that may be difficult to document.

The words listed in the following group also indicate causality, but a causality that is clearly qualified:

contributed to

is associated with

is a function of

facilitated

enabled

influenced

increased

decreased

improved

You are better off using words such as these when the causality you propose is not certain. By using such terms, you are both indicating causality and admitting *some* degree of uncertainty.

ACTIVITIES (8.5)

For two of the following examples, write a paragraph on each indicating what would be needed to make the causal argument more convincing. This additional material may include establishing facts, reporting the process of determination, describing motives, demonstrating the independence of two elements in a proportional correlation, or adding qualifying language, though other steps may also be necessary to make the argument credible.

1. Bill's alleged cheating on the exam was certainly a result of his low grades early in the semester and his desire to be accepted into a reputable law school.

2. Police report the arrest of Hubert Midas, the oil and gas billionaire, for shoplifting a thirty-five-dollar shirt from a downtown department store. Midas must have forgotten to pay for the shirt.

3. As more women have entered the workforce, the number of families without children has risen proportionally. The increasing number of women in the workforce has caused this rise in childless families.

4. Without Martin Luther King, Jr.'s charismatic personality, the civil rights movement of the 1960s would not have had the impact it did.

5. The Roman Empire fell because of the moral decadence of many of its citizens.

SUMMARY

Supporting Causal Claims

- To support a cause, you must establish the factuality of cause and effect; identify an acceptable motivation in cases where human actions are at least part of the cause; usually report how you determined the causes; if necessary, qualify your assertions about the certainty of your argument.

ARGUING EFFECTS

Because arguments of effect are concerned with the future, with events that haven't yet occurred, their claim to certainty is even less absolute than arguments of cause. Even the most carefully constructed argument of effect, one firmly grounded in the principles of causality and in experience in the relevant field, can go awry. We have only to look at the accuracy rate of weather forecasters and political analysts to recognize how frequently the future refuses to cooperate with our plans for it. But if executed carefully and according to certain principles, arguments of effect *can* be reasonable and convincing, serving as useful guidelines for many courses of action.

Claims of arguments of effect can be stated in a number of ways, as in the following:

1. If John continues to drink heavily and drive, it's only a matter of time before he will have a serious accident.

2. The number of high school graduates will continue to decline for the next five years, then begin to stabilize.

3. I will not see a woman president in my lifetime.

4. Consumers are so comfortable with certain companies that they will buy almost anything carrying those companies' logos.

While they may seem quite different, these four claims share certain features common to all arguments of effect. Most obviously, all predict that something will happen in the future (or in the case of the third claim, that something will not happen). Claims 1 and 4—John's heavy drinking, and brand appeal—also identify a causal relationship between a current condition and a future event. Claims 2 and 3 don't identify a current condition that will lead to the effect the writer predicts. In order to make them qualify as arguments of effect rather than mere assertions, the writer will have to identify current conditions that might lead to these effects and claim that the conditions and effects are causally linked. For Claim 2, those conditions could be certain demographic trends that have persisted over time; for Claim 3, those conditions could be the conservative disposition of most voters, or perhaps a poll indicating strong opposition to a woman president among teenagers and young voters. These current conditions and trends set the ground for an argument of effect. An argument of effect demonstrates that the existence of these conditions and trends is enough to cause a particular future effect. Lacking identified causes, these kinds of claims are nothing more than random predictions, similar to the bizarre predictions on the covers of the sensational magazines found in supermarkets: "Psychic Foresees Economic Collapse Following Landing of Martians on White House Lawn!"

Determining and Supporting a Probable Effect

The processes of determining and supporting a probable effect overlap considerably. If you identify a future effect through sound methods, the best supporting strategy will be to report these methods, which we discuss in the following paragraphs.

Applying the Principles of Causality.   To argue an effect, you need to identify a sufficient cause for the effect and prove that this cause exists or could exist. Are the causes that are currently operating (or that might be set in place) enough to bring about the effect? If you can identify an existing sufficient cause or causes for the effect, your prediction is probably a good one.

Let's take the case of a publishing house editor trying to decide whether to publish a book submitted to her on personal relationships. The editor will accept the book if she thinks it will sell well; her job is to decide whether current circumstances will make the book a best-seller. In other words, the projected effect is excellent sales. The circumstances operating are as follows: the market for books on this topic has been very strong; the writer has written popular books on this subject before; the book itself, in the view of this experienced editor, is interesting, original, and provocative. An analysis of these circumstances reveals that all are sufficient causes; in the absence of the other two, one cause alone would be sufficient to create the effect. The editor's experience with bookselling makes her a good judge of the sufficiency of these causes. She also knows how important these three circumstances are because she has seen them again and again. In projecting any effect, the arguer must understand the principles of the subject matter.

Missing from this list of current circumstances is a necessary cause, one that has to operate in order for the effect to occur. The absence of a necessary cause does not make the projected effect implausible; often it is the sufficient causes that create the necessary cause. In this example, the necessary cause of high sales would simply be that people buy the book, and they will buy the book in the presence of one or more of these sufficient causes.

Causal Chains.   In some situations, you can argue a future effect by revealing a chain of causes that plausibly connects Cause A with Future Effect D. To demonstrate the connection between a past or present cause and a future effect, you need to make a series of arguments of effect; if A is the remote cause and D the predicted effect, you will argue that A will cause B, which will cause C, which finally will cause D.

The field of economics often uses causal chains as a basis for future action. A classic example is the Federal Reserve Bank's setting of interest rates on money it lends to banks, which in turn affects the interest rates banks and other financial institutions charge customers on mortgages and other loans and the interest they pay to customers for savings and other deposits. One key step the Federal Reserve Bank can take to reduce consumer spending is to raise its interest rates, which means the banks will raise their rates, and customers will find that it costs more to get a mortgage on a house, to finance a car loan, or to buy other items on credit. Faced with these rising costs, consumers will decide to spend less. Also, because these same banks are now paying more interest for deposits, consumers have an incentive to save rather than spend—another reason why they will reduce spending. Visually, the causal chain looks like this:

(A) higher government interest rates➤(B) higher bank interest rates➤
(C) lower consumer spending

This causal chain can be extended, since lower consumer spending may lead to a lower inflation rate or to less importing of consumer goods from other countries. With causal chains, however, the greater the length of the chain, the less predictable become the effects.

Sometimes causal chains simply don't work the way they are supposed to. When Prohibition became law in 1919, its proponents predicted that alcohol consumption would decrease and along with it a host of evils, including crime, broken homes, and absenteeism from work. They did not foresee a roaring 14 years of speakeasies, bathtub gin, and bootleg whiskey before Prohibition was abolished in 1933. Especially when trying to predict human behavior through elaborate causal chains, you should always keep in mind the adage about the road to hell being paved with good intentions.

Comparable Situations.   You can also determine the probable future result of current conditions by examining comparable situations in which this cause and effect have already occurred. In trying to raise the educational standards of American primary and secondary schools, teachers, school administrators, and government policymakers look to the experience of other countries. The average scores of students from some other industrialized countries are higher than the average scores of American students on certain standardized achievement tests in areas such as math and science. In some of these countries, notably Japan, children spend much more of the year in school, and the schools introduce rigorous academic material earlier in the student's academic career. Some proponents of reform argue that the same methods used here will improve students' performance.

This comparison method will work only if the situations being compared are *significantly* similar. In arguing that the United States should follow Japan's example, advocates of these changes also need to look carefully at what each country expects from its schools and how these expectations relate to the general culture. What seems comparable at first may turn out to be more complicated on closer inspection, since the American and Japanese cultures have very different expectations about the role of the individual in society.

The more comparable the situations you find, the more convincing your argument of effect will be. If you can demonstrate that a certain cause has had the same result over and over again, and that the current conditions you are considering are truly similar to these other causes, your identification of effect will be well supported.

ACTIVITIES (8.6)

1. For two of the following actions, project two effects that might be caused by the action. State whether the action would be necessary or sufficient to the effect.
   Example action: Graduating *summa cum laude*.
   Possible effects: Being accepted into a prestigious graduate school (sufficient); receiving eight job offers (sufficient).
   a. Getting an A in a course
   b. Arranging a date with someone you don't know
   c. Reducing the danger of theft at your college or in your community
   d. Finding a good place to live
   e. Being stopped by the police for speeding

2. Write a two- to three-page essay describing a causal chain for some area or activity with which you are familiar (for example, gaining or losing weight, saving money, raising your grades).

3. For the following five predictions, cite a truly comparable activity or situation that can be used to support your prediction.
   Example: Extending the academic year in primary and secondary education in the United States. A comparable situation could be the long academic year in Japan, to support the prediction of higher test scores for American students.
   a. Being governor of a state
   b. Student success in graduate school
   c. Decreasing alcohol consumption at fraternity parties at your school
   d. Being removed from academic probation
   e. Making the varsity lacrosse team

TWO SAMPLE CAUSAL ARGUMENTS

The following argument is a sample of causal analysis. Written by college student Cassandra Bjork, the essay considers both the effects and causes of obesity in the United States. As you study the essay, see if you can locate where Cassandra establishes the factuality of her causes and her effects. What other methods for determining and arguing cause and effect do you find in the essay?

AMERICANS: BIGGER BY THE DAY

CASSIE BJORK

Why are Americans getting bigger by the day? And what's so bad about that anyway? Studies have shown that there are many negative effects associated with obesity. Obesity has been accused of contributing to many long-term conditions, such as heart disease, stroke, high blood pressure, osteoarthritis, diabetes and cancer (Pennybacker 15). Along with the fact that obesity is the most common form of malnutrition in the Western world, it also affects sixty-four percent of Americans (Pennybacker 15; Brownell 1). Obesity is one of today's most visible, yet neglected conditions affecting more Americans each day.

According to the Merriam-Webster Dictionary, the definition of obesity is "a condition characterized by excessive bodily fat" (Merriam-Webster). Moreover, the Centers for Disease Control and Prevention labels the obesity problem as an "epidemic" (Brownell 1). Basically, obesity is the long-term result of a diet that delivers more calories in than are consumed through daily activity. Nevertheless, obesity is a serious medical condition that impacts a high percentage of Americans and should be treated with concern.

There are many possible factors for the rise in the number of overweight and obese Americans. Brownell outlines these factors very well in *Food Fight* and writes, "The reasons for this growing problem are simple and complex at the same time. People eat too much and exercise too little..." (Brownell 2). Furthermore, by taking a look at the modem lifestyle of our world today, one could say it does not discourage obesity in the least way. One obstacle Americans need to overcome is to find the time in their busy schedules to exercise. It is much too easy to travel in cars, as opposed to walking or biking. Many people sit all day in an office, and do not get much physical activity at all. The conveniences and technology of today contribute to a very sedentary lifestyle for much of the population. According to *Food Fight*, one study found that 23 percent of all deaths from major chronic disease could be attributed to sedentary lifestyle (Brownell 70). The lack of exercise is one of the main causes of obesity in the United States.

Another possible contribution to obesity, which is still in the process of being further researched, is genetics. According to the Office of Genomics & Disease Prevention, studies indicate that inherited genetic variation is an important risk factor for obesity. It was also pointed out that genetic factors are starting to be questioned in the degree of effectiveness of diet and physical activity interventions for weight reduction (Obesity and Genetics I). Learning how genetic variations effect obesity will make it much easier to prevent and treat the condition of obesity.

In addition to the many different causes of obesity, fast food receives much of the blame. With the continual growth of the fast food industry in the United States, obesity is becoming a bigger problem everyday. The connection between fast food and obesity is one of the primary criticisms in the book, *Fast Food Nation*, written by Eric Schlosser. Due to the high-calorie, high-fat food choices offered at many restaurants, both consumers and experts are quick to point their fingers at fast food restaurants. In the book, he states, "If you look at the rise of the obesity rate in the United States, it's grown pretty much in step with the rise of fast-food consumption...and now it's the second leading cause of death in the United States, after smoking" (Schlosser 1). When McDonald's was asked to respond to former charges by Schlosser, they stated that forty-five million customers make the choice of dining at McDonald's every single day (CBS News). The point they were trying to get across is that the fast food restaurant customers are responsible for the persistent growth of the fast food industry. They are the ones choosing to put this type of food into their digestive systems. These restaurants would not be so profitable if it were not for the high demand for their food products by consumers. Another source provided a statement from Dr. Cathy Kapica, Global Director of Nutrition for McDonald's, regarding the responsibility of the customer: "It is not where you eat, but the food choices you make, and especially how much you eat." She then addressed the fact that McDonald's offers a wide variety of different foods, and portion styles that can be a significant part of a healthy diet ("Meet McDonald's").

An opposing opinion on the correlation between fast food and obesity came from *HealthDay Reporter* magazine. According to Amanda Gardner in *HealthDay Reporter,* a study was conducted on individuals' dietary habits. There were 3,301 adults surveyed between ages eighteen and thirty. The results showed that individuals who ate fast food more than twice a week gained an extra ten pounds in just six months, and had a twofold greater increase in insulin resistance than people who ate it less than once a week (Gardner 2). The outcome of the study indicates that eating a high fat diet can lead to weight gain and eventually, obesity.

Although fast food is often blamed because of its high caloric content, it is simply a contributing factor. Obesity is caused by overeating, poor food choices, genetics and lack of exercise as well. Whether it is from fast food or not, extra weight is put on by not burning as many calories as the number taken in. Dining in restaurants can encourage this unhealthy habit by providing enough food for two or more people on a single plate. Frequent visits to restaurants can then compound the effect of too much food, too often. According to Kelly Brownell, more than 40 percent of adults eat at a restaurant on a typical day. The frequency of eating out is associated with higher calorie and fat intake and increased body weight, while eating meals at home is associated with better calorie intake (Brownell 36). When it comes to healthy eating, it can be easier for one to make better healthful choices in his or her own kitchen.

In our world today, obesity affects people of all ages. A common misconception is that obesity is only an adult problem. In the United States, more children suffer from obesity than ever before. The Centers for Disease Control estimate that 23 percent of American children are overweight, in comparison to only four percent in the 1960s. Obesity causes the young to be at risk for problems that used to be common only in adults, such as cardiovascular disease, high cholesterol and blood pressure, and type two diabetes (Pennybacker).

There are many different suggestions for the prevention of and fight against obesity. The first and most obvious recommendation is to lose weight. Because obesity is a condition requiring continuous attention, any behavior changes required to maintain weight loss must be lifelong. In order to lose weight, it is necessary to decrease caloric intake, increase caloric expenditure, or do both (CBS News). According to Greg Critser in *Fatlands,* the response is simple, but not always easy: We need to burn at least as many calories as we take in (Schlosser 2). It has been proven that physical activity is a vital component of a healthy lifestyle, whether a person is overweight or not. It is recommended to participate in moderate levels of physical activity for thirty to forty minutes, three to five times each week (Mathur). It can be difficult to meet this recommendation, but it eventually causes a positive long-term result.

Obesity is one of today's most visible, yet most neglected conditions affecting more Americans each day. The possible causes of obesity include fast food, genetics and lack of physical activity. Although it is a growing problem, today we have the resources and knowledge available to overcome obesity. It is up to Americans to assist in the prevention of this condition that affects such a high percentage of its people.

WORKS CITED

Brownell, Kelly D. *Food Fight*. Boston: The McGraw-Hill
    Companies, 2004.

"Fast Food, Fat Children." CBS News. 21 Apr 2001. Available
    www.cbsnews.com.

Gardner, Amanda. "Fast Food Linked to Obesity." *HealthDay Reporter*. 30 Dec 2005.

Mathur, Ruchi. Obesity (Weight Loss). 22 July 2003. Available http://www.medicinenetcom.

"Meet McDonald's Nutrition Expert, Dr. Cathy Kapica." Retrieved http://www.rmhc.com/usa!_eat/nutritionisthtml.

"Obesity and Genetics." Office of Genomics & Disease Prevention, Centers for Disease Control and Prevention. 31 Aug 2005. Available http://www.cdc.gov/genomics/info/perspectives/files/obesity.html.

"Obesity." Merriam-Webster Dictionary. 20 Oct 2005. Available http://www.m-w.com/.

Pennybacker, Mindy. "Reducing 'Globesity' Begins at Home." *World Watch*. (Sep/Oct 2005): 15.

Schlosser, Eric. *Fast Food Nation: The Dark Side of the All American Meal*. Boston: Houghton Mifflin, 2001.

"What is Obesity?" 2000. Retrieved http://www.hateweightcom/what_is_obesity.html.

Composition Merit Awards Journal Online 2006. http://www.intech.mnsu.edu/mcclur/CMAJO/CMAJO%202006/CMAJO%202006%20prize)winners.htm

The following argument, "I, Too, Am a Good Parent," combines elements of a causal argument and a recommendation. The author, Dorsett Bennett, claims that the continuing custom of granting child custody to the mother is a result of the prejudice of older male judges who continue to dominate the courts. Is the cause Bennett identifies necessary or sufficient? Is it adequately supported by facts and examples? Do you find any further causal arguments embedded in the essay? What are they?

I, TOO, AM A GOOD PARENT

Dads Should Not Be Discriminated Against

DORSETT BENNETT

1   Divorce is a fact of modern life. A great number of people simply decide that they do not wish to stay married to their spouse. A divorce is not a tremendously difficult situation unless there are minor children born to the couple. If there are no minor children you simply divide the assets and debts. But you cannot divide a child. The child needs to be placed with the appropriate parent.

2   In my own case, my former wife chose not to remain married to me. That is her right and I do not fault her decision. My problem is that I do not believe it is her right to deny me the privilege of raising our children. Some fathers want to go to the parent/teacher conferences, school plays, carnivals, and to help their kids with homework. I have always looked forward to participating on a daily basis in my children's lives. I can no longer enjoy that privilege— the children live with their mother, who has moved to a northern Midwest state.

3   I tried so hard to gain custody of my children. I believe the evidence is uncontradicted as to what an excellent father (and more important, parent) I am. My ex-wife is a fairly good mother, but unbiased opinions unanimously agreed I was the better parent. Testimonials were videotaped from witnesses who could not attend the out-of-state custody hearing. I choose to be a father. When I was 3 years old, my own father left my family. While I've loved my father for many years, I did and still do reject his parental pattern.

4   A couple of centuries ago, a father and mother might have shared equally in the care and raising of children above the age of infancy. But with the coming of the Industrial Revolution the father went to work during the day, leaving the full-time care of the young to the mother, who stayed at home. It was easier to decide who should get child custody under those circumstances. That would be true today even if the mother were put into the position of working outside the home after the divorce.

5   Now, a majority of married mothers are in the workplace—often because the family needs the second income to survive. With the advent of the working mother, we have also seen a change in child care. Not only have we seen an increase in third-party caregivers; there is a decided difference in how fathers interact with their children. Fathers are even starting to help raise their children. I admit that in a great many families there is an uneven distribution of childcare responsibilities. But there are fathers who do as much to raise the children as the mother, and there are many examples where men are full-time parents.

6   But, because we have this past history of the mother being the principal child caregiver, the mother has almost always been favored in any contested child-custody case. The law of every state is replete with decisions showing that the mother is the favored custodial parent. The changes in our lifestyles are now being reflected in our laws. In most, if not all, states, the legislature has recognized the change in childcare responsibilities and enacted legislation that is gender blind. The statutes that deal with child custody now say that the children should be placed with the parent whose care and control of the child will be in the child's best interest.

7   This legislation is enlightened and correct. Society has changed. We no longer bring up our children as we did years ago. But it is still necessary to have someone make the choice in the child's best interest if the parents are divorcing and cannot agree on who takes care of the kids. So we have judges to make that enormous decision.

8   The state legislature can pass laws that say neither parent is favored because of their gender. But it is judges who make the ultimate choice. And those judges are usually *older males* who practiced law during the time when mothers were the favored guardians under the law. These same judges mostly come from a background where mothers stayed home and were the primary caregivers. By training and by personal experience they have a strong natural bias in favor of the mother in a child-custody case. That belief is regressive and fails to acknowledge the changed realities of our present way of life. Someone must be appointed to render a decision when parents cannot agree. I would ask that those judges who make these critical decisions re-examine their attitudes and prejudices against placing children with fathers.

9   After the videotaped testimony was completed, one of my lawyers said he had

"never seen a father put together a better custody case." "But," he asked me, "can you prove she is unfit?" A father should not be placed in the position of having to prove the mother is unfit in order to gain custody. He should not have to prove that she has two heads, participates in child sacrifice, or eats live snakes. The father should only have to prove that he is the more suitable parent.

10   Fathers should not be discriminated against as I was. It took me three years to get a trial on the merits in the Minnesota court. And Minnesota has a law directing its courts to give a high priority to child-custody cases. What was even worse was that the judge seemed to ignore the overwhelming weight of the evidence and granted custody to my ex-wife. At the trial, her argument was, "I am their mother." Other than that statement she hardly put

on a case. Being the mother of the children was apparently deemed enough to outweigh evidence that all the witnesses who knew us both felt I was the better parent; that those witnesses who knew only me said what an excellent parent I was; that our children's behavior always improved dramatically after spending time with me; that my daughter wished to live with me; and that I had a better child-custody evaluation than my wife.

So I say to the trial judges who decide   11 these cases: "Become part of the solution to this dilemma of child custody. Don't remain part of the problem." It is too late for me. If this backward way of thinking is changed, then perhaps it won't be too late for other fathers who should have custody of their children.

Source: *Newsweek,* July 4, 1994.

SUGGESTIONS FOR WRITING (8.7)

1. Write an essay describing the necessary and sufficient causes for a major event in your life. Be sure to indicate to the reader how you determined that these causes were operating. Make the essay as long as necessary to describe fully the causes of this event.

2. Analyze at least three persons or organizations that share major common traits, and determine what similar causes, if any, made them the way they are. As examples, you could analyze successful or unsuccessful teams in some sport, or successful or unsuccessful television shows. Report your analysis in an essay of approximately four pages.

3. Analyze two persons or situations that share significant traits but that have ended up differing in some major way. What caused this major difference? For this essay, you might analyze why you and a close friend or a sibling chose different colleges or majors or why you performed differently in two similar classes. Report your analysis in an essay of approximately four pages.

4. Examine two trends that you believe may be causally related to see if there is any proportional correlation between them. An example might be the national crime rate and the national unemployment rate, or the national unemployment rate and the inflation rate. If you expect to find a correlation and you do not, speculate on why the correlation is not present. For the most current information available, your library will probably have the *Statistical Abstracts of the United States* in database format, but you may also be able to retrieve any government statistical data you may need through the Web site at http://www.census.gov/statab/www/ . Report your analysis in an essay of approximately four pages.

5. Fewer and fewer college students are completing bachelor's degrees in the traditional four-year period. Do some research at your own institution, and find out the average time students are taking to graduate. Then write a four- to five-page essay that explores possible causes of this phenomenon. Make sure that the causes you suggest originate in the same time period as the effect.

ILLUSTRATIVE ARGUMENTS IN PART II: ARGUING CAUSE

9

Arguing Evaluations

EVALUATIVE SUBJECTS AND TERMS

All evaluations include a subject to be judged and an evaluative term that is applied to the subject. In the claim "John is a good writer," *John* is the subject, and *good writer* is the evaluative term; in "Miles Davis was a gifted musician," *Miles Davis* is the subject and *gifted musician* the evaluative term. Some evaluative claims include only partial evaluative terms, but their context should suggest the missing parts. In the claim "Capital punishment is immoral," the full evaluative term is *immoral act,* and in "Rembrandt was a master," the evaluative term is *master painter.*

To make a successful evaluative argument, you need to lay some careful groundwork. First, you must define the evaluative term. In the claim "John is a good writer," where *good writer* could mean different things to different people, you'll want to specify your understanding of the term. In many cases, you can do this by a shorthand definition: "John is a good writer; he communicates ideas clearly and gracefully" (see Chapter 4 for a discussion of shorthand definitions). This definition establishes clarity and grace in the communication as the criteria by which John's writing will be judged.

Sometimes evaluations are expressed negatively, as in "John is a poor writer," or "The instructions for this camera are useless." A negative evaluation can either imply its opposite as the standard of judgment or establish a definition of the negative term itself. The writer of the claim "William Faulkner's *Fable* is a failed novel" could work from a definition of *successful novel,* showing how this novel falls short of that definition, or could establish criteria for the term *failed novel* and apply those to the subject.

The second piece of groundwork necessary to most successful evaluations is gaining your readers' agreement about your definition of the evaluative term. If your readers' understanding of the criteria for good writing do not agree with yours, however clearly you have presented them, your argument won't get very far. Perhaps they agree that John's writing is clear and graceful, but because their understanding of good writing includes rich ideas and original expression, they will never be convinced by your argument that John is a good writer. In this situation, and in many evaluations, you will need to argue the definition of your evaluative term, convincing your readers that the criteria by which you define the term are reasonable and complete. Only then can you proceed to the heart of your evaluation: demonstrating the match between your subject and your evaluative term.

ACTIVITIES (9.1)

1. What is the evaluative term (implied or stated) in the following assertions?
   a. Mark Twain's *Adventures of Huckleberry Finn* is an American classic.
   b. When Roger Bannister broke the four-minute mile barrier in 1954, he accomplished one of the greatest athletic feats of this century.
   c. Calvin Coolidge was a mediocre president.
   d. Calculators are a real boon to mathematics students.
   e. The terrible losses in wars in the twentieth century show the bankruptcy of nations' using war as an extension of foreign policy.
2. Write a paragraph giving a brief definition of one of the evaluative terms you identified in Activity 1.

ESTABLISHING THE DEFINITION
OF THE EVALUATIVE TERM

How much space and energy you devote to establishing your term's definition will depend on your audience and the nature of the term. There is so little dispute about some terms that an extensive definition is unnecessary—an honest bank teller, for example, or a reliable car. And in cases where you are very confident about your readers' values, about what is important to them and why, you may not need to argue or even propose a definition. A doctor writing to other doctors about the unprofessional behavior of a certain physician could probably assume agreement among her readers about the definition of unprofessional behavior. But when the following conditions apply, you should define your evaluative term and argue its definition:

- When your audience consists of people with expertise and/or values different from yours
- When your definition of the evaluative term is unconventional or controversial
- When there are different definitions of the term

Whether or not you define the evaluative term explicitly, remember that very vague or inflated evaluations are usually harder to argue than those that are limited and precise. It would be far easier to convince an audience that "Indigo Girls are ingenious lyricists" than that "Indigo Girls are the best songwriters ever."

Presenting the Definition

In most cases, the actual definition of the term can be stated quite briefly, usually as part of or directly following the claim: "Alison is the ideal management trainee: she is intelligent, ambitious, congenial, and hardworking"; "In his highly original and influential reflections on the American spirit, reflections that affected common citizens as well as fellow philosophers, Ralph Waldo Emerson proved himself to be a great thinker."

When defining an evaluative term, you are proposing a *stipulative* definition—a definition that restricts the understanding of a term to a particular meaning appropriate to your context. (See Chapter 4 for a full discussion of definition.) In the argument about John's writing skills, the definition of good writing as the clear and graceful communication of ideas is stipulative: it asks readers to accept this particular and limited definition of the term for the context of this argument. In most cases, your definition will take the shorthand, sentence form identified in Chapter 4, although if the term is very difficult, you might want to provide an extended definition.

As in all definitions, the explanation you offer must be clear and precise. Your definition will be useless if it offers only broad or abstract generalizations. If you write, "The brilliance of the film *Citizen Kane* lies in its wonderful structure," but you fail to define *wonderful structure,* you will leave readers guessing. Try also to avoid definitions that include highly subjective terms. If you define a "talented soprano" as one whose voice is beautiful at all points in her vocal range, you have not done much to clarify the evaluative term. What is beautiful to one listener may be mediocre, or heavy, or thin to another; "beautiful" is a measurement that frequently provokes disagreement. So if you wish the term to be useful, define it by offering comparatively objective standards, like fullness, or clarity, or fluidity. While these, too, are subjective terms, they are more precise and are less a matter of personal taste than a term like *beautiful.*

The following are three examples of promising opening definitions; each is clear, precise, and informative.

- A good argument is one that directly identifies its central proposition; supports that proposition with reasonable, relevant, and concrete evidence; and admits the possibility of alternative points of view.
- A dedicated mother devotes herself to her children because she knows she should; a good mother devotes herself to her children because she can't imagine doing otherwise.
- A good education will prepare a student not only for a career but for a fulfilling life outside a career. As important as careers are in our lives, they do not and should not occupy all of our time and energy. The well-educated person is the one who can view life outside work with zest, knowing that there are many other interests aside from a career.

While the qualities included in your proposed definition should be as clear and precise as possible, the very nature of evaluations will not always allow you to avoid subjective terms. In the last of the three preceding examples, the term *fulfilling life* is inherently subjective, yet it is not meaningless. There are certain qualities and activities we can identify that constitute a fulfilling life, including having friends, having hobbies or other recreational interests, and being curious about the past, the future, and the world. It may not be easy to measure each of these qualities or activities precisely, but they do exist, and they can be gauged on some comparative scale.

ACTIVITIES (9.2)

Using the preceding definitions as a model, give a brief but useful definition of the following. After you have written your definitions, compare them with the definitions written by two other students in your class. How much agreement is there among your definitions? How do you account for the differences that exist?

1. A safe automobile
2. An inspiring professor
3. An honest politician
4. A natural athlete
5. The perfect roommate

Arguing the Definition

Based on your assessment of their backgrounds, needs, and values, you may conclude that your readers will not automatically agree with your definition of the evaluative term. In such cases, you have one more job before you move to the evaluation per se: to *argue* that your definition is just, that the criteria you have assigned to a term such as *necessary war, master craftsman,* or *inspired teacher* are reasonable and complete. You can argue the justness of your definition using any of the methods for supporting definitions presented in Chapter 4, including appeal to assumed values, identification of effect, appeal to authority, and comparison.

To illustrate the application of these methods, let's work with the following example: as a branch manager for a local bank, you are asked to write a formal evaluation of three new management trainees. Your reader will be the bank's vice president of personnel. There is no fixed evaluation form or criteria to work from; *you* must decide which qualities constitute promising performance in a new trainee. The qualities you settle on (in unranked order) are (1) honesty, (2) the ability to foresee the consequences of decisions, (3) attention to detail, and (4) courtesy to customers. Because you have created this list, you will need to justify it, however briefly, to the vice president. Your justification for each item on the list could use the following methods of argument:

- *Honesty:* appeal to assumed value. You wouldn't have to say much about this quality. For obvious reasons, bankers place a premium on honesty in their employees.
- *Ability to foresee the consequences of decisions:* identification of effect. This criterion may not be as obvious as the first, but bankers must base decisions about lending money, setting interest rates, and making investments on the probable consequences of these decisions. You could briefly point out the positive results of having this ability and the negative results of lacking it.

- *Attention to detail:* appeal to assumed value. Like honesty, the importance of this quality doesn't have to be argued to bankers.
- *Courtesy to customers:* identification of effect. You can easily demonstrate that good customer relations lead to good business. For many bankers, this criterion would be an assumed value.

You can buttress these criteria with other support. To bolster the third criterion, attention to detail, you might cite recognized authorities who stress this quality and the grave risks banks run when they hire employees who lack it. To support the fourth criterion, courtesy to customers, you might use the method of comparison, pointing to the success of a competing bank that stresses good customer relations.

If you can make a reasonable argument for your definition of the evaluative term, your readers are likely to accept the qualities you cite. But they may still object to your definition on the basis of omission: your definition is acceptable as far as it goes, but you have omitted one quality critical to them. Without the inclusion of that quality, they cannot accept your evaluation of the subject. So, in formulating your definition, try to anticipate the reactions of your readers; if they are likely to be concerned about the omission of a certain quality, you must explain why you chose to omit it. Any of the methods previously identified will help you make this explanation. For example, you could justify your omission of a knowledge of computer programming as a criterion for judging trainees by using the identification of effect, pointing out that few bank employees do any programming anyway and that it is cheaper and more efficient to hire outside programming experts when they are needed. In this case, you are pointing out that no bad effects are caused by these trainees' inexperience with programming.

Ranking the Qualities in Your Definition

In some evaluative arguments, it is not enough to establish a list of qualities constituting your evaluative term; often you will need to indicate the relative importance of these qualities by ranking them. Ranking is almost always necessary in evaluations of multiple subjects. If you are evaluating four models of home coffee brewers, for example, you might establish the following qualities as essential: reasonable price, good-tasting coffee, a quick-brew cycle, and an automatic timer. A reader may agree with each of these qualities yet disagree with your final choice of brewer. The reason for the disagreement would be that you and your reader rank the four qualities differently. If a quick-brew cycle is most important to you but least important to your reader, he or she will not accept your final evaluation of the three machines.

In some evaluations, particularly those that are likely to directly affect your reader, you may have to justify the relative value you place on each quality. If you are evaluating dormitory life as a valuable freshman experience, you will let your readers (incoming freshmen) know which of the criteria you cite is most important and which is least important. Suppose you rank the qualities as follows: (1) quiet study atmosphere, (2) good social opportunities, (3) proximity to campus, and (4) comfortable surroundings. You could argue the importance of the first quality, a quiet study atmosphere, by a number of familiar methods: appeals to value or authority, comparison, or identification of effect. Regardless of the method you choose, you must be able to demonstrate that without a quiet study atmosphere, one that allows students to work hard and succeed academically, all of the other qualities are meaningless. If a student flunks out of school the first year, the other three qualities will have been useless. Thus the first quality is the most important because, in your view, it is the *essential* quality.

ACTIVITIES (9.3)

For one of the following subjects, list in order of importance the criteria you would include in its definition. Compare your definition with your classmates' criteria, and based on any disagreement you find, write a two-page essay justifying your selection and ranking of the criteria.

1. A college or university
2. A musical concert
3. A campus newspaper
4. A church or synagogue
5. A textbook for a college course

ARGUING THE EVALUATION

Having laid the necessary foundation for a successful evaluation, you're ready to make the evaluative argument.

The evaluation itself will be largely *factual.* By verifying data and presenting concrete examples, you will argue that your subject possesses the criteria you have cited. Establishing this match is especially important when your subject is a service—a travel agency, a long-distance phone service—or a functional object, such as a coffee brewer or a pickup truck. In these cases, where the evaluative term is defined by objectively measurable qualities (for example, speed, efficiency, accuracy, and price), your job is to verify the existence of those qualities in your subject.

Suppose you were evaluating portable MP3 players. For college preparation, your grandparents offered to purchase a portable CD player in the $150 price range. You don't want to take all of your CDs to your dorm room because you won't have enough storage space, and you are worried about some of your favorites disappearing. Your computer has enough memory to store your CDs and a good speaker system, so you really don't need a portable CD player, but you would like to have a stable MP3 player that will allow you to listen to music while you are in the library or walking to class. You see an ad for a *Walkme3* that is comparable in price to the CD player your grandparents suggested. You don't want to hurt their feelings because they thought they were being "hip" by offering to purchase the CD player, and they are not completely "up" on computers. So you prepare an evaluation to show them how the MP3 player will benefit you and provide you with the listening pleasure that they want you to have. Your evaluation will be convincing if the MP3 player will be better for you than a CD player. You evaluate the Euphony Walkme3 as a *good portable MP3 player.* Your evaluation will be convincing as long as you can establish the following three facts: the suggested retail price of the Walkme3 is below $150; it offers good quality sound; it holds a reasonable number of songs.

These facts can be convincingly established through reference to your own experience, provided you present yourself as reliable and objective. (Other supporting sources—the experience of friends or impartial analyses of the Walkme3 found in consumer guides—could be referred to as well.) You could cite the actual price of the Walkme3 at three local stores to verify the first fact. The second, which is the most subjective, can be verified by your physical description of the Walkme3's sound quality—full tones, adjustable balance treble and bass levels, clear reproduction of the original CDs—a description of what you require for your listening pleasure. The third fact can also be established by reference to the number of songs you want to be able to select. "When I'm studying at home in my own room, I like familiar classical music that doesn't interfere with my reading. But when I'm walking around, I like a wide variety, including folk, rock, alternative, and even heavy metal on occasion. I need enough storage space for at least three hours of listening, and the Walkme3 provides four hours of storage." As with all factual arguments, the key to success in arguing evaluations is to cite reliable and authoritative experience and observations and to include specific, concrete examples of general statements. Your grandparents will happily support your choice, allowing you to purchase the Walkme3 player instead of a CD player.

Not all evaluations are as neat and objective as the preceding example. Let's look at a very different example involving more subjective measurement and see how the principles of factual argument apply. This evaluation argues that your friend Ellen knows how to be a good friend: she respects her friends, accepting and loving them for who they are, and she expects the same treatment from them. Because the definition included in the claim is not a standard definition of friendship, it requires some preliminary support (see the preceding section on "Arguing the Definition").

Once supported, the definition must be applied to the subject, your friend Ellen. The quality of respecting others—a key criterion of your evaluative term— cannot be measured as objectively or established as definitively as the price of a radio or the fuel efficiency of an automobile. Yet general agreement exists about what constitutes respectful behavior: it is attentive, considerate, accepting behavior. The best way to demonstrate the applicability of the quality to your subject is through specific examples illustrating such behavior. As in any factual argument, you must *describe* the experience faithfully and objectively. Because you want to establish that Ellen's respectful treatment of her friends is habitual, not occasional, you should cite a number of examples.

Beyond citing the examples, you might also need to point out what is respectful in the examples cited, particularly if your readers might interpret the behavior differently. But in general, the more concrete and immediate your presentation of examples, the less explicit commentary you will need.

Testing Your Evaluation Through the Syllogism

A good evaluative claim falls very neatly into the basic syllogistic model presented in Chapter 5. Once you have come up with your claim, you can test its reasonableness and completeness by rewriting it in syllogistic terms. The definition of the evaluative term will be the major premise, the application of the defining criteria will be the minor premise, and the claim itself will be the conclusion. The preceding example regarding Ellen's friendship would compose the following syllogism:

> **Major premise:** A good friend respects her friends, accepts them and loves them for who they are, and expects the same treatment from them.
> **Minor premise:** Ellen respects me, accepts me and loves me for who I am, and expects the same from me.
> **Conclusion:** Ellen is a good friend.

The major premise establishes characteristics that constitute friendship; the minor premise applies those same characteristics to Ellen; and the conclusion makes a very specific claim derived from the relationship between the two premises. This syllogism tells us that the claim is valid, but we can accept it as true only if the two premises are also true. If the major premise (the definition of friendship) does not appear to be immediately acceptable, it will have to be argued in the ways we have suggested. Similarly the truth (or probability) of the minor premise may have to be established through a factual argument that provides examples of Ellen's behavior toward you. While you may not be able to *prove* the absolute truth of both premises, you can strengthen them by providing appropriate support, thus moving the entire argument much closer to a position of soundness.

ACTIVITIES (9.4)

Working from the definitions you created for Activity (9.2), compose a specific claim from each. Then turn the definition and the claim into a syllogism. To what extent would the major and minor premises of each syllogism need further support?

FURTHER METHODS OF SUPPORTING EVALUATIONS

Definition and factual argument are central to evaluations, but there are other ways to support these arguments. The tactics that follow can be used along with definition and factual arguments or by themselves.

Identification of Effect

Since an action, policy, or object is generally considered valuable if its effects are valuable, a good way to support evaluations is by identifying the positive effects of the subject. Freedom of speech is good because it encourages the widest exchange of ideas, which is more likely to lead to the truth or to solutions to problems. Child abuse is bad because it causes physical and mental anguish in children. Of course, such a causal support of evaluations will work only if it accords with the principles of causality discussed in Chapter 8, and if your audience agrees with your assessment of the effect. If you anticipate any disagreement from your audience, you'll need to argue, if only briefly, your evaluation of the effect.

Appeal to Authority

You can support any evaluation by appealing to the similar judgment of a recognized authority. If Maria Sharapova has publicly expressed her admiration for the tennis game of Kim Clijsters, this statement would be effective support for your argument that Clijsters is the finest tennis player on the women's tour. Just be sure, when you cite the judgment of an expert, that that person truly qualifies as an authority on this particular subject.

Comparison

You can often support your evaluation by showing similarities between your subject and one that your audience is likely to evaluate in the same way. For example, many feminists have supported their arguments against sexual discrimination by comparing it to racial discrimination. The two forms of discrimination are similar in many ways: both base inequitable treatment on irrelevant and immutable characteristics—race and gender. An audience that would object to racial discrimination would, when the similarities were pointed out, be likely to object to sexual discrimination as well. But as with any comparative argument, make sure the similarities between the two subjects are essential, not peripheral.

ACTIVITIES (9.5)

With a small group of your classmates, identify which kinds of support (factual argument, identification of effect, appeal to authority, comparison) would be most appropriate for two of the following evaluative claims. Discuss your reasons for choosing each form of support.

1. Shakespeare is one of the world's greatest writers.
2. Mercedes-Benz makes many of the world's best cars.
3. Failure to build a water treatment plant for the city would be a serious mistake.
4. Strato Airlines has the best customer service record of any airline in America.
5. Military involvements by major powers in small countries are usually unwise in terms of lives lost, money wasted, and the increased suspicion of other small countries.

THE VARIETIES OF EVALUATIONS

By now, you realize that different kinds of evaluations demand different kinds of support. While there are no hard-and-fast rules in this area, if you can identify the *kind* of evaluation you're arguing, you'll have a better sense of how to support it.

Evaluations usually fall into one of three main categories: ethical, aesthetic, or functional. Included in this section is a fourth subclass as well: the interpretation. Strictly speaking, interpretations are not evaluative arguments, but since they are argued in much the same way as evaluations, they are addressed here.

Ethical Evaluations

The word *ethical* is one of those terms that we all understand in a vague way yet might be hard pressed to define precisely. To avoid confusion, consider the following definition: *ethical* describes behavior that conforms to an ideal code of moral principles—principles of right and wrong, good and evil. That code may be derived from any number of cultures: religious, professional, national, or political.

All of us operate within many cultures: we are members of families, communities, organizations, religions, professions, and nations. Each one of these cultures has its own set of ethical standards. For example, among the many ethical principles of Judaism and Christianity are the Ten Commandments. As United States citizens, we are subject to other standards of conduct, such as those recorded in the Constitution—including the Bill of Rights—and the Declaration of Independence. Your college also operates by certain standards that it expects its members to follow: respect for school property, respect for faculty, and academic honesty. In most cultures, these standards are formally recorded, but in some instances they remain implicit. There also exist certain ethical ideals common to virtually all cultures—ideals such as fair play, kindness, and respect for others.

Because individuals are tied to a number of different cultures, clashes between standards are inevitable. Some pacifist groups, for example, see a clash between the religious commandment "Thou shall not kill" and the government's standard that citizens must be prepared to defend their country in time of war. Sometimes conflicts occur between standards of the same culture. Such clashes are commonplace in law. What happens, for example, when the right of free speech collides with the right of a person to be free from libel? Free speech cannot mean that someone has a right to say anything about another person, regardless of how untrue or harmful it is. On the other hand, protection from libel cannot mean protection from the truth being told about mistakes or misdeeds, particularly when they have some impact on the public. Throughout our history, the courts have struggled to find a balance between these two competing claims, sometimes slightly favoring one value, sometimes the other, but always denying that either value can have absolute sway over the other.

Defining the Evaluative Term in Ethical Arguments.   Whenever you evaluate a subject in terms of right or wrong conduct, you'll be appealing to certain ethical values or standards that you believe your audience holds. When asserting that "Hitler was an evil man," or "Ms. Mead is an honorable lawyer," or "The coach used unfair tactics," you are assuming that your readers both *understand* what you mean by the evaluative term and *agree* with that meaning. As in all evaluations, if you have reason to doubt your readers' understanding of the term, you'll have to define it, and if you're uncertain about their agreement with the definition, you'll have to support it.

The Argument in Ethical Evaluations.   Most ethical arguments concentrate on demonstrating what is unethical or immoral about the subject being evaluated. At the center of these evaluations, then, is a factual argument. In arguing that Hitler was evil, your focus would be on documenting the behavior you identify as evil, and on demonstrating that your evaluative term fits the examples you are citing.

You can also strengthen your evaluation through other supporting methods, including comparison (Hitler was as bad as or worse than certain other dictators) or identification of effect (in addition to all of the bad he did in his life, the war Hitler started led to the division of Europe into two opposing camps, or to a pervasive sense of victimization among Jews of later generations).

ACTIVITIES (9.6)

Using one of the following evaluative assertions (from Activities 9.5) as your claim, write a two-page "Letter to the Editor" of your local city newspaper. Or create your own claim derived from a current local or national controversy.

1. Shakespeare is one of the world's greatest writers.
2. Mercedes-Benz makes many of the world's best cars.
3. Failure to build a water treatment plant for the city would be a serious mistake.
4. Strato Airlines has the best customer service record of any airline in America.

Aesthetic Evaluations

Writing a convincing evaluation of a work of art—a poem, an opera, a painting—is not as futile a task as many believe, provided you understand the goals of such an argument. Just as personal tastes in clothes or food are usually immune to reasonable argument, aesthetic preferences—liking Chopin's music and despising Mahler's—are often too much matters of personal taste to be arguable. There is much truth in the Latin saying *De gustibus non est disputandum:* there is no arguing about taste. Nevertheless, while changing aesthetic tastes or opinions is difficult, it is possible and often useful to convince an audience to *appreciate* the strengths or weaknesses of a work of art by giving them a greater understanding of it. A successful aesthetic evaluation may not convince a reader to like Rubens or to dislike Lichtenstein, but it will at least give a reader reasons for approving of or objecting to a work.

All artistic fields have their own sets of standards for excellence, standards about which there is surprising conformity among experts in the field. Most literary critics, for example, would agree on the standards for a successful short story: coherence of the story, careful selection of detail, avoidance of digression, an interesting style. When critics disagree, and of course they do so regularly, they usually disagree not about identified standards of excellence but about the application of those standards. Often such disagreements are matters of a personal preference for one kind of artist over another. Even professional critics are not immune to the influence of their personal tastes.

When you argue an aesthetic evaluation, you should work from standards currently accepted within the field, though you may not have to do more than briefly or implicitly refer to them. Your evaluation is likely to fail if you ignore these standards, or if you try to effect an overnight revolution in them. Like ethical standards, aesthetic standards usually change gradually, though there have been periods of revolutionary change, as occurred in artistic tastes in the early twentieth century.

Usually, then, your chief task is to demonstrate that these standards apply (or don't apply) to your subject. This demonstration consists of careful description and concrete examples, as in the following excerpt from an essay on the famous comedians the Marx Brothers ("From Sweet Anarchy to Stupid Pet Tricks"). In this excerpt, Mark Edmundson gives a description and examples from a particular scene in a Marx Brothers film and then presents his criteria for rich "antiestablishment comedy."

> Groucho always rebels against his own success. When it seems that Trentino might treat him on equal terms, as a gentleman, Groucho stages an imagined encounter between himself and the Sylvanian ambassador that ends in disaster. "I'll be only too happy," Groucho pledges in most statesmanlike tones, "to meet Ambassador Trentino and offer him, on behalf of my country, the right hand of good fellowship." But then, Groucho worries, maybe the ambassador will snub him (stranger things have happened). "A fine thing that'll be! I hold out my hand and he refuses to accept it! That'll add a lot to my prestige, won't it? Me, the head of a country, snubbed by a foreign ambassador! Who does he think he is that he can come here and make a sap out of me in front of all my people?" Then, rising to a boil, "Think of it! I hold out my hand and that hyena refuses to accept it! . . . He'll never get away with it, I tell you! . . . He'll never get away with it."
>
> Enter Trentino, looking haughty. Groucho, raging now, "So! You refuse to shake hands with me, eh?" Groucho slaps Trentino with his gloves. This means war!
>
> It's Groucho's contempt for his own high-mindedness and posing— "I'll be happy to meet Ambassador Trentino and offer him the right hand," blah, blah, blah—that sends him into a spin. Groucho was about to act decorously, something for which he cannot forgive himself. As his predecessor Thoreau put it, "What demon possessed me that I behaved so well?"
>
> Our current outsider comics—Roseanne, Eddie Murphy, Martin Lawrence—attack incessantly, and they sometimes score. But what they don't generally do is what Groucho does so superbly, turn the lens back, dramatize their own flaws. The richness of Groucho's antiestablishment comedy is that it compels us not only to challenge social hypocrisy but to consider our own. And it's that double vision, it seems to me, that helps make Groucho and the Marx Brothers as indispensable now as they were in the 1930s.

Edmundson's chief measure of the success of antiestablishment comedians is what he calls their "double vision," their ability to "turn the lens back, dramatize their own flaws." With the criterion clearly identified, the reader can discover it easily in the detailed description of the film scene.

As with all arguments, when composing an aesthetic evaluation, be sure to consider your readers' level of knowledge—both of the subject being evaluated and of the field in general (comedy, tragedy, jazz, autobiographies, etc.). Edmundson assumes that his readers are familiar with Marx Brothers' films, but he also reviews individual scenes in some detail to ensure that his points are made. In cases where your subject and your evaluative criteria may be less familiar to your audience, you may want to offer not only a careful description of the subject, but also a lucid explanation of the criteria. People often fail to appreciate what they don't understand, so if your evaluation can teach them about the standards of a particular field, it will have a better chance of convincing them that your subject meets (or fails to meet) those standards.

Another useful tactic when arguing a positive evaluation to an inexperienced audience is to relate your subject to one with which they are more familiar. If, for example, you want to convince an audience familiar with and appreciative of modern abstract art that the art of ancient Egypt is also interesting, you might point out the similarities between the two: "Although they are widely separated in time, modern abstract art and ancient Egyptian art both concentrate on the essence of a person or object, not the surface appearance." In taking this approach, you are borrowing from your readers' appreciation of modern abstract art, shining its positive light onto the subject of your evaluation.

ACTIVITIES (9.7)

For each of the following forms of art or entertainment, list at least three standards by which you would judge the quality of a specific work of this type. Then, for one of the categories, write a two- to three-page essay demonstrating how a specific work of that type does or does not fit your standards of excellence. (You should make these standards explicit in your essay.)

1. An action film
2. A mystery novel
3. A jazz recording
4. A portrait photograph
5. An abstract painting

Functional Evaluations

Functional evaluations stand a better chance of changing readers' minds than do ethical and aesthetic evaluations. It is easier to convince a reader that her views about turbo engine cars are inaccurate than that her views about abortion are wrong. While people do form sentimental attachments to objects and machines, they can usually be convinced that however powerful that attachment, it has nothing to do with the subject's actual performance; an audience's preconceptions about performance quality are less matters of cultural values and personal tastes than of practical experience, assumptions, or hearsay.

Functional evaluations always work from a definition of ideal standards: like evaluating MP3s, you can't demonstrate that Sony makes an excellent CD player without some criteria for measuring the player's performance. Some functional evaluations require an explicit presentation of evaluative criteria and some can safely assume reader familiarity with the relevant criteria. Certainly, if your criteria are unusual or innovative ("The most important feature of a car for me is that it *look* good"), you'll have to state them explicitly and argue their relevance and completeness (using any of the methods discussed earlier in this chapter).

Sometimes functional evaluations work best from a ranked list of criteria. For example, a lawnmower can be evaluated in terms of safety features, cost, and noise, but the three criteria may not be equally important. To justify your evaluation, you should explain and support the relative weights you've assigned to each criterion.

Any of the other supporting methods discussed earlier in this chapter (identification of effect, appeal to authority, comparison) can also be used in a performance evaluation. Of these, the most valuable is identification of effect. "Virginia Wensel is a good violin teacher" because she has produced a number of fine players; "My college provides an excellent education" because 85 percent of its graduates go on to graduate school. In each case, the subject is judged in terms of its positive effects. Note that sometimes the effect you identify as an evaluative criterion must be argued. Why, for example, does acceptance into graduate school mean you have received an excellent undergraduate education?

If the effect you are citing has already occurred, your support will be a factual argument. In arguing that "Virginia Wensel is a good violin teacher," you would cite the number of fine players she has produced and briefly support your positive judgment of those players. In other cases, where the effect has not yet occurred, your argument is necessarily more speculative: "Based on the evidence we have, this car is likely to give you years of reliable service."

ACTIVITIES (9.8)

List in ranked order at least three standards by which you would judge the performance of the following. Then, for one of the categories, write a two- to three-page essay demonstrating how well one person or object in that category meets your standards of performance.

1. An automobile for a family with three small children
2. A president of a college or university
3. A personal computer
4. A United States senator
5. A college reference librarian

Interpretations

The purpose of an interpretation is to disclose the meaning of a particular subject—often a meaning not immediately obvious to a casual observer or reader. At some time or other, all students must practice interpretive arguments in literature classes. The following are examples of possible claims for literary interpretations: "Beneath the apparently modest and conventional surface of Christina Rossetti's lyrics lie fiery manifestoes of independence and rebellion"; "In placing the last scene of *Tess of the d'Urbervilles* at Stonehenge, Thomas Hardy reminds us that Tess is a pagan, not a Christian, heroine." But interpretations are not solely the province of literature; we make interpretive arguments all the time about the behavior of people we know ("Paul says he craves a close relationship with a woman, but it's easy to see he's terrified of intimacy") and about the productions of popular culture ("Television advertisements are selling one thing: sex").

Interpretations are often paired with explanatory causal arguments. In claiming that "Hamlet's indecisiveness is a symptom of his unresolved Oedipal complex," we are really making two claims, both of which propose an increased understanding of the play *Hamlet*. First, we are identifying the *cause* of Hamlet's indecisive behavior (his unresolved Oedipal complex), and second, we are claiming that an unresolved Oedipal complex can be discovered within Hamlet's character. Now, if you've read the play, you know that Shakespeare is never explicit about the oddities of Hamlet's relationship with his mother. No character ever says to Hamlet, "Oh Hamlet, cast thy infantile and possessive love of thy mother off." But keen readers who recognize some of the telltale symptoms of the Oedipal complex detect one in Hamlet's words and actions. And that detection is the interpretive argument: the demonstration of meaning beneath the surface. You will remember that causal claims are always somewhat speculative; this brand of causal claim is even more so, because the cause it identifies is interpretive, not factual.

Interpretations can imply a positive or a negative evaluation, but they are not evaluations per se. Nevertheless, the processes for arguing the two are very similar. The subject of an interpretive argument is the visible surface we wish to understand or explore further; it is the behavior, data, or event that openly exists for all to observe. The interpretive term is the summarized explanation of the reality beneath the visible surface. In the interpretive claim "The current baseball cap craze among boys expresses their rejection of tradition and authority," the subject is *current baseball cap craze among boys,* and the interpretive term is *rejection of tradition and authority.*

As in evaluations, your central task in interpretive arguments is to demonstrate a match between the subject and the interpretive term. But also as in evaluations, you will need to lay some groundwork. Most solid interpretations satisfy the following requirements: (1) the interpretive term is clearly defined; (2) the interpretive term and the subject are matched—that is, demonstrated to be equivalent or coincident; and (3) evidence is supplied to support the interpretation.

Defining the Interpretive Term.   Like evaluative arguments, interpretations work from assumptions about definition—about what elements make up a certain condition or reality. In interpretations, we are stating that X (the subject) is Y (the interpretation). To prove or support this assertion, we must define Y in such a way that it restates X or restate X in such a way that it coincides with Y. In the interpretive claim "Television news broadcasting is no longer news; it is entertainment," we must demonstrate the coincidence of our definition of entertainment on the one hand with what we see of television news on the other.

In the following passage, we see a similar assertion of coincidence, where Sigmund Freud equates literature (the subject) with the play of children:

> Now the writer does the same as the child at play; he creates a world of phantasy which he takes very seriously; that is, he invests it with a great deal of affect, while separating it sharply from reality. Language has preserved this relationship between children's play and poetic creation. It designates certain kinds of imaginative creation, concerned with tangible objects and capable of representation, as "plays"; the people who present them are called "players."

The first step in assembling an interpretive argument is to consider whether to define the interpretive term and argue your definition. As with evaluative arguments, you should define the term if you are using it in an unusual or controversial way, and you should justify that definition if you think your audience is likely to object to it. In the first example, the term *entertainment* probably should be defined, as it is a very broad and even subjective term. You might define the term as "any brief, self-contained, sensually pleasing performance that amuses but does not challenge." If your audience is likely to disagree with this definition, you will have to support it with the methods discussed in the preceding section titled "Arguing the Definition" in this chapter.

Of course, you can work from an unstated definition, provided your argument clearly reveals the elements of that definition. The following example illustrates this tactic:

> Much of television news broadcasting is no longer news; it is entertainment. Most local and national news broadcasts, news shows like *60 Minutes* and *20/20*, and even public television news are putting out slick, superficial performances that are usually neither challenging nor controversial, but that capture huge audience shares.

Here the definition of entertainment is contained in the characterization of television news.

Extensive interpretations of a series of events or continuing behavior work somewhat differently, though the basic principles are the same. In these cases— for example, an interpretation of a character's actions in a novel or of quarterly stock market activity—the subjects are usually explained in terms of a coherent and preestablished theory, system of thought, or belief. Instead of demonstrating the coincidence or equivalence of the subject and a single concept (like children's play or entertainment), these more ambitious interpretations reveal the existence of a series of related concepts—an entire system—behind the visible activity of the subject. The system identified could be Christianity, Marxism, Jungian psychology, feminism, Freudian drive theory, capitalism, semiotics—virtually any set of facts or principles logically connected to form a coherent view of the world.

Examples of this kind of systematic interpretation are especially prevalent in artistic and literary interpretations, though they are not limited to these contexts. A feminist interpretation of a literary figure like Emily Dickinson would work from a thorough understanding of feminist theory. The interpretation might explain Dickinson's poems in terms of the tension between her vocation as a poet and the very different expectations that nineteenth-century society had for women.

However compelling such an interpretation, readers are not likely to be swayed if they strongly object to the interpretive system—to the Freudian, or Marxist, or feminist model of human behavior. Even if the construct used to explain the subject is not formally named, the principles contained in that construct must seem at least plausible to your readers. If you interpret modern American history on the basis of tensions and conflicts between different social and economic classes, your readers may not give your interpretation fair consideration if they are opposed to this set of principles. On the other hand, a good interpretation often helps readers gain sympathy for a philosophy or point of view they were previously hostile to or ignorant of. When you write interpretations, you should be sensitive to your audience's beliefs and prepared at least to acknowledge their probable objections as you proceed. In doing so, you may convince some hostile readers, bringing them to accept not only your interpretation but also at least some aspects of your underlying point of view.

Establishing Coincidence.   All interpretations must demonstrate coincidence between the subject and the interpretive term. *Coincidence* in this context can mean equivalence (as in "Television news is the same as entertainment"), substitution ("Although marriage looks like a romantic partnership, it is often a formalization of female dependence"), or revelation ("Behind Jack's warmth and friendliness is a cold and impenetrable shield of defenses"). The challenge of interpretations is in demonstrating these coincidences.

When the interpretive term is concrete, this task is comparatively easy. We recognize such concepts as entertainment or economic dependence; they are verifiable. Once we agree on the meaning of the term, a simple factual argument will demonstrate the applicability of the term to the subject. If we know what economic dependence is, we can detect it in a relationship with little difficulty or little guesswork, provided we have the necessary facts.

But what about detecting a "cold and impenetrable shield of defenses" in an acquaintance? There is no sure way to verify the existence of such a "shield," so how do we argue its existence? Remember in Chapter 8 on causal arguments the principle of a generally accepted link between cause and effect? Just as a cause and its effect must be linked by some acceptable motivational principle that agrees with human experience and observation, so must the interpretation (the less visible reality) relate to the subject (the visible reality) according to an acknowledged principle of experience.

Let's take the case of Jack's misleading warmth and friendliness. Basically we want to demonstrate that his apparent friendliness is an expression of his need to protect himself. First, we'll have to recast the subject or the interpretive term so that the two are shown to be equivalent. We can do this by elaborating on the friendliness: "Jack is as friendly to a grocery clerk as he is to a lifelong friend. He is completely indiscriminate in how he relates to people. This may be good for the grocery clerk, who enjoys Jack's friendly manner, but not so good for the friend, who, in fact, has never gotten to know Jack any better than the grocery clerk has," and so forth. Having established the coincidence or equivalence of this brand of friendliness and defensiveness, you'll want to assure yourself (and your readers, if necessary) that the equivalence you cite agrees with the principles of human behavior that we generally accept: indiscriminate behavior (even friendliness) often expresses its opposite.

Documenting the Interpretation.   Interpretations need documentation, or evidence. As well as explaining your subject through an acceptable principle of experience, you'll have to document your claim through examples taken from your subject. Different arguments will provide different kinds of evidence, so it is difficult to generalize about the best kind of evidence. In literature papers, professors are looking for examples from the literary work that support the claim. For example, in a paper arguing "Behind Othello's seeming self-confidence is a collection of debilitating insecurities," the student would need to cite a number of passages in the play that suggest these insecurities. In the student paper at the end of this chapter, an interpretation of popular media, the writer documents his interpretation of a magazine ad by carefully describing the visual details of the ad.

The Possibility of Multiple Interpretations.   Most subjects lend themselves to a number of different interpretations, and these interpretations are not necessarily mutually exclusive. Widely varied and equally convincing interpretations of Shakespeare's *Hamlet* have been written through the centuries; it is a testament to the brilliance of the play that it can accommodate so many different readings. Because of the likelihood of multiple interpretations of any subject, try to resist adopting a dogmatic and inflexible tone in your arguments. You don't need to constantly acknowledge the possibility of other interpretations, nor should you present your own interpretation too tentatively; on the other hand, don't lay out your argument as if it were immutable, inarguable dogma.

ACTIVITIES (9.9)

1. Write a brief interpretation (approximately one page) of a recent event. Your interpretation should include the interpretive term, the kind of coincidence, and the supporting evidence. Then write a second interpretation of the same event, again including all the necessary elements of an interpretation. Give both essays to a classmate to read, and then discuss with him or her which is the most plausible interpretation and why. Some possible events: a recent election, a political scandal, a friend's recent success or failure in some endeavor, an athletic contest.

2. Find in a magazine an interpretation of a film that you have seen recently. Many magazines that offer movie reviews and criticisms can be found online: *Boxoffice, Entertainment Weekly, Premiere, Film Journal, FilmMaker:*

The Magazine of Independent Film, Shock Cinema, MovieMaker, and *Beatdown: British Film Magazine* are just a few. Be sure to support your argument with concrete references to the film itself. (Give your instructor a copy of the magazine review whether you found the review online or in hard copy.)

SUMMARY

Arguing Evaluations

- All evaluations include a subject to be judged and an evaluative term applied to the subject.

- Before you argue the evaluation, consider whether your readers will recognize and accept your definition of the evaluative term. When their acceptance seems questionable, you'll want to argue your particular definition. Definitions can be argued by appeals to assumed reader values, appeals to authority, identification of effect, and comparison. When evaluating more than one subject against a single set of criteria, you may have to rank the criteria and justify that ranking.

- Applying the syllogistic model to your evaluative claim can help you test its reasonableness.

- Evaluations are made in ethical, aesthetic, or functional terms. *Ethical* evaluations focus on applying the ethical standard (evaluative term) to the subject, or on arguing a stipulative definition of that standard. *Aesthetic* evaluations typically work from standards currently accepted within the field, demonstrating their applicability to your subject. *Functional* evaluations typically work from a number of ranked criteria in terms of which the subject is measured.

- *Interpretations* closely resemble evaluations in structure. They establish coincidence or equivalence between the subject and the interpretive term by linking them through an acknowledged principle of experience.

SAMPLE FUNCTIONAL EVALUATION

The following essay, written by college student Karin Conrad, is a recommendation based upon a comparative functional evaluation. Karin's comment about the essay's origin confirms the importance of writing about topics (or perspectives on topics) that are meaningful to you:

> When Professor Squitieri first assigned the evaluation memo, he recommended that we choose a topic that is interesting and meaningful. I

racked my brain for days trying to figure out the perfect topic, rejecting one idea after the other. While volunteering at St. Mary's Hospital, I was discussing the project with a nurse, and she gave me the idea of researching accidental needle injuries. As a nursing student and daughter of a nurse, I couldn't have imagined a topic more relevant to my life.[1]

ST. MARY'S MEDICAL CENTER

MEMORANDUM

TO: Anthony J. Soprano, Director of Infection
                Control and Employee Health

FROM: Karin Conrad, Supervisor of Infection Control

DATE: 30 November 2004

SUBJECT: Recommendation to Implement Use of the
                VanishPoint® Retractable Needle in the Operating
                Room and Emergency Room to Prevent Accidental
                Needle Injuries

DISTRIBUTION: Ken Steele, Hospital President
                Michelle Angeles, Head of Surgery
                Dana Sue Nelson, Head of Emergency Room/Cast Room
                Suzanne Naito, Director of Hospitalist Program
                Tae Abate, Director of Finance

In response to your memo of 02 November 2004, I have carefully evaluated two different syringes based on their safety devices and recommend that we implement the VanishPoint® Retractable Syringe in the Emergency Room (ER) and Operating Room (OR). This memo covers the dangers and prevention of accidental needle injuries, evaluates the recommended syringe in relation to the BD SafetyGlide™ Hypodermic Needle, and includes a cost analysis of implementing my recommendation.

CONSEQUENCES AND PREVENTION OF ACCIDENTAL
NEEDLE INJURIES IN HOSPITALS

Accidental needle injuries (ANIs) negatively affect the staff and the hospital.

---

[1]http://www.usfca.edu/rhetcomp/journal/conrad2004.pdf

Occurrence and Repercussions of Accidental Needle Injuries on
Hospital Staff

This year alone workers in our hospital sustained twenty-one
reported needle injuries. Nurses suffered the most ANIs, then
doctors, and finally environmental services (non-users of
needles). Most of these injuries occurred in the ER and OR [1].
Sharps accidents pose a serious threat of transmitting bloodborne
pathogens like hepatitis B, hepatitis C and HIV to the victim.
In fact, an estimated 1,000 healthcare workers contract such
serious infections annually [2]. Even if a needlestick victim
does not contract a disease, needlesticks cost him/her time
(extensive testing must be done) and emotional anguish (results
can take months to get back).

Repercussions of Accidental Needle Injuries on the Hospital

Hospitals suffer many losses when an ANI occurs. Extensive
testing for diseases must be done for both the victim of the
needlestick and the patient who used the needle first. This
testing reportedly costs between $2,200 and $3,800 per accident
[3]. Worse still, if the victim does catch a disease, the
hospital must cover the cost of treatment. Hepatitis C costs
about $1,700 per month to treat, plus a possible liver transplant
costs $500,000, and HIV treatments cost up to $6,000 per month
[2]. Diseases spread by ANIs cost the hospital not only money
but also manpower. Nurses sustain the most ANIs, but there is a
huge nursing shortage. Losing nurses to needlestick injuries
makes the hospital understaffed, drags down the quality of
care, and creates an even higher demand for nurses and more
competitive wages; all of these factors help inflate the
hospital's operating expenses.

Prevention of Accidental Needle Injuries in the Hospital

Accidental needlesticks are preventable. The costs of
victims and hospitals don't have to be paid because safety
syringes such as the VanishPoint® retractable syringe and the
BD SafetyGlide™ hypodermic needle are available. These devices
work to protect nurses and other staff from accidental needle
injuries and infectious disease.

EVALUATION OF VANISHPOINT® AND SAFETYGLIDE™ SYRINGES

The evaluation includes the criteria used to judge the safety devices and the actual comparison of the two.

Criteria Used to Evaluate the Safety Syringes

I used six criteria in comparing the two safety needle options to determine which best suits the needs of St. Mary's Medical Center.

1. Active vs. Passive   4. Training Requirement
2. Protection Against ANI   5. Time to Activate
3. Ease of Use/One-handed   6. Cost

Comparison of SafetyGlide™ Hypodermic Needle and VanishPoint® Retractable Needle

1. These syringes represent two different types of safety devices: active and passive [4]. The SafetyGlide™ hypodermic needle is active because it requires the healthcare worker to activate a safety device once the needle has been used. During use, the VanishPoint® retractable syringe triggers the safety device automatically, classifying it as passive. See Figures 1a and 1b to see how the safety mechanisms are deployed.

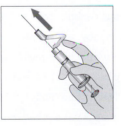

Figure 1a. [5] SafetyGlide™ Hypodermic Needle

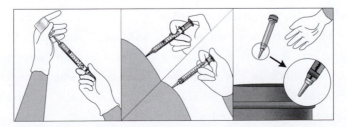

Figure 1b. [6] VanishPoint® Retractable

2. The VanishPoint® syringe is 100% effective at protecting workers from accidental needle injuries [5]. ANIs most typically occur when the user does not trigger the safety mechanism and/or tries to recap the needle [1]. The VanishPoint® prevents both of these incidents from happening since the needle is retracted while still inside the patient.

3. The SafetyGlide™ syringe is 90% more effective at preventing ANIs than the syringe currently in use because the SafetyGlide's safety device is easier to use. However, there is still the risk of an ANI because the user must remember to activate the mechanism. As mentioned above, a user's failure to activate the safety mechanism is one of the leading causes of ANIs.

4. Both syringes require only one hand to use, and there is virtually little change in technique from the old syringes to the new [5; 6]. One-handed use is important because the user should always keep both hands behind the needle to prevent an ANI. It is also vital that the technique for using the syringe remains approximately the same because learning a new technique takes away a nurse's or doctor's valuable time.

5. Since the techniques for use remain about the same, there is little training requirement for either syringe. This factor saves the hospital money and time.

6. Sliding the sheath over the needle instead of just keeping the finger on the plunger (this action retracts the needle) is more involved. Thus, the SafetyGlide™ syringe requires a few more seconds to activate than the VanishPoint® retractable needle.

7. A 3cc VanishPoint® retractable needle costs $0.50 [7]. A 3cc SafetyGlide™ hypodermic needle costs $0.35. The initial expenditures for safer syringes will be higher than current spending. However, over time costs will become lower than current costs as the expenses caused by accidental needle injuries diminish. Tables 1a and 1b illustrate comparative syringe costs with and without ANIs.

Table 1a. Cost of Syringes
(in dollars)

Table 1b. Real Costs of
Syringes and ANIs (in dollars)

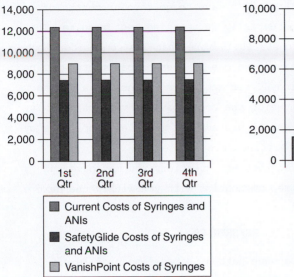

Legend:
- Current Costs of Syringes and ANIs
- SafetyGlide Costs of Syringes and ANIs
- VanishPoint Costs of Syringes

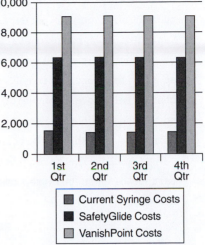

Legend:
- Current Syringe Costs
- SafetyGlide Costs
- VanishPoint Costs

As you can see in the tables, once the ANIs are calculated, safer syringes are the best option, and there is only a minor difference in cost between the SafetyGlide™ syringe and VanishPoint® syringe.

RECOMMENDATION TO IMPLEMENT VANISHPOINT® RETRACTABLE
NEEDLES IN OR AND ER

After carefully considering the strengths and weaknesses of these two devices, I strongly recommend the VanishPoint® retractable needle to be used in the Emergency Room and Operating Room. The VanishPoint® retractable needle will initially cost more than the SafetyGlide™ needle to implement, but what makes the VanishPoint® syringe far superior to the SafetyGlide™ is an impressive array of compensatory factors. First, time is extremely valuable in the hospital and the extra seconds that the SafetyGlide™ sheath takes to deploy add up quickly throughout the day; thus, the VanishPoint® will save time. Moreover, the VanishPoint® safety mechanism is passive and 100% effective, meaning that our hospital staff will no longer be subject to ANIs due to human error or carelessness.

Nurses, doctors, and environmental staff will be able to work better and more effectively because they won't be afraid of being accidentally stuck. They won't have to go through months of turmoil waiting for potentially devastating test results. The VanishPoint® syringe costs $0.15 more than its competitor, but it guarantees saved lives; no one in these departments will be at risk for contracting HIV or Hepatitis C. The extra monetary costs truly do not outweigh the costs paid by victims of ANIs, so we should do our best to protect our priceless employees by using the VanishPoint® retractable needle.

I would like to address any questions you may have and further discuss this recommendation with you within the next few days.

REFERENCES

[1]   J. Dimech, "Bloodborne pathogens baseline profile of sharps injuries," San Francisco, CA, St. Mary's Medical Center, 2004.

[2]   American Nurses Association. (1999). Nursing Facts. Retrieved November 11, 2004, from <http://www .nursingworld.org/readroom/fsneedle.htm>.

[3]   Safe Needles are money in the bank. (1999, May). *Nursing Management 30* (12). Retrieved from Proquest database.

[4]   K. Rosenthal and P. Shelton, "Sharp's injury prevention: select a safer needle," *Nursing Management 30,* pp. 28–29, June 2004.

[5]   Syringe use and application. (2004). Retrieved November 12, 2004, from <http://www.retractabletechnologies.com/ instructions.asp?section=hc>.

[6]   Step-by-step safety. (2004). Retrieved November 29, 2004, from <http://www.bd.com/safety/pdfs/BD_safetyglide _syringe_brochure.pdf>.

[7]   Cost analysis. (2004). Retrieved November 12, 2004, from <http://www.retractabletechnologies.com/ costanalysis.asp?section=purch>.

SUGGESTIONS FOR WRITING (9.10)

1. Write a two- to three-page evaluation of a course you have taken or are taking in college. Your evaluation will be primarily a functional evaluation, one of the crucial questions being whether the course actually achieves its intended goals.

2. Write a three- to four-page argument for or against a subject that requires evaluation—i.e., sexual harassment policies, ethnicity issues, Distance Learning, or even euthanasia—based on your reading of the sample student paper at the end of the section on evaluation. Have you established a clear definition? What about the other supporting arguments? Are there other arguments for the stand you have taken or do you have what you believe are more powerful arguments against it?

3. Write a combination interpretation and evaluation (three to four pages) of a recent artistic or entertainment event you enjoyed: a film, play, novel, concert, or something similar. Your evaluation will be primarily aesthetic, but it may be ethical as well.

ILLUSTRATIVE ARGUMENTS IN PART II: ARGUING EVALUATIONS

10

Arguing
Recommendations

At one time or another, most of us—whether student, professional, or concerned citizen—will have to argue a *recommendation* (sometimes called a *proposal*). A recommendation is a written request for change of some sort: cable TV in the dorms, paternity leave in a company, or a new major in a university. Recommendations vary in format from a simple one-page letter to an elaborate minivolume with strictly prescribed components. But despite the many variations in format, all recommendations argue for change.

Recommendations are the hybrids of argument, drawing on the principles and practices of factual, causal, and evaluative arguments. So, for the most part, writing a successful recommendation is a question of applying what you have already learned about the different kinds of argument and their support.

All recommendations establish a current situation (how things are now) and a probable future situation (how they would be if the change were instituted). In other words, recommendations rely on arguments of fact and arguments of effect. How central either type of argument is to your recommendation will depend on the emphasis demanded by the particular situation.

If you focus on the current situation, which usually means showing that things have gotten so bad that change must be considered, much of your argument will be factual. Let's say you want to impress the authorities with the inadequacy of parking facilities at your commuter campus. You figure it's up to them to come up with the answer to the problem, but you know they won't do it without being convinced that a serious problem *does* exist. In this case, your recommendation would begin with a factual argument that establishes exactly what the current situation is.

But if you are the contractor asked to submit a proposal for new parking lots, your focus will be on the future effects of your particular plan and predicting its ability to solve the current problem. In this case, the recommendation will be largely causal, establishing the probable effects of the implemented recommendation.

Regardless of their emphases, all recommendations also make evaluative arguments; they include a judgment of the current situation (the parking situation is inadequate or unfair) and/or an evaluation of the proposed change (parking will be more available, more convenient, etc.).

AUDIENCE NEEDS AND VALUES

By now you've learned how important it is when making any kind of argument to know as much about your audience as possible. Nowhere is this knowledge more critical than in writing recommendations. Most recommendations ask readers to *do* something, not merely to give their armchair agreement to a claim. Human nature being what it is, people are more likely to take action if there is a possibility that the action will benefit them in some way. Thus, a powerful way to support any recommendation is to appeal to the needs, values, and desires that you have identified in your readers. Making such an appeal means paying particular attention to the early stage of audience consideration: who is your audience? what are their needs and values likely to be regarding your claim? can you responsibly appeal to these in your recommendation? Luckily, it is usually fairly easy to answer these questions when you're preparing a recommendation, because in most cases, you're addressing a very specific audience (often a single individual).

For example, suppose your favorite professor is denied tenure, and you and a number of other students write a letter to the dean arguing for a reconsideration of the decision. What kinds of appeals would most likely move the dean? To answer the question, you have to know what the dean's priorities and responsibilities are, which, in fact, you're never thought about. In speaking with faculty members, you learn that your dean is determined to enhance the academic reputation of the college as a way of attracting and retaining good students. Knowing this, you're not going to get far arguing that Professor Morris be granted tenure because he's a good shortstop on the faculty-student softball team or an easy grader. You'll need to find a way to demonstrate just how valuable Professor Morris is to students in the *classroom,* perhaps including testimonials from students.

Though you'll always need to be aware of the needs and values of your readers, you will rarely identify them explicitly in the recommendation. In the case of Professor Morris's tenure, you will identify the positive effects on students of granting him tenure, but you probably won't need to identify which of the dean's needs or priorities will be addressed by this action. Provided your assumption about these priorities is correct, you can trust her to recognize that the change you are proposing would satisfy them.

When Your Values Differ from Assumed Reader Values

Recommendations actually work with two sets of values: the reader's *and* the writer's. While a successful recommendation must appeal to the appropriate reader values, it will originate in values held by the writer. Indeed, most recommendations are born in the writer's experience of *dissonance,* that sense of mismatch between one's values and a current situation (see Chapter 2).

Often the values that move you to recommend a certain change will be the same as those that will move your reader to accept your recommendation. But sometimes writer and reader values do not coincide. Usually, as long as the two values or sets of values are somehow related and not directly opposed, their lack of coincidence will not weaken your recommendation. But you do need to be aware of the difference between them.

Suppose you are a commuter student who takes the city bus to get to campus each day. This term, you have an 8 A.M. class, the early bus from your stop has been overcrowded and unreliable, and you have been late to class a number of times. You decide to write a letter to the local transit authority recommending improvements in bus service. Your letter derives from your own experience of dissonance—your frustration at not making it to class on time—and it seeks to satisfy your rights to good service as a paying customer (your needs and values).

But you realize that these values are not necessarily going to move your audience—the transit authority—to make the necessary improvements to the service. The manager of customer service may not care much about your rights as a paying customer, but he does care about the value of *customer satisfaction.* No business, even one that holds a virtual monopoly, as most transit authorities do, can afford to ignore the importance of customer satisfaction.

In this example, the values of customer rights and customer satisfaction are not identical, but they can comfortably coexist in the recommendation because they are not in conflict, and they are *causally* connected: if your rights are being served, you will be satisfied.

Your letter to the transit authority might look like this:

Mr. Brian Rose
Manager, Customer Service
Metro Transit Authority
Collegetown, USA

Dear Mr. Rose:

I am writing to complain about the quality of the morning bus service on Bus 15, which runs from Main and Winton to the community college. By the time the bus scheduled to stop at 7:21 A.M. gets to the stop at Main and Winton, it is usually late (in October, by an average of 15 minutes) and always overcrowded, with standing room only. Two days in October (the ninth and the fifteenth) the bus was so crowded that some people could not get on at all. I have tried to take the 7:04 bus, but the situation is essentially the same, and I cannot take a later bus because I have an 8:00 A.M. class at the college.

I and a number of others who rely on bus service are very unhappy. We are being cheated of the service we deserve, given the high fares we pay, and we would like some action taken to improve the situation. I am enclosing with this letter a petition signed by eight other students who depend on Bus 15 to get them to campus.

Now that you are aware of this problem, I hope you will take action to correct it. I look forward to hearing from you about what that action might be.

Very truly yours,

Patrick Booth

This letter has a good chance of influencing its reader because the values from which it is written and the values to which it appeals are related and compatible. In cases where there is clear conflict between your values and your readers', you must search for other values to appeal to. You couldn't convince an audience of cigarette smokers that cigarette sales should be restricted because smoking is, as you believe, a stinking, filthy habit. But you might make some headway with an argument citing the risks of secondary smoke to loved ones—a risk that might concern even the most committed of smokers.

ACTIVITIES (10.1)

1. In each of the following cases, the value cited to win the audience's acceptance of the recommendation is not appropriate. With a small group of your classmates, identify alternative values that are more appropriate. Then discuss your list with the entire class.

   Sample recommendation: A longer school year for elementary and secondary students
   Audience: Elementary and secondary teachers
   Inappropriate value: More work from teachers
   Alternative value: A greater opportunity to ensure students' mastery of skills

   a. **Recommendation:** Earlier closing of a college cafeteria
      Audience: College students
      Inappropriate value: Shorter hours and fewer headaches for cafeteria staff
   b. **Recommendation:** A new federal tax on gasoline
      Audience: Truck drivers
      Inappropriate value: Reduced reliance on trucks for transporting goods
   c. **Recommendation:** A curfew for everybody under the age of sixteen
      Audience: Those under sixteen
      Inappropriate value: Those under sixteen can't be trusted
   d. **Recommendation:** A law requiring motorcyclists to wear helmets
      Audience: Motorcyclists
      Inappropriate value: Reduced claims against insurance companies and therefore increased profits for insurance companies
   e. **Recommendation:** A shorter work week
      Audience: Employers
      Inappropriate value: More leisure time for employees

2. With the same small group of classmates, identify values that would be shared by the following pairs, or that would be compatible.
   Example: Republicans and Democrats
   Common value: Concern for the national interest—the country as a whole
   a. Planners of a new highway; homeowners whose property is in the path of the new highway
   b. Managers of a company; workers on strike against that company

c. Parents planning to take away a child's allowance as punishment for bad behavior; the child in question
d. Planners of a large rock concert; neighborhood groups opposed to the concert because of noise
e. Proponents of legislation restricting the use of handguns; opponents of this legislation

RECOMMENDATIONS EMPHASIZING THE PRESENT

Some recommendations, like Patrick Booth's letter to the transit authority, concentrate on problems in a current situation, leaving a detailed proposal for change to another argument. The goal of such arguments is to demonstrate more *that* something needs to be done than *what* exactly that something is.

To accept this kind of recommendation, your readers need an accurate and, usually, detailed picture of the current situation. They must grasp the situation as it is before they can agree or disagree with your evaluation of it. Recommendations emphasizing the present usually open with a factual argument.

Establishing the Current Situation

Booth's letter to the transit authority does a good job establishing the current situation through facts and figures that he collected: the average tardiness of the bus, the number of times the bus had to leave customers behind, and so on. Establishing these details is critical to the recommendation for a couple of reasons. First, readers are likely to take exact figures more seriously than irate vagueness. Exaggerations like "Huge numbers of people are regularly prevented from riding the 7:21 bus" are far less effective than exact figures.

Second, misrepresenting the facts, whether intentionally to strengthen your case or negligently through sloppy research, will be detected. The recipient of any recommendation is going to investigate the situation before taking action, and if the results of that investigation differ substantially from your figures, your recommendation will have reached a dead end.

Evaluating the Current Situation

All recommendations contain some evaluative elements. In recommendations emphasizing the present, the subject of the evaluation is the current situation. If you have a good understanding of your audience and their needs and values, you probably won't need to write a full-blown evaluation complete with a defined evaluative term. The transit authority letter, for example, doesn't require an explicit judgment of the situation presented. Any reader, whether an official of the transit authority or an occasional passenger, will recognize that the conditions described are undesirable. You could point to this fact for rhetorical emphasis, but the judgment is implicit within the factual presentation.

Sometimes your recommendation will be addressed to readers who may not immediately recognize the problems in the current situation. In these cases, you'd be wise to identify *what* is wrong by providing a clear and limited evaluative term. For example, a professor's schedule of assignments on a syllabus is unfair to students or hopelessly unrealistic. You can then proceed to match the subject (the syllabus) with the evaluative term according to the suggestions in Chapter 9, remembering the importance of considering audience needs and values.

Applying the Toulmin Model

The Toulmin logical model is especially useful when you're composing a recommendation. Placing your claim and support in the Toulmin paradigm (see Chapter 6) will help you detect any weaknesses of reasoning or wording in your argument and will suggest the secondary claims you'll need to support the central claim. Assume that an outside consultant, hired to analyze the employee benefits package of Quick-Stop Copy (the current situation), recommends that the company provide a benefits package more competitive with those of comparable companies (central claim). The consultant's recommendation would fit into the Toulmin model as follows:

Data
The current benefit package at Quick-Stop Copy is not competitive with those of comparable companies.

Claim
Quick-Stop Copy should institute a more competitive benefits package.

Warrant
Companies should have competitive benefits packages.

Remember that in the Toulmin model, the warrant is equivalent to the major premise in a syllogism; it is the general statement about a class that enables the data (or the minor premise in a syllogism) to justify the claim (or conclusion in a syllogism). As noted in Chapter 6, sometimes both data and warrant need further support. Indeed, one of the virtues of the Toulmin system is that once you have stated your argument in its terms, you can recognize what further support (backing) your argument will need. In this example, you realize that the argument will need a breakdown of facts and figures to back the data (i.e., how the Quick-Stop package actually compares with those of other companies'). And you should recognize as well that the warrant will need further backing if it is not self-evident to the reader that companies should have competitive benefits packages. Depending on the reader's point of view, the consultant may want to strengthen the warrant by supporting it with a secondary argument of effect—that is, demonstrating the negative results of the inferior benefits package to employees and to the company.

ACTIVITIES (10.2)

1. For two of the following current situations, what kind of facts would be necessary to convince readers that some change is necessary? Make a list of all the kinds of factual evidence you can think of.
   a. Traffic at an intersection
   b. Someone's physical appearance
   c. A friend's choice of career
   d. A company's health care benefits
   e. The local court system

2. Using the material you developed for Activity 1, create two claims of recommendation. Then state your argument in terms of the Toulmin model, indicating what additional support or backing is necessary.

RECOMMENDATIONS EMPHASIZING THE FUTURE

When your recommendation emphasizes the probable future effects of its proposed changes, you'll have to move beyond the current problems and the general claim that something must be done; you'll also have to identify, reasonably and convincingly, *what* that something is. A recommendation emphasizing the future will be effective if it can demonstrate (1) that your proposal is likely to produce desirable effects and (2) that the proposal is feasible.

Presenting the Recommendation

The recommendation itself—the proposed plan for change—must be crystal clear. Obviously, readers can't agree with a plan they don't understand. Some situations will call for a rather general recommendation, leaving the details to others, whereas in other cases, particularly when you have some responsibility for implementing the plan, a detailed recommendation will be necessary.

Kate Quill is a second-year student at Carlson College, a small liberal arts college in Maine. Carlson has operated on a trimester calendar for years, with three ten-week terms per academic year. It is common knowledge at Carlson that many students are unhappy with the trimester system: they feel rushed and overworked by the short terms. Kate and a number of her friends think it's time to do something about this dissatisfaction, so they decide to write a letter to the college administration recommending that a committee of faculty and students look at alternatives to the trimester calendar. The letter they write, which follows, is an example of a *general* recommendation emphasizing the future.

Dr. Dale Hill
President, Carlson College
Carlson, Maine

Dear Dr. Hill:

It should be no surprise to you that students feel considerable dissatisfaction with the trimester calendar used at Carlson. Faculty report that students have complained about the excessively fast pace of courses for years. Given this long history of dissatisfaction, we feel it is time for a formal examination of alternative calendars. Such an analysis should determine once and for all whether our current trimester calendar is the best system for Carlson.

We recommend that you put together a calendar committee consisting of students, faculty, and administration to conduct such an examination. This group could research the calendars used by comparable institutions, determining the advantages and disadvantages of each case. If the committee concludes that our current system is the best, we believe that the current level of student dissatisfaction would be reduced. Similarly, if a different calendar more suitable to Carlson were discovered and implemented, students would be much happier.

Any of the students signing this letter would be eager to serve on such a committee. We appreciate your time in considering this proposal.

> Very truly yours,
>
> Kate Quill and Carlson Students

Let's assume that President Hill has been hearing complaints about the trimesters for years and decides, on reading this letter, to take its recommendation seriously. After consulting with the deans and vice presidents, the president decides to constitute a "blue ribbon" committee to investigate the calendar issue. While Quill's recommendation was appropriately general (it's not a student's job to dictate details to a college president), the review process President Hill recommends to the chairperson of the Calendar Committee must be detailed and specific. This letter might read as follows:

Professor Rachel Eisenberg
Chair, Calendar Committee
Department of English
Carlson College

Dear Rachel:

Thank you for agreeing to serve as chair of the Calendar Committee. As you know, the calendar issue is extremely controversial; it is my hope that under your competent leadership the committee will put to rest once and for all the question of what calendar is the most appropriate for Carlson.

It is not my intention to direct the committee's work, but I hope you will allow a few suggestions about process and objectives:

- It will be critical to your deliberations to identify and verify the most common student complaints about our trimester system and the most common faculty complaints. This information can be obtained through survey instruments and through individual or group interviews.
- When exploring the alternative calendars currently used by other colleges, you should try to select schools whose size and mission are closely comparable to Carlson's.
- Please do not forget to factor in the budgetary implications of the various alternatives. While our primary concern should be with the quality of the education we deliver, an extremely costly calendar implementation could actually jeopardize our educational quality.
- While the final action taken on the basis of your report will be determined by the Carlson Board of Trustees, it would be helpful if the report included a ranking of the alternative calendars.
- The format and style of the final report I leave up to the committee, but bear in mind that it will be distributed to a number of different campus groups, so brevity and readability will be important.

Again, I thank you for agreeing to take on this challenging and important task. If there is any way that my office can help the work of the committee, don't hesitate to let me know.

Very truly yours,

Dale Hill

President

The preceding examples illustrate only two possibilities; recommendations can be more or less detailed than the second example. Generally, the more concrete your recommendation, the more effective it will be, provided your plan reflects a sound understanding of the operations of the group that will implement it. But there are times when a great deal of detail is inappropriate. Most editorials make recommendations without much detail; most politicians give few details in their speeches to general audiences. In deciding how much detail to include, be sure to consider your audience's capacity for and interest in the details, as well as their proposed role in carrying out the recommendation.

ACTIVITIES (10.3)

1. The following sample recommendations are extremely general. The writers have given no indication of how they expect their plans to be implemented. For each, provide at least three specific recommendations that will help an audience understand how the plans can be carried out. If you like, instead of working with the claims provided, create your own general recommendations (the kind that might come out of a conversation with friends), and then provide more specific recommendations for each.
   Example: We need a city with cleaner air.
   Specific recommendations: (1) Encouragement of "park-and-ride" lots for commuters to decrease automobile traffic, (2) tighter inspection standards for automobiles' exhaust emission systems, and (3) restrictions on the burning of leaves and trash.
   After you have made this list of recommendations, write a short essay (250–500 words) briefly explaining each of the recommendations and how they relate to the general recommendation.
   a. Our college needs more school spirit.
   b. Americans need to be more tolerant of racial and ethnic diversity.
   c. Adolescents must be made more aware of the dangers of alcohol.
   d. American industry needs to put more emphasis on the quality of its products.
   e. Students and professors must learn to see each other as human beings.

2. In your student or local newspaper, find an example of a recommendation that you think is good, but that is too general to be implemented. Write a letter to the editor suggesting specific ways that the recommendation might be developed further.

Arguing the Effects of Your Recommendation

Recommendations with future emphasis always identify and evaluate the probable effects of the proposed plan. Identifying probable effects will take the form of an *argument of effect* and will follow the steps presented in Chapter 8. This part of your recommendation will be strong if you can show that the proposed changes (the causes) are related to the results you predict (the effects) through established causal principles.

In the example of the Carlson College calendar, the Calendar Committee might predict the following short causal chain: converting to a semester calendar (cause) will give students more classroom contact with their faculty (first effect), which in turn is likely to make students feel more satisfied with their college experience (second effect). Readers would be likely to accept the first causal link: a semester course meets something like 45 hours per term, whereas a trimester course meets approximately 30 hours per term. Unless faculty use the additional time showing films and bringing in guest lecturers, the increase in hours will result in increased contact with faculty.

To support the second link in the chain, the committee needs to identify a linking behavioral principle. In this case, the principle linking increased student-faculty contact and student satisfaction has to be spelled out explicitly. That principle might be stated as follows: young people go to college to receive an education and to become adults; faculty not only provide that education but offer a new brand of adult relationship based on mature, intellectual foundations. Thus, substantial contact with faculty will meet a primary objective of many students. The committee report might also want to support this second effect in the chain by citing existing higher education studies that have discovered this connection between student-faculty contact and student satisfaction.

ACTIVITIES (10.4)

With a small group of your classmates, discuss the likelihood of the projected results of the following three recommendations. Have one student write up the reasons for your judgment of each. Submit this write-up to your instructor.

1. **Recommendation:** Increase the price of tickets to films at the college theater from $2.00 to $2.50.
   Projected results: No significant decline in attendance; more revenue from tickets to allow the theater to rent better films, which will eventually lead to higher attendance.

2. **Recommendation:** Allow students to take one course pass-fail.
   Projected results: Students will feel under less pressure about grades and more willing to take tough courses; the students will work just as hard in the courses they take pass-fail as they would have if they had taken the course for a regular grade.

3. **Recommendation:** Increase school taxes to subsidize new athletic facilities at the high school.
   Projected results: Greater community involvement in and identification with high school athletic teams; improvement in high school image; increased student enrollment.

Judging Effects in Terms of Assumed Needs and Values

In developing your recommendation, you will probably identify several probable effects, only some of which will meet the needs and values of your readers. Suppose you support your recommendation to faculty of a pass-fail grading option by predicting the effect of students' doing less work in their courses. Such an effect isn't likely to appeal to faculty values. This does not mean that you should deny the effect if it seems probable, but at the same time, there is no reason to emphasize it.

You may not always have to evaluate the probable effects explicitly nor identify the needs and values that those effects will satisfy. But at a minimum, you must be aware of the values that the probable effects of your implemented recommendation will satisfy.

When Some Effects Are Undesirable.   Few recommendations can promise exclusively positive results. But as long as the desirable effects outweigh the undesirable ones, your recommendation is worth making. When you know that along with the positive effects there may be some less desirable repercussions, you should acknowledge them in your argument. Provided you can demonstrate that the negative effects are less significant than the positive ones, you will not weaken your argument by mentioning them. In fact, an argument that acknowledges and measures its own weaknesses is usually more effective than one that fails to admit what any intelligent reader will recognize.

If you are on a committee recommending the building of a new expressway, you should admit that the building of the new expressway, whatever its ultimate advantages, will cause inconveniences. This is a more effective and responsible approach than ignoring altogether the obvious negative consequences of your recommendation. You will enhance your credibility by admitting what many people will know or suspect anyway.

Implementation.   To be successful, your recommendation must pass one further test: it must be feasible. Even the most brilliant recommendation will be rejected if its implementation is fraught with difficulties. While a detailed implementation plan is not required of all recommendations, some indication of the feasibility of your plan will strengthen your argument. At the least, you must provide a general indication that the recommendation *is* feasible. There is no point in advancing a recommendation that your audience will see as totally impractical, regardless of how desirable the results might be. Sometimes, your audience will expect a very detailed implementation plan, including a list of activities and the name of the person responsible for each activity, the dates for beginning and completing each activity, and the likely costs of each activity.

A crucial element of a general or detailed implementation plan is an analysis of costs. Many great ideas born in the heat of inspiration have failed to materialize because of a lack of cold cash; programs that many judge worthwhile (such as human exploration of Mars) have been delayed because of their expense. Whenever you present a proposal and outline its benefits, you also need to project its costs as accurately as you can. Remember that these costs often include not only the expense of constructing a new building or starting a new program but also the continuing costs once the proposal is a reality. Your community may need a new and larger airport, or a new bus service for the elderly, or new day care facilities, but once these are established, there may be additional costs of keeping the services going from day to day. The new and larger airport, for example, may need more employees to maintain it and may cost more to heat and cool than the old one did. These continuing expenses are easy to overlook or to minimize; the great temptation in making a recommendation that you believe in strongly is to overstate the benefits and understate the costs. You need to fight this temptation, remembering that some of your readers will be expecting just such a miscalculation.

People tend to accept recommendations that can be implemented within existing systems more readily than those requiring radical changes. Most of us are reluctant to make major changes on the strength of what *might* happen, however convincingly the probabilities are argued. Other things being equal, people usually prefer the least disruptive course of action.

On the other hand, sometimes existing structures need to be shaken up and disruptive measures taken. Much of our world, including the very existence of this country, is a result of radical changes. You should at least consider whether a drastic change will not be more effective ultimately and easier to implement than a piecemeal one. Sometimes piecemeal recommendations are like putting money into an old car that is going to break down anyway, or like eighteenth-century Americans hoping King George III and the British government would see the error of their ways. One test here, though a difficult one, is whether the piecemeal changes will improve the situation enough to justify the time and cost of the changes: the old car may not be worth keeping; on balance, it was easier to leave King George than to reform him.

Applying the Toulmin Model

The Toulmin model will help you evaluate the reasonableness and completeness of recommendations emphasizing the future. Applying the Toulmin format to the Carlson College example, we get a look at what kinds of secondary arguments the recommendation calls for.

Data	Claim
Carlson College does not operate on a semester calendar.	Carlson College should adopt a semester calendar to achieve greater opportunities for student-faculty contact.

Warrant
Colleges operating on semester calendars provide the most opportunities for student-faculty contact.

Laying the recommendation out this way shows us what additional support the argument will need. The data in this case will need minimal backing (all the readers will accept it as true), but the warrant is clearly not self-evident and thus calls for backing. Depending on your assessment of the readers' needs, that backing may follow at least two directions. On the one hand, you'll probably want to support the generalization with a secondary factual argument that compares the number of student-faculty contact hours in semester and trimester systems: "Students at Rusk College, which operates on a semester system, meet in class with their course faculty four hours per week for fourteen weeks, as opposed to Carlson's three hours per week for ten weeks."

A second issue raised by the warrant is the unstated assumption that student-faculty contact is a good thing. If you think your readers need to be convinced of this assumption, then you'll want to provide a secondary evaluative and/or causal argument demonstrating the positive elements and results of student-faculty contact. Here, you can resort to anecdotal evidence, but your best bet is to cite some of those higher education studies demonstrating the merits of this contact.

ACTIVITIES (10.5)

1. The following are recommendations that many believe are good ideas. For at least two of these claims, make a list of possible drawbacks to the recommendation that the writer would need to admit. Compare your list with those of some of your classmates. If you like, you may come up with your own recommendations—changes you would like to see occur—and consider the possible drawbacks.
   a. Sending astronauts to explore Mars
   b. Passing elementary and secondary students from one grade to another only after they have passed strict competency tests
   c. Prohibiting smoking in all public facilities
   d. Increasing the school year by an average of one month for all elementary and secondary schoolchildren
   e. Abolishing fraternities and sororities on your campus

2. Prepare an implementation plan for some change you would like to make in your own life, such as studying harder, learning a new sport or hobby, or exploring a possible career. Your implementation plan should include the sequence of activities you will undertake, the dates you plan to begin and end each activity, and the costs, if any, of the project. See the recommendation report "A Proposal for a Computer Facility in Marshall Dormitory" at the end of this chapter for a sample implementation plan.

3. Derive a claim of recommendation from three issues that you feel strongly about. Then place each claim within the Toulmin model, providing data and warrant. For each claim, where will you need additional backing? On the basis of your answer to this question, prepare an outline of a four- to five-page paper that would argue this recommendation.
   Example: Our staggering divorce rate suggests that a course in marriage and relationships should be mandatory for all high school students.

RECOMMENDATIONS THAT CONSIDER PRESENT AND FUTURE

The two types of recommendations we have discussed rarely occur in pure form; many recommendations contain some discussion of both the current situation and the future possibilities. Obviously, such recommendations combine the strategies discussed in this chapter: they present and evaluate the current situation, lay out the recommendation, and finally identify and evaluate the probable results of the recommendation. Because these arguments consider what currently exists and what could exist, they provide the groundwork for a useful comparative evaluation. After you have examined both the present and future elements of your argument, you may wish to compare the two explicitly—to demonstrate that the probable effects will be preferable to the current situation. If you have an accurate grasp of your audience's needs and values, you should be able to make this comparison effectively.

S U M M A R Y

Arguing Recommendations

- Recommendations emphasizing present conditions include the following:

  –A presentation of the current situation, policy, and/or practice (a factual argument).

  –An evaluation of this situation in terms of the values and needs important to your audience. The judgment expressed and the value appealed to may be stated or implied.

  –When applicable, a presentation of the existing effects (causal argument) and a judgment of these effects.

  –When applicable, a presentation of the probable future effects (argument of effect) and a judgment of these effects.

- Applying the Toulmin model will help you identify the supporting secondary claims your argument will need to make.

- Recommendations emphasizing the future include the following:

  –Presentation of the recommendation. The degree of detail in this presentation is usually dictated by your degree of responsibility for implementing the recommendation.

  –Identification of probable effects of your recommendation if it is implemented.

  –Evaluation of these effects (both desirable and undesirable) in terms of audience needs and values.

  –In some cases, a suggested implementation plan and an analysis of costs.

  Whether or not you include such a plan, those recommendations requiring minor changes to existing structures are generally more acceptable, though not necessarily more valuable, than those requiring radical restructuring.

- Recommendations considering present and future include the following:

  –Presentation and evaluation of the current situation.

  –Presentation of the recommendation.

–Identification and evaluation of the probable results of the recommendation.

–In many cases, a demonstration that the probable effects of the implemented recommendation will be preferable to the current situation.

TWO SAMPLE RECOMMENDATIONS

The following sample recommendation report considers both the current situation and probable results of its implementation. The report is an example of what a student might include in a recommendation for a computer room in the dormitory. The format of the report, outlined here, is one of several possible formats for a recommendation report:

   I. STATEMENT OF PROBLEM
  II. STATEMENT OF RECOMMENDATION
 III. ADVANTAGES OF RECOMMENDATION
 IV. DISADVANTAGES OF RECOMMENDATION
  V. COSTS AND IMPLEMENTATION PLAN

Many organizations and many professors have a preferred format for such reports; you would be wise to check whether there are such preferred formats before you begin to write this kind of report either at work or for a class.

This recommendation is briefer and more general than many. If a report with the same proposal were prepared by the university's office of computing, it would undoubtedly include more detail on the scheduling of the project, the nature of the renovations, and the kind of equipment that would be purchased. But a recommendation like this one—proposed by a student to an administrator—need not include an implementation plan (although some suggestions about implementation might impress the audience with how carefully the writer has thought about her recommendation).

A PROPOSAL FOR A COMPUTER FACILITY IN MARSHALL DORMITORY

Prepared for

Dr. Hector Martinez,

Assistant Vice President for Student Life

by Elaine Weston,

Chair, Marshall Dormitory Student Committee

February 13, 2007

Statement of Problem

Currently many students living in Marshall Dormitory have difficulty getting access to a computer. The college's main computer facility is located over a mile away on the other end of campus, and that facility is often overcrowded; many students find that they can use a computer only after eleven at night or before ten in the morning. Some students bring their own computers with them to college, but not all students here can afford their own computers. I surveyed all students living on the third floor of Marshall and found that only 25 percent had their own computers, while another 50 percent said they use computers frequently for course work. Of this 50 percent, 45 percent said that they have sometimes found it hard to get access to one of the college's computers, and 35 percent frequently had this problem. Clearly, this lack of access to needed computers is a serious problem for Marshall students. When I spoke with Helen Borshoff, the Vice President for Computing, she confirmed the severity of the problem and said that her organization is trying to deal with the problem within the constraints of its limited resources.

RECOMMENDATION

We recommend that the Office of Student Life work with the Office of Computing to convert the student lounge at the west end of the second floor of Marshall into a computer facility equipped with seven PCs connected to the central campus computer system and three printers: our discussions with the Office of Computing indicate that the number of computers and printers is the maximum that would fit into the amount of space available and that this range of equipment would be most appropriate for student needs. Since the need for more computers and more access to computers is so pressing, we recommend that the necessary renovations take place this summer so that the facility will be ready by the beginning of the next academic year on September 6, 2007.

ADVANTAGES OF RECOMMENDATION

If our recommendation is implemented, students who live in Marshall will be able to use college-owned computers without having to go all the way to the college facility. There will also be more computers available than there are now, and students without the means to buy their own computers will be at less of a disadvantage than they currently are. For students, then, there are significant educational advantages if this proposal is implemented.

For the administration, there are several other advantages as well. Construction of this facility will alleviate at least some of the overwhelming pressure on the main computer facility. Since the space for this new facility already exists, renovating this space will be less costly than adding new space somewhere on campus. This new facility will also show the administration's concern about increasing student access to computers, and it will therefore help to reduce the growing tension between students and administrators over this issue.

DISADVANTAGES OF RECOMMENDATION

Our recommendation does have some disadvantages. Probably the most significant is the security risk of having a small facility so far removed from the central computer facility, which means that it would not make financial sense to have someone on duty to guard the equipment. Another disadvantage is that some space devoted to student relaxation would be taken and used for another purpose. The placing of a computer facility in a dormitory also raises some new policy questions for the college, including whether only students in the dormitory can use the facility, or whether the facility would be open to all students of the college.

These disadvantages are real, but they can be dealt with. The Vice President for Computing assures us that new electronic security devices reduce the need for security personnel. In a poll taken two weeks ago, the Marshall students indicated that they preferred to see the current lounge converted into a computer facility, with 68 percent expressing this preference, 18 percent opposing it, and 14 percent expressing no opinion. Finally, while this proposal does raise some new questions of policy, these questions must be addressed at some point in the

near future anyway, as computers and computer facilities become
more pervasive in the college.

COSTS AND IMPLEMENTATION PLAN

The following is a tentative and very general outline of the
costs of the project as well as an implementation plan. These will
have to be refined by the Offices of Student Life and Computing as
they begin to work on the project. The Vice President for Computing
has assured us, however, that the costs and implementation plan we
have outlined here seem reasonable. On her advice, we have not
included personnel costs for the time of administrators, since
these costs are difficult to calculate and are not usually
included in the budgets for small projects of this kind.

Activity	Dates	Costs
Initial planning with students, Student Life, and Computing administrators	March	—
Work requests for construction; orders for equipment	April	—
Renovation of lounge	June–July	$30,000
Installation of security devices	Early August	$ 6,000
Purchase and installation of computer equipment	Late August	$30,000
Total initial costs		$66,000
Ongoing costs; maintenance of equipment		$ 3,000 per year

The following recommendation is a more general argument than the preceding
formal proposal, but like the preceding argument, its central claim calls for a new
course of action.

THE SIDE EFFECTS OF AFFIRMATIVE ACTION

PAMELA J. HSU

1 In the 1960s, the civil rights movement said people could not be denied things like employment based on race. In the 1970s, affirmative action injected women and minorities into the workplace. In the 1980s, diversity programs stressed appreciating differences among all people. But are we starting to see some negative side effects in the 1990s?

2 During the past several decades, many programs have promoted the education and employment of women and minorities. Minority scholarships are readily available in just about every field. And most corporations track hiring, retention, and promotion of women and minorities, and aim to improve performance in these areas.

3 As a 24-year-old Chinese woman, I benefit from these programs. I received a generous minority internship/scholarship package from a major corporation one summer during college. When I applied to graduate school, one university offered me a fellowship specifically for minorities entering that particular field of study.

4 I know that these opportunities have provided a boost in my career. I appreciate them. But there are times when I wish I could have competed against everyone else. I believe my ability would have made me at least a strong contender against all applicants.

5 I know we have not reached that ideal scenario. I realize that problems still exist and that economic and social conditions prevent some children from getting any chance at all. But we need to look at some of the actions taken in the name of fighting discrimination and promoting diversity to see if they are solving these problems—or just creating different ones.

6 I'm noticing a growing number of white males who say they are now being discriminated against. I'm talking about the professor who warns his white male students that a particular graduate program may be difficult to get into because they are favoring women and minority candidates. I'm talking about a former employer who ran a department one person short for months, even though many applied for the job, because the position had to be filled by a minority. There's a difference between fairness and force fitting.

7 Daniel J. Boorstin, the Pulitzer Prize–winning historian and best-selling author, said it best: "We must give everybody a fresh start and not try to compensate for past injustices by creating present injustices."

8 A growing number of groups are voluntarily segregating themselves from others to preserve ethnic identity. Just take a look at the average college campus, and you'll find Greek houses for minorities and organized student groups for just about every ethnic population. But some may be developing blanket beliefs about their own ethnic group. I've heard that you aren't being true to yourself if you "act" white or you aren't really happy if you've assimilated. The fact that I'm Chinese in blood and American in behavior rubs some people the wrong way. They dub me a Twinkie—yellow on the outside but white on the inside.

9   I was raised to assimilate, and I don't regret that. Just because I live an American lifestyle doesn't make me any less Chinese. It's ironic that groups which intend to promote an appreciation of their culture among others sometimes fail to reciprocate the respect among their own.

10   Competition between minority groups may be breeding another problem. One minority group complains that a university gave such-and-such group this much money, and how come they didn't get the same? Columnist William Raspberry pointed out that more students these days search for "discrimination nuggets" because if they find enough of them, they can trade in at the administration building for an ethnic sensitivity course or a minority student center.

It's time to step back and refocus on our ultimate goal. The idea that minority status equals money needs to change. Financial assistance should be available for those who need a chance. Ethnic groups should preserve traditions but not alienate those who do things differently. Sharing traditions with other people and encouraging those who are interested to get more involved—even if they do not belong to that ethnic group—would truly promote diversity.   11

Source: *Detroit News*, Sunday, 22 May 1994.

SUGGESTIONS FOR WRITING (10.6)

1. Following the form of the first sample recommendation, write a recommendation report to improve some aspect of your college or university. Possible areas for improvement include dormitories or apartments, the library, the call for more online courses, requiring faculty and students to use laptop computers for class work, the curriculum in your major, or the food service. Make your recommendation as realistic as possible by interviewing people with some responsibility for that area. From these people, you should try to learn why the situation exists in its current form and how feasible your recommendation is as well as to get some sense of the costs of the project. The length of this report will vary with the complexity of the problem and your recommendation, though it might be wise to limit yourself to a maximum of approximately ten pages.

2. Almost every community has its share of white elephants: elaborate projects or expensive buildings that ultimately had to be abandoned or converted to some alternative use because their cost greatly exceeded their benefit to the community. Look for a white elephant in your community and analyze why the project never met its original intentions. Your professor can help you get started. You will almost certainly have to consult the local newspapers and then perhaps the local archives. Since your time is limited and there may be a great deal of documentation, you might have to restrict your research to newspaper accounts of what happened and why. As with Suggestion 1, the maximum length should be approximately ten pages.

3. Working from the outline you prepared for Activity (10.5.3), write a four- to five-page general recommendation emphasizing the future (along the lines of the preceding Hsu sample above). Be sure to include and support all the secondary claims suggested by the Toulmin model.

ILLUSTRATIVE ARGUMENTS IN PART II: ARGUING RECOMMENDATIONS

11

Writing and Image

In our contemporary society of sound bites and spin doctors, the concept of *image* has developed something of a negative flavor, suggesting superficiality and deceit. Public personalities pay a great deal of money to have distinctive images packaged and popularized—images that may bring them enormous success but that bear little relationship to the real people behind them.

This book uses the term *image* differently and more positively, to suggest the ways in which writing honestly reflects to the reader the kind of person the writer is. In successful arguments, writers project an image of intelligence, probity, and trustworthiness. There is nothing false or superficial about this kind of image: these qualities cannot be created out of thin air; they must be true *reflections* of the writer and thus are developed over time and through experience. But whenever you write, you should strive to project such an image, while also being aware that this image will need to be slightly adjusted to fit the context of a given argument.

Image consists of many elements. Most obviously, the quality of the argument itself—its intelligence, honesty, and accuracy—will impress your readers. But image is projected on a smaller scale as well—by your argument's word choice, sentence construction, and figures of speech; by its spelling, punctuation, and physical format; even by its *sound*.

This chapter focuses on some of the conscious choices you'll be making about your image as a writer of argument—choices about voice, diction, metaphor and analogy, emotive language, and the sound of your prose. As you'll see in this chapter, the choices you make will vary from one argument to the next, depending on your subject, your purpose, and your audience.

THE ROLE OF VOICE

A writer's *voice* is the role that he or she takes for a particular occasion, almost like an actor taking a part in a new play. To many inexperienced writers, voice suggests insincerity or fakery, but all of us continually "play" different roles. We behave one way in a classroom, another way playing basketball; we talk to our parents in one way and to our friends in another. Voice is simply the written manifestation of this adaptability.

The following simple example demonstrates the variability of voice:

```
Dear Mr. Jones:

At the suggestion of Ms. Hawkins, I am writing to inquire about

an opening as an electrical engineer in your firm.


Dear Mom and Dad:

Hi and help! You won't believe this but I'm broke again. Boy,

were my textbooks expensive this quarter!
```

The same student wrote both of these openings and was completely sincere in both cases but the voices differ markedly. In the first case, the student was formal, polite, and restrained. In the second, she was informal and very direct. In cases like these, the choice of a particular voice seems natural; the student did not spend much time or effort choosing these voices. But you can improve your writing by being conscious of the available choices and using them effectively. One crucial choice is between the formal and the informal voices—the voices of the first and second letters, respectively. Using an informal voice in a formal situation may have disastrous effects. What would happen to our student if she wrote to Mr. Jones (whom she presumably does not know) in the following manner?

```
Dear Mr. Jones:

Hi and help! I ran into somebody Hawkins—I forget her first

name—and she says you've got jobs. Boy, do I need one!
```

The Importance of Ethos

As the Greek philosopher Aristotle noted, a major element of a successful image is the *ethos* projected by the writer. The ethos is the impression of the writer's character that the reader gets; a positive ethos is one reflecting sincerity and trustworthiness. Readers are likely to accept arguments written by someone who comes across as honest, upright, and unselfish; they will distrust the claims of one known to be dishonest or selfish, or whose voice suggests these traits. So, in your own arguments, try to write from the most principled, unselfish part of yourself. And try not to emulate the ethos projected by the angry writer of the following letter to his campus newspaper:

> The grading policies of this college are rotten, just like everything else here at State. How can the administration put a student on probation for failing a course outside of his major? That's just outrageous. When I got an F in physics, they put me on probation even though I received at least a C in the courses in my major. I didn't want to take physics anyway, and the professor really stunk. Now I'm not eligible to play basketball! When are we students going to force the administration to get rid of this stupid policy?

The reasoning in this letter has many weaknesses, but the writer's failure to establish a respectable ethos also destroys its effectiveness. He presents himself as lacking balance (is *everything* at State rotten?) and as concerned only about himself (what about the effect of the probation policy on others?). Almost all readers, including fellow students, would dismiss this letter as the howl of outrage that it is; certainly they would not be likely to join forces with the writer in an attempt to change school policy.

When Aristotle urged writers of argument to establish an effective ethos, he was not urging hypocrisy. In creating an ethos, you will present your best side, but this side is still part of you; it is not wholly fabricated. Our outraged student in the preceding example is doubtless capable of balance and concern for others. Before writing that letter, he should have given himself the time to move from outrage to a broader perspective, using his anger to inspire dissonance but recognizing that hurt feelings and the impulse to dodge responsibility don't advance arguments.

A writer's ethos can be enhanced by the confidence with which his ideas are expressed. You should always appear confident about your claims, though not more confident than their support warrants. A credible ethos finds a balance between dogmatism and apology. Readers suspect writers, such as our angry student, who make sweeping claims (everything at State is rotten) and writers who make forceful statements that they can't possibly support ("the governor is the dumbest woman in the state"). On the other hand, readers will also suspect arguments that seem too wishy-washy: "I think it is probably true that this policy may lead us in the wrong direction."

Let's take a look at how the disgruntled student might create an ethos that works *for,* rather than *against,* him.

> After a painful experience with the academic probation policy here at State, I have concluded that the college should consider revising it. The policy states that any student whose grades fall below a C average will be placed on probation, so that that student will be ineligible for many extracurricular activities. The policy appears reasonable, but its effect is to place too much emphasis on courses outside a student's major. Many students, including three of my acquaintances, have found themselves ineligible to participate in extracurricular activities even though they were doing solid work in their majors. I now find myself in a similar situation, being ineligible to play basketball yet earning grades of C or higher in my major.

Here, the student comes across as someone who is honest about his own situation and also concerned for others, someone who allows for an apparently reasonable opposing view while remaining firm in his own.

ACTIVITIES (11.1)

1. Write a one-page letter to your parents or a friend asking for a loan to help with college expenses. Then write a letter to your college's financial aid office asking for the same loan. With two to three of your classmates, make a list of the differences in the two letters.

2. Go back to Chapter 8 and reread Dorsett Bennett's essay "I, Too, Am a Good Parent." In a one- to two-page essay, characterize the argument's ethos. Your instructor may want to devote some class time to a discussion of the effectiveness of Bennett's ethos.

THE VIRTUES AND LIMITATIONS OF PLAIN WRITING

Most writing teachers and most writing textbooks encourage students to make their writing clear and straightforward, without distracting embellishments. Perhaps the most famous advocate of this plain style was British writer George Orwell, who formulated the following six stylistic rules in one of the most famous essays about writing style, "Politics and the English Language":

   (i) Never use a metaphor, simile or other figure of speech which you are used to seeing in print.

  (ii) Never use a long word where a short one will do.

 (iii) If it is possible to cut a word out, always cut it out.

 (iv) Never use the passive where you can use the active.

  (v) Never use a foreign phrase, a scientific word or a jargon word if you can think of any everyday English equivalent.

 (vi) Break any of these rules sooner than say anything outright barbarous.

The plain style Orwell urges arose as a reaction against the bloated and often dishonest prose of modern bureaucratic society, where military first strikes are called "anticipatory retaliations," visual materials in school curricula become "integrated systems learning designs," and simple sentences and direct expression disappear behind clouds of vague pomposity: "Please contact my secretary about an appointment regarding the project slippages in implementing the new online system." The writer could have said, "Please see me about the delays in starting the new online system," but to too many writers today, the first version seems more official, more important. A plain style of writing is an antidote to this swollen prose.

But plain writing carries its own risks, as Orwell notes in his sixth rule. Writers who use the plain style exclusively risk prose that is clear but undistinguished, serviceable but dull. To help you avoid this extreme, here are some friendly amendments to Orwell's rules:

(i) Don't be afraid to use metaphors, similes, or other figures of speech, provided they are not overworked.
(ii) When a long word is the best one, use it.
(iii) Use long sentences for variety and when they best suit your needs.
(iv) Dare to try something different.
(v) Break any of these rules rather than confuse your reader.

The following passage from Annie Dillard's book *The Writing Life* is a good sample of writing that succeeds by going beyond the plain style. The marginal annotations mark instances of enriched prose.

Effective exaggeration— dare to be different	It should surprise no one that the life of the writer—such as it is—is colorless to the point of sensory deprivation. Many writers do little else but sit in small rooms recalling the real world.
Varied sentence length	This explains why so many books describe the author's childhood. A writer's childhood may well have been the occasion of his only firsthand experi-
Inventive language	ence. Writers read literary biography, and surround themselves with other writers, deliberately to enforce in themselves the ludicrous notion that
Ironic humor	a reasonable option for occupying yourself on the planet until your life span plays itself out is sitting in a small room for the duration, in the company of pieces of paper.

FIGURES OF SPEECH

A figure of speech involves a "turn" on the literal use of words, or using words to suggest something related to but different from their literal meaning. Two of the most common figures of speech are *metaphor* and *analogy*. A metaphor is an implicit comparison of two unlike subjects so that some aspects of one (usually concrete and familiar) illuminate aspects of the other (usually more abstract or unfamiliar). "The twilight of her career" is a metaphor comparing something concrete and familiar, the end of a day, to something more abstract, in this case the end of someone's career. "Global village" is another metaphor, where the abstract concept of the globe or world (the entire population of the earth) is compared to the more familiar and concrete idea of a village. A *simile*, a variant of a metaphor, is an explicit comparison, where the two subjects are linked by *like* or *as:* "Falling in love is like getting caught in a warm spring rain."

Analogy is like metaphor in that dissimilar subjects are compared, but in analogy, the comparison is usually extended through several points. The "global village" becomes an analogy when the world is compared to a village in several respects—for example, the need for certain agreed-upon laws and the importance of communication and cooperation among those in the community.

The following passage by historian Barbara Tuchman shows the value of metaphor in argument. In the first paragraph of "History as Mirror," Tuchman compares history to a mirror reflecting our own image:

> At a time when everyone's mind is on the explosions of the moment, it might seem obtuse of me to discuss the fourteenth century. But I think a backward look at that disordered, violent, bewildered, disintegrating and calamity-prone age can be consoling and possibly instructive in a time of similar disarray. Reflected in a six-hundred-year-old mirror, a more revealing image of ourselves and our species might be seen than is visible in the clutter of circumstances under our noses.

Tuchman could not have made her point about history so succinctly without this metaphor. What aspects of history are clarified through its comparison to a mirror?

The following passage by psychoanalyst Carl Jung contains an effective use of analogy. Here Jung describes the collective mind of twentieth-century humanity through the analogy of a building:

> We have to describe and to explain a building the upper story of which was erected in the nineteenth century; the ground-floor dates from the sixteenth century, and a careful examination of the masonry discloses the fact that it was reconstructed from a dwelling-tower of the eleventh century. In the cellar we discover Roman foundation walls, and under the cellar a filled-in cave, in the floor of which stone tools are found and remnants of glacial fauna in the layers below. That would be a sort of picture of our mental structure.

Of course, Jung could have described the characteristics of the mind in more abstract language, but his description would have been less memorable than this picture of a house with a buried cave underneath. This example demonstrates how analogies crystallize abstract ideas into a sharp picture that both clarifies the ideas and makes them memorable.

Metaphors can also be valuable means of discovery—doors that lead you to important ideas and arguments. We are all naturally disposed to notice correspondences, to see the threads of similarity that unify experience. We have all had the experience of being spontaneously struck by similarities between two seemingly different subjects. Usually our minds hit on such a comparison because it is apt, because it contains a truth that we may not consciously recognize. On close examination, these correspondences or metaphors that come to us may reveal important truths about both subjects and may generate and even structure a theory or argument. When the noted computer scientist Edward Fredkin was struck by the correspondences between the operation of computers and the operation of the universe, he followed up that metaphor, creating a controversial but intriguing theory of digital physics from the implications of a seemingly simple metaphor. Like Fredkin and others, you should be alive to the generating power of your natural metaphor-making tendency, letting it work for you in the ideas you develop and the arguments you write.

Some Cautions About Figures of Speech

Metaphors, similes, and analogies can illuminate and generate ideas, but they can't prove a point; they offer clarification, not evidence. (See Chapter 6 for a discussion of false analogy as an informal fallacy.) Calling the world a village doesn't prove the need for world government. Ultimately all analogies break down if pursued too far; the two subjects of an analogy are, finally, *different* subjects. The world may be a village, but it is a village with more than five billion inhabitants, speaking thousands of different languages and following countless different customs and beliefs. Some village!

Analogies are risky if people take them too literally, as they did the "domino theory" analogy in the 1960s and 1970s. The domino analogy compared countries in Southeast Asia to a row of dominoes. When dominoes are placed on their ends in a row, they will fall down one by one if the first in the series is pushed. According to the domino theory, these countries would fall to communism in the same manner. The domino theory was a major reason for American involvement in Vietnam; American strategists believed that the fall of South Vietnam to the communists would lead to communist control of all of Southeast Asia and perhaps all of Asia. South Vietnam and some other parts of Southeast Asia are now communist, but other countries in Southeast Asia are not and do not seem to be in any danger of falling under such control. The domino theory may not always be this faulty, yet the theory cannot become an excuse for failing to analyze the particular complexities of a specific situation. Real countries are always more complicated than dominoes.

ACTIVITIES (11.2)

1. For one of the following analogies, write a one-page essay analyzing how the analogy illuminates aspects of the situation and how it does not. Our discussion of the "domino theory" in the previous section is one example of this kind of analysis.
   a. Sexual politics
   b. The family of humanity
   c. The game of life
   d. The war of ideas
   e. The corporate ladder

2. Write a paragraph that develops an analogy. You may use one of the analogies in Activity 1, provided it is not the one you used in that exercise. The paragraph by Carl Jung previously cited is one model for this kind of development.

3. Read a classmate's paragraph from Activity 2 while he or she reads yours. Evaluate the effectiveness of the analogy, and discuss your evaluation with your partner.

CONNOTATIVE LANGUAGE AND SLANTING

Good writers must be aware not only of the *denotations* of words but of their *connotations* as well. The denotation of a word is its explicit meaning, its dictionary definition; the connotation of a word is the meaning or meanings suggested by the word, the word's emotional associations. The denotation of the words *apple pie* is a baked food made with apples. In our society, the connotations of "apple pie" are family life, patriotism, and innocence. Writers of arguments need to be sensitive to the connotations of words and to use these connotations appropriately. A writer urging the development of a suburban tract of land for offices and factories is more likely to succeed by describing it as a "high-tech park" than as an "industrial development area"; the term *high-tech* has a certain vogue, while "*industrial development*" smells of factory smokestacks. And have you noticed how frequently suburban office complexes are called something like Corporate Woods, even when there are few trees anywhere in sight? Beyond a certain point, words used for their connotative value cease to have any meaning at all; there are very few woods in Corporate Woods and nothing fresh in "lemony fresh" soap or in "fresh frozen" juice. And what is so natural about many of the products that advertise themselves as "naturally delicious"? Connotation is an inescapable element of argument, but it should not be used without regard to denotation. Some advertising disregards denotation and gets away with it, but most readers demand higher standards for other kinds of written arguments.

Writers are often tempted to use not only connotation but also blatantly emotional terms as illegitimate supports for their arguments. Suppose you were arguing for a new recreation center on your campus. You might refer to the necessity of having a place "where students can use their free time constructively, letting off the frustrations and pressures caused by rigorous scholastic demands." Here you are portraying students and their needs in a positive way: we tend to respect anyone subjected to "rigorous scholastic demands." But if you were arguing against the recreation center, you could completely alter this impression by using words with negative connotations: "Do our spoiled and spoon-fed students really need another service catering to their already well-satisfied needs?" The respectable students of the first argument have become the undeserving parasites of the second. Words like *spoiled, spoon-fed,* and *catering* are negative words, and their application to the students in question affects a reader's impression of the issue. The words used *slant* the argument, even in the absence of sound evidence. As a writer of responsible arguments, *you* must not fall into the trap of letting such language suggest conclusions your argument does not support.

The temptation to slant is probably strongest in arguments of ethical evaluation; of all the arguments you write, these are the most personal, the most self-revealing, and thus the most important to you. For these reasons, they may tempt you to resort to irrational means to convince your audience. You are not likely to invest high emotional stakes in arguing that four-wheel-drive cars are superior to other kinds of cars, but you can be passionately committed to an argument for or against capital punishment or abortion. Slanting, while almost unavoidable in such cases, must not become a substitute for sound support of your argument.

(See Chapter 6 for a discussion of "Emotive Language" and "Circular Argument" as informal fallacies.)

ACTIVITIES (11.3)

With one other student in your class, select a subject to describe. Each of you should then write a description of that subject—one favorable, one unfavorable. Some possible topics are: city life, a particular television show, a book you both have read. Before you write your descriptions, agree on certain qualities to refer to in your descriptions.

THE MUSIC OF LANGUAGE

Any writer who ignores the importance of *sound* in argument is overlooking a valuable tool. We all know the power of advertising's jingles and catch phrases, which linger in our minds even when we wish they wouldn't. Less obvious but powerfully convincing is prose that holds our attention because of a fresh and pleasing combination of sounds. Such prose contains euphony and rhythm.

Euphony, a term that comes from Greek roots meaning "good sound," is a pleasing combination of sounds. We usually think of euphony as a characteristic of poetry or some kinds of prose fiction, but it can and should be present in written arguments as well. Euphony, of course, depends on the ear of the reader or listener, but ears can be trained to become sensitive to this quality of prose, just as we learn to be sensitive to different qualities of music.

Rhythm is a recognizable pattern of sounds through time. In prose, rhythmical units are often divided by grammatical pauses such as commas or periods, though a rhythmical break may also occur at some other place where we would pause to catch our breath if we were reading aloud. "I came, I saw, I conquered" is a simple example of prose rhythm, with three short, rhythmical units divided by commas. All of us have a rhythm to our prose just as we have a rhythm to our breathing or walking, and this rhythm varies with the situation, just as our walking rhythm does. Good prose writers learn to know their prose rhythms, to develop them as they gain experience in writing, and to recognize and use the appropriate rhythm for a specific purpose.

The following passage is from Jeff Greenfield's "The Black and White Truth About Basketball." Note Greenfield's sensitivity to euphony and rhythm:

> Basketball is a struggle for the edge: the half step with which to cut around the defender for a lay-up, the half second of freedom with which to release a jump shot, the instant a head turns allowing a pass to a teammate breaking for the basket. It is an arena for the subtlest of skills: the head fake, the shoulder fake, the shift of body weight to the right and the sudden cut to the left. Deception is crucial to success; and to young men who have learned early and painfully that life is a battle for survival, basketball is one of the few pursuits in which the weapon of deception is a legitimate tactic rather than a source of trouble.

For one thing, this passage makes effective use of the stylistic element of parallelism. Parallelism is the principle that equivalent thoughts demand equivalent expression. Notice how the actions described in the first and second sentences are presented in the same grammatical form: a noun modified by a verbal phrase ("the half step with which to cut around the defender for a layup, the half second of freedom with which to release a jump shot"). In addition to the grammatical parallelism within each of these sentences, Greenfield has made the two sentences parallel to each other: in each, two shorter phrases are followed by a third, longer phrase.

As well as parallelism, Greenfield also makes use of repetition ("half step" and "half second"; "the head fake" and "the shoulder fake") and opposition ("the shift of body weight to the *right* and the sudden cut to the *left*"). The overall effect of these strategies is one of balance—a rhetorical balance that nicely mirrors the physical balance of the intricate choreography of basketball.

The sound of your prose *will* affect how readers react to your argument, even if they are not conscious of the role sound plays in written prose and even if they have not developed the skill to create sound-pleasing prose themselves. As the rhetorician Kenneth Burke has noted, audiences tend to identify with skilled speakers and writers and are likely to be carried along simply by the very structure of the prose. A solid argument that is also aurally effective is hard to beat.

ACTIVITIES (11.4)

Read the following passages and choose the one whose prose style you find most memorable or striking. Write a one- to two-page evaluative argument demonstrating what is effective about the style and why.

1. You know how it is, you want to look and you don't want to look. I can remember the strange feelings I had when I was a kid looking at war photographs in *Life*, the ones that showed dead people or a lot of dead people lying close together in a field or a street, often touching, seeming to hold each other. Even when the picture was sharp and cleanly defined, something wasn't clear at all, something repressed that monitored the images and withheld their essential information. It may have legitimized my fascination, letting me look for as long as I wanted; I didn't have a language for it then, but I remember now the shame I felt, like looking at first porn, all the porn in the world. (Michael Herr. *Dispatches*. London: Picador, 1978. 23.)

2. Wandering through the old rooms, I have, on occasion, felt as if I were on an archaeological dig. In the bathroom cabinets there are vials of aspirin whose contents expired more than a decade ago. In the front hall closet, four different eras of life jackets jostle for space. On the utility room shelves, I find five rusty cans of Drano, six cans of lighter fluid (all with prices of less than a dollar a quart), two cans of weed killer whose toxic contents clearly predate Rachel Carson's *Silent Spring*, and five half-empty tubes of Sea & Ski from the innocent era, before people worried about skin cancer, when it was called not sunblock but suntan oil. Why have we saved these artifacts? (George Howe Colt. *The Big House*. New York: Scribner, 2003, 125.)

3. The stars awaken a certain reverence, because though always present, they are inaccessible; but all natural objects make a kindred impression, when the mind is open to their influence. Nature never wears a mean appearance. Neither does the wisest man extort her secret, and lose his curiosity by finding out all her perfection. Nature never became a toy to a wise spirit. The flowers, the animals, the mountains, reflected the wisdom of his best hour, as much as they had delighted the simplicity of his childhood. (Ralph Waldo Emerson. "Nature." *Ralph Waldo Emerson and Margaret Fuller. Selected Works.* Ed. John Carlos Rowe. Boston: Houghton Mifflin Company, 2003, p. 25.)

4. Dividedness is a personal pathology, but it soon becomes a problem for other people. It is a problem for students whose teachers "phone it in" while taking cover behind their podiums and their power. It is a problem for patients whose doctors practice medical indifference, hiding behind a self-protective scientific facade. It is a problem for employees whose supervisors have personnel handbooks where their hearts should be. It is a problem for citizens whose political leaders speak "with forked tongue." (Parker J. Palmer. *A Hidden Wholeness.* San Francisco: Jossey-Bass, 2004, 7.)

5. Yes, Virginia, there is a Santa Claus. He exists as certainly as love and generosity and devotion exist, and you know that they abound and give your life its highest beauty and joy. Alas! how dreary would be the world if there were no Santa Claus. It would be as dreary as if there were no Virginias. There would be no child-like faith then, no poetry, no romance to make tolerable this existence. We should have no enjoyment, except in sense and sight. The eternal life with which childhood fills the world would be extinguished. (Francis Pharcellus Church. *New York Sun,* 1897.)

SUMMARY

Writing and Image

- The image you project through your writing is the result of a number of conscious choices you make about your style, your voice, and your use of language.

- You should write clearly, but you should also use various strategies to enrich your prose, including metaphors, similes, and other figures of speech, as well as long words and sentences when appropriate. In general, dare to try something different.

- Metaphor and analogy are valuable for illuminating and generating an argument, but they can never prove a point.

- You must be sensitive to the connotations of words, but you must defend your position with adequate support, not merely with connotation or open slanting.

- You should be sensitive to, and use, euphony and rhythm in your prose.

SUGGESTIONS FOR WRITING (11.5)

1. Write a one-page description of a friend for another friend. Then rewrite the description as a speech describing your friend at a ceremony where he or she will be receiving an award. Have a classmate read both versions and identify the stylistic details of each version.

2. Choose a famous brief essay or speech such as Kennedy's Inaugural Address, Lincoln's Gettysburg Address, or Martin Luther King, Jr.'s, "I Have a Dream." Each of these speeches and many others can be found online reproduced by reliable sources. Using this essay or speech as a model, try to capture some of the spirit of the original while using your own words and ideas on some topic of your choice in a two- to three-page essay. Pay particular attention to frequently recurring patterns of sentences, and try to use some similar patterns in your own essay. (Give your instructor a copy of the speech you select as a model.)

ILLUSTRATIVE ARGUMENTS IN PART II: WRITING AND IMAGE

12

Introductions and Conclusions

Because your argument's introduction and conclusion are the first and last impression you will make on your readers, they require careful attention. Conclusions—whether a general closing or a specialized summary—are, of course, almost always composed late in the writing process, when you know exactly what it is your argument has concluded. Some writers compose introductions before they write the actual argument, but many delay until the last stage of the first draft, when they know more clearly what is to be introduced. This chapter discusses the importance of effective openings and closings and makes some suggestions for writing them.

INTRODUCTIONS

Because it is your readers' initial experience with your argument, your introduction must be particularly appealing to them. Regardless of what form your introduction takes, it is the hook that draws your readers into your argument.

The style and content of your introduction will be influenced by your argument's context (the occasion and audience for which it is written) and by its length, tone, and level of complexity. But no matter how you choose to open your argument, the basic purpose of any introduction is the same: to engage your readers. Usually an introduction succeeds in engaging readers if it is clear and inviting. Of these two features, clarity—the precise and accurate expression of carefully considered ideas—is probably the easiest to achieve, though for many writers it comes only with careful thought and considerable revision. To be inviting, your introduction must stimulate your readers' interest, as well as arouse their curiosity about the rest of the argument. Since being inviting is, for most of us, a learned skill, we offer some strategies for writing engaging introductions.

Strategies for General Introductions

Introduction by Narrative.   Writers of "general interest" arguments (nontechnical arguments intended for a broad audience) often gain their readers' attention by opening their essay with a specific anecdote or short narrative. This kind of opening engages readers in two ways: first, in its narrative approach, it satisfies our delight in being told a story, and second, it gains our interest by its *particularity*—its details about people, places, and events that give readers a firm footing as they enter an unknown text. An essay entitled "Boring from Within," by English professor Wayne C. Booth, begins with the following paragraph:

> Last week I had for about the hundredth time an experience that always disturbs me. Riding on a train, I found myself talking with my seat-mate, who asked me what I did for a living. "I teach English." Do you have any trouble predicting his response? His face fell, and he groaned, "Oh, dear, I'll have to watch my language." In my experience there are only two other possible reactions. The first is even less inspiring: "I hated English in school; it was my worst subject." The second, so rare as to make an honest English teacher almost burst into tears of gratitude when it occurs, is an animated conversation about literature, or ideas, or the American language—the kind of conversation that shows a continuing respect for "English" as something more than being sure about *who* and *whom, lie* and *lay*.

Booth's essay, addressed to high school English teachers, goes on to identify the ways in which English is mis-taught and to suggest alternative teaching methods. As a renowned college professor addressing high school teachers about the problems of high school instruction, Booth must be careful not to alienate his audience by coming across as superior or critical. He does this in part by opening the essay (initially an oral address) with this personal anecdote, which immediately, but tacitly, says "I am one of you." As well as disarming his audience with the personal references, Booth captures their attention with the simultaneous specificity and universality of effective narrative.

Introduction by Generalization.   Good introductions can also begin with a strong, unambiguous generalization related to the readers' experiences, as in the following opening paragraph of an article by David Brown published in a medical society journal:

> Few honorable professions have as much inherent hostility toward one another as medicine and journalism. Ask a doctor to describe journalists and you are likely to hear adjectives such as "negative," "sensationalistic," and "superficial." Ask a journalist about doctors, and you will probably hear about "arrogance," "paternalism," and "jargon."

Broad statements such as this should be limited and developed in succeeding sentences or a succeeding paragraph. In the second paragraph of this essay, the writer both justifies and develops the generalization made in the first paragraph.

> The descriptions are the common stereotypes and not wholly inaccurate, for the two professions occupy distant worlds. Physicians are schooled in confidence and collegiality; journalists seek to make knowledge public. Physicians speak the language of science; journalists are largely ignorant of science. Physicians inhabit a world of contingencies and caveats; journalists inhabit a world where time and audience require simplification. Physicians are used to getting their way; journalists are used to getting their story.

This paragraph's development of the idea contained in the initial paragraph is echoed by the writer's syntax (the arrangement of his words): the last four sentences, neatly divided by semicolons into opposing clauses, emphasize the focus on this professional opposition.

Introduction by Quotation.   Some introductions begin with quotations that are eventually connected to the topic of the essay. While perhaps overused and overtaught, this technique *does* work if practiced thoughtfully. The writer using an opening quotation must be sure that it can be made to apply to the subject in an interesting way, and that the quotation is interesting, provocative, or well written (preferably all three). The following paragraph in an essay by Marilyn Yalom is a successful example of this technique:

> When Robert Browning wrote his famous lines "Grow old along with me!/The best is yet to be,/The last of life, for which the first was made," he was undoubtedly not thinking about women. The poet's Victorian optimism is difficult enough to reconcile with the realities of old age for men, and virtually impossible when we consider the condition of older women in the nineteenth century.

As in the article about the antagonism between the medical and journalistic professions, the initial statement here is immediately explained and developed in the succeeding sentence. Here, in fact, the explanatory sentence is also the claim of this essay on the older woman in Victorian England and America.

Other Types of Introductions.   There are a number of other strategies for making arguments inviting to your readers: startling statistics, a brief historical survey of the topic (which can have the same charm as the narrative introduction), a particularly startling or shocking statement (provided, of course, that it is relevant to the content of your argument), and even a direct announcement of the argument's subject (as in "This is an article about bad writing"). Any of these tactics will work as long as it connects in some way with the body of the argument.

Introductions in Professional Writing

Introductions written in a professional context according to established formats don't need to be as inviting as the previous examples, largely because readers of professional reports usually don't have much choice about whether or not to read a given report. Rather than trying to engage their readers, on-the-job writers are concerned about serving the needs of a known audience who will make some use of the report. In these cases, introductions are successful if they accurately represent the report's content. Company policy often dictates the form of a preliminary summary: some companies require an initial outline, others an abstract, still others a summary reflecting both organization and content. When the form is not dictated, the most useful is a simple summary of organization and content.

Take as an example an analysis of problems in customer relations assigned to a customer service representative of a local grocery chain. In her report, the representative first identifies, describes, and documents the different conditions she has found to be damaging to good customer relations: inadequate customer check-cashing privileges, a time-consuming refund policy, impolite carryout personnel, and inaccurate advertising of sale prices. She then estimates the loss of business resulting from each problem. Finally, she recommends possible solutions to the problems she has identified. Her report is clearly written and organized, but it is also lengthy and somewhat complex; it needs an introduction that will prepare its readers not only for the content of the report but also for the arrangement of its material. The preliminary summary will prepare readers for the sequence of the argument's main points, and it will serve as a useful reference should the readers become confused while reading the full report.

Our customer service representative introduces her report with the following preliminary summary:

> This report examines the recent quarterly decline in business at the seven Goodbelly stores. It attributes this loss of revenue to at least four remediable problems in the area of customer relations: (1) inadequate check-cashing privileges, (2) a time-consuming refund policy, (3) lack of concern for customers by carryout personnel, and (4) inaccurate advertising of sale prices. It is estimated that these difficulties may have cost Goodbelly's as much as $300,000 in revenue in the past three months. This report concludes by recommending specific personnel and policy measures to be taken to ease these difficulties and to regain the lost business.

Without being painstakingly mechanical, this brief paragraph identifies the central claim of the report (that the decline in revenue is due to poor customer relations) and prepares the reader for the organization and content of the argument. While an introduction such as this one may not engage a reader who has neither an interest in nor an obligation to the company, its concise and accurate representation of the report's content will be extremely useful to the obligated reader.

General Suggestions About Introductions

Finally, you may find these general suggestions about writing introductions useful:

1. Try writing your introduction *after* you've written your first draft. Often, there's no point in agonizing over a preliminary summary for a professional report or a catchy introduction for a general interest argument before you know

exactly how the argument is going to evolve. Even if you're working from a detailed outline, your organization and content will change as you compose.

2. On those rare occasions when a catchy opening sentence or paragraph comes to you early, giving you a hold on the overall structure, tone, and style of your argument, don't let this opening get away!

3. Don't make your introduction too long. Even the most interesting, captivating introduction is going to seem silly if it's twice as long as the argument itself. The turbot, a variety of anglerfish, has a head that takes up half of its total body length and is one of the silliest looking fish on the planet. Don't follow its example.

4. Make sure your introduction is truly representative of the entire argument. If you are writing a preliminary summary, be sure all the main points of the argument are covered in the introduction. In a less formal argument, don't let your desire to be engaging lure you into writing an introduction that is stylistically or tonally inconsistent with the rest of the argument. In short, the opening paragraph should never look as if it has been tacked on merely to attract reader interest, with no thought about its relationship to what follows. Rather, it should resemble an operatic overture, beautiful in its own right, but always preparing its audience for what is to follow.

ACTIVITIES (12.1)

1. For one of the following writing tasks, write two different introductory paragraphs using two of the tactics discussed in the preceding section: narrative, generalization, quotation, startling statistics, a brief historical survey, a startling statement, or an outright announcement of claim. Then write a two- to three-sentence description of the different effects of the two introductions.
   a. An essay on a relative whom you admire
   b. An essay on a law or policy of the federal government that you strongly support or oppose
   c. An essay on your favorite food
   d. An editorial in your local newspaper opposing teenage curfew
   e. A report to your supervisor (or a parent or a friend) explaining why you have failed to accomplish all the goals you set for yourself six months ago
2. For one of the arguments you have already written for this class, write (or rewrite) an introductory paragraph following the suggestions offered in the preceding discussion.
3. Working on a different argument written for this course, compose an opening paragraph that begins at a general level and ends with the argument's claim.

CONCLUSIONS

Once you have selected and presented the best possible support for your argument, you may feel that you have nothing more to say on the subject. But you're not finished yet. Until you have provided a final closing, a conclusion that rounds out your argument, your argument is incomplete. Most readers need to feel closure in all kinds of writing: letters, imaginative literature, and arguments.

Conclusions are not always easy to write, particularly because by the time we get around to thinking about writing an ending, we're often tired of the whole project. But you don't need to be a master rhetorician to write an effective ending. A conclusion that is direct, precise, and appropriate to the occasion will do the job just fine. Depending on the context, it can be as short as a paragraph or as long as a chapter.

Types of Conclusions

Arguments can have three basic types of conclusions: the findings or results of an investigation, a recommendation or set of recommendations, or a more general closing reflecting on the argument or raising other considerations related to the central claim.

Findings.   The findings or results conclusion usually ends an argument of fact, such as the reporting of a scientific experiment or a case study. Some causal arguments, such as certain historical studies, may also end with findings or results. Actually, these findings are the argument's claim, which may be given in general form early in the argument and then with more detail at the end, or they may be given only at the end. The following paragraph (the second-to-last paragraph of an essay titled "Particle Accelerators Test Cosmological Theory") exemplifies the findings type of conclusion:

> Preliminary results from the machines indicate that there are at most five families of elementary particles. David B. Cline of the University of California at Los Angeles and the University of Wisconsin at Madison . . . has shown that the lifetime of the $Z°$ boson [a subatomic particle] is approximately what one would expect with just three families. Experimental uncertainties, however, allow for two additional kinds of neutrinos [another subatomic particle] and hence two additional families. . . . For the first time accelerators are counting neutrino types and getting a small number, one that was predicted by cosmological theory.

Recommendation.   Not surprisingly, recommendations typically conclude arguments of recommendation. Their purpose is to tell readers exactly what the argument expects of them. If the findings conclusion tells readers what they should *know,* the recommendation conclusion tells them what they should *do.* An example of this type of conclusion is found at the end of the St. Mary's Medical Center Memorandum in Chapter 9 of this book. The proposal ends with an implementation recommendation that states explicitly what the writer wants the reader to do. Since the recommended action is relatively straightforward, she has appropriately chosen to summarize the most salient support of her argument. In many other cases, the most appropriate conclusion is a general recommendation, as in this last paragraph from an essay titled "U.S. Economic Growth":

> Only if we increase investment in both capital and technology in all sectors of the U.S. economy (particularly manufacturing) and improve the quality of labor at all levels can the American standard of living rise at an acceptable rate. In the present highly competitive world market, the U.S. has some historically demonstrated advantages, but it must take the longer view and pursue those seemingly trivial increases of a few tenths of a percentage point in growth rate each year.

General Closing.   The general closing is what we usually think of when we think of conclusions. This type of conclusion can work in several ways: it can move from the specific argument to a statement of the argument's broader significance, it can suggest future directions for research, or it can raise related issues. The general closing suggests a movement *onward* (where we go from here) or a movement *outward* (how this specific argument relates to other arguments), though the emphasis in any case will vary between these two elements.

The following paragraph (the closing of Mike Messner's "Sports and the Politics of Inequality") exemplifies a conclusion that moves to a consideration of an argument's broader significance:

> If this discussion of sports and inequality seems to make contradictory points, it is because sports plays a contradictory role in the larger politics of inequality. On an ideological level, sports strengthens and legitimates class and ethnic inequalities in society while simultaneously providing cultural space where ideologies supporting inequalities can be challenged and debunked. And for participants, sports offers a place where class and ethnic antagonisms and prejudices can be destructively played out *and* it can offer a space where participants can experience transcendent moments of play which are relatively free from the larger social inequities. In this space, it is possible to discover ourselves and each other as human beings. What all this means is that the role sports will play in the politics of inequality will be determined by "how we play the game," both individually and collectively.

The final paragraph of "Particle Accelerators Test Cosmological Theory" (cited previously) demonstrates the concluding strategy of pointing to new directions and future possibilities:

> The next step promises to be even more exciting. As new accelerators are completed and begin producing more data with fewer uncertainties, the cosmological limit of three or at most four families will be checked with extreme accuracy. . . . The machines will probe the early universe with an effectiveness that no telescope will ever match.

A conclusion that raises related issues is found in the last two paragraphs of George Orwell's famous essay "Politics and the English Language." Throughout most of the essay, Orwell gives examples of bad English. But toward the end of the essay, he suggests connections between corrupt language and corrupt political systems. The final paragraph addresses this connection directly:

> One ought to recognize that the present political chaos is connected with the decay of language, and that one can probably bring about some improvement by starting at the verbal end. If you simplify your English, you are freed from the worst follies of orthodoxy. You cannot speak any of the necessary dialects, and when you make a stupid remark its stupidity will be obvious, even to yourself. Political language—and with variations this is true of all political parties, from Conservatives to Anarchists—is designed to make lies sound truthful and murder respectable, and to give an appearance of solidity to pure wind. One cannot change this all in a moment, but one can at least change one's own habits, and from time to time one can even, if one jeers loudly enough, send some *melting pot, acid test, veritable inferno,* or other lump of verbal refuse—into the dustbin where it belongs.

A conclusion can contain more than one of the three basic types described previously. The second-to-last paragraph of "Particle Accelerators Test Cosmological Theory" presents the results of the research, whereas the very last paragraph presents a statement on the future directions of this research. A results or recommendation conclusion may be supplemented with a more general conclusion that opens the argument outward.

A word of caution about all conclusions: the conclusion must not lie outside the boundaries of what you can legitimately claim in your argument. You should not, for example, turn an argument about the weakness of a certain school's curriculum into a conclusion uniformly condemning all schools, though your conclusion may suggest that the case you have examined is not an isolated one. In other words, don't overgeneralize from the evidence you used to support your argument. Nor should you use your conclusion as the place to launch a whole new argument or to make claims that do not have some basis in what has preceded.

SUMMARIES

A conclusion is different from a *summary,* which is a restatement of the main points of your argument. Most short or medium-length arguments (five hundred to five thousand words) do not require a summary; final summaries are typically found in very long essays, in essays with difficult subject matter, or in books. This book, for example, uses sentence summaries at the end of each chapter to stress certain key points to an audience new to much of this material.

Writers of arguments sometimes provide a summary of the basic points *preceding* the argument. Such summaries are usually either separate from or at the very beginning of the argument. Typically they take one of two forms: the *abstract,* often used in academic or technical research, and the *executive summary,* often used in business reports and proposals.

An abstract is a summary, typically in paragraph form, that states the essential points of the essay so that readers can grasp these points without having to read the essay; in other words, the good abstract can stand alone, being meaningful by itself. If the readers read only the abstract, they will of course miss much of the argument, especially its support, but they will at least know what the argument's main claims are. With the flood of information confronting us all, abstracts have the obvious value of helping us decide what research needs further investigation and what can be left alone.

The following summary by King-Kok Cheung of her essay on Alice Walker's *The Color Purple* and Maxine Hong Kingston's *Woman Warrior* is a good example of an abstract for academic writing:

> *The Color Purple* and *The Woman Warrior* exhibit parallel narrative strategies. The respectively black and Chinese American protagonists work their way from speechlessness to eloquence by breaking through the constraints of sex, race, and language. The heroines turn to masculine figures for guidance, to female models for inspiration, and to native idioms for stylistic innovation. Initially unable to speak, they develop distinctive voices by registering their own unspoken grief on paper and, more important, by recording and emulating the voices of women from their respective ethnic communities. Through these testimonies, each written in a bicultural language, Walker and Kingston reveal the obstacles and resources peculiar to minority women. Subverting patriarchal literary traditions by reclaiming a mother tongue that carries a rich oral tradition (of which women are guardians) the authors artfully coordinate the tasks of breaking silence, acknowledging female influence, and redefining while preserving ethnic characteristics.

Here is an example of an abstract introducing a technical argument, "Cutting into Cholesterol," written by Bruce P. Kinosian and John M. Eisenberg:

> We performed an analysis of the cost-effectiveness of treating individuals with significantly elevated levels of total serum cholesterol (>6.85 mmol/L [>265 mg/dL]), comparing treatment with three alternative agents: cholestyramine resin, colestipol, and oat bran (a soluble fiber). We simulated a program for lowering cholesterol levels that was similar to that of the Coronary Primary Prevention Trial, and then used the outcomes of the trial to calculate the incremental cost per year of life saved (YOLS) from the perspective of society. Our findings suggest that the cost per YOLS ranges from $117,400 (cholestyramine resin packets) to $70,900 (colestipol packets) and $17,800 (oat bran). Using bulk drug reduces the cost per YOLS to $65,100 (cholestyramine resin) and $63,900 (colestipol). Targeting bulk colestipol treatment only to smokers has a cost per YOLS of $47,010; the incremental cost of treating nonsmokers would be $89,600 per additional YOLS. Although pharmacologic therapy has substantial costs, it may be more cost-effective when low-cost forms are applied to particular high-risk groups, such as smokers. However, a broad public health approach to lowered cholesterol levels by additional dietary modification, such as with soluble fiber, may be preferred to a medically oriented campaign that focuses on drug therapy.

Executive summaries are often longer than abstracts, though they should not usually be longer than a page. Like abstracts, they give the main points of an argument, but they may also contain some background on why the report was written and on the scope of the original study. If the executive summary is of a recommendation report, the major recommendation should be included in it. Like abstracts, executive summaries should be written to stand alone; readers should be able to get the major points of the report without referring to the report itself.

The following is a sample executive summary with a format that might be used by a group auditing the overall effectiveness of a university computer center:

> The audit completed a review of the Johnston Computer Center in February 2006. The Johnston Computer Center is one of three academic computing centers at the university and contains terminals and micro-computers for up to 200 on-site users, with access also available for up to 50 off-site users, so that it is second largest of such centers at the university.
>
> The objectives of our review were to determine whether present and planned center operations are fulfilling user needs and are in compliance with university policies and procedures for computer security.
>
> In our opinion, the center's operation is satisfactory in meeting the needs of its users and in using its internal resources to meet these needs, but unsatisfactory in meeting security policies and procedures.
>
> Our survey of Johnston Computer Center users indicated that user satisfaction is high and that center personnel are responsive to user needs. While system response time has deteriorated in the last six months because of an unexpected increase in user demand, center man-agement has addressed this problem by encouraging users to use the system during nonpeak hours and by recommending a hardware upgrade to the Vice President for Systems and Computing.
>
> Our review of security showed that unauthorized users could gain access to and change another user's files. Since the center's computers are not directly connected to the university's administrative computers, which do contain other security safeguards, the university does not face a risk to its financial and personnel records because of these deficiencies. The student and faculty academic files contained in the center's computers are at risk, however. The center has reported three instances of tamper-ing in the last six months. Center management is eager to address this problem but will need additional resources to purchase software and to obtain the necessary technical assistance.

Executive summaries have become increasingly common as business execu-tives and other managers find themselves confronted with an overwhelming number of reports to read. The executive summary allows readers to decide if they want to read further, or if the summary alone provides enough information. Unlike abstracts, which are often intended for a specialist audience, executive summaries usually have a nonspecialist audience of higher managers who may be very far removed from the technical details of the report. The executive summary should allow for the audience's lack of familiarity with these details by avoiding specialized vocabulary whenever possible and by defining any specialized terms that are used. In other words, executive summaries demand great attention to the readers' needs and great precision in wording. Typically they are written after the report is finished, when the writer knows all its twists and turns.

ACTIVITIES (12.2)

1. Return to an argument you have written for this course, and write two differ-ent conclusions for it: first, a general closing, and second, a conclusion re-stating the argument's findings or results. Give your argument and these two conclusions to a classmate to read; discuss with him or her which of the two conclusions seems more appropriate to its context.

2. Find a different argument from the one you used in Activity 1, and write a 250-word abstract (one double-spaced page) of the argument.

SUMMARY

Introductions and Conclusions

- The context of your argument will influence the style, content, and length of your introduction, but all introductions should be clear, engaging, and appropriate to the occasion.

- Some useful tactics for general introductions are:
  - Introduction by narrative
  - Introduction by generalization
  - Introduction by quotation

- Introductions of arguments in formal, professional writing should be precisely representative of the content of the report.

- Conclusions are usually one of three basic types: findings or results, a recommendation or set of recommendations, or a general closing. Which type of conclusion you use depends on the type of argument. Findings or results typically conclude reports of scientific experiments or case studies. Recommendations conclude recommendation reports. General closings are used for other types of arguments, especially interpretations and evaluations. The general closing has three sub-types: a statement of significance, suggested directions for research, and a raising of related issues.

- Do not confuse a conclusion with a summary. A summary is a restatement of the main points of your argument. There are three types of summaries: the ending summary, the abstract, and the executive summary. Ending summaries are typically found in books and in very complex or very long essays or reports. Abstracts and executive summaries are typically found at the beginning of or separate from the arguments on which they are based. Readers should be able to understand an abstract or an executive summary without referring to the report or essay on which it is based.

SUGGESTIONS FOR WRITING (12.3)

1. Locate a section of a newspaper or magazine that presents several editorial or opinion essays. The Sunday *New York Times* op-ed page is an excellent source; your local Sunday paper may have its own version. Or, if you choose a reputable newspaper or magazine resource online, note that you need to select their op-ed section for your articles. (This is one exercise that might be easier to conduct using hardcopy because all of the op-ed pieces can usually be found on one or two pages of your newspaper of choice.) Examine the types of conclusions used for three pieces, and write an essay of two to three pages describing the type of each conclusion, its effect on readers, and its overall effectiveness. Which of the three do you find the most effective? Why? Be sure to give your instructor a copy of the op-ed articles you use for this assignment.

2. Write a one-paragraph executive summary using one of your last papers, making sure that your readers will be able to understand the summary without reading the paper. When you hand in this assignment, give your instructor both the summary and the paper on which it is based.

ILLUSTRATIVE ARGUMENTS IN PART II: INTRODUCTIONS AND CONCLUSIONS

13

Revising

Finally, you've finished your argument. It has an introduction and a conclusion, a claim and appropriate support, and you're ready to hand it over to your instructor with a sigh of relief.

But not so fast. You've certainly earned a break—writing is hard work—but if you want your paper to be as good as it can be, you've got to find the time and the energy for another crucial step in the writing process: revising.

Revising your argument means stepping back from it and seeing it whole. As the word's Latin roots (*re*—"again," and *visere*—"to look at") indicate, to revise is to see again, to have a new vision of the entire work. Sometimes this new vision leads to dramatic changes in any part of the argument, though the more attention you pay to the content and organization of your argument as you're writing the first draft, the fewer the major changes you will need to make (yes, that paper you've just finished is only a first draft, not a finished argument). But even the most carefully composed first draft will require some changes. So, if you're not in the habit, it's time to make a practice of allowing plenty of time and attention for revision. It will pay off. Some people revise *as* they write, adjusting earlier parts of the argument to fit better with what they've just written or are about to write. This is a perfectly good practice that can save you time later on, but it shouldn't take the place of the revising process outlined in this chapter.

WRITING A FIRST DRAFT, REVISING, AND EDITING

Don't confuse revising with editing. Editing is a careful check of the spelling, grammar, punctuation, and overall consistency of a manuscript. Revising, as noted, is a more profound look at the argument's entire content, shape, and style.

Revising involves considerable judgment on your part, because questions about claim, support, and style rarely have simple right or wrong answers. On the other hand, most questions about editing do have right or wrong answers; there are only so many ways to spell a word or to punctuate a sentence correctly.

Writing your first draft, revising, and editing require different attitudes and use somewhat different skills. Writing the first draft requires energy and egoism to keep you going through the bumpy parts; revising calls for detachment and reflection; and editing demands close attention to detail. Attempting a "perfect" first draft is actually one of the most dangerous and laborious ways to write. It is dangerous because you will lack the necessary distance to judge the quality of your argument, and laborious because you are trying to combine these three separate tasks. To some extent, of course, revising and editing occur during the writing of any draft; we all make minor changes in wording, organization, and mechanics even in the early stage of writing, and sometimes we decide on major changes as we write. Inserting these changes then makes sense, but you still need to set aside time for revising and editing, making each your major preoccupation in a separate review of the manuscript.

Many college students feel that they don't have time for anything but a first draft; in fact, they usually do. Students of roughly equal ability and with roughly the same amount of time available work in amazingly different ways, some finishing their work with plenty of time to spare, others doing everything at the last minute. Most students who claim that they were forced to write their papers just before the due date mean that writing the paper was not their highest priority and they could get motivated to write it only by the pressure of a deadline. Especially with word processing, writers who write a first draft, leave it for a while, and then revise it, do not spend any more time writing than those who try to write just one polished draft.

SOME SUGGESTIONS FOR SUCCESSFUL REVISING

Offered here are some suggestions aimed at making your revising stage as effective as possible. These suggestions are based on years of writing experience, but they are only suggestions, not ironclad rules.

Suggestion 1: Give Yourself Some Breathing Space

After you've finished your first draft, give yourself some time—at least 24 hours—before you begin the revising process. This "breathing space" gives you some distance from your work, which you will need in order to review it objectively. And it gives your unconscious an opportunity to mull over the material, so that when you return to the argument, you'll find you have fresh ideas about how to make it more effective. You've probably had the experience of rereading a graded paper and wondering how you could have missed the problems that seem so obvious to you now (and that were far too obvious to your instructor). Putting some distance between the first draft and the revision gives you an opportunity to gain this fresh perspective, and to put it to use *before* your paper is graded.

Suggestion 2: Avoid the Red Pen

As you're reviewing your first draft, avoid the lure of the red pen or typing in any changes if you are reading from the screen—the temptation to make small editorial changes before you have reread and assimilated the argument as a whole. Reread with your hands tied behind your back (figuratively, that is), and you'll get a much better sense of how the draft works as a whole.

Suggestion 3: Review Your Original Purpose and Audience

In writing your first draft, you've been intent on coming up with the right word and composing individual sentences. It's easy at this level to lose touch with your original purpose and intended audience. So an important question to ask yourself as you're rereading and revising is whether you've fulfilled your original purpose for your intended audience (of course, your original purpose and audience may have changed during the first draft, but that should be your conscious choice, not an accident).

It can be helpful to review your argument pretending that you're one of its intended readers. From this perspective, you can ask yourself: do I understand the purpose and claim of this argument? are the vocabulary and specialized terms clear to me? is the argument meaningful to me? am I convinced by the argument?

Suggestion 4: Review Your Organization

In reviewing the effectiveness of your argument, you'll need to consider not only your purpose and audience, but also the overall organization of what you've written, making sure that the parts fit together well and are logically sequenced, that nothing crucial is omitted, and that the structure is lean, with a minimum of repetition. If it's hard to keep the organization in mind, try reproducing it in outline form, as in the following model. Remember, you're outlining what you actually wrote, not what you intended to write. If you actually wrote your draft from an outline, don't look at it until you have completed this new one.

    I. Introduction (if appropriate)
   II. Claim (if appropriate)
 III. Supporting arguments:
      A.
      B.
      C.
      D.
 IV. Conclusion or summary (if appropriate)

If you have trouble constructing this new outline, your argument probably has organizational problems that need attention.

This is also a good time to review the effectiveness of your claim and your introduction. Ask yourself these questions: if I have an explicit claim, is it clearly stated? if it is implied, will my readers recognize it? does my introduction prepare my readers for what follows? should it be more interesting?

Suggestion 5: Review Your Argument's Coherence

Even the most carefully organized argument will puzzle readers if the relationship between its parts is not indicated in some way. In certain professions and businesses, standard formats include headings like "Introduction," "The Problem," "History," and so on. But such headings are inappropriate in many settings. You can make the elements of your argument *coherent*—establish their relationship to one another and to the whole—by using simple transitional words and expressions that indicate the nature of the relationship.

Words like *therefore, thus, so,* and *consequently* identify a conclusion and its evidence. Words like *but, however,* and *on the other hand* indicate exceptions to a stated point. You can alert your reader to the introduction of each new piece of support by using indicators such as *first . . . , second . . . , and furthermore, and finally.* Transitional words and expressions such as these are enormously useful to readers of arguments, particularly when the argument is long or elaborate. They help readers understand how one statement or section that may otherwise seem a digression or an irrelevancy relates to what has gone before or what might come later.

As well as using such brief signposts, you can also be quite direct about the role of different parts of your argument. Public speakers are often very explicit about the function of crucial parts of their speeches: "Let me give you two reasons why this land should be developed," or "To conclude, I'd like to remind you of a few lines by Walt Whitman." Such obvious signs are crucial when there is no written text for an audience to follow and ponder. But indicators such as these can be used in written argument as well, especially when the parts are many and complex.

Suggestion 6: Review Your Style

The revising stage is the time to consider the effectiveness of your argument's style: its tone, word choice, and general treatment of the reader. As discussed in Chapter 11, style is a crucial component of argument, often playing a major role in convincing or alienating readers. Poor style is just as damaging to an argument as a vague or unsupported claim; an effective style is just as convincing as compelling evidence. And while you're considering your style, think about the ethos projected by your argument: does the argument reflect a writer who is fair, open-minded, and appropriately confident?

This is also a good time to ask yourself if you have followed Orwell's rules for clarity, along with the friendly amendments offered in Chapter 11. Finally, check your draft to see if you have (1) used connotation effectively, (2) avoided slanting, (3) used metaphor and analogy effectively, and (4) paid attention to the sounds of words. Some of these questions will naturally occur during your consideration of claim (if you have one) and the organization of its support, as well as during your review of audience and purpose.

Suggestion 7: Review Your Argument for Faulty Reasoning

Chapter 6 introduced some basic principles of logic that will help you set up a reasonable argument. The "informal fallacies" presented there are most easily detected during the revision stage. As a final step in reviewing your argument, read it through to detect any unwitting fallacies, paying special attention to those that are particularly common in the kind of argument you've written.

Suggestion 8: Use a Word Processor

Fortunately (some students would say unfortunately), revising may lead to a drastic overhaul of your argument. But if you want your argument to be as good as it can be, you won't ignore the opportunity to make these major changes. Most students now write their papers on computers, which make large- and small-scale revising much easier than any other method. With a computer and a good word-processing program, you can switch entire sections of a draft around with ease; change words swiftly and even "globally," so that one word replaces another throughout an entire essay; and make corrections with no trace of erasures or correction fluid. Virtually all campuses have computer labs for their students, which save the expense of purchasing your own computer. And while a computer will not make you a better writer, it will give you the chance to make yourself a better writer. So get wired!

ACTIVITIES (13.1)

1. Write an outline of a paper or a draft of a paper that you have written for this class, using the format given in Suggestion 4. Then exchange this paper or draft with one of your classmates, while keeping your outline. Now prepare an outline of your classmate's paper, again using the same format, and then exchange outlines with your classmate. Compare your classmate's outline with your own. Do the two outlines agree on what the claim is and what the supporting arguments are? If there are disagreements, discuss these with your classmate. Find out why he or she saw your argument working in a different way than you did. Remember that if there is disagreement, you cannot simply assume that your classmate is wrong and you are correct: the purpose of your argument is to convince the reader, not yourself. After this discussion, make a list of the changes or possible changes you would make in your paper in the next draft.

2. Have a classmate read a clean copy of one of the papers you have written for this course. Ask him or her to write a one-page description of the overall image reflected in that paper and a one-page evaluation of that image. Do the same for a paper written by your classmate.

SUMMARY

Revising

- You should plan to spend separate portions of time writing a draft, revising, and editing.

- Allow breathing space between writing a draft and revising it. In your first review of the draft, concentrate on how the draft works as a whole.

- In revising, review your original purpose and audience, your organization, the adequacy and logic of your support, and your style.

- Knowing the principles of logic is a significant help in reviewing your draft.

- Using a word processor makes revising much easier.

AN EXAMPLE OF REVISION

Having read your manuscript all the way through at least once, and preferably twice, you are now ready to make major changes if they are needed. By avoiding the red pen until you have reviewed the entire manuscript, you are more likely to recognize the need for such major changes, and less likely to get lost in grieving over minor errors.

The following sample student essay is a good example of how to correct major problems in an argument. What follows is the first draft of the essay, along with the student's notes for revision, which he wrote in the margins during a second and third reading of the draft.

EMPHASIZE TEACHING, NOT TECHNOLOGY

(first draft)

Vague—what does this mean? →

Surely it is a step in the right direction to utilize technology in the classroom. It helps educate the students about the "real world" by

claim is too narrow for content of argument →

making it possible for them to do assignments on computers. However, this "progress" is actually becoming a problem. Teachers are focusing so much attention on making projects fun and technologically sound that they are losing focus on their curriculum.

Really 2 intro. ¶'s. Use one or the other. →

Such was the case at my high school, and over the course of my four years at East Greenwich High School in East Greenwich, Rhode Island, I noticed this problem becoming more of an issue with the coming of every September. This is a predicament on a number of levels: for students, teachers, and for the future of our nation. The dilemma is not the usage of technology, but rather the ignorance that many teachers have when they decide to assign these projects; they are lessening the standards of education in order to include technology. The emphasis on utilizing technology in projects throughout high school has, in fact, diminished the focus on the educational aspect of the classes.

Rep. and still not broad enough

At the high school level, projects using technology are assigned too frequently when a more traditional assignment would be more beneficial. Milton Chen, executive director of the George Lucas Education Foundation, recently said "[t]he more we, who see the promise of technology, talk about it just as technology, the more it leads us away from issues of teaching and learning" (Vojtek 1). As we try to incorporate technology just for the sake of incorporating technology, the quality of education will continue to fall. Concurrently, students are becoming less interested in doing these "creative assignments" because of the time commitment and sheer volume of technology projects being assigned. Although common sense tells us otherwise, it is surprising that students actually would prefer to write a paper than complete a technology project 71% of the time (Denice). Education experts and students alike recognize that solely incorporating technology instead of improving education is devastating for our schools. Teachers must realize the same soon.

Start with specific, move to general

Really a separate idea; use later as another negative example.

Some people claim that projects are beneficial because they are more creative than regular assignments and incorporate technology into the classroom to prepare students for the world outside. While these points appear to be true, projects still make each class easier for students to pass. Technological projects are often too casual, requiring less thinking about the subject matter, despite the fact that teachers are more ready to give an "A" to a project than to a paper. Too often our teachers are amazed by the creativity and the technological aspects of projects (Tomei 37). They should be looking for the educational value as

Counter-argument—put at end of reason #1

related to the curriculum, but instead are dazzled by the animation and polish that accompany technological projects. And due to the fact that it would require a great amount of self-discipline *for a student to ask for a* more challenging assignment, this problem will likely go unaddressed from within the classroom. As teachers continue to assign technological projects to simply use technology, they are making their classes easier. This has long-term repercussions; our nation will face serious problems when our schools move backwards as other nations' schools are becoming more rigorous.

Wordy—use "because"

Delete—I can't really prove this & never followed up

I can say that projects make school easier because I have gone through public school for thirteen years and have seen the difference in difficulty between technological projects and other assignments. When teachers assign a PowerPoint slideshow, I have found that it is actually more difficult to get lower than a "C" on it than getting an "A" on a paper. My senior-year British Literature class was assigned a final project (rather than an exam) that had to "use technology in a practical and useful manner." Our group chose to create a website about British Literature and to summarize what we had learned throughout the year. Another group chose to make a DVD reenacting scenes from various works we had read.

Support for reason #1

Contrastingly, in my history class junior year, we had to write a three- to five-page paper every week about a topic we covered in our notes. I can honestly say that I can recall more from that "boring, old fashioned" history class than any other class from high school. Writing a paper every week was not necessarily fun, but it forced us to learn the material thoroughly. Having to create a webpage earned me an "A" on the project, but I can barely recollect anything from the class (despite creating ten webpages summarizing everything I supposedly learned just four months ago). It is clear from a student's perspective that projects, specifically those that focus on technology, allow mediocrity to be graded as creativity, where more traditional teaching methods prove more productive.

awk

Specific support for # 1

Despite teachers' expectations that their projects be completed using the newest technology, often schools are unable to provide the materials needed. While 67% of projects were required to use technology, only 13% of students said the materials and help they needed to complete the project were provided by their school (Denice). At my high school, the only digital video camera was owned by the Student Council, but since it could not be

Support for # 3

taken over the weekend, there was often difficulty gaining access. Despite this, I alone had to create at least one video project in ten different classes over the four years of high school. After the first few projects, my family ended up buying a $200 camera to ease the burden of having to schedule around borrowing the school's one camera with everyone else in the class. Often, technology usage comes down to the haves and have-nots, leaving underprivileged students behind because they do not have the access to technology (Wright 33).

However, it is also a problem if the teachers assigning the projects are unable to provide assistance. In fact, a recent report, "Technology Quality: A Report on the Preparation and Qualifications of Public School Teachers," said

Out of place; this is a new result (#2)

only 20% of teachers felt very well prepared to employ educational technology in the classroom (Vojtek 2). There is no value in giving work to students that teachers themselves do not confidently know how to use. If the school cannot provide the materials and help for technological projects to students, teachers simply cannot expect the students to use it.

The debate of technological haves and have-nots, known as the "Digital Divide," is a major problem that our educational system faces today (Attewell 251). It has caused great controversy because the

(#3)

"haves" tend to be affluent, suburban, white schools while the "have-nots" are the underprivileged, urban, minority-populated schools (Attewell 252). Many have labeled the divide "cyber-segregation" (Attewell 252). All of these names, the sayings, and new terms signal just how awkward technology is making the educational world feel. Already faced with plentiful troubles, these "have-not" schools now have been criticized for not being able to provide technological access (Wright 34). Putting these schools under the microscope for yet another reason can add no positive impact to the already awkward situation.

Now, critics are using racism as the excuse why these schools do not have computer access. They are saying that politicians and administrators do not put proper emphasis on improving these schools because of the high minority population in the student body. Clearly, this is a very controversial attack. It is damaging because there is a huge need for upgrading the schools' technology and education, while neither are seeing any significant improvements. If this one issue, the issue of adding technology into classrooms, proves so controversial, then it should make us ask just how necessary this over-emphasis on technology really is.

Specifically regarding young children, computer usage is rarely linked to success, despite ongoing misconceptions that claim otherwise. In fact, computer usage in children is proved to cause problems ranging from vision problems to bad posture. But the real loss here is that computers are seen to "displace authentic childhood learning experiences" (Attewell 254). This childhood problem transitions to a crisis for high school students because it is related to the "cognitive and emotional development" of young adults (Attewell 254). Specifically, many experts believe that it may cause disorders like ADD (Attention Deficit Disorder) and ADHD (Attention Deficit Hyperactivity Disorder) in children. Just going room-to-room for the poll I conducted, I learned that 100% of the 45 people I polled in my dormitory found it more difficult to concentrate while using a computer than just sitting at a desk (Denice). As it appears, technology may not only have fewer advantages than planned, but may actually cause more problems than we ever expected for our children.

Many projects that are assigned place a burden on the students to get access to the numerous devices for their work. And despite the good intention of trying to implement technology into the classroom, assignments designed to use certain materials make busywork out of important lessons. Creating a website should never be substituted for

Another negative result: # 4

taking a final exam; on no level do the two require
the same thought process. And contrary to what many
students are expected to say, I was not in that
British Literature class to learn how to create a

Personal support
for # 1

website or make a DVD. I was there with the rest of
the class to study British Literature. While I got
an "A" on my final project, I know I would have been
lucky with a "C" if I had taken a written exam. I
did not learn the material I was responsible for in
the curriculum, nor did I need to, apparently. It is
alarming that teachers are making such a grand
effort to incorporate technology into their classes
that they are forgetting that students are in the
class to learn about the course material, not to
practice using the newest gadgets. With 82% of
students saying that doing projects with technology
was more work and 67% saying that they actually
retained less information doing a project compared
to a paper, students feel like these new assignments
are wasting their time (Denice).

Teachers should be more practical with their
expectations of using technology and assigning
projects and should realize that their focus should
be on their curriculum. Technology should be used
for the purpose of creating shortcuts and saving
time, not wasting it when students should be
learning. Nobody ever asked how to implement the
pencil or chalkboard into lessons, so why should we
do so now that the medium of technology has
changed? This overzealous attitude of teachers to
"keep up with technology" is not making education
any more profound but rather lowering the quality
of what is being taught while simultaneously making
the classes easier, as they also make homework more
time-consuming (Kent 11). It is one more way we are
"dumbing down" our schools, only this time it is a
by-product of trying to advance them.

If teachers were more practical in their
applications of technology, then it would not be a
problem at all. They should stop worrying about how

Repeats previous
¶, which is a
punchier
conclusion.

much technology they make their students use and
should instead think about how to improve the
quality of education overall. Also, until the
teachers are masters of the technology themselves,
they should not being assigning projects that they

themselves could not complete. Technology continues to develop in order to create shortcuts in activities that would normally take more time and effort. Despite the earnest goal of society to be more technologically savvy, it is foolish to force a burden on students to use technology while simultaneously reducing the quality of the actual subject material being taught in our schools. Today, while the technological projects teachers assign may be more fun and different from the expected, the reality of the situation is that these projects are more disadvantageous for everyone in the long-run.

First drafts (and final drafts, for that matter) are never perfect, as our student has recognized on carefully reviewing his. Here is a list of the problems that his review has discovered:

1. *Claim.* My claim is a combination causal/evaluative claim: I identify negative results of an over-reliance on technology in schools. But I identify more results than are included in my claim, so I have to broaden the claim statement.

2. *Organization.* My organization is my big problem. I move all over the place in stating negative effects and supporting them. The organization should be simpler, like this:

   Claim statement

   Reason 1: technology projects not educational

   Reason 2: teachers don't know enough about technology

   Reason 3: students don't like doing these projects

   Support (my survey)

   Reason 4: Students who can afford technology do better

   Support (camera example from my school)

   Reason 5: ADD and other results

   Conclusion (which includes a recommendation of what teachers should do)

3. Support. I have basically 3 kinds of support: 1) my own personal experience; 2) the results of my survey; 3) general support from outside sources. I need to present the 3 kinds in the same order under each of the four reasons/examples: personal; survey; general.

4. Style. I don't see many problems here, but my introduction could be punchier, as well as broader to match the rest of the paper.

In his second draft, the student carefully attended to this list, ending up with a much stronger version of the paper.

EMPHASIZE TEACHING, NOT TECHNOLOGY

Christopher Denice

Argument 301

Surely it is a step in the right direction for teachers to utilize technology in the classroom. In particular, it is important for students to learn to use the computer-based tools they will rely on in college and their careers. But there are downsides to this "progress" that can compromise the educational experience of students.

In thirteen years in Rhode Island public schools, I saw the reliance on technology as a "teaching tool" increase and can personally attest to its counter-educational effects. Technology-based projects are simply easier to do than other more traditional assignments. When teachers assign a PowerPoint slideshow, it is more difficult to get lower than a "C" grade than it is to get an "A" on an essay.

My senior-year British Literature class was assigned a final project (rather than an exam) that had to "use technology in a practical and useful manner." Our group chose to create a website about British Literature and to summarize what we had learned throughout the year. Another group chose to make a DVD reenacting scenes from various works we had read. I earned an "A" on the website project, but I can barely recollect anything from the class. In my junior-year history class, we had to write a three- to five-page paper every week about a topic we covered in our notes. I recall more from that "boring, old-fashioned" history class than from any other class from high school. Writing a paper every week was not necessarily fun, but it forced me to learn the material thoroughly. In my experience, then, technology-based projects allowed mediocrity to be graded as creativity while more traditional teaching methods proved to be truly educational.

At my college, 67% of students surveyed reported that they retained less information doing a project than writing a paper. Furthermore, 82% of this same group of students found that technology-based projects take them more time than traditional assignments. Surely, if students see that such an educational approach is a waste of time, our teachers should realize it as well (Denice).

Milton Chen, executive director of the George Lucas Education Foundation, recently said "[t]he more we, who see the promise of technology, talk about it just as technology, the more it leads us away from issues of teaching and learning" (Vojtek 1). As we try to incorporate technology just for the sake of incorporating technology, the quality of education will continue to fall.

Some people claim that projects are beneficial because they are more creative than regular assignments and incorporate technology into the classroom to prepare students for the world outside. While these points appear to be true, projects still make each class easier for students to pass. Technological projects are often too casual, requiring less thinking about the subject matter, despite the fact that teachers are more ready to give an "A" to a project than to a paper. Too often our teachers are amazed by the creativity and the technological aspects of projects (Tomei 37). They should be looking for the educational value as related to the curriculum, but instead are dazzled by the animation and polish that accompany technological projects.

Another problem with this over-reliance on computer-based assignments is that teachers themselves don't always understand the technology that they assign. A recent report, "Technology Quality: A Report on the Preparation and Qualifications of Public School Teachers," said only 20% of teachers felt very well prepared to employ educational technology in the classroom (Vojtek 2). There is no value in giving work to students that teachers themselves do not confidently know how to do.

Assigning projects requiring computers and other digital technology can also end up being unfair to those students who may not have access to these tools. At my high school, the only digital video camera was owned by the Student Council, but since it could not be taken home over the weekend, there was often difficulty gaining access. After about the fourth assignment requiring a video camera, my family ended up buying a $200 camera to ease the burden on me. But not every family could do this, which means that good grades were actually being based upon the student's financial situation, not his or her performance.

The debate of technological haves and have-nots, known as the "Digital Divide," is a major problem that our educational system faces today (Attewell 251). It has caused great controversy because the "haves" tend to be affluent, suburban, white schools while the "have-nots" are the underprivileged, urban, minority-populated schools (Attewell 252). Many have labeled the divide "cyber-segregation" (Attewell 252). Already faced with plentiful troubles, these "have-not" schools now have been criticized for not being able to provide technological access (Wright 34). Putting these schools under the microscope for yet another reason can add no positive impact to an already difficult situation.

Finally, using computers can actually be physically and behaviorally harmful. Computer usage in children has been proven to result in problems ranging from poor vision to bad posture to ADD (Attention Deficit Disorder) and ADHD (Attention Deficit Hyperactivity Disorder) (Attewell 254). Such problems follow children into young adulthood and beyond. In my poll of college students living on my dormitory floor, I found that 100% of the 45 people I polled in my dormitory found it more difficult to concentrate while using a computer than just sitting at a desk (Denice).

Technology should be used for the purpose of creating shortcuts and saving time, not wasting it when students should be learning. This overzealous attitude of teachers to "keep up with technology" is not making education any more profound but rather lowering the quality of what is being taught while simultaneously making the classes easier, as they also make homework more time-consuming (Kent 11). It is one more way we are "dumbing down" our schools, only this time it is a by-product of trying to advance them. When we consider the educational inequities and developmental risks also associated with the marriage of technology and education, can we really come up with any good reasons for incorporating technology into teaching and learning?

WORKS CITED

Attewell, Paul. "The First and Second Digital Divides."
    Sociology of Education 74 (July 2001): 252–259.

Denice, Christopher. Poll: Boston College Freshman High School
    Projects Survey. 25 September 2005.

Kent, W., and Robert F. McNergney. *Will Technology Really
    Change Education: From Blackboard to Web*. Thousand Oaks,
    California: Corwin Press, Inc.: 1999.

Tomei, Lawrence A. *Challenges of Teaching with Technology
    Across the Curriculum: Issues and Solutions*. Hershey,
    Pennsylvania: IRM Press, 2003.

Vojtek, Bob and Rosie O'Brien Vojtek 'Not a blunt instrument':
    An interview with Milton Chen. *Journal of Staff
    Development*, Summer 1999. 24 September 2005.
    http://www.nsdc.org/library/publications/jsd/vojtek203.cfm.

Wright, Cream, ed. *Issues in Education & Technology: Policy
    Guidelines and Strategies*. London: Commonwealth
    Secretariat, 2000.

Paper adapted from "Emphasize Teaching, Not Technology," by Christopher Denice
(http://www.newcommave.com/denice1).

ACTIVITIES (13.2)

Read the following draft of a student's essay (actually a composite of several essays), and make a list of what you feel the major revisions need to be. Compare your list with those of your classmates; then revise the essay in accordance with your list. Compare your revision with some of those done by your classmates.

STUDENT GOVERNMENT: WHY NO ONE CARES

Being an engineering student here at High Tech, I have
very little free time. My time is entirely devoted to academics.
Occasionally I will have a few hours free on the weekend, but
then I work part time at odd jobs. Tuition here is very high.

I am one of many busy students here who simply doesn't
have the time to take an interest in student government. This
same fact is true for most of us. Most of us don't even know
one person who is in student government and could not tell
you what student government actually does.

We are very ignorant about student government and what
role we can play in it. Speaking for myself, even if I saw
posters announcing a meeting about student government, I would
not attend. Most of my fellow students would not either. What
can just one student do? None of us has much of a voice in how
things are run. The administration really runs the show here at
High Tech, not the students. I believe that if the student
government started putting up more posters and getting out more
publicity about its activities, students would be more interested
in its activities even if they did not attend them.

It is a whole lot simpler to just ignore what's going on
and to assume that the student government is looking out for
our interests than to take the trouble to get involved.
Besides, life isn't all that bad around here, so why should we
spend a lot of time and effort trying to improve a situation
most of us already find satisfactory? By the time we solved
some problem, we would be ready to graduate anyway.

SUGGESTIONS FOR WRITING (13.3)

1. Revise a paper you wrote earlier in this course, following the advice outlined
   in this chapter. Make a list of the major differences between the original paper
   and your new version, and indicate very briefly why you made these changes.

2. For this assignment, the class should be divided into groups of three or four.
   Each group will collectively write a three- to four-page paper (750 to 1,000
   words) on the general question "What are the three things that infuriate me
   most about this campus?" Each group will brainstorm ideas that lead it to a
   working claim for an evaluative paper concerning student life at your school.
   From this working claim, the group will compose an outline; then each student
   will write a particular section of the paper. When the first draft is written,
   the group will discuss it and each student will revise his or her own section.
   Finally, the group will discuss this second draft and choose one student to
   prepare and edit a final version consistent in style and tone.

3. Write a description of the steps you typically follow when writing arguments.
   Start with the step of coming up with ideas and move through writing the first
   draft to whatever steps you take before you arrive at a final edited version.
   How efficient is this typical process in terms of time spent? How effective is it
   in helping you compose a convincing argument? Do you think the process can
   be improved so that you can write better arguments in a reasonable amount of
   time? Give the description to your instructor for comments and suggestions.

4. If you selected activity number one in this section, write a complete paper
   incorporating your resources. Be sure to give your instructor copies of your
   resource materials along with your first draft and notes you made concerning
   the draft.

PART II

READING
ARGUMENTS

Athletic coaches know the value of practice drills that require players to switch positions. In soccer and basketball, a player will be a more effective dribbler if he practices stealing the ball. A tennis player will hit more ace serves if she practices receiving against a powerful server. The principle applies equally to writing arguments, where a writer attempts to convince a reader of an arguable position. While writer and reader are not exactly opponents, they are, like server and receiver, engaged in a transitive act where the action of one affects the reaction of the other.

Part II of *Everyday Arguments* is based upon the premise that careful reading contributes to successful writing. "Reading" in this context means a great deal more than scanning for the main ideas—what in a novel we would call the plot. A careful reader of argument moves well beyond content comprehension to an analysis of *technique*—how structure, logic, evidence, and style enhance or detract from the reasonableness of the claim. The readings that follow offer you abundant examples of how the strategies of argument laid out in Part I are actually applied in the real-life arguments that people write every day. A wide range of writers is represented in these readings—some famous, others unknown. Likewise, the forms and contexts of these arguments vary widely—from the formal and methodical to the casual and offhand. But all the selections in this section share the defining characteristics of argument: they promote a position with the intent of convincing an audience through reasonable methods.

The commentaries accompanying the first argument of every unit are detailed analyses of the argument technique. The discussion questions following every argument will guide you in making your own careful analyses—a critical skill if you want to become a truly effective writer. And the suggestions for writing following each reading will give you the opportunity to experiment with the techniques you've analyzed and to engage with the subject matter and claims you've read.

The readings are divided into six subject units, which address such contemporary topics as today's college students, sports, popular culture, the Internet, the diet industry, and the world of work. These topics may at first sight not appear to be the stuff of argument, and they certainly are different from the subject areas typically addressed in writing anthologies. But each satisfies criteria that are critical for arguments designed as practical illustrations of the do's (and sometimes don'ts) of written argument. First, all six units revolve around subjects that are part of the air that today's college students breathe. You can scarcely pick up a newspaper, have a conversation with a friend, or turn on the television without confronting one of these topics. And while as such, they may seem too unexceptional to inspire model arguments, they model one of the central claims of this book: that argument informs virtually all of the writing we encounter—regardless of its subject, its writer, or its audience.

There is another important reason for this particular choice of subject areas. Because they surround us on a daily basis, we tend not to subject them to the same rigorous analysis and interrogation that we might apply to a Supreme Court decision on affirmative action or a call to action by a renowned world leader. But precisely because of their *dailiness*, these are the arguments that we must scrutinize, taking care to question and challenge the seemingly harmless claims that, if uncritically accepted, form cultural values that will serve only the organizations and individuals that make them, not the general population that unthinkingly accepts them. So these readings ask you to develop the habit of examining *how* the claims of our society are made, to accept or reject them on the basis of the principles of reasonable argument presented in the first half of this book. As in the sports analogy above, you have to be a critical reader of argument to be an effective writer of argument, and there's no better place to start reading critically than these popular issues that daily clamor for our acceptance but sometimes evade our careful scrutiny.

14

Today's College Student

INTRODUCTION

Had this book been written in the 1980s, it would have been much easier to generalize about "today's college student," who at that time tended to be U.S.-born, unmarried, largely middle-class, 18–22 years old, and enrolled in college full time. Recently, this "typical" student has been joined by very different populations of students—adults, single parents, citizens of different countries, part-time students, and students from a wider range of ethnic and economic backgrounds. While responsible generalizations—inductive arguments—about the subgroups comprising today's more diverse student population are still possible, the days of all-encompassing generalizations are past.

Because you are all automatic experts on "today's college student," and because induction plays such an important element in written argument, a set of inductive arguments describing you and your fellow students seems like an excellent place for this argument anthology to begin. The selections that follow—all of which use the inductive method to some degree—don't cover all the major populations of college students, but they do describe at least a representative sampling: the traditional 18–22-year-old full-time undergraduates, adult female students (a quickly growing segment of the undergraduate student population), underprivileged students, and others. The arguments contained here come from an equally diverse set of vantage points—from education specialists, students, professors, and reporters. If you were to write your own all-inclusive description of today's college student, these arguments would give you much, though certainly not all, of the material you would need.

As you read these arguments, be mindful of the mistakes to which generalizations are prey: insufficiently limited claims; inadequate supporting data; and unsubstantiated facts, to name a few. You may find yourself being particularly critical of those arguments that describe the group to which you belong; it can be an unsettling experience to hear yourself described without having had any opportunity to contribute to or approve that description. The suggestions for writing after each argument will give you ample opportunity to formulate and argue your responses to these essays.

RETREAT FROM INTIMACY

ARTHUR LEVINE AND JEANETTE S. CURETON

Arthur Levine, Ph.D., is one of the nation's top experts on college students. For 30 years, he has been studying and writing on the topic, winning in the process a host of prestigious awards for his work. When Hope and Fear Collide *(1998), from which this essay is taken, is a follow-up to his 1980 study of college students,* When Dreams and Heroes Died. *Levine is currently president and professor of education at Teachers College, Columbia University.*

Jeanette S. Cureton has collaborated with Levine on a number of higher education studies. She holds an M.A.T. from Johns Hopkins and a Master's in Education from Harvard. Her career in higher education research has provided her a wide view of college and university campuses across the country.

COMMENTARY

This argument uses an introductory strategy similar to the one illustrated in the essay by David Brown in Chapter 12. It is a breathtaking generalization that captures readers' attention simply by virtue of its magnitude. Generalizations like these are engaging in part because readers automatically see them as dares that they could win: "I dare you to prove this," we say to the writer.

The essay is a combination factual and causal argument. The opening sentence does double duty: not only is it an attention-grabbing opener, it is also the argument's opening claim—a factual generalization that is then broken down into general examples, which in turn are supported through data and supporting quotations from experts. Just as outlining your own arguments after they are written can help you judge their organizational strengths and weaknesses, performing the same exercise with other people's arguments is an excellent way to judge the reasonableness of that argument's evolution. An outline of the opening factual argument might look like this:

Claim #1: "Today's students are frightened" (factual generalization)

    A. Example 1: "They are afraid of getting hurt" (supporting factual generalization) (Par. 1)
        1–3: Supporting data (Par. 1)
    B. Example 2: "Students are also frightened about their economic prospects"(Par. 2)
        1–5: Supporting data (Par. 2)

C. Example 3: "Relationships were another source of concern for students" (Par. 3)
1–x: Supporting data (Par. 3–5)
D. Summary: "The bottom line is that students are coming to college overwhelmed and more damaged than those of previous years" (Par. 6)
1. Supporting data (Par. 6)
2. Supporting expert opinions (Par. 6)

Once the authors have established the reasonableness of their original factual claim, they introduce the central causal claim of the essay: "The effect of the accumulated fears and hurts that students have experienced is to divide and isolate them" (Par. 7). Par. 8 and 9 support this claim through citing linking behavioral principles: the effect (isolation) is linked to the cause (fear) through such universal human behaviors as withdrawal and escape.

In order for this causal claim to be credible, further support is necessary. First, we need verification of the effect (the first section of the argument has amply verified the cause). And second, because this is a causal generalization, we need evidence that the isolation is a widespread phenomenon.

Both verifications are offered in the second section of the argument, "Having Fun?" Like much of the factual support in this essay, the verifications come in the form of data obtained through interviews and surveys of college students and student affairs professionals. In this case, that data is presented in tabular form (Tables 14.2 and 14.3). Supplementing the tables are quoted statements from students interviewed for the study (Par. 13).

The final three paragraphs turn to a concluding causal argument proposing three reasons for the increased social isolation of college students: the high numbers of students working while attending school (Par. 14); conforming to "a national trend of disengagement" (Par. 15); and the "wiring" of dorm rooms. Each of these proposed causes is amply documented by a variety of strategies.

Overall, the argument by Levine and Cureton is a solid, well-documented inductive argument. The writing, while not stylistically memorable, is clear and serviceable; the organization is sensible and easy to follow. Stylistic moderation and structural predictability are appropriate to an argument that makes such vast and ambitious claims.

RETREAT FROM INTIMACY

Fear and Pain

1 Today's students are frightened. They are afraid of getting hurt. Nearly half of all undergraduates (46 percent) worry about becoming victims of violent crime. Among women the proportion is even higher (54 percent) (Undergraduate Survey, 1993). We asked a female junior on a suburban campus in an affluent area why she was afraid. She could not think of any incidents that had occurred on her campus. Instead, she told us the college had recently introduced emergency phones,

stronger outdoor lighting, and nighttime escort services. For her, cause and prevention were the same thing. Both fueled her fears.

2   Students were also frightened about their economic prospects. Many have had financially unstable lives. More than one-fifth (21 percent) of the undergraduates surveyed reported the ultimate instability: someone who helped pay their tuition had been unemployed during their college years (Undergraduate Survey, 1993). The students saw their own economic futures as uncertain too. They told us over and over again that they were worried about whether they could pay their college tuition. In an age in which students are taking average loans of $3,210 per year at two-year colleges and $4,790 per year at four-year colleges (U.S. Department of Education, 1996c), three college students out of every ten are uncertain whether they have enough money to complete college; this is more than a 50 percent increase since 1976. In fact, only 25 percent of undergraduates were confident of having sufficient funds to pay for college (Table 14.1). They were equally frightened about whether they would be able to repay their college loans, whether they could find a decent job after college, and whether they could afford a home and a family—or would have to move back home with their parents.

3   Relationships were another source of concern for students. Nearly one-third of all college freshmen (30 percent) grew up with one or no parent (Sax, Astin, Korn, and Mahoney, 1996). Even those students who lived with both parents usually experienced divorce up close by seeing it in the lives of their friends and neighbors. These students often told us of unhappy relationships between their own parents. The result is that current undergraduates worry a great deal about divorce. As one dean of students put it: "They want a nurturing and caring environment. They want security. They don't want divorce to happen to them." They are desperate to have only one marriage, and they want it to be happy. They don't know whether this is possible anymore.

4   Again and again, deans of students reported on the growing rate of dysfunctional families among their students. They talked of violence; instability; blended families; and emotional, sexual, and financial problems. As one dean put it, "It's hard to send a student home, when home is the problem."

5   In interviews, students alluded to such difficulties, often very subtly. Others were more concrete, particularly in regard to the feeling of not having a home. Startlingly, 27 percent of the students surveyed had moved four or more times while growing up; 16 percent had moved more than five times. Among students of color, the proportions were even higher, 36 percent and 20 percent respectively (Undergraduate Survey, 1993). For these students, there were frequently no roots, no sense of place, and no strong relationships. They yearned deeply for all of these things but feared they would never have them.

Table 14.1.   Student concern about ability to finance a college education: 1976, 1993.

Financial concern	Percentage reporting	
	1976	1993
Confident they will have sufficient funds	38	25
Probably will have enough funds	43	45
Not sure they will have enough funds to complete college	19	30

Source: Undergraduate Surveys (1976, 1993).

6   The bottom line is that students are coming to college overwhelmed and more damaged than those of previous years. Six out of ten chief student affairs officers (60 percent) reported that undergraduates are using psychological counseling services in record numbers and for longer periods of time than in the past; this is true at 69 percent of four-year schools and 52 percent of two-year colleges. Eating disorders are up at 58 percent of the institutions surveyed. Classroom disruption increased at a startling 44 percent of colleges, drug abuse at 42 percent, alcohol abuse at 35 percent of campuses. Gambling has grown at 25 percent of the institutions, and suicide attempts have risen at 23 percent (Student Affairs Survey, 1997). Deans of students concluded:

"Students carry more baggage to college today."

"Dealing with more developmentally delayed or disabled students."

"Much more time devoted to emotionally ill students."

"We deal with a greater number of dysfunctional students and dysfunctional family situations."

"Dealing with more psychopathology among students of all levels and all backgrounds."

"Students bring more nonacademic-related issues. We are becoming a secondary social service agency."

"I spend more time dealing with student discipline, stalking, harassment, and domestic violence."

"Students expect the community to respond to their needs—to make 'right' their personal problems and those of society at large." (Student Affairs Survey, 1997)

7   The effect of the accumulated fears and hurts that students have experienced is to divide and isolate them. Undergraduates have developed a lifeboat mentality of sorts. It is as if each student is alone in a boat in a terrible storm, far from any harbor. The boat is taking on water and believed to be in imminent danger of sinking. Under these circumstances, there is but one alternative; each student must single-mindedly bail. Conditions are so bad that no one has time to care for others who may also be foundering. No distractions are permitted. The pressure is enormous and unremitting.

8   This situation has resulted in a generation often too busy or too tired to have a social life. It has produced students who fear intimacy in relationships. Withdrawal is easier and less dangerous than engagement. It has led to undergraduates who want things to be different; escaping from the campus physically and from life via a bottle are both popular.

9   Social life is an area in which student fears loom larger than their hopes. Their behavior differs in this realm from that in the political arena. Though fears and doubts about politics, politicians, and government are extremely high, students have chosen to engage, albeit through the local and more informal approach of community service. In part, the reason stated for their involvement is that they had no choice; they had to embrace the political agenda or it would engulf them. In contrast, a social life is viewed by undergraduates as optional. To be intimately involved is a higher-stakes game than politics. It presents a far greater potential for getting hurt, for adding to one's burden, or for personal failure.

Having Fun?

10   We asked students what they did for fun. We had asked the same question in the prior study, but this time the answers were very different (Table 14.2).

11   We also asked the same question of deans of students, who responded similarly regarding the most popular activities but tended to give greater preference to more wholesome pursuits (Table 14.3).

12   With many students, the question drew a wide-eyed stare or a look of bemusement, as

Table 14.2. What college students do for fun, according to students: 1979, 1993.

Activities	Percentage of students reporting	
	1979	1993
Drinking	77	63
Clubs and bars	—	59
Off-campus	—	52
Parties	38	41
Sports and intramurals	54	33
No social life, commuter	27	30
Theater	—	26
Music	27	22
Movies	27	22
Concerts	12	22
Fraternities and sororities	19	15
Study	—	21
Travel and trips	8	11
Dances	58	11
Drugs	54	a
Sleep	—	11
Residence hall activities	19	—
Cards, backgammon	12	—
Running	12	—

[a]Students talked about drugs regularly, but most often in the negative, saying drug use on campus was less popular than alcohol use.
Source: Campus Site Visits (1979, 1993).

Table 14.3 What students do for fun, according to deans of students: 1997.

Activities	Percentage of deans reporting		
	Two-year schools	Four-year schools	Total
Party	17	52	34
Sports	48	51	50
Drink	9	50	29
Socialize	39	36	37
Games	30	15	23
Video	13	30	21
Outdoor	13	24	18
Comedy or other entertainment	22	7	15
Clubs	13	16	14
Music	9	15	12
Greek	—	9	5
Date	—	2	7

Source: Student Affairs Survey (1997).

if to ask the interviewer, What are you talking about? What planet do you come from? On nearly one-third of the campuses (30 percent) at which we conducted focus group interviews, students said they had no social life. This is only a small increase (27 percent) from the earlier study, but for the first time students (11 percent) listed "sleeping" as a form of recreation. The students at the University of Colorado who selected "tired" as the best adjective to describe their generation apparently knew what they were talking about.

13   Studying was another leisure activity making a first-time appearance on the fun list. It was cited on more than one-fifth of the campuses (21 percent). Undergraduates told us again and again:

> "I don't have a social life."
> "There is no free time."
> "My whole life is juggling."
> "Study, that's all we ever do."
> "I'm always behind. I never catch up."
> "I feel run down."
> "People's lives are dictated by their jobs."
> "The high cost means I have to work forty to fifty hours per week, and it's killing me. Sometimes I fall asleep in class."

14   For many undergraduates, "life is just work, school, and home." There may be time to gulp the coffee, but there is absolutely "no time to smell the coffee." This is no surprise given the dramatic rise in the proportion of students who work while attending college (now about 60 percent) or the growing percentage who are working full-time (currently 24 percent overall and as high as 39 percent at two-year colleges) (Undergraduate Survey, 1993). During the 1990s, 71 percent of the colleges surveyed reported increases in the proportion of students working while attending college (Student Affairs Survey, 1997). The increase in part-time attenders and students with families is also a factor. Today almost one in five college students (18 percent) has dependent children (Undergraduate Survey, 1993). With all the demands on their time, something has got to give. They have elected to sacrifice social life.

15   But not all of the retreat from social life is time-based. Chief student affairs officers describe students more often as loners than in the past. Requests for single dormitory rooms have skyrocketed. The thought of having a roommate is less appealing than it once was. Perhaps this desire to withdraw simply mirrors the national trend of disengagement from groups that once connected individuals with a broad swath of other people who shared similar interests. Across the country we are losing our "social capital"—the networks and norms of society—as civic organizations once as commonplace and popular as the Boy Scouts and local bowling leagues have suffered huge declines in membership; so laments Robert Putnam in his thought-provoking essay "Bowling Alone" (1995).

16   Similarly, group activities that once connected students on college campuses are losing their appeal and are becoming more individualized. For instance, the venue for television watching has moved from the lounge to the dorm room. Film viewing has shifted from the theater to the home VCR. As one student put it, these days dormitory rooms come "fully loaded." A dean of students said he was worried about wiring; can it support the electronic menagerie behind each residence hall door? Equally important is whether college can afford to support financially the needed upgrades in wiring, cable, and other technological infrastructure demanded and expected by current undergraduates. Student rooms have microwaves, televisions, VCRs, computers, CD players, tape decks, phones, answering machines, refrigerators, coffee makers, and who knows what else. The dean said, "Everything is right there." He could not imagine a reason, other than eating or attending class, why a student would need to leave his or her room.

17   That is the point. Increasingly, students are living their lives in ways that allow them not to venture out.

Source: Arthur Levine and Jeanette S. Cureton, "Retreat From Intimacy," in *When Hope and Fear Collide: A Portrait of Today's College Student.* Jossey-Bass, 1998, pp. 93–101.

DISCUSSION QUESTIONS

1. After carefully reading this argument at least twice, work through it with a classmate and see if you can identify any unsupported claims. Then compare your findings with other pairs in your class. Does the existence of these inadequately supported claims (if you found any) weaken the credibility of the argument? Could the claims have been documented?

2. The authors do not provide any lists of the questions that were asked in their surveys and interviews. Yet the wording of such questions can influence the answers obtained. With a small group of your classmates, compose two lists of interview questions that you would ask a group of students at your school about a well-defined topic—for example, the food in the cafeteria, entertainment on campus, parking facilities, and so on. In the first list, try to keep the wording as neutral as possible; in the second, create "leading" questions that attempt to get at predetermined answers.

3. Conduct two sets of interviews of the rest of your class with these questions. How different are the answers? How do these differences reflect upon the authors' decision to omit their interview and survey questions from the text?

4. Levine and Cureton do not identify their intended audience. Based upon this part of their argument, how would you identify that audience? What clues have you based your identification on? What, if anything, do you think the authors want their audience to do as a result of reading the argument?

5. The authors present their data in a number of ways: as part of the text, in tabular form, and as quotations from interviews. Which of these formats do you find most effective? Could all the data have been presented in a single format? What would the effect have been?

SUGGESTIONS FOR WRITING (14.1)

1. College campuses today may be more troubled by alcohol abuse than Levine and Cureton suggest was true in the mid-'90s. Using your own school as subject, write a three- to five-page causal analysis of this phenomenon. Remember to establish the factuality of your effect and cause(s). Assume that the readers of this argument are your student peers.

2. Write a letter to your college president recommending steps to alleviate the drinking problem on your campus. If you are not aware of such a problem, select another one and write a letter to your president recommending solutions.

3. Using the other students in this class as a sample, create two surveys designed to determine what these students do "for fun." In the first, provide open-ended questions that one half of the class must answer without prompts. In the second, provide a list of alternative activities that the other half must choose from. Compare the results of the two surveys.

   Write a two-page causal analysis speculating on the reasons for the different responses.

4. While Levine and Cureton may be experts on the topic of today's college student, they write from an outside perspective. Those of you who belong to the generation they describe have first-hand experience that the authors cannot claim. Based upon your familiarity with your college peers, write a five-page argument assessing the accuracy of Levine and Cureton's claims. The support for the generalizations you make may be personally experienced facts, but be sure to supply enough of these to make your generalizations credible.

COLLEGE, MY WAY

KATE ZERNIKE

Each year, the Sunday New York Times *publishes an Education supplement that consists of articles, advertisements, and recent statistics related to the current state of higher education. This article, by national* Times *correspondent Kate Zernike, describes the increasingly common phenomenon of college students attending multiple institutions. The article cites a number of individual student cases as at least partial support for the factual claim that "These days, a majority of students take a . . . nomadic path to a degree."*

1   Erin Madden laughs a little self-consciously referring to what she calls "my college tour." Not the kind that high school students take to look at potential campuses; hers started after she went to college and discovered she didn't like her choice. She transferred to another, and another, and another, and another, ultimately ending up with five colleges on her transcript when she graduated last year.

2   It wasn't collegiate life as she once imagined it. But it wasn't so unconventional, either. These days, a majority of students take a similarly nomadic path to a degree; about 60 percent of students graduating from college attend more than one institution, a number that has risen steadily over at least the last two decades.

3   In large part, those numbers reflect the growing population of nontraditional-age students, adults who go to college later in life and often start at a two-year institution. But even traditional students like Ms. Madden—

those who head to a four-year college right out of high school—are approaching the experience in a nontraditional way.

4   They transfer to get a more agreeable major or social life, or take classes at a college back home during the summer to get a leg up on the next year's credits. They take an online class, or earn credits during the year at a nearby community college where they find a required course cheaper, less demanding, or at a more convenient hour. Or they do some of each.

5   College officials call it swirling, mix and match, cut and paste, grab and go. Whatever the term of art, it makes sense for the so-called millennial generation, students famously lacking in brand loyalty, used to having things their way, and can-do about changing anything they don't like. As with other commodities, students are looking for that magic combination of quality, affordability, and convenience. They shun CDs to

create their own iPod playlists; is it any surprise they shape their own course catalogs?

6   "Everybody can customize it the way they want it," says Ms. Madden, now 24 and working at a Cape Cod media company that runs radio stations and a website. "In the world we live in, with the Internet making things so accessible, we try to find what we like."

7   Some college officials see all this as the behavior of an overindulged generation, raised by helicopter parents and lacking in resiliency.

8   "These millennial kids are the most loved, most wanted kids ever, and they want things to be immediately perfect," says Jacqueline Murphy, director of admissions at St. Michael's College in Vermont. "They want to get things done, and maybe they decide that if things aren't going their way they'd rather be elsewhere where things are going their way. Some of it is: if there's a little adversity or things aren't as promised, I'll take my tent and go elsewhere."

9   "Personally," she continues, "I don't think it's the best way to deal with things. In life you have good days and bad days, and learning to establish that even keel is important."

10   The new nomads are creating challenges for colleges and universities, which have spent years shaping what they believed to be a signature experience only to have students try to take it apart. Researchers and college officials worry that students who campus-hop to check off all their required courses may be getting a degree, but not an education.

11   The numbers surprise even people who make a life of studying the behavior of college students. Federal statistics and several studies have documented a rise over the last two decades in students attending more than one college—59 percent of those graduating from four-year colleges in 1999–2000, compared with 53 percent in 1992–93. More than 16 percent attended three colleges; 8 percent went to four or more.

12   How students move between institutions has changed, too. In decades past, students who attended more than one institution were more likely to attend only four-year colleges. Now, they are more likely to attend a four-year college and a community college, either transferring between them or enrolling at both at the same time.

13   Of those who start their college careers at four-year institutions, about a third transfer for a desired program, according to a study released last May by the National Center for Education Statistics. Another third transfer for better location or more prestige, and almost 10 percent for financial reasons. Then, college officials say, there are other reasons not tracked in the survey: homesickness or to be near a high school girlfriend or at less of a party school.

14   "Families all over this country can tell stories like this," says Clifford Adelman, a senior researcher with the United States Department of Education, "and families all over this country who are parents of high school students ought to be prepared for this kind of thing to happen."

15   Ms. Madden started off at American University, which had been her second choice, and it soon disappointed her. The university lacked school spirit, she says, and seemed too politically charged. (It was the autumn of the 2000 elections.) She found herself shying away from campus activities, unlike the student she had been in high school. She felt uncertain about her classes, and sometimes overwhelmed.

16   "I wanted to know myself before my parents were spending $30,000 on an education," she says. "I wanted to know what I wanted to do with my life, and I didn't." She went home to Cape Cod, and resisting suggestions from her parents that she go to community college—"I was too proud"—decided to enroll in two institutions in Boston at the same time. She took classes during the day at the University of Massachusetts and evening classes at the Massachusetts College of Art, to try out an interest she had not explored in high school.

17   But she was lonely, still uncertain about what she wanted to do. So she moved home to the Cape and, swallowing her pride, began classes at the local community college. She found some direction in a marketing class and decided to pursue a communications

degree at Suffolk University in Boston, where she was in good company: transfers make up 24 percent of new students. But she had landed a job during her time at home, at the media company, and when her bosses offered to make it full time, she decided to finish her degree at Suffolk's Cape Cod campus.

18   Other students say they were simply unprepared to leave the comforts of home.

19   "You're used to having everything on a silver platter," says Brian Donnelly of Yorba Linda, Calif. "You just expect things to be there, so when you go to college, you're not ready. You don't know how to do your laundry, you don't know how to do your food, you don't know how to care for yourself. It's a shock."

20   Mr. Donnelly, 23, started at the University of Colorado, Boulder, where by his own account he spent most of his time snowboarding and playing golf, and ended up with a 2.5 grade point average; he remorsefully calls it the $40,000 vacation. So he withdrew and moved back to California, where he went to two junior colleges and raised his grades to a 4.0, high enough to get into Boston College. He will graduate there this spring. "It was just awesome as soon as I got here," he says. "There's a fit."

21   Glossy catalogs and the heated admissions process have increased the sense that there is such a thing as the perfect fit and that much depends on finding it.

22   "There's pressure from parents, there's pressure from your peers, to find the right fit," says Eric Smith, 22. "I was one of those kids who thought, I deserve better." He

Brian Donnelly, Fall 2001–May 2006
University of Colorado, Boulder
Santa Monica College
Santiago Canyon College
Boston College

doesn't see it as being spoiled; it's simply squeezing the most out of the experience.

23   Mr. Smith, who started taking college courses in high school in a special program at Syracuse University, had his heart set on the State University of New York at Purchase. Purchase accepted him but could not offer housing the first semester, so he went to a community college. He was interested in journalism, but when he finally arrived at Purchase second semester, those classes were already filled. He wasn't terribly impressed, anyway, with what his roommate was doing in his journalism classes. He transferred to Pace University for a broader program.

24
25   Even there, he feared it wasn't the right fit. "I got so used to not really settling in," he says. His mother convinced him to try at least one college for more than a semester, and gradually he found the fit. Still, he indulged a bit of wanderlust last fall; he wanted to study abroad but could not afford it, so he enrolled in a semester exchange program at American University, which included an internship at a local television station.

26   "If I'm investing all my time and energy," he says, "I'd better like it and be getting something out of it."

27   Interests change, too, Erika Cowley points out. She had started at the College of Wooster in Ohio, thinking she would major in international relations. After a trip with the National Outdoor Leadership School, an Outward Bound-like experience, she longed to do something that would allow her to be outside, perhaps environmental studies. Then she heard about a major in adventure recreation at Green Mountain College in Vermont, where she is now a sophomore. "I honestly started thinking I wouldn't transfer," she says. "I just realized I would be happy doing this."

28   For many students, swirling between different colleges is not about finding themselves. It's about efficiency. In the 2005 National Survey of Student Engagement, which found that about half of all college

Number of colleges attended

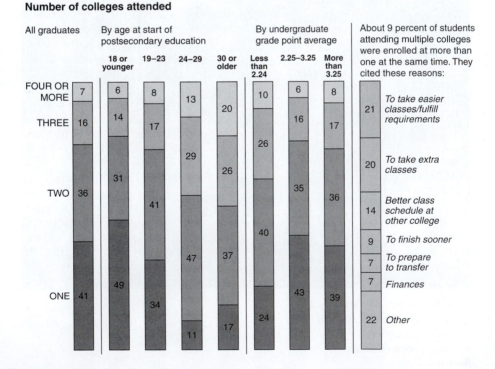

seniors had taken a class elsewhere, 47 percent said they had done so to complete their requirements sooner.

29   "There's all the pressure to graduate in four years," explains Meighan Ruby, a senior at Drake University who began the race in high school by taking classes at a community college in her hometown, Des Moines.

30   In her sophomore year at the University of Iowa in Iowa City, she decided to change her major from communications to finance, so she went back to the community college in summer months to make up the credits she would need for her degree. The community college made it easy: she could do much of the course work online and still keep her summer job at an arts festival.

31   Then, in her senior year, she moved back to Des Moines for a cooperative education semester working with a commercial real estate company. She intended to return to Iowa City after five months but ended up loving her work and getting hired full time. So she transferred to Drake in Des Moines, taking some credits over the summer at the community college to make up for ones that she lost in the move. She will "walk" at commencement in May, meeting her four-year deadline, and finish a couple of courses over the summer.

32   In Iowa City, she had been a member of a sorority and other campus groups, and she missed her friends after transferring. Still, she says, "I wouldn't make a different decision. I like to know what's ahead of me, I like to be very organized, and this was an interest where I saw myself wanting to build a career. It was hard to leave, but I kept thinking, am I going to go back to school just to hang out with my friends?"

33   Educators, though, worry that students jumping from place to place are missing out on the campus experience—and the student engagement survey backs them up. Transfer students report spending less time with teachers, being less involved in campus activities, and getting less out of college than their peers.

34   "What we want is for students to feel like this is the single best place for them to achieve what they need to in the near term and beyond," says George Kuh, a professor of higher education at Indiana University Bloomington and director of the survey. "That doesn't happen just in the classroom; it's about the other students who are there. For a transfer student who's moving from campus to campus, it's not the same as 'We're all new here; this is what we learn to do together.'"

35   Others say they miss out academically, too.

36   "One of the consequences is some loss of coherence, and a loss of the college's ability to understand what all of their students have learned," says Alexander C. McCormick, a researcher at the Carnegie Foundation for the Advancement of Teaching, who has studied the patterns of transfer students.

37   A professor teaching a higher-level course, for example, cannot count on all the students having read the same books or learned the same material if some have taken the prerequisites at a community college.

38   "There's the question of whether someone who is just taking these courses to get them out of the way is really learning," says Carol Geary Schneider, president of the Association of American Colleges and Universities. "They're trying to get through their education with the greatest efficiency, and as a result, they're just cobbling something together. They're not following a curriculum."

39   Colleges and universities have traditionally placed most of their emphasis on the first year, Ms. Schneider says, but those efforts are wasted if most students arrive later.

40   Many colleges are reshaping the curriculum to make sure that even transfer students have a common experience, moving required courses and "signature" programs to the last two years so that everyone goes through them. Portland State University, where two-thirds of new students are transfers, was one of the first to do this. It redesigned its curriculum in fall 1995, threading general education requirements throughout all four years, and requiring seniors to complete a "capstone" project, working with students

from other majors around a community issue—industry, schools, the environment. "Part of the thinking was to actively engage transfer students with the university through their course work and with the community," says Terry Rhodes, vice president for curriculum and undergraduate studies.

41   With so many students moving among its campuses or arriving from community colleges, the California State University system now requires students to take at least nine specified advanced courses in their final two years. San Jose State, where a third of the 22,000 undergraduates are transfers, demands that those advanced courses be taken on its campus, not at another Cal State branch. And it is creating a transfer-student version of the general education program now required for all incoming freshmen.

42   Ms. Schneider, though, says creating too many new requirements could backfire. "American students like choice," she says. "The less said about what's required, the better."

43   The students themselves admit that there are drawbacks, but many speak of a significant upside: if they weren't resilient when they arrived, they are when they leave. "It set me up for things to come," says Eric Smith, who will graduate from Pace next month. "I know that nothing is certain. I hope to have more of a stable lifestyle, but if for any reason things don't go as expected, I have the ability to move quickly."

44   Erin Madden started out expecting that she'd feel loyalty to a campus where she'd spend four glorious years, a place with quadrangles and fountains and football games. Instead, she is loyal to Suffolk, a commuter school, for the close friendships she developed with professors and classmates of a range of ages, and because it set her on a career path.

45   "Looking at it now from the other side and having been at my job for three years, it's all fallen into place very nicely," she says. "I don't regret going to American or going to Boston or having five schools on my transcript. All in all I had a good experience. I figured out a lot about myself. Which is what the college experience is about, whether you have 1 or 5 or 10 schools on your transcript."

Source: Kate Zernike, "College, My Way; Lost, Alone and Not a Freshman" from *The New York Times*, Education Life Supplement Section, 4/23/06 issue, page 28.

DISCUSSION QUESTIONS

1. In Par. 5, Zernike describes the "so-called millennial generation" as "students famously lacking in brand loyalty, used to having things their way, and can-do about changing anything they don't like." Is the support provided for this generalization adequate? What is it?

2. Why do you think the author describes the experience of individual students through both paraphrase and direct quotation?

3. What are the reasons cited by Zernike for the transfer phenomenon? How reasonable are these causal arguments (according to the principles of causality discussed in Chapter 8)?

4. The original article included color photographs of three of the students interviewed and, under the photograph, a list of the schools the student attended. Eric Smith's list looks like this:

   Eric Smith, Fall 2002–May 2006
   Syracuse University (in high school, 2001)
   Onondaga Community College
   State University of New York, Purchase
   American University
   Pace University

Why do you think these lists were included? Would the argument have been equally effective without the lists?

5. Do a Web search on Kate Zernike. Share the information you locate with a few of your classmates. Do her experience and credentials make her a credible authority on the topic?

SUGGESTIONS FOR WRITING (14.2)

1. In Par. 10, Zernike suggests that some of today's "nomadic" students "may be getting a degree, but not an education." Write a one-page definition that distinguishes the two terms.

2. Design a graph that illustrates the data presented in Par. 11. In one paragraph, discuss why you think the graph style is an effective choice.

3. Select an activity that is typically popular with college students—sports, listening to a particular kind of music, playing computer games—and write a five-page paper following Zernike's strategy of referring to specific students and to summarized data. Use the students in this writing class as your sample, and create interview questions and a survey that will yield the type of information you need.

4. Interview one fellow student extensively about how his or her college choice was made. Write a two- to three-page description of the process, including paraphrase, direct quotation, and some causal speculation about whether he or she is likely to stay at this institution through graduation.

5. Write a three- to four-page argument of effect speculating on the disadvantages of repeated college transfers.

SUPER EGOS

PETER FRANCESE

This essay appeared in August of 1997 in a marketing research magazine called Marketing Tools. *Peter Francese is a market analyst for Dow Jones & Co. In other words, he is in the business of making and relying on highly generalized portraits of large groups of people. Here, Francese interprets results from a national survey of college freshmen.*

1   For all the fretting about self-esteem that marked their high school years, today's college sophomores feel pretty good about themselves. Nearly 58 percent of last year's incoming freshmen rated themselves "above average" or "highest 10 percent" in academic ability, compared to 31 percent of incoming freshmen in 1971, according to a 1996 survey conducted by the UCLA Higher Education Research Institute. A majority of 1996 freshmen (54 percent) also expressed above-average levels of intellectual self-confidence, compared to only 35 percent in 1971.

2   UCLA researchers have been surveying college freshmen annually for 31 years, and they have never before recorded such across-the-board high levels of self-confidence. Specifically, last year's freshmen gave themselves unprecedented high marks for their

abilities in leadership, public speaking, mathematics, artistic endeavors, and writing.

3   This uncommon aplomb may be based on uncommonly good grades. Nearly one-third (31.5 percent) told UCLA researchers that they had "A" averages in high school, more than twice the number that reported top grades in 1966. The 1996 report attributes the increase to "grade inflation," a polite term for what happens when teachers feel pressured to bestow an "A" on B-plus work.

4   What is remarkable about this study is the disconnection between what freshmen said and the reality of their lives in college. Last year's freshmen also set a record for frequently or occasionally oversleeping and missing class or an appointment (34 percent, compared to 19 percent in 1968). Nevertheless, half of the 1996 respondents (49 percent) expect to make at least a "B" average, and two-thirds (66 percent) plan to go to graduate school. It appears that these students feel a sense of entitlement to good grades and a place in graduate school regardless of the amount of effort they expend during their undergraduate careers.

5   The gap between self-image and reality has profound implications for the service sector. First, some college graduates are going to be very disappointed to find that employers demand a lot more from them than their teachers and professors. Second, many employers are going to find it hard to sustain high performance with entry-level

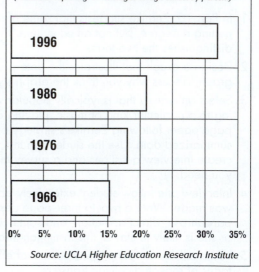

All the Children Are Above Average

The UCLA study has noted a hefty increase in the number of "A" students over the past 30 years.

(Freshman reporting "A" averages in high school by percent)

1996	
1986	
1976	
1966	

0%   5%   10%   15%   20%   25%   30%   35%

Source: UCLA Higher Education Research Institute

managers who may be more focused on nurturing their egos than on taking care of customers.

6   The contrast between image and reality also suggests problems for the market research industry. When researchers ask for customer input on a product or service, will they get the true picture, or nice words to make them feel good about themselves?

Source: Peter Francese, "Super Egos," *Marketing Tools*. 1997, p. 64.

DISCUSSION QUESTIONS

1. In Par. 4, Francese makes the following interpretive claim: "It appears that these students feel a sense of entitlement to good grades and a place in graduate school regardless of the amount of effort they expend during their undergraduate careers." Identify the support for this claim and discuss with your classmates whether this support is sufficient.

2. Identify the causal claims of this argument and discuss the adequacy of their support.

3. Search the World Wide Web for information on Francese and the work he does. Do his credentials qualify him to interpret this UCLA data?

4. How helpful is the graphic included in Francese's article? Would the point have been made as clearly without it? Are there other facts that would have been clarified by a similar chart?

SUGGESTIONS FOR WRITING (14.3)

1. Make a copy of this article. Then go over it as if you are the professor and Francese is one of your students who has written an assigned factual argument about trends in college grades. Identify all the strengths and weaknesses of the essay, provide comments and questions, and give the paper a grade.

2. Working with a small group of your classmates, create a one-page survey for your class designed to identify (a) their musical preferences; (b) their post-graduation ambitions; or (c) their political persuasion. Ask the class to fill out the survey and to identify their age, gender, and ethnicity. Then write a one- to two-page argument in which you make generalizations about your findings including patterns of responses in certain subpopulations. Conclude the essay with speculations about causes for the survey results. Attach the survey and tabulated results to your argument.

3. Consider possible alternative interpretations of the contradictory data cited in Par. 4. In a one-page outline, identify how you would support this interpretation— that is, what kind of support, how much, in what order?

4. Francese is clearly writing about traditional-aged college students. In a two-page argument, compare Francese's characterization of these students with your own characterization of working adult students.

WHO IS A TEACHER?

CELESTE M. CONDIT

You may be used to hearing your fellow students complain about their treatment by professors, but it may surprise you to hear this writer, a college professor, complain about her treatment by students. Celeste Condit, professor of Communications at the University of Georgia, is a seasoned teacher whose experience has led her to some less than favorable generalizations about her students.

Clearly originating in the author's experience of dissonance, this argument was written for an audience of other professors. Even for this audience, however, the claims are provocative and unexpected.

Who Is a Teacher?

1   In any speaking situation (and teaching is invariably a speaking situation), all speakers arrive with and develop what classical rhetoricians called "ethos." One's ethos is one's perceived character or persona. It is who the audience thinks you are. Ethos is derived from social roles, personal appearance, voice quality, management of language, selection of reasons, and a complex

amalgam of expectations and behavioral interactions. It strongly influences both the nature of the affective relations between speaker and audience and the persuasiveness of the message that the speaker offers.

2   Those who wish to impose cutting edge theories on teaching practices generally presume a certain kind of ethos for the teacher. They presume that the teacher is powerful, probably excessively powerful, and that the teacher has high credibility with the students. They worry that the teacher's power and credibility will cow the students and take away the students' ability to find their own identity or develop their own "voice." In this version of the ivory tower, the professor is in control. Even when the professor decides to "share power" and engage in a collaborative model of teaching, it is the professor who makes that decision. Moreover, this teacher is a rational animal. The teacher rationally and thoughtfully matches theory to practice. Even when the professor decides to abdicate authority and engage in dialogue, this is only a strategy. It is still the teacher, in conversation with other theorists, who decides what rationally devised "theory" is to be presented (or embodied) in the classroom.

3   I do not live in this theoretical university. When teaching undergraduates, I often feel less like a confident, rational professor than a battered woman who cannot escape a bad marriage. For me, undergraduate teaching is not a matter of thoughtful direction of delicate student minds, but more like a desperate attempt to make a relationship work while the other party maneuvers energetically and angrily to shell me. The regnant theories of teaching thus fail me, and call me to search for some alternatives.

4   To reach for these alternatives requires that I share with you some of my experiences from the classroom. To some extent, these experiences are grounded in gendered experience. To a large extent, however, these gendered experiences raise a more general set of issues about the power of the teacher. Unfortunately, like most members of most oppressed groups, I am not good at drawing the line between those experiences—it is all too easy to see all trauma as gendered. So I will leave it to the men to say which experiences they share. Before I begin, I want to mention that the teaching experiences I describe below will appear very bleak, and that they do not constitute an accurate picture of all of my teaching experience—there are many joyful moments in teaching. However, it is important to attend to the bad side of teaching, and I have had too many of these bad experiences at the University of Georgia, a large Southern "research" university, named by *Money* magazine as one of the "best buys" in the nation.

5   When I came to teach at Georgia, I came to an entirely new set of experiences of teaching. One of the most shocking elements of that experience was the repeated nonverbal behaviors of male students. Most notably, whenever they wanted me to change their grade or give them an "excused absence," they would put their arms around my shoulders or place their hands on my knee. The first time this happened to me, in the middle of a classroom, with other students milling around, I was so stunned I could not react other than by shrugging and backing away. Later, I was to get angry and tell them not to touch me, for which I was verbally accosted. Later still, I learned to give them a quiet, unthreatening explanation about nonverbal behavior and professional gender norms. But as I watched the world around me, I discovered that this mannerism was a routine way in which white Southern males exhibit their dominance over females. Because it was so routine, there was no way (other than submission) that I could react to this behavior without being labeled a "bitch." In the worst cases, that label is overtly used; a female colleague of mine has even been chased by a male student down the hall yelling at her for assigning him a low grade. I myself have been physically threatened and have had to ask for the protection of campus police.

6   These are the clearest examples of male control in the classroom to which I can point, but they are not the only type of control that is exercised, and probably not the most important one; gender manifests itself in a variety of ways. On a regular basis, male students challenge not only my arguments, but my right to tell them what to do. It is difficult to describe the nonverbal behaviors by which these challenges are made. It is a glare, a lifted chin, a defiance. Occasionally these gestures break out into verbal form, as with the eighteen-year-old who told me (a middle-aged full professor), "you have to earn my respect." The control is also issued in other ways. Male students talk more, and they make it very difficult for me to address female students and raise issues that I perceive are more salient for female students.

7   When I walk into the classroom each quarter, I dread the new term, for I know that, each time, I am going to have to go through a battle establishing my authority; and in classrooms with a hundred students, authority is a necessity. This is not the game I came to the role of teacher to play. It is not the role that my feminist theory would have me play. But I have learned that I am forced to play it, or I cannot be a teacher here. I am now fairly good at waging this battle. I do not lose very often anymore, but I am sapped, and I flinch from teaching undergraduates so that I can avoid these battles.

8   I believe that this "battle of the sexes" that plays itself out in the South is merely an extreme form of something that goes on in most classrooms in America. To put it bluntly, students are not our pawns. They are not sheep that we decide to teach "actively" or "passively." They are highly motivated, highly skilled, and enormously self-interested people who feel themselves forced to share a classroom with us, often against their desires, and they intend to minimize the pain we cause them, and sometimes to maximize the pain they inflict on us.

9   The ethos of "student" has probably always contained more resistance to teachers than our formal theorizing has recognized. The records show that students at Georgia were throwing things at professors and spitting in classrooms and skipping classes in the nineteenth century, and of course demonstrations against the authority of the university were common and loud in the sixties even in the South. However, there are a variety of institutional factors that seem to enhance this power in our own era.

10   The first institutional support for student power is the use and character of teaching evaluations. Let me say first that I believe that students have a right to give anonymous feedback, and, except in exceptional circumstances, I tend to get high teaching evaluations numerically. However, I do this *not* by being a good teacher, but by catering to the prejudices of the students and avoiding irritating their prickly tempers. Nonetheless, I have been attacked in the "open-ended comments" on teaching evaluations, and my younger female peers are even more prone to punishment via this means. Repeatedly, women-oriented content (it needn't be "feminist") garners the ire of male students. They readily report on teaching evaluations that one is "too feminist" or is "biased." This is not in any way an objective evaluation. Even by introducing two or three speeches by women and another two or three speeches by blacks, a female teacher in a speech class can earn this sobriquet on her evaluations. "Too feminist" means simply that one expresses the view that women speakers have had special problems and were historically silenced. It does not mean that one enacts the speaking style or values and arguments of Andrea Dworkin. In other words, for these students, any equality is too much equality.

11   In my experience, male colleagues do not take this kind of abuse. If they do teach feminist content, they are not suspected of being a "biased special interest" (my geologist husband gleefully calls all dinosaurs "she" in his class, and students never complain about his feminism). If males teach conservative content instead of objective or liberal (as in

the "liberal arts") content, this is taken as "natural" or "objective" and so not commented on. But even if men do receive political attacks for their perspectives, note two things. First, the point is the same. *Students are exercising enormous power in controlling what is taught in the classroom.* Second, the uses to which these comments are put by administrators are different. Female teachers have their raises and promotions threatened by these comments. Department heads put these comments into year end evaluations as signs of failures of teaching. (I am reporting actual incidents here, not engaging in general hand wringing.) I do not believe the same happens for men. (This may be hand wringing.)

12   This problem is even greater for female graduate students. I have now had to counsel a parade of female graduate students who received bad course evaluations. In every case, I have gone to observe their teaching in the classroom, only to find them well organized, well prepared, and giving substantive lectures. In each case, the students saw the women as "biased" and "unfair." I believe they did so primarily because of the women's gender. The graduate supervisor, in one case, commented that *he* never had problems with this. Students never challenged his politics. But of course, he fit the profile of a "professor" and its gender expectations, and he sported relatively conservative politics. Judging from his reactions to my graduate students' comprehensive examination papers, I do not think that he is any less biased in the classroom, but he certainly is perceived as less biased. The minute a woman instructor walks into a Southern classroom in pants and short hair she is branded as outside the bounds of the normal—a liberal, a feminist, or a dyke. There is little she can do to dispute that automatic rejection. Male professors have to work a little harder to earn that kind of rejection.

13   So what happens to the female graduate students? I counsel them to learn to "perform objectivity" for their students, and to drop all the examples that matter to them and their female students. I teach them to lie low, hide themselves and their interests and politics until they become full professors and can tolerate the salary hits. In other words, the vocal, white, male, upper-middle-class undergraduate students get their way.

14   The misuse of teaching evaluations is, unfortunately, not the sole factor in this battering of the college teacher. There are higher administrative structures that participate in this game as well. One notes first the reward structure of the university. Our university takes great pride in the fact that it "takes teaching seriously," but this means only that it rewards those teachers who please students. Good teaching, in my view, requires a lot of hard work focused on writing and speaking exchanges that require extensive feedback (i.e., lots of time outside the classroom). This kind of good teaching, however, is in no way recognized by the institution. Moreover, many students resent both the time they have to put into such assignments and the fact that your feedback to them inevitably asks them to improve (and therefore implies that they are not perfect just as they are). Thus the university definition of good teaching as catering to the lowest common denominator among student pleasure represents a double whammy to the would-be good teacher. Your salary is imperiled and no awards are forthcoming if you do not soothe the students, and if you do teach well, this will take time away from your research responsibilities, and you will be further imperiled.

15   All these problems are further exacerbated by the fact that administrations across the country are pushing for larger and larger classes. The battles of one professor against thirty-five are magnified tenfold when it becomes one professor against the anonymous hundred. Here the culture of student resistance becomes enormously powerful. It makes it impossible to run a democratic classroom or an active one. Students, when told to think and argue, break out into the chaos of a mob, and the

instructor is chastised for "losing control of the classroom." The culture of resistance enabled in this environment has taught students to challenge every grade structure and every administrative decision of a professor as "unfair" (where fair is defined as "to my advantage").

16   Finally, there are "staff" functions, those efforts to "improve teaching," that also batter the (woman) teacher. When faced with the task of teaching classes exceeding a hundred students I diligently began to attend the "large lecture discussion group" on campus. In only a few sessions I learned my lesson. If one admits, before such a body, that one has any type of difficulty teaching, one is immediately attacked for one's bad teaching. One is "at fault." There are no systemic problems, no basic gender difficulties, no bad students. There are only bad teachers. The purpose of these groups is to share successes, which means that elderly male business professors sit around and tell everyone about their wonderful models and many successes, as they bid against each other for this year's teaching awards.

By now it should be clear that I see the   17 professor who would well and truly teach as being required to respond to a powerful student culture, and I see a variety of university structures complicit in enhancing student power over teachers. I see female instructors as particularly vulnerable to this power, but I recognize that the same forces are at work against male instructors (they simply have a few more tools to deal with the problems). To some extent, we are all Doonesbury's Professor Deadmon.

Source: Celeste M. Condit, "Theory, Practice, and the Battered (Woman) Teacher," in *Teaching What You're Not: Identity Politics in Higher Education*, Katherine J. Mayberry, ed. New York University Press, 1996, pp. 156–162.

DISCUSSION QUESTIONS

1. Into what class or classes of argument does Condit's essay fall? Identify the central claim or claims.

2. Condit's arrangement of supporting arguments is thoughtful and effective. After carefully reading the argument at least twice, prepare an outline that reflects the kind of support used and its arrangement (use Chapter 4 as a reference for the varieties of support).

3. With a group of your classmates, make a list of changes you would make in the tone, language, and style of this essay if its audience were male college students.

4. Because so much of her argument relies on personal experience, it is critical that Condit project a balanced, objective image. To what extent is she successful in portraying herself in this way?

5. Condit's argument contains much more modest generalizations than some of the other essays in this unit. But even modest generalizations must be warranted by specific examples. Discuss with your classmates the degree to which the writer's general conclusions are credible and reasonable.

SUGGESTIONS FOR WRITING (14.4)

1. Using your own experience and observations as support, write a three- to four-page argument in support or contradiction of Condit's argument about student behavior.

2. Write a letter to Professor Condit recommending, from the student's point of view, strategies she might develop to ease the difficulties she has experienced with students.

3. In Par. 14, Condit offers the following definition of "good teaching": "Good teaching, in my view, requires a lot of hard work focused on writing and speaking exchanges that require extensive feedback (i.e., lots of time outside the classroom)." Create your own extended definition of "good teaching" (approximately two to three pages).

4. Write a general portrait of college professors at your school. Assume that your audience is the upper administration (i.e., president, provost, deans) of the institution. You may limit your support to your own experience and the experiences reported by your acquaintances, but be sure the support is adequate to support the breadth of the claim(s).

A LOST MOMENT RECAPTURED

SARA RIMER

As Sara Rimer demonstrates in this article from the New York Times *(January 9, 2000), the 18–22-year-old post-adolescent is no longer the "typical" college student. Increasingly, traditional-aged students are finding themselves in classes with students closer to their parents' ages than their own. As Rimer points out, 25 percent of today's undergraduates are 30 years and older, as compared with 11 percent in 1972. The Smith College program written about here, which accepts mature women as full-time, residential students, is one of the more extraordinary approaches to what used to be called "adult education."*

1   At 43, Sandy Colvard did not simply go back to college. She did something far more daring: she quit her job as a logistician with the United States Navy, packed up a U-Haul, drove from her home in Virginia to Smith College in Massachusetts and moved into a dormitory with 84 other undergraduates.

2   Her room measures all of 9 feet by 9 feet, big enough for a bed, desk and chair. She shares a bathroom with 14 women—and, on weekends, their boyfriends. Some of the women are messy. They leave hair in the sink. This fall, a chocolate bar landed in the dryer in the laundry. Dorm food is hardly haute cuisine, and dinner is served ridiculously early, at 5:30. Cutter House, four stories of cinder blocks unadorned by a single ivy vine, is considered one of the ugliest buildings on campus. Ms. Colvard, however, is not complaining.

3   Though her parents had been opposed to her going to college and had refused to fill out financial aid forms, she enrolled at the University of Maryland anyway after high school. But she had to quit within a year: she ran out of money and found herself homeless.

4   Twenty-four years later, Smith College accepted Ms. Colvard into its Ada Comstock Scholars Program, which was begun in 1975 to allow nontraditional-age students to complete their undergraduate degrees.

5   "When I got the letter that I had been accepted, I sat on the floor of my living room and I cried," said Ms. Colvard, whose

stepfather was a sheet-metal worker and mother a bookkeeper. Neither went to college.

6   Ms. Colvard's story is not unusual, despite the advances women have made in higher education (8.4 million women versus 6.7 million men were enrolled in college in 1996, according to the Department of Education's latest statistics). Many of the "Adas," as they are known, have had families who discouraged their academic aspirations, said Eleanor Rothman, who shepherded hundreds of students through the program during her 23 years as its director. "I got a call once from a Hispanic woman in California whose 45-year-old daughter was here," Mrs. Rothman recalled. "She said, 'I don't know what you people are doing. What does she think she's going to do when she comes home with her fancy degree?'"

7   This year, there are 207 women in the program, which is named for Ada Comstock Notestein, who died in 1973 and had been a professor, dean and trustee of Smith and a president of Radcliffe College. While most Adas rent apartments off campus or commute, some prefer the cheaper option of a dorm. This fall, Cutter House is home to 14 older women.

8   In a way, the program demonstrates that it is possible to recapture a lost moment. "One of the missions of women's colleges has always been to allow women to think of themselves as individuals and not just in terms of social or familial roles," said Ellen Fitzpatrick, a historian at the University of New Hampshire in Durham, who has studied women in higher education.

9   "Young women are there to learn and to think about who they are and what they can contribute in an environment more free of gendered expectations. Older women who come back to college return with lives already shaped by these expectations, some of them low expectations. It's a situation of unusual freedom to strip away those expectations, to find out what they want to do, to explore different aspects of liberal education and to examine again their own sense of

self. It can be, and often is, an exhilarating experience."

10   Kathi Legare got married at 19 and became a foster parent at 20. She worked as a waitress and helped run the office of her husband's plumbing business. She was 37 when she entered Smith. She and her husband, Brian, had seven children at home, six of them adopted. She hoped a degree would help her find a career, and commuted two hours each day from Connecticut. She graduated in 1996, earned her master's degree from the Smith College School of Social Work, and is now a social worker.

11   "I went to Smith without a clear understanding of what anything in the world was about," Mrs. Legare said. "I knew reality from the blue-collar standpoint, but I had no idea about social policy—other than how it affected my children—about world politics, about local politics, the courts, the way others lived in general. My eyes opened wide when I got there. I was reading books I never knew existed."

12   Alyssa Mahoney, 36, a former hospice caregiver, is juggling her studies at Smith as a premed student with her responsibilities as the single parent of a 4-year-old boy. "One of the most common responses of Adas when they get into Smith is, 'They made a mistake,'" said Ms. Mahoney, who is from the Mission Hill neighborhood of Boston and, like most Adas, attended community college. "In your heart, you think, 'I'm here under false pretenses.'"

13   Smith is an intensely demanding college. On a recent night at Cutter House, the Adas and the trads, as traditional-age students are called, were mostly engaged in studying. Sandy Colvard was bent over precalculus textbooks in her room. On one wall was a poster with the Smith motto "Where Women's Minds Matter."

14   It was a half-hour before dinner, and Ms. Colvard was glad for the interruption when several young dormmates wandered by to admire her new short haircut and chat about the grueling workload. While

dressed unremarkably in blue jeans and a Smith sweatshirt, Ms. Colvard did not wear the sweatshirt quite as casually as the younger students. On her, it held particular resonance; she had waited a quarter century to go to college, and a prestigious liberal arts one, no less.

15   To the trads, the Adas seem worldly. Shannon Friedrichs, a 21-year-old senior who hopes to work in the media, has become friendly with Kimberly B. Marlowe, 42, who came to Smith from *The Seattle Times*, where she was a staff writer. "Most of us have led very cloistered lives," Ms. Friedrichs said. "To have a woman who's been in the work force, who can give you advice about how to go about negotiating the work world, has been very helpful."

16   Occasionally, Ms. Friedrichs said, the older women can be dismissive. "They'll write us off because we're only 21, and we haven't had the life experience," she said.

17   Anne C. Martindell has had plenty of life experience. At 85, she is the oldest Ada on campus. She spent a year at Smith, from 1932 to '33, but was forced by her father to withdraw. "He wanted me to get married, and he thought it was a complete waste of time for me to be here," Mrs. Martindell said. "He thought I'd scare men off by being overeducated."

18   She did get married, and raised four children. But she also became active in New Jersey Democratic politics—as a state senator —and was appointed the first female ambassador to New Zealand, under President Jimmy Carter in 1979. Now Mrs. Martindell is back to finish her degree in American studies and write her memoirs.

19   Liz Land, 72, was a 16-year-old freshman when she arrived in Northampton from Manhattan in 1943. At the end of her sophomore year, she married a chemical engineer and graduate of the Massachusetts Institute of Technology. A week later, Smith returned her deposit for the next year; married women were not considered appropriate in the campus mix. Mrs. Land, who has four grown children, five grandchildren and two step-grandchildren, spends four days a week

in Northampton and three days in Westport, Conn., with her husband, Gay.

20   While high-school seniors struggle to dredge up sufficient experiences to round out their admissions essays, midlife students have more than enough to write about. They often have trouble containing their complicated lives—husbands, children, jobs, volunteer work, setbacks, failures, illness, death—within the essay's allotted length. In hers, Mrs. Colvard wrote how, at about the time she left college, someone informed her mother and stepfather that she was a lesbian.

21   "When my stepfather broke my jaw and threatened to kill me, I had to leave quickly," she wrote in her essay. "So, at 19 years of age, for about six months, I found myself homeless. I survived. I lived in my car, sleeping during the day and driving at night to stay warm."

22   During the next 10 years, she held a number of jobs—as part of a road construction crew, a delivery person, convenience-store clerk, truck driver, warehouse worker and secretary. She also described in the essay the all-women country rock band she started, Big Night Out.

23   Like many Ada scholars, Ms. Colvard received generous financial aid to attend Smith.

24   "We've had women who have overcome child abuse," Mrs. Rothman said. "They've overcome addictions. They've overcome serious mental illness and families that were hostile to the idea of college. We've had some women who, when they graduate, there is no one from their family to watch them graduate."

25   Many of the 1,375 Ada graduates have become social workers, teachers, school administrators and lawyers. They are more likely than younger graduates to choose the helping professions, according to Mrs. Rothman. "Many have had a hard time, and they want to help someone else," she said.

26   The Adas are part of a steadily growing trend of adults returning to college. The Census Bureau reports that more than

25 percent of today's undergraduates are age 30 or older, an increase of some 11 percent since 1972; 63 percent of those students are women. Half of nontraditional students study at community colleges, half at four-year colleges, and most attend near their homes, according to the Office of Adult Learning Services for the College Board.

27   While the majority of older students are seeking credentials and skills that can help their careers, those students at Smith and other elite women's colleges, like Mount Holyoke in South Hadley, Mass., and Bryn Mawr in Pennsylvania, seem more focused on gaining the knowledge that comes with a liberal arts degree.

28   "I wish I could take at least one class in every subject," said Ms. Colvard, whose parents had pushed her to settle into a job as a legal secretary when she was in high school and earning straight A's. "I want to learn Latin and Greek. I always thought it would be so wonderful to read *The Odyssey* in Greek. I want to take a theater class, and more literature. There's nothing much I'm not interested in."

29   Ms. Colvard, who plans to major in religion with a minor in music, is still earning mostly A's. The Adas traditionally get higher grade point averages than undergraduates, and also graduate with a high rate of honors.

30   "Before, I would have been thrilled to get a B minus," said Ms. Marlowe, who is majoring in American studies, recalling the year she spent in college after high school. "Now, if I got a B minus, I'd hang myself."

31   Ms. Marlowe and other Adas—Mrs. Martindell, Mrs. Land, Roberta Jordan, 60, Cypriane Williams, 35—were sparkling recently in Daniel Horowitz's core class in American studies, an examination of methods of looking at American culture. With 27 students seated around him in a circle, Professor Horowitz was leading a discussion of the week's reading assignment, a book about African-American culture—dress, music, language—written by two Australians.

32   While younger students were hardly shy about expressing their opinions, the Adas could not contain their enthusiasm. Several commented that this sort of cultural study was relatively new. Mrs. Martindell, with her ambassador years in New Zealand, said that the Australian authors must have brought to their examination knowledge of Aborigines and their body painting. Ms. Williams questioned the legitimacy of two white men from Australia writing about African-Americans. Ms. Marlowe said the book should carry a disclaimer: Anyone reading it should have already studied slavery.

33   Adas always do the reading, turn in papers on time and have much to say. "Everyone talks about race, class, and gender, but here you've got age, said Professor Horowitz, the author of a recent biography of a 1942 Smith graduate, Betty Friedan. "It really does add depth and perspective. I think of them as not unlike the men who came back to school on the G.I. Bill after World War II. They've been in battle, and boy, the education means something. That sets the tone for the discussion."

34   The Adas, of course, have had to make major adjustments to the rigors of academic life.

35   "My first semester, I was somewhat intimidated," said Ms. Jordan, whose father made it clear to her when she was a teenager that with seven brothers, she was not going to be the one to go to college. "There was a trad who sat next to me in Gothic literature last year who was 16, and she would speak right up. I was just intimidated. But I realized as the weeks went by that I had something to contribute that the trads didn't have."

36   Ms. Jordan raised two daughters mostly by herself—she was divorced—and helped put them through college partly by working her way up from secretary to vice president at a New Hampshire real-estate firm. She remarried in 1990; her husband, a landscape painter, died three years later.

37   "I didn't even know whether to use pen and paper in class," Mrs. Land said. "I didn't know how to prepare a paper. Should it be double-spaced? Where do you put your name?"

38   Campus life also has its uncertainties.

39   Adrienne McAlpine, 41, said she found dating a challenge, given her living situation at Cutter House. "What do you say to a guy? 'How would you like to come over to . . . my dorm?'"

40   She recalled: "I was in the bathroom brushing my teeth, and all of a sudden, there was a man coming out of the stall. I thought, 'Wow, when I was their age, I would have been petrified if that happened.'"

41   Last year, Ms. Jordan and Ms. Marlowe lived on the fifth floor of the Northrup House dormitory. Ms. Marlowe's room was 7 feet by 9 feet. There was no elevator. "It's like military service," she said. "I'm proud I served, but I wasn't crazy enough to reup for another term."

42   "Half the time they're driving me crazy," Ms. Marlowe said, referring to the trads. "They have purple hair, their music is loud. But the other half I think, 'The country is in good hands.'"

43   As for the tattooing and piercing common among the trads, Mrs. Land said she barely notices that anymore. "It's a good learning experience," she said. "It's a lot like when we used to wear our sweaters backward, and my father never could understand."

44   This year, Ms. Jordan and Ms. Marlowe are sharing a spacious two-bedroom apartment just off campus. Mrs. Land and Mrs. Martindell have apartments in the same building.

45   Mrs. Land's sunny one-bedroom, filled with secondhand furniture—her husband's M.I.T. chair, her son Stephen's desk, her son David's chair. Most Thursdays, she collects her books, closes up the apartment and drives two hours home to Westport. There, she resumes her responsibilities as a wife, doing her husband's laundry and the grocery shopping and cooking. Since her husband stays in Manhattan while she is at Smith, she prepares food he can take back to the city in small containers, like chicken Parmesan, chicken salad, applesauce and hash.

46   She might go to a craft show with her daughter Ellie, or kayak with Stephen. It can be hard to find time to study.

47   Mrs. Land—who has been president of a P.T.A. and the Westport Young Women's League, served on the board of a regional mental health organization and worked with unmarried teenage mothers in Bridgeport, Conn.—made the dean's list last year. She will graduate this spring, three years after her granddaughter Elizabeth Humphries finished.

48   For Ms. Colvard, graduation is, thankfully, several years off. "If I had my druthers, I'd spend the next 10 years here," she said. "All the trads are talking about what they're going to do when they get out of here. I've been out of here. I've done out of here. I want to be in here for a while."

Source: Sara Rimer, "A Lost Moment Recaptured," *New York Times.* January 9, 2000, pp. 21–23 and 40.

DISCUSSION QUESTIONS

1. How would you classify this argument? What is the major claim (or claims) and by what kind of secondary arguments is it supported?

2. Isolate three examples of inductive reasoning used here. Using the criteria for sound induction presented in Chapter 6, evaluate the soundness of these claims and their support.

3. Much of the support for this argument consists of personally experienced facts—specifically, interviews Rimer conducted with individual Ada scholars. How does the author establish an image of credibility in her reporting of these interviews?

4. Use the World Wide Web to investigate Sara Rimer's professional credentials. What do you learn through this search about credibility?

5. Could the material in this article support an evaluative major claim? How might such a claim read?

SUGGESTIONS FOR WRITING (14.5)

1. According to the examples in this article, adults tend to be better students than 18–22 year olds. With a group of your classmates, brainstorm about possible reasons for this. What kind of evidence would you need to support these hypotheses?

2. Choose the most plausible and defensible of the hypotheses developed in Suggestion #1 as the working claim for a six- to eight-page causal argument and do the research necessary to support this claim, or a modified version of it (be careful to keep your claim limited, so you won't have to range too widely in the research stage). Hand your (probably revised) claim into your instructor with a bibliography.

3. Taking into consideration any comments made by your instructor about your claim from Suggestion #2, draft a six- to eight-page argument supporting the claim. What changes have you made to your original working claim through the drafting process?

4. After receiving input from a classmate on your draft argument, write a final version, complete with references (using the APA citation format).

STUDENTS BEHAVING BADLY

RICHARD FLACKS

Richard Flacks is a professor of sociology at the University of California, Santa Barbara. In this argument and in book-length studies, Flacks combines his interest in the students he teaches with his own expertise in the field of sociology in creating generalized profiles of "today's college student." Here, he focuses on the special attributes and successes of nontraditional students—those students who do not fit the mold of the middle-class, Caucasian, 18–22 year old. While his findings are similar to Sara Rimer's ("A Lost Moment Recaptured") and, in a way to Celeste Condit's ("Who Is a Teacher?"), the methods that lead him to his conclusions are quite different.

1 Professors have been complaining about the lack of connection between faculty and students at least since the 1980's, with growing dismay at poor lecture attendance and attention, reading assignments that students suddenly find too onerous and courses that must be "dumbed down." Such disengagement, along with the binge-drinking party culture that predominates at many universities today, seems to be part of a broader pattern— a general decline in academic, intellectual and community life on campus.

2 I began to wonder several years ago about who these disconnected students

were. My political-sociology class at the University of California, Santa Barbara, had turned in a particularly weak set of essays, yet there were a few papers of polished writing and obvious effort. Those papers had not come from the typical Santa Barbara student, who attends good schools and has high test scores and parents with advanced degrees. They had come from students with demanding and difficult personal lives—a single father of a young child who worked full time and commuted 40 miles a day, a single mother of two school-age children and an older student who had grown up in the inner city and entered college after serving time in prison.

3   In fact, the most active, responsive students in my classes fit this profile. Many were not admitted on the basis of their test scores but had managed to get here by shining in junior college or by dint of affirmative-action admissions policies.

4   In 1995, my colleague Scott Thomas and I began a study to explore whether there was a relationship between student disengagement and social background. We surveyed nearly 1,000 Santa Barbara students, about half white, a quarter Asian and 25 percent underrepresented minorities; 50 students provided diaries and were interviewed in depth.

5   At the extremes, 15 percent had family incomes below $25,000 and 15 percent above $125,000. The latter group's SAT scores averaged almost 200 points higher than those of the disadvantaged students. While their dismal scores would suggest the poor students were unprepared for the demands of college, their grade point averages were only slightly lower than those of the more privileged students: 2.80 versus 2.95.

6   The poor students reported studying 16 to 20 hours a week; students with household incomes of more than $125,000 said they studied fewer than 10 hours a week to maintain their higher grades. They also inhabited U.C.S.B.'s notorious social scene. For most of its 50-year history, the university has been labeled a party school. On any given weekend, music blares and drunken teenagers spill into the streets of the densely populated student enclave, Isla Vista.

7   About 75 percent of the high-income students reported binge drinking (five drinks in one sitting) at least once a month, and 40 percent imbibed excessively three to five times a month. At the same time, 70 percent of the poor students said they never binged. We found similar patterns whether adversity was defined by race, income or family educational levels.

8   In their spare time, the privileged students seemed to keep their distance from the intellectually challenging opportunities the campus offers. Instead, they worked out in the beautiful fitness facilities that were recently opened on campus or they watched television. A typical diary entry recounts a group of friends sitting on a couch watching sitcoms about a group of friends sitting on a couch.

9   Meanwhile, the students taking leadership roles in student government, tutoring in local high schools, attending the performance of a visiting theater troupe or a conference on the global economy were disproportionately from working-class or minority backgrounds.

10   These highly motivated, striving students call to mind earlier moments in American higher education, when conventional assumptions about class, merit and intellectual passion were challenged.

11   From the 20's through the 50's, New York's city colleges ranked among the top in the nation as producers of future Ph.D.'s; City College was reputed to have one of the most intellectually vibrant student bodies in the country. Its students were overwhelmingly from working-class backgrounds, the first in their families to go to college and often first- and second-generation immigrants. In the 20's and 30's, the college's only admission requirement was a high school average of 60 percent (a C), and after World War II, 80 percent.

12   From 1945 through 1948, with the G.I. Bill of Rights luring students who would never have contemplated college before, two million veterans thronged the city system. A

study by the Educational Testing Service in 1952 determined that veterans' college grades tended to be higher than non-veterans' when SAT scores were matched.

13 In the early 20th century, according to Nicholas Lemann's book *The Big Test: The Secret History of the American Meritocracy,* pioneers of testing thought they were creating a fairer basis for college admissions: if selection were based on test scores, working-class students could compete with graduates of prep schools, and colleges would have a solid way to measure the aptitudes of applicants.

14 But studies show that test scores are closely correlated to family income, which determines the quality of a student's schooling and a family's ability to pay for test preparation. There is also growing evidence that scores are affected by biases built into test content and by the emotional effect of the test-taking experience.

15 Conventional wisdom says that tests predict who will succeed in higher education. Accordingly, the best colleges recruit the highest scorers; to upgrade, they raise SAT requirements of the freshman class. Another prevailing assumption is that efforts to increase access and create a more diverse student body will result in admitting students who are unprepared for a college curriculum.

16 Such assumptions now pervade efforts for academic reform. Standardized testing has become the primary way to measure the achievement of individual students, schools and school systems. Teachers and administrators are driven by both sticks and carrots to set and fulfill test score targets. "Teaching to the test" is the newest look in pedagogy.

17 Preparation for college certainly entails mastery of subject matter and the discipline to study and learn; and standardized testing may be a useful tool for assessing educational outcomes. But to exploit the opportunities of higher education, students must be motivated not only to get the right test scores but also to test their values and assumptions, and to stretch their minds.

18 The students of sacrifice, the less-prepared but hungry students who have struggled to get and stay in college, see it as a precious opportunity for self-realization. They are the ones, at least at U.C.S.B., who are making the best use of what higher education has to offer, and at the same time invigorating the intellectual climate of the campus.

Source: Richard Flacks, "Students Behaving Badly," *New York Times.* January 9, 2000.

DISCUSSION QUESTIONS

1. In his first paragraph, Flacks offers a series of generalizations about faculty complaints about their students and then summarizes these complaints as "a general decline in academic, intellectual and community life on campus." Chapter 12 of this book tells you that generalizations can be effective introductory strategies. Discuss the effectiveness of Flacks's generalized introduction. Are the broad statements he makes supported elsewhere in the argument? Do they need to be? What effect does his opening paragraph have on his overall credibility?

2. Flacks's claim, which can be classified as a generalized evaluation, is explicitly stated in the last paragraph of the argument. It is supported by a series of narrower factual generalizations gleaned from a 1995 study of 1,000 Santa Barbara students. Discuss with your classmates and instructor the adequacy of the supporting evidence to the claim. You may want to review the section on "Factual Generalizations" in Chapter 7 of this book. Does Flacks's sample of 1,000 Santa Barbara students pass the three criteria

identified there? Do you need more information about his survey to answer these questions? Is the movement from factual to evaluative generalization reasonable?

3. You know that Richard Flacks is a professor of sociology at UC Santa Barbara. Is this enough information to convince you of his authority and credibility? Where would you go to learn more about him and his reputation as a sociologist?

4. In terms of argument strategy, what purposes are served by the discussions of New York's City College (Par. 11), the G.I. Bill (Par. 12), and test scores (Par. 13–15)? Would Flacks's argument have been equally effective without this material? Why or why not?

5. Presumably, Flacks is summarizing the lengthier findings of his 1995 study. How would you go about finding the full-length study? Conduct your own search and then compare it with the process followed by a few of your classmates.

SUGGESTIONS FOR WRITING (14.6)

1. Using the observations of Flacks, Condit, Rimer, Levine and Cureton, as well as your own as support, write a five- to seven-page characterization of contemporary college students. Your claim will be some form of generalization (factual, causal, evaluative, etc.); given its breadth, you will need to provide adequate qualifiers (as Flacks does in the final sentence of his argument). Provide references using the APA format. (You might want to consult the website of the National Center for Education Statistics. You may need to include two or more groups in your characterization.)

2. Select a subpopulation of the student body at your institution—for example, students in a particular major, students in a particular class, students in a particular group—and conduct a series of interviews designed to gather information about their backgrounds, their goals, or their attitudes toward their college experience. Write a three-page summary of your findings (the summary will be a factual generalization).

3. Go to the UC Santa Barbara website (Hint: begin with http://www.california .edu). Based upon the information contained there, write a three-page description of the school to an audience of prospective students.

4. In your view, what does it take to be a successful college student? Write a fully supported causal argument answering this question, being sure to provide an extended definition of the term "successful student."

5. Interview one of your favorite professors. Based upon this interview and your own observations of the professor, write a description of "a day in the life of Professor X." Your argument will rely solely upon firsthand experience (your own observations) and the information obtained from the professor, so you will need to report this information carefully, accurately, and authoritatively (see Chapter 7).

15

The Internet

INTRODUCTION

When the idea for creating an anthology of readings featuring "everyday arguments" was conceived back in 1997, the original plan was to include a section of arguments on a variety of technologies informing contemporary life. Our intention was to find exemplary arguments on the familiar and often taken-for-granted devices that quietly influence our lives—from the microchip to the mechanical pencil.

But by the time I began selecting and organizing readings, the century's technological wonder—the Internet—had become at the same time so dominant, so "everyday," and so revolutionary that we scrapped the initial set of readings in favor of the following collection of diverse arguments revolving around that single topic. In looking for arguments on technologies simultaneously commonplace and extraordinary, I realized the Internet was made to order for my purposes. Everything about it is breathtaking: the speed with which it has evolved from a novel toy to a dominating medium of human interaction; the grand scale on which those interactions are taking place; the variety of transactions conducted there— from e-commerce to matchmaking to education.

It was not that there was no Internet back in 1997. It existed, it was already powerful, and it was widely used. In 1994, then Vice President Al Gore had called for a "Global Information Infrastructure" built upon the Internet; that infrastructure is now well on its way to full development. But within the relatively short span of time since 1997 (although by Internet time, twelve years is a lifetime), what had arisen through "an accidental history" in which "the most important parts of the Net piggybacked on technologies that were created for very different purposes"[1] had

[1] Howard Rheingold. *The Virtual Community: Homesteading on the Electronic Frontier.* Reading, MA: Addison Wesley (1983), 67.

265

become a global phenomenon dominating the activities of information distribution, communication, and commerce. Overnight—or so it seemed—the Internet was everywhere and everyone was on the Internet. And they were on the Internet in multiple capacities: as users, producers, consumers, and merchants.

Given what you'll learn in other sections of this anthology about the susceptibility of all social phenomena to endless commentary, argument, and discussion, it should be no surprise to learn that the Internet and its attendant technologies and capabilities have become the occasion for what amounts to a new industry of publications. New magazines like *Wired* and *Internet World* are gaining impressive circulations; bookstore and library shelves are groaning with new tomes on the information superhighway; and, of course, the Internet itself is becoming the repository of countless commentaries on itself.

Some of this print material (both hard copy and electronic) falls within the category of "how-to" writing; but a good deal of it is interpretive, speculative, predictive, and evaluative. The Net is a controversial, complicated, and multifaceted phenomenon that has attracted the attention of countless thoughtful people who are excited, troubled, and disturbed by its endless implications. In short, as the following collection of readings demonstrates, the Net is the stuff of argument—good, bad, and indifferent. And while these readings represent only a minuscule slice of what people are writing and arguing on the subject, they do give some sense of the variety of perspectives that are out there. As with all the readings in this anthology section, you should read these arguments carefully and critically, analyzing each in terms of the principles and practices of effective argument.

DAEMON SEED

DAVID S. BENNAHUM

This argument about the accessibility of e-mail first appeared in the May 1999 issue of Wired *Magazine. Bennahum is a contributing editor to* Wired *as well as the author of a number of books on contemporary computer technology. You'll learn more about the author and the magazine in the following commentary.*

COMMENTARY

"Daemon Seed," by David S. Bennahum, appeared in the May 1999 issue of *Wired Magazine*. The essay is almost entirely a factual argument, and like all factual arguments, its success depends on the quality of the factual framework that supports it and on the reputation of the writer and the publisher.

So before analyzing the argument itself, let's do a little checking on the career and reputation of David Bennahum and on the history, advertisers, and circulation of *Wired Magazine.* As noted in Chapter 6 on Factual Arguments, these reputational issues can themselves operate as effective support for factual claims.

Given the topic of this section of the anthology, it seems appropriate to do these background checks on the Internet. It is a good guess that *Wired Magazine* has a website, and we know that it's a commercial journal, so its URL will end in ".com." Before using a Web search tool, I make a guess about the full URL and type in http://www.wired.com to see. This gets me to the website of Wired Digital, which is the company that owns *Wired Magazine.* There is a link on the home page to the magazine. If my guess had been incorrect, I could have used any of the search engines available through my university Internet server.

Here's some of what I learned about *Wired Magazine* from its website. The home page is a trove of information about the magazine, though of course the information will have a certain bias. But the list of awards is impressive. With a circulation of 425,000, *Wired* is directed at "high-tech professionals and the business savvy . . . the forward-looking, the culturally astute, and the simply curious." Translated, the typical *Wired* reader is intelligent, relatively young, professionally successful, creative, and innovative. I also take a close look at a hard copy of the magazine and learn that its advertisers are big-name, Internet-related computer and digital electronic companies like Cisco and Toshiba, and that the magazine itself is glossy and slick and full of visual distractions (much like the WWW).

According to the article itself, David Bennahum is a contributing editor to *Wired Magazine.* I don't find anything more about him on this website, so I use a search engine, which takes me first to the Amazon.com site, where I learn that David S. Bennahum has written a number of books on cybertechnology. Amazon has provided quotes from professional reviews of Bennahum's book, *Extra Life: Coming of Age in Cyberspace,* and they are all positive (Amazon *does* include negative reviews of its books, by the way). There is also a good bit of information about Bennahum himself in the review section, all of which strongly suggests that he is an intelligent, reputable, responsible writer.

The bottom line of this "context check" is that we have no reason to suspect the reliability of the facts reported in "Daemon Seed." The essay appears in a reputable and respected magazine that has won a variety of awards, and the writer is an established voice in the field with the respect of his colleagues. Of course, the context check doesn't guarantee that the argument will be absolutely free of mistakes or untruths, but it does tell us that they are unlikely.

"Daemon Seed" opens with an anecdotal introduction that begins *in medias res*—in the middle of things: "It's almost impossible to hide your e-mail from John Jessen." With its casual implication that the reader is somehow a participant in the anecdote, the first paragraph successfully engages our attention. The next four paragraphs give the necessary background on John Jessen and his business, preparing us for the central claim—a factual generalization—in Par. 5: "Jessen's thriving business is a by-product of our growing dependency on e-mail in the workplace—e-mail that is increasingly important in civil lawsuits, criminal investigations, and libel law." This movement from the specific to the general is exactly the tactic presented in the example of an anecdotal introduction presented in Chapter 11. It is a favorite tactic of journalists, who, rarely blessed with captive audiences, must capture their readers' attention at the outset.

While the first part of the claim might appear to be causal ("Jessen's thriving business is a by-product of our growing dependency on e-mail in the workplace"), one thorough reading of the entire argument discovers that its focus is not on the cause-and-effect relationship between Jessen's business and our e-mail dependency, but on the legal liabilities of e-mail (the second part of the sentence). Bennahum is betting that we will accept the assumptions about the proliferation of workplace e-mail and its causal relationship between businesses like Jessen's as self-evident (later, in Par. 19, Bennahum does offer documentation of the growth of e-mail).

The success of a factual generalization depends upon both the quality and quantity of its supporting facts. Supporting facts must be recent, reliable, concrete, and verifiable; and they must be sufficient in number to warrant the generaliza-tion. Most extended factual arguments consist of a series of secondary factual claims in support of the central claim, with each of these secondary claims sup-ported by more detailed and concrete facts. The *quantity* of supporting facts must be sufficient to warrant the generalization (see the section "Applying the Princi-ples of Induction" in Chapter 6).

We won't put every factual support to the test in this analysis, but let's look at a sampling. In Par. 6–13, Bennahum offers concrete, directly quoted verification of the inductive factual claim that e-mail has increasing legal implications. He first cites the incriminating role played by Microsoft employee e-mail in the Microsoft antitrust case, then moves beyond this narrower but still general reference to supply the text of some of the actual e-mails (Par. 9–12).

The introduction of Joan Feldman in Par. 16 provides another example in sup-port of the original generalization about the legal implications of e-mail. Here, Bennahum relies on summary rather than direct examples: "For more than 1,000 clients in six years, Feldman has turned to e-mail as an invaluable record of mis-deeds, prevarication, plots, and sometimes tragedy." Since we have Feldman's name and the name of her company, we can assume the accuracy of the summary.

A third instance of e-mail's legal implications appears in Par. 21 with the ref-erence to incriminating e-mail discovered by an ethics panel investigating the United States Olympic Committee in its attempt to bring the 2002 Winter Games to Salt Lake City.

Beginning in Par. 24, the argument turns to the legal history of e-mail. While this factual summary is not absolutely necessary to verify the central claim, it is useful in providing historical context for the claim. The background also serves to break up the marshalling of evidence for the central claim—not so much inter-rupting the train of supporting examples as offering some variation in the diet.

A similar tactic is employed in Par. 42 with the introduction of the film *You've Got Mail*. Here, Bennahum breaks away from the journalistic arrangement of facts to wax interpretive and philosophical about the film's meaning. He offers no sup-port for his interpretation—his aim here seems to be merely to lend variety and rhythm to a rather long factual argument. This strategy reveals Bennahum's awareness of his audience, of the need to keep them interested as well as to con-vince them of his argument.

I have cited three of Bennahum's factual examples in support of his original claim, but there are many more. And since some of these examples themselves summarize literally hundreds of instances, we can conclude that the generalization is sufficiently supported. With the validity of the central claim established, Bennahum moves in the last part of his argument to coverage of possible solutions to the very real risks that employee e-mail poses to businesses. He reintroduces Jessen and Feldman and their recommendation of e-mail "centralization" (Par. 50), and cites at some length the e-mail containment strategies recommended by the Electronic Messaging Association (Par. 51–55). At this point, Bennahum is reporting recommendations, not supporting them, so he needn't launch into a full-blown argument of recommendation.

Bennahum skillfully concludes his argument with an implicit reference to its title—"Daemon Seed." While the analogy is never directly made, Bennahum is suggesting similarities between e-mail and this legendary seed that manages to sprout despite all attempts to contain it. There may be solutions out there for making employee e-mail less of a risk to companies, but the "seed" will grow in spite of the best precautions. And he supports this comparison by the final reference to Microsoft. Despite the legal damage done by Microsoft e-mail, employees continue to use it as they always have—indiscriminately and impulsively; e-mail at Microsoft remains "like a hallway conversation."

DAEMON SEED

1 It's almost impossible to hide your email from John Jessen. To him, the word *delete* is an invitation. Jessen can restore email from magnetic tapes that have been overwritten several times, resuscitating information off "deleted" files. He can read email and documents from obsolete computer systems. Jessen can capture phantoms; he understands the foibles of wordprocessing programs that leave undo lists and backups of old edits in hidden parts of files and disks.

2 "You see everything," he says, "from high and low comedy to human tragedy."

3 Jessen started reading email professionally out of his basement in 1988, when he launched a career as a "computer forensics" specialist, digging through disk drives to find incriminating words. Today, he's the president and CEO of Electronic Evidence Discovery in Seattle, a 50-person company whose additional offices include New York, Los Angeles, Chicago, and Washington, DC. Working with a team of computer programmers, behavioral scientists, and retired police detectives, Jessen ferrets out emails that people believe, mistakenly, are long gone.

4 "For every email system around, we've developed a piece of software that can find each hidden element and read it," he says, "like header and routing information. Our software goes in, finds it, strips it out with any attachments, and puts it into a searchable database."

5 Jessen's thriving business is a by-product of our growing dependency on email in the workplace—email that is increasingly important in civil lawsuits, criminal investigations, and libel law. In high-stakes corporate litigation, it has become routine to demand access to the company email dating back 10 to 20 years.

6 "If you're not prepared to deal with email, it's one of the most devastating liabilities in corporate America today," Jessen says. "Which is why everyone is so afraid of it."

7 Electronic Evidence's business is booming partly because of well-publicized email gaffes at neighboring Microsoft. Over the past

year, as internal Microsoft email has gone public in federal court, the shock value of intemperate messaging has sent many companies scurrying to Jessen for advice on protecting themselves. David Boies, the Justice Department's leading attorney in the antitrust trial, has shaken corporate America with his relentless digging for Microsoft messages, evidence that's been used to argue, with alarming specificity, that Gates & Co. tried to crush Netscape by forcing vendors to use Internet Explorer as the default browser on their systems.

8   The email trove has been ugly: "The threat to cancel MacOffice 97 is certainly the strongest bargaining point we have, as doing so will do a great deal of harm to Apple immediately," a senior Microsoft executive wrote in email to Bill Gates, allegedly hoping to force Apple to incorporate Internet Explorer. An internal mail from AOL, reportedly recounting a meeting with Gates, described him as saying, "How much do we need to pay you to screw Netscape?" Then there's the oft-quoted portion of an email from Gates to other Microsoft executives: "Do we have a clear plan on what we want Apple to do to undermine Sun?"

9   Over the years, Jessen has collected plenty of big-mouth emails, ones that very quickly settled the lawsuits involved. He sends me a few samples, with identifying characteristics blotted out. They read like parodies, but they're real:

> Yes I know we shipped 100 barrels of [deleted], but on our end, steps have been taken to ensure that no record exists. Therefore it doesn't exist. If you know what I mean. Remember, you owe me a golf game next time I'm in town.

> Did you see what Dr. [deleted] did today? If that patient survives it will be a miracle.

> Hi David, please destroy the evidence on the [litigation] you and I talked about today. Thx Laura
> ***Evidence Destroyed***

> Hi Laura ack yr msg. and taken care of. Aloha David.

> [National retail chain] would like 2,500 free units of [our product] in order to conduct a test marketing study. If the study goes well, they will place an order for 100,000 units. I recommend we provide the free units for the following reasons:
> 1. 2,500 free units is cheap compared with the profit from an order for 100,000 units.
> 2. They will provide the names and addresses of the stores involved in the study so that we can drop-ship the product.
> 3. Since we will know where the product will be, I will send someone around to buy all of it, thereby ensuring a successful test.

10   What's most astonishing about these messages is, of course, their unequivocal honesty. Email is a truth serum. That's why it's scary—and why it's irresistible.

11   Every morning, I come to my computer, sit down, launch my email program. I'm an email pack rat, a compulsive saver and correspondent. I've kept every message—sent and received—since March 1994. My email folder contains 226 Mbytes of mail. That's around 14,811,136 characters, or approximately 300,000 words, lodged in more than 75,000 messages. I save them because I can

(I have an external drive connected to my PC for this sole purpose). My mail stays with me wherever I go, because endless possibility resides in the medium: An innocuous message might one day be exciting; an exciting message might become essential.

12   Joan Feldman, president of Computer Forensics in Seattle, and a colleague and competitor of Jessen's, tells me I am on the outer edge of compulsion. "Maybe 15 percent of the online population keeps as much as you do," she says.

13   From her office in Seattle, Feldman has a clear window on the collective psyche of the email nation, an exploding web of 96 million interconnected Americans. Where her forensic predecessors studies corpses, measuring time of death by the congealing of blood, Feldman studies the particularities of electromagnetic fields on digital media, gleaning the patterns that form words. "Dig deeper. Dig harder," she says with relish, describing her m.o. "When people are looking at me and lying, that gives me an extra incentive to look further." And look she has.

14   For more than 1,000 clients in six years, Feldman has turned to email as an invaluable record of misdeeds, prevarication, plots, and sometimes tragedy. In hundreds of lawsuits, Feldman has been called in to find hidden evidence, taking her to offices around the nation, people's homes, and vast warehouses where thousands of backup tapes containing millions of email messages are the digital equivalent of formaldehyde, a medium where nothing decays.

15   Meanwhile, the growth of email is relentless. In 1991, according to the Electronic Messaging Association, an industry trade group that helps corporations establish email policies, 8 million Americans had access to email. In 1997, the number grew to 67 million. Now, 96 million Americans use email. By next year, that number is expected to increase to 108 million, with office workers exchanging 25.2 billion messages daily. With nearly a third of the country sending messages to one another, hauls of electronic mail under subpoena have become

more than a nuisance; they've exposed us all to the gnawing sense that anything we write may one day be held against us. It's led companies to want immunity from the human propensity to write what we think in electronic correspondence; a 1997 survey by the Society for Human Resource Management showed that 20 percent of US businesses reported they check employee email randomly.

16   "It's like insurance—people don't want to think about it until their house burns down. In the Microsoft case, they saw their neighbor's house burn down," says Feldman, who has seen demand for her preventive services—rules and procedures for systematically retaining or deleting company mail—increase by 50 percent over the last year.

17   The cost of uncontainable email is most obvious in the workplace. Daily, more revelations of email's truth-telling power are revealed; think of *The New York Times* headline about the Salt Lake City Olympics scandal: E-MAIL TRAIL ADDS DETAILS TO U.S.O.C.'S ROLE. The story reprinted emails sent among officials of the United States Olympic Committee who were angling to bring the 2002 Winter Games to Utah. An ethics panel dug up email describing, with casual nonchalance, the way votes were collected by granting favors to visiting representatives of the International Olympic Committee. Referring to a quid pro quo in which Sudanese votes were traded for airfare, room and board, and other amenities for their athletes, one official wrote simply: "A lot of promises were made to secure votes."

18   The technology of electronic communications is moving so quickly that it has outpaced both the law and our own sense of propriety. In a weird and still unclear turn, our vast pools of saved email have mutated into personal surveillance mechanisms. Big Brother isn't some dark figure of distant, central control. He's us: the decentralized record of all our thoughts and feelings, preserved in the electronic platters of hard disks on desktops and in archives across the country.

19   For companies, email's permanence and seductive call to intimacy means facing a question: How can it be contained?

20   Federal law says that all email sent or received using a company's mail system is company property. The law, the Electronic Communications Privacy Act, dating from 1986, made perfect sense when email was still a novelty, confined mainly to large corporations with expensive, time-shared mainframes. But it makes little sense today.

21   In 1986, electronic mail moved through one of three types of networks. In the forefront were corporate email systems running off proprietary mainframes and terminals. Companies like Xerox interconnected thousands of employees within a vast local-area network. Sending an electronic message from, say, Xerox to General Motors was impossible. The systems were closed off, separate. The Internet was another type. Though it was growing rapidly in the '80s—with several hundred thousand users, interconnecting universities, government agencies, and companies involved in federally funded research—it remained explicitly noncommercial until 1991, when restrictions were lifted and Internet email started becoming a mass phenomenon. The third type was for general communications use. Systems like CompuServe, MCI Mail, and FidoNet, which linked privately run bulletin board systems, also had thousands of users.

22   In this world of separate computer networks, the ECPA allowed for an easy distinction between "open" and "closed" systems. The former provided email to paying customers; the latter gave people access to email as part of their employment. In a closed system, it is permissible for an employer, the system's owner, to treat all electronic mail like any other form of property, no different from printed letters. In an open system, messages are considered personal property, and private. But what happens when the once "closed" system of corporate email becomes connected to the "open" Internet? In a strictly legal interpretation, the answer is: Nothing changes. Any email composed at work and sent to the Internet

emanates from a closed system, and is therefore company property.

23   Tora Bikson, a researcher specializing in issues of access to electronic communications with the Rand organization, says that the ECPA approach doesn't add up anymore. "What do you mean by open or closed?" she asks. "There are no longer any closed systems, since with the Internet you can connect almost every system with any system. The real question is, How much privacy do you want to trade for connectivity?"

24   Complicating matters are services like Hotmail—which gives workers free Web-based email accounts—and the increasing use of freelancers in the workplace.

25   "Say a company has an email system, hires temporary employees, and gives them an email account because they'll be there for several months," says Jessen. "Now you have nonemployees using the system. Does that mean you've switched from being closed to open?" Jessen's solution is what he calls "the consent rule—you put consent language in employee contracts that says by using the system you agree to have your email read by the company."

26   That doesn't sound very appetizing, but employees have little recourse when it comes to keeping email private on the job. Courts have consistently upheld the idea that constitutional rights to freedom of speech end when an employee arrives at the office. "It's the employer's workplace, and he's master of his domain," explains Jeremy Gruber, an attorney with the American Civil Liberties Union in New Jersey. For the past two years, Gruber has worked on the ACLU's Workplace Rights Project. Every week, he receives six or seven calls from people upset about workplace monitoring of their email and Internet use. Typical cases involve workers exchanging personal messages disparaging the boss or their superiors. When the employer finds out, the underling can be fired.

27   The Workplace Rights Project supports legislation requiring employers to tell employees whether their electronic communications are being monitored. It's a modest ambition, yet in the current Congress no

legislation has been proposed. Gruber's ideal scenario is one where "employers would have no right to intrude on your Internet use or email without just cause," but that possibility seems remote. For now, at least, the employer's concerns are getting more attention, and employers are frantic—justifiably—that problematic emails might cause them trouble.

28 "There isn't a single case I have that does not deal with email," says Claude Stern, an attorney with Fenwick & West in Palo Alto, California. Stern specializes in representing high tech companies, including Symantec, Intuit, Electronic Arts, and Broderbund. "One hundred percent of my lawsuits now have significant amount of time focused on emails and Internet communications, like discussion boards and chat rooms." The first thing Stern does in a lawsuit is request the other side's electronic mail. "Emails tend to contain very candid, and not particularly socially sensitive, remarks. We see it time and time again, making email the Achilles' heel of every party in litigation."

29 In 1998, for instance, several players of *Ultima Online* sued Electronic Arts, claiming the game was defective. Stern succeeded in getting the case thrown out thanks partly to email he'd lassoed. "One of these people had contacted customer support by email and admitted they loved the game. They said the real problem was not with the game, but with another player who had killed them and stolen all their stuff."

30 In another case, a man filed a wrongful termination suit against one of Stern's clients, claiming he'd been unfairly fired because of his age. Stern obtained the plaintiff's computer and email, which he used to identify key witnesses and support the company's argument that the plaintiff was terminated based on performance. A California court threw out the suit.

31 Stern, trained to see email as a booby trap, sees potential trouble almost anywhere. For instance, he says companies that rely on email to communicate with customers are opening themselves up to whole new varieties of liability.

32 "One of the greatest vulnerabilities for companies is tech support and customer service," he explains. "When customers are mad, they send in very frank email. The tech-support people tend to be very candid in their replies." Thus, a company selling a defective product, while officially claiming the product works fine, might find its defense destroyed in email from an honest support employee. A canny attorney will eventually find those tech-support messages.

33 "We have a company where the tech-support person admitted the product had problems, that they knew it for six months, and wished someone would finally get around to fixing it. You would think they would want to filter that."

34 Newsrooms are especially vulnerable to the danger of frank email, since successful libel suits are based on the premise that a journalist knowingly produced a story that was false—that is, with malice going in. "With respect to newspapers, email is going to be a very key part of libel cases," says James Goodale, an attorney with Debevoise & Plimpton who has represented *The New York Times* in libel cases. To win, the plaintiff has to show the journalist's state of mind while reporting the story. "It's difficult for courts to decide what someone is thinking when they are looking at a story," says Goodale. "The chances of having someone say something out loud is very slim. The substitute for that will be email."

35 The first high-profile libel cases based on email are just now taking shape. Goodale expects email to play a key role in a suit by retired military officers against CNN. The news broadcaster aired a report on Operation Tailwind alleging that the US military used chemical weapons during the Vietnam War, a story CNN later retracted.

36 Newspapers, like other big corporations, aren't adequately prepared. "We don't really have an email policy," admits a senior executive for *The New York Times,* who requested anonymity. The *Times* policy is limited to controlling workplace atmospherics. In a recent internal memo, circulated by email to all *Times* employees, the staff was told that

sending "messages with sexual implications, or which reflect offensively on another's age, race, sex, sexual orientation, national origin or disability, among other things" would not be tolerated. Even though the paper is sued for libel a dozen times a year, the exec says, "most lawyers are not sophisticated enough to ask for email. I've never had to do a real comprehensive email search.

37   "We've just been lucky," he says. "Courts have no sympathy when you say, 'I have no way to search my system except by hand.'"

38   The subtext of *You've Got Mail,* Nora Ephron's recent movie, is that authenticity, stripped of the social conventions of everyday life, is revealed in the world of email. Somehow the medium permits the characters in the movie to share truths about themselves, to reveal parts of themselves, that in the physical world would remain hidden. When we see the characters as antagonists in physical space, we squirm, knowing that they are meant to be with each other—that in fact they are electronic soulmates. And that if they are to become lovers, they must transcend the identities they've ascribed meaning to in the real world.

39   When I emailed Ephron (who's been online since 1995) asking about her email, she wrote back, explaining, "What interests me about it—besides all the obvious things (it brings back letter-writing, et cetera)—is that it's a form of communication unlike any other and yet the second you start doing it you understand it." The conundrum of email is that it's a shortcut to self-expression, but it's also a language of its own. It invites both the mere passing of information and the sharing of secrets, longings, emotions. There's a certain permissiveness to it that real-world addresses on paper letters don't offer.

40   One thing everyone gets right away is flirting. "The main thing about email is that it's God's gift to the adulterer," a well-known writer tells me, adding, "It is a little delicate, because I am in the middle of a divorce." The author is afraid that his wife's lawyers could go after his emails. "The notion that everything you say on email can be subpoenaed ought to give pause to everybody," he says.

41   He may be relieved to know that truth hunting can be expensive. "We were involved with a case with 300 people and all their email going back four years," Jessen says. "It was a live email system with 16 backup tapes. The final email count was a couple million messages." That's relatively small, yet because the company was unprepared for electronic discovery, management had to hire 60 temps to sit at 60 workstations and pick through each message; relevant messages were forwarded to one of 20 attorneys. Those were cataloged and delivered to the opposition, under court order. "In nine months they had looked through not even a fraction of the live mail, let alone the backup tapes," Jessen says. "They had put in $700,000 at this point."

42   Jessen's solution was to copy all the mail to a central server and have an algorithm sort and search the mail for keywords. He billed the company $200,000, pushing the total cost of making email available to the plaintiff to $900,000.

43   Jessen cites another case where the two sides had a combined email volume of 1 *billion* messages. Each individual message had to be indexed and made available for either side in discovery. Putting that document count in perspective, Jessen says it dwarfs that of one of the largest litigations in US history—the Justice Department's 13-year antitrust suit against IBM—which involved 30 million documents.

44   "Think about a company with a volume of 50 million emails a month," Jessen says. "It does not take very long to hit those astronomical numbers. So the bottom line is that it costs a heck of a lot to deal with email in litigation." This fact, he asserts, can lead companies to consider a settlement. "If it costs less to settle, then you settle. A company that is not prepared is in an adverse settlement position."

45   Being prepared for electronic discovery requires a radical restructuring of the email mind-set. Email use tends to be concentrated in personal computers—and personal computers invariably become perceived as "belonging" to an employee, even though the vast majority of messages may be stored

on a central mail server. So companies under subpoena must retrieve files that contain all sorts of personal stuff that gets scooped up in the net, opening doors to potential embarrassment, or even more lawsuits, as new traces of malfeasance are discovered.

46 The solution Jessen and Feldman embrace is a move toward further centralization. They believe employees should not be allowed to save mail on workplace PCs. Messages would be saved on central servers and automatically deleted. (Jessen recommends deleting after 90 days at the most.) Rules on what mail should be saved indefinitely would be defined by specific corporate "retention policies."

47 The Electronic Messaging Association publishes a booklet, *Message Retention Toolkit*, that outlines the basics of what it considers a sound email-retention policy. At its simplest, the EMA recommends that companies identify all the different kinds of email employees write, identify how long various types of messages should be saved (say, seven years for tax-related emails, 50 years for certain SEC-related mails, et cetera), and save them in a central archive. All other mail should be deleted quickly, the recommendations say, and employees should be given a thorough briefing on the retention files. That way, when a company is sued, management can get to the relevant messages quickly and inexpensively.

48 A retention policy can't do anything about calling back sent mail once it's left the company. And erased internal email may linger for a while as ghost fragments that can be reconstructed by the likes of Feldman and Jessen. When it comes to using email in lawsuits, "deletion" has a special meaning. It doesn't mean gone forever. It means, "Not our problem anymore." Assuming that deleting mail is done as part of a long-standing set of rules—rather than in a last-minute, frantic all-night purge—retrieving deleted mail falls to the other side. The adversary has to hire the forensic specialists and convince the judge to allow a peek into the opponent's computers, something that's hard to do without just cause.

49 The EMA Toolkit was written by a committee with representatives from a who's-who of corporate America: Texaco, Boeing, Chevron, Citigroup, and Hewlett-Packard. Yet, when contacted, many of the booklets authors refused to comment. "It's just that the moment we hear the word 'litigation' we get very uncomfortable discussing email," says one of the Toolkit's writers. "It's just not a good idea."

50 One contributor to the EMA booklet, Marion Weiler, did agree to talk about it. Responsible for crafting Chevron's email-retention policy, Weiler is in the midst of a $1 million review of how this 35,000-person corporation should handle email. "We're creating a whole set of rules for how long email has to be saved," Weiler says. "There are entire classes of email we are required to keep, like taxes and contracts describing oil-field rights. Dealing with email retention goes beyond deleting things that are not needed. It goes into organizational issues and structures that may not even exist yet."

51 Weiler estimates that Chevron's new retention policy—storing mail in central archives and establishing clear rules about what mail should and should not be saved—will save the company 30 percent on related costs, including email retrieval, in future litigation, savings expected to exceed the cost of devising the policy. Harder to quantify are the savings from avoiding catastrophic litigation and multimillion-dollar settlements. "In the worst-case scenario, you find yourself in litigation that revolves around some electronic records, and because you can't find them, you lose the full judgment," Weiler says. "And if that judgment is high, it could be worse than dealing with Y2K bugs in terms of cost."

52 Helping companies decide how to centralize email is itself now a booming trade. One popular approach is server-based programs that specifically allow for high levels of email filtering and saving based on centralized, company-controlled rules. A firm called Worldtalk in Santa Clara, California, has seen sales of its email-retention software, WorldSecure, increase 524 percent from 1997 to 1998. The company expects sales to

double this year. "In the last six months demand has really exploded," says company spokesperson Dawn Harris, attributing the boom to "the Monica Lewinsky subpoena and the Bill Gates subpoena."

53   Worldtalk targets companies in the insurance, finance, health care, and legal industries. WorldSecure generates 80 percent of the company's revenues. It can be configured to force messages emanating from senior executives to be encrypted. (Encryption can prevent email impersonation and provide protection from snoopers; encrypted mail, under subpoena, must be decrypted and made available.) WorldSecure can screen outbound mail for keywords like "hot stock tip" or "insider trading." It can also screen for words the company decides are sexist or racist, halting the message's delivery. WorldSecure can also be configured to limit who in the company can use email.

54   "To reduce risk, not everyone needs access to Internet mail," Harris explains. "The people in the mail room do not need it." Worldtalk's customers include 25 of the 100 largest US law firms, as well as Nike, OppenheimerFunds, and Catholic Healthcare West, one of California's largest health care providers.

55   In January, Compaq released a product that competes with WorldSecure. Vault is designed to keep continuous email archives, seamlessly integrating new messages with old ones stored on backup media like CD-ROM. Using the AltaVista search engine, Vault lets companies search their old mail by subject, keyword, and author, and has viewing capabilities to handle attachments in formats that, inevitably, will be obsolete in a few years. Prices for Vault and WorldSecure vary, depending on the amount of mail to be stored or the number of users sending mail. Vault, for instance, charges a onetime fee of $325 for the initial gigabyte of archived mail, with prices declining as the gigabytes increase. Individual user licenses to access the stored mail cost $15 to $41, with discounts for increased usage. A hypothetical Vault customer with 10,000 employees and 6 Gbytes of mail daily might buy a license to store 20 terabytes, with the archive

accessible to all company employees. The total cost: $185,000.

56   But, Jessen argues, there is only so much these programs, with their keyword searches and retention rules, can do to keep email under control.

57   "The single biggest impediment to companies cutting down their risk is culture," Jessen explains. "More than money or anything else, it's a cultural issue."

58   Email has a tone of intimate candor that's hard to imagine appearing in a secret business memo. It's a long-noted phenomenon, going as far back as the earliest studies of how electronic mail affects us. What's really eerie is how little our behavior has changed, even though email has been around for years. We still seem stuck in the same cycle of naivete and seduction, willing ourselves to believe that because email is electronic it is also somehow impermanent, equivalent to the temporary vibrations of air molecules when we speak.

59   In 1985, Robert Anderson, an analyst at Rand, cowrote (with Norman Shapiro) a seminal study on the social effects of email, called "Towards an Ethics and Etiquette for Electronic Mail." Writing at a time when fewer than a million Americans were exchanging messages, Anderson described email's greatest "phenomenon" as its propensity to lead to "misinterpretation." He warned of "the strange permanency yet volatility of electronic messages," and issued cautionary statements that still sound applicable; "Never say anything . . . you wouldn't want appearing, and attributed to you, in tomorrow morning's front-page headline in *The New York Times*"; "Assume that any message you send is permanent"; "Avoid responding while emotional"; and the very prescient "Consider alternative media."

60   Anderson, still at Rand, is a bit dismayed at how few people followed his advice. "So much for what I write! No one pays attention." He is particularly fascinated by email's mutation into a corporate problem. "In 1985, we saw email largely as individual to individual. All of our cautions were about how an individual could be affected," he says. "I have been taken by the Microsoft case—how

much of the day-to-day business of the company is done by email. Thus the organization's history literally becomes only available through email. That puts companies in a dilemma. Either they keep the email, so it can all be discoverable and appear on the front page of the *Times* the next day, or they scrub the files so nothing can be discovered in court, at the expense of their own corporate history."

61   Scrubbing the files, of course, does not ensure that intrepid computer specialists won't discover readable fragments, or that the recipient's copy won't reemerge one day from another computer system.

62   What would Anderson do about it? His proposed solution is rather quaint. "I would have a rule that anyone who creates email with corporate interest print it out and put it in a folder," he says. The rest he would delete—at least the copies he still had access to.

63   Out of curiosity, I share Anderson's idea with a Microsoft employee who prefers to stay anonymous. "Ted" is proud to tell me that his current email volume is a modest 100 messages a day—down from 900 last year—and he laughs at Anderson's idea. Call in the dump trucks! I got a lotta mail to print out!" A Microsoft program manager, he has been at the company for several years. He remembers the days before Windows could handle email, when the entire company was networked through PCs running Xenix, a version of Unix. At every employee's desk was a diminutive terminal, generally a VT-52, with a monochrome screen and text-only interface.

64   Like most Microsoft employees, Ted now has two PCs: one for testing software, one for writing email and documents. Part of his job is serving as a human email filter, relaying messages between the programmers developing a product and the marketers selling it. Last year, he typically filtered 500 messages daily—"We are tapping into the great collective mind of everybody."

65   Maybe it should come as no surprise that he's seen no impact, internally, on the way email is handled at Microsoft because of the antitrust suit. "I haven't noticed a chilling effect," he says. "I do not pay much attention to the outcomes of what I write. When you look at the number of messages we exchange here, it's like a hallway conversation—in a medium that's stored."

66   He says controlling Microsoft email would be impossible. With thousands of "alias" lists—the equivalent of internal mailing lists—everyone's life is lived on email. When asked if he knows Microsoft's official position on what's appropriate use of email, he says, "I think it's in the handbook." Has the company ever sent around a memo about the policy? No. "It would be pretty funny if they did," he adds. "Everyone would comment on it." By email, naturally.

Source: David S. Bennahum, "Daemon Seed," *Wired Magazine*. May 1999, pp. 101–111.

DISCUSSION QUESTIONS

1. See if you can find a definition of the meaning and history of the term "daemon seed" through the Internet.

2. Did you find any other statements in this essay that might also qualify as the central claim? What are they?

3. The purpose of factual arguments is often to give useful information to an audience. In the case of "Daemon Seed," what is the information? How useful would it be to the audience inferred in the preceding commentary?

4. What kind of relationship does Bennahum seem to assume with his readers? What is your evidence for your answer?

5. Could Bennahum's argument have been made as effectively in less space? If so, what could have been eliminated? If you were Bennahum's editor, would you recommend these deletions? Why or why not?

SUGGESTIONS FOR WRITING (15.1)

1. Adapting the *persona* of a department manager in a small business, write a memorandum cautioning your employees against indiscriminate use of e-mail. Use at least three facts from the Bennahum essay to support your recommendation.

2. Some think that the very nature of e-mail—its impersonality, its speed, its ease of use—encourages impulsive and thoughtless communication. In a three-page causal argument, support or challenge this view.

3. Write an e-mail evaluating the course in which this book (*Everyday Arguments*) is assigned to another student not currently taking the course. You needn't worry about support or evidence, but do be sure your evaluation is clear and helpful.

4. Write a two- to three-page letter to your instructor evaluating the course, using the e-mail from Suggestion #3 as a starting point. In this case, be sure all your points are adequately supported and that your evaluative term is clearly defined, if necessary.

STOP ME BEFORE I SHOP AGAIN

JAMES GLEICK

This argument appeared in the May 24, 1999 issue of The New Yorker *magazine. James Gleick, a frequent contributor to* The New Yorker *and a prolific commentator on emerging technologies, writes here about the Internet phenomenon of eBay—an enormously popular virtual auction site. If you haven't ever visited that site (http://www.ebay.com), you might want to do so before you read Gleick's essay.*

1   Stuff has been lying dormant in the world's attics and garages—stuff we might call "junk," like that Early American iron steam whistle, that 1938 Luzianne coffee tin (three inches tall and apparently used as a piggy bank), that 1962 Geiger counter, with its original yellow carrying strap, and all the rest of the detritus of our productive little species. Suddenly, this stuff is on the move. It's churning through the Internet's new auction bazaars like water through Hoover Dam, maybe just destined for future attics and garages but providing considerable entertainment along the way. Economists have used the concept of velocity, *V,* to measure the turnover of the money supply. Now our flotsam and jetsam seem to be acquiring a velocity of their own. Look at eBay, the biggest of the auction sites that have sprung up on line. This place, if it is a place, is a billion-acre garage sale. Two million sixty-nine thousand seven hundred and forty-three auctions are under way right now, in real time. More than eight hundred of them involve, specifically, Collectibles–Advertising–Candy–M&M—boxes, cards, molds, planters, and an orange die-cast Reese's Pieces airplane bank ("only 5,000 were made," way back in 1992, the seller assures us). Pass them on. Then pass them on again.

2   It's not just old stuff. New retail merchandise is flowing in along with the antiques and "collectibles," and it's easy to get

hooked. I'd never bought a laser pointer—I'd never even desired a laser pointer—but I suddenly couldn't resist. I found myself at a "Featured Auction," happening before my eyes. The flashing blue icon said "COOL." This laser pointer was made of metal, not plastic, and the seller, one selwine@ix.net-com.com, stressed that it has been banned in many urban school systems. Also, it is vital in business presentations. Also, if you have pets, "they love to chase the little dot." But mainly I felt a hankering to own one of the century's essential pieces of technology, a powerful, pulsating energy machine that would surely have cost a lot more a few years ago. The ineffable Selwine called for bids of at least $13.99. He promised that in six days, at precisely 8:19:17 A.M. P.D.T., he would award a laser to each of the four hundred highest bidders. So, what to bid? Being new to this auction thing, I decided to type in a crafty "$14."

3 Then I waited. And browsed a few of the other ongoing auctions, here in the land of exclamation points. The eBay Webmasters have organized and recognized this cornucopia into "1,627 categories now!"—a giant directory, always in flux. Anyone can sign up and list an item for sale, and then everyone else can start bidding. The process is meant to be easier than the average arcade game. You choose a suitably cute or mysterious User ID ("muscles" or "buygonetrading" or "lulu32"). You type in a few sentences of description and, if you wish, put digitized photographs of the merchandise on line. (This makes the Erotica categories especially popular for browsing.) For a two-dollar fee, you can add a boldface title to your listing. For $99.95, you can buy a place in the rotating list of featured auctions. (You didn't think eBay was choosing these on the basis of merit, did you?) Sellers specify a minimum bid, and the eBay computers handle the rest. So here is a Drop Dead!!! one-of-a-kind Art Nouveau bronze chandelier with floral detail and mermaid cutouts, acquired from a Bel Air estate. I could bid on any one of the two thousand seven hundred and sixty-five Furbys for sale today. Or a car. Or a house. Or "Soul of a 15-year-old girl, somewhat depleted and abused but still in good shape! Comes in an attractive cigarette box!"

4 The people at eBay aren't scrutinizing the offerings. They stay away from shipping and handling, settling payment—that sort of thing. They're just lending us their virtual back yard for a vast, free-floating, never-ending tag sale. They estimate that they get eight million unique visitors a month. More than five hundred million dollars' worth of stuff got sold in the first quarter of this year, and the number has been almost doubling from quarter to quarter. Of course, eBay takes a piece of the action: from one and a quarter to five per cent of every deal. Pretty much the entire human experience seems to be for sale, at eBay or some other Internet bazaar. Did you need "Las Vegas Rms New Yrs Eve 1999 for 3 nights"? How about a tee time for next Sunday morning—the 8:50 at the Heritage Palms Golf Club, in Indio, California, is available. The current bid: ninety-one dollars.

5 The new, on-line retailers of books, recorded music, and computer equipment have invaded their respective business territories to much greater fanfare. And with reason: the flow of goods through the mercantile world has never before been rerouted so dramatically, so fast. The news that Amazon.com, formerly a bookstore, has bought chunks of Drugstore.com and Pets.com should make one wonder whether it was ever that much fun trudging to real-world shops to stand in line for vitamins, laxatives, condoms, or dog food. But these retail enterprises, powerful though they will grow, are not the truest harbingers of the economy of the twenty-first century. That role falls to an assortment of odd marketplaces—auction bazaars with names that drive copy editors mad. Besides eBay, there are uBid, Onsale, AuctionBuy, AuctionInc., AuctionPort, AuctionAddict.com, bid4it, Up4Sale, Bidaway, EZbid. Now Amazon, too, is starting an auction service and is buying a company called LiveBid. Just as the World Wide Web seems to

be turning every computer owner into a "content provider"—publisher, broadcaster, artist, commentator—the auction sites promise to make all of us merchants. "We have to partner with thousands of sellers, even millions of sellers, over time," says Amazon's sportive founder and C.E.O., Jeff Bezos. "Our customers in a way are now able to compete with us."

6   Call these outfits junkmongers or facilitators of electronic commerce. Either way, Wall Street is having trouble coming to grips with them. When eBay went public eight months ago, for eighteen dollars a share, *Forbes* warned investors to watch out for the hype, the outrageous ratio of price to earnings, and the scent of "a bogus bill of goods." This was fair. Three years earlier, eBay had been nothing more than a personal World Wide Web page belonging to a bearded, bespectacled software engineer named Pierre Omidyar, who had also written a free program for playing chess on line. Luckily for people who ignored *Forbes,* eBay not only has failed to collapse but has climbed tenfold. Now the financial markets assign to this little San Jose, California, company a value greater than the combined worth of K mart, United Airlines, Apple Computer, and U.S. Steel. Unlike some Internet companies, eBay actually makes a profit. Anyway, the people driving up the stock price aren't the pros; they're day traders, sitting at home computers, hopping in and out of the stock with an attention span measured in minutes. Their mental arithmetic goes, *Take all global commerce and multiply by one and a quarter to five percent.* . . . And when the market closes and they need to cool down, they point their computers to eBay and trade sports memorabilia: cards, autographed balls, Olympic hand-me-downs. Maybe someone, somewhere, will actually bid $9.99 for this "glass Snickers commemorative canister type candy jar" from the 1992 Olympic Games in Barcelona. It might have some kind of personal meaning.

7   The eBay people see their service as a counterforce to an overcommoditized world, with Gaps and Starbucks in every downtown.

They talk about using technology in the cause of individualism—as though we were a race of people defined by our fetishes. Certainly the world has never before seemed so full of tchotchkes and curios. Omidyar, who is thirty-two, started the company because his girlfriend collected Pez dispensers and needed an on-line forum for trading them. One eBay vice-president collects Monopoly games and Depression glass; another collects hand-painted toy soldiers. "People are at a certain fundamental level prewired to love collecting things," Steve Westly, the V.P. with toy soldiers, says. "They want to return to their childhood or memories that have had a special meaning." Either that or we're bid dumb squirrels who can't stop gathering nuts.

8   Executives at eBay and Amazon alike say that they are really building communities, composed of people who could never before have found so many secret fellow-obsessives on the trail of Barbie shoes or Wonder Woman figurines. They have auction cheerleaders to egg people on. "Express Yourself," urge the managers of eBay's jewelry neighborhood. "If you could have any piece of jewelry that you wanted, money (and any other types of reality) being no object, what would it be and why? Click here to share your thoughts." Hundreds of people do click there: "I think it would be great to have a piece of jewelry from everyone in the world so that you could spend every day looking at different jewelry. Now, that isn't too much to ask, is it?"

9   No, it isn't too much to ask. People who care about nothing so much as jewelry can spend every day looking at different jewelry. They can buy, and sell, and buy, and sell, or, at least, bid on, or view pictures of, or dream of, something not too far short of "jewelry from everyone in the world." The same goes for people who prefer antique microscopes, Beanie Babies, camera lenses, duck stamps, erotic photographs, or French brocade pillow covers. Or guns: eBay, reacting to criticism, has stopped providing a venue for the trading of firearms, but scores of less fastidious sites have leaped in to perform this service.

10   For human beings as shoppers, barterers, traders, collectors, and hagglers, the on-line bazaars represent a rapid retreat of the horizon. In olden days, someone in need of a Teddy bear would, at most, explore for it as far as the handful of stores near home. The consumer's reach grew with mail-order catalogues and the Yellow Pages. We have telephone ordering and FedEx. Still, the options were limited. Suddenly, the marketplace for Teddy bears is truly global—not to mention the marketplace for Furbys. Not only buyers can reach farther; so can sellers.

11   Charles Chiarchiaro, a Maine antique dealer who has been obsessed with old steam whistles since he was a boy of seven, now trades them on eBay, simultaneously buying from and selling to a larger peer group than he had ever imagined possible. He's waiting to see if eleven hundred dollars will win him the variable-tone Crane Mockingbird fire whistle being auctioned. He sees it as a "technological icon, a representation of technology and industrial art." Even when he travels to real flea markets, as he still does, he brings his P.C. along and monitors his eBay auctions through his car phone. I know how he feels. It turns out that I could have called RadioShack or the Sharper Image and got a laser pointer for anywhere from thirty-nine to ninety-nine dollars, but that's a bit pricey. And, besides, I hadn't realized I wanted one. Meanwhile, U.S. Pawn Inc., an operator of old-fashioned pawnshops, is rushing to open its own global on-line pawnshop-cum-auction service.

12   The auction process is a loopy kind of entertainment that is even more hypnotic than the Home Shopping Network. It's a participant sport. Bonnie Burton, a compulsive shopper who has started an "eBay Weirdness Mailing List," says she is reliving her childhood in daily auctions of pop-culture toys— Little Miss No Name, Spirograph, Talking View-Master. She finds herself getting frenzied over a small, waiflike plastic doll: "I started at twenty-five dollars, but ten minutes before the auction ended I got outbid over and over again by some pesky old-man collector. I wanted to e-mail him during the bidding to ask him what the hell an old man needed a little dolly for? Was he a perv? Could I make him ashamed, so he'd let me win? Yeah, right. One thing you have to remember on eBay: no one has any shame, ever!" She hung in and won the doll, for sixty dollars. In theory, bidders can avoid this kind of undignified last-minute craziness. You can tell eBay what you are "really" willing to pay, and the computers will increment your bid for you as is necessary, keeping your bottom-line number secret from the other bidders. In reality, though, people seem to prefer making their own heat-of-the-moment decisions, costly though that can be. "You start thinking of different ways to outsmart other bidders so you can get that mint-condition Super Spirograph," Burton says. "It's sick, and we're all happy to be addicts."

13   The average sale price for an item at eBay is modest—under fifty dollars. If I want to get more serious about this, maybe I should look at the on-line auctions that are underway over at Butterfield & Butterfield, the venerable San Francisco auction house, which is now trying, as they put it, to "leverage our traditional model to the Internet world." Past meets present, and past keeps on meeting present. I could bid on first editions of Nabokov's "Lolita" and Madonna's "Sex" (the latter guaranteed to be unopened). Sotheby's is preparing to open a sothebys.com auction business this summer. Christies.com hopes to start Internet auctions in September, notwithstanding its scorn for certain unnamed "recent on-line auction initiatives." ("It is not surprising," Christie's C.E.O., Christopher Davidge, declared recently, "that these initiatives have come under considerable criticism and raise concerns of potential fraud.")

14   All these houses stress their old-line virtues. They appraise and authenticate and stand behind the merchandise that passes through their doors, even if the doors are virtual. George Noceti, Butterfield's senior vice-president for Internet strategy, says that the people who really know auctions are the old, old auction firms. Those mini-auctions over

at eBay just barely qualify as auctions. "They're glorified classified ads in most cases," Noceti says. "But the matching they do is the best I've ever seen—people who want to buy with people who want to sell. Everybody can participate: you can put something on sale for a dollar, you can put something on sale for a hundred dollars." Or a thousand, or a hundred thousand. It hardly needs to be added that after a hundred and thirty-four years in the business Butterfield & Butterfield filed for an I.P.O. this year. But they have already cancelled it. Instead, eBay is buying the whole company.

15   It's worth remembering that the auction and all its variants, including formal and informal haggling, predate fixed pricing in economic history. Academics have long argued about whether auctions—dynamic, raucous, and equilibrium-seeking as they are—lead to fair prices. Why shouldn't they, as long as they are open and honest? Because we humans aren't robots. Richard H. Thaler, a University of Chicago economist, argues in his provocative book "The Winner's Curse" that people who win auctions almost automatically overpay. If you take a jar of coins to a bar, he says, and auction it off to the assembled patrons, the average bid will probably be less than its real value but the winning bid will be greater—because everybody is guessing, and some people will guess too high. And if the online world is like a bar it's very, very big and very, very crowded. Then again, not everything has a "true" value. It's easier to put a rational price on a jar of coins than on a vintage Little Miss No Name. Our obsessions and irrationalities aside, the global online auction does seem to represent a leap forward in price-setting efficiency, if only because of the sheer volume of information now sloshing around the world at high speed. There are few secrets here. Thousands of laser pointers are up for sale on eBay at any given moment: *Liquidation! Blowout! Incredible closeout!* All these mercurial transactions establish a knowledge-driven marketplace. In another eBay auction, you can buy for a dollar a list of fifty wholesale laser-pointer distributors.

So sellers like on-line auctions because 16 they get a flood of new bidders, and thus better prices for their merchandise. The bargain-crazed consumers who populate the auctions feel that they, too, are getting better prices. Can this be real? Kevin Kelly, the author of "New Rules for the New Economy: Ten Radical Strategies for a Connected World," sees a remarkable illusion of loaves-and-fishes happening here. "The miracle of both sellers' and buyers' doing better at once is really a statement about how clumsy and full of fat the usual way of buying something is," he says. "I don't think this paradoxical state where both buyer and seller gain together is sustainable in the long term. I think it is a sudden and temporary 'gift.' The techniques used in auctions will benefit ordinary retail outlets; the bidding for things and the taking of bids will become so routine that they disappear into the background, done mostly by programs."

One tiny detail: payment is still not quite 17 frictionless. The people at eBay just don't get involved, so people have to fuss with checks and money orders. Amazon.com, by contrast, is setting up a system using credit cards. At the less well-organized end of the spectrum, some people will think that E-auctions will lead to E-barter. A person with, say, a surplus of Beanie Babies and a need for outdoor furniture could find ways to trade and cut out the middleman. "Barter, sufficiently lubricated by electrons," Kelly says, "bypasses the inefficiencies in money itself." Maybe the whole mercantile economics of the past few millennia will turn out to have been a passing phase. People find themselves as addicted to selling junk as to buying it.

What's really flowing freely, of course, is 18 information. We see now that high profits all along the distribution chain from producer to consumer have depended on pockets of darkness—places where information failed to penetrate. That's why local realtors and car dealers guard their price lists so jealously. It is why retailers have been slow to sell directly on line, where they inevitably compete with their own distributors. It is why pure Information is a major eBay category:

wholesale lists; how to make money on government C.D.s; best "Secret Info Sellers Don't Want U to See!" ($9.95); and plenty of vaporous get-rich-quick schemes. In the auction bazaars of the Internet, there will always be someone with a lower price. "The world as we know it today is going to change," says George Noceti, at Butterfield's. "I don't expect us to have new-car lots anymore. Everybody knows that you can get a better price online than from a dealer." The auction model has begun to transform the business-to-business supply chain as well. Industrial procurement of coal, machine parts, plastic moldings, cosmetics ingredients, and specialty steel has all turned to real-time, interactive, on-line bidding, which saves money and cuts out middlemen.

19   Jeff Bezos, at Amazon.com, doesn't think electronic commerce means the end of stores, any more than television meant the end of cinema. He finds himself in the enviable position of being able to condescend to what we used to call reality. "The fact of the matter is, the physical world is the best medium ever," he says. "It's an amazing medium. You can do more in the physical world than you can do anywhere else. I love the physical world!" Hey, don't we all? But it's 8:19:17, and, lucky me, I have won a laser pointer. (In E-auction world, we don't buy things; we win them.)

20   Selwine@ix.netcom.com steps out from behind the curtain and reveals himself as Spencer Zink, a sometime wine salesman from Torrance, California. Only thirty-six people bid on this lot of several hundred laser pointers, so we all pay the same as the lowest winning bidder—in this case, the original $13.99. Plus shipping and handling, of course. We're inclined to trust Zink and cheerfully mail off our personal checks, because he rates well in eBay's feedback system, where users can both praise and slander our fellows, for all to see. Talk is cheap, and there are plenty of shady buyers and sellers trying out various scams on line. Consumer-fraud bureaus in many localities have been struggling to find a way of dealing with the eBay phenomenon, but it isn't easy, because, after all, they are in localities. Anyway, almost a thousand of Zink's past buyers have posted comments like "Great seller, excellent deal, superfast shipping— I'll bid again!" He started about a year ago, with some wine he happened to have on hand. Then he looked around, "did some homework," and found cheap sources of merchandise, like laser pointers, wholesale, from Taiwan. Sometimes he uses the more traditional auction style, starting off with a minimum bid as low as a dollar. He tries to double his money while undercutting the retailers by fifty percent or more. He has sold about seven thousand items in this manner, and he is just a piker.

21   So go back to eBay's home page. A genuine five-hundred-billion-dinar note from the former Yugoslavia can be yours for $9.95. (Eleven zeroes! Be a billionaire!) If you're an adult, or are willing to pretend you're an adult, you can bid on pornographic pictures from all eras, in all media, not to mention leather whips, chains, handcuffs, vinyl, and more mysterious technologies. Several dozen Internet users in the United States and Canada are vying for a few cases of military-surplus meals—chili with beans, chunky beef stew. They have a five-year shelf life, and are "a must for those preparing for Y2K." And, lo and behold, Spencer Zink has a new auction under way. It seems he has some pointers to sell.

Source: James Gleick, "Stop Me Before I Shop Again!" *The New Yorker*. May 24, 1999, pp. 42–47.

DISCUSSION QUESTIONS

1. Identify the central claim(s) and its (their) argument class(es). Compare your answers with those of three of your classmates. If there is a discrepancy, can you reconcile it through discussion among you?

2. Characterize the tone of Gleick's argument.

3. How does the tone as you've described it in Question #2 work for or against the success of the argument? (Note: you will need to identify Gleick's intended audience to answer this question.)

4. Use the World Wide Web to get information about James Gleick. Record both your route to that information and a summary of the information itself. Then compare both with the search results of two students in your class.

5. What point does Gleick seem to be making in his final two sentences?

SUGGESTIONS FOR WRITING (15.2)

1. Spend some time on the eBay site and write your own one- to two-page description (first-person factual argument) of the experience.

2. Exchange descriptions from Suggestion #1 with a classmate and see if you can detect an implicit, nonfactual claim within his/her argument. Your classmate will do the same. Then modify your initial description to an argument that clearly supports the claim your classmate has identified. (If your classmate has not found an implicit nonfactual claim, convert your original description to an evaluation of the eBay site.)

3. Choose a particular phenomenon of the Internet and write a three- to five-page interpretation of it. (Possible topics: chat rooms; automobile "lots"; singles sites; newspages; travel agents.)

4. In Par. 18, George Noceti, Senior Vice President for Internet strategy at the venerable auction house Butterfield & Butterfield, is quoted as follows: "The world as we know it today is going to change." Specifically, he is referring to changes brought about by electronic commerce. Using Noceti's prediction as your central claim, write your own prediction (causal argument) of changes likely to evolve from the explosion of buying and selling over the Internet. You may cite several instances of probable changes and support them briefly, or you may concentrate on one. (Note: if you have trouble coming up with focused examples of changes, see the section "Finding a Claim" in Chapter 3.)

5. Write an extended two-page definition of electronic commerce. The purpose of your definition is to clarify the term to readers not familiar with it.

THOUGHTS ON FACEBOOK

TRACY MITRANO

"Thoughts on Facebook" appears on the Cornell University Office of Information Technologies website. Tracy Mitrano is Director of IT Policy at Cornell University. Since 85 percent of college students use Facebook, chances are you're familiar with this "online directory that connects people through social networks."[1] If not, before reading this article, go to http://www.facebook.com.

[1]"Welcome to Facebook," http://www.facebook.com/

Introduction

1   Facebook, like much of the Internet, is a great innovation! It offers you an opportunity to interact with an extraordinarily expansive universe of new people. You can sculpt your online identity and learn more about how the Internet and its various programs work to create new relationships and communities. For the entrepreneurially minded, it might be an introduction into business as you think of how to "market" yourself. Individuals with particular social identities or hobbies, say as a Christian gay person or someone who likes a narrow range of military online games, can use it to find friends with common interests. Facebook is a cool tool.

2   People make the technology, not only in the fundamental sense of discovery and invention, but also in the sense that they make it happen and that they contour it in ways that reflect our basic humanity. Our basic humanity is for better or for worse, however. It is vulnerable to context, circumstance, and interpretation. And so it is important to remember that Facebook is malleable and creates as many obligations as it does opportunities for expression. Below are five concepts to keep in mind when you use Facebook, if not other programs of personal creativity such as chat rooms or MySpace, on the Internet.

Five Things to Think About When Using Facebook

I. Invincibility

3   A long time ago, well before the advent of Facebook, there was a student at an it-shall-go-unnamed university who used a chat room to post some facts about the size of his penis. What a surprise when he went for his first job interview, all nicely tailored in a new suit and armed with a good G.P.A. He was rejected. Fortunate for him, there was a friendly alumnus on the search committee who told him the reason. The HR person on the hiring committee had looked him up on the Internet and found the boasting posting! Frantically, the student called the university officials asking them to remove it.

Alas, they could not help him, because a commercial ISP was the domain of the posted information. In time, the student learned about the labyrinthine procedure in which he had to engage in order to have the posting removed. It never occurred to him that a relatively harmless boast could cause him so much trouble.

4   This example is just one of many. Other examples from around the country include students whose posted pictures of themselves partying bolstered the administration's case when the underage students were charged with alcohol abuse; a student who applied to be a resident advisor but was rejected because staff reviewing applications found material the student had posted on Facebook sites inappropriate; or the students reprimanded for extreme and possibly libelous statements that they made about a professor on their Facebook postings.

> **Thought:** Think about not only your marketability today as a cool guy or girl in your college social circle, but who you might want to be in five or ten years when posting an "identity" on the Internet. Remember, just because it is a new technology does not absolve you of the responsibility to use it in legal and appropriate ways—including taking into account your obligations regarding proper conduct as a citizen of the university.

II. Caching

5   In the days before Google became the dominant search engine for the Internet, ISPs that sported chat rooms had policies regarding caching information. Nowadays, Google is the main corporate entity with which one deals when it comes to cached information. To date, Google has tended to be good about removing material within a certain number of days pursuant to a proper request. But let's take a step back and see what caching means.

6   Caching, in effect, means that if you post something on Facebook, let's say for a day or two, just to be funny or to make a point,

even if you take it down or change it, it remains accessible to the rest of the world on the Internet anyway.

7   Take a moment to think about how you want to "brand" yourself on the Internet. Almost everyone is more complex of a person than a single label can explain, but for most people it takes time and effort, if not real friendship, to get to know people's complexities. Don't give people an excuse to think of you in a single-dimensional way. Instead of trying just to fit into a single group, think about yourself as an interesting person with depth of personality and character. What you put out on Facebook about yourself should be an invitation to the rest of the world to get to know you better.

8   Then consider what it takes to get something removed from Google. You must go through their policy process[1] for removing information from their caching technology. Not only is that a lot of bureaucracy, but also you should know that while Google is the dominant search engine on the Internet today, it might not be tomorrow. Moreover, other search engines operate currently on the Internet and so it is not just Google whom you might have to contact in order to remove a page.[2]

> **Thought:** Think about how much you would be willing to have to go through the bureaucracies of at least three to five search engine companies to remove cached material before you post something about yourself online.

III. CU IT Policy: Freedom: No monitoring the network for content

9   Cornell University is very proud of its policy against monitoring the network for content as a practice. That policy has put the university in good light not merely as a response to content industries that have requested that we monitor in order to enforce their intellectual property rights, but more important as a statement about its role in higher education as research university. Because Cornell is a private not for profit entity, it is not required to observe the First Amendment on free speech. No bother, because as a research institution it prizes free inquiry, and free speech is a prerequisite to that exercise. Thus, for Cornell University, free speech is a part of our values as an important center for research, teaching and outreach internationally.

10   I am sure you have all heard that with freedom comes responsibility. Facebook is an excellent example of that adage. No official at Cornell is going to monitor your posting and make suggestions to you about it, good or bad, either way. Most entering freshmen are young adults and we treat you that way. It is time for you to be away from your families and make your own decisions about who you want to be. This is not because Cornell University does not care; its officials care deeply about you and your development. It is just that we all believe you are of an age and maturity that it is time you learned about freedom and responsibility for yourself. It also means, however, that it is up to you to set your own limits and create your own identity and to be responsible for the consequences, given that you live in the real world of rules, judicial discipline, employers with their own interests as well as other people who, like it or not, will make judgments about what they see.

IV. CU IT Policy: Responsibility: No limiting authorized viewers from your site on Facebook or other Internet expressions of your identity.

11   Here is the responsibility part: no one is going to limit those people who are authorized to use the Internet or view Facebook postings from seeing what you post online. The Internet is an open, unlimited international

---

[1]Google offers a Privacy questions/Removing information from Google's search results page, as well as removal information for webmasters.
[2] You may also want to check whether the material has been stored in the Internet Archive's Wayback Machine.

community (that is why it is such an exciting innovation!). Facebook is open generally to .edu addresses and specifically to anyone with a Cornell NetID address. That authorization includes faculty and staff—as well as alumni. Such people might be members of your family, your parent's neighbors, the local bank manager where you want to get a loan for a new car, your insurance agent, an advertising industry in NYC with whom you might want a summer internship, or a law firm where you want to work your second summer of law school—anyone, worldwide! Thus, if you are applying for a job as a resident advisor there is nothing keeping the residence hall staff from looking you up. Got JAed[3] for alcohol abuse? The JA can look you up as well. Trying to get a deal on car insurance? Who knows, maybe that little Geico went to Cornell! Do you really want him seeing a photograph of you bombed out of your mind? In other words, there is nothing to keep just about anyone from looking you up. On Facebook, you have absolutely no expectation of privacy.

12 You also might want to take a moment and reflect on the physical safety of this tool when posting information about yourself. No expectation of privacy combined with the full range of humanity represented in these forums means that you may be exposing yourself to someone who may not have the same values, assumptions about appropriate behavior or may even have a mental defect or disease which could put you at risk as a victim of criminal behavior. Very likely you would not place a placard in the front of your house or dorm describing intimate details of your personal life, private sexual matters, detailed comings and goings, or anything else that someone less careful and competent than you might construe as an invitation for communication or even harassment and stalking that could prove dangerous. Use physical space as your guide. What you wouldn't put on a poster on your dorm room door you might want to think two or three times about posting on-line.

> **Thought:** With the freedom to post what you want comes the responsibility to do so in your interests not only for today, but also for who and what you want to be tomorrow. And also think of your personal safety. Cyberspace can have the effect of creating an illusion of intimacy that could prove dangerous for you in reality. Use the manners and mores of behavior in physical space both in how you present yourself and how you interpret other people online as a guide.

V. The Law

13 Most of the time when we talk about Facebook it is a very individual matter. There is yet another angle to consider: the privacy of others. "Privacy" is a complicated matter in American law. It evokes everything from the right to family planning through Fourth Amendment search and seizure to torts, or civil rights, "to be let alone" in our person.

14 Watch what you say! If you post an alleged fact about someone that proves incorrect, you may be liable for damages under either defamation or libel. Moreover, if you post photographs or information about someone that can be construed to be an "invasion of their privacy" (say while they were sleeping in their own bed), or "false light" (say suggesting that they are of one sexual persuasion when they are of another), or "misappropriation of likeness" (a claim usually reserved for celebrities, but then again we have them here at Cornell too!) then you may be liable for a tort under the broad rubric of "privacy."

> **Thought:** Think not only about what identity you create for yourself online, but also how you

---

[3]JA stands for "Judicial Administrator" at Cornell. Being "JAed" means being brought up on disciplinary charges. [author's note]

represent others. At the very least, be sure that you take their feelings into account. You would not want to find yourself as a defendant in a tort case that alleged you invaded their privacy.

Conclusion

15 Facebook, along with much of the Internet, is a great innovation that allows users to express their humanity and an opportunity to create new communities. As such it represents a forum in which one can make choices about their identity, at least insofar as one chooses to represent themselves publicly. That freedom does not suggest that one can do so with impunity, however. Because we live in a society in which expression is judged in legal, policy and even personal ways, it is important to remember the consequences of that expression no matter how ephemeral or fun in the moment it might seem to be.

This essay offers some things to contemplate when using Facebook, all of which can be summed up easily in a "Golden Rule." Don't say anything about someone else that you would not want said about yourself. And be gentle with yourself too! What might seem fun or spontaneous at 18, given caching technologies, might prove to be a liability to an ongoing sense of your identity over the longer course of history. Have fun and make productive use of these new, exciting technologies, but remember that technology does not absolve one of responsibility. Behind every device, behind every new program, behind every technology is a law, a social norm, a business practice that warrants thoughtful consideration. 16

Tracy Mitrano
Director of IT Policy and Computer Policy & Law Program, Cornell University
April, 2006
Last modified: June 23, 2006
©2006 Cornell University

Source: Cornell University's office of Technologies website

DISCUSSION QUESTIONS

1. Describe the image that Mitrano projects through her writing and trace that image to specific elements of the article. Do you find the image appropriate for the audience—college students?

2. What purpose do the "Thought" boxes serve in this argument? Think about recent papers that you have written; would a similar strategy have been useful in any of these? Why or why not?

3. Chapter 12 of this book offers the following caution about using figures of speech in your arguments: "Metaphors, similes, and analogies can illuminate and generate ideas, but they can't prove a point; they offer clarification, not evidence. . . . ultimately, all analogies break down if pursued too far; the two subjects of an analogy are, finally, *different* subjects." Apply this caution to the extended analogy developed in Par. 12 of the Cornell piece. Has the author over-used the analogy between Facebook and physical space? In a conversation with a fellow student, consider the strengths and weaknesses of this extended analogy.

4. Arguments of recommendation always involve secondary causal claims. Identify as many of the supporting causal claims as you can and discuss with a classmate how effectively these secondary claims are supported.

5. Does Mitrano acknowledge any counterarguments to her claim(s)? If yes, do they strengthen her claim? If no, what might an effective counterargument be?

SUGGESTIONS FOR WRITING (15.3)

1. Write a three- to four-page evaluation of Facebook. Use one of the following "evaluative terms" or come up with one of your own: "effective social network"; "agency of democracy"; "great tool for shy people"; "hazard to all who use it."

2. Using APA format, write a three- to four-page paper cautioning first-year college students against using online "paper mills"—services that sell papers to students. Use at least one personally-experienced or -observed fact to support the argument and at least three secondary sources. Feel free to use any of the material cited in this book to support your argument (with proper attribution, of course).

3. Write a one- to two-page interpretation of Mitrano's assertion that the people who make technology "contour it in ways that reflect our basic humanity" (Par. 2). Include two or three examples of this "contouring."

4. Construct a questionnaire that measures the amount of time per week a group of students uses Facebook. Provide options like "1–2 hours per week," "5–6 hours per week." Then create a graph that illustrates your findings. Submit both the questionnaire and the graph to your instructor.

5. There are many privileges that offer freedom while requiring responsible use— for example, a driver's license, a college education, an Internet connection, an MP3 device. Select one of these (or one of your choice), and write a causal paper about the dangers of irresponsible use.

THE REAL DIGITAL DIVIDE

ECONOMIST.COM

This essay comes from the website of Economist.com, the online version of The Economist *magazine. It appeared in the print edition on March 10, 2005 and is not attributed to any author. According to* Wikipedia, The Economist *"is a weekly news and international affairs publication. . . . It takes a strongly argued editorial stance on many issues . . . it thus practices advocacy journalism" (September 2006).*

1   It was an idea born in those far-off days of the internet bubble: the worry that as people in the rich world embraced new computing and communications technologies, people in the poor world would be left stranded on the wrong side of a "digital divide". Five years after the technology bubble burst, many ideas from the time—that "eyeballs" matter more than profits or that internet traffic was doubling every 100 days—have been sensibly shelved. But the idea of the digital divide persists. On March 14th, after years of debate, the United Nations will launch a "Digital Solidarity Fund" to finance projects

that address "the uneven distribution and use of new information and communication technologies" and "enable excluded people and countries to enter the new era of the information society". Yet the debate over the digital divide is founded on a myth— that plugging poor countries into the internet will help them to become rich rapidly.

The lure of magic

2   This is highly unlikely, because the digital divide is not a problem in itself, but a symptom of deeper, more important divides: of income, development and literacy. Fewer people in poor countries than in rich ones own computers and have access to the internet simply because they are too poor, are illiterate, or have other more pressing concerns, such as food, health care and security. So even if it were possible to wave a magic wand and cause a computer to appear in every household on earth, it would not achieve very much: a computer is not useful if you have no food or electricity and cannot read.

3   Yet such wand-waving—through the construction of specific local infrastructure projects such as rural telecentres—is just the sort of thing for which the UN's new fund is intended. How the fund will be financed and managed will be discussed at a meeting in September. One popular proposal is that technology firms operating in poor countries be encouraged to donate 1% of their profits to the fund, in return for which they will be able to display a "Digital Solidarity" logo. (Anyone worried about corrupt officials creaming off money will be heartened to hear that a system of inspections has been proposed.)

4   This sort of thing is the wrong way to go about addressing the inequality in access to digital technologies: it is treating the symptoms, rather than the underlying causes. The benefits of building rural computing centres, for example, are unclear (see the article in our Technology Quarterly in this issue). Rather than trying to close the divide for the sake of it, the more sensible goal is to determine how best to use technology to promote bottom-up development. And the answer to

that question turns out to be remarkably clear: by promoting the spread not of PCs and the internet, but of mobile phones.

5   Plenty of evidence suggests that the mobile phone is the technology with the greatest impact on development. A new paper finds that mobile phones raise long-term growth rates, that their impact is twice as big in developing nations as in developed ones, and that an extra ten phones per 100 people in a typical developing country increases GDP growth by 0.6 percentage points (see Economics focus, page 94).

6   And when it comes to mobile phones, there is no need for intervention or funding from the UN: even the world's poorest people are already rushing to embrace mobile phones, because their economic benefits are so apparent. Mobile phones do not rely on a permanent electricity supply and can be used by people who cannot read or write.

7   Phones are widely shared and rented out by the call, for example by the "telephone ladies" found in Bangladeshi villages. Farmers and fishermen use mobile phones to call several markets and work out where they can get the best price for their produce. Small businesses use them to shop around for supplies. Mobile phones are used to make cashless payments in Zambia and several other African countries. Even though the number of phones per 100 people in poor countries is much lower than in the developed world, they can have a dramatic impact: reducing transaction costs, broadening trade networks and reducing the need to travel, which is of particular value for people looking for work. Little wonder that people in poor countries spend a larger proportion of their income on telecommunications than those in rich ones.

8   The digital divide that really matters, then, is between those with access to a mobile network and those without. The good news is that the gap is closing fast. The UN has set a goal of 50% access by 2015, but a new report from the World Bank notes that 77% of the world's population already lives within range of a mobile network.

9   And yet more can be done to promote the diffusion of mobile phones. Instead of

messing around with telecentres and infra-structure projects of dubious merit, the best thing governments in the developing world can do is to liberalise their telecoms markets, doing away with lumbering state monopolies and encouraging competition. History shows that the earlier competition is introduced, the faster mobile phones start to spread. Consider the Democratic Republic of Congo and Ethiopia, for example. Both have average annual incomes of a mere $100 per person, but the number of phones per 100 people is two in the former (where there are six mobile networks), and 0.13 in the latter (where there is only one).

Let a thousand networks bloom

10 According to the World Bank, the private sector invested $230 billion in telecommu-nications infrastructure in the developing world between 1993 and 2003—and countries with well-regulated competitive markets have seen the greatest investment. Several firms, such as Orascom Telecom (see page 80) and Vodacom, specialise in providing mobile access in developing countries. Handset-makers, meanwhile, are racing to develop cheap handsets for new markets in the developing world. Rather than trying to close the digital divide through top-down IT infrastructure projects, governments in the developing world should open their telecoms markets. Then firms and customers, on their own and even in the poorest countries, will close the divide themselves.

Source: *The Economist*, March 10, 2005.

DISCUSSION QUESTIONS

1. Can you find an explicit claim statement in this argument? If so, what is it? If not, what is the implied central claim?
2. By opening with the claim that "the debate over the digital divide is founded on a myth," this article uses a variant of the supportive technique of "acknowledging the counterargument" (see Chapter 4). How effective is the strategy of opening the argument this way, as opposed to citing and arguing against the counterargument in the body of the essay?
3. Is there evidence in the argument or tone of this essay that *The Economist* is, as *Wikipedia* states, an example of "advocacy journalism"?
4. What logical fallacy or fallacies are implicit (according to the author) in the "myth that plugging poor countries into the Internet will help them to become rich rapidly." Make a list of the fallacies you find and compare the list with a classmate's.
5. Spend some time on websites like http://www.digitaldivide.org or "Falling Through the Net" (http://www.ntia.doc.gov) in order to determine whether the author's characterization of "the digital divide" at the end of Par. 1 as a "myth" is accurate.

SUGGESTIONS FOR WRITING (15.4)

1. Select an argument you have written for this course that includes a counterargument. Revise the argument so that it opens with the counterargument as this article does.
2. As this article suggests, the concept of "the digital divide" has changed over time. Using a combination of Web and print sources, research the history of the term and write a three- to four-page factual argument tracing the development of the term.

3. Consider, in a group discussion, ways in which the cell phone has a negative impact on your peers (who, presumably, have considerable access to technology). Then create an outline for an argument of effect identifying and supporting three probable effects of cell phone use for your contemporaries.

4. Develop two or three analogies that the author of this argument might have used—for example, "Giving a Macintosh powerbook to an illiterate child in Bangladesh is like. . . ." Do you think such analogies would have furthered the argument here?

5. Based upon the tone, references, and content of this argument, what can you reasonably speculate about its author? Create a list of five descriptors (e.g., political party, gender, age, education) that you think might characterize the author. For each descriptor, identify the major and minor premise of a logical syllogism supporting it. For example, if you describe the writer as holding an advanced degree, the major premise might be

> **Major premise:** "Those holding advanced degrees tend to be well-informed on a variety of topics."
> **Minor premise:** "The following references in this argument come from a variety of topics, such as _____, _____. and _____."
> **Conclusion:** "Therefore, the author probably holds/does not hold an advanced degree."

INFORMATION LITERACY:
THE WEB IS NOT AN ENCYCLOPEDIA

This page from The University of Maryland's website serves a dual purpose in this book. First, it exemplifies an argument of recommendation. Second, its content—the cautions and recommendations regarding the World Wide Web—are valuable to anyone who uses the Web as a research tool.

1   In this Information Age it is important to pay attention to issues of information literacy in traditional, media, and computing arenas. I use the term information literacy to mean the ability of people to:

- know when they need information
- find information
- evaluate information
- process information
- use information to make appropriate decisions in their lives

2   The Internet has added a new dimension to traditional information literacy issues—especially in the exploding growth of the World Wide Web. Nearly a mix between all other media, the Web democratizes information ownership, provision, and retrieval. The federal government is leading the way in publishing its vast array of information on the Web. On many campuses every student may publish a webpage.

3   The Web allows us to speak directly to the purveyors of information in every imaginable field. Few reference librarians, teachers, publishers, or other mediating forces stand between us and information on the Internet, and specifically, the Web. While this does have great advantages in expanding our information base and providing more accurate and timely information at the "click of a mouse," it also means, perhaps, more intellectual effort on the part of the information consumer to develop valuable critical

thinking skills and to evaluate the sources, quality, and quantity of that information. It also means serious attention should be paid to intellectual property and appropriate use issues.

4   The Web is **not** a huge book written by multiple authors. There is no definitive table of contents for the Web and no definitive index. To some it seems more like a giant reference collection.

5   While it is true that many fine reference materials are available on the Web, it is **not** an encyclopedia. Encyclopedias have subject experts writing refereed articles that pass through editors and style guides before publication. The Web has these same experts, and many non-experts, creating non-refereed webpages on a vast array of topics at a vast range of quality and depth. Some people consider the Web to be a digital library full of materials of varying quality and format.

6   The Web is **not** one large digital library. Libraries have trained professionals who carefully evaluate, select, organize, and index materials from credible sources.

7   The Web **IS** an electronic repository for books, data collections, encyclopedias, libraries, **AND** any disparate piece of text, graphic, or sound byte that someone chose to put on-line. And some of it is inaccurate, biased, out-of-date, shallow, and inappropriate for academic use.

8   In evaluating information on the Internet, one should consider many of the same elements that would be considered when selecting resource material in other formats, and a new one: permanence. As when judging any kind of publication, much is subjective. However, keeping the following elements in mind will assist users to identify resources of value to meet their information needs.

- Scope
- Authority and Bias
- Accuracy
- Timeliness
- Permanence
- Value Added Features
- Presentation

Information Literacy Issues: Content Scope

Evaluate the scope of the site

9   Identifying the scope of material presented is the basic breadth and depth question of **what's covered** and in **what detail.** The scope should reflect the purpose of the site and its intended audience. Evaluating scope includes reviewing topical aspects of a subject on which the site is focused and noting if there are any key omissions from the subject area.

10   Many Web sites have abstract levels of current information but no archives or information in depth. Users should look for specific information included on the website that describes the intended scope and audience. If this information is not available, and it usually is not, one can look for clues in key headings and follow links to estimate the scope of the material.

11   Things to look for:

- Is there a stated purpose of the site
- Who is the intended audience for the site
- Are there statements of scope and any limitations which may apply
- What is the site comprehensiveness

Authority and Bias

Evaluate the authority and bias of the Internet site

12   Sometimes it is very difficult to discover who actually provided the information available at a Web site. One can always check if the site is officially mandated by an organization or institution. Is it an individual's page or is it institutionally supported? Was it created by a subject area expert or by an undergraduate student doing a class project?

13   Checking the publisher of the information may be helpful. Sites in the .edu (education) or .gov (government) domains have often built important databases in specific topic areas and/or have public information and services available on-line. Sites in the .com (commercial) and .org (organization) domains are usually selling something—a product or a point of view.

14   Bias can be introduced in any Web site furthering a political or social philosophy and in any domain, however, it is most prevalent in organization Web sites (.org).

15   Email, web chats, threaded conversations, provide special cases for consideration. Electronic communication in these formats may provide valuable archives of conversations between or from experts, but does the informal nature lessen its value as an authoritative reference?

16   Things to look for:

- Who provided the information and why
- What credentials do they have
- Is the provider affiliated with a known organization
- Is a point of view being "sold" to the user
- Can you find explicit statements of authority—such as a statement of institutional support
- For "advocacy" pages see *Checklist for an Advocacy Web Page* from Widener University.

Information Literacy Issues: Accuracy

Evaluate the accuracy of the site

17   Unless you already have a base knowledge of a particular field and its experts, how do you tell if information is "good"? One way is to measure it against information on the same topic in other formats. Or you may have found a rich source of information on your chosen topic by following a link from a page you judge to contain accurate information.

18   It is helpful to know if you are at a site that is referenced by other sites for its content. It may not be a citation in a printed bibliography, but it *may* mean that someone thought well enough of it to provide a link to it. Not many institutional sites provide links to badly constructed websites with inaccurate information.

19   Things to look for:

- Is the topic appropriate for the site
- Is the source of the information clearly posted
- Who is the author/creator/publisher and what are his/her/their credentials

- Are there references from other resources on the same or related topics
- Has the site been reviewed by a professional organization or your peers

Information Literacy Issues: Timeliness

Evaluate the timeliness of the site

20   Printed media is often considered to be out of date before it reaches its audience. Some data gathered by electronic means can be displayed immediately on the Internet while other information was translated from printed materials that already fit the "out of date" description. If a government manual is on-line, it can be edited within minutes of new policy implementation, but was it?

21   With the exception of archival information, all sources should be checked for currency. Email sent to a Listserv is dated. Many websites post the date and, sometimes, the time of the last modification to the information. This may be included in a stated policy for the site or be given on individual files. Sometimes you will find relevant information in a document header or footer. This may help you determine if you revisit the site in the future for additional or newer information.

22   Things to look for:

- Posting and revision dates
- Policy statements for information maintenance
- Link maintenance—do the hyperlinks work?

Information Literacy Issues: Permanence

Evaluate the permanence of the site

23   Here today and gone tomorrow! There is no guarantee that a particular file of information will reside in the same location today that it did yesterday. On the Internet, files move from server to server, undergo on-line editing or deletion, and otherwise change their form and/or their location routinely. It is important to note the date and time that a site is visited if one plans to use the information and a citation is taken. In some cases,

the researcher may wish to download, or otherwise capture the file or the section of the file being cited, for on-site reference.

24   Things to look for:

- Explicit statements of temporary or changing location of servers or files
- Author's relationship to the server infrastructure
- Impermanent or transitory nature of the information

Information Literacy Issues: Value Added Features

Evaluate any 'Value Add' service of the site

25 What can be considered a valuable addition to a Web site? Generally, anything that helps the user find the information needed. Here are some examples: Web sites moderated by trained professionals who receive and respond to feedback; evaluation or rating of informational content or presentation on this or other sites; provision of text-only formats, search engines, navigational and help tools.

26   Things to look for:

- Evidence of a content manager with appropriate credentials
- Clear navigation bars
- Index and/or search facilities
- Descriptions of site structure beyond the table of contents (site maps)
- About or help information

- Summaries or abstracts
- Ratings and/or evaluations
- Feedback mechanisms

Information Literacy Issues: Presentation and Organization

Evaluate the presentation and organization of the site

Presentation issues include page or site **lay-**   27 **out,** clarity or intuitiveness of the site's organizational design, and help/example sections. Presentation issues may, or may not, impact the information provided. If a citation of the source means that others will visit the site, the citation should be annotated to include information about the site presentation and organization. If a site is very difficult to use, it might be better to not use it as a reference.

Things to look for: 28

- Intuitive site organization for the appropriate audience
- Clear headings and textual references
- Appropriate use of graphics and multimedia
- Help and example sections appropriately placed
- Navigational links provided back to starting points or table of content pages

Source: "Information Literacy: The Web Is Not An Enclyclopedia." http://www.inform.umd.edu/LibInfo/literacy/

DISCUSSION QUESTIONS

1. The URL for this website is http://www.inform.umd.edu/LibInfo/literacy/. Find the site and determine, based upon the cautions and recommendations contained in the article, the reliability of the source.

2. What is the purpose of the initial bulleted definition? To clarify? To introduce? To interpret? To argue? What in the rest of the article leads you to this conclusion?

3. This website is essentially a set of recommendations for getting the most out of the World Wide Web as an information resource. Working from what you learned in Chapter 10 on writing arguments of recommendation, discuss, with two or three of your classmates, the effectiveness of the recommendations.

4. Find three or four other college or university websites with similar pages on using the WWW (Hint: check your school's library link). How similar are the principles and recommendations included in these sites to those presented here?

SUGGESTIONS FOR WRITING (15.5)

1. Using three different search tools, search for information on a single topic of your or your instructor's choice. For each tool, note the usefulness of the search tips, the number of "hits" for your topic, the range of hits, the reliability of sites, and so on. Then, in a three- to four-page argument, recommend one of these tools (comparing all three) to a first-time Internet user doing research on your topic.

2. Select two of the criteria discussed in this site (i.e., Scope, Authority and Bias, Accuracy, etc.). For each, study one of the linked sites (on the Web site itself) and write a brief, bulleted evaluation of the site in terms of the criterion.

3. Write a one-page extended definition of "information," using at least three of the definitional strategies in Chapter 4.

4. Write a one-page extended definition of "knowledge," in which you contrast it with "information."

DIGITAL DIVIDE

WIKIPEDIA

This extended definition of the term "digital divide" was taken from Wikipedia *on 8 September, 2006 at 2:44 p.m.* Wikipedia *is a "free encyclopedia that anyone can edit"* (Wikipedia *main page). In all likelihood, the definition below will have been significantly revised by the time you read it here.*

1   The **digital divide** is the gap between those with regular, effective access to digital technologies and those without.

2   The digital divide is related to social inclusion and equality of opportunity. It is seen as a social/political problem and has become increasingly relevant as the industrialized nations have become more dependent on digital technologies in their democratic and economic processes. Larry Irving, a former United States Assistant Secretary of Commerce and technology adviser to the Clinton Administration, made the term digital divide popular in a series of reports in the mid 1990's. The **digital divide** results from the socio-economic differences between communities that in turn affects their access to digital information mainly but not exclusively through the Internet. Broadly speaking, the difference is not necessarily determined by the size or depth of the user group. Any digital media that different segments of society can use, can become the subject of a digital divide.

3   With regard to the Internet, ease of access is a fundamental aspect, but it is not the sole factor. Effective access also depends on ability to use ICT (Information and Communications Technologies) effectively, and on the quality of digital content that is available and can be provided. The quality of connection, auxiliary services and other factors that affect effective use are also important (Davison and Cotten, 2003). Access can be through a range of devices (MSN TV, Webphone, PDA, mobile phone) and each provides a different level of support. Once an appropriate level of access is achieved, the individual then requires an education that includes literacy and technological

skills to make effective use of it. From this point on, participation becomes possible because of the wealth of usable information that becomes available coupled with the equally important capacity to provide information to others.

4   The digital divide is often discussed in an international context because of the widely varying social and economic conditions in different countries. The concept of a digital divide has resonance with views that the revolutionary power of the Internet and the emerging utopian information society is also subject to a downside but this has to be balanced by the evidence of rapidly increased take up of the Internet in the developing world.

National Interest and Social Benefit

5   There are a variety of arguments about why closing the digital divide is important. The major arguments are as follows:

1. **Economic equality:** Some think that access to the Internet is a basic component of civil life that some developed countries aim to guarantee for their citizens. Telephone service is often considered important for the reasons of security. Health, criminal, and other types of emergencies may indeed be handled better if the person in trouble has access to a telephone. Also important seems to be the fact that much vital information for education, career, civic life, safety, etc. is increasingly provided via the Internet, especially on the Web. Even social welfare services are sometimes administered and offered electronically.

2. **Social mobility:** If computers and computer networks play an increasingly important role in continued learning and career advancement, then education should integrate technology in a meaningful way to better prepare students. Without such offerings, the existing digital divide disfavors children of lower socio-economic status, particularly in

light of research showing that schools serving these students in the USA usually utilize technology for remediation and skills drilling due to poor performance on standardized tests rather than for more imaginative and educationally demanding applications.

3. **Social equality:** As education integrates technology, societies such as in the developing world should also integrate technology to improve the girl-child life. This will reduce the gender inequalities. Access to information through Internet and other communication tools will improve her life chances and enable her to compete globally with her contemporaries even in the comfort of her rural settings.

4. **Democracy:** Use of the Internet has implications for democracy. This varies from simple abilities to search and access government information to more ambitious visions of increased public participation in elections and decision making processes. Direct participation (Athenian democracy) is sometimes referred to in this context as a model.

5. **Economic growth:** The development of information infrastructure and active use of it is inextricably linked to economic growth. Information technologies in general tend to be associated with productivity improvements even though this can be debatable in some circumstances. The exploitation of the latest technologies is widely believed to be a source of competitive advantage and the technology industries themselves provide economic benefits to the usually highly educated populations that support them. The broad goal of developing the information economy involves some form of policies addressing the digital divide in many countries with an increasingly greater portion of the domestic labor force working in information industries.

Source: *Wikipedia,* September 8, 2006.

DISCUSSION QUESTIONS

1. In an article on *Wikipedia* published in the July 31, 2006 *New Yorker,* author Stacy Schiff writes, "the entries can read as though they had been written by a seventh grader: clarity and *concision* [sic] are lacking." How well does Schiff's characterization apply to this definition?

2. Which of the strategies for extending a definition are used here? Compare your answer with a classmate's. Are there missing strategies that could have been effectively included?

3. How well does the sentence definition of the term satisfy the requirements of a formal sentence definition discussed in Chapter 4?

4. Conduct a Web search on "digital divide." Create an annotated bibliography of five useful sites, indicating why you believe they are reliable and well-informed.

5. Discuss with a small group of your classmates the pros and cons of a service like *Wikipedia*. For whom is it likely to be useful? Would you ever cite it in a formal paper for this course? Why or why not?

SUGGESTIONS FOR WRITING (15.6)

1. Look up "argument" in *Wikipedia*. With a classmate, create an addition to the definition and, after clearing it with your instructor, post it on *Wikipedia*.

2. Paragraph 3 states that "effective access" depends upon "the quality of digital content that is available and can be provided." In other words, access to inappropriate or misunderstood Internet material could have negative consequences. Discuss this idea with a few of your classmates, citing possible examples of this phenomenon. Then select one of these examples and write a three- to five-page evaluation of the situation. Your claim will read something like: "In certain situations, unlimited access to Internet material could be . . . " [fill in the blank with an evaluative term]. Remember that evaluative arguments always involve definition of the evaluative term and secondary causal arguments.

3. After perusing the *Wikipedia* cite, write a two-paragraph extended definition of "*Wikipedia*."

4. Write an account (three pages) of how the quality of your life would be different (better or worse) if you did not have Internet access. This is a broad topic, so be sure to limit it to a manageable claim. Be sure to use concrete examples to support your claim(s).

5. Develop a multiple choice questionnaire that will survey how and how often your classmates use the Internet. Give them multiple answers for each question (e.g., "1–2 hours per day," "2–4 hours per day," etc.) Create a bar graph summarizing the results of the survey.

16

Sports

INTRODUCTION

Last year on a Sunday evening in January, my daughter and I made our customary weekly trip to the nearby frozen yogurt shop for dessert. When we arrived at the little strip mall where the shop—part of a national chain—is located, we were surprised to find it closed. It took us a minute to figure out the reason, and when we did, we were both amused and appalled: it was Super Bowl Sunday. As we drove home on a normally busy suburban artery, we realized the streets were as empty as if it had been 8:00 on Christmas morning. A football game some 3,000 miles away had effectively closed down a large eastern city.

This personal anecdote demonstrates a fact that few Americans could argue: sports are a dominant force in American culture, regularly touching the lives of even those most determinedly uninterested in them. From nursery schools to nursing homes, sports saturate our lives, defining our language, our values, our image of ourselves and others, and the patterns of our days and nights.

The term "sports" is a broad one. To define it for the purposes of this reading unit, I borrow from Norbert Elias, an early sociologist of sport. According to Elias, sports are those "leisure activities demanding bodily exertion . . . with a framework of rules, including those providing for 'fairness,' for equal chances to win for all contestants."[1] Elias's definition makes no distinction regarding the participants of sports; children playing stickball in the street are engaging in sports, as are Barry Bonds and David Beckham.

[1]Norbert Elias, "An Essay on Sport and Violence." *Quest for Excitement: Sport and Leisure in the Civilizing Process.* Ed. Elias, Norbert and Eric Dunning. Oxford: Blackwell (1986), p. 151.

If you need evidence of the ubiquity of sports in our lives, consider how fully its language has been incorporated into all our vocabularies. Unruly toddlers are required by parents and caretakers to take "time-outs," with adults who have never watched a football or basketball game using the referee's hand signal; contemporary businesses are requiring all their employees to work as "teams"; more and more of us are joining life in "the fast lane"; an uncontested victory of any kind is a "slam dunk"; criminals are discouraged by a "three strikes and you're out" policy. In 10 minutes, even the least athletic-minded of you could come up with your own lengthy list of examples.

Or, if you need further proof of the high profile of sports, look at the front page of any newspaper on any day—not the sports page, but the front page. A recent Wednesday morning edition of my local paper proclaimed on the front page in underscored red letters above the paper's masthead, "Notre Dame thumps Syracuse." Well below the basketball headline was the headline "Bush lays out school reforms."

Explanations for the omnipresence of sports in modern life abound, from the economic (sports is a multibillion dollar industry) to the sociological (sports is a social microcosm) to the political (sports is an empire built upon an intricate power structure). But however you account for its dominant position, whatever perspective you view the phenomenon of modern sport from, there is no denying that it is an infinitely rich and instructive subject from which we can learn a great deal more than rules, records, wins, and losses.

We often think of sports as a mindless activity reserved for those times when we need to let down. This is equally true for the television jock who "veges out" in front of Sunday afternoon football and for the overloaded student who runs five miles at the end of a full day to clear her head. But the arguments in this unit—while varying widely in subject and argument class—share an implicit claim about another, very different appeal of sports: to a thoughtful, reasonable mind, sports are an uncommonly rich and provocative field of inquiry. The arguments you will read here cover a variety of athletic subjects from a variety of angles, but they all discover considerable meaning and resonance within the seemingly simple, "mindless" domain of sports. Like all of the topics in this readings section, sports contain as much meaning and as many implications as the eye of their observer is inclined to discover there.

LITTLE GIRLS IN PRETTY BOXES

JOAN RYAN

By the author's own admission, Joan Ryan's book Little Girls in Pretty Boxes *emerged from an experience of powerful dissonance. A reporter for the* San Francisco Examiner, *Ryan initially intended to write a single newspaper article about female gymnasts and figure skaters. But as she says, "I couldn't close my notebook." Her discovery of the painful sacrifices made by these young girls was disturbing enough to prompt her to take a year's leave from the newspaper to continue her investigation. The product of this dissonance is the much discussed book Little Girls in Pretty Boxes:* The Making and Breaking of Elite Gymnasts and Figure Skaters *(1995). The following is the full "Introduction" to the book.*

COMMENTARY

Joan Ryan's "Introduction" to her *Little Girls in Pretty Boxes* models a successful introduction to a lengthy—in this case, book-length—argument. As discussed in Chapter 11, the goals for such introductions are at least two: (1) to engage the reader, to draw him or her into reading the entire book; and (2) to clearly represent the content of the full argument. This second goal can be especially tricky, as introductory summaries can become tedious, causing the reader to skip them altogether, or worse, to put the book aside permanently. While introductions such as this one might best be classified as hybrid arguments that represent the many claims of the book, they also contain an implicit argument, which could be stated as "You will find this book compelling and clearly organized."

The opening paragraphs of Ryan's introduction skillfully engage the reader's interest and attention. The essay begins with two detailed anecdotes—brief but vivid narratives of a gymnastic and a figure skating competition. In the third paragraph, this concrete detail gives way to a more general claim about the popularity of the two sports, which includes both familiar and startling evidence. Finally, the fourth paragraph applies the "hook": "Yet while gymnastics and figure skating are among the most-watched sports in the country, the least is known about the lives of their athletes." Few readers who have read this far are likely to put the book down; they have, in effect, been drawn into a mystery and will stay the course until they know more.

Having engaged her reader's interest and attention, Ryan now moves to her second introductory task: previewing the content of the book. Paragraph 7 serves as a summary (albeit a rather sensationalistic one) of all the worst discoveries Ryan encountered in her research on elite gymnasts and figure skaters: broken bodies, sexual abuse, anorexia, self-mutilation, parental ambition, and sadistic coaches. These discoveries will become the major claims of the book; each will have a chapter dedicated to it. (The subtitles of the chapters are as follows: (1) Injuries; (2) Eating Disorders; (3) Image; (4) Pressure; (5) Parents; (6) Politics and Money; and (7) Coaches.)

The strategy of the rest of the introduction is to pick up each one of these subjects and provide more, but still tantalizing, detail about them. While the introduction reads as a self-contained argument in its own right, it is also successful in beckoning the reader to the succeeding chapters that will provide still further details about the plight of these young female athletes.

While it may seem unlikely that you will ever be writing a complete book requiring an introduction of such length and completeness, many undergraduate college students end up writing senior and/or honors theses in their majors. These theses can be as many as 50 to 75 pages in length, and will require thorough and strategic introductions.

LITTLE GIRLS IN PRETTY BOXES

1   The little girls marched into the Atlanta arena in single file, heads high, shoulders back, bare toes pointed. Under hair ribbons and rouged cheeks, their balletic bodies flowed past bleachers where expectant fathers craned forward with videocameras. Small and pretty in their shimmery leotards, the girls looked like trinkets from a Tiffany box. They lined up facing the crowd, and when the announcer summoned the winners of the Peachtree Classic, the gymnasts stepped forward and bowed their heads as soberly as Nobel laureates to receive their medals. Mothers with scoresheets tucked under their arms clapped until their hands hurt, shooting hopeful glances at the ESPN cameras roving among the girls. Along velvet ropes strung across the base of the bleachers, awestruck seven- and eight-year-olds stretched toward the winning gymnasts clutching programs and gym bags for them to sign.

2   On the opposite coast, at a skating rink in Redwood City, California, one fifteen-year-old skater—in a ponytail, braces and baby-blue sequins—stood at the edge of the rink, eyes wide, listening to her coach's last-minute instructions as her parents held hands in the bleachers, packed solid for the Pacific Coast Sectional Championships. She glided to the center of the ice. Then, as her music began, she spun like a jewel-box ballerina, executing the intricate choreography of leaps and footwork she had practiced nearly every day for as long as she could remember. On her ¼-inch skate blades rode her hopes of qualifying for the U.S. Figure Skating Championships, moving her one step closer to the Winter Olympic Games.

3   In gyms and rinks across the country, the air is thick with the scent of the Olympics. And the parents, coaches and young athletes chase it like hounds, impatient for the rewards of the sports that captivate American audiences as no others do. Gymnasts and figure skaters hold a unique and cherished place among American athletes. Gymnasts are the darlings of the Summer Games, figure skaters the ice princesses of the Winter Games. Every four years they keep us glued to our televisions for two weeks with their grace, agility, youth and beauty. They land on magazine covers, Wheaties boxes, the "Today" show. Television ratings for Olympic gymnastics and figure skating events rank among the highest for any sport on television. Helped by the Tonya Harding–Nancy Kerrigan saga, the women's technical program at the 1994 Winter Games drew the fourth-highest rating of any show in the history of television, placing it up there with the final episode of "M*A*S*H." But even at the controversy-free 1992 Winter Games, women's figure skating attracted a larger television audience than either the final game of the 1992 World Series or the 1992 National Collegiate Athletic Association basketball championship game between Michigan and Duke. Americans are so enchanted by gymnasts and figure skaters that in a 1991 survey they chose gymnast Mary Lou Retton and skater Dorothy Hamill—both long retired—as their favorite athletes, beating out the likes of Chris Evert, Michael Jordan and Magic Johnson.

4   Yet while gymnastics and figure skating are among the most-watched sports in the country, the least is known about the lives of their athletes (with the exceptions, of course, of Harding and Kerrigan). We watched thirteen-year-old Michelle Kwan, an eighth grader, land six triple jumps to finish second at the 1994 U.S. Figure Skating championships. We see sixteen-year-old Shannon Miller soar above the balance beam as if it were a trampoline to win a silver medal at the 1992 Olympics. But we know little about how they achieve so much at such a young age or what becomes of them when they leave their sport.

5 Unlike women's tennis, a sport in which teenage girls rise to the highest echelon year after year in highly televised championships, gymnastics and figure skating flutter across our screens as ephemerally as butterflies. We know about tennis burnout, about Tracy Austin, Andrea Jaeger, Mary Pierce and, more recently, about Jennifer Capriati, who turned pro with $5 million in endorsement contracts at age thirteen and ended up four years later in a Florida motel room, blank-eyed and disheveled, sharing drugs with runaways. But we hear precious little about the young female gymnasts and figure skaters who perform magnificent feats of physical strength and agility, and even less about their casualties. How do the extraordinary demands of their training shape these young girls? What price do their bodies and psyches pay?

6 I set out to answer some of these questions during three months of research for an article that ran in the *San Francisco Examiner*, but when I finished I couldn't close my notebook. I took a year's leave to continue my research, focusing this time on the girls who never made it, not just on the champions.

7 What I found was a story about legal, even celebrated, child abuse. In the dark troughs along the road to the Olympics lay the bodies of the girls who stumbled on the way, broken by the work, pressure and humiliation. I found a girl whose father left the family when she quit gymnastics at age thirteen, who scraped her arms and legs with razors to dull her emotional pain and who needed a two-hour pass from a psychiatric hospital to attend her high school graduation. Girls who broke their necks and backs. One who so desperately sought the perfect, weightless gymnastics body that she starved herself to death. Others—many—who became so obsessive about controlling their weight that they lost control of themselves instead, falling into the potentially fatal cycle of bingeing on food, then purging by vomiting or taking laxatives. One who was sexually abused by her coach and one who was sodomized for four years by the father of a teammate. I found a girl who felt such shame at not making the Olympic team that she slit her wrists. A skater who underwent plastic surgery when a judge said her nose was distracting. A father who handed custody of his daughter over to her coach so she could keep skating. A coach who fed his gymnasts so little that federation officials had to smuggle food into their hotel rooms. A mother who hid her child's chicken pox with makeup so she could compete. Coaches who motivated their athletes by calling them imbeciles, idiots, pigs, cows.

8 I am not suggesting that gymnastics and figure skating in and of themselves are destructive. On the contrary, both sports are potentially wonderful and enriching, providing an arena of competition in which the average child can develop a sense of mastery, self-esteem and healthy athleticism. But this book isn't about recreational sports or the average child. It's about the elite child athlete and the American obsession with winning that has produced a training environment wherein results are bought at any cost, no matter how devastating. It's about how our cultural fixation on beauty and weight and youth has shaped both sports and driven the athletes into a sphere beyond the quest for physical performance.

9 The well-known story of Tonya Harding and Nancy Kerrigan did not happen in a vacuum; it symbolizes perfectly the stakes now involved in elite competition—itself a reflection of our national character. We created Tonya and Nancy not only by our hunger for winning but by our criterion for winning, an exaggeration of the code that applies to ambitious young women everywhere: Talent counts, but so do beauty, class, weight, clothes and politics. The anachronistic lack of ambivalence about femininity in both sports is part of their attraction, hearkening back to a simpler time when girls were girls, when women were girls for that matter: coquettish, malleable, eager to please. In figure skating especially, we want our athletes thin, graceful, deferential and cover-girl pretty. We want eyeliner, lipstick and

hair ribbons. Makeup artists are fixtures backstage at figure skating competitions, primping and polishing. In figure skating, costumes can actually affect a score. They are so important that skaters spend $1500 and up on one dress—more than they spend on their skates. Nancy Kerrigan's dresses by designer Vera Wang cost upward of $5000 each.

10   Indeed, the costumes fueled the national fairy tale of Tonya and Nancy. Nancy wore virginal white. She was the perfect heroine, a good girl with perfect white teeth, a 24-inch waist and a smile that suggested both pluck and vulnerability. She remained safely within skating's pristine circle of grace and femininity. Tonya, on the other hand, crossed all the lines. She wore bordello red-and-gold. She was the perfect villainess, a bad girl with truckstop manners, a racy past and chunky thighs. When she became convinced Nancy's grace would always win out over her own explosive strength, Tonya crossed the final line, helping to eliminate Nancy from competition. The media frenzy tapped into our own inner wranglings about the good girl/bad girl paradox, about how women should behave, about how they should look and what they should say. The story touched a cultural nerve about women crossing societal boundaries—of power, achievement, violence, taste, appearance— and being ensnared by them. In the end, both skaters were trapped, Tonya by her ambition and Nancy by the good-girl image she created for the ice—an image she couldn't live up to. The public turned on Nancy when foolish comments and graceless interviews made it clear she wasn't Snow White after all.

11   Both sports embody the contradiction of modern womanhood. Society has allowed women to aspire higher, but to do so a woman must often reject that which makes her female, including motherhood. Similarly, gymnastics and figure skating remove the limits of a girl's body, teaching it to soar beyond what seems possible. Yet they also imprison it, binding it like the tiny Victorian waist or the Chinese woman's foot. The girls aren't allowed passage into adulthood. To survive in the sports, they beat back puberty, desperate to stay small and thin, refusing to let their bodies grow up. In this way the sports pervert the very femininity they hold so dear. The physical skills have become so demanding that only a body shaped like a missile—in other words, a body shaped like a boy's—can excel. Breasts and hips slow the spins, lower the leaps and disrupt the clean, lean body lines that judges reward. "Woman's gymnastics" and "ladies' figure skating" are misnomers today. Once the athletes become women, their elite careers wither.

12   In the meantime, their childhoods are gone. But they trade more than their childhoods for a shot at glory. They risk serious physical and psychological problems that can linger long after the public has turned its attention to the next phenom in pigtails. The intensive training and pressure heaped on by coaches, parents and federation officials—the very people who should be protecting the children—often result in eating disorders, weakened bones, stunted growth, debilitating injuries and damaged psyches. In the last six years two U.S. Olympic hopefuls have died as a result of their participation in elite gymnastics.

13   Because they excel at such a young age, girls in these sports are unlike other elite athletes. They are world champions before they can drive. They are the Michael Jordans and Joe Montanas of their sports before they learn algebra. Unlike male athletes their age, who are playing quarterback in high school or running track for the local club, these girls are competing on a worldwide stage. If an elite gymnast or figure skater fails, she fails globally. She sees her mistake replayed in slow motion on TV and captured in bold headlines in the newspaper. Adult reporters crowd around, asking what she has to say to a country that had hung its hopes on her thin shoulders. Tiffany Chin was seventeen when she entered the 1985 U.S. Figure Skating Championships as the favorite. She was asked at the time how she would feel if she didn't win. She paused, as if trying not to consider the possibility.

"Devastated," she said quietly. "I don't know. I'd probably die."

14 Chin recalled recently that when she did win, "I didn't feel happiness. I felt relief. Which was disappointing." Three months before the 1988 Olympics, Chin retired when her legs began to break down. Some, however, say she left because she could no longer tolerate the pressure and unrelenting drive of her stern mother. "I feel I'm lucky to have gotten through it," she said of skating. "I don't think many people are that lucky. There's a tremendous strain on people who don't make it. The money, the sacrifices, the time. I know people emotionally damaged by it. I've seen nervous breakdowns, psychological imbalances."

15 An elite gymnast or figure skater knows she takes more than her own ambitions into a competition. Her parents have invested tens of thousands of dollars in her training, sometimes hundreds of thousands. Her coach's reputation rides on her performance. And she knows she might have only one shot. By the next Olympics she might be too old. By the next *year* she might be too old. Girls in these sports are under pressure not only to win but to win quickly. They're running against a clock that eventually marks the lives of all women, warning them they'd better hurry up and get married and have children before it's too late. These girls hear the clock early. They're racing against puberty.

16 Boys, on the other hand, welcome the changes that puberty brings. They reach their athletic peak after puberty when their bodies grow and their muscles strengthen. In recent years Michael Chang and Boris Becker won the French Open and Wimbledon tennis titles, respectively, before age eighteen, but in virtually every male sport the top athletes are men, not boys. Male gymnastics and figure skating champions are usually in their early to mid twenties; female champions are usually fourteen to seventeen years old in gymnastics and sixteen to early twenties in figure skating.

17 In staving off puberty to maintain the "ideal" body shape, girls risk their health in ways their male counterparts never do. They starve themselves, for one, often in response to their coaches' belittling insults about their bodies. Starving shuts down the menstrual cycle—the starving body knows it cannot support a fetus—and thus blocks the onset of puberty. It's a dangerous strategy to save a career. If a girl isn't menstruating, she isn't producing estrogen. Without estrogen, her bones weaken. She risks stunting her growth. She risks premature osteoporosis. She risks fractures in all bones, including her vertebrae, and she risks curvature of the spine. In several studies over the last decade, young female athletes who didn't menstruate were found to have the bone densities of postmenopausal women in their fifties, sixties and seventies. Most elite gymnasts don't begin to menstruate until they retire. Kathy Johnson, a medalist in the 1984 Olympics, didn't begin until she quit the sport at age twenty-five.

18 Our national obsession with weight, our glorification of thinness, have gone completely unchecked in gymnastics and figure skating. The cultural forces that have produced extravagantly bony fashion models have taken their toll on gymnasts and skaters already insecure about their bodies. Not surprisingly, eating disorders are common in both sports, and in gymnastics they're rampant. Studies of female college gymnasts show that most practice some kind of disordered eating. In a 1994 University of Utah study of elite gymnasts—those training for the Olympics—59 percent admitted to some form of disordered eating. And in interviewing elites for this book, I found only a handful who had not tried starving, throwing up or taking laxatives or diuretics to control their weight. Several left the sport because of eating disorders. One died. Eating disorders among male athletes, as in the general male population, are virtually unknown.

19 "Everyone goes through it, but nobody talks about it, because they're embarrassed," gymnast Kristie Phillips told me. "But I don't put the fault on us. It's the pressures that are put on us to be so skinny. It's

mental cruelty. It's not fair that all these pressures are put on us at such a young age and we don't realize it until we get older and we suffer from it."

20   Phillips took laxatives, thyroid pills and diuretics to lose weight. She had been the hottest gymnast in the mid-1980s, the heir apparent to 1984 Olympic superstar Mary Lou Retton. But she not only didn't win a medal at the 1988 Summer Games, she didn't even make the U.S. team. She left the sport feeling like a failure. She gained weight, then became bulimic, caught in a cycle of bingeing and vomiting. Distraught, she took scissors to her wrists in a botched attempt to kill herself. "I weighed ninety-eight pounds and I was being called [by her coach] an overstuffed Christmas turkey," Phillips said in our interview. "I was told I was never going to make it in life because I was going to be fat. I mean, in *life*. Things I'll never forget."

21   Much of the direct blame for the young athletes' problems falls on the coaches and parents. Obviously, no parent wakes up in the morning and plots how to ruin his or her child's life. But the money, the fame and the promise of great achievement can turn a parent's head. Ambition gets perverted. The boundaries of parents and coaches bloat and mutate, with the parent becoming the ruthless coach and coach becoming the controlling parent. One father put gymnastics equipment in his living room and for every mistake his daughter made at the gym she had to repeat the skill hundreds of times at home. He moved the girl to three gyms around the country, pushing her in the sport she came to loathe. He said he did it because he wanted the best for her.

22   Coaches push because they are paid to produce great gymnasts. They are relentless about weight because physically round gymnasts and skaters don't win. Coaches are intolerant of injuries because in the race against puberty, time off is death. Their job is not to turn out happy, well-adjusted young women; it is to turn out champions. If they scream, belittle or ignore, if they prod an injured girl to forget her pain, if

they push her to drop out of school, they are only doing what the parents have paid them to do. So, sorting out the blame when a girl falls apart is a messy proposition; everyone claims he was just doing his job.

23   The sports' national governing bodies, for their part, are mostly impotent. They try to do well by the athletes, but they, too, often lose their way in a tangle of ambition and politics. They're like small-town governments: personal, despotic, paternalistic and absolutely without teeth. The federations do not have the power that the commissioners' offices in professional baseball, football and basketball do. They cannot revoke a coach's or an athlete's membership for anything less than criminal activity. (Tonya Harding was charged and sentenced by the courts before the United States Figure Skating Association expelled her.) They cannot fine or suspend a coach whose athletes regularly leave the sport on stretchers.

24   There simply is no safety net protecting these children. Not the parents, the coaches or the federations.

25   Child labor laws prohibit a thirteen-year-old from punching a cash register for forty hours a week, but that same child can labor for forty hours or more inside a gym or an ice skating rink without drawing the slightest glance from the government. The U.S. government requires the licensing of plumbers. It demands that even the tiniest coffee shop adhere to a fastidious health code. It scrutinizes the advertising claims on packages of low-fat snack food. But it never asks a coach, who holds the lives of his young pupils in his hands, to pass a minimum safety and skills test. Coaches in this country need no license to train children, even in a high-injury sport like elite gymnastics. The government that forbids a child from buying a pack of cigarettes because of health concerns never checks on the child athlete who trains until her hands bleed or her knees buckle, who stops eating to achieve the perfect body, who takes eight Advils a day and offers herself up for another shot of cortisone to dull the pain, who drinks a bottle of Ex-Lax because her coach

is going to weigh her in the morning. The government never takes a look inside the gym or the rink to make sure these children are not being exploited or abused or worked too hard. Even college athletes—virtually all of whom are adults—are restricted by the NCAA to just twenty hours per week of formal training. But no laws, no agencies, put limits on the number of hours a child can train or the methods a coach can use.

26 Some argue that extraordinary children should be allowed to follow extraordinary paths to realize their potential. They argue that a child's wants are no less important than an adult's and thus she should not be denied her dreams just because she is still a child. If pursuing her dream means training eight hours a day in a gym, withstanding abusive language and tolerating great pain, and if the child wants to do it and the parents believe it will build character, why not let her? Who are we to tell a child what she can and cannot do with her life?

27 In fact, we tell children all the time what they can and cannot do with their lives. Restricting children from certain activities is hardly a revolutionary concept. Laws prohibit children from driving before sixteen and drinking before twenty-one. They prohibit children from dropping out of school before fifteen and working full-time before sixteen. In our society we put great value on protecting our children from physical harm and exploitation, and sometimes that means protecting them from their own poor judgment and their parents' poor judgment. No one questions the wisdom of the government in forbidding a child to work full-time, so why is it all right for her to train full-time with no rules to ensure her well-being? Child labor laws should address all labor, even that which is technically nonpaid, though top gymnasts and figure skaters do labor for money.

28 In recent years the federations have begun to pay their top athletes a stipend based on their competition results. The girls can earn bonuses by representing the United States in certain designated events. Skaters who compete in the World Figure Skating Championships and the Olympic Games, for example, receive $15,000. They earn lesser amounts for international competitions such as Skate America. They also earn money from corporate sponsors and exhibitions. The money might not cover much more than their training expenses, which can run $75,000 for a top skater and $20,000 to $30,000 per year for a top gymnast, but it's money—money that is paid specifically for the work the athletes do in the gym and the skating rink.

29 The real payoff for their hard work, however, waits at the end of the road. That's what the parents and athletes hope anyway. When Mary Lou Retton made millions on Madison Avenue after winning the gold medal at the 1984 Olympics, she changed gymnastics forever. "Kids have agents now before they even make it into their teens," Retton says. Now the dream is no longer just about medals but about Wheaties boxes and appearance fees, about paying off mom and dad's home equity loans and trading in the Toyota for a Mercedes. It doesn't seem to matter that only six girls every four years reach the Olympics and that winning the gold once they get there is the longest of long shots. Even world champion Shannon Miller didn't win the all-around Olympic gold in 1992.

30 Figure skating, even more than gymnastics, blinds parents and athletes with the glittering possibilities, and for good reason. Peggy Fleming and Dorothy Hamill are still living off gold medals won decades ago. Nancy Kerrigan landed endorsements with Reebok, Evian, Seiko and Campbell's soup with only a bronze medal in 1992. With glamorous and feminine stars like Kerrigan and Kristi Yamaguchi to lead the way, the United States Figure Skating Association has seen the influx of corporate sponsorship climb 2000 percent in just five years. Money that used to go to tennis is now being shifted to figure skating and gymnastics as their popularity grows. The payoff in money and fame now looms large enough to be seen from a distance, sparkling like the Emerald City,

driving parents and children to extremes to reach its doors.

31   I'm not suggesting that all elite gymnasts and figure skaters emerge from their sports unhealthy and poorly adjusted. Many prove that they can thrive under intense pressure and physical demands and thus are stronger for the experience. But too many can't. There are no studies that establish what percentage of elite gymnasts and figure skaters are damaged by their sports and in what ways. So the evidence I've gathered for this book is anecdotal, the result of nearly a hundred interviews and more than a decade of covering both sports as a journalist.

32   The bottom line is clear. There have been enough suicide attempts, enough eating disorders, enough broken bodies, enough regretful parents and enough bitter young women to warrant a serious reevaluation of what we're doing in this country to produce Olympic champions. Those who work in these sports know this. They know the tragedies all too well. If the federations and coaches truly care about the athletes and not simply about the fame and prestige that come from trotting tough little champions up to the medal stand, they know it is past time to lay the problems on the table, examine them and figure out a way to keep their sports from damaging so many young lives. But since those charged with protecting young athletes so often fail in their responsibility, it is time the government drops the fantasy that certain sports are merely games and takes a hard look at legislation aimed at protecting elite child athletes.

33   It is also my hope that by dramatizing the particularly intense subculture of female gymnastics and figure skating, we can better understand something of our own nature as a country bent on adulating, and in some cases sacrificing, girls and young women in a quest to fit them into our pretty little boxes.

Source: Joan Ryan, *Little Girls in Pretty Boxes*. New York: Time Warner, 1995, pp. 1–15.

DISCUSSION QUESTIONS

1. Is the implicit claim identified in the "Commentary" on this argument ("You will find this book compelling and clearly organized") amply supported in the essay? By what methods? Give specific examples.

2. Ryan makes frequent use of metaphors, similes, and analogies to stress her points. Identify some of these and discuss their effectiveness in terms of argument.

3. Ryan makes a number of factual generalizations in her essay. Identify three or four of them and consider whether they are adequately supported by specific examples. In an introduction of this type, is full support necessary?

4. Describe Ryan's implied audience; what does Ryan assume to be their needs and values? Where does she appeal to these?

SUGGESTIONS FOR WRITING (16.1)

1. Ryan is writing about what she calls "elite" athletes, whose training and goals are very different from those of the average high school or even college varsity athlete. Yet the abuses Ryan exposes are not limited to the elite level. Write a factual argument exposing training abuses you have experienced or witnessed in high school, college, or amateur athletics.

2. Based on this introduction, which faithfully represents the contents of the book, write a 250-word abstract of the book.

3. In Par. 18, Ryan refers to "our national obsession with weight, our glorification of thinness." Based upon your own personal observations, compose an inductive argument that supports one of the following, more modest generalizations: "My own experience and observations lead me to conclude that at least among my acquaintances, there is (or is not) an obsession with weight, a glorification of thinness." You may adapt the suggested conclusion, but be sure to qualify it and support it with an appropriate number of specific examples.

4. Participate in a discussion with three or four of your classmates in which you brainstorm about the advantages and/or disadvantages of the participation of girls and young women in organized (not professional) athletics. Based upon the discussion, create your own list of advantages or your own list of disadvantages. Then write a working claim that would introduce an evaluation of this participation.

WHERE HAVE ALL THE HEROES GONE?

STEPHEN D. MOSHER

This article was first published in the Ithaca College Quarterly *(Winter 1998). The head note to the article reads as follows:*

> *Racism. Sexual assault. Biting an opponent's ear. These are the actions of our "national heroes"? Why do we make sports figures into heroes, anyway? Do athletes have any responsibility to act as role models? We asked associate professor of exercise and sport sciences Stephen D. Mosher to give us a little background on sport in the United States, so we can make up our own minds.*

If you want to find out more about Stephen Mosher, visit his Web page on the Ithaca College site at http://www.ithaca.com.

1   In the opening scenes of Robert Redford's *The Natural*, Roy Hobbs's father teaches his son how to pitch a baseball but also warns him, "You have a gift, Roy. But if you rely too much on your gift, you'll fail."

2   During one of the endless bus rides through the North Carolina League in *Bull Durham*, veteran catcher Crash Davis tells rookie Nuke Lalouche, "You don't respect yourself, which is your problem; but you don't respect the game, and that's my problem."

3   When we survey the contemporary American sport landscape, we are struck by the almost never-ending displays of immaturity (the frustrated American Olympic men's ice hockey team trashing their hotel rooms in Nagano), shameless self-promotion (the NBA/WNBA's two-ball fiasco during the 1998 all-star weekend), blatant profit taking (Wayne Huizenga's dismantling of the Florida Marlins less than two weeks after they won the 1997 World Series), elitist protectionism (the PGA, trying to prevent Casey Martin from joining its ranks by claiming that walking is integral to golf), overtly racist slurs (Fuzzy Zoeller's comments on Tiger Woods's eating habits, John Rocker's condemnation of virtually all non-white New Yorkers, Payne Stewart's tasteless imitation of "Chinese" Ryder Cup golfers), and personal violence (Latrell

Sprewell's attack on Golden State coach P.J. Carlesimo), never-ending streams of drug abuse (Darryl Strawberry's tragic addiction to cocaine), and even participation in deadly street fights (the Baltimore Ravens' Ray Lewis on Super Bowl night 1999) or, perhaps the most disturbing example, North Carolina Panthers' Ray Carruth's hiring hit men to commit murder.

4   We ask ourselves: Where have all the heroes gone? Where is the nobility of the sport? Who holds true to the ideals of the game? Who cares about sportsmanship and playing fair? Is it all just about winning?

5   The best athletes we can come up with to be role models for our children are those like Cal Ripken Jr. and Tara Lipinski. What exactly does Ripken do to have earned his hero status? Go to work every day and do his job just like countless other citizens? What advice for living life can come from the mouth of Lipinksi? She's not even 19, has spent over half her life skating, and already she's written *two* autobiographies?

6   They are, however, reminders that celebrity is not fame. Moreover, the most honest athlete today may be Charles Barkley, who insists, "I am not a role model!"

7   Wherever did we come up with the belief that sport builds character or that it teaches us teamwork and how to be "good sports," how to be modest in victory and gracious in defeat? We must understand this before we can even ask our athletes to be our heroes.

8   Sport has not always been considered a good thing in American life. The Puritans, in their attempt to reform the Church of England, sought to squelch virtually all forms of organized rituals, holy days, pageantry, symbols, and play associated with the Roman Catholic church. Sporting pastimes in early America involved gambling (horse racing, bowling), violence (gouging, cockfighting), or both (boxing); all those directly connected with Catholic holidays were discouraged. However, the Puritans did approve "lawful" sport that could "refresh the spirit" or better prepare people to fulfill their religious duties. Lawful sports included fishing, hunting, and swimming. Children's play was also tolerated.

9   Nonetheless, the sporting traditions of the citizenry remained impossible to fully regulate. These activities were the province of the poor, the working class, children, and single, young men. But starting in the 1850s, as an outgrowth of the Second Great Awakening, social reformers again sought to govern the recreation of the greater society. Catharine Beecher's concept of womanhood—the "cult of domesticity"—and Thomas Higginson's concept of manhood—"muscular Christianity"—were the first sports-specific manifestations of this movement. The ideas gained momentum because advances in science, medicine, and technology, as well as the move away from an active agrarian lifestyle, meant that people no longer had physical activity, with its side perks of endurance and stamina, built into their daily lives. People were becoming sedentary.

10   For the first time in modern history, sport was seen to serve a purpose in developing the character of both boys and girls. Sport and physical exercise would assist girls in becoming healthy homemakers and nurturers and would prepare boys to enter the professional world. Basketball itself was invented by Dr. James Naismith, who'd been charged with creating a game that could be played indoors during the winter and would embrace all of the ideals of the Muscular Christian movement regarding teamwork, self- sacrifice, obedience, self-control, and loyalty.

11   The mottoes of the play movement organizations reveal volumes about their underlying purpose: "Mind, Body, Spirit" (YMCA), "Wohelo"—Work, Health, Love (Campfire), "Be Prepared" (Girl and Boy Scouts), "Head, Heart, Hands, Health" (4-H). The pledges of these movements are even more revealing. 4-H's pledge is *I pledge/ My Head to clearer thinking,/My heart to greater loyalty,/My Hands to larger service, and/My Health to better living,/for my club, my community, my country, and my world.* Even Little League Baseball has its own reformist pledge and motto: "Character, Courage, Loyalty."

12   Perhaps the most important key to understanding the problem of asking athletes

to be role models is found in the modern Olympic movement. There is no doubt that the ideals of amateurism established in Britain at the end of the 19th century and promulgated through the Olympic Games served to separate people by social class. Many people fondly talk of the nobility of the "taking part," the "inclusion of all" in the Olympics. But the amateur code actually sought to prevent the working class from corrupting the sporting diversions of the wealthy. Simply put, the requirement that competitors be amateurs meant those who had to work for a living could not compete. Consequently, the "civilized gentlemen" of the ruling elite were able to exclude from sport virtually anyone they wanted.

13   In America, the self-described classless society, amateurism was met with some initial resistance (the early days of college sport were full of paid players and pseudostudents), but slowly took hold in the middle class. The morality of privilege, however, had little influence among those who were born to poverty and struggle or were immigrants; sport soon took on the looks of its new practitioners and was no longer cloaked simply in hunting suits and riding boots.

14   To expect sports as they exist today to teach children to play games, become physically healthy, and also build character may be unrealistic. In fact, the results of sport participation fall far short of these expectations. Competitive sports actually have little effect on the development of positive social characteristics. Research shows that competitive team sports are more likely to teach children that "winning is the *only* thing" and that "the end justifies the means" rather than that hard work, dedication, and self-sacrifice are the true payoffs. There are no convincing data to support the belief that sport prevents juvenile delinquency or reduces drug abuse. There are, however, data that suggest that male athletes develop a view of gender superiority that may explain their higher rates of promiscuity and sexual abuse than those of nonathletes. (There is also ample research showing that athletes are significantly less altruistic than nonathletes.) It is certainly quite clear that

in most high schools varsity athletes enjoy higher status than those students who excel in art, music, and even academics.

15   We are quick to condemn the behavior of Mike Tyson, as if we can separate the champion boxer from the street thug. We are disgusted by Latrell Sprewell's assault on an authority figure, as if P. J. Carlesimo's long history of bullying players is irrelevant. We are horrified by Ray Lewis's and Ray Carruth's crimes and countless incidents of domestic violence, but overlook the fact that the teams in the National Football League actually scout for players in prisons and deliberately seek out personnel with violent tendencies. On the other hand, Arthur Ashe was certainly a hero, but it wasn't tennis that led him to fight for greater awareness of HIV/AIDS, write *A Hard Road to Glory*, or protest the racist government in South Africa. Muhammad Ali was certainly a warrior king, but it wasn't boxing that prompted him to sacrifice his career when he said, "I ain't got no quarrel with them Viet Cong."

16   The heroism found in sports is powerful, legitimate, and sometimes even magical, but it is a heroism that is quite different from that of everyday people. When Gatorade urges us to "Be like Mike," are they talking about Michael Jordan the basketball player, the husband and father, or the endorser of a company that has been accused of exploiting child labor in the third world? Are we really supposed to believe Andre Agassi when he says for Canon cameras, "Image is everything"? Earl Woods has said that his son is literally capable of *saving the world*. Isn't it enough to simply marvel at Tiger's heroic golfing ability? Why do we insist on turning this young man's good manners into heroism? In recent years, as Woods replaces Michael Jordan as America's version of the global sporting icon, his political actions become eligible for public scrutiny. In the summer of 2000, Woods, a member of the Screen Actors Guild, crossed the strike line by filming Buick commercials in Canada for telecast during the Sydney Olympic Games. And like Jordan, his predecessor as Nike's dominant global spokesperson, Woods has yet to follow through on his

promise to examine in person the working conditions at Nike's alleged sweatshops in southeast Asia.

17 One of the most tragic figures in recent American sport is Pete Rose. The ultimate symbol of hard work and determination overcoming a perceived lack of talent, Rose nonetheless remains the disgraced and fallen hero, clueless as to why he can't get into baseball's hall of fame on the basis of his heroic diamond feats alone. Rose's hubris really knows no limits. He would be well served to heed Crash Davis's advice: "You have to play this game with fear and arrogance." Rose, like so many of our celebrity athletes, has the arrogance but lacks the fear. Like those celebrities who refer to themselves in the third person, Rose—the self-proclaimed "Hit King"—places himself above the game. Also known as "Charlie Hustle," Rose betrayed those who depended on him when, as manager of the Cincinnati Reds, he gambled on baseball. Rose's greatest "hustle" was trying to convince the public he loved the game more than he loved himself. Rose still does not recognize that heroes must fear letting us down.

18 The responses of public grief to the tragic deaths of Payne Stewart and Dale Earnhardt reveal a nation starving for people to admire. But is the nation looking in the wrong direction? Stewart's blatantly conservative racial politics of exclusion, his reputation as an out of control youth sport parent, and his dedication to consumer capitalism is somehow overwhelmed by the images of a "WWJD" (What would Jesus do?) bracelet and the ghost plane crashed in the South Dakota farmland. Dale Earnhardt's death in the 2001 Daytona 500 received unprecedented media attention, but through it all there was never a mention that his nickname—"The Intimidator"—was earned through a career of *deliberately* running his NASCAR opponents off the race track, putting them at death's door.

19 Roy Hobbs's home run at the end of *The Natural* brings us joy and hope, not because he saves the world but because he saves himself. Ray Kinsella eases our pain at the end of *Field of Dreams*, not because he demonstrates the moral superiority of baseball but because he finally has the chance to tell his father he's sorry.

20 Perhaps Cal Ripken Jr., Tiger Woods, and Sammy Sosa are heroes. They are certainly marvelous athletes. But to ask them—or any other athletes—to be the fathers of the nation is unfair. They have enough of a burden being fathers to their own children or children who can make their parents proud. For us to get anything more than that from them is simply a blessing.

Source: Stephen D. Mosher, "Where Have All the Heroes Gone?" *Ithaca College Quarterly*. Winter 1998.

DISCUSSION QUESTIONS

1. Go to Stephen Mosher's Web page on the Ithaca College site at http://www.ithaca.com. Without clicking on any links, what do you learn about Mosher from the contents, design, and graphics of the website? How are these clues borne out by the article itself?

2. Mosher uses the third person plural pronoun, "we," throughout his argument (for example, "When we survey the contemporary American sport landscape, we are struck by the almost never-ending displays of immaturity," Par. 3). What effect do you think Mosher was trying to achieve through this rhetorical strategy? In considering this, you might think of how different the argument might have been if Mosher had used "I" or "one" or "you" instead of "we."

3. Par. 14 claims that "Competitive sports actually have little effect on the development of positive social characteristics." How convincingly is this generalization supported? Given what you know about Mosher's credentials and the nature of the publication for which his argument is written, is the support sufficient? Why or why not?

4. In which category of argument would you place "Where Have All the Heroes Gone?"? Where do you find the best statement of the central claim?

5. How does Mosher's detour into the history of sport (Par. 10–13) contribute to his argument? Is this historical survey necessary to the success of the argument?

SUGGESTIONS FOR WRITING (16.2)

1. Write an outline for a four- to five-page direct refutation of Mosher's argument. (To do this, you must be very clear about the answers to Question #4.) You may use any of the other arguments in this section as support for your counterargument.

2. Exchange outlines with a fellow student and review the structure of each other's outline. Is the central claim clear? Will it be supported by appropriate secondary claims and support? Will there be adequate support for each claim? Is the order of the argument sensible? Write a one-page set of comments and recommendations for your partner.

3. With the comments from Question #2 in mind, draft your counterargument and hand it in to your instructor, who will hold it for two days, then return it to you for revision.

4. Write a final draft of your argument including an introduction and conclusion. Try to follow Mosher's use of introductory and closing anecdotes.

THE CHOSEN ONE

GARY SMITH

Gary Smith is a senior writer for Sports Illustrated *and has won the National Magazine Award for feature writing, an honor not often conferred upon sports journalists.*

This essay on Tiger Woods first appeared in Sports Illustrated *in December 1996, before Woods won his first major tournament, the Masters. "The Chosen One" was included in the prestigious anthology* The Best American Sports Writing *(1997), an annual collection of each year's finest sports writing.*

1 It was ordinary. It was oh so ordinary. It was a salad, a dinner roll, a steak, a half potato, a slice of cake, a clinking fork, a podium joke, a ballroom full of white-linen-tablecloth conversation. Then a thick man with tufts of white hair rose from the head table. His voice trembled and his eyes teared and his throat gulped down sobs between words, and everything ordinary was cast out of the room.

2 He said, "Please forgive me . . . but sometimes I get very emotional . . . when I

talk about my son. . . . My heart . . . fills with so . . . much . . . joy . . . when I realize . . . that this young man . . . is going to be able . . . to help so many people. . . . He will transcend this game . . . and bring to the world . . . a humanitarianism . . . which has never been known before. The world will be a better place to live in . . . by virtue of his existence . . . and his presence. . . . I acknowledge only a small part in that . . . in that I know that I was personally selected by God himself . . . to nurture this young man . . . and bring him to the point were he can make his contribution to humanity. . . . This is my treasure. . . . Please accept it . . . and use it wisely. . . . Thank you."

3   Blinking tears, the man found himself inside the arms of his son and the applause of the people, all up on their feet. In the history of American celebrity, no father has ever spoken this way. Too many dads have deserted or died before their offspring reached this realm, but mostly they have fallen mute, the father's vision exceeded by the child's, leaving the child to wander, lost, through the sad and silly wilderness of modern fame.

4   So let us stand amidst this audience at last month's Fred Haskins Award dinner to honor America's outstanding college golfer of 1996, and take note as Tiger and Earl Woods embrace, for a new manner of celebrity is taking form before our eyes. Regard the 64-year-old African-American father, arm upon the superstar's shoulder, right where the chip is so often found, declaring that this boy will do more good for the world than any man who ever walked it. Gaze at the 20-year-old son, with the blood of four races in his veins, not flinching an inch from the yoke of his father's prophecy but already beginning to scent the complications. The son who stormed from behind to win a record third straight U.S. Amateur last August, turned pro and rang up scores in the 60s in 21 of his first 27 rounds, winning two PGA Tour events as he doubled and tripled the usual crowds and dramatically changed their look and age.

5   Now turn. Turn and look at us, the audience, standing in anticipation of something different, something pure. Quiet. Just below the applause, or within it, can you hear the grinding? That's the relentless chewing mechanism of fame, girding to grind the purity and the promise to dust. Not the promise of talent, but the bigger promise, the father's promise, the one that stakes everything on the boy's not becoming separated from his own humanity and from all the humanity crowding around him.

6   It's a fitting moment, while he's up there at the head table with the audience on its feet, to anoint Eldrick (Tiger) Woods—the rare athlete to establish himself immediately as the dominant figure in his sport—as *Sports Illustrated*'s 1996 Sportsman of the Year. And to pose a question: Who will win? The machine . . . or the youth who had just entered its maw?

7   Tiger Woods will win. He'll fulfill his father's vision because of his mind, one that grows more still, more willful, more efficient, the greater the pressure upon him grows.

8   The machine will win because it has no mind. It flattens even as it lifts, trivializes even as it exalts, spreads a man so wide and thin that he becomes margarine soon enough.

9   Tiger will win because of God's mind. Can't you see the pattern? Earl Woods asks. Can't you see the signs? "Tiger will do more than any other man in history to change the course of humanity," Earl says.

10   Sports history, Mr. Woods? Do you mean more than Joe Louis and Jackie Robinson, more than Muhammad Ali and Arthur Ashe? "More than any of them because he's more charismatic, more educated, more prepared for this than anyone."

11   Anyone, Mr. Woods? Your son will have more impact than Nelson Mandela, more than Gandhi, more than Buddha?

12   "Yes, because he has a larger forum than any of them. Because he's playing a sport that's international. Because he's qualified through his ethnicity to accomplish miracles. He's the bridge between the East and

the West. There is no limit because he has the guidance. I don't know yet exactly what form this will take. But he is the Chosen One. He'll have the power to impact nations. Not people. Nations. The world is just getting a taste of his power."

13   Surely this is lunacy. Or are we just too myopic to see? One thing is certain: we are witnessing the first volley of an epic encounter, the machine at its mightiest confronting the individual groomed all his life to conquer it and turn it to his use. The youth who has been exposed to its power since he toddled onto *The Mike Douglas Show* at 3, the set of *That's Incredible!* at 5, the boy who has been steeled against the silky seduction to which so many before him have succumbed. The one who, by all appearances, brings more psychological balance, more sense of self, more consciousness of possibility to the battlefield than any of his predecessors.

14   This is war, so let's start with war. Remove the images of pretty putting greens from the movie screen standing near the ballroom's head table. Jungle is what's needed here, foliage up to a man's armpits, sweat trickling down his thighs, leeches crawling up them. Lieut. Col. Earl Woods, moving through the night with his rifle ready, wondering why a U.S. Army public information officer stationed in Brooklyn decided in his mid-30s that he belonged in the Green Berets and ended up doing two tours of duty in Vietnam. Wondering why his first marriage has died and why the three children from it have ended up without a dad around when it's dark like this and it's time for bed—just as Earl ended up as a boy after his own father died. Wondering why he keeps plotting ways to return to the line of fire—"creative soldiering," he calls it—to eyeball death once more. To learn once again about his dark and cold side, the side that enables Earl, as Tiger will remark years later, "to slit your throat and then sit down and eat his dinner."

15   Oh, yes, Earl is one hell of a cocktail. A little Chinese, a little Cherokee, a few shots of African-American; don't get finicky about measurements, we're making a vat here. Pour in some gruffness and a little intimidation, then some tenderness and some warmth and a few jiggers of old anger. Don't hold back on intelligence. And stoicism. Add lots of stoicism, and even more of responsibility—"the most responsible son of a bitch you've ever seen in your life" is how Earl himself puts it. Top it all with "a bucket of whiskey," which is what he has been known to order when he saunters into a bar and he's in the mood. Add a dash of hyperbole, maybe two, and to hell with the ice, just whir. This is one of those concoctions you're going to remember when morning comes.

16   Somewhere in there, until a good fifteen years ago, there was one other ingredient, the existential Tabasco, the smoldering why? The Thai secretary in the U.S. Army office in Bangkok smelled it soon after she met Earl, in 1967. "He couldn't relax," says Kultida (Tida) Woods. "Searching for something, always searching, never satisfied. I think because both his parents died when he was young, and he didn't have Mom and Dad to make him warm. Sometimes he stayed awake till three or four in the morning, just thinking."

17   In a man so accustomed to exuding command and control, in a Green Beret lieutenant colonel, *why?* has a way of building up power like a river dammed. Why did the Vietcong sniper bracket him that day (first bullet a few inches left of one ear, second bullet a few inches right of the other) but never fire the third bullet? Why did Earl's South Vietnamese combat buddy, Nguyen Phong—the one Earl nicknamed Tiger, and in whose memory he would nickname his son—stir one night just in time to awaken Earl and warn him not to budge because a viper was poised inches from his right eye? What about that road Earl's jeep rolled down one night, the same road on which two friends had just been mutilated, the road that took him through a village so silent and dark that his scalp tingled, and then, just beyond it . . . hell turned inside-out

over his shoulder, the sky lighting up and all the huts he had just passed spewing Vietcong machine-gun and artillery fire? He never understands what is the purpose of Lieutenant Colonel Woods's surviving again and again. He never quite comprehends what is the point of his life, until . . .

18   Until the boy is born. He will get all the time that Earl was unable to devote to the three children from his first marriage. He will be the only child from Earl's second marriage, to the Thai woman he brought back to America, and right away there are signs. What other 6-month-old, Earl asks, has the balance to stand in the palm of his father's hand and remain there even as Daddy strolls around the house? Was there another 11-month-old, ever, who could pick up a sawed-off club, imitate his father's golf swing so fluidly, and drive the ball so wickedly into the nylon net across the garage? Another 4-year-old who could be dropped off at the golf course at 9 A.M. on a Saturday and picked up at 5 P.M., pockets bulging with money he had won from disbelievers ten and twenty years older, until Pop said, "Tiger, you can't do that"? Earl starts to get a glimmer. He is to be the father of the world's most gifted golfer.

19   But why? What for? Not long after Tiger's birth, when Earl has left the military to become a purchaser for McDonnell Douglas, he finds himself in a long discussion with a woman he knows. She senses the power pooling inside him, the friction. "You have so much to give," she tells him, "but you're not giving it. You haven't even scratched the surface of your potential." She suggests he try EST, Erhard Seminars Training, an intensive self-discovery and self-actualizing technique, and it hits Earl hard, direct mortar fire to the heart. What he learns is that his overmuscular sense of responsibility for others has choked his potential.

20   "To the point," says Earl, "that I wouldn't even buy a handkerchief for myself. It went all the way back to the day my father died, when I was 11, and my mother put her arm around me after the funeral and said,

'You're the man of the house now.' I became the father that young, looking out for everyone else, and then she died two years later.

21   "What I learned through EST was that by doing more for myself, I could do much more for others. Yes, be responsible, but love life, and give people the space to be in your life, and allow yourself room to give to others. That caring and sharing is what's most important, not being responsible for everyone else. Which is where Tiger comes in. What I learned led me to give so much time to Tiger, and to give him the space to be himself, and not to smother him with do's and don'ts. I took out the authority aspect and turned into companionship. I made myself vulnerable as a parent. When you have to earn respect from your child, rather than demanding it because it's owed to you as the father, miracles happen. I realized that, through him, the giving could take a quantum leap. What I could do on a limited scale, he could do on a global scale."

22   At last, the river is undammed, and Earl's whole life makes sense. At last, he sees what he was searching for, a pattern. No more volunteering for missions—he has his. Not simply to be a great golfer's father. To be destiny's father. His son will change the world.

23   "What the hell had I been doing in public information in the army, posted in Brooklyn?" he asks. "Why, of course, what greater training can there be than three years of dealing with the New York media to prepare me to teach Tiger the importance of public relations and how to handle the media?"

> Father: Where were you born, Tiger?
>
> Son, age 3: I was born on December 30, 1975, in Long Beach, California.
>
> Father: No, Tiger, only answer the question you were asked. It's important to prepare yourself for this. Try again.
>
> Son: I was born in Long Beach, California.
>
> Father: Good, Tiger, good.

The late leap into the Green Berets? "What the hell was that for?" Earl says. "Of course, to prepare me to teach Tiger mental toughness."

24 The three children by the first marriage? "Not just one boy the first time," says Earl, "but two, along with a girl, as if God was saying, 'I want this son of a bitch to really have previous training.'"

25 The Buddhist wife, the one who grew up in a boarding school after her parents separated when she was 5, the girl who then vowed that her child would know nothing but love and attention? The one who will preach inner calm to Tiger simply by turning to him with that face—still awaiting its first wrinkle at 52? Whose eyes close when she speaks, so he can almost see her gathering and sifting the thoughts? The mother who will walk every hole and keep score for Tiger at children's tournaments, adding a stroke or two if his calm cracks? "Look at this stuff!" cries Earl. "Over and over you can see the plan being orchestrated by someone other than me because I'm not this damn good! I tried to get out of that combat assignment to Thailand. But Tida was meant to bring in the influence of the Orient, to introduce Tiger to Buddhism and inner peace, so he would have the best of two different worlds. And so he would have the knowledge that there were two people whose lives were totally committed to him."

26 What of the heart attack Earl suffered when Tiger was 10 and the way the retired lieutenant colonel felt himself floating down the gray tunnel toward the light before he was wrenched back? "To prepare me to teach Tiger that life is short," Earl says, "and to live each day to the maximum, and not to worry about the future. There's only now. You must understand that time is just a linear measurement of successive increments of now. Anyplace you go on that line is now, and that's how you have to live it."

27 No need to wonder about the appearance of the perfect childhood coach, John Anselmo; the perfect sports psychologist, Jay Brunza; the perfect agent, Hughes Norton; the perfect attorney, John Merchant; and the perfect pro swing instructor, Butch Harmon. Or about the great tangle of fate that leads them all to Tiger at just the right junctures in his development. "Everything," says Earl, "right there when he needs it. Everything. There can't be this much coincidence in the world. This is a directed scenario, and none of us involved in the scenario has failed to accept the responsibility. This is all destined to be."

28 His wife ratifies this, in her own way. She takes the boy's astrological chart to a Buddhist temple in Los Angeles and to another in Bangkok and is told by the monks at both places that the child has wondrous powers. "If he becomes a politician, he will be either a president or a prime minister," she is told. "If he enters the military, he will be a general."

29 Tida comes to a conclusion. "Tiger has Thai, African, Chinese, American Indian, and European blood," she says. "He can hold everyone together. He is the Universal Child."

30 This is in the air the boy breathes for twenty years, and it becomes bone fact for him, marrow knowledge. When asked about it, he merely nods in acknowledgment of it, assents to it; of course he believes it's true. So failure, in the rare visits it pays him, is not failure. It's just life pausing to teach him a lesson he needs in order to go where he's inevitably going. And success, no matter how much sooner than expected it comes to the door, always finds him dressed and ready to welcome it. "Did you ever see yourself doing this so soon?" a commentator breathlessly asks him seconds after his first pro victory, on October 6 in Las Vegas, trying to elicit wonder and awe on live TV. "Yeah," Tiger responds. "I kind of did." And sleep comes to him so easily: in the midst of conversation, in a car, in a plane, off he goes, into the slumber of the destined. "I don't see any of this as scary or a burden," Tiger says. "I see it as fortunate. I've always known where I wanted to go in life. I've never let anything deter me. This is my purpose. It will unfold."

31   No sports star in the history of American celebrity has spoken this way. Maybe, somehow, Tiger can win.

32   The machine will win. It must win because it too is destiny, 5 billion destinies leaning against one. There are ways to keep the hordes back, a media expert at Nike tells Tiger. Make broad gestures when you speak. Keep a club in your hands and take practice swings, or stand with one foot well out in front of the other, in almost a karate stance. That will give you room to breathe. Two weeks later, surrounded by a pen-wielding mob in La Quinta, California, in late November, just before the Skins Game, the instruction fails. Tiger survives, but his shirt and slacks are ruined, felt-tip-dotted to death.

33   The machine will win because it will wear the young man down, cloud his judgment, steal his sweetness, the way it does just before the Buick Challenge in Pine Mountain, Georgia, at the end of September. It will make his eyes drop when the fans' gaze reaches for his, his voice growl at their clawing hands, his body sag onto a sofa after a practice round and then rise and walk across the room and suddenly stop in bewilderment. "I couldn't even remember what I'd just gotten off the couch for, two seconds before," he says. "I was like mashed potatoes. Total mush."

34   So he walks. Pulls out on the eve of the Buick Challenge, pulls out of the Fred Haskins Award dinner to honor him, and goes home. See, maybe Tiger can win. He can just turn his back on the machine and walk. Awards? Awards to Tiger are like echoes, voices bouncing off the walls, repeating what a truly confident man has already heard inside his own head. The Jack Nicklaus Award, the one Jack himself was supposed to present to Tiger live on ABC during the Memorial tournament last spring? Tiger would have blown it off if Wally Goodwin, his coach at Stanford during the two years he played there before turning pro, hadn't insisted that he show up.

35   The instant Tiger walks away from the Buick Challenge and the Haskins dinner, the hounds start yapping. See, that's why the machine will win. It's got all those damn heel-nippers. Little mutts on the PGA Tour resenting how swiftly the 20-year-old was ordained, how hastily he was invited to play practice rounds with Nicklaus and Arnold Palmer, with Greg Norman and Ray Floyd and Nick Faldo and Fred Couples. And big dogs snapping too. Tom Kite quoted as saying, "I can't ever remember being tired when I was twenty," and Peter Jacobsen quoted, "You can't compare Tiger to Nicklaus and Palmer anymore because they never [walked out]."

36   He rests for a week, stunned by the criticism—"I thought those people were my friends," he says. He never second-guesses his decision to turn pro, but he sees what he surrendered. "I miss college," he says. "I miss hanging out with my friends, getting in a little trouble. I have to be so guarded now. I miss sitting around drinking beer and talking half the night. There's no one my own age to hang out with anymore because almost everyone my age is in college. I'm a target for everybody now, and there's nothing I can do about it. My mother was right when she said that turning pro would take away my youth. But golfwise, there was nothing left for me in college."

37   He reemerges after the week's rest and rushes from four shots off the lead on the final day to win the Las Vegas Invitational in sudden death. The world's waiting for him again, this time with reinforcements. Letterman and Leno want him as a guest; *GQ* calls about a cover; Cosby, along with almost every other sitcom you can think of, offers to write an episode revolving around Tiger, if only he'll appear. Kids dress up as Tiger for Halloween—did anyone ever dress up as Arnie or Jack?—and Michael Jordan declares that his only hero on earth is Tiger Woods. Pepsi is dying to have him cut a commercial for one of its soft drinks aimed at Generation Xers; Nike and Titleist call in chits for the $40 million and $20 million contracts he signed; money managers are eager to know how he wants his millions invested; women walk onto the course during a practice round and ask for his hand in

marriage; kids stampede over and under ropes and chase him from the 18th hole to the clubhouse; piles of phone messages await him when he returns to his hotel room. "Why," Tiger asks, "do so many people want a part of me?"

38   Because something deeper than conventional stardom is at work here, something so spontaneous and subconscious that words have trouble going there. It's a communal craving, a public aching for a superstar free of anger and arrogance and obsession with self. It's a hollow place that chimes each time Tiger and his parents strike the theme of father and mother and child love, each time Tiger stands at a press conference and declares, "They have raised me well, and I truly believe they have taught me to accept full responsibility for all aspects of my life." During the making of a Titleist commercial in November, a makeup woman is so moved listening to Earl describe his bond with Tiger that she decides to contact her long-estranged father. "See what I mean?" cried Earl. "Did you affect someone that way today? Did anyone else there? It's destiny, man. It's something bigger than me."

39   What makes it so vivid is context. The white canvas that the colors are being painted on—the moneyed, mature, and almost minority-less world of golf—makes Tiger an emblem of youth overcoming age, have-not overcoming have, outsider overcoming insider, to the delight not only of the 18-year-olds in the gallery wearing nose rings and cornrows, but also—of all people—of the aging insider haves.

40   So Tiger finds himself, just a few weeks after turning pro at the end of August, trying to clutch a bolt of lightning with one hand and steer an all-at-once corporation—himself—with the other, and before this he has never worked a day in his life. Never mowed a neighbor's lawn, never flung a folded newspaper, never stocked a grocery shelf; Mozarts just don't, you know. And he has to act as if none of this is new or vexing because he has this characteristic—perhaps from all those years of hanging out with his dad at tournaments, all those years of

mixing with and mauling golfers five, ten, twenty, thirty years older than he is—of never permitting himself to appear confused, surprised, or just generally a little squirt. "His favorite expression," Earl says, "is, 'I knew that.'" Of course Pop, who is just as irreverent with Tiger as he is reverent, can say, "No, you didn't know that, you little s—." But Earl, who has always been the filter for Tiger, decides to take a few steps back during his son's first few months as a pro because he wishes to encourage Tiger's independence and because he is uncertain of his own role now that the International Management Group (IMG) is managing Tiger's career.

41   Nobody notices it, but the inner calm is beginning to dissolve. Earl enters Tiger's hotel room during the Texas Open in mid-October to ask him about his schedule, and Tiger does something he has never done in his twenty years. He bites the old man's head off.

42   Earl blinks. "I understand how you must feel," he says.

43   "No, you don't," snaps Tiger.

44   "And I realized," Earl says later, "that I'd spent twenty years planning for this, but the one thing I didn't do was educate Tiger to be the boss of a corporation. There was just no vehicle for that, and I thought it would develop more slowly. I wasn't presumptuous enough to anticipate this. For the first time in his life, the training was behind the reality. I could see on his face that he was going through hell."

45   The kid is fluid, though. Just watch him walk. He's quick to flow into the new form, to fit the contour of necessity. A few hours after the outburst he's apologizing to his father and hugging him. A few days later he's giving Pop the O.K. to call a meeting of the key members of Tiger's new corporation and establish a system, Lieutenant Colonel Woods in command, chairing a two-and-a-half-hour teleconference with the team each week to sift through all the demands, weed out all the chaff, and present Tiger five decisions to make instead of five hundred. A few days after that, the weight forklifted off

his shoulders, at least temporarily, Tiger wins the Walt Disney World/Oldsmobile Classic. And a few weeks later, at the Fred Haskins Award dinner, which has been rescheduled at his request, Tiger stands at the podium and says, "I should've attended the dinner [the first time]. I admit I was wrong, and I'm sorry for any inconvenience I may have caused. But I have learned from that, and I will never make that mistake again. I'm very honored to be part of this select group, and I'll always remember, for both good and bad, this Haskins Award; for what I did and what I learned, for the company I'm now in and I'll always be in. Thank you very much." The crowd surges to its feet, cheering once more.

46   See, maybe Tiger can win. He's got the touch. He's got the feel. He never writes down a word before he gives a speech. When he needs to remember a phone number, he doesn't search his memory or a little black book; he picks up a phone and watches what number his fingers go to. When he needs a 120-yard shot to go under an oak branch and over a pond, he doesn't visualize the shot, as most golfers would. He looks at the flag and pulls everything from the hole back, back, back . . . not back into his mind's eye, but into his hands and forearms and hips, so they'll do it by feel. Explain how he made that preposterous shot? He can't. Better you interview his knuckles and metacarpals.

47   "His handicap," says Earl, "is that he has such a powerful creative mind. His imagination is too vivid. If he uses visualization, the ball goes nuts. So we piped into his creative side even deeper, into his incredible sense of feel."

48   "I've learned to trust the subconscious," says Tiger. "My instincts have never lied to me."

49   The mother radiates this: the Eastern proclivity to let life happen, rather than the Western one to make it happen. The father comes to it in his own way, through fire. To kill a man, to conduct oneself calmly and efficiently when one's own death is imminent—a skill Earl learns in Green Beret

psychological training and then again and again in jungles and rice paddies—one removes the conscious mind from the task and yields to the subconscious. "It's the more powerful of the two minds," Earl says. "It works faster than the conscious mind, yet it's patterned enough to handle routine tasks over and over, like driving a car or making a putt. It knows what to do.

50   "Allow yourself the freedom of emotion and feeling. Don't try to control them and trap them. Acknowledge them and become the beneficiary of them. Let it all outflow."

51   Let it all because it's all there: the stability, almost freakish for a close-of-the-millennium California child—same two parents, same house all his twenty years, same best friends, one since second grade, one since eighth. The kid, for god's sake, never once had a baby-sitter. The conditioning is there as well, the two years of psychological boot camp during which Earl dropped golf bags and pumped cart brakes during Tiger's backswings, jingled change and rolled balls across his line of vision to test his nerves, promising him at the outset that he only had to say "Enough" and Earl would cut off the blowtorch, but promising too that if Tiger graduated, no man he ever faced would be mentally stronger than he. "I am the toughest golfer mentally," Tiger says.

52   The bedrock is so wide that opposites can dance upon it: the cautious man can be instinctive, the careful man can be carefree. The bedrock is so wide that it has enticed Tiger into the habit of falling behind—as he did in the final matches of all three U.S. Junior Amateur and all three U.S. Amateur victories—knowing in his tissue and bones that danger will unleash his greatest power. "Allow success and fame to happen," the old man says. "Let the legend grow."

53   To hell with the Tao. The machine will win, it has to win, because it makes everything happen before a man knows it. Before he knows it, a veil descends over his eyes when another stranger approaches. Before he knows it, he's living in a walled community with an electronic gate and a security

guard, where the children trick-or-treat in golf carts, a place like the one Tiger just moved into in Orlando to preserve some scrap of sanity. Each day there, even with all the best intentions, how can he help but be a little more removed from the world he's supposed to change, and from his truest self?

54 Which is . . . who? The poised, polite, opaque sage we see on TV? No, no, no; his friends hoot and haze him when they see that Tiger on the screen, and he can barely help grinning himself. The Tiger they know is perfectly a fast-food freak who never remembers to ask if anyone else is hungry before he bolts to Taco Bell or McDonald's for the tenth time of the week. The one who loves riding roller coasters, spinning out golf carts, and winning at cards no matter how often his father accuses him of "reckless eyeballing." The one who loves delivering the dirty joke, who owns a salty barracks tongue just a rank or two beneath his father's. The one who's flip, who's downright cocky. When a suit walks up to him before the Haskins Award dinner and says, "I think you're going to be the next great one, but those are mighty big shoes to fill," Tiger replies, "Got big feet."

55 A typical exchange between Tiger and his agent, Norton:

"Tiger, they want to know when you can do that interview."

"Tell them to kiss my ass!"

"All right, and after that, what should I tell them?"

"Tell them to kiss my ass again!"

"O.K., and after that . . ."

56 But it's a cockiness cut with humility, the paradox pounded into his skull by a father who in one breath speaks of his son with religious awe and in the next grunts, "You weren't s— then, Tiger. You ain't s— now. You ain't never gonna be s—."

57 "That's why I know I can handle all this," Tiger says, "no matter how big it gets. I grew up in the media's eye, but I was taught never to lose sight of where I came from. Athletes aren't as gentlemanly as they used to be. I don't like that change. I like the idea of being a role model. It's an honor. People took the time to help me as a kid, and they impacted my life. I want to do the same for kids."

58 So, if it's a clinic for children instead of an interview or an endorsement for adults, the cynic in Tiger gives way to the child who grew up immersed in this father's vision of an earth-altering compassion, the 7-year-old boy who watched scenes from the Ethiopian famine on the evening news, went right to his bedroom and returned with a $20 bill to contribute from his piggy bank. Last spring busloads of inner-city kids would arrive at golf courses where Tiger was playing for Stanford, spilling out to watch the Earl and Tiger show in wonder. Earl would talk about the dangers of drugs, then proclaim, "Here's Tiger Woods on drugs," and Tiger would stagger to the tee, topping the ball so it bounced crazily to the side. And then, presto, with a wave of his arms Earl would remove the drugs from Tiger's body, and his son would stride to the ball and launch a 330-yard rocket across the sky. Then Earl would talk about respect and trust and hard work and demonstrate what they can all lead to by standing ten feet in front of his son, raising his arms and telling Tiger to smash the ball between them—and, *whoosh*, Tiger would part not only the old man's arms but his haircut too.

59 They've got plans, the two of them, big plans, for a Tiger Woods Foundation that will fund scholarships across the country, set up clinics and coaches and access to golf courses for inner-city children. "I throw those visions out there in front of him," Earl says, "and it's like reeling in a fish. He goes for the bait, takes it, and away he goes. This is nothing new. It's been working this way for a long time."

60 "That's the difference," says Merchant, Tiger's attorney and a family friend. "Other athletes who have risen to this level just didn't have this kind of guidance. With a father and mother like Tiger's, he has to be real. It's such a rare quality in celebrities nowadays. There hasn't been a politician

since John Kennedy whom people have wanted to touch. But watch Tiger. He has it. He actually listens to people when they stop him in an airport. He looks them in the eye. I can't ever envision Tiger Woods selling his autograph."

61   See, maybe Tiger can win.

62   Let's be honest. The machine will win because you can't work both sides of this street. The machine will win because you can't transcend wearing sixteen Nike swooshes, you can't move human hearts while you're busy pushing sneakers. Gandhi didn't hawk golf balls, did he? Jackie Robinson was spared that fate because he came and went while Madison Avenue was still teething. Ali became a symbol instead of a logo because of boxing's disrepute and because of the attrition of cells in the basal ganglia of his brain. Who or what will save Tiger Woods?

63   Did someone say Buddha?

64   Every year near his birthday, Tiger goes with his mother to a Buddhist temple and makes a gift of rice, sugar, and salt to the monks there who have renounced all material goods. A mother-of-pearl Buddha given to Tiger by his Thai grandfather watches over him while he sleeps, and a gold Buddha hangs from the chain on his neck. "I like Buddhism because it's a whole way of being and living," Tiger says. "It's based on discipline and respect and personal responsibility. I like Asian culture better than ours because of that. Asians are much more disciplined than we are. Look how well behaved their children are. It's how my mother raised me. You can question, but talk back? Never. In Thailand, once you've earned people's respect, you have it for life. Here it's, What have you done for me lately? So here you can never rest easy. In this country I have to be very careful. I'm easygoing, but I won't let you in completely. There, I'm Thai, and it feels very different. In many ways I consider that home.

65   "I believe in Buddhism. Not every aspect, but most of it. So I take bits and pieces. I don't believe that human beings can achieve ultimate enlightenment, because humans have flaws. I don't want to get rid of all my wants and desires. I can enjoy material things, but that doesn't mean I need them. It doesn't matter to me whether I live in a place like this"—the golf club in his hand makes a sweep of the Orlando villa—"or in a shack. I'd be fine in a shack, as long as I could play some golf. I'll do the commercials for Nike and for Titleist, but there won't be much more than that. I have no desire to be the king of endorsement money."

66   On the morning after he decides to turn pro, there's a knock on his hotel room door. It's Norton, bleary-eyed but exhilarated after a late-night round of negotiations with Nike. He explains to Tiger and Earl that the benchmark for contract endorsements in golf is Norman's reported $2½ million-a-year deal with Reebok. Then, gulping down hard on the yabba-dabba-doo rising up his throat, Norton announces Nike's offer: $40 million for five years, 8 mil a year. "Over three times what Norman gets!" Norton exults.

67   Silence.

68   "Guys, do you realize this is more than Nike pays any athlete in salary, even Jordan?"

69   Silence.

70   "Finally," Norton says now, recalling that morning, "Tiger says, 'Mmmm-hmmm,' and I say, 'That's it? Mmmm-hmmm?' No 'Omigod.' No slapping five or 'Ya-hooo!' So I say, 'Let me go through this again, guys.' Finally Tiger says, 'Guess that's pretty amazing.' That's it. When I made the deal with Titleist a day later, I went back to them saying, 'I'm almost embarrassed to tell you this one. Titleist is offering a little more than $20 million over five years.'"

71   On the Monday morning after his first pro tournament, a week after the two megadeals, Tiger scans the tiny print on the sports page under Milwaukee Open money earnings and finds his name. Tiger Woods: $2,544. "That's my money," he exclaims. "I earned this!"

72   See, maybe Tiger can win.

73   How? How can he win when there are so many insects under so many rocks? Several more death threats arrive just before the

Skins Game, prompting an increase in his plainclothes security force, which is already larger than anyone knows. His agent's first instinct is to trash every piece of hate mail delivered to IMG, but Tiger won't permit it. Every piece of racist filth must be saved and given to him. At Stanford he kept one letter taped to his wall. Fuel comes from the oddest forms.

74   The audience, in its hunger for goodness, swallows hard over the Nike ad that heralds Tiger's entrance into the professional ranks. The words that flash on the screen over images of Tiger—"There are still courses in the United States I am not allowed to play because of the color of my skin. I've heard I'm not ready for you. Are you ready for me?"—ooze the very attitude from which many in the audience are seeking relief. The media backlash is swift: the Tiger Woods who used to tell the press "The only time I think about race is when the media ask me"—whoa, what happened to him?

75   What happened to him was a steady accretion of experiences, also known as life. What happened, just weeks before he was born, was a fusillade of limes and BBs rattling the Woods house in Cypress, California, one of the limes shattering the kitchen window, splashing glass all around the pregnant Tida, to welcome the middle-class subdivision's first non-Caucasian family.

76   What happened was a gang of older kids seizing Tiger on his first day of kinder-garten, tying him to a tree, hurling rocks at him, calling him monkey and nigger. And Tiger, at age 5, telling no one what happened for several days, trying to absorb what this meant about himself and his world.

77   What happened was the Look, as Tiger and Earl came to call it, the uneasy, silent stare they received in countless country-club locker rooms and restaurants. "Something a white person could never understand," says Tiger, "unless he went to Africa and suddenly found himself in the middle of a tribe." What happened was Tiger's feeling pres-sured to leave a driving range just two years ago, not far from his family's California home, because a resident watching Tiger's drives rocket into the nearby protective netting reported that a black teenager was trying to bombard his house.

78   What happened was the cold shoulder Earl got when he took his tyke to play at the Navy Golf Course in Cypress—"a club," Earl says, "composed mostly of retired naval personnel who knew blacks only as cooks and servers, and along comes me, a retired lieutenant colonel outranking 99 percent of them, and I have the nerve to take up golf at 42 and immediately become a low handicap and beat them, and then I have the audacity to have this kid. Well, they had to do some-thing. They took away Tiger's playing privi-leges twice, said he was too young, even though there were other kids too young who they let play. The second time it happened, I went up to the pro who had done it and made a bet. I said, 'If you'll spot my 3-year-old just one stroke a hole, nine holes, play-ing off the same tees, and he beats you, will you certify him?' The pro started laughing and said, 'Sure.' Tiger beat him by two strokes, got certified, then the members went over the pro's head and kicked him out again. That's when we switched him to another course."

79   Beat them. That was his parents' solution for each banishment, each Look. Hold your tongue, hew to every rule, and beat them. Tiger Woods is the son of the first black baseball player in the Big Seven, a catcher back in the early '50s, before the conference became the Big Eight. A man who had to leave his Kansas State teammates on road trips and travel miles to stay in motels for blacks; who had to go to the back door of restaurant kitchens to be fed while his teammates dined inside; who says, "This is the most racist society in the world—I know that." A man who learned neither to extinguish his anger nor spray it but to quietly convert it into animus, the determi-nation to enter the system and overcome it by turning its own tools against it. A Green Beret explosives expert whose mind natu-rally ran that way, whose response, upon hearing Tiger rave about the security in his new walled community, was, "I could get in.

I could blow up the clubhouse and be gone before they ever knew what hit them." A father who saw his son, from the beginning, as the one who would enter one of America's last Caucasian bastions, the PGA Tour, and overthrow it from within in a manner that would make it smile and ask for more. "Been planning that one for twenty years," says Earl. "See, you don't turn it into hatred. You turn it into something positive. So many athletes who reach the top now had things happen to them as children that created hostility, and they bring that hostility with them. But that hostility uses up energy. If you can do it without the chip on the shoulder, it frees up all that energy to create."

80   It's not until Stanford, where Tiger takes an African-American history course and stays up half the night in dormitories talking with people of every shade of skin, that his experiences begin to crystallize. "What I realized is that even though I'm mathematically Asian—if anything—if you have one drop of black blood in the United States, you're black," says Tiger. "And how important it is for this country to talk about this subject. It's not me to blow my horn, the way I come across in that Nike ad, or to say things quite that way. But I felt it was worth it because the message needed to be said. You can't say something like that in a polite way. Golf has shied away from this for too long. Some clubs have brought in tokens, but nothing has really changed. I hope what I'm doing can change that."

81   But don't overestimate race's proportion in the fuel that propels Tiger Woods. Don't look for traces of race in the astonishing rubble at his feet on the Sunday after he lost the Texas Open by two strokes and returned to his hotel room and snapped a putter in two with one violent lift of his knee. Then another putter. And another. And another and another—eight in all before his rage was spent and he was ready to begin considering the loss's philosophical lesson. "That volcano of competitive fire, that comes from me," says Earl. A volcano that's mostly an elite athlete's need to win, a need far more immediate than that of changing the world.

82   No, don't overestimate race, but don't overlook it, either. When Tiger is asked about racism, about the effect it has on him when he senses it in the air, he has a golf club in his hands. He takes the club by the neck, his eyes flashing hot and cold at once, and gives it a short upward thrust. He says, "It makes me want to stick it right up their asses." Pause. "On the golf course."

83   The machine will win because there is so much of the old man's breath in the boy . . . and how long can the old man keep breathing? At 2 A.M., hours before the second round of the Tour Championship in Tulsa on October 25, the phone rings in Tiger's hotel room. It's Mom. Pop's in an ambulance, on his way to a Tulsa hospital. He's just had his second heart attack.

84   The Tour Championship? The future of humanity? The hell with 'em. Tiger's at the old man's bedside in no time, awake most of the night. Tiger's out of contention in the Tour Championship by dinnertime, with a second-round 78, his worst till then as a pro. "There are things more important than golf," he says.

85   The old man survives—and sees the pattern at work, of course. He's got to throw away the cigarettes. He's got to quit ordering the cholesterol special for breakfast. "I've got to shape up now, God's telling me," Earl says, "or I won't be around for the last push, the last lesson." The one about how to ride the tsunami of runaway fame.

86   The machine will win because no matter how complicated it all seems now, it is simpler than it will ever be. The boy will marry one day, and the happiness of two people will lie in his hands. Children will follow, and it will become his job to protect three or four or five people from the molars of the machine. Imagine the din of the grinding in five, ten, fifteen years, when the boy reaches his golfing prime.

87   The machine will win because the whole notion is so ludicrous to begin with, a kid clutching an eight-iron changing the course of humanity. No, of course not, there won't be thousands of people sitting in front of tanks because of Tiger Woods. He won't

bring about the overthrow of a tyranny or spawn a religion that one day will number 300 million devotees.

88   But maybe Pop is onto something without quite seeing what it is. Maybe it has to do with timing: the appearance of his son when America is turning the corner to a century in which the country's faces of color will nearly equal those that are white. Maybe, every now and then, a man gets swallowed by the machine, but the machine is changed more than he is.

89   For when we swallow Tiger Woods, the yellow-black-red-white man, we swallow something much more significant than Jordan or Charles Barkley. We swallow hope in the American experiment, in the pell-mell jumbling of genes. We swallow the belief that the face of the future is not necessarily a bitter or bewildered face; that it might even, one day, be something like Tiger Woods's face: handsome and smiling and ready to kick all comers' asses.

90   We see a woman, 50-ish and Caucasian, well-coiffed and tailored—the woman we see at every country club—walk up to Tiger Woods before he receives the Haskins Award and say, "When I watch you taking on all those other players, Tiger, I feel like I'm watching my own son" . . . and we feel the quivering of the cosmic compass that occurs when human beings look into the eyes of someone of another color and see their own flesh and blood.

Source: Gary Smith, "The Chosen One," in *The Best American Sports Writing*, ed. George Plimpton. Boston: Houghton-Mifflin, 1997, pp. 297–316.

DISCUSSION QUESTIONS

1. Smith develops a number of metaphors to express his views on Tiger Woods. Of these, the most extended is the metaphor of the "machine." What, exactly, does the "machine" stand for? How appropriate is this metaphor for Smith's purposes? How effective do you find his repeated references to the machine? Identify other examples of extended metaphors in this argument and discuss their effectiveness.

2. From what point of view does Smith write—that is, personal, impersonal, first person or third person, formal or familiar, and so on? Do you think this choice of perspective was strategic on Smith's part, intended to create a particular effect or support a particular position? Discuss.

3. Summarize Smith's major claim in a sentence or two. To what class of argument does this claim belong?

4. Smith makes a number of secondary causal arguments—some indicating why the "machine" will win, others, why Tiger will win. Identify three or four of these secondary arguments and discuss with your classmates the adequacy of their support.

5. Characterize the overall tone of Smith's writing. Then, conduct a World Wide Web search for other writing by Smith and obtain two or three other samples. Is the tone similar in all the pieces? If not, why do you think he has adopted this particular tone to write about "The Chosen One"?

SUGGESTIONS FOR WRITING (16.3)

1. You are a senior editor of *Sports Illustrated* submitting Gary Smith's "The Chosen One" to George Plimpton, editor of *The Best American Sports Writing*, for inclusion into the annual collection. Selection is highly competitive, and, as Smith's editor, you have to point out the merits of his article. Write a one-page

cover letter to Plimpton evaluating Smith's writing and recommending it for inclusion.

2. Earl Woods, Tiger's father, claimed that his son "is the Chosen One. He'll have the power to impact nations. Not people. Nations." Construct an outline for a causal argument (an argument of effect) claiming that "Tiger Woods will impact nations." Indicate in your outline the kind of information and support you would need to argue this claim effectively. Don't forget Mill's tests for causality as possible support (see Chapter 8).

3. Smith has created an interesting device for presenting argument and counter-argument ("The machine will win. . . . Tiger will win."). Write your own argument of effect about the future of a young person you know or know about, using Smith's model for presenting the counterargument. Note: your claim need not be as ambitious as Smith's. For example, you could claim that a sibling will be a varsity athlete or that a popular movie star will be a flash in the pan.

4. Do you think that the particular sport a person plays can tell us something about that person? For example, is Tiger Woods's choice of golf or Michael Jordan's choice of basketball (or, briefly, baseball, for that matter) significant in our attempt to understand each? Select an athlete you know or know about (professional, amateur, or recreational) and write a two- to three-page argument demonstrating what we learn about this person through his or her athletic activity. Your argument may be interpretive or causal. Be sure you are clear which it is before you begin supporting it.

Because this assignment is relatively sophisticated, you should show a draft to your instructor to make sure you're on the right track.

PUBLIC USE OF NATIVE AMERICAN NAMES, SYMBOLS, AND MASCOTS

RICHARD P. MILLS

Richard Mills is the Commissioner of Education for the State of New York. This argument was written in the form of a memorandum to presidents of boards of education and superintendents of public schools in New York State.

According to the N.Y. State Education website, "As Commissioner of Education, Mills serves as chief executive officer of the Board of Regents, which has jurisdiction over the most comprehensive state educational system in the nation. The system encompasses every education endeavor in the State, including public and non-public elementary, middle, and secondary education; public and independent colleges and universities; museums, libraries, historical societies, and archives; the vocational rehabilitation system; and responsibility for the licensing, practicing, and oversight of 38 professions."

April 5, 2001
TO: Presidents of Boards of Education and Superintendents of Public Schools
FROM: Richard P. Mills
SUBJECT: Public Schools Use of Native American Names, Symbols, and Mascots

1   Some time ago, I directed Department staff to study the use of Native American mascots by public schools. I would like to share with you the results of that work.

What I conclude:

2   Our review confirmed that the use of Native American symbols is part of time-honored traditions in some of our communities, and that there are deeply felt, albeit conflicting, ideas about them. Some members of these communities believe that the mascots honor or pay tribute to Native Americans and their culture. However, most Native Americans appear to find the portrayal by others of their treasured cultural and religious symbols disparaging and disrespectful. Many [others] who have looked at this issue concur.

3   After careful [thought] and consideration, I have concluded that the use of Native American symbols or depictions as mascots can become a barrier to building a safe and nurturing school community and improving academic achievement for all students. I ask the superintendents and presidents of school boards to lead their communities to a new understanding of this matter. I ask boards to end the use of Native American mascots as soon as practical. Some communities have thought about this and are ready to act. Others already have acted and I commend them. Yet, in others, more reflection and listening is needed, and so I ask that these [discussions] begin now. I believe that local leaders can find the right way to inquire into this matter and resolve it locally. Next year I will formally evaluate the progress on this issue.

4   Here is my reasoning.

What we found:

5   There has already been extensive statewide discussion of this issue. Some of it is eloquent. We sought the views of local superintendents. Many wrote directly and many others expressed their thoughts through District Superintendents. I have had extended conversations with a few of them. We contacted representatives of Native American communities. We also asked the counsel of District Superintendents. We researched the literature on this subject and read legal documents from other states. We examined New York law, regulation, and Regents policy. In addition, many citizens wrote to us.

6   The use of Native American names, symbols, and mascots is such a significant issue that it is being looked at in other states, in professional sports, at the collegiate level, as well as at the local level in some New York school districts. The Society of the Indian Psychologists of the Americas has raised the concern that the use of these mascots and symbols creates an "unwelcome academic environment" for Native American students. Organizations such as the NAACP, and the NEA have issued statements calling for an end to the use of mascots. The U.S. Census 2000 issued a resolution stating that it would not include teams that used these symbols as part of its promotional program. over the last 30 years, more than 600 colleges, universities and high schools have changed or eliminated their use of Native American mascots. For example, the Los Angeles school board required its junior high and high schools to drop Native American-themed names and mascots, and 20 high schools in Wisconsin followed suit. Collegiate institutions such as Miami University of Ohio, St. John's University, Siena College and Stanford University have changed their school logos. In the professional sports world, objections have also arisen, and it is clear that recent expansion teams in professional baseball, hockey, football and basketball have avoided the use of Indian-themed names or mascots.

7   In 1999, the United States Department of Justice Civil Rights Division investigated a North Carolina school district to determine if the high school's mascot and nicknames violated Federal Civil Rights Law by creating a racially hostile environment. That

investigation was closed after the school district's board of education decided to eliminate the use of Native American religious symbols.

8   In August 2000, Attorney General Elliot Spitzer [reviewed] this issue as it related to a New York State school district. The Attorney General raised serious concerns that certain uses of Native American mascots and symbols could violate the Federal Civil Rights Act of 1964. His opinion identified many factors that school districts should consider in examining their use of these symbols and mascots, particularly areas such as stereotypical nicknames, images, gestures and use of historical and religious symbols such as feather headdress, face-paint, or totem poles.

9   Clearly, many of those who are thinking deeply about this issue are concerned that the use of these symbols should end.

The argument:

10   Schools must provide a safe and supportive environment that promotes achievement of the standards for all children. The use of Native American mascots by some schools can make that school environment seem less safe and supportive to some children, and may send an inappropriate message to children about what is or is not respectful behavior toward others. For that reason we must question the use of such mascots. If children and parents in the school committee are offended or made to feel diminished by the school mascot, what school leader or board would not want to know that and correct the situation? School mascots are intended to make a statement about what the school values. School leaders and communities may not be aware that the statement heard can be contrary to the one intended.

11   Here are some thoughts from a student: "Today this school promotes respect, responsibility, compassion, [honesty,] and tolerance. When you use words like these, you need to teach by example. The resigning of this mascot would be a great example of these character education words. I would like to see my brother, sister, and cousins go to a school that shows respect and toler-

ance for other cultures. I don't want them to feel the confusion that I have felt going to this school. It has taken me a couple of years to come to understand Native American stereotypes and their effects on me. By keeping [this] mascot the principal lesson the students, staff, and community learn is how to tolerate stereotypes."

12   Some argue that such mascots honor Native Americans. Most Native American representatives do not share that view.

13   Some would argue that mascots that are problematic could be made dignified through some state review process. It is difficult to imagine how to craft criteria to make such a judgment process feasible on a statewide basis. Most people would recognize and deplore mocking, distorted representations of minority group members. However, fair-minded people might view these mascots as respectful without realizing that the representation included religious symbols that Native American observers would find distressing when used in that manner.

14   Some urge keeping the status quo. That is not realistic either. Collegiate sports and newer professional teams have recognized changing public attitudes and decided not to use Native American mascots. The same changes that affected them will eventually overtake schools. It would be better [to] resolve the matter now. The central role of sports in this issue is advantageous. Few areas of American life are as concerned about fairness and respect for individual value and achievement as is the world of sport. We can turn to those values as we think about mascots.

15   Some call for an immediate and statewide halt to the use of these mascots. That approach is not advisable. People in many communities haven't had an opportunity to talk about this and listen to one another. There are cherished traditions surrounding many of the mascots. There are even significant costs involved: consider mascots on team uniforms and gymnasium floors, to cite obvious examples. In any case, local remedies should be exhausted first. Many communities have engaged the issue and

made changes. Many other communities will now do so.

16   Still others believe this is a local matter. I cannot agree that it is *only* a local matter. There is state interest in providing a safe and supportive learning environment for every child. The use of Native American mascots involves a state responsibility as well.

17   Here are some questions that might help local communities consider how to approach the issue. I have adapted them from ideas suggested by a New York School Superintendent and they seem like a good place to begin.

- Do Native Americans and non-Native Americans perceive the mascot differently?
- Is there a significant difference between how the mascot may have been intended and how it is interpreted?
- How should an organization respond if its well-intentioned actions unintentionally offend a member of the group's [religious] or ethnic beliefs?

- Are there other symbols that represent the school's values that could be used in place of the existing mascot?

18   I call upon school leaders in communities that use Native American symbols, names, or mascots to pose these questions to their communities and lead them in a discussion of the right path to take. It is important that our students learn about the diversity of our communities so that they will understand and respect our differences and draw strength from them in becoming good citizens and productive adults. School administrators, staff, parents, and community members play a critical role in modeling behavior that celebrates and honors traditions and beliefs of our fellow citizens. As educators, we have an obligation to inform communities so that they might come to understand the pain, however unintentionally inflicted, these symbols cause.

Source: Richard P. Mills, "Public Schools Use of Native American Names, Symbols, and Mascots." http://earnestman.tripod.com/ fr.2001nysed.htm

DISCUSSION QUESTIONS

1. Under the heading *"What we found,"* Mills concludes "Clearly, many of those who are thinking deeply about this issue are concerned that the use of these symbols should end." Is this an example of the *ad populum* fallacy?

2. Is the factual support Mills introduces to support his argument adequate? Why or why not?

3. Discuss with two or three of your classmates how appropriate Mills's diction, tone, references, etc., are to his intended audience.

4. Place the claims made in the first paragraph under the heading *"The argument"* into the syllogistic model. With a group of your classmates, consider whether each element of the syllogism is adequately supported.

5. Mills makes a number of inductive conclusions that lack support through individual examples. Identify two or three of these and consider whether they weaken his overall argument.

SUGGESTIONS FOR WRITING (16.4)

1. Create an analogy to the use of Indian mascot names that might be used in an argument supporting their discontinuance—i.e., "Using mascot names like 'the Braves' or 'the Redskins' would be like calling a team xxx or xxx." Make sure your analogy satisfies the criteria of a reasonable comparison.

2. Regardless of your own views on this topic, write a three-page argument supporting the use of team mascots with Indian names. Be sure to identify the type of claim you are making and to support it as reasonably as possible.

3. Assume you are the principal of a high school with a long tradition of using a "Redskin" mascot. Write a one-page letter to your athletic teams supporting your decision to discontinue use of this mascot. You may use Commissioner Mills's memo as support.

4. Write a three- to four-page causal argument speculating on the reasons for the widespread adoption of Indian mascot names for sports teams.

SOMETIMES, A GAME MEANS MUCH MORE THAN THE SCORE

JOHN FEINSTEIN

Well-known sportswriter John Feinstein has published a number of books on contemporary sports, including A Season on the Brink, A Good Walk Spoiled, *and* The Last Amateurs. *Feinstein is a regular commentator for National Public Radio and writes for AOL and* Golf *Magazine. This article was posted on America Online on December 2, 2004. In 1999, Feinstein published a book on the history of the Army-Navy football game titled* A Civil War: Army v. Navy.

1 One of the questions I am frequently asked is: "If you could only go to one event in sports every year, which one would it be?"

2 Most people expect my answer to be The Final Four or The Masters or perhaps Wimbledon or The World Series. I love each of those events and consider myself fortunate to have covered them often through the years. But the answer to the question is simple: Army-Navy.

3 There's just nothing like the Army-Navy football game. Not because of the quality of the football game, but because of the quality of the people playing the football game. And because of the quality of the people who have played in the game in the past. Saturday, when Army and Navy play for the 105th time, the day will be special. Not because Navy is 8-2 and going to a bowl game for a second straight season. Not because Army is 2-8 but well on the way back to respectability under the leadership of Bobby Ross. Not because Navy fullback Kyle Eckel

is a good enough player that pro scouts say he could be a third or fourth round draft pick this spring.

4 That's all well and good. It is also well and good that, regardless of the size and speed of the players—or lack thereof—the game will be played very hard, with great intensity and emotion and a minimum of trash-talking. The nature of Army-Navy is best summed up by a brief moment three years ago when President Bush conducted the coin toss just 10 weeks after the tragedies of 9-11. When he tossed the coin into the air, Navy captain Ed Malinowski made the call on behalf of his team:

5 "Heads SIR!" he said, loud and clear for everyone in the packed stadium to hear. We all smiled at that moment because only at Army-Navy would you hear a future marine tell the President of the United States, "Heads SIR!" during the coin toss.

6 Saturday, when the coin is tossed, Malinowski will be in Iraq. So will a number

of players who were on the field that day along with many others who have played in Army-Navy games in the recent past. They will be on the minds of all of us in the stadium throughout the day. Scott Zellem, Ron Winchester, J.P. Blecksmith and Kevin Norman will also be on our minds. All played football at Army and Navy. All graduated and went overseas to fight for their country. In the last year, all died for their country. They aren't the first and, sadly, they won't be the last. When Norman died last spring, Jim Cantelupe, his roommate at West Point, talked about what he and all of those who attend the academies know and understand about life in the military.

7   "You never want to think you're going to die overseas," he said. "But you know that it's possible. Every day that you're there, you're preparing for the possibility that you may have to fight for your country. You don't want to have to do it, but you have to be ready, willing and able to do it. We all are. We know that's why we're there."

8   If you are ready, willing and able to fight for your country, then you must accept the possibility that you may die for your country. When Pat Tillman, the one-time Arizona Cardinals defensive back died in Afghanistan last spring, much was made—properly—of the fact that he died a hero because he died fighting for his country. But what made Pat Tillman a hero wasn't the fact that he died for his country, it was that he was WILLING to die for his country.

9   Every player on the field Saturday will be like Pat Tillman: willing to die for his country. Sure, Pat Tillman gave up a lot of money and glory when he left the NFL to volunteer for the Army. The players at Army and Navy may not be as gifted or as wealthy as Tillman was, but they made a decision similar to his: they are all good enough students that they could have gotten into almost any college; almost all are good enough players that they could have gotten scholarships at Division 1-AA schools (at least). All could have left Army or Navy after two years, no harm, no foul, and gone to school someplace else.

All elected to stay, knowing—especially now—that they might very well find themselves in harm's way soon after graduation.

10   Zellem graduated from Navy in 1991. He was long past his five year commitment when he died earlier this year. The same was true for Norman, Army class of 1996, who steered his plummeting airplane away from a populated area and crashed into a bridge so only he and his co-pilot would die. Winchester and Blecksmith were younger, but understood—and embraced—the risks they faced.

11   This week, the football players at Notre Dame faced a crisis: their coach was fired quite suddenly. Should they agree to play in the Insight.com Bowl? The players at Auburn may face the unfairness of finishing a season undefeated and yet not being allowed to compete for the national championship. The players at Rutgers just went through a 12th straight losing season.

12   Adversity? Sure. But not exactly adversity that matches what Zellem, Winchester, Blecksmith, Norman and their families have faced this year. Not exactly the adversity that many of the players who will play in Philadelphia on Saturday may be facing a few months from now.

13   Almost every college football team likes to post some kind of inspirational message over the door of its locker room. Things like, "Winners never quit and quitters never win." As the players exit the locker room, they all reach up and touch the sign to remind themselves to try to live up to the words. More often than not, the message changes when the coach changes. But at Army, for as long as anyone can remember, the sign over the locker room door has been the same: "I lay me down to bleed awhile but I will rise again to fight."

14   Think about those words. In many way they sum up exactly what our country—regardless of how one feels about the war in Iraq—has done since 9-11. They also explain perfectly the mentality of those who play football at Army and Navy. Knock me down and I will get up. Knock me out and I will still get up. Kill me and others will rise to

take my place. I may lose a battle, but I will never surrender.

15   Perhaps that's all just too corny to even ponder in a sports world dominated today by Ron Artest and on-field brawls in so-called, "rivalry" games and multi-millionaire athletes wrestling for money with billionaire owners. But it is what Army and Navy has always been about and always will be about.

16   You see, I want to be at Army-Navy on Saturday because Tyson Stahl will be there. Tyson Stahl is a Navy senior. His older brother Hoot, also a Navy football player, is currently on his second tour of duty in Iraq. A year ago, Navy assistant coach Jeff Monkton received an American flag from a friend, who happened to be an ARMY officer stationed in Baghdad. The flag had flown over the Baghdad Airport shortly after the American takeover of the city. Monkton's friend wondered if the Navy football team might have some use for the flag.

17   It did. Prior to each game that flag, carried by Tyson Stahl, has led the Navy team onto the field. Thinking about his brother as he carries the flag, Tyson Stahl says that each time he carries it with his teammates behind him, "It is the proudest moment of my life."

18   I wouldn't miss seeing that moment in a stadium filled with people who feel as I do; people who will be thinking of Hoot Stahl and Ed Malinowski and Scott Zellem and Ron Winchester and J.P. Blecksmith and Kevin Norman, for anything else but sports.

Not this year. Not any year.

Source: AOL sports.

DISCUSSION QUESTIONS

1. Feinstein's claim is the answer to the question: "If you could only go to one event in sports every year, which one would it be?" Summarize his answer and its class of argument.

2. In Par. 15, Feinstein suggests that his argument might be "just too corny." Presumably, a "corny" argument would rely more on emotion and sentiment than on reason. Do you think this is the case with this argument? Discuss your reasons with your classmates.

3. What stylistic similarities do you find in this argument by Feinstein and in Smith's "The Chosen One?"

4. How would you identify Feinstein's purpose in writing this article? Is he trying to convince his readers to agree with his views on the Army-Navy game? Or is he using the opportunity of the article merely to express his own views or to praise the players or to praise all who fight for their country? Is the article really an argument? Why or why not?

5. Feinstein's essay is set very specifically in time (the 2004 Army-Navy game) and his writing is filled with references to very specific people, many of whom will not be playing football when you read this article. What are some of the effects of these specific references? Consider, among other possibilities, whether they "date" the article, making it less relevant to a contemporary reader; whether they make the article more real, more vivid.

SUGGESTIONS FOR WRITING (16.5)

1. In his book *A Civil War,* Feinstein discusses the ways in which football is like war. Some would argue that many team sports have war-like elements. In two pages, compare a sport you know well with war or battle. Your comparison will combine elements of factual and interpretive argument.

2. One of Feinstein's gifts as a writer is his ability to describe sports competitions without lapsing into cliché. He does this by using original language and imagery and by keeping the pace of his descriptions sharp and quick. See if you can write a one-page description of a moment in sports that you saw or experienced personally. This description will be a factual argument based upon your own personal experience and observation.

3. Feinstein's argument answers the question "If you could only go to one event in sports every year, which one would it be?" Write your own three-page answer to this question (a causal argument). You may exchange a sports event for any other large public event (e.g., music concert, play, public lecture).

4. Rewrite the argument you wrote for #3 above, including appeals to the reader's sentiment. That is, you have permission to be "corny," as Feinstein puts it, or emotional, or sentimental. With a classmate, consider which paper is more effective at achieving its purpose (and the purposes may be different) and why.

5. Write a three-page argument to a fictitious reader with no interest in sports recommending the experience of being a sports fan. If you personally have no interest in sports, write a recommendation to a sports fanatic, arguing (recommending) a life without sports.

BIZBALL

HARVEY ARATON

This argument was the feature story in a Sunday New York Times Magazine *issue devoted entirely to sports (October 1998). Harvey Araton is a sports columnist for the* New York Times. *The cover of this issue of the magazine carried the following teaser/abstract: "For the Murdochs and the Disneys, sports is no game. It's a hot, global entertainment product—and that's changing all the rules."*

1 Once every spring, I get a telephone call from my friend Michelle, who informs me she has received her invoice for Knicks season tickets and will be faxing news of the latest increase in the price of her two seats in the front row, directly behind the team's bench. This year, despite the lockout that threatens to delay the start of the National Basketball Association's season, the markup is $20 per ticket. That's the lowest since Pat Riley began modeling Armani at Madison Square Garden in 1991, at the expense of Michelle's once-perfect sight lines. The other good news is that Jeff Van Gundy—considerably shorter than his predecessor, with much less hair and given to the occasional midgame squat—remains the coach.

2 For the amount she is sacrificing to support her decades-old basketball habit, Michelle Musler prefers to see for herself

why her beloved Knicks haven't won the championship in a quarter-century. On the other hand, she can no longer afford the unobstructed view she had when the Knicks' bench was across the way, where Spike Lee holds court, in a camera-friendly seat that will cost the he's-gotta-have-it filmmaker $1,350 per game this year, or $116,100 for his two season tickets. Comparatively, at $220 a pop, or $9,460 per season ticket, Michelle is in the cheap seats.

3   She also sends me the welcome-back letter that annually accompanies the bill and is signed by David W. Checketts, the Garden's chief executive officer. For years, Michelle has indignantly scrawled in the margin, "No reference to price increase!" Lo and behold, a corporate conscience emerged last spring, albeit one line's worth, near the bottom of a cheerful, go-team epistle. "In such a competitive marketplace," Checketts wrote, "please be aware that you will notice an increase in your 1998–99 ticket renewal package."

4   Her five adult children were typically trenchant when their mother's tickets went up again. (The cost was a Broadway bargain at $45 as recently as 1991.) When, they wondered, would she outgrow this draining obsession and pay more attention to her retirement savings? A single woman in her early 60's, Michelle loves basketball, though, from the pregame buzz to the fourth-quarter buzzer. She holds stubbornly to the illusion of the extended team family, despite evidence all around her that the big sports daddies are more concerned with the construction of intricate global networks and taxpayer-financed stadiums that feature club seats and luxury suites, set conveniently apart from the rabid riffraff.

5   I have known few, if any, more involved fans during my sportswriting career than Michelle, who, to me, represents the endangered spirit of an industry that keeps getting bigger and, admittedly, better in many qualitative ways. When Riley's Knicks went to Houston in June 1994 with a chance to win that elusive championship, Michelle procured a ticket, booked a flight, ditched a client and went down with the ship. Now she wonders where many of the other committed loyalists from her Section 15 have gone.

6   "So many people I knew dropped out," she says ruefully. Like Dennis, the postal worker who brought priests from his community, and Danny, who though legally blind knew more about basketball than anyone Michelle has known. Her friends from down the row, the Coplands and the Tamans, were told by the man who'd sold them tickets for 20 years to get lost when he realized he could extract a lot more from brokers than he could from them.

7   "I'm embarrassed to tell people what I pay for basketball tickets," says Michelle, a professional coach herself, of corporate executives, who lives comfortably, not luxuriously, in Stamford, Conn. "They think you're rich or crazy."

8   Sometimes, it does seem as if the world has gone, well, sports crazy. Like the runaway cost of Michelle Musler's tickets, there appears to be no stopping this locomotive industry, as it has merged with the entertainment game to create a television-fueled explosion of expansion and wealth. Who could have imagined a decade ago that a single player, even one as breathtaking as Michael Jordan, could reel in a reported $80 million in salary and endorsements in a single year? That a media and entertainment baron would bid $1 billion to own a single team, as Rupert Murdoch offered recently for England's world-famous Manchester United soccer club? A year ago, Murdoch paid $311 million for the Los Angeles Dodgers, after *Financial World* magazine estimated the value of the team and its assets at about $180 million. That all-time-high price for a sports team had little of the endurance of Roger Maris's home run record. Compared with the $530 million Alfred Lerner recently agreed to pay for football's expansionist Cleveland Browns, it's a bargain.

9   Once derided as an Australian interloper and muckraker, Murdoch is now the most influential man in sports. He has made himself the face on the corporate invasion, steering his Fox Sports tank across the

American landscape, removing competitors from his path by shooting off serious denominations of cash. "Murdoch and Fox changed the economics of sports when he took football away from CBS five years ago," says Robert M. Gutkowski, Checketts's predecessor at the Garden and now C.E.O. of the Marquee Group, a New York-based sports-marketing company.

10   When Fox lifted rights to the National Football Conference from CBS for $1.58 billion in 1993, Murdoch recognized the heightened appeal of live programming in a saturated market of taped family entertainment. If a sports deal lost money, it could nonetheless pull strong demographic groups to a network's mainstream programming. According to a report in *Barron's*, the Fox Network is worth about $4 billion more than it was when it struck its original N.F.L. deal, on which it lost $350 million.

11   By the time CBS paid $4 billion to regain a share of N.F.L. rights this season, some media analysts said it was banking its very future on football's power to draw male viewers back to the slumping network. Early in the fall TV season, it's looking like a good bet: CBS won the ratings race the opening two weeks, the first time it had led in any week since—take a guess—1993.

12   "Sports at the highest level is what people want to see," says Chet Simmons, who was the first president of ESPN and is currently a consultant for the Marquee Group. "And it's no different anywhere you go." The beauty of sports is that you don't have to go anywhere. Images of the games, bouncing off satellites, cross not only cultures but also continents. The world has become a playground for the media conglomerates as they pursue live, unscripted programming that is more valuable than ever on an increasingly crowded dial.

13   As a result, television money is pouring into the mainstream leagues as never before. The turn-of-the-century deals for national rights are staggering. N.F.L.: $17.6 billion over eight years in various network and cable deals. N.B.A.: $2.4 billion over four years. Even the National Hockey League, a sport with limited American appeal and a

television audience that has been in sobering retreat, reeled in a five-year, $600 million deal from ABC/ESPN—more than four times its previous Fox deal.

14   "Twenty years ago, we all thought the numbers couldn't get any higher," Simmons says. "There was a time in my career when I recommended the company not spend more than the previous year. I don't think that way anymore."

15   Given recent developments, it is no wonder that men like Checketts find it difficult to imagine a ceiling to this expanding universe, particularly as long as people wait on lists for Michelle Musler to follow her old friends out the Garden door.

16   "People have warned me and warned me that anger was building over the Knicks tickets and that the real fans were gone," Checketts says. "I have to tell you that I used to feel stronger about this than I do now. We raised Knicks prices 11 percent after a year when we got trounced in the second round, haven't been able to make any moves to significantly better the team and had a season-threatening lockout all summer. And guess what? We had a 96 percent season-ticket renewal rate, an all-time high."

17   Back in the early 1980's, when there were nights Michelle couldn't give her tickets away, I was an eager young beat reporter for *The New York Post*, dispatched on my Murdochian mission to search and distort. We were both drawn to the sport by the Knicks' 1970 and 1973 championship teams of Willis Reed and Walt Frazier. Sportswriters not much younger than myself look at me as if I'm 100 when I tell them how the Knicks' mid-1980's star, Bernard King, would playfully punch a computer key as he strolled by me to his seat on the plane, or how the coaches might look up from a Robert Ludlum novel to recommend the chicken over the steak. Today's coaches might be more inclined to allow a terrorist aboard the private jet than a reporter.

18   It wasn't that long ago that we could all feel closer to sports, more in touch, less likely to be shooed away by an executive bodyguard or a player's entourage. The players are richer, the arenas are nicer and the

telecasts are better, but the financial and ideological divide has grown. Michelle has waiter service at her seat but rare is the player or coach who will turn around and chat, as their predecessors did not long ago.

19   This distancing process began decades ago with the rise of the sports unions. But the perception of professional athletes as Our Guys was forever shattered when the sports agent David Falk walked into Nike headquarters one day in the mid-1980's and soon after Michael Jordan evolved from basketball icon to global marketing superman with a dollar sign on his chest. The old-school consensus was that such power handed to the players—though obviously extreme in Jordan's case—would be the death knell of professional sports. Free agency for players granted by the courts in the 1970's would damage fan loyalties, curtail interest. It sounded logical, but failed to foretell fundamental social and technological changes that transformed the way information is received.

20   Detailed reports of athletes who use drugs, commit acts of violence or father children out of wedlock are finally making corporate America more circumspect in choosing its jock-celebrity pitchmen, though it wasn't as if the public had begun looking elsewhere for action heroes. A dozen Chris Webbers, players pathologically drawn to trouble, are obscured by one Jordan, who is treated by the media and the public as Presidents once were.

21   By and large, the young channel surfers don't look at sports through a boys-of-summer prism. They have learned to define change as a way of life, and in a nation of so many single-parent homes, what's the big deal, anyway, of having a sports hero walk out after a championship season when Daddy has already traded in Mom? The bottom line: The more players have moved, the more off-season rumors have flowed, the more there has been to gossip about on another relatively new phenomenon, all-sports talk radio. Murdoch's formula has become the industry model. Stretch the story. Inflate the value. Cross the promotion.

22   Aging Americans may bristle at the manufactured noise and rank commercialism at sporting events and mourn the dearth of affordable seats and free autographs. But there is actually something right with this picture. Today's young sports fan has a much more sophisticated menu of options from which to choose—and learn. In the new world order, there are no more cold-war collisions between the Patriots and the Reds. The once-hated Russians skate on our fancy capitalist ponds and Europeans drop routinely into the N.B.A. Our football gladiators rumble in Europe, and you're no true baseball fan unless you can match the Hispanic superstar with his Caribbean home. There are competing professional women's basketball leagues. The ice hockey women were a bigger story at the Nagano Olympics last winter than the men. The world's hottest young tennis players are named Martina and Venus and Anna. The good old days may be gone for Michelle Musler, but there is no argument about this being a far better time for women and girls to get in the game.

23   And no matter how many overhyped jocks curse the adoring multitudes and spit on umpires, there seems no end to the fans' appetite for the games. As Mark McGwire and Sammy Sosa sprayed record-setting home-run balls around the nation's bleachers, we opened our hearts to baseball after years of watching it stumble into foul territory. The national media celebrated baseball's return to its pastime pedestal, while a recent USA Today/Gallup poll gave the game its highest approval ratings since before the 1994 season-ending strike.

24   The breaking of Maris's 37-year-old record was the equivalent of a large dose of Prozac, temporarily lifting the country from depressing developments in the capital. McGwire and Sosa, day after day, were an example of sports in all its galvanizing splendor, its knack for unifying a society polarized by politics, by gender, by religion and by race. And we saw it all, every at-bat, every pitch, shown live and a

hundred times more on 24-hour sports networks and Internet sites by the end of the night.

25   Some have speculated that declining television ratings—even the near-monolithic National Football League is down 22 percent over the past decade—is an ominous message that working- and middle-class families and fans are less frequently able to afford the games and are gradually losing interest in watching them. An equally plausible generalization is that lower ratings are resulting from the far greater number of choices available today than a decade ago. Satellite dishes provide more games in a year than most could watch in a lifetime, while the more conventional airwaves are saturated with pro and college games and a variety of events for the most eclectic tastes. The sports cable networks never sleep, and when they run short of viable programming, they can always make something up, as ESPN has done with its Extreme, or X, Games, a virtual Olympics "R" Us.

26   "It's quite successful, how's that?" the ABC/ESPN sports president, Steven Bornstein, said when I recently asked how much money the Extreme Games make.

27   It is the unpredictable nature of sports that makes it unique to the television audience. But maintaining that quality requires a delicate competitive balance, or at least the sense of a level playing field. More and more, the immediate future of sports looks like a half-dozen media titans bulking up in the gym for interminable rounds of corporate chess, with the same player sometimes controlling competing pieces on the board. For instance, under an umbrella Murdoch has walked with John Malone's TeleCommunications, Fox-Liberty has what Checketts calls "direct equity interest" in the Cablevision-owned Garden and its basketball and hockey teams. Murdoch this year has also acquired part ownership in a new Los Angeles arena, along with options to purchase minority shares of basketball's Lakers and hockey's Kings, in addition to their television rights. Given Murdoch's dual involvement, how can the Lakers ever make a trade with the Knicks without raising the issue of impropriety?

28   The trend of the elite sports teams and television rights being bought up by the many-headed media conglomerates like Fox, Turner and Disney is creating a nightmare of hidden agendas and potential conflicts. Several major-market teams reportedly opposed the lockout orchestrated by the N.B.A. commissioner, David Stern, last June because it was designed to protect smaller, poorer teams. "We may be getting $150 for a club ticket, but we have to have compelling teams coming in on a Tuesday night," Checketts says.

29   In other words, he is saying that sports has a class crisis in ownership that mirrors the one in the stands. There must be room for the smaller market within the process, if not necessarily the little guy inside Madison Square Garden.

30   Recently, Paul Allen, the Portland Trail Blazers' owner, went against the inflationary grain and slashed season-ticket prices an average of 14 percent, a kickback to his most loyal fans. As television and other revenues increase, this is the formula that would seem to be the most prudent long-term strategy to protect a team's fan base. Yet the big-market teams have habitually driven up player salaries (and forced once-thriving small-market teams to atrophy) by overspending. Then they pass this payroll burden on to ticket holders. On and on it has gone, with the average player salary now more than $2.6 million in basketball, $1.4 million in baseball and $1.2 million in hockey. Meanwhile, *Team Marketing Report* estimates the cost of basketball, football and hockey games for a family of four at between $214 and $245.

31   I recently commented to Checketts that my own family of four had attended just one major-league game last summer but a dozen games at Yogi Berra Stadium (ticket price: $4 to $8) on the campus of Montclair State University in New Jersey, one of the many minor-league operations that have flourished in recent years on the periphery of major-league markets. We also made a

couple of summer visits to the Garden to see the Liberty of the Women's National Basketball Association, which was more affordable, family-oriented and, to our pleasant surprise, far more integrated than any Knicks' game of the past decade I have been to.

32   Checketts said he understood what I was getting at, but added that this was not distressing news. No matter which events my young children are taken to, he said, they are being turned into sports fans. They will, before long, spend their own money at the ball parks and arenas. Or they will ante up to watch on pay TV, another unavoidable 21st-century revenue stream that men like Murdoch and Cablevision's Charles Dolan and Disney's Michael Eisner are factoring into their expansion outlay. As long as there is a next generation, Checketts was saying, there will be a game.

"I'm not trying to defend sports as   33 untouchable," he said. "But sometimes it seems as if there's an insatiable appetite for more."

And in such a competitive marketplace,   34 please be aware that you will notice an increase in your bill, because it is generally assumed that you are crazy for sports—or rich.

Source: Harvey Araton, "Bizball," *New York Times Sunday Magazine*. Oct. 18, 1998.

DISCUSSION QUESTIONS

1. Araton embeds his explicit central claim within his lengthy introductory narrative regarding sports fan Michelle: "I have known few, if any, more involved fans during my sportswriting career than Michelle, who, to me, represents the endangered spirit of an industry that keeps getting bigger and, admittedly, better in many qualitative ways." But these introductory paragraphs (Par. 1–7) also implicitly reflect a considerable amount of information about Araton's position. What elements of style, tone, diction, and figurative language are clues to this position?

2. In Par. 15–21, Araton provides a thumbnail survey of how sports have changed in recent decades. One of his examples concerns the changing attitudes toward sports heroes among young fans. In Par. 21, Araton writes of these fans ("the young channel surfers"): "They have learned to define change as a way of life, and in a nation of so many single-parent homes, what's the big deal, anyway, of having a sports hero walk out after a championship season when Daddy has already traded in Mom?"

   As support to the secondary factual argument that sports have changed, how reasonable and effective is this statement? Do you find the lack of evidence acceptable? Are there other examples in the argument of similarly supported statements?

3. Discuss with some classmates the effectiveness of Araton's reference to himself, his friends, his family. How does this affect your response to the argument? If Araton had written from the "we" point of view (as Mosher does in "Where Have All the Heroes Gone?"), would the effect have been different?

4. In Par. 25, Araton offers two causal explanations to the ratings decline in televised sports. What are the two explanations? How would both of these speculations need to be supported in order to be reasonable causal arguments?

5. What do you think are the strongest parts of this argument? The weakest?

SUGGESTIONS FOR WRITING (16.6)

1. Choose a sports event that was particularly memorable to you—as a spectator or participant. Write a two-page argument (probably interpretive, evaluative, or causal) explaining its significance to you. Your argument should include a factual description of the event.

2. Using the steps included in Suggestion #2 of "Finding a Claim" in Chapter 3, derive a focused working claim regarding the differences between professional and amateur sports. Submit your list of increasingly narrowed claims to your instructor.

3. Write a one-paragraph description of the audience Araton seems to have addressed.

   Then write a one-paragraph description of an audience different in every regard (age, gender, education level, etc.). Make a list of the changes you would make in Araton's argument for this audience (keeping the central claim the same).

4. Do you think the huge salaries in mainstream professional sports make it easier or harder for sports stars to be true heroes? Beginning with a stipulative definition of "hero," write a causal argument answering this question.

17

Earning Your Living

INTRODUCTION

Of all the subjects treated in this reader, perhaps the one that you take least for granted is the subject of work—particularly as it applies to your future. In fact, most of you are in college and even taking this course in order to prepare for your full-time entry into the world of work. Some people know from an early age what they're going to do when they grow up; others graduate from college and even graduate school still uncertain about what line of work they are going to commit some 80,000 hours of their waking lives to. It's one of the most difficult decisions we make in our lives, and in this new millennium, the decision is getting harder and harder. Now more than ever in history, with breathtaking developments in technology, the global economy, and knowledge in general, certainties about how you will earn your living are hard to come by. The only thing that seems certain about work these days is its uncertainty. Predictions like the following abound: "the career for which you're currently preparing may be obsolete in ten years"; "your life's work may not even have been conceived of yet"; "you will change careers multiple times during your lifetime."

The first three readings of this chapter are personal narratives of career choice. While heavily autobiographical, all exemplify different types of argument. And all make the point that despite the most careful, conscious planning, one's choice of career is often the result of chance and timing.

Unlike the retrospective arguments that open this section, the middle two readings are prospective—they look to careers of the future. Both of these essays have a bearing on the career opportunities and decisions facing most college students, and we hope you'll find them useful. The section concludes with a look at the much cited phenomenon of "job stress," and is an excellent example of an argument that challenges a commonly held assumption.

340

WHY I WRITE

GEORGE ORWELL

You read an excerpt from George Orwell's Politics and the English Language *in Chapter 11. George Orwell (1903–1950) was an English writer who, through his penetrating political essays and novels* (Animal Farm *and* 1984), *became one of the most influential voices of the 20th century. In* Why I Write, *a timeless essay despite its topical historical references, Orwell examines his choice of career.*

COMMENTARY

In this largely autobiographical narrative, George Orwell considers both why he became a writer and why his style and subject matter evolved in certain ways. The essay contains elements of evaluation and interpretation, but the dominant arguments are causal.

Analyzing causal arguments usually begins in an examination of the factuality of the cause(s) and of the effect(s). Before determining whether the relationship between cause and effect is logical, we must be assured that the cause and the effect are plausible. As Chapter 8 of this book states, "While in most causal arguments you will write, the causal relationship you propose between two events will rarely be certain and verifiable, there can be no room to doubt the certainty of the events you are linking; they *must* be true if your argument is to be meaningful and plausible" (*Everyday Arguments*, p. 129). Because Orwell's argument is a wholly personal one, the causes and effects he presents are largely unverifiable. But the manner in which he describes the personally experienced "facts" that constitute his causes and effects gives us little reason to suspect them (beyond the inevitable dubiousness of any personal memory, that is). For example, the causes of his childhood loneliness (later cited as a major reason for his becoming a writer) are succinctly and unemotionally recounted: "I was the middle child of three, but there was a gap of five years on either side, and I barely saw my father before I was eight." (Par. 2)

Orwell moves from the personal examination of his own motives for writing (Par. 1–4) to a series of causal generalizations explaining why all writers write: "Putting aside the need to earn a living, I think there are four great motives for writing, at any rate for writing prose" (Par. 5). In other words, from a sample of one (himself), he moves to a generalization encompassing all. The inductive leap is a huge one, with no immediate explicit support beyond his personal experience (a sample of one). While he doesn't adduce the experiences of other writers to bridge the leap, we can assume that such a seasoned and famous literary figure bases his generalization on more than his single experience.

In paragraphs 6 and 7, Orwell explicitly offers the human motivations linking cause and effect that are often only implied in causal arguments (see "Identifying an Acceptable Motivation" in Chapter 8). An obvious, though hardly foolproof, way to test the reasonableness of these motives is simply to consider whether they comport with what you know about human behavior and motivation. It would be especially useful to ask the question, "Is it likely that a writer would write in the absence of any of these four motives?"

In the remainder of the essay, Orwell returns to his own career as a writer, and particularly to an examination of how the fourth motive—"political purpose"— operates in his writing. His support through personal example of this motive is a powerful confirmation of our identification, in Chapter 2, of "the value of disso-nance" as a starting point for an effective written argument. Orwell writes, "When I sit down to write a book, I do not say to myself, 'I am going to produce a work of art.' I write it because there is some lie that I want to expose, some fact to which I want to draw attention, any my initial concern is to get a hearing'." (Par. 9)

While on first reading the essay might seem guilty of a certain amount of meandering, there is an underlying and no doubt quite purposeful structure. Orwell draws us into his topic by that most seductive of introductory tech-niques—the narrative. Imagine how much less engaging the essay would have been had it begun with a statement like "I think there are four great motives for writing." From the specific (his own childhood experience), Orwell moves on to the very general. Finally, to support the motive that he admits to be the least likely, he returns to his own career and examples of the political motivations of his writing.

WHY I WRITE

1   From a very early age, perhaps the age of five or six, I knew that when I grew up I should be a writer. Between the ages of about seventeen and twenty-four I tried to abandon this idea, but I did so with the con-sciousness that I was outraging my true na-ture and that sooner or later I should have to settle down and write books.

2   I was the middle child of three, but there was a gap of five years on either side, and I barely saw my father before I was eight. For this and other reasons I was somewhat lonely, and I soon developed disagreeable mannerisms which made me unpopular throughout my schooldays. I had the lonely child's habit of making up stories and hold-ing conversations with imaginary persons, and I think from the very start my literary ambitions were mixed up with the feeling of being isolated and undervalued. I knew that I had a facility with words and a power of fac-ing unpleasant facts, and I felt that this cre-ated a sort of private world in which I could get my own back for my failure in everyday life. Nevertheless the volume of serious—i.e. seriously intended—writing which I pro-duced all through my childhood and boy-hood would not amount to half a dozen pages. I wrote my first poem at the age of four or five, my mother taking it down to dictation. I cannot remember anything about it except that it was about a tiger and

the tiger had 'chair-like teeth'—a good enough phrase, but I fancy the poem was a plagiarism of Blake's *Tiger, Tiger*. At eleven, when the war or 1914–18 broke out, I wrote a patriotic poem which was printed in the local newspaper, as was another, two years later, on the death of Kitchener. From time to time, when I was a bit older, I wrote bad and usually unfinished 'nature poems' in the Georgian style. I also attempted a short story which was a ghastly failure. That was the total of the would-be serious work that I actually set down on paper during all those years.

3   However, throughout this time I did in a sense engage in literary activities. To begin with there was the made-to-order stuff which I produced quickly, easily and without much pleasure to myself. Apart from school work, I wrote *vers d'occasion*, semi-comic poems which I could turn out at what now seems to me astonishing speed—at fourteen I wrote a whole rhyming play, in imitation of Aristophanes, in about a week—and helped to edit a school magazine, both printed and in manuscript. These magazines were the most pitiful burlesque stuff that you could imagine, and I took far less trouble with them than I now would with the cheapest journalism. But side by side with all this, for fifteen years or more, I was carrying out a literary exercise of a quite different kind: this was the making up of a continuous 'story' about myself, a sort of diary existing only in the mind. I believe this is a common habit of children and adolescents. As a very small child I used to imagine that I was, say, Robin Hood, and picture myself as the hero of thrilling adventures, but quite soon my 'story' ceased to be narcissistic in a crude way and became more and more a mere description of what I was doing and the things I saw. For minutes at a time this kind of thing would be running through my head: 'He pushed the door open and entered the room. A yellow beam of sunlight, filtering through the muslin curtains, slanted on to the table, where a match-box, half-open, lay beside the inkpot.

With his right hand in his pocket he moved across to the window. Down in the street a tortoiseshell cat was chasing a dead leaf', etc. etc. This habit continued until I was about twenty-five, right through my non-literary years. Although I had to search, and did search, for the right words, I seemed to be making this descriptive effort almost against my will, under a kind of compulsion from outside. The 'story' must, I suppose, have reflected the styles of the various writers I admired at different ages, but so far as I remember it always had the same meticulous descriptive quality.

4   When I was about sixteen I suddenly discovered the joy of mere words, i.e. the sounds and associations of words. The lines from *Paradise Lost* —

So hee with difficulty and labour hard
Moved on: with difficulty and labour hee.

5   which do not now seem to me so very wonderful, sent shivers down my backbone; and the spelling 'hee' for 'he' was an added pleasure. As for the need to describe things, I knew all about it already. So it is clear what kind of books I wanted to write, in so far as I could be said to want to write books at that time. I wanted to write enormous naturalistic novels with unhappy endings, full of detailed descriptions and arresting similes, and also full of purple passages in which words were used partly for the sake of their own sound. And in fact my first completed novel, *Burmese Days*, which I wrote when I was thirty but projected much earlier, is rather that kind of book.

6   I give all this background information because I do not think one can assess a writer's motives without knowing something of his early development. His subject matter will be determined by the age he lives in—at least this is true in tumultuous, revolutionary ages like our own—but before he ever begins to write he will have acquired an emotional attitude from which he will never completely escape. It is his job, no doubt, to discipline his temperament and avoid getting stuck at some immature

stage, in some perverse mood; but if he escapes from his early influences altogether, he will have killed his impulse to write. Putting aside the need to earn a living, I think there are four great motives for writing, at any rate for writing prose. They exist in different degrees in every writer, and in any one writer the proportions will vary from time to time, according to the atmosphere in which he is living. They are:

(i) Sheer egoism. Desire to seem clever, to be talked about, to be remembered after death, to get your own back on the grownups who snubbed you in childhood, etc., etc. It is humbug to pretend this is not a motive, and a strong one. Writers share this characteristic with scientists, artists, politicians, lawyers, soldiers, successful businessmen—in short, with the whole top crust of humanity. The great mass of human beings are not acutely selfish. After the age of about thirty they almost abandon the sense of being individuals at all—and live chiefly for others, or are simply smothered under drudgery. But there is also the minority of gifted, willful people who are determined to live their own lives to the end, and writers belong in this class. Serious writers, I should say, are on the whole more vain and self-centered than journalists, though less interested in money.

(ii) Aesthetic enthusiasm. Perception of beauty in the external world, or, on the other hand, in words and their right arrangement. Pleasure in the impact of one sound on another, in the firmness of good prose or the rhythm of a good story. Desire to share an experience which one feels is valuable and ought not to be missed. The aesthetic motive is very feeble in a lot of writers, but even a pamphleteer or writer of textbooks will have pet words and phrases which appeal to him for non-utilitarian reasons; or he may feel strongly about typography, width of margins, etc. Above the level of a railway guide, no book is quite free from aesthetic considerations.

(iii) Historical impulse. Desire to see things as they are, to find out true facts and store them up for the use of posterity.

(iv) Political purpose. Using the word 'political' in the widest possible sense. Desire to push the world in a certain direction, to alter other peoples' idea of the kind of society that they should strive after. Once again, no book is genuinely free from political bias. The opinion that art should have nothing to do with politics is itself a political attitude.

It can be seen how these various impulses must war against one another, and how they must fluctuate from person to person and from time to time. By nature—taking your 'nature' to be the state you have attained when you are first adult—I am a person in whom the first three motives would outweigh the fourth. In a peaceful age I might have written ornate or merely descriptive books, and might have remained almost unaware of my political loyalties. As it is I have been forced into becoming a sort of pamphleteer. First I spent five years in an unsuitable profession (the Indian Imperial Police, in Burma), and then I underwent poverty and the sense of failure. This increased my natural hatred of authority and made me for the first time fully aware of the existence of the working classes, and the job in Burma had given me some understanding of the nature of imperialism: but these experiences were not enough to give me an accurate political orientation. Then came Hitler, the Spanish Civil War, etc. By the end of 1935 I had still failed to reach a firm decision. I remember a little poem that I wrote at that date, expressing my dilemma:

A happy vicar I might have been
Two hundred years ago
To preach upon eternal doom
And watch my walnuts grow;
But born, alas, in an evil time,
I missed that pleasant haven,
For the hair has grown on my upper lip
And the clergy are all clean-shaven.
And later still the times were good,
We were so easy to please,
We rocked our troubled thoughts to sleep

On the bosoms of the trees.

All ignorant we dared to own

The joys we now dissemble;

The greenfinch on the apple bough

Could make my enemies tremble.

But girl's bellies and apricots,

Roach in a shaded stream,

Horses, ducks in flight at dawn,

All these are a dream.

It is forbidden to dream again;

We maim our joys or hide them:

Horses are made of chromium steel

And little fat men shall ride them.

I am the worm who never turned,

The eunuch without a harem;

Between the priest and the commissar

I walk like Eugene Aram;

And the commissar is telling my fortune

While the radio plays,

But the priest has promised an Austin Seven,

For Duggie always pays.

I dreamt I dwelt in marble halls,

And woke to find it true;

I wasn't born for an age like this;

Was Smith? Was Jones? Were you?

8   The Spanish war and other events in 1936–37 turned the scale and thereafter I knew where I stood. Every line of serious work that I have written since 1936 has been written, directly or indirectly, *against* totalitarianism and *for* democratic socialism, as I understand it. It seems to me nonsense, in a period like our own, to think that one can avoid writing of such subjects. Everyone writes of them in one guise or another. It is simply a question of which side one takes and what approach one follows. And the more one is conscious of one's political bias, the more chance one has of acting politically without sacrificing one's aesthetic and intellectual integrity.

9   What I have most wanted to do throughout the past ten years is to make political writing into an art. My starting point is always a feeling of partisanship, a sense of injustice. When I sit down to write a book, I do not say to myself, 'I am going to produce a work of art.' I write it because there is some lie that I want to expose, some fact to which I want to draw attention, and my initial concern is to get a hearing. But I could not do the work of writing a book, or even a long magazine article, if it were not also an aesthetic experience. Anyone who cares to examine my work will see that even when it is downright propaganda it contains much that a full-time politician would consider irrelevant. I am not able, and do not want, completely to abandon the world view that I acquired in childhood. So long as I remain alive and well I shall continue to feel strongly about prose style, to love the surface of the earth, and to take a pleasure in solid objects and scraps of useless information. It is no use trying to suppress that side of myself. The job is to reconcile my ingrained likes and dislikes with the essentially public, non-individual activities that this age forces on all of us.

10   It is not easy. It raises problems of construction and of language, and it raises in a new way the problem of truthfulness. Let me give just one example of the cruder kind of difficulty that arises. My book about the Spanish civil war, *Homage to Catalonia*, is of course a frankly political book, but in the main it is written with a certain detachment and regard for form. I did try very hard in it to tell the whole truth without violating my literary instincts. But among other things it contains a long chapter, full of newspaper quotations and the like, defending the Trotskyists who were accused of plotting with Franco. Clearly such a chapter, which after a year or two would lose its interest for any ordinary reader, must ruin the book. A critic whom I respect read me a lecture about it. 'Why did you put in all that stuff?' he said. 'You've turned what might have been a good book into journalism.' What he said was true, but I could not have done otherwise. I happened to know, what very few people in England had been allowed to know, that innocent men were being falsely

accused. If I had not been angry about that I should never have written the book.

11   In one form or another this problem comes up again. The problem of language is subtler and would take too long to discuss. I will only say that of late years I have tried to write less picturesquely and more exactly. In any case I find that by the time you have perfected any style of writing, you have always outgrown it. *Animal Farm* was the first book in which I tried, with full consciousness of what I was doing, to fuse political purpose and artistic purpose into one whole. I have not written a novel for seven years, but I hope to write another fairly soon. It is bound to be a failure, every book is a failure, but I do know with some clarity what kind of book I want to write.

12   Looking back through the last page or two, I see that I have made it appear as though my motives in writing were wholly public-spirited. I don't want to leave that as the final impression. All writers are vain, selfish, and lazy, and at the very bottom of their motives there lies a mystery. Writing a book is a horrible, exhausting struggle, like a long bout of some painful illness. One would never undertake such a thing if one were not driven on by some demon whom one can neither resist nor understand. For all one knows that demon is simply the same instinct that makes a baby squall for attention. And yet it is also true that one can write nothing readable unless one constantly struggles to efface one's own personality. Good prose is like a windowpane. I cannot say with certainty which of my motives are the strongest, but I know which of them deserve to be followed. And looking back through my work, I see that it is invariably where I lacked a political purpose that I wrote lifeless books and was betrayed into purple passages, sentences without meaning, decorative adjectives and humbug generally.

1946

Source: George Orwell, "Why I Write" from *Such, Such Were the Joys*, 1953.

DISCUSSION QUESTIONS

1. Consider Orwell's list of the four motives for writing. With one or two of your classmates, evaluate the reasonableness of each of these causes according to the principles presented in Chapter 7.

2. Review Orwell's list of stylistic rules (Chapter 10) and discuss with your classmates whether he follows his own advice in "Why I Write."

3. Why do you think Orwell included his early poem describing his "dilemma" about choosing a career? Would a brief summary of what he was experiencing at the time have been more or less effective? Why?

4. Discuss with your classmates the probable audience of Orwell's essay.

5. In what ways does this personal, reminiscent essay constitute an argument?

SUGGESTIONS FOR WRITING (17.1)

1. Interview one of your professors, focusing on the question, "Why did you become a college teacher?" Then write a two- to three- page essay explaining his or her choice of career.

2. Orwell writes that "every book is a failure." Write a one- to two-page interpretation of this statement.

3. Orwell's historical and literary references are not explained—for example, Blake's *Tiger, Tiger; vers d'occasion;* the Spanish Civil War. Through Internet research, create explanatory footnotes for every unfamiliar reference, using MLA citation form.

4. Write an extended definition of the word "career," including at least four of the strategies discussed in Chapter 4.

5. Write an interpretation of Orwell's statement in the last paragraph, "Good prose is like a windowpane."

FASTEST GROWING OCCUPATIONS

DANIEL E. HECKER, BUREAU OF LABOR STATISTICS

The text and table below were published in the November 2001 edition of the Monthly Labor Review, *a periodical published by the Bureau of Labor Statistics, an agency of the U.S. Department of Labor. The text is excerpted from a longer article titled "Occupational Employment Projections to 2010," by Daniel E. Hecker.*

1   While the education and training requirements of the workforce continue to increase, in 2000, only 21 percent of jobs were in occupations generally requiring a bachelor's degree or more education. However, these jobs will account for 29 percent of total job growth from 2000 to 2010. Occupations generally requiring a postsecondary vocational award or an associate degree, which accounted for 8 percent of all jobs in 2000, will account for 13 percent of the job growth over the 2000–2010 period. Occupations generally requiring only work-related training, which accounted for 71 percent of all jobs in 2000, will account for 58 percent of the job growth over the 2000–2010 period.

2   All seven categories generally requiring a postsecondary award are projected to have faster-than-average employment growth over the 2000–2010 period. These categories are made up mostly of professional and related occupations, projected to grow the fastest, along with a number of faster-than-average growing management, business, and financial occupations. All four work-related training categories are expected to have slower growth. These categories include many slow growing or declining production, office and administrative support, and other occupations.

3   The largest education and training category, short-term on-the job training, with 53 million workers in 2000, accounted for 37 percent of total employment and is projected to account for 35 percent of job growth. It is the fastest growing of the four categories requiring work-related training, and includes large faster-than-average-growing occupations such as security guards, teacher assistants, and combined food preparation and serving workers, including fast food. More than half of the 30 occupations with the largest numerical job growth fall into this category. These workers had the lowest earnings of any education and training group in 2000—60 percent as much as the mean for all wage and salary workers.

4   Occupations generally requiring moderate-term on-the-job training, including medical assistants and painters, construction and maintenance, accounted for 28 million workers, or 19 percent of total employment in 2000, and are projected to account for 14 percent of new jobs. These workers earned 88 percent as much as the mean for all wage and salary workers in 2000.

5   The long-term on-the-job training category is projected to grow the slowest. It accounted for 8.5 percent of total employment in 2000, but should account for only 4.2 percent of new jobs. It includes slow growing occupations, such as carpenters, and declining ones, such as butchers and meatcutters, and farmers and ranchers. These workers

earned the mean for all workers in 2000. An additional 7.2 percent were employed in occupations requiring experience in another occupation that generally did not require postsecondary education or training; these are projected to account for 5 percent of new jobs. Most workers in these occupations are first-line supervisors or managers, so it is not surprising that they earned 24 percent more than the mean for all workers.

6   The postsecondary vocational award category accounted for 4.6 percent of total employment in 2000 and should account for 5.5 percent of new jobs. This group includes automobile service technicians and mechanics; licensed practical nurses; and hairdressers, hairstylists, and cosmetologists. They earned 95 percent as much as the mean for all workers in 2000. Occupations generally requiring an associate degree is the fastest growing group; it includes computer support specialists, paralegals and legal assistants, and many fast growing health occupations. It accounted for 3.5 percent of all jobs in the base year but is expected to account for 7.3 percent of total growth. More than two-fifths of the workers in this group are registered nurses.

7   The bachelor's degree category accounted for 12 percent of all workers in 2000 and is projected to account for 18 percent of job growth. Most computer occupations are in this group. In addition, jobs in which workers generally need experience in another occupation requiring at least a bachelor's degree before getting their current job accounted for another 5 percent of all workers in 2000 and should account for 6.4 percent of job growth. Almost all workers in this category were in management, business, and financial occupations. Many of the fastest growing occupations and those with the largest projected numerical increases require a bachelor's degree. Mean earnings of occupations generally requiring a bachelor's degree were 46 percent more than the mean for all wage and salary workers and

for those in occupations generally requiring work experience plus a bachelor's or higher degree, 111 percent more.

About 3.4 percent of workers are employed in occupations that generally require more education than a bachelor's degree, including those requiring a first professional degree (1.4 percent), doctoral degree (1 percent), or master's degree (1 percent). Together, these three categories are projected to account for 4.8 percent of job growth. The first professional degree category, which includes lawyers, physicians and surgeons, and pharmacists, had the highest average earnings of any group in 2000—2.8 times as much as the mean for all wage and salary workers. The doctoral degree category earned 58 percent more than the mean; most workers in this group are postsecondary teachers. Those in the master's degree category earned 32 percent more than the mean, not as much as occupations requiring a bachelor's. This group includes librarians and several counseling occupations.

9   The share of total job openings resulting from both employment growth and net replacement needs in each of the education and training categories differs from job openings resulting from employment growth alone. In general, occupations requiring the least amount of education and training account for a greater share of net replacement needs—and total job openings—because workers in them have less job attachment than workers in other occupations. While occupations requiring a postsecondary vocational award or an academic degree should generate 42 percent of jobs from growth alone, they should generate only 30 percent of total job openings. Occupations requiring work-related training should generate 58 percent of openings due to growth, but 70 percent of total openings.

Source: Daniel E. Hecker, "Occupational Employment Projections to 2010," *Monthly Labor Review*. November 2001.

Fastest Growing Occupations, 2000–2010
(Numbers in thousands of jobs)

Occupation	Employment		Change		Quartile rank by 2000 median hourly earnings[1]	Education and training category
	2000	2010	#	%		
Computer software engineers, applications	380	760	380	100	1	Bachelor's degree
Computer support specialists	506	996	490	97	2	Associate degree
Computer software engineers, systems software	317	601	284	90	1	Bachelor's degree
Network and computer systems administrators	229	416	187	82	1	Bachelor's degree
Network systems and data communications analysts	119	211	92	77	1	Bachelor's degree
Desktop publishers	38	63	25	67	2	Postsecondary vocational award
Database administrators	106	176	70	66	1	Bachelor's degree
Personal and home care aides	414	672	258	62	4	Short-term on-the-job training
Computer systems analysts	431	689	258	60	1	Bachelor's degree
Medical assistants	329	516	187	57	3	Moderate-term on-the-job training
Social and human service assistants	271	418	147	54	3	Moderate-term on-the-job training
Physician assistants	58	89	31	53	1	Bachelor's degree
Medical records and health information technicians	136	202	66	49	3	Associate degree
Computer and information systems managers	313	463	150	48	1	Bachelor's or higher degree, plus work experience
Home health aides	615	907	291	47	4	Short-term on-the-job training
Physical therapist aides	36	53	17	46	3	Short-term on-the-job training
Occupational therapist aides	9	12	4	45	3	Short-term on-the-job training
Physical therapist assistants	44	64	20	45	2	Associate degree
Audiologists	13	19	6	45	1	Master's degree
Fitness trainers and aerobics instructors	158	222	64	40	3	Postsecondary vocational award

(Continued)

Fastest Growing Occupations, 2000–2010
(Numbers in thousands of jobs)

Occupation	Employment		Change		Quartile rank by 2000 median hourly earnings[1]	Education and training category
	2000	2010	#	%		
Computer and information scientists, research	28	39	11	40	1	Doctoral degree
Veterinary assistants and laboratory animal caretakers	55	77	22	40	4	Short-term on-the-job training
Occupational therapist assistants	17	23	7	40	2	Associate degree
Veterinary technologists and technicians	49	69	19	39	3	Associate degree
Speech-language pathologists	88	122	34	39	1	Master's degree
Mental health and substance abuse social workers	83	116	33	39	2	Master's degree
Dental assistants	247	339	92	37	2	Moderate-term on-the-job training
Dental hygienists	147	201	54	37	1	Associate degree
Special education teachers, preschool, kindergarten, and elementary school	234	320	86	37	1	Bachelor's degree
Pharmacy technicians	190	259	69	36	3	Moderate-term on-the-job training

[1]The quartile rankings of Occupational Employment Statistics annual earnings data are presented in the following categories: 1 = very high ($39,700 and over), 2 = high ($24,760 to $39,660), 3 = low ($18,500 to $25,760), and 4 = very low (up to $18,490). The rankings were based on quartiles using one-fourth of total employment to define each quartile. Earnings are for wage and salary workers.

DISCUSSION QUESTIONS

1. This excerpt has the look of a factual argument, yet it makes repeated use of the word "projected," which would suggest an argument of effect. Which is it?

2. Each paragraph of the argument summarizes a portion of the large amount of data presented in the table. Give each paragraph a "title," based upon the data it summarizes.

3. Who is the intended audience for this material?

4. Consider with a small group of your classmates whether the table could stand alone, with no textual commentary accompanying it.

5. Do you find the table to be an absolutely necessary support to the text, or could the text stand alone?

SUGGESTIONS FOR WRITING (17.2)

1. Conduct some research on how labor projections are developed. Based upon what you learn, write a two-page factual description of the process.

2. Using the data provided in the table, create a bar chart whose title would be: "Percent change in number of jobs by most significant source of education or training, projected 2000–2010."

3. Using the data in this chart and any personal experience you have, write a three- to four-page argument recommending that high school students go to college.

4. Create a single graph or table displaying the income quartiles of jobs requiring a bachelor's degree.

5. Pick one of the jobs listed in the table that is unfamiliar to you. Conduct research on the job and write a detailed factual argument (three to five pages) explaining the job to a peer.

ON DUMPSTER DIVING

LARS EIGHNER

Lars Eighner is a graduate of the University of Texas at Austin. He began writing soon after college, publishing articles and a volume of short stories. In 1988, he became homeless, a three-year experience that he wrote about in his book Travels with Lizbeth *(1993). After publishing his first novel,* Pawn to Queen Four, *in 1995, Eighner became homeless again.*

1   I began Dumpster diving about a year before I became homeless. I prefer the term *scavenging.* I have heard people, evidently meaning to be polite, use the word *foraging,* but I prefer to reserve that word for gathering nuts and berries and such, which I also do, according to the season and opportunity.

2   I like the frankness of the word *scavenging.* I live from the refuse of others. I am a scavenger. I think it a sound and honorable niche, although if I could I would naturally prefer to live the comfortable consumer life, perhaps—and only perhaps—as a slightly less wasteful consumer owing to what I have learned as a scavenger.

3   Except for jeans, all my clothes come from Dumpsters. Boom boxes, candles, bedding, toilet paper, medicine, books, a typewriter, a virgin male love doll, coins sometimes amounting to many dollars: all came from Dumpsters. And, yes, I eat from Dumpsters, too.

4   There is a predictable series of stages that a person goes through in learning to scavenge. At first the new scavenger is filled with disgust and self-loathing. He is ashamed of being seen.

5   This stage passes with experience. The scavenger finds a pair of running shoes that fit and look and smell brand-new. He finds a pocket calculator in perfect working order. He finds pristine ice cream, still frozen, more than he can eat or keep. He begins to understand: people do throw away perfectly good stuff, a lot of perfectly good stuff.

6   At this stage he may become lost and never recover. All the Dumpster divers I have known come to the point of trying to acquire everything they touch. Why not

take it, they reason, it is all free. This is, of course, hopeless, and most divers come to realize that they must restrict themselves to items of relatively immediate utility.

7   The finding of objects is becoming something of an urban art. Even respectable, employed people will sometimes find something tempting sticking out of a Dumpster or standing beside one. Quite a number of people, not all of them of the bohemian type, are willing to brag that they found this or that piece in the trash.

8   But eating from Dumpsters is the thing that separates the dilettanti from the professionals. Eating safely involves three principles: using the senses and common sense to evaluate the condition of the found materials; knowing the Dumpsters of a given area and checking them regularly; and seeking always to answer the question "Why was this discarded?"

9   Yet perfectly good food can be found in Dumpsters. Canned goods, for example, turn up fairly often in the Dumpsters I frequent. I also have few qualms about dry foods such as crackers, cookies, cereal, chips, and pasta if they are free of visible contaminants and still dry and crisp. Raw fruits and vegetables with intact skins seem perfectly safe to me, excluding, of course, the obviously rotten. Many are discarded for minor imperfections that can be pared away.

10   A typical discard is a half jar of peanut butter—though nonorganic peanut butter does not require refrigeration and is unlikely to spoil in any reasonable time. One of my favorite finds is yogurt—often discarded, still sealed, when the expiration date has passed—because it will keep for several days, even in warm weather.

No matter how careful I am I still get   11
dysentery at least once a month, often in warm weather. I do not want to paint too romantic a picture. Dumpster diving has serious drawbacks as a way of life.

I find from the experience of scavenging   12
two rather deep lessons. The first is to take what I can use and let the rest go. I have come to think that there is no value in the abstract. A thing I cannot use or make useful, perhaps by trading, has no value, however fine or rare it may be.

The second lesson is the transience of   13
material being. I do not suppose that ideas are immortal, but certainly they are longer-lived than material objects.

The things I find in Dumpsters, the love   14
letters and rag dolls of so many lives, remind me of this lesson. Now I hardly pick up a thing without envisioning the time I will cast it away. This, I think, is a healthy state of mind. Almost everything I have now has already been cast out at least once, proving that what I own is valueless to someone.

I find that my desire to grab for the   15
gaudy bauble has been largely sated. I think this is an attitude I share with the very wealthy—we both know there is plenty more where whatever we have came from. Between us are the rat-race millions who have confounded their selves with the objects they grasp and who nightly scavenge the cable channels for they know not what.

I am sorry for them.   16

Source: From Lars Eighner, *Travels with Lisbeth* New York: Bedford/St. Martin's, 1993.

DISCUSSION QUESTIONS

1. With a group of your classmates, make a list of adjectives that describe the tone of this essay. For each adjective, attach an example quoted from the text. Is there consensus within the group about the essay's tone? If not, how do you account for the different responses?

2. What are Eighner's definitions of the terms *scavenging* (Par. 1) and *foraging* (Par. 2)? Are the definitions complete and clear? What do you think about their placement in an essay that describes finding a living from garbage dumpsters?

3. What is the central claim here. Is it explicit or implicit?

4. Based upon your careful reading of this essay, compose, with a few of your classmates, a character portrait of Eighner. What kind of man does he seem to be? Does he have a sense of humor or is he very serious? Is he intelligent? Would you like to know him? Be sure to point to those parts of the essay that led you to your portrait.

5. Do you think Eighner finds satisfaction in his work? What evidence do you have for your answer?

6. Is Eighner's essay just about Dumpster diving, or can you attach further significance to it? Participate in a full class discussion of this question.

SUGGESTIONS FOR WRITING (17.3)

1. Write a "how-to" essay on an activity that most people would find very unappealing.

2. In a half page, characterize the tone of your "how-to" essay.

3. Write a two-page argument of any type about a job you've had. Do not state the claim explicitly, but make sure that it is clear to your readers. After you've written the essay, give it to two or three of your classmates and ask them to state the implicit claim.

4. Write a factual argument describing how your preconceptions about the homeless have changed (or stayed the same) based on Eighner's essay.

LESSONS FROM 2 GHOSTS

SCOTT M. FISHER

In this causal argument, Scott Fisher, an instructor of English at Rock Valley College, identifies the reasons for his career choice. Fisher assumes that his readers are familiar with the political situation of the late 1960s, when the Vietnam war was raging and young American men lived in the shadow of the military draft. This was a time when the war in Vietnam was the preoccupation of all young men, many of whom went to incredible and often self-destructive lengths to avoid the "1-A" draft status that guaranteed a military stint in the dangerous Vietnam conflict. Throughout America's involvement in the war (1965–1972), full-time undergraduate students were automatically exempted from the draft.

This essay first apeared in June of 1996 in the Chronicle of Higher Education, *a weekly publication covering higher education issues for college and university faculty, administrators, and graduate students.*

1   I know many educators who, like me, spend scores of extra hours planning, developing, and evaluating ideas and materials for their courses. I admire my colleagues for being so dedicated to their students and their profession. I wish I could say my reasons for my long hours were as altruistic. In fact, I often wish I had more time to read for pleasure, hike in the mountains, or go to more baseball games.

2   The truth is that there are ghosts in my office that force me to stay there and work, even when I'd rather be somewhere else. Oh, they let me go home and get enough rest and nourishment to sustain my body. But they know I'll be back, and they're always waiting for me when I unlock the door to my office. As Poe would have asked: "You think me mad?" Maybe I am.

3   I've known these ghosts—there are two of them—for about 25 years. That's longer than I've been teaching, although they really only started haunting me on my first day as a student teacher. Every day since then, they've been standing right behind or on either side of me. Heck, I knew them before they were ghosts. They were young men once, as I was.

4   Their names are (were) Pritchard and Simplett. We were classmates—freshmen— in the late '60s at a teachers' college in the Midwest. Pritchard was the kicker on our football team. He could make field goals from any angle, off any surface, in any temperature, in rain, snow, or high winds. If the ball was inside the 30-yard line, Pritch could nail it dead center every time. He didn't miss a single field goal or extra point all season. I can testify to that, because I was his holder (I was too small and slow to start in any other position). We weren't a powerhouse team, by any means, but Pritchard's foot made the difference in some of our games.

5   Simplett and I were on the baseball team that year. He was an outstanding shortstop, with a rifle arm (excuse the cliche). He could go into the hole, drop to his knees, and fling a runner out at first base by two steps. I was a fourth-string catcher, used almost exclusively when the game was not in doubt and the coach didn't want to risk injury to any of his "good" players. That was also when Simp got his chance to pitch. He was magnificent—about one-third of the time. The other two-thirds, his blazing fastball had a mind of its own. Also, Simp had a little trouble reading his catcher's signs. He couldn't see too well from 60 feet away. That's why nobody wanted to catch for him. I tried everything—flashing the signs very slowly, wrapping white adhesive tape around my fingertips—but nothing worked. We finally agreed that he would just "throw 'em," and I'd try to "catch 'em," which worked out about as well as anything else. We didn't win many games, but we had fun.

6   Pritch, Simp, and I had a couple of other things in common besides sports. For one thing, we all liked to write. I liked research and writing historical narrative—essays on the Old West, sports teams of the 1930s, classic airplanes, that kind of thing.

7   Pritch was into fantasy. He could weave a wonderful tale, gripping readers with his spellbinding tales of planets and sorcerers, which he illustrated deftly with bizarre, intriguing drawings.

8   Simp was a poet. His mind worked in metaphor; even in the dugout he would call umpires the "traffic cops of the basepaths" and the pain of a batter's hands when the bat connected on a cold day "the sweet sting of spring." And he loved all kinds of music. He lived across the hall from me in the dorm, and on Thursday nights ("rave" nights, when it was okay to make a little more noise), he'd bring over his Country Joe McDonald records, and we'd sing along at the top of our off-key voices. "And it's one, two, three, what're we fightin' for? Don't ask me, I don't give a damn; next stop is Vietnam."

9   Just as I admired their athletic ability, I was in awe of my friends' talents and creativity, both in writing and in living. While I had to work for each ounce of strength, both on the athletic field and at the typewriter, Pritch and Simp had natural gifts. I was envious, but also proud to know them. Their talents inspired me to work harder to improve myself.

10   It may sound corny now, but those guys were preparing themselves to be skilled educators in every activity they pursued. They often helped out in the tutoring lab in the evenings and volunteered to coach elementary-school teams on weekends. They loved taking kids from the town on field trips to nearby farms or sporting events. I was amazed at how both of them could motivate even the shyest youngster. They were natural

leaders and role models. Kids seemed to be drawn to them instinctively.

11   The only time all three of us were together regularly was in "Old Man" Rivers's (Professor Rivers, that is) English-composition class. Now, in retrospect, I can corroborate what we thought then: He was a complete jerk. He seems to be about 160 years old, wore black suits, starched white shirts, bow ties, black wingtip shoes, and white socks. He was a fanatical Freudian and expected all our writing to reflect Freud's theories. Even though I did my best to work them into my narrative essays, short-story analyses, and research thesis, my papers always came back with a C, if I was lucky. Although I had been praised as a clear and insightful writer in high school, Old Man Rivers made it clear to me that I had no writing talent and that perhaps I should consider hiring a tutor or retaking the class in the summer.

12   I was too immature and unclear about my role as a future teacher to care all that much about what an eccentric English professor thought of me. But for Simp and Pritch it was different. They saw Professor Rivers for what he really was—a "scholarly bully," Simp called him. (Pritch's description was more profane, as I recall.) They often challenged (respectfully, at first) his weird interpretations of the stories, poems, and essays that we discussed in class. Of course, this did not please Rivers one bit, although their arguments made perfect sense to me.

13   Some of the more "intellectually needy" members of the class, including me, often tried to get some extra help from the old duffer, but he always was too busy to bother with "ignorant freshmen," especially if he was working on his latest textbook. He was particularly cool to us athletes, because he thought college sports were a waste of time and didn't like the fact that we had permission to miss classes when we had games at other colleges.

14   Most of us decided just to go with the flow, earn our solid C's, and get on with our lives. But Pritchard and Simplett were not about to go that route. They each spent hours preparing for the essays we had to write in class, looking up literary critical analysis that even doctoral candidates wouldn't want to read, just so they could prove their points with logic that Rivers couldn't refute. Yet Rivers was such a pedant that my two friends didn't stand a chance.

15   Those two guys spent all year—freshmen were stuck with Rivers for both semesters—trying to show him up. They each received D's the first semester, which threatened to put them on academic probation. By April, the situation had deteriorated to the point that they no longer even tried to suppress their snide comments in class. Pritch drew some hilarious, obscene sketches of Rivers expounding on Freudian aspects of fiction. And Simp concocted a tune about what a dirty old man Rivers was. Both of these creative scholarly works were published in the local forum—the men's bathroom in the athletic building.

16   Pritch and Simp each were called in by the dean at various times and told to knock it off. They were reminded that we "boys" were all 1-A in the eyes of Uncle Sam, and that without their educational deferments, they would quickly find themselves in the military.

17   But that wasn't enough of a threat for them, because they had very different ideas of what education was supposed to be. They continued to rebel against Old Man Rivers, and they continued to be reprimanded. In they end, they both failed Rivers's class the second semester and were placed on academic probation, with the understanding that they could make up the credits during summer session. But guess who taught all the summer composition classes?

18   There was a lot I didn't quite grasp back then. I couldn't understand how a teacher at the college to which we were paying such high tuition could be so aloof and arrogant. I also couldn't understand how a published author of English textbooks could fail to recognize the talents of two gifted writers, right under his own nose. But neither could I understand why two intelligent guys would keep trying to buck the system when they knew Rivers wasn't going to change. Didn't they get it? They could just get

through the class and pursue their own ideas after they graduated, with their own students.

19   But they just laughed in disgust at any notion of compromise. Each of them, separately, refused to take the summer-school makeup course from Rivers and decided to head back to their respective hometowns. They planned to take their chances with the draft, maybe start again at another college the following year or when they got out of the service, should they be drafted.

20   Within 18 months, Pritchard and Simplett were dead. Pritch was blown apart by a land mine during an infantry patrol. A few months later, the Army helicopter in which Simp was riding crashed and burned, leaving no survivors.

21   Of course, it's really not Old Man Rivers's fault that my friends died. It was just a cruel trick of timing. Still, I can't help thinking that by sticking around my office after hours, I might help some student stay on track. I feel the presence of my two old friends, and I see traits of theirs, such as their eagerness to ask challenging questions and explore opposing viewpoints, in a lot of my students. Some of them may go on to make a difference in young people's lives in a way in which my ghostly friends cannot. I hope they do.

22   So I just keep plugging away, like a fourth-string catcher, giving extra help where I can. It's not because I'm a great humanitarian, or that I'm gifted or even dedicated.

23   I'm just haunted.

Source: Scott M. Fisher, "Lessons From 2 Ghosts," *The Chronicle of Higher Education.* June 14, 1996. p. A56.

DISCUSSION QUESTIONS

1. "Lessons From 2 Ghosts" proceeds through retrospective narrative, with the author describing his two friends and their eventual fates. Yet it also qualifies as a causal argument, in which a given effect (the author's own dedication to his teaching job) is accounted for by an identified cause (the influence of his two friends). Assuming that one of Fisher's main purposes here is to demonstrate cause, consider the level of narrative detail in the essay. For example, are the stories about the pair's athletic talents necessary (Par. 4–5)? Do we need to know about their literary talents (Par. 7–8) and other "natural gifts" (Par. 8–9)? In other words, from the point of view of argument, how necessary are these details?

2. Identify the unstated motivational link between cause and effect in this essay.

3. What does Fisher mean when he claims that he is "haunted" by the ghosts of his friends?

4. Describe the image of the writer that comes through in this essay. How does that image affect your response to the essay?

SUGGESTIONS FOR WRITING (17.4)

1. Interview one of your professors about his or her reasons for choosing a career in teaching. Then write a three-page causal argument on the subject. Before the interview, think carefully about the questions you want to ask, and prepare them in such a way that they don't determine the answers.

2. If you were one of these two "ghosts," what advice might you have for today's young college students? Write a three-page recommendation from Pritchard's or Simplett's point of view that makes use of their own experience during and after college.

3. Write your own two- to three-page personal narrative about a high school friendship that taught you something important. After providing background information about your friend and the relationship, relate one important thing you learned from that friend. In effect, this will be a factual argument based upon personal experience. Your challenge will be to make the narrative engaging, but also credible and realistic.

REVENGE OF THE RIGHT BRAIN

DANIEL H. PINK

Author of Free Agent Nation *(2001) and* A Whole New Mind *(2005), Daniel Pink has earned a national reputation as a writer and speaker about the capacities needed to succeed in 21st century work. Pink has become a sought-after speaker by higher education and professional organizations. This essay, adapted from* A Whole New Mind, *appeared in the February 2005 edition of* Wired *magazine, for whom Pink is a contributing editor.*

1   When I was a kid—growing up in a middle-class family, in the middle of America, in the middle of the 1970s—parents dished out a familiar plate of advice to their children: Get good grades, go to college, and pursue a profession that offers a decent standard of living and perhaps a dollop of prestige. If you were good at math and science, become a doctor. If you were better at English and history, become a lawyer. If blood grossed you out and your verbal skills needed work, become an accountant. Later, as computers appeared on desktops and CEOs on magazine covers, the youngsters who were *really* good at math and science chose high tech, while others flocked to business school, thinking that success was spelled MBA.

2   Tax attorneys. Radiologists. Financial analysts. Software engineers. Management guru Peter Drucker gave this cadre of professionals an enduring, if somewhat wonky, name: knowledge workers. These are, he wrote, "people who get paid for putting to work what one learns in school rather than for their physical strength or manual skill." What distinguished members of this group and enabled them to reap society's greatest rewards, was their "ability to acquire and to apply theoretical and analytic knowledge." And any of us could join their ranks. All we had to do was study hard and play by the rules of the meritocratic regime. That was the path to professional success and personal fulfillment.

3   But a funny thing happened while we were pressing our noses to the grindstone: The world changed. The future no longer belongs to people who can reason with computer-like logic, speed, and precision. It belongs to a different kind of person with a different kind of mind. Today—amid the uncertainties of an economy that has gone from boom to bust to blah—there's a metaphor that explains what's going on. And it's right inside our heads.

4   Scientists have long known that a neurological Mason-Dixon line cleaves our brains

into two regions—the left and right hemi-spheres. But in the last 10 years, thanks in part to advances in functional magnetic res-onance imaging, researchers have begun to identify more precisely how the two sides divide responsibilities. The left hemisphere handles sequence, literalness, and analysis. The right hemisphere, meanwhile, takes care of context, emotional expression, and synthesis. Of course, the human brain, with its 100 billion cells forging 1 quadrillion connections, is breathtakingly complex. The two hemispheres work in concert, and we enlist both sides for nearly everything we do. But the structure of our brains can help explain the contours of our times.

5   Until recently, the abilities that led to success in school, work, and business were characteristic of the left hemisphere. They were the sorts of linear, logical, analytical talents measured by SATs and deployed by CPAs. Today, those capabilities are still necessary. But they're no longer sufficient. In a world upended by outsourcing, del-uged with data, and choked with choices, the abilities that matter most are now closer in spirit to the specialties of the right hemisphere—artistry, empathy, seeing the big picture, and pursuing the transcendent.

6   Beneath the nervous clatter of our half-completed decade stirs a slow but seismic shift. The Information Age we all prepared for is ending. Rising in its place is what I call the Conceptual Age, an era in which mas-tery of abilities that we've often overlooked and undervalued marks the fault line be-tween who gets ahead and who falls behind.

7   To some of you, this shift—from an econ-omy built on the logical, sequential abilities of the Information Age to an economy built on the inventive, empathic abilities of the Conceptual Age—sounds delightful. "You had me at hello!" I can hear the painters and nurses exulting. But to others, this sounds like a crock. "Prove it!" I hear the program-mers and lawyers demanding.

8   OK. To convince you, I'll explain the rea-sons for this shift, using the mechanistic language of cause and effect.

9   The effect: the scales tilting in favor of right brain-style thinking. The causes: Asia, automation, and abundance.

Asia

10   Few issues today spark more controversy than outsourcing. Those squadrons of white-collar workers in India, the Philippines, and China are scaring the bejesus out of software jockeys across North America and Europe. According to Forrester Research, 1 in 9 jobs in the US information technology industry will move overseas by 2010. And it's not just tech work. Visit India's office parks and you'll see chartered accountants preparing American tax returns, lawyers researching American lawsuits, and radiologists reading CAT scans for US hospitals.

11   The reality behind the alarm is this: Outsourcing to Asia is overhyped in the short term, but underhyped in the long term. We're not all going to lose our jobs tomorrow. (The total number of jobs lost to offshoring so far represents less than 1 per-cent of the US labor force.) But as the cost of communicating with the other side of the globe falls essentially to zero, as India be-comes (by 2010) the country with the most English speakers in the world, and as devel-oping nations continue to mint millions of extremely capable knowledge workers, the professional lives of people in the West will change dramatically. If number crunching, chart reading, and code writing can be done for a lot less overseas and delivered to clients instantly via fiber-optic cable, that's where the work will go.

12   But these gusts of comparative advan-tage are blowing away only certain kinds of white-collar jobs—those that can be reduced to a set of rules, routines, and instructions. That's why narrow left-brain work such as basic computer coding, accounting, legal research, and financial analysis is migrat-ing across the oceans. But that's also why plenty of opportunities remain for people and companies doing less routine work—programmers who can design entire systems, accountants who serve as life planners, and

bankers expert less in the intricacies of Excel than in the art of the deal. Now that foreigners can do left-brain work cheaper, we in the US must do right-brain work better.

Automation

13 Last century, machines proved they could replace human muscle. This century, technologies are proving they can outperform human left brains—they can execute sequential, reductive, computational work better, faster, and more accurately than even those with the highest IQs. (Just ask chess grandmaster Garry Kasparov.)

14 Consider jobs in financial services. Stockbrokers who merely execute transactions are history. Online trading services and market makers do such work far more efficiently. The brokers who survived have morphed from routine order-takers to less easily replicated advisers, who can understand a client's broader financial objectives and even the client's emotions and dreams.

15 Or take lawyers. Dozens of inexpensive information and advice services are reshaping law practice. At CompleteCase.com, you can get an uncontested divorce for $249, less than a 10th of the cost of a divorce lawyer. Meanwhile, the Web is cracking the information monopoly that has long been the source of many lawyers' high incomes and professional mystique. Go to USlegalforms.com and you can download—for the price of two movie tickets—fill-in-the-blank wills, contracts, and articles of incorporation that used to reside exclusively on lawyers' hard drives. Instead of hiring a lawyer for 10 hours to craft a contract, consumers can fill out the form themselves and hire a lawyer for one hour to look it over. Consequently, legal abilities that can't be digitized—convincing a jury or understanding the subtleties of a negotiation—become more valuable.

16 Even computer programmers may feel the pinch. "In the old days," legendary computer scientist Vernor Vinge has said, "anybody with even routine skills could get a job as a programmer. That isn't true anymore. The routine functions are increasingly being turned over to machines." The result: As the scut work gets offloaded, engineers will have to master different aptitudes, relying more on creativity than competence.

17 Any job that can be reduced to a set of rules is at risk. If a $500-a-month accountant in India doesn't swipe your accounting job, TurboTax will. Now that computers can emulate left-hemisphere skills, we'll have to rely ever more on our right hemispheres.

Abundance

18 Our left brains have made us rich. Powered by armies of Drucker's knowledge workers, the information economy has produced a standard of living that would have been unfathomable in our grandparents' youth. Their lives were defined by scarcity. Ours are shaped by abundance. Want evidence? Spend five minutes at Best Buy. Or look in your garage. Owning a car used to be a grand American aspiration. Today, there are more automobiles in the US than there are licensed drivers—which means that, on average, everybody who can drive has a car of their own. And if your garage is also piled with excess consumer goods, you're not alone. Self-storage—a business devoted to housing our extra crap—is now a $17 billion annual industry in the US, nearly double Hollywood's yearly box office take.

19 But abundance has produced an ironic result. The Information Age has unleashed a prosperity that in turn places a premium on less rational sensibilities—beauty, spirituality, emotion. For companies and entrepreneurs, it's no longer enough to create a product, a service, or an experience that's reasonably priced and adequately functional. In an age of abundance, consumers demand something more. Check out your bathroom. If you're like a few million Americans, you've got a Michael Graves toilet brush or a Karim Rashid trash can that you bought at Target. Try explaining a designer garbage pail to the left side of your brain! Or consider illumination. Electric lighting was rare a century ago, but now it's commonplace. Yet in the US, candles are a $2 billion a year business—for

reasons that stretch beyond the logical need for luminosity to a prosperous country's more inchoate desire for pleasure and transcendence.

20   Liberated by this prosperity but not fulfilled by it, more people are searching for meaning. From the mainstream embrace of such once-exotic practices as yoga and meditation to the rise of spirituality in the workplace to the influence of evangelism in pop culture and politics, the quest for meaning and purpose has become an integral part of everyday life. And that will only intensify as the first children of abundance, the baby boomers, realize that they have more of their lives behind them than ahead. In both business and personal life, now that our left-brain needs have largely been sated, our right-brain yearnings will demand to be fed.

21   As the forces of Asia, automation, and abundance strengthen and accelerate, the curtain is rising on a new era, the Conceptual Age. If the Industrial Age was built on people's backs, and the Information Age on people's left hemispheres, the Conceptual Age is being built on people's right hemispheres. We've progressed from a society of farmers to a society of factory workers to a society of knowledge workers. And now we're progressing yet again—to a society of creators and empathizers, pattern recognizers, and meaning makers.

22   But let me be clear: The future is not some Manichaean landscape in which individuals are either left-brained and extinct or right-brained and ecstatic—a land in which millionaire yoga instructors drive BMWs and programmers scrub counters at Chick-fil-A. Logical, linear, analytic thinking remains indispensable. But it's no longer enough.

23   To flourish in this age, we'll need to supplement our well-developed high tech abilities with aptitudes that are "high concept" and "high touch." High concept involves the ability to create artistic and emotional beauty, to detect patterns and opportunities, to craft a satisfying narrative, and to come up with inventions the world didn't know it was missing. High touch involves the capacity to empathize, to understand the subtleties of human interaction, to find joy in one's self and to elicit it in others, and to stretch beyond the quotidian in pursuit of purpose and meaning.

24   Developing these high concept, high touch abilities won't be easy for everyone. For some, the prospect seems unattainable. Fear not (or at least fear less). The sorts of abilities that now matter most are fundamentally human attributes. After all, back on the savannah, our caveperson ancestors weren't plugging numbers into spreadsheets or debugging code. But they were telling stories, demonstrating empathy, and designing innovations. These abilities have always been part of what it means to be human. It's just that after a few generations in the Information Age, many of our high concept, high touch muscles have atrophied. The challenge is to work them back into shape.

25   Want to get ahead today? Forget what your parents told you. Instead, do something foreigners can't do cheaper. Something computers can't do faster. And something that fills one of the nonmaterial, transcendent desires of an abundant age. In other words, go right, young man and woman, go right.

Source: Daniel H. Pink, "Revenge of the Right Brain," *Wired* magazine 2/2005, 1st serial adaptation.

DISCUSSION QUESTIONS

1. Review Chapter 11 of this book—particularly the sections on "Figures of Speech" and "The Music of Language." See how many figures of speech and instances of rhythm, alliteration, and euphony you can find in this argument. With a few of your classmates, consider the effect of these strategies on the argument as a whole.

2. Conduct some research on *Wired* magazine and characterize its typical reader. Is the overall tone of Pink's argument—its diction, level of formality, humor—appropriate to this imputed reader?

3. Using the Internet and a search engine like Google, check Pink's facts in Par. 15. Has he provided sufficient support for these statements? Why or why not?

4. In Par. 19, Pink makes the causal claim that the material abundance of our age has resulted in our placing "a premium on less rational sensibilities— beauty, spirituality, emotion." What evidence does Pink present for this claim (largely in Pars. 19–20)? Is the evidence adequate? If not, what additional kinds of evidence are required?

5. Identify three stipulative definitions in this argument.

SUGGESTIONS FOR WRITING (17.5)

1. This essay is filled with generalizations—from "more people are searching for meaning" (Par. 20) to "Any job that can be reduced to a set of rules is at risk" (Par. 17) to "now that our left-brain needs have largely been sated, our right-brain yearnings will demand to be fed." Select two generalizations and, doing the necessary research, support them with as many specific instances as you think are necessary to support the generalizations adequately.

2. Write a one- to two-page evaluation of this article, with "reasonable argument" as your evaluative term. Be sure to provide a clear definition of this term before applying it to the subject (Pink's article).

3. Think of someone you know well who works in a "left-brain" job. In two-three pages, argue how the capacities of "high concept" and "high touch" (defined in Par. 23) would change his or her job (for better or worse).

4. Pink assumes that anyone can be trained to use the "right brain" more fully. Drawing on your own experience and that of people you know or know about, agree or disagree with this proposition. Your support will consist largely of specific examples of your claim.

5. Conduct enough Internet research on Daniel Pink to write a balanced three-page biography of his life and career.

THE STRESS MYTH

RICHARD REEVES

"The Stress Myth" is a chapter in Richard Reeves's book Happy Mondays: Putting the Pleasure Back into Work *(2001). As its title suggests,* Happy Mondays *argues that work is or should be a pleasure, not a necessary evil. In the course of his book, Reeves debunks many common and negative assumptions about work. This chapter refutes the assumption that work is destructively stressful. Reeves is British, and his reference points are likewise British. He is a member of the Industrial Society and the head of its Futures Domain.*

1   The latest chapter in the history of anti-work spin focuses on stress. Work, it seems, is stretching us beyond human limits, demanding punishing hours and eroding personal relationships. It is stressing us out. Some U.S. commentators argue that work is taking on some of the characteristics of a religious cult, turning previously normal people into obedient workaholic zombies with deteriorating health and imploding families. work faces a serious charge: causing dangerous levels of stress.

2   Survey after survey appears to support the prosecution. Pick a number and you can probably find a survey to match. One in four British workers say they are "highly stressed" at work, according to one poll. Another finds that nine out of ten Londoners experience stress at work (*Evening Standard*, 13 September 2000). One in ten workers are "in despair", says the International Labor Organization.

3   A report from the International labor Organization (*Guardian*, 12 October 2000) warns that stress and anxiety at work are risky. Depression is ranked second after heart disease in terms of impact on work. "In the UK," reports the *Guardian*, "as many as three in 10 employees experience mental health problems," and "higher stress levels" are losing firms 80 million working days every year, at a cost of more than £5 billion.

4   Professor Cary Cooper, one of Britain's leading voices on workplace trends, warns that workplace stress is the "21st century plague." Workaholism has been outed as the new addiction of the middle classes. The title of Diane Fassel's book, *Working Ourselves to Death*, sums up the expert consensus.

5   But the literature on workaholism undermines its legitimacy when it lists "thinking about work outside working hours" and "consistently working more than forty hours a week" as symptoms. On this basis, Archimedes, Einstein, Shakespeare, Picasso and one in four British workers were or are in the grip of the disease. It seems unlikely.

6   And most of the scare stories about stress are just that. Indeed, stress is now a pretty useless word. It has been distorted and expanded. It has become a catch-all description for everything from deadline pressure to an off-day. Life contains some stress and life contains work—the only question begged by the London survey is who are the 10 percent who never experience stress at work? What kind of jobs do they have?

7   It is true that each survey seems to show an increase in stress levels, but it is doubtful that we have mutated from a nation of chilled-out yoga teachers to a society of screaming, semi-suicidal basket-cases in the space of a couple of decades. What has happened with stress is an overload of surveys. People get surveyed to ask how they feel about something, the results are plastered all over the papers, and then another set of people—who have read the articles—are surveyed on the same subject. It is now so well-established that anyone who is anyone is "stressed," that every one of us will tell the clipboard-wielding pollster that, yes, we are too, before sneaking around the corner for a latte with friends.

8   There is no "stress epidemic" in Britain's workplaces. Sometimes we feel stretched, or under pressure, or anxious, or busy at work, and we have fallen into the trap of labelling all these natural and positive feelings as stress. Take the London survey again, in which nine out of ten people experienced stress at work; half of them also said that they were happy at work. It is perfectly possible to be "stressed" and happy. In fact the only people whose mental health is really being hit by work are those who are out of it; unemployment is where the highest price is paid. As a trade unionist once said, "the trouble with unemployment is you never get a day off."

9   For some people, stress is used in an entirely upbeat way. As one of the participants in a Channel Four programme, *The Joy of Stress*, put it, "it is hard work but it's a buzz." Most people want activity, they want challenge. It is not stress, it's a buzz.

10   It's true that the intensity of work has increased. More people report deadline pressure and having to work faster and harder. This is often seen as bad news, as if it would

somehow be better for us if we all worked more slowly and with less effort. The legacy of work as punishment, unrewarding toil and necessary evil suffuses debates about work intensity. If work was empty drudgery, of course it would be bad news that we're putting more effort into it. But work isn't like that every day; it is becoming even less like that. Maybe people are putting more effort into work because work has become more worthwhile.

11   And a little pressure often goes a long way. Adrenaline fuels success. James Thurber, after having 20 stories successively rejected by the *New Yorker*, was asked by his wife one afternoon in 1927 if he wasn't "ruining those stories by spending so much time on them." She advised him to give himself a 45-minute time limit for his next story. Thurber did just that, sent off his piece— and received an acceptance letter in a matter of days.

12   Any life worth living is full of "stresses." A life with a wide range of choices, aspirations, paths and challenges, and with stretching and demanding work, feels more challenging than one with predictable, repetitive, dull jobs and activities, and limited horizons. And thank God for that. As Kierkegaard put it, "Anxiety is freedom."

This is not to say that there aren't some   13 workplaces that damage mental health— simply that the vast majority do not. The real issue is control. As long as we feel in control of our work our psychological health is unlikely to suffer. Self-generated pressure to produce the best presentation is not stress; it is personal pride and ambition. And pride and ambition are good for you.

For many centuries work has been la-   14 belled curse, punishment, religious instruction, necessary evil, survival course, time bandit, marriage-wrecker and depressant. And the spin continues to the present day. A long list of maladies is linked to work; we are more anxious and less horny; more rushed and less homely; more sick and less polite; more addicted and less happy than ever before. And work is supposedly to blame. There is an anti-work case being put in persuasive terms on an almost daily basis. There is only one problem with it. It's bunkum. Work is simply the scapegoat. For the truth, whisper it softly, is that as far as work is concerned, we've never had it so good.

Source: Richard Reeves, *Happy Mondays: Putting the Pleasure Back Into Work*, London: Pearson, 2001.

DISCUSSION QUESTIONS

1. How would you classify "The Stress Myth"?

2. Characterize the image projected by this argument. Does this image contribute to the argument's effectiveness?

3. Where and how effectively does Reeves address the counter-argument to his position?

4. Reeves does not define the term "stress" anywhere in this chapter. Would an extended or shorthand definition have strengthened his argument? Why or why not?

5. In Par. 2, Reeves refers to "survey after survey" that support the dangers of work-related stress. Would his argument have benefited from the inclusion of one or more of these surveys? Why or why not?

SUGGESTIONS FOR WRITING (17.6)

1. Create an outline of Reeves's argument, identifying major and secondary claims and their support. What strengths or weaknesses does your outline reveal?

2. Create an outline for an argument based upon personal experience supporting the central claim that "Any life worth living is full of 'stresses'" (Par. 12). What would the class of this argument be? What would be the best ways to support your central and secondary claims?

3. Compose your own survey about the stresses associated with college. Before writing the questions, be sure you are clear about what you want to find out. Administer the survey to the rest of your class and write a summary of the results.

4. Write a one-page stipulative definition of the term "stress."

5. Write a two-page letter to a college administrator arguing how certain stresses of college life could be eliminated or reduced.

18

Diet

INTRODUCTION

Of all the subject units in this anthology of arguments, this one on "Diet" may seem the most curious.

The term "diet," which derives from the Latin *dies,* or "days," means simply "daily fare"—the combination of food and drink that we consume from day to day. More specifically, we use the term "diet" to refer to habits of food consumption directed toward a particular goal. One can be on a diet for weight gain, a diet for improved memory, a diet for increased energy. But as members of a culture that prizes thinness above all body shapes, many of us immediately associate the term "diet" with weight loss strategies—with calorie counting, low-fat food, and self-imposed hunger. It is largely with this use of the word diet that this unit is concerned.

If at this point you're wondering what the literature of diet, with its preoccupation with calorie counting and fat reduction, could possibly teach about writing reasonable and effective arguments, consider the following.

First, the very *dailiness* of diet qualifies it for the attention of this book. Like every other unit in this reader—popular culture, the Internet, work, sports, and so on—diet, in all senses of the word, is everywhere. It has spawned numerous industries that barrage us daily with their marketing ploys; it requires constant decisions that consume huge amounts of our time, whether we are counting fat grams or picking a restaurant; and it is the occasion of countless conversations (try counting the number of conversations you overhear or participate in, in a single day that revolve around eating—you'll be amazed). In other words, diet has become a kind of ever-present, ambient noise that we hear but don't always listen to. We need to pay attention to the noise once in a while, to analyze those claims and conclusions that too often we unthinkingly accept.

Second, as you will see in some of the following readings, arguments concerning diet seem to be particularly susceptible to flawed reasoning. One can hypothesize a number of explanations for this susceptibility. For one, when it comes to body-sculpting through diet, our own credulity, fueled by our desperation to emulate those impossible models in magazines, probably encourages advertisers to indulge in careless reasoning (not that advertising in any area is distinguished by reason).

Third, the universality of diet—the fact that it is something all of us engage in on a daily basis—tends to make us behave like experts on the subject. Just as we are all doctors when it comes to the common cold, we are dietitians when it comes to eating. Though we often lack rigorous scientific studies to back up our claims, experience, and intuitions, few of us can resist adding to the abundant supply of unwarranted pronouncements about diet. When was the last time you contributed to this store of "common knowledge" about diet?

And finally, arguments about diet are unreliable because the subject is anything but an exact science. Even the experts—the nutritionists, dieticians, and physiologists—disagree about the facts. Look at the parade of claims, revisions, and counterclaims that regularly come out of medical center laboratories and double-blind studies. When publications as prestigious as the *New England Journal of Medicine* and the *Journal of the American Medical Association* come out with directly contradictory claims about diet—as they did, for example, about the disputable benefits of oat bran in the 1980s,[1] how can we expect lucidity and reason in the popular literature about diet?

But not all the readings in this section are examples of argument gone awry. For while the subject of diet may tempt misguided and misguiding reasoning, it is also, like all the topics represented in this reader, a fascinating and provocative phenomenon that, when given our (unaccustomed) attention, yields a wealth of information about who we are, what we value and why, where we locate our identities, and how we construct meaning. Diet, it turns out, is a remarkably rich site at which to extend your understanding of argument, readily offering cautionary examples of faulty argument and worthy instances of original, well-reasoned thinking.

THE DIET BIZ

DONALD JACKSON

Reading Donald Jackson's "The Diet Biz" may give you a jaundiced view of the "diet industry" of the last century. This survey of the history of dieting, which originally appeared in the Smithsonian *magazine in November 1994, highlights some of the more crackpot diet plans in a business not noted for following scientific principles.*

---

[1] Kinosian, Bruce P., M.D. and John M. Eisenberg, M.D. M.B.A. "Cutting Into Cholesterol." *Journal of the American Medical Association,* April 15, 1988, Vol. 259, No. 15. Swain, Rouse, Curley, Sacks. "Comparison of the Effects of Oat Bran on Serum Lipoprotein Levels and Blood Pressure." *New England Journal of Medicine,* Jan. 18, 1990, Vol. 322, No.3.

COMMENTARY

The essay's claim, which appears at the outset in large bold and italicized print, is a factual generalization: "The art of wishful shrinking has made a lot of people rich. But it has not made many thin—or at least not for long. Diet sensations come and go but excess weight seems to hang on forever." The body of the essay consists of a series of factual examples that support the opening generalization.

The organization of the many examples is chronological. Paragraphs 3–16 provide numerous examples of diet conjurers, beginning with William Banting in the mid-nineteenth century and ending with Gayelord Hauser in the 1930s. Paragraphs 17–22 offer examples of diet devices. Finally, paragraphs 23–24 detail examples of the development of diet organizations like Weight Watchers and dieting "methods" like Atkins and Scarsdale.

Writing an exclusively factual survey of the bizarre history of dieting would challenge even the most objective and humorless writer. Jackson is not at all reluctant to offer his evaluative take on the subject matter, though his evaluations are not argued at any length. Rather, they are expressed through the use of strongly connotative language and a consistently ridiculing tone. Terms like "diet hustling" (Par. 3), "dietmeister-showman-mogul" (Par. 15), "glop" (Par. 25), and "talkaholic" (Par. 28) reveal pretty clearly what the author thinks of this "diet roadshow" (Par. 13). As Chapter 11 cautions, connotative language, slanting, and sarcasm do not make arguments, though they can certainly influence a careless reader. In the case of this essay, however, the silliness and deceit of the diet industry is sufficiently obvious (a diet, for example, that claims thorough chewing causes weight loss) to warrant Jackson's shorthand judgments.

THE DIET BIZ

1   Any day now it's coming, you can bank on it—the ultimate no-pain, no-sacrifice, no-hunger, eat-all-you-want diet, guaranteed medically and nutritionally sound, effortless, and did I say *guaranteed*, that's right, and all in a book for a mere $24.95, your money back if not delighted and transformed into a new, wonderful, slimmer you in, oh, three weeks tops. Listen—hear that tapping in the far reaches of the doctor's office? He's finishing it now, publication is a couple of months off; they're just buttoning up paperback rights.

2   The author-promoter of the next diet sensation will take his or her place in a long, gaudy and intermittently felonious procession of gurus and messiahs who have lived well while dispensing weight-loss wisdom, more or less. Happily for them, there has ever been a huge reservoir of pudgy people ready and willing to snap up the latest offerings. As the apostles of slenderness know full well, rare is the overweight individual who will not do almost anything to improve his or her appearance—and, of course, the less a diet requires one to do, the more likely one is to try it. This is why dieting has become such a big business. In 1993, Americans spent around $30 billion on books, video tapes, nutritional aides, reducing salons and other diet-related goods and services. If some would-be dieters are hanging back now

because of the latest scientific reservations about the long-term value of self-denial, just wait until the new book comes out. They'll find it impossible to resist.

3   Doctors have been the most conspicuous promoters, especially in recent years, but diet hustling is an equal-opportunity field. Tycoons and housewives have had a go at it, as have self-styled "nutritionists" of a dozen different shadings, preachers and writers and actors and a few with no credentials whatever, people who seemed to wander in off the street to conjure up a diet plan. One of the first such savants in the historical record, as it happens, was a mid-19th-century London undertaker.

4   His name was William Banting, and his problem was that at age 65 he had 14 stone 6 (202 pounds) of lard lumpily distributed on his 5-foot-5 frame. He couldn't tie his shoes or descend a staircase frontally, and he was going deaf. Banting tried rowing and horseback riding, purgatives and diuretics and Turkish baths, but nothing worked until his doctor prescribed a diet free from sugar and starch. When he dropped 52 pounds on a regimen of lean meat, vegetables, dry toast and soft-boiled eggs (with a daily alcoholic toddy), when his hearing improved and he could again navigate a stairway with dignity, Banting the pioneer dieter became Banting the promoter, producing a book that had sold 58,000 copies by the time he died in 1878.

5   In this country, Horace Fletcher attained early dietary eminence as "The Great Masticator." Fletcher parlayed a fanatical dedication to the act of chewing, a serene self-assurance and some remarkable physical exploits into a career as a self-taught expert on diet and health just after the turn of the century. Fletcher was a cosmopolitan businessman who made a fortune in ink and imports only to find himself at age 40 unable to buy life insurance because he was a white-haired, 217-pound blob.

6   The turning point came when a friend told him about former British prime minister William Gladstone's conviction that proper and prolonged chewing precluded overeating and led to good health. It was not a totally novel notion, since vigorous chewing had been viewed as an aid to digestion for years, but Fletcher embraced it like a sinner saved. Gladstone had counseled 32 chews per morsel, one for each tooth in a normal mouth, but Fletcher, soon known as "the chew chew man," raised the dental ante and urged that all food be munched until it turned to liquid. Never mind if it was liquid already—soup and milk were to be "chewed" as well. Fletcher argued further that any food that did not liquefy under such relentless mastication should be spit out. That eliminated roughage and thus made constipation a problem to be reckoned with.

7   Fletcher, by now 65 pounds lighter and down to one noisy, drawn-out meal a day, did what all diet mavens do: he wrote a book. *The AB-Z of Our Own Nutrition.* He dressed in white suits, bought a house in Venice and churned out articles claiming that 200,000 families in the United States lived by his precepts. Students at Yale and West Point "fletcherized" their meals. The faithful in Britain had "munching parties"; John D. Rockefeller solemnly fletcherized. Fletcher's own weight fluctuated—one professor described him at 55 as "rather plump than otherwise"—but he now appeared to be mostly muscle. At 58 he performed the astonishing feat (or so he claimed) of lifting 300 pounds dead weight 350 times with his right leg, double a previous record.

8   Fletcher eschewed meat, alcohol, coffee and tea. His meals ran to potatoes, cornbread, beans, sometimes eggs and toast, and the occasional stewed tomato. His guidelines were light on specific food groups but heavy on the attitude the eater brought to the table. Rule No. 1 was "wait for a true, earned appetite." A diner could eat what he wanted as long as he chewed till the food "swallowed itself," and no "depressing or diverting feelings" were to intrude at mealtime. The consequences would be complete and easy digestion, perfect health, and a farewell to eczema, headaches, pimples, boils and "that foggy feeling."

9   In his sunset years, the man once denounced as a food crank became a venerated figure, but the Great Masticator's star eventually faded. Early adherents like Dr. John Harvey Kellogg, of the Battle Creek, Michigan, cereal Kelloggs, defected over the roughage issue, adding the gratuitous observation that Fletcher's breath was "highly malodorous."

10   A little book printed a year before Fletcher's death at 70 in 1919 showed that in dieting, as in other difficult but rewarding pastimes, the best advice is not always the latest word. Dr. Lulu Hunt Peters, who wrote *Diet and Health, with a Key to the Calories,* had a precocious grasp of the awful truth that millions would ultimately spend billions to avoid: successful dieting was a hard, demanding, lifelong commitment. Having pared her own weight from 200 to 150, she told her readers that "no matter how hard I work—no matter how much I exercise, no matter what I suffer, I will always have to watch my weight, I will always have to count my calories."

11   Calorie-counting was still a novelty when Dr. Peters, a physician in Los Angeles who wrote a syndicated health column, introduced it in her book. (A calorie is a unit of measurement representing the energy-producing value of food.) Addressing herself mainly to women, then as now the foot soldiers in the diet forces, she instructed them to use the word "calorie" as routinely as they used "pound," "gallon" or "yard." "Hereafter you are going to eat calories of food," she wrote. "Instead of saying one slice of bread or a piece of pie, you will say 100 calories of bread, 350 calories of pie."

12   Her diet began with a fast to show the body who was boss, then imposed a 1,200-calorie daily limit, followed by a more relaxed but permanent—as in *forever*—maintenance plan. The Peters preachments of self-denial and self-discipline won the endorsement of government agencies while selling two million books, making hers the first and one of the best in a long and often odious line of American diet-book best-sellers.

13   Two other leading lights of the diet roadshow in the 1920s and '30s took a different approach. Dr. William Howard Hay and Gaylord Hauser were forerunners of what was waiting down the road in the wide-open, largely unregulated diet biz. Promoters of soft, semiscientific hustles that defied the medical establishment while profiting from Americans' nutritional gullibility, they were early masters of the art of wishful shrinking.

14   Hay, who operated out of a resort he called Pocono Hay-ven, Pennsylvania, decreed that proteins, starches and fruits had to be eaten separately to avoid acidosis, which drained vitality and led to fat. One food category per meal was the best way—plus a daily enema to flush out the poison. Henry Ford obediently chomped down on fruit at breakfast, carbohydrates for lunch and proteins at dinner. Critics churlishly pointed out that nature had already mixed proteins and carbohydrates in many foods, and that the digestive system handles the mix with minimal difficulty, but Hay diets still lured millions.

15   Hauser was one of the earliest dietmeister-showman-moguls, a suave, charismatic European with a vaguely academic background. (He was an N.D., or doctor of naturopathy, a system of treatment that uses natural substances to help the body heal itself.) He enjoyed showy cars and the company of film stars like Greta Garbo and Paulette Goddard. He lectured, wrote best-sellers (*Look Younger, Live Longer*), developed his own lucrative line of special foods and supplements, and for a time indulged a Fletcher-like preference for white suits.

16   His 10- and 28-day diets stressed his five vitamin-B-heavy "wonder foods"—brewer's yeast, wheat germ, yogurt, powdered skim milk and blackstrap molasses. Hauser agitated medical hackles with pronouncements like his claim that we all have both an "appestat," which he defined as an acquired appetite for the wrong stuff, and a "hungerstat," or craving for nutritionally correct foods. He and Garbo sometimes shared hungerstat-driven lunches of wild-rice burgers and broiled grapefruit.

17   By the time Hay and Hauser bestrode the diet whirlwind, the public was beginning to flinch under a baffling bombardment of confusing claims. One expert, for example, plumped for a breakfast of whole-wheat pancakes with maple syrup, another advised vegetable soup, and a third urged melon, peaches or berries, a baked potato and broiled fish. Special combinations of foods, "magic pairs" like lamb chops and pineapple, were touted as bearers of unique "fat-burning" properties, a notion debunked by two generations of scientists.

From belts to creams to salts to . . .

18   In such an atmosphere it was little wonder that almost any device, instrument or lotion that promised weight loss without the bother of stress or sacrifice found a ready market. As far back as the 1890s, a Boston druggist had peddled a corsetlike "obesity belt" bearing electrically charged disks that purportedly dispelled intestinal gas, disintegrated fat and dispersed tumors. By the 1930s, dieters could rub away flab with "reducing creams," melt it away with bath salts, or jiggle it away on a "Slendro Massager Table" or "the magic couch."

19   Slenderella reducing salons, which first appeared in 1950, invited women into curtained booths where they listened to piped-in music and quivered fully clothed on a specially designed vibrating table. They remained clad because of founder Larry Mack's belief that the "only place a respectable woman ever took her clothes off was her bedroom." Customers were given low-calorie diets disingenuously labeled "menu adjustments" to preserve the illusion that nothing so taxing as a diet was called for. By 1955, more than 16,000 women were shimmying daily in more than 100 Slenderella salons and shelling out $2 for each of the 30 to 150 sessions. Despite a Food and Drug Administration (FDA) warning that no device was effective for "spot reducing, melting away fat or breaking up fatty deposits," it was the Internal Revenue Service and not customer discontent that

brought Slenderella down in 1959. The name was later sold to a company that made low-cal jelly.

20   Dieting, the American Medical Association (AMA) declared in the mid-1950s, had become a national neurosis. Thinner was better—more attractive, more youthful, healthier, more productive. And if a product could deliver thinness in a reasonably palatable form, the possibilities were limitless. At least that's how it looked for the Mead Johnson drug company and the product Metrecal—short for "metered calories"—in 1960.

21   Metrecal came as a powder made from milk, soya flour, starch, corn oil, yeast, vitamins, coconut oil and chocolate, vanilla or butterscotch flavoring. A $1.59 can contained 900 calories and when mixed with four glasses of water provided a day's nourishment. (Metrecal was also sold in a premixed, liquid form.) It satisfied hunger, and it seemed to satisfy the medical establishment, which detected no nutritional Achilles' heel. A dieter didn't even have to count calories and commonly dropped about ten pounds in two to three weeks. All of this accompanied by a smooth advertising campaign produced a bonanza: Mead Johnson's profits rocketed from $5.5 million to $13.3 million in a year.

22   Then, suddenly, consumers stopped buying. Nothing happened—no revelation, no assault in the courts. People simply got tired of swilling the same stuff meal after meal. Profits went south in 1962 and '63 while the company scrambled up a Metrecal cookie that failed to halt the plunge. Somebody suggested that Metrecal palled because people missed chewing; the Great Masticator may have been on to something after all.

23   Metrecal's boom and bust, like the profusion of exercise salons and the swelling numbers of diet books (from 60 in the 1960s to 260 in the '70s), diet foods, diet doctors and especially diet pills, was another sign that the diet biz was now a big-ticket enterprise. A 25-cent calorie-counter book that first appeared in 1951 had sold 17 million

copies by 1973. Diet pills in one form or another had been around for decades. A pamphlet one drug company distributed to doctors illuminated the ethics of the diet-pill trade: recommend NO diet or exercise, the company advised, prescribe plenty of tablets and demand payment in cash.

Take these whether you need 'em or not

24 In 1968, when *Life* magazine dispatched reporter Susanna McBee to visit ten "fat doctors" as an undercover patient, the FDA estimated that as many as 7,000 such practitioners were doling out more than two billion diet pills annually, including diuretics, barbiturates, amphetamines, thyroid tablets and laxatives. McBee, at about 5-feet-6 and 125 pounds, was anything but obese. Every one of her ten doctors prescribed pills, most after only a cursory examination and conversation; one saw her for three minutes and gave her 150 capsules. Her total haul from the ten healers was 1,479 pills.

25 The vilest potion concocted in the name of weight reduction was doubtless the liquid protein mixture popularized by Dr. Robert Linn in his 1970s book *The Last Chance Diet*. Like Banting and Fletcher in dieting's more innocent era, Linn presented himself as an ex-portly advertisement, claiming he had dropped 83 pounds while subsisting on his syrup. It was a loathsome blend of crushed animal horns, hooves and hides mixed with enzymes, tenderizers—one would hope so—and fruit flavoring. The idea was that 300 to 400 calories a day of this glop would sustain a person who was otherwise fasting. The AMA warned of side effects like renal and coronary disease. The FDA and the Centers for Disease Control investigated several dozen deaths among liquid protein consumers, but an estimated two million to four million hard-core dieters tried it anyway.

26 Esther Manz of Milwaukee became a diet-club pioneer after learning about the Alcoholics Anonymous network. She had no product or plan to hustle, just a consignment of fat to shed and the belief that it would be more pleasant to lose it amid an agreeable, mutually supportive group. She nourished the idea during a year of therapeutic weekly meetings with a few friends, lost 45 pounds and emerged with TOPS—for Take Off Pounds Sensibly (some called it Tomorrow Or Pretty Soon)—the first national dieting organization.

27 The TOPS clubs that blossomed around the country gave themselves good-natured names like Button Busters, Zipper Rippers, Thick 'n Tired and InvisiBelles. Members followed individual diets under the supervision of their doctors and met regularly to fuss over one another when they lost and shame one another when they gained. Backsliders were tried at a "Court of Weights and Measures" and deposited fines in piggy banks; the worst offender in one club was crowned "Queen Pig" and honored with a bouquet of weeds. By the late 1950s, the 60,000 members were losing an average of 15 pounds a year, but studies suggested that group dieters were not much more successful than solo, unsupervised reducers in keeping lost weight off.

28 Jean Nidetch, the Brooklyn-born talkaholic who founded Weight Watchers in 1963, was another overextended housewife who couldn't jettison pounds in solitude and, like Manz, she found Nirvana in a support group. Initially Weight Watchers differed from TOPS in that its members all followed the same diet, which involved no calorie-counting. Treating overeating almost as an addiction ("I used to hide chocolate cake in the laundry hamper," Nidetch confessed), it permitted unlimited gnoshing of certain vegetables while banning other foods altogether. Weight Watchers also differed from TOPS in that it was a profit-making business, and the proceeds from such products as frozen foods, desserts, cookbooks, scales and other goods were so rich that the company was gobbled up by the H. J. Heinz Company 16 years ago.

29 The somewhat startling truth about dieting is that, for all its up-and-down, cash-and-carry history, nothing much changes.

Elizabeth Sharon Hayenga puts it this way in her doctoral dissertation titled "Dieting Through the Decades": "Virtually everything . . . cottage cheese diets, low-carbohydrate diets, diet pills, diet clubs, fasting, liquid diets—is reincarnated with a new title, author or brand name decade after decade. And each new incarnation produces new sales records."

30   In the 1960s and '70s, the boffo diets came attached to doctors' names but most owed their high-protein, low-carbohydrate regimen to William Banting, the London undertaker who had beaten that old devil corpulence with a low-carbohydrate diet in the 1860s. One after another the white-coated savants appeared in the center ring clutching nutritional salvation between hard covers—Dr. Herman Taller with *Calories Don't Count* in 1961, Dr. Irwin Stillman with *The Doctor's Quick Weight-Loss Diet* in 1967, Dr. Robert Atkins with *Dr. Atkins' Diet Revolution* in 1972, and Dr. Herman Tarnower with *The Complete Scarsdale Medical Diet* in 1978.

High-fat fraud, extra-light fine

31   The Romanian-born Taller, a gynecologist, contended that his book reflected "new knowledge" that polyunsaturated fats "soft-ened" body fat, which then melted away quicker. He promoted a high-fat diet supplemented with vegetable oil capsules, but he veered into trouble when he mentioned a particular mail-order company as a source for the capsules. To federal prosecutors, this sounded like an advertisement and, when it turned out that the doctor owned an interest in the capsule company, they indicted him for mail fraud, conspiracy and mislabeling. Convicted of 12 counts in 1967, Taller was given a suspended sentence and fined $7,000, probably far short of a month's royalties for his book.

32   Stillman, who was a medical consultant at Coney Island Hospital, advocated a regimen similar to Taller's but lower in fat and cholesterol, in deference to evidence linking high cholesterol to heart disease. He urged

lean meats, cottage cheese, hard-boiled eggs and eight ten-ounce glasses of water a day. Atkins' diet was another spin of the same tune, spiced with the identification of a previously (and still) unknown substance he called FMH (for "fat mobilizing hormone"), which he said "moves fat around the body." His tolerance of high-cholesterol bacon, cream and mayonnaise appalled the medical establishment—one critic called it "planned malnutrition"—but went over big with dieters.

33   Tarnower's Scarsdale diet marked a return to the traditional low-calorie, low-fat, low-carbohydrate discipline, with meals precisely spelled out in a 14-day plan. But Tarnower, too, was prone to gild biology a bit, declaring on no particular authority that the food combination in his plan stimulated a unique metabolic change that diminished fat. He had little time to enjoy his celebrity as a diet maven. He was shot to death by a jealous lover in 1980—but that's another story.

34   Not until the late 1980s did disaffection with the received wisdom that thinner was better begin to simmer beneath a surface still littered with diet books (300 were in print in 1984). Researchers commenced taking potshots at long-accepted theories (*Smithsonian*, January 1986): heredity and metabolism might have more to do with rotundity, they suggested, than overeating: "yo-yo" dieting, the chronic swings endured by many dieters, could do more long-run harm than good; some scientists contended that each of us has a "set point" weight that the body finds ways to maintain, diet or no. Was dietmania, after booming for a century or so, on the wane? Probably not, but last year *Consumer Reports* concluded an article on weight-loss methods with these heretical words: "The majority of dieters would probably do better to forget about cutting calories, focus on exercising and eating a healthful diet, and let the pounds fall where they may."

35   Let them fall where they may? You mean all those diets, all that self-denial

and self-discipline, all that ingenuity and imagination and hustle and con—all that was in vain? No more belts, rainbow pills or diet books? No more salons, clubs and obnoxious concoctions? That can't be right. Don't forget: I still hear somebody tapping away out there, cranking up yet another best-seller. This expert is laying the foundation of the diet revolution of all time. Really. It's the next big thing.

Notes: *Never Satisfied: A Cultural History of Diets, Fantasies and Fat* by Hillel Schwartz, Macmillan, 1986.

"Losing Weight: What Works, What Doesn't," *Consumer Reports,* June 1993.

"The Diet Biz" by Bonnie Blodgett, *Glamour,* January 1991.

Source: Donald Dale Jackson, "The Art of Wishful Shrinking Has Made a Lot of People Rich," *Smithsonian*. November 1994.

DISCUSSION QUESTIONS

1. Do you agree with the commentary's appraisal of Jackson's use of connotative language? Is his use of language warranted by the evidence, or is it a sleight-of-hand tactic that should be avoided?

2. How different would the essay's effect be if the author had avoided all connotative language? You might want to rewrite one or two of the paragraphs that are especially slanted, using the most impartial, objective language.

3. With a classmate or two, divide up the sources cited at the end of the article and investigate the expertise of the authors cited and the reputation of the publication. Consider whether these sources pass the tests of reliability, impartiality, and currency. Is the number of sources cited adequate? If not, what further kinds of sources would be useful?

4. Has this essay influenced your thinking on the subject? What features of the argument do you think are responsible for that (e.g., the number of examples, the sources cited, the organization of support, the connotative language, etc.)?

SUGGESTIONS FOR WRITING (18.1)

1. Write a three- to four-page causal argument speculating on the reasons for the public's willingness to believe the impossible when it comes to one of the following: dieting; get-rich-quick-schemes; exercise equipment; age-defying potions.

2. Conduct research for a five- to seven-page factual survey of a pastime that you find silly or a waste of time or senseless (e.g., gambling, bridge, golf, computer games, etc.). Including at least four sources you located, write an objective factual argument laying the background and evolution of this activity. In your argument, do not follow Jackson's example: avoid slanted, evaluative language. Use the APA form for your notes and bibliography.

3. Write an evaluation of one of the activities suggested in the preceding question. You may use slanted or connotative language, provided it is supported. Be sure to define your audience carefully so you can appeal to appropriate needs and values. Also, if necessary, define your evaluative term carefully.

INTUITIVE EATING

EVELYN TRIBOLE AND ELYSE RESCH

Intuitive Eating, by Evelyn Tribole and Elyse Resch, is one of the many dieting "how to" books available on bookstore shelves. The book as a whole is an extended recommendation claiming that those who want to lose weight should not diet ("lose the diet mentality"). Instead, would-be dieters should rely on their own nutritional intuition to tell them when and what to eat.

Tribole and Resch are registered dietitians. Both are regular contributors to the growing literature of dieting.

Step I: Recognize and Acknowledge the Damage That Dieting Causes

1   There is a substantial amount of research on the harm that dieting causes. Acknowledge that the harm is real, and that continued dieting will only perpetuate your problems. Some of the key side effects gleaned from major studies are described below in two categories, biological and emotional. As you read, take a personal inventory and ask yourself which of the problems you are already experiencing. Recognizing that dieting is the problem will help you break through the cultural myth that diets work. Remember, *if dieting is the problem, how can it be part of the solution?*

Damage from Dieting: Biological and Health

2   In every century, famine and human starvation has existed. Sadly, this is true even today. Survival of the fittest in the past meant survival of the fattest—only those with adequate energy stores (fat) could survive a famine. Consequently, our bodies are still equipped in this modern age to combat starvation at the cellular level. As far as the body is concerned, dieting is a form of starvation, even though it's voluntary.

3   Chronic dieting has been shown to:

- *Teach the body to retain more fat when you start eating again.* Low-calorie diets double the enzymes that make and store fat in the body. This is a form of biological compensation to help the body store more energy, or fat, after dieting.

- *Slow the rate of weight loss* with each successive attempt to diet. This has been shown to be true in both rat and human studies.

- *Decrease metabolism.* Dieting triggers the body to become more efficient at utilizing calories by lowering the body's need for energy.

- *Increase binges and cravings.* Both humans and rats have been shown to overeat after chronic food restriction. Food restriction stimulates the brain to launch a cascade of cravings to eat *more*. After substantial weight loss, studies show that rats prefer eating more fat, while people have been shown to prefer foods both high in fat and sugar.

- *Increase risk of premature death and heart disease.* A thirty-two-year study of more than 3,000 men and women in the Framingham Heart Study has shown that *regardless of initial weight,* people whose weight repeatedly goes up and down—known as weight cycling or yo-yo dieting—have a higher overall death rate and twice the normal risk of dying from heart disease. These results were independent of cardiovascular risk factors, and held true regardless if a person was thin or obese. The harm from yo-yo dieting may be equal to the risks of staying obese.

  Similarly, results of the Harvard Alumni Health Study show that people who lose and gain at least eleven pounds within a decade or so, don't live as long as those who maintain a stable weight.

- *Cause satiety cues to atrophy.* Dieters usually stop eating due to a self-imposed limit rather than inner cues of fullness. This, combined with skipping meals, can condition you to eat meals of increasingly larger size.
- *Cause body shape to change.* Yo-yo dieters who continually regain the lost weight tend to regain weight in the abdominal area. This type of fat storage increases the risk of heart disease.

4   Other documented side effects include headaches, menstrual irregularities, fatigue, dry skin, and hair loss.

Damage from Dieting: Psychological and Emotional

5   Psychological experts reported the following adverse effects at the landmark 1992 National Institutes of Health, Weight Loss and Control Conference:

- Dieting is linked to eating disorders.
- Dieting may cause stress or make the dieter more vulnerable to its effects.
- Independent of body weight itself, dieting is correlated with feelings of failure, lowered self-esteem, and social anxiety.
- The dieter is often vulnerable to loss of control over eating when violating "the rules" of the diet, whether there was an actual or *perceived* transgression of the diet! The mere perception of eating a forbidden food, regardless of actual calorie content, is enough to trigger overeating.

6   In a separate report, psychologists David Garner and Susan Wooley make a compelling case against the high cost of false hope from dieting. They conclude that:

- Dieting gradually erodes confidence and self-trust.
- Many obese individuals assume they could not have become obese unless they possessed some *fundamental character deficit*. Garner and Wooley argue

that while many obese individuals may experience binge eating and depression, these psychological and behavioral symptoms are the *result of dieting*. But these overweight individuals easily interpret these symptoms as further evidence of an underlying problem. Yet, obese people do not have inordinate psychological disturbances compared to normal weight people.

Step 2: Be Aware of Diet-Mentality Traits and Thinking

7   The diet mentality surfaces in subtle forms, even when you decide to reject dieting. It's important to recognize common characteristics of the diet mentality; it will let you know if you are still playing the dieting game. Forget about willpower, being obedient, and failing. The general difference in the ways the dieter versus the nondieter views eating, exercise, and progress are summarized by a chart at the end of this chapter.

8   *Forget Willpower.*   While no doctor would expect a patient to "will" blood pressure to normal levels, physicians frequently expect their overweight patients to "will" their weight loss by restricting their food, according to Susan Z. Yanovski, M.D. This is also a prevailing attitude among our clients and many Americans—all you need is willpower and a little self-control. In a 1993 Gallup poll, the most common obstacle to losing weight cited by women was willpower.

9   For example, Marilyn is a highly successful lawyer who climbed to the top of the corporate ladder. She credits determination, willpower, and self-discipline as being responsible for her success. Yet, when she tried to use these exemplary principles in her dieting attempts, she always failed. Whatever success she had achieved in her professional life was dulled by her sense of failure with eating.

10   Why was Marilyn able to be so disciplined in one area of her life but not in the other? The word "discipline" derives from the word "disciple." According to Stephen

Covey's work, if you are a disciple to your own deep values that have an overriding purpose, it's likely that you'll have the *will* to carry them out. Marilyn believed deeply that writing exacting contracts and keeping immaculate records were requisites to building confidence with her clients and her law firm. But, somehow, hearing that bread was wrong on one diet and anything with sugar was wrong on another, did not engender the same kind of deep beliefs. Try as she might, she couldn't really believe that chocolate chip cookies were that evil!

11   *Willpower* can be defined as an attempt to counter natural desires and replace them with proscriptive rules. The desire for sweets is natural, normal, and quite pleasant! Any diet that tells you you can't have sweets, is going against your natural desire. The diet becomes a set of rigid rules, and these kinds of rules can only trigger rebellion.

12   *Willpower does not belong in Intuitive Eating.* As Marilyn became an Intuitive Eater, she found that listening to her personal signals reinforced her natural instincts, rather than fighting them. She had no one else's proscriptive rules to follow or to rebel against. Marilyn has stopped fighting the phantom willpower battle and she has lost all the weight with which she had been struggling.

13   ***Forget Being Obedient.*** A well meaning suggestion by a spouse or significant other, such as: "Honey, you should have the broiled chicken . . ." or "You shouldn't eat those fries . . ." can set off an inner food rebellion. In this type of food combat, your only weapon to fight back becomes a double order of fries. Our clients call this *forget-you eating.*

14   In physics, resistance always occurs as a reaction to force. We see this principle in action in society as riots often erupt when the force of authority becomes too great. Similarly, the *simple act of being told what to do* (even if it's something you want to do) can trigger a rebellious chain reaction. Just like "terrible two year olds," or teenagers who revolt to prove they are independent, dieters can initiate rebellious eating in response to the act of dieting, with its set of rigid rules dictating what to eat. And so, it's not surprising to hear from our clients that breaking the rules of a diet makes them feel just like they did when they were defiant teens.

15   But take heart, rebellion is a normal act of self-preservation—protecting your space or personal boundaries.

16   Think of a personal boundary as a tall brick fence surrounding you, with only one gate. Only you can open that gate, if you choose. Therefore, no one is allowed inside, unless you invite the person in. Within your fence reside private feelings, thoughts, and biological signals. People who *assume* they know what you need and tell you what to do are picking the lock to your gate, or invading your boundaries. No one could possibly know what's inside unless you tell him, by inviting him in.

17   What diet or diet counselor can possibly know when you are hungry or how much food it will take to satisfy you? How can anyone but you know what texture and taste sensations will be pleasing to your palate? In the world of dieting, personal boundaries are crossed at many levels. For example, you are told what to eat, how much of it to eat, and when to eat it. These decisions should be personal choices, with respect for individual autonomy and body signals. While food guidance may come from elsewhere, *you* should ultimately be responsible for the *when, what,* and *how much* of eating.

18   When a diet doctor or a diet plan invades your boundaries, it's normal to feel powerless. The longer you follow the food restrictions, the greater the assault to your autonomy. Here is where the paradox lies. When dieting, you will likely rebel by eating more—to restore your autonomy and protect your boundaries. But the act of rebelling can make you feel as out of control as a city riot. Instead, you have an inner food fight on your hands. But once the food rebellion is unleashed, its intensity reinforces feelings of lack of control and the belief that you don't possess willpower. Ultimately you begin to drown in a sea of self-doubt and shame. *What begins as a psychologically healthy behavior, ends in disaster.* Ultimately, weight loss is sabotaged as a result of personal boundary protection.

With Intuitive Eating, there is no need to rebel, because you become the one in charge!

19   Boundaries are also invaded when someone makes comments about your weight or how you should look. Again, you are bound to rebel by overeating. It's a way of saying "forget you" once again; "You have no right to tell me what to weigh."

20   Rachel is an artist who had dieted all of her life. She was married to a successful lawyer who wanted to show off his beautiful *slim* wife to all of his colleagues. He'd continually make subtle remarks that she wasn't as thin as she could be. He would even go so far as to give her dirty looks when she reached for a rich dessert at a party. Rachel rebelled against her husband by sneaking foods behind his back (free from his evil eye). While going through the Intuitive Eating process, Rachel discovered that she was actually keeping extra weight on as the ultimate form of rebellion toward her husband.

21   But instead of feeling strong and powerful from her rebellion, she found that she actually felt weak, out of control, and miserable. She knew that she would feel better at her natural, lower weight, but "something" kept making her turn to the hidden extra foods. Rachel had been trapped in a game of control, boundary invasion, and rebellion all her life. Her husband and the world of dieting had been trying to control this free spirited woman. To protect her boundaries, she would fight the diets by overeating and fight her husband's inappropriate demands by staying overweight.

22   Eventually, Rachel stood up to her well meaning husband and told him that he had no right to make comments about her food or her weight. Although initially resistant, he began to respect her boundaries. She also made a firm commitment to give up dieting. As a result, Rachel was shocked to find that her secret eating disappeared, as did her self doubt, and she began to lose weight without a struggle.

23   ***Forget About Failure.*** All of our chronic dieters walk into our offices feeling as if they are failures. Whether they are highly placed executives, prominent celebrities, or straight A students, they all talk about their food experiences shamefully, and they doubt whether they'll ever be able to feel successful in the area of eating. The diet mentality reinforces feelings of success or failure. You can't fail at Intuitive Eating—it's a learning process at every point along the way. What used to be thought of as a setback, will instead be seen as a growth experience. You'll get right back on track when you see this as progress, not failure.

Step 3: Get Rid of the Dieter's Tools

24   The dieter relies on external forces to regulate his eating, sticking to a regimented food plan, eating because it's time, or eating only a specified (and measured) amount, whether hungry or not. The dieter also validates progress by external forces, primarily the scale, asking "How many pounds have I lost? Is my weight up or down?" It's time to throw out your dieting tools. Get rid of the meal plans and the bathroom scales. If all it took was a good "sensible" calorie-restricted meal plan to lose weight, we'd be a nation of thin people—free meal plans are readily available from magazines, newspapers, and even some food companies.

25   ***The Scale As False Idol.*** "Please, please, let the number be . . ." This wishful number prayer is not occurring in the casinos of Las Vegas, but in private homes throughout the country. But just like the desperate gambler waiting for his lucky number to come in, so is it futile for the dieter to pay homage to the "scale god." In one sweep of the scale roulette, hopes and desperation create a daily drama that will ultimately shape what mood you'll be in for the day. Ironically, "good" and "bad" scale numbers can *both* trigger overeating—whether it's a congratulatory eating celebration or a consolation party.

26   The scale ritual sabotages body and mind efforts; it can in one moment devalue days, weeks, and even months of progress, as illustrated with Connie.

27   Connie had been working very hard at Intuitive Eating and refrained from weighing herself, which in itself was a feat since she originally weighed in daily, and sometimes

even twice a day at home. But Connie felt she had made so much progress in three months that she was certain she had lost a significant amount of weight. To "confirm" her progress, Connie stepped on the scale. But the number of pounds she had lost was disappointing, compared to how great she felt. The momentary brush with the scale boomeranged Connie right back to the diet mentality. That week, Connie cut back on her food intake, which resulted in a large binge. Stepping on the scale was a step back into the diet mentality. It was no surprise that Connie countered her scale experience with a dieting approach. She also thought, "I must be doing something wrong." Her newfound trust began to erode—all with a single trip to the scale.

28   So much power is given to the almighty scale that it ultimately sabotages our efforts. But in the case of Sherry, she found the weighing process to be so humiliating that she had postponed going to doctors for fifteen years! At the age of fifty-five, Sherry had not had a mammogram or other essential physical exams because she did not want to be weighed at the doctor's office (although she weighed in at home daily). In this case, the scale was getting in the way of Sherry's health. She was at risk for breast cancer because it ran in her family. Getting the mammogram was more important than any number on the scale, but Sherry couldn't face the routine admonishments from the nursing staff. It was standard procedure— weigh the patient regardless of the reason for the appointment. Sherry did not realize that she had the right to refuse to be weighed. She finally got the courage after our work together. She made a doctor's appointment and refused to be weighed since it was not an essential component of her medical care at the moment. Fortunately her physical exam results were healthy.

29   We have found that the "weigh-in" factor usually detracts from a person's progress. In the "old days" when we used to weigh all patients, we found that sessions were often spent on why the weight went up or did not move at all, and they became scale-counseling

sessions. Our patients also dreaded the weighing-in part as much as we did.

When a Pound Is Not a Pound.   Many fac-   30 tors can influence a person's weight which do not reflect that person's body fat. For example, two cups of water weigh one pound. If you tend to retain water or bloat, the scale can easily rise a few pounds without a change in what you have eaten. But for the oft guilt-ridden dieter, the consequences of water weight can seem severe. For example, we have had many patients feel bad about eating an extra dessert over the weekend and weigh themselves on the following Monday. The scale shoots up five pounds— and they *believe* they gained five pounds of *fat*. Since many dieter-clients are quick with the calorie calculator, we ask, "Did you eat an *extra* 17,500 calories over the weekend?" Of course not, would be their retort. Yet to make five pounds of fat requires a calorie *excess* of 17,500 calories above normal eating (one pound of fat is equivalent to 3,500 calories).

So how do you explain the weight gain?   31 Water weight. Any time the scale suddenly rises or falls, it is usually because of a fluid shift in the body. Eating high-sodium foods can also provoke water retention (not fat retention) in salt-sensitive individuals. Yet how easily chronic dieters believe they did something wrong; they must have single-handedly gobbled five pounds worth of food! No! No! No!

Similarly, losing two pounds immedi-   32 ately from an hour of aerobics is not a two pound fat loss. Rather, it's mostly water loss from sweat.

Jubilant dieters who think that they have   33 lost ten pounds in a week may be in for an unwanted surprise. While it may be true that the scale indicated ten pounds less than when they weighed one week ago, the question is, what *kind* of weight did they lose? To lose ten pounds of fat in one week requires an energy deficit of 35,000 calories, or a deficit of 5,000 calories each day! The average woman only eats about 1,500 to 1,600 calories per day. The sad reality is that this person

Summary: The Diet Mentality Versus the Nondiet Mentality

Issue	Diet Mentality	Nondiet Mentality
Eating/Food Choices	• Do I deserve it? • If I eat a heavy food, I try to find a way to make up for it. • I feel guilty when I eat heavy foods. • I usually describe a day of eating as either good or bad. • I view food as the enemy.	• Am I hungry • Do I want it? • Will I be deprived if I don't eat it? • Will it be satisfying? • Does it taste good? • I deserve to enjoy eating without guilt.
Exercise Benefits	• I focus primarily on the calories burned. • I feel guilty if I miss a designated exercise day.	• I focus primarily on how exercise makes me feel, especially the energizing and stress-relieving factors.
View of Progress	• How many pounds did I lose? • How do I look? • What do other people think of my weight? • I have good willpower.	• While I'm concerned with my weight, it is not my primary goal or indicator of progress. • I have increased trust with myself and food. • I am able to let go of "eating indiscretions." • I recognize inner body cues.

is losing a lot of water weight, usually at the expense of their muscles, due to the process of *muscle-wasting*. Muscle is made up mainly of water (about 70 percent).

34   When a hungry body is not given enough calories, the body cannibalizes itself for an energy source. The prime directive of the body is that it must have energy, at any cost—it's part of the survival mechanism. The protein in muscles is converted to valuable energy for the body. When a muscle cell is destroyed, water is released and eventually excreted—there's your precious weight loss. The whittled-away muscle contributes to lowering your metabolism. Muscles are metabolically active tissue—generally the more muscle we have, the higher our metabolic rate. That's one of the reasons men burn more calories than women—they have more muscle mass.

35   Increased muscle mass, while metabolically more active and desirable, weighs more than fat. Muscle also takes up less space than fat. While this is certainly beneficial, a chronic dieter often gets frustrated by the rising, or unchanging, scale number. *The scale does not reflect body composition*—just like weighing a piece of steak at the butcher's does not tell you how lean the meat is.

Weighing in on the scale only serves to   36 keep you focused on your weight, it doesn't help with the process of getting back in touch with Intuitive Eating. Constant weigh-ins can leave you frustrated and impede your progress. Best bet—stop weighing yourself.

Works Cited: Associated Press (Washington). Vitamin retailer to pay fine. *AP Online*, April 29, 1994.
Berdanier, C.D., and McIntosh, M.K. Weight loss—weight regain: A vicious cycle. *Nutrition Today* 26, 5(1991):6.
Berg, F.M. *The Health Risks of Weight Loss.* Hettinger, N.D.: Healthy Living Institute, 1993.
Blackburn, G.L., et al. Weight cycling: The

experience of human dieters. *American Journal of Clinical Nutrition* 49(1989):1105.

Why and how to stop weight cycling in overweight adults. *Eating Disorders Review* 4, 1(1993):1.

Ciliska, D. *Beyond Dieting*. New York, N.Y.: Brunner/Mazel, 1990.

Foreyt, J.P., and Goodrick, G.K. *Living Without Dieting*. Houston, TX.: Harrison, 1992.

Weight Management Without Dieting. *Nutrition Today* March/April (1993):4.

Gallup Organization. Women's Knowledge and Behavior Regarding Health and Fitness. Conducted for American Dietetic Association and Weight Watchers, June 1993.

Garrow, J.S. Treatment of obesity. *Lancet* 340(1992):409–13.

Goodrick, G.K., and Foreyt, J.P. Why treatments for obesity don't last. *Journal of the American Dietetic Association* 91, 10(1991):1243

Grodner, M. Forever dieting: Chronic dieting syndrome. *Journal of Nutrition Education* 24, 4(1992):207–10.

Hartmann, E. *Boundaries in the Mind. A New Psychology of Personality*. New York, N.Y.: Basic Books, 1991.

Hill, A.J., and Robinson, A. Dieting concerns have a functional effect on the behaviour of nine-year-old girls. *British Journal of Clinical Psychology* 30(1991):265–67.

Katherine, A. *Boundaries—Where You End and I Begin*. Park Ridge, Ill. Parkside Publishing, 1991.

Kern, P.A., et al. The effects of weight loss on the activity and expression of adipose-tissue lipoprotein lipase in very obese humans. *New England Journal of Medicine* 322,15(1990):1053–59.

National Research Council *Diet and Health* National Academy Press, Washington, D.C., 1989.

Polivy, J., and Herman, C.P. Undieting: A program to help people stop dieting. *International Journal of Eating Disorders* 11, 3(1992) 261–68.

Rodin, J., et al. Weight cycling and fat distribution. *International Journal of Obesity* 14(1990): 303–10.

Wilson, G.T. Short-Term Psychological Benefits and Adverse Effects of Weight Loss. NIH Technology Assessment Conference: Methods for Voluntary Weight Loss and Control, March 30–April 1, 1992.

Wooley, S.C., and Garner, D.M. Obesity treatment. The high cost of false hope. *Journal of the American Dietetic Association* 91, 10(1991) 1248.

Yanovski, S.Z. Are anorectic agents the magic bullet for obesity? Editorial *Arch Family Medicine* 2(1993)1025–27.

Source: Evelyn Tribole, *Intuitive Eating: A Recovery Book for the Chronic Dieter*. M.S., R.D. & Elyse Resch, M.S., R.D., New York: Bedford/St. Martin's, 1995, pp. 49–60.

DISCUSSION QUESTIONS

1. This argument of recommendation emphasizes the future. After reviewing Chapter 11 on writing recommendations, identify and evaluate the effectiveness of the argument's support.

2. What are the needs and values being appealed to in this set of recommendations? (Hint: the list will be considerably longer than the obvious value of thinness.)

3. The authors present a number of brief case studies to illustrate their arguments about the negative effects of dieting. Discuss with your class the effectiveness of these examples. What, if anything, do they add to the argument?

4. Discuss the reliability of facts in this essay (be sure to study the references listed at the end). As a reader, are you confident that the third-party facts supporting this recommendation are authoritative, sufficiently recent, and reasonably objective?

5. Do you find the table on p. 379 to be a helpful summary of the argument's content? Would the argument be as effective without this table?

SUGGESTIONS FOR WRITING (18.2)

1. Write your own set of recommendations for losing weight, based upon your own experience or that of someone you know. Your audience will be a group of your peers who have struggled with their weight. Be sure that the causal connection between your recommendation and the future effect is plausible.

2. With a group of your classmates, discuss possible reasons for our worship of thinness. Then, using the best ideas generated by this discussion, write a three-page causal argument speculating on the causes of the high value we place on thinness.

3. Select a popular fashion magazine (e.g., *Vogue, GQ*). After studying the photographs carefully, write an inductive factual argument describing the body type prized by this magazine.

4. Write a one- to two-page letter to a friend recommending the argument by Tribole and Resch. Be sure to identify to yourself the emphasis of your recommendation (present, future, or combination). Your argument should include a secondary evaluative argument.

INCLUDE ME OUT: A REFLECTION ON "ICE TEA"

FRED CHAPPELL

Believe it or not, there is a recognized sub-genre of nonfiction writing known as "food writing," of which Fred Chappell's essay is an example. This essay first appeared in the food magazine Gastronomica *and was subsequently included in the anthology of food writing* Best Food Writing *(Marlow & Co., 2002). Chappell is the former poet laureate of North Carolina.*

1 There are people who eat cold pasta salad. They enjoy despoiling their greenery with gummy, tasteless squiggles of tough, damp bread dough that are usually made palatable only when heavily disguised with hot tomato sauce and a stiff mask of Parmesan cheese. This salad does have the virtue of economy. Wednesday leftovers can be marketed to Thursday customers of perverse taste.

2 It is probably perversity also that accounts for the prevalence of ice tea in our American south. It was Edgar Allan Poe who first diagnosed this immitigable contrariness of human nature in his short story, *The Imp of the Perverse*, and he undoubtedly saw it as a normal trait of Dixie character. But please include me out. I am one southerner who detests that dirty water the color of oak-leaf tannin and its insipid banality. When I am offered ice tea by one of our charming southern hostesses, I know I'm in for a long afternoon of hearing about Cousin Mary Alice's new babe and its genius antics in the playpen.

3 Hot tea makes sense. It can relax as well as stimulate and in fact may be sipped as a soporific. It can offer a bouquet pungent or delicate and causes us to understand why the Chinese designated certain strains of flowers as "tea roses." It can be a topic of conversation, too, as southerners revive the traditional English debate as to whether the boiling water should be brought to the pot or the pot fetched to the water. Such palaver reassures us that all traces of civilization have not disappeared under the onslaughts of video games and e-mail.

4   But if you ice the stuff down it cannot matter in the least whether the water or the pot has journeyed. Any trace of the tea's bouquet is slaughtered and only additives can give this tarnished liquid any aroma at all. There is, of course, plenty of discussion about these added condiments. Even the mildest of southern ladies may bristle and lapse into demotic speech when they consider that a glass of ice tea has been improperly prepared.

5   Notice that we say, "ice tea." Anyone who pronounces the successive dentals of "iced tea" is regarded as pretentious. And if you say "Coca-Cola" you will be seen as putting on airs, just as obviously as if you employed "you" as a collective pronoun. Down here we say "you-all," "CoCola," and "ice tea" and collect monetary fines from strangers who misspeak. Ignorance before the law is no excuse.

6   In recent years some enterprising women have seen the futility of the pot/water controversy and have begun making "sun tea," a beverage that is never acquainted with either stove or teapot. They simply fill a gallon jug with water, drop in a flock of tea bags, and set the collocation out on the back porch to brew in the broiling August sunshine. If this method does not make the kitchen more cheerful, it does at least lessen the hypocritical chatter about proper procedure. Ice cannot harm sun tea; it is created beyond the reach of harm or help.

7   Now as to the recipe for ice tea:

8   Lemons are essential and should be of the big thick-skinned variety, cut into sixths. They are never—repeat: *never*—squeezed but only plumped into the pitcher, four or five slices. Extra slices are offered on a cut-glass plate six inches in diameter. Mint may be added, but it is always submerged in the pitcher and never put into a glass where it would glue to the interior side like a Harley-Davidson decal.

9   And sweetening is the soul of this potation. The sugar bowl passes from hand to hand at a pace so dizzying it is like watching the rotating label on an old 78-rpm record. Southerners demand sweetness. The truly thoughtful hostess shall have already sweetened the tea for her guests with a simple sugar syrup that excludes the possibility of unpleasant graininess from bowl sugar. Sugar syrup for ice tea is concocted by adding one pound of Dixie Crystal sugar to a tablespoon of water.

10   In the south sweetened ice tea is taken for granted, like the idea that stock car racing is our national pastime and that the Southern Baptist church is a legitimate arm of the Republican Party. If you order ice tea in a restaurant it will arrive pre-sweetened. If you want it unsweetened you must ask for it. Actually, you must demand it with pistol drawn and cocked. And you will have to repeat your demand several times, because tea unsweetened is as abstruse a proposition to most servers as a theorem of Boolean algebra. Even then you can't be sure. My wife Susan once ordered unsweetened, but it arrived as sweet as honey. The waitress pleaded for understanding. "We couldn't figure out how to get the sugar *out*," she said.

11   Why southerners are so sugar-fixated may be a mystery, but it is an indisputable fact. We are a breed who makes marmalades of zucchini, tomatoes, onions, and even watermelon rinds. Our famous pecan pie ("puhKAWN pah") is a stiff but sticky paste of boiled Karo corn syrup studded with nuts. Since this is not sweet enough, it will likely be served with a gob of bourbon whipped cream dusted with cocoa powder and decorated with vegetable-peeler curls of milk chocolate.

12   "Do you want ice tea with that?"

13   "Oh yes. Sweetened, please."

14   Well, I'll confess that, though born in North Carolina, I make a poor example of a southerner. I don't even capitalize the name of the region. I'm a Democrat, a non-Baptist, and don't care what kind of car I drive. To me, adding broiled marshmallows to yams is like putting raspberry jam on porterhouse. I once spotted a recipe in the magazine *Southern Living* for CoCola cake and had to fight down a surge of nausea. I flee as if pursued from fatback, spoon bread, barbecue, grits, and—ice tea.

15   Susan tells me I need sweetening.

Source: *Best Food Writing—2002*, New York: Marlow and Company, 2002.

DISCUSSION QUESTIONS

1. The *Literary Encyclopedia* describes Chappell's writing as "rich with surprising paradoxes that make it both rewarding and challenging for the reader" (http://www.litencyc.com/php/speople.php?rec=true&UID=825). Discuss with some classmates whether you think this is an accurate description of this essay.

2. Does this essay qualify as an argument? That is, do you think Chappell is trying to convince his readers of a particular proposition? Give specific reasons for your answer. If you see the essay as an argument, what is the central claim? To what category does this claim belong?

3. Is "Include Me Out" an essay about more than "ice tea"? Compare your answer with those of your classmates.

4. Identify three figures of speech in this essay. How effective are they?

5. Describe the image that this essay projects of the author. Does this image contribute to the effectiveness of the article?

SUGGESTIONS FOR WRITING (18.3)

1. This essay may be as much about southern culture or values as it is about "ice tea." Write a one- to two-page interpretation of the essay, identifying its implicit argument. Support your interpretation with references to the text itself.

2. Using Chappell's essay as a model, write a rough draft of an essay that makes an argument about your school's culture by discussing a popular food on your campus (pizza, wings, beer). Discuss the draft with a classmate, concentrating on whether you have succeeded in "hiding" an argument in your first draft.

3. Using the discussion suggested in #2 above, revise the draft and submit it to your instructor.

4. Write a brief (one- to two-page) argument demonstrating what a particular food trend (fast-food, designer coffee shops, microwave popcorn, for example) reveals about contemporary culture.

5. Using four different Internet sources, write a three-page biography of Fred Chappell. Be prepared to explain to your instructor or classmates how you decided which details to include.

MY STORY: BOB

DANIEL SLOSBERG

While the vast majority of those who suffer from eating disorders (anorexia nervosa, bulimia nervosa, binge eating) are female, these disorders can afflict men as well, as Bob's story illustrates. This reading was found within a World Wide Web site titled "Males and Eating Disorders" which was copyrighted by Daniel Slosberg in 1998.

1   When I was about fifteen, a freshman in High School, and slightly overweight, I went on a diet so that, ostensibly, I wouldn't have to move from the "C" division to the "B" division on my swimming and water polo teams. I alternately starved myself (in a relative sense—I ate, but not nearly enough to sustain my activity level) and binged (donuts and halvah were favorites at the time).

2   Thus began about ten years of bulimia during which I exercised more and more so that I could eat as much as I wanted. No one ever knew I had a problem; people just thought that I was a good athlete. I eventually became one of only five people ever to complete a double-crossing of the Catalina Channel (Catalina's an island off the coast of California), and I became one of the first people to compete in the Iron-Man Triathlon in Hawaii. And I did it all out of fear: I couldn't stop or I'd get *fat*, a fate worse than death or having to live far from the beach.

3   My sister, a year and a half younger than I, began her own eating disorder about the time I did, maybe a little earlier. She binged and purged for about fourteen years. After many attempts to deal with her eating disorder, including residential treatment and different drug therapies, she committed suicide. This happened about seven years ago.

4   I got into short-term therapy after a close friend died. I had previously felt like something was wrong, but I couldn't put my finger on it. I couldn't have said, "I have an eating disorder," or, "I've been depressed," even though I clearly was both. Opening up about my eating disorder (and other stuff) seemed to begin the process of sloughing it off.

5   I have since been to two other therapists, the most current one I began seeing shortly after we adopted my first son four years ago. After my son's birth, I went into the deepest depression I'd ever experienced, kind of a fear-of-fatherhood crisis. Perhaps this occurred because I didn't have the food to hide behind; perhaps the depression was, in a sense, a more constructive coping mechanism. Anyway, I found a therapist who's been very helpful, and I've been dealing with the issues which led to the eating problems (and the depression) in the first place. These issues include both familial and cultural issues which left me empty and unable to cope.

6   I figure that something must be working because, when our twins arrived two years after my son, I didn't get depressed—just exhausted. The twins turned two in May, five months after the birth of our fourth child, Noah. Though I remain exhausted, I never cease feeling incredibly lucky to be part of my family.

Source: Daniel M. Slosberg, "My Story."
http://www.primenet.com/

DISCUSSION QUESTIONS

1. Does Bob's narrative account qualify as argument? If so, what kind? If not, how would you describe or categorize it?

2. What do you think Bob wanted to accomplish by writing this account and posting it on the website? Do you have any evidence for your theory? Identify Bob's intended audience. Again, cite any evidence you find within the text.

3. What image of the author is projected within this account? What evidence can you cite for this image?

4. Do your own Web search on males and eating disorders. List the sites you discover and compare your list with the lists of a few of your classmates.

SUGGESTIONS FOR WRITING (18.4)

1. Write a one-page personal account of a "condition" you have suffered from (the condition can be as mild as laryngitis or as severe as Bob's eating disorder). Before you write, identify to yourself your motive for writing the paper (other than that your instructor has assigned it)—that is, to instruct, to confess, to vent, to sympathize. At the end of the paper, identify the motive for your instructor.

2. We all know that females are particularly susceptible to eating disorders. The subject has received so much public attention lately that most of us know the most frequently cited hypotheses for this susceptibility: the pressure to conform to fashion norms; a search for control; a reluctance to grow up. Given the scant public attention paid to the subject of males and eating disorders, we are more at a loss to explain this phenomenon. In a two-page speculative argument, identify two or three possible causes for eating disorders in men. Concentrate on establishing a probable motivational link between the causes you identify and their effect.

3. Write a two-page review (i.e., evaluation) of one of the websites you identified in Question #4. Consider such factors as visual layout, content, expertise of website owner, accessibility of links, and so on.

BED CONFESSIONS

K.D. ELLIOTT

The "BED" in the title of this reading doesn't refer to the place you sleep at night; it is an acronym for a condition known as Binge Eating Disorder. This argument was found on the Healthgate website, one of the many sites devoted to physical and mental health issues.

While "My Story" (the preceding reading), is a painful personal confession of an eating disorder victim, "BED Confessions" is an objective and dispassionate description of a related disorder.

1   BED. It's something shared by men and women in more ways than one. BED, or Binge Eating Disorder, has become an emotional and health concern for men across the United States. This eating disorder, which affects more than 1 million men in America, has only recently been recognized by the American Psychiatric Association as a disorder of its own, that needs further study.

2   Ninety-five percent of the U.S. population has cravings for "pleasure" or "comfort" foods. The other five percent crave alcohol, cigarettes, or some other addictive substance. Having cravings, and fulfilling them, is natural human instinct.

3   But BED is more than an occasional craving for a sweet snack. At first, eating may satisfy cravings. But eventually the eating becomes more and more frequent, and higher in calories and fat. This overeating leads to feelings of self-disgust and guilt, which may cause a person to eat even more.

4   A typical binge may include eating anywhere from 1000 to 15,000 calories at a

time. In fact, it is not uncommon to actually have a "food hangover" the day following an especially large binge. The foods consumed are usually high in fat and are eaten in a relatively short period of time, putting an enormous amount of stress on the digestive and endocrine systems. BED is different from the two other characteristic eating disorders, anorexia and bulimia. Anorexia is a condition of slow, self starvation; bulimia is a binging and vomiting syndrome.

5   BED is formally characterized by the American Psychiatric Association in the Diagnostic and Statistical Manual for Mental Disorders (DSM-IV) according to the following five criteria:

1. Recurring binge eating episodes. An episode of binge eating is characterized by both of the following:

   • eating an amount of food that is definitely larger than most people would eat in a similar amount of time under similar circumstances
   • a sense of lack of control over eating during the episode

2. The binge eating episodes are associated with three or more of the following:

   • eating much more rapidly than you usually would
   • eating until you feel uncomfortably full
   • eating large amounts of food when you don't physically feel hungry
   • eating alone because of embarrassment at how much you are eating
   • feeling disgusted with yourself, depressed, or very guilty after overeating

3. Binge eating causes emotional and physical stress or remorse.

4. The binge eating occurs, on average, at least two days a week for six months or more.

5. The binge eating is not followed by other inappropriate behaviors such as purging, fasting, excessive exercise and does not occur exclusively during episodes of other eating disorders, such as anorexia nervosa or bulimia nervosa.

BED is a unique eating disorder, especially   6 when it comes to men. While only 5% to 10% of people with anorexia and bulimia nervosa are male, it is estimated that BED affects a much greater proportion of men. According to Dr. Anne Becker of the Harvard Eating Disorders Center, "The ratio of females to males with this disorder is about 1.5 to 1.0 or about 40% men." Dr. Becker adds, "Binge eating disorder has become more recognizable by doctors as more attention is given to weight control in the clinical setting."

There are some underlying common   7 characteristics of men who have BED. Most are overweight, with a history of depression, low assertiveness, and poor self-esteem. Similar to all people with eating disorders, men with BED view themselves in a negative light and allow food to control their lives in order to compensate for their lack of control in other areas such as work or family matters.

Another common characteristic of men   8 with BED is that they fail to address their own personal needs, and instead, turn to food. For these men, food can be a great sedative and a means of suppressing feelings of anger, guilt, despondency, and sadness. Men with eating disorders tend to eat in private, not wanting to alert others to their habit. This increases the feelings of isolation and sadness, and creates another vicious cycle.

Unlike bulimia, where people eat and   9 then purge, there is no counteraction to bingeing. Therefore, weight gain is a likely effect. As noted above, men with BED are often overweight to begin with. The effects of BED on health include all the possible consequences of overweight or obesity—diabetes, hypertension, and heart disease.

An ever more serious consequence is   10 death. According to Dr. Ken Stephenson, a psychotherapist who specializes in treating males with eating disorders, "People with eating disorders have the highest mortality rate of all psychiatric patients." Isn't that a good enough reason to seek help now?

11 Men with symptoms of BED need to seek treatment as soon as possible. The longer a person waits, the greater the risk to their health. Treatment of the disorder generally includes cognitive-behavioral or interpersonal therapy performed by a licensed clinician. Cognitive-behavioral therapy teaches patients techniques to monitor and change their eating habits as well as to change the way they respond to difficult situations. Interpersonal psychotherapy helps people examine their relationships with friends and family and to make changes in problem areas.

12 Treatment with medications such as antidepressants may be helpful for some individuals. Self-help groups also may be a source of support. Researchers are still trying to determine which method or combination of methods is the most effective in controlling binge eating disorder. The type of treatment that is best for an individual is a matter for discussion between the patient and his or her health care provider.

13 Professional and confidential treatment and information can be sought through the following organizations:

The National Eating Disorders Organization
6655 South Yale Avenue
Tulsa, OK 74136
918-481-4044
http://www.laureate.com/

Overeaters Anonymous
PO Box 44020
Rio Rancho, New Mexico 87174
505-891-2664
http://www.overeatersanonymous.org/

Other resources

Males and Eating Disorders
http://www.primenet.com/~danslos/males/links.html

Source: K.D. Elliot, "Bed Confessions."
http://www.healthgate.com/

DISCUSSION QUESTIONS

1. Using the guidelines contained in the reading "Information Literacy" (page 292) in the "Internet" section of these readings, evaluate the reliability of the Healthgate website (http//www.healthgate.com). Do you find any reason not to trust the material on this site as accurate and authoritative?

2. The first part of this article is an extended definition of Binge Eating Disorder. How many strategies of definition are used here (see Chapter 4 of this book for a list of possible strategies)? Compare your findings with those of two classmates.

3. Discuss with your classmates what the overall purpose of this argument is. Is that purpose fulfilled? Support your answer.

4. The final two paragraphs contain a recommendation. What is the emphasis of this recommendation? Present or future? Can you place the recommendation into the Toulmin model presented in Chapter 10?

5. Discuss the overall tone of this article. Do you find any evidence of slanted or connotative language? Is the tone appropriate to the apparent purpose of the article? How do you think it would affect someone suffering from the disorder?

SUGGESTIONS FOR WRITING (18.5)

1. With a classmate, draw up a list of speculations about why men are more af-flicted with BED than any other eating disorder. Choose two of the most plausi-ble explanations and brainstorm together how you would go about turning this speculation into an effective causal argument.

2. While men are not generally assumed to be preoccupied with how their bodies look to others, ten minutes in the weight room of any gym might contradict this assumption. After going through the necessary preliminary steps outlined in Chapters 2 and 3, write an argument comparing male interest in muscle-building with female interest in thinness. Your comparison can be evaluative, interpretive, causal, or a hybrid of two classes.

3. Most of us have friends who engage in worrisome behavior—for example, unhealthy eating or drinking habits, too much time on the computer, poor relationship choices. Write a three-page recommendation to a friend that attempts to modify such risky behavior. Your recommendation can be in letter form, but it must follow the principles of effective recommendations presented in Chapter 10. Be sure that you can document any of the physical or mental consequences of your friend's risky behavior.

4. Identify with a group of classmates some of the most prevalent risky behaviors on your campus. Pick one of these and compose a formal proposal for reduc-ing that behavior that would be submitted to administrators on your campus. Be sure that the behavior you choose is something you are actually con-cerned about. Follow the model of the computer facility proposal presented in Chapter 10.

19

Reading Popular Culture

INTRODUCTION

For most of you, formal reading lessons began in first grade, when you were launched on an elementary school curriculum that taught you what words say. By fifth or sixth grade, as primers and readers give way to "real" literature, reading became more complicated; you were expected not only to understand what the words *said,* but also what they *meant.* At this point, you learned that writers have all sorts of tricks for meaning more than they appear to say—tricks like symbols, imagery, and setting. Throughout high school, especially in your English classes, you probably became skilled at interpreting these literary techniques, at discovering and unpacking the multiple meanings they allow. By the time you entered college, you knew perfectly well that the kind of reading assigned in an English course would be entirely different from the reading you do for recreation in your increasingly limited spare time. The first requires energy, creativity, and active, alert thought; the second, not much more than passive, relaxed attention.

At this point in your education, you also know that the skills of careful reading you've been practicing for at least the last 12 years are not exclusive to written texts. If you've taken a course in art history, film studies, or music appreciation, you're aware that other art forms contain rich and diverse meaning that, like literature, reveals itself to students with the right analytical tools.

The following unit of essays, entitled "Reading Popular Culture," contains arguments that extend the practice of close reading from the productions of what some call "high" culture (Rembrandt's paintings, Shakespeare's plays) to those of popular culture (television shows, horror movies, even clothing fashion—any artifact with mass appeal). In recent years, the activity of reading or interpreting popular culture has grown in popularity and legitimacy within academic circles. Indeed, your college or university probably offers courses in popular culture, possibly even a minor or a major. There are also academic associations and conferences in this new area, and it's even possible to receive a Ph.D. in Popular Culture.

But why, just when you might think your lessons in reading are behind you, should you worry about the subtle meanings contained in television sitcoms and trashy novels? And what does reading popular culture have to do with writing arguments?

Let's look at the first question: why study popular culture? For one thing, "reading" a popular artifact, uncovering subtle messages and patterns of meaning in a magazine ad or a soap opera, is like looking into a cultural mirror—one that reflects the often unadmitted values and priorities of its audience. There is a good deal to be learned about a culture with a seemingly insatiable taste for war movies, or a generation glued to a Thursday night television lineup featuring shallow, sex-based relationships.

But there is more than knowledge about ourselves and others to be gained from seriously attending to popular culture; we also can become conscious of the ways in which the brokers of popular culture use cultural productions to manipulate their audience. As college student Kevin Maloney says in his argument reproduced in Chapter 9, "Being unable to recognize the sometimes hidden messages of . . . [popular culture] is like being in a foreign country where you don't speak the language. In both cases, you can easily fall prey to individuals eager to take advantage of your ignorance, to manipulate you into doing what they want you to do." Close readers of popular culture are agents capable of forming their own opinions and withstanding the powerful but often unreasonable suasions of the popular culture industry. The essays included in this unit model this kind of reading for you.

And finally, why include readings of popular culture in a textbook on argument? Because multiple layers of arguments, both explicit and implicit, faulty and reasonable, reside in every production of contemporary popular culture. And all the essays in this unit are in the business of revealing and evaluating these arguments. By reading these "readings," by learning through them to detect hidden as well as manifest arguments, you will become that much more effective in your own creation of reasonable, ethical arguments.

POPULAR CULTURE AND THE FAMILY: HOW MASS-MEDIATED CULTURE WEAKENS THE TIES THAT BIND

KENNETH A. MYERS

Kenneth Myers is a former producer of National Public Radio's "All Things Considered." He currently produces "Mars Hill Tapes," a bimonthly audio magazine. Myers is also the author of All God's Children and Blue Suede Shoes: Christians and Popular Culture *(Crossway).*

The journal Family Policy, *where this essay first appeared, is published bimonthly by the Family Research Council, a tax-exempt social policy research, educational, and advocacy organization chartered in 1983.*

COMMENTARY

As its subtitle suggests, "Popular Culture and the Family" is primarily a generalized causal argument linking the phenomenon of popular culture with a dissolution of communal values. As a causal argument, the essay combines organizational and stylistic strengths with a number of those same weaknesses in reasoning and strategy you've been cautioned against in the first part of this book.

Following an engaging, albeit highly slanted anecdotal introduction that takes us on a tour of contemporary magazine stands, Myers introduces his central claim in Par. 9: "popular culture as known today is a complete novelty in human history. Its very nature, not simply its content, coupled with its role in American life, pose great challenges to the work of families in shaping the moral character of children."

Immediately following the claim, Myers proceeds with a survey of the decline of traditional culture—from the pre-Freudian age when, Myers attests, culture was a force of moral guidance largely in the hands of the family and its immediate community, to contemporary society, ruled by mass-distributed, liberationist popular culture. The historical survey consists of factual generalizations supported by appeals to authority—a wide range of individuals whom Myers presumes his readers will recognize as distinguished experts on the subject of culture and morality (T.S. Eliot, Philip Rieff, Allan Carlson, etc.). The brief references to the experts are Myers's only support for generalizations about entire eras—generalizations like the one found in Par. 13: "Empowering people to be all that they can be, to express all that they feel, and to obtain all that they desire is now seen to be the proper function of cultural institutions, including the family."

Myers then enlists this unsupported characterization of the post-Freudian decline in values to serve as the "factual" foundation of the succeeding causal argument. This is an example of how arguments can be built on sand, with unsupported generalizations being treated as justified conclusions that are then promoted to serve as springboards for new claims.

The next four sections of the argument identify the many losses brought about by popular culture—the losses of "the local," of "moral authority," of "tradition," and of "moral seriousness." These sections constitute the heart of the causal argument, identifying popular culture as the cause of a number of deficiencies in contemporary life. Yet the plausibility of the causal argument is extremely hard to measure because of the vagueness of the primary causal agent: popular culture itself. The failure to offer a clear definition of the term, which is the very subject of the essay, is probably its gravest flaw. In Par. 10, Myers borrows from T.S. Eliot and David Wells to offer a definition of culture as "the outward discipline in which inherited meanings and morality, beliefs and ways of behaving are preserved." Yet no such succinct definition of "popular culture" is ever offered, and though Myers implies a certain understanding of the term, he never defines it clearly, and we are left at the mercy of inference and speculation. Is popular culture the same as "culture," but popular? Is popular culture "mass mediated culture," as he says in Par. 16? Is popular culture really just television, as paragraphs 18 and following seem to imply?

As Chapter 8 of this book demonstrates, reasonable causal arguments link two clearly established phenomena through any number of causal principles. Forgetting for a moment that the causal agent (popular culture) lacks a clear definition, let's take a look at the manner in which Myers links cause and effect. In the section "The Loss of Moral Seriousness," he tells us that popular culture, or "the forms in which it is presented," "discourage depth, reflection, and moral seriousness." He then quotes media critic Todd Gitlin's characterization of television's glib, superficial conversational style as an instance of one example of popular culture. While Gitlin's quote does help us to understand one of the "forms in which [popular culture] is presented" (i.e., television), it does nothing to warrant the causal connection between popular culture and a lack of moral seriousness. Presumably, we are to assume that those who watch superficial television become superficial. Myers is using an implied linking principle here to connect his cause and effect. This strategy works fine as long as the linking principle—in this case the principle of "monkey see, monkey do"—is universally accepted. But in this case, the linking principle hardly qualifies as universally accepted: volumes have been written about the effects of television on behavior and no definitive conclusion on the topic has yet been reached.

Myers's argument is a causal generalization, and causal generalizations are two-step arguments. First, the claim that A causes B must be established according to principles of causality; and second, the generalization that A causes B on a large scale must be established through principles of inductive reasoning. As you learned in Chapter 6, inductive claims—which tend to be most convincing when they are qualified—are best supported through the citing of numerous specific examples. Yet Myers does very little in the way of offering specific instances of his generalizations. Look, for example, at the following paragraph:

> The frame of mind encouraged by modern entertainment is one which is suspicious of any legacy or inheritance, and which is committed to the assertion of the sovereignty of the self. It is a mentality that evokes a mood of restlessness and blocks out the reflection necessary for acknowledging its disease and then seeking a remedy. It is a sensibility rooted only in the present, ignoring the past, indifferent to the future.

How many specific supporting examples for these sweeping generalizations do you find?

In sum, while Myers makes a number of fascinating and provocative claims in this argument, his failure to clarify critical terms of the argument, to apply the principles of causality, and to support his generalized claims seriously undermine the plausibility of those claims.

POPULAR CULTURE AND THE FAMILY: HOW MASS-MEDIATED CULTURE WEAKENS THE TIES THAT BIND

1   On a recent visit to a local grocery store, I passed by the magazine rack. Such a place is not the source of most of my reading material, but I stopped long enough to check out some titles. I noticed that *Jane,* a magazine pitched to adolescents, carried a feature on "summer clothes sexier than going naked." Another teen publication, *ym* ("young and modern"), was

distributed with a free booklet: "your 8-page school-year love horoscope." The issue also ran an article "love at first sight—what makes him fall?" Though I did not even glance at the articles in question, I doubt the girls who purchase such magazines are likely to gain wisdom about love or about their own identities.

2 Meanwhile, *American Woman,* a periodical for older but not necessarily more mature readers, teased shoppers seeking fresh produce or ginger snaps: "Discover his private pleasure zones and drive him wild with desire! SEXUAL ECSTASY: naughty tricks that *always* work." The magazine also contained a QUIZ: "How do you rate in bed?" Then there were the fan magazines, one carrying a cover shot of gender nightmare Marilyn Manson; the computer game magazines, several extolling heavy doses of virtual violence and imaginary sex; and the venerable *Rolling Stone*—once the saucy bad boy of newsstands—now, given the raucous competition, looking rather conservative, with a cover photograph of Madonna less provocative than most celebrity photographs from the 1940s.

3 At the checkout counter, I was greeted with the usual assembly of lurid tabloids and soap-opera magazines, each with promises of predictably provocative and pitifully tawdry trash. The cover of *Redbook* featured a photograph of Harrison Ford juxtaposed with screaming headlines in large type heralding an inside feature revealing "46 things to do to a naked man." One might safely assume that "Tell him to get dressed or get out" is not numbered among the suggestions.

4 These may not be the worst examples of magazine covers parents and children see regularly in public; most city newsstands and bookstores display magazines even more blatant in their commitment to radical liberation. But the matter-of-factness of such display in a family neighborhood *grocery* store, for all passing eyes to see, is a profoundly disturbing fact of life in late twentieth-century America. Certainly *ym* or *Jane* are nowhere near 2 Live

Crew in morally destructive megatonnage. Nor does *Redbook* and its ilk rate with the disgusting lyrics in rap music, degrading dialogue in television shows, and detestable violence in movies. Yet the question arises: does not our culture invite the extremities of celebrity vulgarists and blasphemers because it is so blasé about the everyday desensitizing by enticements such as "naughty tricks that *always* work" and "summer clothes sexier than going naked" displayed in the same aisle as Betty Crocker and Mrs. Butterworth?

5 Whatever the connection between the two, Protestant theologian David F. Wells pulls no punches in his astute assessment of our cultural situation:

> The moral hedges that surrounded our collective life have been trampled down. That is the paramount truth. What once was sublimated is now, in all of its raw and often violent nature, spewed forth in the name of liberty or self-expression. What once had to be private is now paraded publicly for the gallery of voyeurs. The virtues of the old privacy, such as reticence and modesty, are looked upon today as maladies. What was once unseemly is now commonplace.[1]

6 Perhaps no class of American citizens feels the consequences of cultural regress more forcefully than parents, many of whom believe that popular culture is the most powerful carrier of this decline. A 1995 *New York Times* poll indicated that Americans blame television more than any single factor for teenage sex and violence.[2] So parents and other authority figures, quite naturally, try to restrict children's access or exposure to some "artifacts" of popular culture. Or they may patronize only "sanitized" artifacts of popular culture, whether G-rated movies and television programming or rock music whose lyrics have been cleaned-up or attached to a good cause.

---

[1] David F. Wells, *No Place for Truth, or, Whatever Happened to Evangelical Theology?* (Grand Rapids: Wm. B. Eerdmans Publishing Co., 1993), p. 168.

[2] Elizabeth Kolbert, "American Despair of Popular Culture," *New York Times,* August 20, 1995, Section 2.

7   Consider how schools—public and private—have within a generation moved from virtually ignoring popular culture to blessing it. Dana Mack, in *The Assault on Parenthood: How Our Culture Undermines the Family,* writes:

> In a misguided effort to make school "relevant" to children's lives outside of school, educators often bring popular culture into the classroom in the form of literature, music and social instruction. In fourth grade, for example, my own child was assigned to write a "rap" poem as part of her language-arts program. Not surprisingly, children take this emphasis on popular culture as an endorsement and end up clinging to the tastes of the marketplace rather than expanding their horizons toward more sophisticated work with a longer shelf life.[3]

8   Mack notes that "even in affluent suburban schools, art education is based far more on contemporary models taken from popular culture than on historical models of high art or folk culture.[4]

9   With blessings from schools, churches, and other historically normative institutions, popular culture is assumed to be a perfectly normal attribute of life. But let the buyer (or parent) beware: popular culture as known today is a complete novelty in human history. Its very nature, not simply its content, coupled with its role in American life, pose great challenges to the work of families in shaping the moral character of children.

The Function of Culture

10   Historically, culture has had an intrinsically moral dimension. Borrowing from T. S. Eliot, David F. Wells defines culture as "the set of values, the network of beliefs that are institutionalized in a people's collective life and that govern their behavior. Culture, then, is the outward discipline in which inherited meanings and morality, beliefs and ways of behaving are preserved.[5]

11   Since they communicate moral content from one generation to the next, and because human beings are inherently in need of correction and guidance, cultures have always been mechanisms of restraint. Cultural institutions, traditions, and artifacts developed as means of encouraging members of a society to respect its taboos, to obey its laws, and to become the sort of persons whose characters served the common good by conforming to a view of the good that the society held in common. In theological terms, cultures are thus instruments of common grace or natural law that keep people from doing everything that they want to do. Cultures are by nature communal—not individualistic—and deliberately intergenerational; cultural artifacts are ways of handing down to the coming generation the commitments and beliefs of the passing generation. Culture by its nature transmits morals, and families by their nature transmit culture. Those two laws of social life seem to be at work throughout history around the world.

12   The family, of course, has been the key. As T. S. Eliot has argued "the primary vehicle for the transmission of culture is the family."[6] Even as forces seek to redefine it, the family remains "a constant expectation for all humanity, past, present, and future," according to Allan C. Carlson.[7] Families, with the aid and support of other cultural institutions, such as church and school, have the primary responsibility of teaching moral principles to the young, not only by

---

[3] Dana Mack, *The Assault on Parenthood: How Our Culture Undermines the Family* (New York: Simon and Shuster, 1997), p. 218.

[4] Ibid.

[5] Ibid., p. 167.

[6] T.S. Eliot, "Notes towards the Definition of Culture," *Christianity and Culture* (New York: Harcourt Brace Jovanovich, 1968), p. 121.

[7] Allan C. Carlson, *From Cottage to Workstation: The Family's Search for Social Harmony in the Industrial Age* (San Francisco: Ignatius Press, 1993), p. 5.

establishing the content of morality in their minds, but by instilling a love for the true and the good in their hearts. This affective role, a critical component of moral instruction, explains why stories and songs are central cultural expressions. The stories we love, and the songs we delight in singing and hearing, are the mechanisms whereby we, as parents and children, commit ourselves to virtue.

13   Since the time of Sigmund Freud, however, the normative and restraining role of culture has been turned inside out. As sociologist Philip Rieff documents in *The Triumph of the Therapeutic,* cultures and specifically cultural institutions in the West have increasingly been redefined as instruments of *liberation* rather than restraint. Since repression is now presumed to be a bad thing, the commonweal is best served, ironically, without any notion of the common good that cultural institutions formerly enforced. Empowering people to be all that they can be, to express all that they feel, and to obtain all that they desire is now seen to be the proper function of cultural institutions, including the family. As Wells puts it: "The external discipline of the culture is now denied in the name of the emancipated self."[8] This helps explain why unprecedented allusions to orgasms greet customers at the supermarket checkout line.

14   The transition from culture to its complete opposite, what some have termed anticulture or postculturalism, has not happened overnight, but has been reinforced in the latter half of the twentieth century by all forms of popular culture, whether sanitized or not. The net result has reaped a far weaker family unit, particularly in its historic role as preserver and transmitter of morals.

The Loss of the Local

15   Some critics and historians argue that popular culture is nothing new, that Shakespeare was the popular culture of his day. That is not quite true. Prior to the invention of modern technologies of communications and travel, all culture was *local* culture. Music, dances, stories, visual representation, and sports all originated from and were sustained by people who were neighbors, who shared large enough amounts of time and small enough amounts of space to build some kind of knowledge of and affection for each other. Since culture was "produced and consumed" locally, the values communicated through cultural forms were values of the local community. Moral notions that did not fit "community standards" were not publicly tolerated.

16   In contrast, most of our cultural life is now defined by distant strangers; today's popular culture is *mass mediated culture.* As such, the moral dynamic of cultural activity has changed radically. We have moved from being creators and participants in culture to being simply consumers of culture. Culture is now a commodity, something we buy, "put on," or appropriate—a matter of fashion or taste, surely not something we receive, a legacy with permanent worth.

17   The extent to which mass mediators of culture were able to disturb the local mediation of culture was restrained until the 1960s. Neighborhoods still maintained their own standards, churches did not feel compelled to emulate television and popular music, and ethnic groups still transmitted some notion of identity that predated the products of mass media. But that local, religious, and ethnic independence is rapidly waning. Partly because of aggressive efforts in the name of free speech and partly because of the carelessness of a generation raised on television, the centrality of local life in the shaping of culture has given way to mass produced culture from Hollywood, New York, and Nashville.

18   Television, the dominant medium of popular culture, has been central to the transition from local to mass-mediated culture. By weaning children from local (specifically parental) authority, television

[8] Eliot, "Notes towards the Definition of Culture," p. 121.

reflects the dynamics of mass-mediated culture in general.

19   Prior to the advent of television, parents were the principal agents in establishing a trajectory for their children's intellectual and moral development. Writing in 1964, sociologists Oscar Ritchie and Marvin Koller argued that the home is the child's "small world" where the "family serves as a screen to the culture of its society and selects only those portions that it deems worthy of attention."[9] In this traditional pattern, the family is supplemented in its role by friends of the family, whose visits bring reports from the outside world that have different perspectives, but which are likely to be consonant with that of the parents. "As a person who lives outside the child's home, the guest functions as a transmitter, bringing into the world of the child new ideas and information, and new and different opportunities for vicarious participation in the outside world."[10]

20   This gentle and sensitive portrait of childhood seems painfully anachronistic today. The family is not the dominant "screen" in the lives of many children, who are given huge daily doses of television almost from birth. Rather than interacting with parents, extended family members, and neighbors, children increasingly interact with one-hundred-thousand watts of whatever network executives and cable companies think can make children buy more candy, toys, or designer clothes.

21   *That* children watch television in such quantity may be more significant than *what* they see. As Joshua Meyrowitz argues, television profoundly alters the moral relationship between parents and children:

> Children who have television sets now have outside perspectives from which to judge and evaluate family rituals, beliefs, and religious practices. Parents could once easily mold their young children's

upbringing by speaking and reading to children only about those things they wished their children to be exposed to, but today's parents must battle with thousands of competing images and ideas over which they have little direct control. . . . Unable to read, very young children were once limited to the few sources of information available to them within and around the home: paintings, illustrations, views from a window, and what adults said and read to them. Television, however, now escorts children across the globe even before they have permission to cross the street.[11]

22   Whether or not the worldview children receive from television conforms to their parents' worldview does not really matter. Parents are simply no longer the dominant sources of moral instruction, thereby weakening their role and changing the perception that children have of parental authority long before they are even able to think about such things.

23   A subtle way television weakens parental authority, according to Meyrowitz, is by exposing "the backstage life" of adults to children. Even family-oriented shows like *Father Knows Best* or *Leave It To Beaver* reveal the behavior of adults when children are not around, including ways parents talk about their children. Meyrowitz says its *content* is less significant than the revelation of the backstage's very *existence*:

> As a result of such views of adulthood, children may become suspicious of adults and more unwilling to accept all that adults do or say at face value. Conversely, adults may feel 'exposed' by television and, in the long run, it may

---

[9] Oscar Ritchie and Marvin Koller, *Sociology of Childhood* (New York: Appleton-Century-Crofts, 1964), p. 86, 109.

[10] Ibid., p. 103.

[11] Joshua Meyrowitz, *No Sense of Place: The Impact of Electronic Media on Social Behavior* (New York: Oxford University Press, 1985), p. 238.

no longer seem to make as much sense to try to keep certain things hidden from children.[12]

24 In addition, popular culture has been able to interfere with local culture and the moral unity of communities by exploiting generational differences. By creating product lines that are intended to define adolescent identity as a deliberate rejection of parental expectations, the producers of popular culture have successfully entrenched the notion of a relatively new concept, youth culture. Our system of education does not help either, segregating young people from adults as well as from children outside a narrow age range, not to mention from infants and the elderly. This tendency is even unwittingly encouraged by many churches—the very institutions that should be the most vigilant in demonstrating that all ages dwell in unity, but which often celebrate the idea of youth culture as something divinely ordained.

25 Given that culture rightly understood is an intergenerational system of communicating moral convictions, the very phrase "youth culture" should be seen as a contradiction in terms. Not only does age segregation weaken the family's ability to pursue the cultural task of moral transmission, the glorification of the present at the expense of honoring the past and preparing for the future all work against the task of sustaining a rich idea of what family is. Among other things, it weakens the understanding of the family as an intergenerational entity that T. S. Eliot believed played a vital culture-shaping role:

> When I speak of the family, I have in mind a bond which embraces a longer period of time than this [that is, the living members of a nuclear family]: a piety toward the dead, however obscure, and a solicitude for the unborn, however remote. Unless this reverence for past and future is cultivated in the home, it can never be more than a verbal convention in the community.[13]

The Loss of Moral Authority

26 Another way popular culture interferes with the local and family mediation of culture is by undercutting the very notion of any properly recognized authority. Children have always challenged parental authority with the time-honored complaint: "But Johnny's mom lets him do it." While a child may not understand the moral reasoning, he is essentially arguing that since other authority figures have looser standards, more stringent standards cannot be justified. On the other hand, a common and worthy parental response is: "I'm not Johnny's mom." That response presumes the parent is the duly constituted authority here, giving her the right to establish local or family standards.

27 Another way of responding is to observe: "*We* don't do that sort of thing." The first person plural pronoun in the subject of that sentence suggests that the child belongs to a moral community, at least as large as the family, with certain received standards. To the degree parents are able to help children identify with that *we,* they can effectively transmit moral convictions, enabling a child to know he should not do such-and-such because it would not be fitting with his religious identity, or because it would give his family a bad name, or because it would poorly represent his hometown. Without this sense of "binding address," moral identity is left undefined and open; moral authority does not seem compelling.

28 By encouraging young people to become fans of whatever is regarded as trendy or hip each week, popular culture makes a morally recognizable *we* especially difficult to maintain. Television, in particular, undermines efforts of parents or other authority figures to establish terms of propriety in several ways. The immediacy of the medium and the easygoing, chumminess of television personalities make formalities of any kind seem alien; everyone is on a first-name basis.

---

[12] Ibid., p. 249.
[13] Eliot, "Notes towards the Definition of Culture," p. 116.

Its programming is equally problematic. By publicly displaying private behavior, television implicitly legitimizes virtually any behavior in any setting. Joshua Meyrowitz believes this leads to the elimination of the idea of moral and social taboos:

> Any topic on any popular situation comedy, talk shows, news program, or advertisement—be it death, homosexuality, abortion, male strippers, sex-change operations, political scandals, incest, rape, jock itch, or bras that "lift and separate"—can be spoken about the next day in school, over dinner, or on a date, not only because everyone knows about such subjects, but also because everyone knows that everyone knows, and everyone knows that everyone knows that everyone knows. In fact, it almost seems strange *not* to talk and write about such things. The public and all-inclusive nature of television has a tendency to collapse formerly distinct situations into one. In a society shaped by the segregated situations of print, people may secretly discuss taboo topics, but with television, the very notion of the "taboo" is lost.[14]

29   Television, of course, is not really all-inclusive. It actually presents a rather narrow range of experiences and personalities. But it gives the impression of being "all things considered," with the result that those aspects of existence not explored by television come to be regarded as more marginal to human experience than they might be otherwise.

30   Nor does television communicate moral accountability the way literature does. According to Meyrowitz,

> A child's book is, in a sense, a "guest" in the house. It makes a "social entrance," that is, it comes through the door and remains under at least nominal parental authority. As a physical object it must be stored somewhere in the house and it can be discarded. The child's television set, in contrast, is like a new doorway [in]to the home. Through it come many welcome and unwelcome visitors: schoolteachers, Presidents, salesmen, police officers, prostitutes, friends, and strangers.[15]

31   All these factors profoundly affect the ability of families to be schools of character. By weakening the consciousness of moral accountability of children to parents and by distressing the prescriptive power of parents, popular culture establishes its own artifacts and celebrities as sources of moral understanding—a moral system that has only one commandment: Fulfill thyself.

The Loss of Tradition

32   The shift from understanding culture as a legacy to be received (on its terms) to a titillation to be consumed (on my terms) has another consequence: the loss of tradition. That may not initially sound so bad; Americans love innovation, change, and progress. Yet cultural conservatives may need to consider to what extent the traditional values they covet can be sustained without tradition, and especially without a more conscious effort to connect with the past. As Edward Shils, a prominent sociologist, wisely warns: "A family which incorporates into itself little of the past, and, of that which it does incorporate, little of high quality—not all of the past was of equal quality—deadens its offspring; it leaves them with a scanty set of categories and beliefs which are not easily extended or elaborated."[16]

---

[14] Meyrowitz, *No Sense of Place,* p. 92.
[15] Ibid., p. 245.
[16] Edward Shils, *Tradition* (Chicago: University of Chicago Press, 1981), p. 172f.

33   While he does not mention popular culture explicitly, Shils believes the family's ability to connect with the past has been weakened by parents who are reluctant to impose their beliefs on their children and who neglect the hard work of mediating tradition to their children because of other preoccupations. Cultural transmission is further weakened among single parents who lack a needed spouse to reinforce family standards. All these factors "make the stream of tradition narrower and shallower." The phenomenon, writes Shils, resembles the aftermath of war which displaces parents from each other and their children: "The offspring are left to define their own standards; this means the acceptance of the norms of their most imposing coevals."[17]

34   By eliminating a sense of cultural legacy, popular culture weakens or destroys the sense of a permanent moral order in creation. One function of traditional culture is to transmit this sense of moral order, with the implication that each person is obligated to discern and obey the laws of Nature and of Nature's God. The modern sensibility, embodied so fully in popular culture, is that reality is something each individual invents. No moral order exists in the nature of things, only *my* will and *my* desires.

35   Traditional cultures work by a sense of prescription. The traditional order is given the benefit of the doubt, not the burden of proof. Living with the habit of submitting to the received order (unless it is perceived to be in violation of some natural law) cultivates a much greater sympathy to belief in moral absolutes. On the other hand, the regime of popular culture—in which one *must* do one's *own* thing—makes relativism much more plausible. In fact, the sort of aculturalism that popular culture encourages seems to prescribe relativism.

36   Not only does it prescribe a state of flux, but popular culture ends up filling the vacuum left by the abandonment of old ways. According to sociologist Daniel Bell:

A society in rapid change inevitably produces confusions about appropriate modes of behavior, taste, and dress. A socially mobile person has no ready guide for acquiring new knowledge on how to live 'better' than before, and his guides become the movies, television, and advertising. In this respect, advertising begins to play a more subtle role in changing habits than in stimulating wants. . . . Though at first the changes were primarily in manners, dress, taste, and food habits, sooner or later they begin to affect more basic patterns: the structure of authority in the family, the role of children and young adults as independent consumers in the society, the pattern of morals, and the different meanings of achievement in the society."[18]

The Loss of Moral Seriousness

37   A final criticism of popular culture is its superficiality. Not only is the content of popular culture often trite, but the forms in which it is presented discourage depth, reflection, and moral seriousness. As media critic Todd Gitlin describes it, television encourages the sensibility of being "flat and happy." Because the pace of television is relentless and because slick production values are more important than content, glibness rules:

On TV both children and adults speak with unprecedented glibness. Thanks to the wonders of editing, no one on television is ever at a loss for words or photogenic signs of emotion. . . . Hesitancy, silence, awkwardness are absent from TV's repertory of behaviors, except in sitcoms or made-for-TV movies where boy meets girl. Yet outside TV, awkwardness and hesitancy often characterize the beginning, and

[17] Ibid.

[18] Daniel Bell, *The Cultural Contradictions of Capitalism* (New York: Basic Books, 1996), p. 68f.

each further development, of interiority, of a person's internal life. On TV, however, speech is stripped down, designed to move. The one-liner, developed for ads, is the premium style. TV's common currency consists of slogans and mockery. Situation comedies and morning shows are in particular obsessed with the jokey comeback. The put-down is the universal linkage among television's cast of live and recorded characters. A free-floating hostility mirrors, and also inspires, the equivalent conversational style among the young who grow up in this habitat.[19]

38   Gitlin quotes fellow critic Mark Crispin Miller who has observed that this knowingly snide attitude is so widespread and automatic that it deserves to be called "the hipness unto death." Earnestness is out, attitude is all, and the development of character that was once the proper goal of cultural life is thus stunted if not exterminated. What remains stands in vivid contrast to the kind of moral imagination that Russell Kirk claims is an essential prerequisite to cultural health:

> One thing we can do is this: to refrain from choking up the springs of the moral imagination. If we stifle the sense of wonder, no wonders will occur among us; and if wondrous remedies are lacking, then indeed the words of doom written on the sky will become as the laws of the Medes and the Persians, ineluctable.[20]

True Entertainment

39   In the 1950s, Martha Wolfenstein foresaw the cumulative effect of popular culture: entire generations who have a need to be constantly entertained. In her telling essay, "The Emergence of a Fun Morality," the sociologist discerned signs of a new morality displacing an emphasis on goodness. A preoccupation with goodness was, after all, demanding, and interfered with self-fulfillment. Fun morality makes its own demands, since not having fun becomes an occasion for anxiety. Wolfenstein writes: "Whereas gratification of forbidden impulses traditionally aroused guilt, failure to have fun now lowers one's self-esteem."[21] Ironically, many parents, teachers, and religious leaders who today might share Wolfenstein's concerns at face value often appear more worried about being a fun person than about being a good person. As products of this new cultural climate, they assume their roles of moral authority with the same inverted sense of what is moral.

40   For these reasons, the moral condition of American society under the regime of popular culture is a serious and radical problem for which no simple solutions exist. One step in addressing the problem might be to define the proper role of entertainment in society, in the family, and in the life of the individual. The Oxford English Dictionary lists the root meaning of the verb *entertain* as: "To keep in a certain state or condition; to keep in a certain frame of mind; to maintain a state of things; to maintain in existence." That original meaning remains surprisingly accurate, as in the television program, *Entertainment Tonight*. The only difference is the state, condition, or frame of mind being sustained by modern entertainment.

41   The condition of our times is one of disorder and relentless, boundless change. Most entertainment serves to render Americans sympathetic to that condition, undisturbed by the losses, and impressed by the pomp and show of bogus "progress." The frame of mind encouraged by modern entertainment

---

[19] Todd Gitlin, "Flat and Happy," *The Wilson Quarterly* (Autumn 1993), p. 53.

[20] Russell Kirk, *The Wise Men Know What Wicked Things Are Written on the Sky* (Washington, D.C.: Regnery Gateway, 1987), p. 128.

[21] Martha Wolfenstein, "The Emergence of Fun Morality," in *Mass Leisure*, ed. Eric Larrabee and Rolf Meyerson (Glencoe, Ill: The Free Press, 1958), p. 86.

is one which is suspicious of any legacy or inheritance, and which is committed to the assertion of the sovereignty of the self. It is a mentality that evokes a mood of restlessness and blocks out the reflection necessary for acknowledging its disease and then seeking a remedy. It is a sensibility rooted only in the present, ignoring the past, indifferent to the future.

42 In the Christian tradition, the Church (the bride of the One who Was and Is and Shall Be) is called to entertain herself with past and future matters: with millennia-long memories of her sovereign and suffering Lord and of her own rich history of loving and obeying him; and with visions of a distant yet certain glory in a time beyond time. The present is where people of faith are called to obey, but it only makes sense when triangulated within the history and future of redemption, from Creation to Consummation.

43 Conversely, the forms of worldly entertainment are marvelously suited to its content. Thanks to mass media, we are sovereign and isolated consumers of entertain- ment, seeking temporary amnesia from the unhappiness and disappointment of reality. To imagine entertainment that is radically different, truer to its root sense, and engages participants in a mutually edifying service of sustaining love is possible. But that sort of entertainment requires serious attention to the recovery of local culture and how the shape of shared life together might recover a richer sort of entertainment.

44 Poet-farmer Wendell Berry's description of families entertaining one another in his essay, "The Work of Local Culture," describes entertainment in the root sense of the word. In Berry's view, the sharing of memories, not the pursuit of forgetting, maintains a people in its existence. Cultural conservatives therefore should be as concerned about the *form* of entertainment as its content. Our social and cultural disorder does not simply spring from the fact that R-rated movies outnumber G-rated movies. It issues equally from parents who are more likely to take or send their children to the movies than tell them stories. Our society suffers not from being over-entertained, but from not being *truly* entertained. Whether we can recover depends to the extent we attend, not just to the words, but to the way the song is being sung.

Source: Kenneth Myers, "Popular Culture and the Family." *Family Policy,* Family Research Council. Sept. 15, 1998. http.//www/frc.org/papers

DISCUSSION QUESTIONS

1. What examples of slanted language can you find in the introductory section of "Popular Culture and the Family"?

2. Throughout his argument, Myers supports his various claims through appeals to authority. Using the World Wide Web, find information on three of the authorities Myers cites. Based upon what you've learned, discuss with classmates the degree of authority these references lend to the argument.

3. Identify a secondary causal claim in the essay (other than the one analyzed in the preceding commentary). Write a brief summary of the strategies used to support this argument.

4. Select two or three of the generalized claims in the essay and consider how many and what kind of specific examples would have supported the generalization adequately.

5. Select another generalized claim and list three or four counterexamples.

SUGGESTIONS FOR WRITING (19.1)

1. Try writing a one-paragraph definition of the term "popular culture" based upon Myers's apparent understanding of the term.

2. Without consulting any outside sources, write an extended definition of "popular culture" that reflects your personal understanding of the term.

3. Using the definition you wrote for Suggestion #2, write a three- to four-page evaluative argument defending or attacking popular culture. You will probably support your evaluation of the concept through causal arguments that demonstrate its positive or negative effects.

4. Trying to be as engaging as possible, write your own three- or four-paragraph description of the magazine rack in a grocery store, using no slanted language at all. Exchange descriptions with a classmate and discuss how successfully each engaged the reader's interest.

LISTENING TO KHAKIS

MALCOLM GLADWELL

The New Yorker's *Website describes this venerated magazine as follows:*

> The New Yorker *is a weekly magazine dedicated to ideas. It is timeless and immediate, energetic and thoughtful, serious and funny.* The New Yorker *is about good writing, a point of view, and a deeper understanding of the world. . . . Contributors to the* New Yorker *include both recognized talents of long standing and newly discovered voices.*

Malcolm Gladwell, the author of this 1997 New Yorker *article, belongs in the first category of* "Recognized Talents of Long Standing." *Gladwell writes for a number of magazines and journals and is a regular contributor to the* New Yorker.

LISTENING TO KHAKIS

What America's most popular pants tell us about the way guys think

1   In the fall of 1987, Levi Strauss & Co. began running a series of national television commercials to promote Dockers, its new brand of men's khakis. All the spots—and there were twenty-eight—had the same basic structure. A handheld camera would follow a group of men as they sat around a living room or office or bar. The men were in their late thirties, but it was hard to tell, because the camera caught faces only fleetingly. It was trained instead on the men from the waist down—on the seats of their pants, on the pleats of their khakis, on their hands going in and out of their pockets. As the camera jumped in quick cuts from Docker to Docker, the men chatted in loose, overlapping non sequiturs—guy-talk fragments that, when they are rendered on the page, achieve a certain Dadaist poetry. Here is the entire transcript of "Poolman,"

one of the first—and, perhaps, best—ads in the series:

> "She was a redhead about five foot six inches tall."
>
> "And all of a sudden this thing starts spinning, and it's going round and round."
>
> "Is that Nelson?"
>
> "And that makes me safe, because with my wife, I'll never be that way."
>
> "It's like your career, and you're frustrated. I mean that—that's—what you want."
>
> "Of course, that's just my opinion."
>
> "So money's no object."
>
> "Yeah, money's no object."
>
> "What are we going to do with our lives, now?"
>
> "Well . . ."
>
> "Best of all . . ."
>
> [Voice-over] "Levi's one-hundred-per-cent-cotton Dockers. If you're not wearing Dockers, you're just wearing pants."
>
> "And I'm still paying the loans off."
>
> "You've got all the money in the world."
>
> "I'd like to at least be your poolman."

2 By the time the campaign was over, at the beginning of the nineties, Dockers had grown into a six-hundred-million-dollar business—a brand that if it had spun off from Levi's would have been (and would still be) the fourth-largest clothing brand in the world. Today, seventy per cent of American men between the ages of twenty-five and forty-five own a pair of Dockers, and khakis are expected to be as popular as blue jeans by the beginning of the next century. It is no exaggeration to call the original Dockers ads one of the most successful fashion-advertising campaigns in history.

3 This is a remarkable fact for a number of reasons, not the least of which is that the Dockers campaign was aimed at men, and no one had ever thought you could hit a home run like that by trying to sell fashion to the American male. Not long ago, two psychologists at York University, in Toronto—Irwin Silverman and Marion Eals—conducted an experiment in which they had men and women sit in an office for two minutes, without any reading material or distraction, while they ostensibly waited to take part in some kind of academic study. Then they were taken from the office and given the real reason for the experiment: to find out how many of the objects in the office they could remember. This was not a test of memory so much as it was a test of awareness—of the kind and quality of unconscious attention that people pay to the particulars of their environment. If you think about it, it was really a test of fashion sense, because, at its root, this is what fashion sense really is—the ability to register and appreciate and remember the details of the way those around you look and dress, and then reinterpret those details and memories yourself.

4 When the results of the experiment were tabulated, it was found that the women were able to recall the name and the placement of seventy percent more objects than the men, which makes perfect sense. Women's fashion, after all, consists of an endless number of subtle combinations and variations—of skirt, dress, pants, blouse, T-shirt, hose, pumps, flats, heels, necklace, bracelet, cleavage, collar, curl, and on and on—all driven by the fact that when a woman walks down the street she knows that other women, consciously or otherwise, will notice the name and the placement of what she is wearing. Fashion works for women because women can appreciate its complexity. But when it comes to men what's the point? How on earth do you sell fashion to someone who has no appreciation for detail whatsoever?

5 The Dockers campaign, however, proved that you could sell fashion to men. But that was only the first of its remarkable implications. The second—which remains as weird and mysterious and relevant to the fashion business today as it was ten years ago—was that you could do this by training a camera on a man's butt and having him talk in yuppie gibberish.

6   I watched "Poolman" with three members of the new team handling the Dockers account at Foote, Cone & Belding (F.C.B.), Levi's ad agency. We were in a conference room at Levi's Plaza, in downtown San Francisco, a redbrick building decorated (appropriately enough) in khaki like earth tones, with the team members— Chris Shipman, Iwan Thomis, and Tanyia Kandohla—forming an impromptu critical panel. Shipman, who had thick black glasses and spoke in an almost inaudible laid-back drawl, put a videocassette of the first campaign into a VCR—stopping, starting, and rewinding—as the group analyzed what made the spots so special.

7   "Remember, this is from 1987," he said, pointing to the screen, as the camera began its jerky dance. "Although this style of film making looks everyday now, that kind of handheld stuff was very fresh when these were made."

8   "They taped real conversations," Kandohla chimed in. "Then the footage was cut together afterward. They were thrown areas to talk about. It was very natural, not at all scripted. People were encouraged to go off on tangents."

9   After "Poolman," we watched several of the other spots in the original group— "Scorekeeper" and "Dad's Chair," "Flag Football" and "The Meaning of Life"—and I asked about the headlessness of the commercials, because if you watch too many in a row all those anonymous body parts begin to get annoying. But Thomis maintained that the headlessness was crucial, because it was the absence of faces that gave the dialogue its freedom. "They didn't show anyone's head because if they did the message would have too much weight," he said. "It would be too pretentious. You know, people talking about their hopes and dreams. It seems more genuine, as opposed to something stylized."

10   The most striking aspect of the spots is how different they are from typical fashion advertising. If you look at men's fashion magazines, for example, at the advertisements for the suits of Ralph Lauren or Valentino or Hugo Boss, they almost always consist of a beautiful man, with something interesting done to his hair, wearing a gorgeous outfit. At the most, the man may be gesturing discreetly, or smiling in the demure way that a man like that might smile after, say, telling the supermodel at the next table no thanks he has to catch an early-morning flight to Milan. But that's all. The beautiful face and the clothes tell the whole story. The Dockers ads, though, are almost exactly the opposite. There's no face. The camera is jumping around so much that it's tough to concentrate on the clothes. And instead of stark simplicity, the fashion image is overlaid with a constant, confusing patter. It's almost as if the Dockers ads weren't primarily concerned with clothes at all—and in fact that's exactly what Levi's intended. What the company had discovered, in its research, was that babyboomer men felt that the chief thing missing from their lives was male friendship. Caught between the demands of the families that many of them had started in the eighties and career considerations that had grown more onerous, they felt they had lost touch with other men. The purpose of the ads—the chatter, the lounging around, the quick cuts— was simply to conjure up a place where men could put on one-hundred-percent-cotton khakis and reconnect with one another. In the original advertising brief, that imaginary place was dubbed Dockers World.

11   This may seem like an awfully roundabout way to sell a man a pair of pants. But that was the genius of the campaign. One of the truisms of advertising is that it's always easier to sell at the extremes than in the middle, which is why the advertisements for Valentino and Hugo Boss are so simple. The man in the market for a thousand-dollar suit doesn't need to be convinced of the value of nice clothes. The man in the middle, though—the man in the market for a forty-dollar pair of khakis—does. In fact, he probably isn't comfortable buying clothes at all. To sell him a pair of pants you have to take him somewhere he is comfortable, and that was the point of Dockers World. Even the apparent gibberish of lines like "'She was a redhead about five foot six inches tall.'

/ 'And all of a sudden this thing starts spinning, and it's going round and round.' / 'Is that Nelson?'" have, if you listen closely enough, a certain quintessentially guy-friendly feel. It's the narrative equivalent of the sports-highlight reel—the sequence of five-second film clips of the best plays from the day's basketball or football or baseball games, which millions of American men watch every night on television. This nifty couplet from "Scorekeeper," for instance— "'Who remembers their actual first girlfriend?' / 'I would have done better, but I was bald then, too'"—is not nonsense but a twenty-minute conversation edited down to two lines. A man schooled in the highlight reel no more needs the other nineteen minutes and fifty-eight seconds of that exchange than he needs to see the intervening catch and throw to make sense of a sinking liner to left and a close play at the plate.

12 "Men connected to the underpinnings of what was being said," Robert Hanson, the vice-president of marketing for Dockers, told me. "These guys were really being honest and genuine and real with each other, and talking about their lives. It may not have been the truth, but it was the fantasy of what a lot of customers wanted, which was not just to be work-focused but to have the opportunity to express how you feel about your family and friends and lives. The content was very important. The thing that built this brand was that we absolutely nailed the emotional underpinnings of what motivates baby boomers."

13 Hanson is a tall, striking man in his early thirties. He's what Jeff Bridges would look like if he had gone to finishing school. Hanson said that when he goes out on research trips to the focus groups that Dockers holds around the country he often deliberately stays in the background, because if the men in the group see him "they won't necessarily respond as positively or as openly." When he said this, he was wearing a pair of stone-white Dockers, a deep-blue shirt, a navy blazer, and a brilliant-orange patterned tie, and these worked so well together that it was obvious what he meant.

When someone like Hanson dresses up that fabulously in Dockers, he makes it clear just how many variations and combinations are possible with a pair of khakis—but that, of course, defeats the purpose of the carefully crafted Dockers World message, which is to appeal to the man who wants nothing to do with fashion's variations and combinations. It's no coincidence that every man in every one of the group settings profiled in each commercial is wearing—albeit in different shades—exactly the same kind of pants. Most fashion advertising sells distinctiveness. (Can you imagine, say, an Ann Taylor commercial where a bunch of thirtyish girl-friends are lounging around chatting, all decked out in matching sweater sets?) Dockers was selling conformity.

14 "We would never do anything with our pants that would frighten anyone away," Gareth Morris, a senior designer for the brand, told me. "We'd never do too many belt loops, or an unusual base cloth. Our customers like one-hundred-per-cent-cotton fabrics. We would never do a synthetic. That's definitely in the market, but it's not where we need to be. Styling-wise, we would never do a wide, wide leg. We would never do a peg-legged style. Our customers seem to have a definite idea of what they want. They don't like tricky openings or zips or a lot of pocket flaps and details on the back. We've done button-through flaps, to push it a little bit. But we usually do a welt pocket—that's a pocket with a button-through. It's funny. We have focus groups in New York, Chicago, and San Francisco, and whenever we show them a pocket with a flap—it's a simple thing—they hate it. They won't buy the pants. They complain, 'How do I get my wallet?' So we compromise and do a welt. That's as far as they'll go. And there's another thing. They go, 'My butt's big enough. I don't want flaps hanging off of it, too.' They like inseam pockets. They like to know where they put their hands." He gestured to the pair of experimental prototype Dockers he was wearing, which had pockets that ran almost parallel to the waistband of the pants. "This is a stretch for us," he said. "If you start putting more stuff on

than we have on our product, you're asking for trouble."

15 The apotheosis of the notion of khakis as nonfashion-guy fashion came several years after the original Dockers campaign, when Haggar Clothing Co. hired the Goodby, Silverstein & Partners ad agency, in San Francisco, to challenge Dockers' khaki dominance. In retrospect, it was an inspired choice, since Goodby, Silverstein is Guy Central. It does Porsche ("Kills Bugs Fast") and Isuzu and the recent "Got Milk?" campaign and a big chunk of the Nike business, and it operates out of a gutted turn-of-the-century building downtown, refurbished in what is best described as neo-Erector set. The campaign that it came up with featured voice-overs by Roseanne's television husband, John Goodman. In the best of the ads, entitled "I Am," a thirtyish man wakes up, his hair all mussed, pulls on a pair of white khakis, and half sleepwalks outside to get the paper. "I am not what I wear. I'm not a pair of pants, or a shirt," Goodman intones. The man walks by his wife, handing her the front sections of the paper. "I'm not in touch with my inner child. I don't read poetry, and I'm not politically correct." He heads away from the kitchen, down a hallway, and his kid grabs the comics from him. "I'm just a guy, and I don't have time to think about what I wear, because I've got a lot of important guy things to do." All he has left now is the sports section and, gripping it purposefully, he heads for the bathroom. "One-hundred-per-cent-cotton wrinkle-free khaki pants that don't require a lot of thought. Haggar. Stuff you can wear."

16 "We softened it," Richard Silverstein told me as we chatted in his office, perched on chairs in the midst of—among other things—a lacrosse stick, a bike stand, a gym bag full of yesterday's clothing, three toy Porsches, and a giant model of a Second World War Spitfire hanging from the ceiling. "We didn't say 'Haggar Apparel' or 'Haggar Clothing.' We said, 'Hey, listen, guys, don't worry. It's just stuff. Don't worry about it.' The concept was 'Make it approachable.'" The difference between this and the Dockers ad is humor. F.C.B. assidu-ously documented men's inner lives. Goodby, Silverstein made fun of them. But it's essentially the same message. It's instructive, in this light, to think about the Casual Friday phenomenon of the past decade, the loosening of corporate dress codes that was spawned by the rise of khakis. Casual Fridays are commonly thought to be about men rejecting the uniform of the suit. But surely that's backward. Men started wearing khakis to work because Dockers and Haggar made it sound as if khakis were going to be even easier than a suit. The khaki-makers realized that men didn't want to get rid of uniforms; they just wanted a better uniform.

17 The irony, of course, is that this idea of nonfashion—of khakis as the choice that diminishes, rather than enhances, the demands of fashion—turned out to be a white lie. Once you buy even the plainest pair of khakis, you invariably also buy a sports jacket and a belt and a whole series of shirts to go with it—maybe a polo knit for the weekends, something in plaid for casual, and a button-down for a dressier look—and before long your closet is thick with just the kinds of details and options that you thought you were avoiding. You may not add these details as brilliantly or as consciously as, say, Hanson does, but you end up doing it nonetheless. In the past seven years, sales of men's clothing in the United States have risen an astonishing twenty-one per cent, in large part because of this very fact—that khakis, even as they have simplified the bottom half of the male wardrobe, have forced a steady revision of the top. At the same time, even khakis themselves—within the narrow constraints of khakidom—have quietly expanded their range. When Dockers were launched, in the fall of 1986, there were just three basic styles: the double-pleated Docker in khaki, olive, navy, and black; the Steamer, in cotton canvas; and the more casual flat-fronted Docker. Now there are twenty-four. Dockers and Haggar and everyone else has been playing a game of bait and switch: lure men in with the promise of a uniform and then slip them, bit by bit, fashion. Put them in an empty room

and then, ever so slowly, so as not to scare them, fill the room with objects.

18   There is a puzzle in psychology known as the canned-laughter problem, which has a deeper and more complex set of implications about men and women and fashion and why the Dockers ads were so successful. Over the years, several studies have been devoted to this problem, but perhaps the most instructive was done by two psychologists at the University of Wisconsin, Gerald Cupchik and Howard Leventhal. Cupchik and Leventhal took a stack of cartoons (including many from the *New Yorker*), half of which an independent panel had rated as very funny and half of which it had rated as mediocre. They put the cartoons on slides, had a voice-over read the captions, and presented the slide show to groups of men and women. As you might expect, both sexes reacted pretty much the same way. Then Cupchik and Leventhal added a laugh track to the voice-over—the subjects were told that it was actual laughter from people who were in the room during the taping—and repeated the experiment. This time, however, things got strange. The canned laughter made the women laugh a little harder and rate the cartoons as a little funnier than they had before. But not the men. They laughed a bit more at the good cartoons but much more at the bad cartoons. The canned laughter also made them rate the bad cartoons as much funnier than they had rated them before, but it had little or no effect on their ratings of the good cartoons. In fact, the men found a bad cartoon with a laugh track to be almost as funny as a good cartoon without one. What was going in?

19   The guru of male-female differences in the ad world is Joan Meyers-Levy, a professor at the University of Chicago business school. In a groundbreaking series of articles written over the past decade, Meyers-Levy has explained the canned-laughter problem and other gender anomalies by arguing that men and women use fundamentally different methods of processing information. Given two pieces of evidence about how funny something is—their own opinion and the opinion of others (the laugh track)—the women came up with a higher score than

before because they added the two clues together: they integrated the information before them. The men, on the other hand, picked one piece of evidence and ignored the other. For the bad cartoons, they got carried away by the laugh track and gave out hugely generous scores for funniness. For the good cartoons, however, they were so wedded to their own opinion that suddenly the laugh track didn't matter at all.

20   This idea—that men eliminate and women integrate—is called by Meyers-Levy the "selectivity hypothesis." Men are looking for a way to simplify the route to a conclusion, so they seize on the most obvious evidence and ignore the rest, while women, by contrast, try to process information comprehensively. So-called bandwidth research, for example, has consistently shown that if you ask a group of people to sort a series of objects or ideas into categories, the men will create fewer and larger categories than the women will. They use bigger mental bandwidth. Why? Because the bigger the bandwidth the less time and attention you have to pay to each individual object. Or consider what is called the invisibility question. If a woman is being asked a series of personal questions by another woman, she'll say more if she's facing the woman she's talking to than she will if her listener is invisible. With men, it's the opposite. When they can't see the person who's asking them questions, they suddenly and substantially open up. This, of course, is a condition of male communication which has been remarked on by women for millennia. But the selectivity hypothesis suggests that the cause of it has been misdiagnosed. It's not that men necessarily have trouble expressing their feelings; it's that in a face-to-face conversation they experience emotional overload. A man can't process nonverbal information (the expression and body language of the person asking him questions) and verbal information (the personal question being asked) at the same time any better than he can process other people's laughter and his own laughter at the same time. He has to select, and it is Meyers-Levy's contention that this

pattern of behavior suggests significant differences in the way men and women respond to advertising.

21   Joan Meyers-Levy is a petite woman in her late thirties, with a dark pageboy haircut and a soft voice. She met me in the downtown office of the University of Chicago with three large folders full of magazine advertisements under one arm, and after chatting about the origins and the implications of her research she handed me an ad from several years ago for Evian bottled water. It has a beautiful picture of the French Alps and, below that, in large type, "Our factory." The text ran for several paragraphs, beginning:

22   You're not just looking at the French Alps. You're looking at one of the most pristine places on earth. And the origin of Evian Natural Spring Water.

23   Here, it takes no less than fifteen years for nature to purify every drop of Evian as it flows through mineral-rich glacial formations deep within the mountains. And it is here that Evian acquires its unique balance of minerals.

24   "Now, is that a male or a female ad?" she asked. I looked at it again. The picture baffled me. But the word "factory" seemed masculine, so I guessed male.

25   She shook her head. "It's female. Look at the picture. It's just the Alps, and then they label it 'Our factory.' They're using a metaphor. To understand this, you're going to have to engage in a fair amount of processing. And look at all the imagery they're encouraging you to build up. You're not just looking at the French Alps. It's 'one of the most pristine places on earth' and it will take nature 'no less than fifteen years' to purify." Her point was that this is an ad that works only if the viewer appreciates all its elements—if the viewer integrates, not selects. A man, for example, glancing at the ad for a fraction of a second, might focus only on the words "Our factory" and screen out the picture of the Alps entirely, the same way he might have screened out the canned laughter. Then he wouldn't get the visual metaphor. In fact, he might end up equating Evian with a factory, and that would be a

disaster. Anyway, why bother going into such detail about the glaciers if it's just going to get lost in the big male bandwidth?

26   Meyers-Levy handed me another Evian advertisement. It showed a man—the Olympic Gold Medal swimmer Matt Biondi—by a pool drinking Evian, with the caption "Revival of the fittest." The women's ad had a hundred and nineteen words of text. This ad had just twenty-nine words: "No other water has the unique, natural balance of minerals that Evian achieves during its fifteen year journey deep within the French Alps. To be the best takes time." Needless to say, it came from a men's magazine. "With men, you don't want the fluff," she said. "Women, though, participate a lot more in whatever they are processing. By giving them more cues, you give them something to work with. You don't have to be so literal. With women you can be more allusive, so you can draw them in. They will engage in elaboration, and the more associations they make the easier it is to remember and retrieve later on."

27   Meyers-Levy took a third ad from her pile, this one for the 1997 Mercury Mountaineer four-wheel-drive sport-utility vehicle. It covers two pages, has the heading "Take the Rough with the Smooth," and shows four pictures—one of the vehicle itself, one of a mother and her child, one of a city skyline, and a large one of the interior of the car, over which the ad's text is superimposed. Around the border of the ad are forty-four separate, tiny photographs of roadways and buildings and construction sites and manhole covers. Female. Next to it on the table she put another ad—this one a single page, with a picture of the Mountaineer's interior, fifteen lines of text, a picture of the car's exterior, and, at the top, the heading: "When the Going Gets Tough, the Tough Get Comfortable." Male. "It's details, details. They're saying lots of different stuff," she said, pointing to the female version. "With men, instead of trying to cover everything in a single execution, you'd probably want to have a whole series of ads, each making a different point."

28   After a while, the game got very easy—if a bit humiliating. Meyers-Levy said that her observations were not antimale—that both the male and the female strategies have their strengths and their weaknesses—and, of course, she's right. On the other hand, reading the gender of ads makes it painfully obvious how much the advertising world— consciously or not—talks down to men. Before I met Meyers-Levy, I thought that the genius of the famous first set of Dockers ads was their psychological complexity, their ability to capture the many layers of eighties guyness. But when I thought about them again after meeting Meyers-Levy, I began to think that their real genius lay in their heroic simplicity—in the fact that F.C.B. had the self-discipline to fill the allotted thirty seconds with as little as possible. Why no heads? The invisibility rule. Guys would never listen to that Dadaist extemporizing if they had to process nonverbal cues, too. Why were the ads set in people's living rooms and at the office? Bandwidth. The message was that khakis were wide-bandwidth pants. And why were all the ads shot in almost exactly the same way, and why did all the dialogue run together in one genial, faux-philosophical stretch of highlight reel? Because of canned laughter. Because if there were more than one message to be extracted men would get confused.

29   In the early nineties, Dockers began to falter. In 1992, the company sold sixty-six million pairs of khakis, but in 1993, as competition from Haggar and the Gap and other brands grew fiercer, that number slipped to fifty-nine million six hundred thousand, and by 1994 it had fallen to forty-seven million. In marketing-speak, user reality was encroaching on brand personality; that is, Dockers were being defined by the kind of middle-aged men who wore them, and not by the hipper, younger men in the original advertisements. The brand needed a fresh image, and the result was the "Nice Pants" campaign currently being shown on national television—a campaign widely credited with the resurgence of Dockers' fortunes.

30   In one of the spots, "Vive la France," a scruffy young man in his early twenties,

wearing Dockers, is sitting in a café; in Paris. He's obviously a tourist. He glances up and sees a beautiful woman (actually, the super-model Tatjana Patitz) looking right at him. He's in heaven. She starts walking directly toward him, and as she passes by she says, "Beau pantalon." As he looks frantically through his French phrase book for a translation, the waiter comes by and cuffs him on the head: "Hey, she says, 'Nice pants.'" Another spot in the series, "Subway Love," takes place on a subway car in Chicago. He (a nice young man wearing Dockers) spots her (a total babe), and their eyes lock. Romantic music swells. He moves toward her, but somehow, in a sudden burst of pushing and shoving, they get separated. Last shot: she's inside the car, her face pushed up against the glass. He's outside the car, his face pushed up against the glass. As the train slowly pulls away, she mouths two words: "Nice pants."

31   It may not seem like it, but "Nice Pants" is as radical a campaign as the original Dockers series. If you look back at the way that Sansabelt pants, say, were sold in the sixties, each ad was what advertisers would call a pure "head" message: the pants were comfortable, durable, good value. The genius of the first Dockers campaign was the way it combined head and heart: these were all-purpose, no-nonsense pants that connected to the emotional needs of baby boomers. What happened to Dockers in the nineties, though, was that everyone started to do head and heart for khakis. Haggar pants were wrinkle-free (head) and John Goodman-guy (heart). The Gap, with its brilliant billboard campaign of the early nineties—"James Dean wore khakis," "Frank Lloyd Wright wore khakis"—perfected the heart message by forging an emotional connection between khakis and a particular nostalgic, glamorous all-Americanness. To reassert itself, Dockers needed to go an extra step. Hence "Nice Pants," a campaign that for the first time in Dockers history raises the subject of sex.

32   "It's always been acceptable for a man to be a success in business," Hanson said,

explaining the rationale behind "Nice Pants." "It's always been expected of a man to be a good provider. The new thing that men are dealing with is that it's O.K. for men to have a sense of personal style, and that it's O.K. to be seen as sexy. It's less about the head than about the combination of the head, the heart, and the groin. It's those three things. That's the complete man."

33   The radical part about this, about adding the groin to the list, is that almost no other subject for men is as perilous as the issue of sexuality and fashion. What "Nice Pants" had to do was talk about sex the same way that "Poolman" talked about fashion, which was to talk about it by not talking about it—or, at least, to talk about it in such a coded, cautious way that no man would ever think Dockers was suggesting that he wear khakis in order to look pretty. When I took a videotape of the "Nice Pants" campaign to several of the top agencies in New York and Los Angeles, virtually everyone agreed that the spots were superb, meaning that somehow F.C.B. had managed to pull off this balancing act.

34   What David Altschiller, at Hill, Holliday/Altschiller, in Manhattan, liked about the spots, for example, was that the hero was naïve: in neither case did he know that he had on nice pants until a gorgeous woman told him so. Naïveté, Altschiller stressed, is critical. Several years ago, he did a spot for Claiborne for Men cologne in which a great-looking guy in a bar, wearing a gorgeous suit, was obsessing neurotically about a beautiful woman at the other end of the room: "I see this woman. She's perfect. She's looking at me. She's smiling. But wait. Is she smiling at me? Or laughing at me? . . . Or looking at someone else?" You'd never do this in an ad for women's cologne. Can you imagine? "I see this guy. He's perfect. Ohmigod. Is he looking at me?" In women's advertising, self-confidence is sexy. But if a man is self-confident—if he knows he is attractive and is beautifully dressed—then he's not a man anymore. He's a fop. He's effeminate. The cologne guy had to be neurotic or the ad wouldn't work. "Men are still abashed about acknowledging that clothing is important," Altschiller said. "Fashion can't be important to me as a man. Even when, in the first commer-

cial, the waiter says 'Nice pants,' it doesn't compute to the guy wearing the nice pants. He's thinking, What do you mean, 'Nice pants'?" Altschiller was looking at a videotape of the Dockers ad as he talked—standing at a forty-five-degree angle to the screen, with one hand on the top of the monitor, one hand on his hip, and a small bemused smile on his lips. "The world may think they are nice, but so long as he doesn't think so he doesn't have to be self-conscious about it, and the lack of self-consciousness is very important to men. Because 'I don't care.' Or 'Maybe I care, but I can't be seen to care.'" For the same reason, Altschiller liked the relative understatement of the phrase "nice pants," as opposed to something like "great pants," since somewhere between "nice" and "great" a guy goes from just happening to look good to the unacceptable position of actually trying to look good. "In focus groups, men said that to be told you had 'nice pants' was one of the highest compliments a man could wish for," Tanyia Kandohla told me later, when I asked about the slogan. "They wouldn't want more attention drawn to them than that."

35   In many ways, the "Nice Pants" campaign is a direct descendant of the hugely successful campaign that Rubin-Postaer & Associates, in Santa Monica, did for Bugle Boy Jeans in the early nineties. In the most famous of those spots, the camera opens on an attractive but slightly goofy-looking man in a pair of jeans who is hitchhiking by the side of a desert highway. Then a black Ferrari with a fabulous babe at the wheel drives by, stops, and backs up. The babe rolls down the window and says, "Excuse me. Are those Bugle Boy Jeans that you're wearing?" The goofy guy leans over and pokes his head in the window, a surprised half smile on his face: "Why, yes, they are Bugle Boy Jeans."

36   "Thank you," the babe says, and she rolls up the window and drives away.

37   This is really the same ad as "Nice Pants"—the babe, the naïve hero, the punch line. The two ads have something else in common. In the Bugle Boy spot, the hero wasn't some stunning male model. "I think he was actually a box boy at Vons in Huntington

Beach," Larry Postaer, the creative director of Rubin-Postaer & Associates, told me. "I guess someone"—at Bugle Boy—"liked him." He's O.K.-looking, but not nearly in the same class as the babe in the Ferrari. In "Subway Love," by the same token, the Dockers man is medium-sized, almost small, and gets pushed around by much tougher people in the tussle on the train. He's cute, but he's a little bit of a wimp. Kandohla says that F.C.B. tried very hard to find someone with that look— someone who was, in her words, "aspirational real," not some "buff, muscle-bound jock." In a fashion ad for women, you can use Claudia Schiffer to sell a cheap pair of pants. But not in a fashion ad for men. The guy has to be believable. "A woman cannot be too gorgeous," Postaer explained. "A man, however, can be too gorgeous, because then he's not a man anymore. It's pretty rudimentary. Yet there are people who don't buy that, and have gorgeous men in their ads. I don't get it. Talk to Barneys about how well that's working. It couldn't stay in business trying to sell that high-end swagger to a mass market. The general public wouldn't accept it. Look at beer commercials. They always have these gorgeous girls—even now, after all the heat—and the guys are always just guys. That's the way it is. We only reflect what's happening out there, we're not creating it. Those guys who run the real high-end fashion ads—they don't understand that. They're trying to remold how people think about gender. I can't explain it, though I have my theories. It's like a Grecian ideal. But you can't be successful at advertising by trying to re-create the human condition. You can't alter men's minds, particularly on subjects like sexuality. It'll never happen."

38   Postaer is a gruff, rangy guy, with a Midwestern accent and a gravelly voice, who did Budweiser commercials in Chicago before moving West fifteen years ago. When he wasn't making fun of the pretentious style of East Coast fashion advertising, he was making fun of the pretentious questions of East Coast writers. When, for example, I earnestly asked him to explain the logic behind having the goofy guy screw up his face in such a—well, goofy—way when he says, "Why, yes, they are Bugle Boy Jeans,"

Postaer took his tennis shoes off his desk, leaned forward bemusedly in his chair, and looked at me as if my head came to a small point. "Because that's the only way he could say it," he said. "I suppose we might have had him say it a little differently if he could actually act."

Incredibly, Postaer said, the people at 39 Bugle Boy wanted the babe to invite the goofy guy into the car, despite the fact that this would have violated the most important rule that governs this new style of groin messages in men's-fashion advertising, which is that the guy absolutely cannot ever get the girl. It's not just that if he got the girl the joke wouldn't work anymore; it's that if he got the girl it might look as if he had deliberately dressed to get the girl, and although at the back of every man's mind as he's dressing in the morning there is the thought of getting the girl, any open admission that that's what he's actually trying to do would undermine the whole unselfconscious, antifashion statement that men's advertising is about. If Tatjana Patitz were to say "Beau garçon" to the guy in "Vive la France," or the babe on the subway were to give the wimp her number, Dockers would suddenly become terrifyingly conspicuous— the long-pants equivalent of wearing a tight little Speedo to the beach. And if the Vons box boy should actually get a ride from the Ferrari babe, the ad would suddenly become believable only to that thin stratum of manhood which thinks that women in Ferraris find twenty-four-dollar jeans irresistible. "We fought that tooth and nail," Postaer said. "And it more or less cost us the account, even though the ad was wildly successful." He put his tennis shoes back up on the desk. "But that's what makes this business fun— trying to prove to clients how wrong they are."

The one ad in the "Nice Pants" campaign 40 which isn't like the Bugle Boy spots is called "Motorcycle." In it a nice young man happens upon a gleaming Harley on a dark back street of what looks like downtown Manhattan. He strokes the seat and then, unable to contain himself, climbs aboard the bike and bounces up and down, showing off his Dockers (the "product shot") but accidentally breaking a mirror on the handlebar. He looks up. The Harley's owner—a huge, leather-clad biker—is looking down at him. The biker glowers, looking him up and down, and says, "Nice pants." Last shot: the biker rides away, leaving the guy standing on the sidewalk in just his underwear.

41   What's surprising about this ad is that, unlike "Vive la France" and "Subway Love," it does seem to cross the boundaries of acceptable sex talk. The rules of guy advertising so carefully observed in those spots—the fact that the hero has to be naïve, that he can't be too good-looking, that he can't get the girl, and that he can't be told anything stronger than "Nice pants"—are all, in some sense, reactions to the male fear of appearing too concerned with fashion, of being too pretty, of not being masculine. But what is "Motorcycle"? It's an ad about a sweet-looking guy down in the Village somewhere who loses his pants to a butch-looking biker in leather. "I got so much feedback at the time of 'Well, God, that's kind of gay, don't you think?'" Robert Hanson said. "People were saying, 'This buff guy comes along and he rides off with the guy's pants. I mean, what the hell were they doing?' It came from so many different people within the industry. It came from some of our most conservative retailers. But do you know what? If you put these three spots up—'Vive la France,'

'Subway Love,' and 'Motorcycle'—which one do you think men will talk about ad nauseam? 'Motorcycle.' It's No. 1. It's because he's really cool. He's in a really cool environment, and it's every guy's fantasy to have a really cool, tricked-out fancy motorcycle."

Hanson paused, as if he recognized that   42
what he was saying was quite sensitive. He didn't want to say that men failed to pick up the gay implications of the ad because they're stupid, because they aren't stupid. And he didn't want to sound condescending, because Dockers didn't build a six-hundred-million-dollar business in five years by sounding condescending. All he was trying to do was point out the fundamental exegetical error in calling this a gay ad, because the only way for a Dockers man to be offended by "Motorcycle" would be if he thought about it with a little imagination, if he picked up on some fairly subtle cues, if he integrated an awful lot of detail. In other words, a Dockers man could only be offended if he did precisely what, according to Meyers-Levy, men don't do. It's not a gay ad because it's a guy ad. "The fact is," Hanson said, "that most men's interpretation of that spot is: You know what? Those pants must be really cool, because they prevented him from getting the shit kicked out of him."

Source: Malcolm Gladwell, "Listening to Khakis," *The New Yorker*.
July 28, 1997.

DISCUSSION QUESTIONS

1. Like most of Gladwell's pieces, this article is (at least for a magazine), long, thoughtful, and fairly complex. It is also typical of *New Yorker* features. Using this article and the *New Yorker* Website description cited earlier, create a speculative description of a typical *New Yorker* reader. Include in your description level of education, type of employment, salary level, marital status, geographical location, and any other descriptors you can think of.

2. After reading the article carefully at least twice, prepare an outline of its structure, making sure to indicate the logical relationships among the parts.

3. Gladwell refers to polls, focus groups, studies, and experiments. In some cases, he cites the specific sources within the text; in others, he does not. He does not provide (and this is standard for the *New Yorker*) a bibliography or list of works cited. Discuss with a group of your classmates whether these omissions detract from the writer's overall credibility. Why do you think the magazine has adopted this editorial policy?

4. Discuss with your classmates the usefulness of an argument such as this. What, if anything, is to be gained by the reader of such an argument? Why would it interest a *New Yorker* reader? Does it go too far in analyzing cultural artifacts?

SUGGESTIONS FOR WRITING (19.2)

1. Select an item of clothing commonly worn on your campus (blue jeans, T-shirts, baseball caps, for example), and write a parody of Gladwell's Dockers interpretation.

2. According to one of Gladwell's sources, "baby-boomer men felt that the chief thing missing from their lives was male friendship." Create a set of interview questions for a group of your male peers designed to identify the chief thing missing from their lives.

3. Gladwell concludes in Par. 28 that "the advertising world—consciously or not—talks down to men." Using this conclusion as your central claim, write a four- to five-page interpretation of three magazine ads clearly designed for men. To be sure you've chosen appropriate ads, look through publications that are clearly male-oriented (e.g., *Sports Illustrated*, *Field and Stream*, etc.).

4. Many believe that our clothes reveal a great deal about us. Using two or three of your closest friends or family members as supporting examples, write a factual argument that agrees or disagrees with this maxim.

THE CONTENTS OF WOMEN'S PURSES: AN ACCESSORY IN CRISIS

DANIEL HARRIS

This "reading" of women's purses and their contents appeared in 1997 in the quarterly journal Salmagundi. *Daniel Harris is a writer whose most recent book is* The Rise and Fall of Gay Culture. Salmagundi *is a decidedly upscale periodical published by Skidmore College. Its contents include original poetry and fiction, book reviews, literary criticism, and cultural reflections like this one by Harris.*

1   Before the twentieth century, when housewives began to spend more time away from home than they had ever spent before, the purse had not yet evolved into the bottomless pit of the contemporary woman's seemingly infinite handbag whose unplumped depths are full of business cards, subway passes, grocery lists, and ATM receipts. Instead, it was a largely optional accessory designed to carry a few basic items for brief excursions to church, the opera, the theater, or other women's houses, places where they could survive quite comfortably on the contents of a draw-string pouch slung around their wrists containing such things as a fan, mirror, handkerchief, smelling

salts, pad of paper, pencil, and powder puff. The collection of objects that women carried during the nineteenth century was far less complex than the odd assortment of mismatched articles that many women now carry in their pocketbooks, which overflow with used Kleenexes, aspirin, hair spray, lip balm, dental floss, peppermint Altoids, charge cards, Lifesavers, gum wrappers, loose jelly beans, parking validations, expired bus transfers, good luck stones, and Walgreen's receipts.

2   As women began to join the work force in ever larger numbers during World War I and dramatically increased the scope of their activities to everything from lobbying for suffrage to engaging in competitive sports, the purse slowly began to bulge with a surfeit of inessentials. Today's working woman needs countless provisions to survive for the prolonged periods of time she is now stranded in public, marooned in anonymous spaces far away from the luxuries of the vanity table and the medicine cabinet. The modern woman's psychologically complicated relationship with her purse is thus directly linked to the enormous improvement in her political and economic status in the course of the struggle for women's rights which freed her from the captivity of her own home, a realm she nonetheless nostalgically clings to by carrying around with her a seemingly inexhaustible stockpile of tweezers, Rolaids, mangled Tampax, eye pencil sharpeners, and hair "thingeys." The purse's own intense and carefully guarded privacy embodies the extreme loss of privacy that occurred in women's lives as they exchanged one role for another, an upheaval whose consequences they have attempted to soften by creating on their own person a microcosm of "home," a cache of talismanic articles suggestive of the domestic world's intimacy and security.

3   The transition from the kitchen to the office was made easier by the revolution in packaging that occurred in the early part of the twentieth century which suddenly miniaturized cosmetics and hygienic products, shrinking them into the minute squeeze tubes and dainty roll-on sticks that could be used anywhere, in a public rest room or even out in the open at the worker's desk. Ironically, however, while consumerism subtly enhanced women's mobility by allowing them to move about more freely and remain in public for longer periods of time it also, until very recently, as we shall see, increased their dependence on their purses, which became reassuring surrogates for the bathroom. These psychological crutches made them more vulnerable to the panaceas of the beauty industry. The modern makeup bag's light-weight, space-saving cover sticks and lip glosses stretched, but carefully refrained from cutting, the now endlessly elastic umbilical cord that tied women to their houses. Although the packaging revolution contributed in a small but important way to the confidence they needed to escape from the shackles of domestic life (as the automobile was later to do on a much larger scale for women living in the suburbs), such products as Wash and Dry hand wipes or tiny tubes of toothpaste ultimately didn't liberate the housewife from the house so much as they did the house from its foundations; in enabling women to venture out into public equipped with a portable comfort station, the tricks of consumerism turned them into white-collar pack rats who carted around with them wherever they went a rudimentary drug store of eye brow pluckers, curling irons, breath fresheners, and "herbal flower rescue remedies." As women became more independent, they paradoxically became more burdened with things, so that in the course of their emancipation they acquired a new and very literal kind of ball and chain, albeit one with a lining of satin and the ebony sheen of a Tignanolla.

Women's almost atavistic memory of the anxiety they once experienced in public, far away from the things that they were accustomed to having immediately at hand, surfaces in a recurrent feminine fantasy in which the modern purse plays a central role. When women discuss their pocketbooks, they frequently boast of the readiness with which they could face unforeseen disasters, claiming that "I could survive for 24 hours out of my purse," "it contains enough stuff that if I were trapped somewhere overnight, I could still get by," or "I carry all the emergency supplies I would need if something were to happen." Such statements reveal that, in comparison with men, many women have a more complex attitude towards being in public, a realm in which they experience a vague sense of aggravation, even fear, a feeling that emerges in the rhetoric of crisis with which they often describe their purses. Even the youngest and most confident of professional women express concern about being trapped in public during an emergency, unable to get home, stranded in the corporate wilderness where their purses, like sofas that fold out into beds or airplane seats that also function as "flotation devices," would magically become survival kits rigged out with flashlights, matches, Swiss Army knives, and other essentials necessary for subsisting under difficult conditions. In every woman's purse, there lurks a hidden survivalist, a crazed Mormon busily stocking her pantry for the coming apocalypse. When women venture out-of-doors, they remain on a permanent state of high alert, of Girl Scout "preparedness" that by now is an important part of the purse's mythology as a bulwark against a hostile world. The psychological roots of this ill-defined feeling of defenselessness are the conditions of insecurity that arose during the difficult transition from the home to the office.

5 　As deceptively commonplace as purses might seem, they are in fact mausoleums in which anachronistic feminine roles have been preserved for all time. When women sought out new opportunities in the work place, they took with them attitudes towards their possessions that had been developed specifically for a pre-industrialized culture but that are irrelevant in the fast-paced environment of corporate America. One of the most distinctive features of the modern purse is the way in which many women unthinkingly stash away in it, with absurd yet affectionate loyalty, all of the refuse of consumerism, which they are strangely reluctant to part with, whether it be ratty Kleenexes, crumpled drinking straw wrappers, or the six dead chapsticks of the physical therapist from North Carolina who admits to having what she calls a "chapstick security issue." In the worst cases, purses become ambulatory compost heaps in whose dark and unfathomable recesses women squirrel away the rubbish of an over-packaged society whose commodities are designed to be used once and then discarded. Just as the purse still retains, in the conspicuous uselessness of its vast collection of accessories, the faint image of the nineteenth-century housewife unaccustomed to remaining in public for sustained periods of time, so it also preserves another sort of archaic woman. The habits of possessiveness of this strange figure were established in a culture of durable goods immune to obsolescence, things that were meant to be treasured and cared for for an entire life. In this older America, one did not throw out one's embroidered handkerchief, as one does one's dirty Kleenexes, nor did one throw out one's fountain pen, as one does one's empty Bic. Try as she might, this quaint Victorian ghost, who still haunts the modern purse, jealously guarding empty Maalox bottles and Tri-dent sugarless gum wrappers, cannot fully overcome her indoctrination as the over-protective curator of her cherished belongings. Having failed to adapt to a culture of instant trash, she cannot throw away the old hotel room key given to her several years ago by a friend visiting from out of town nor can she get rid of the moist towelette she acquired at a barbecue in 1988 or the lint-covered cough drop from last season's cold.

　Women also hoard items like broken eye- 6 glass frames, tarnished belt buckles, gloves without mates, pieces of string, extra curtain rings, mechanical pencils without lead, and shoes with torn straps in the mistaken belief that these things might come in handy at some point in the future. The modern purse is an almost tragic collection of the good intentions of the efficient homemaker who, while she dreams of mending and recycling the avalanche of clutter she carries, simply does not have the time, ingenuity, or will power to carry out the aborted projects and stillborn ideas contained in a bag that, however stylish, frequently amounts to little more than a traveling lost-and-found. Side by side with the pocketbook's resident survivalist and curator is yet another ghost, a figure that the woman aspires to be but whose high standards of organization and resourcefulness she is helpless to attain: the shrewd economizer and conscientious domestic engineer who dutifully tucks away for a rainy day a small arsenal of damaged odds and ends and dilapidated knickknacks, from the stray button, the mystery key, and the broken watchband to the unmatched earring, the bracelet with the missing clasp, and the things-to-remember book that is "empty because I never remember to use it." The purse is thus the crash site in which two roles collided, that of the perfect fifties housewife who found a use for every pencil stub and broken zipper she encountered and that of the busy professional perpetually on the run, dashing from the dry cleaners to the staff meeting to the day-care center, all the while leaving in her wake a path strewn with the wreckage of the ingenious but forever unfinished schemes of a woman she no longer has the time to be. Because her instinct for efficiency is at war with the very conditions of her life, the purse is full of frustrated efforts to reclaim the mythic past of the contemporary career woman's maddeningly competent alter ego whose farsighted practicality and daunting skills in exploiting her limited resources were the first casualties of the modern professional's stressful life as both a mother and a member of the work force.

7   A strange amnesia comes over women when they review the contents of their purses, an inability to remember why they placed things in an accessory that, in the cases of the most absent-minded women, begins to resemble the Freudian subconscious, the psychic realm of forgetfulness in whose darkness objects—like painful memories— are swallowed up, never to appear again. Shaking their heads in disbelief as they sort through their things, they pluck out items they hadn't even realized were there or that

they misplaced months ago, from the pair of earrings they removed at a dance ("so that's where those were!") to the mysterious business card of a lawyer with the note "call Sunday" scrawled in pencil (I haven't the slightest idea who this guy is!"). Many women unpack their purses with a sense of amazement and lack of recognition, totally unable to explain the inclusion of articles they stash away almost unconsciously, as if the purse were not exclusively their own but were held in joint custody with a split personality whose existence they become aware of only in the course of these periodic spring cleanings, which function almost like rites of confession, psychoanalytic unmaskings of the inner-most secrets of their purse's hidden pockets. The irrationality of what ultimately ends up in the purse is highly significant. The decision to incorporate something into one's permanent collection is often determined, less by the needs of the particular individual, than by reflexive and involuntary requirements of archaic social roles. The three abandoned personae that women have largely forgotten, the survivalist, the curator, and the homemaker, have never completely disappeared from the scene but are holed up in her bag where they continue to operate like underground fugitives, leading her to collect things that serve no discernible purpose. Her amnesia is therefore indicative, not just of her inability to remember the reason for a particular object, but of her inability to remember former stages in the evolution of women's roles, which still linger in the purse's collective unconscious like past lives.

The proverbial rat's nest of the purse,   8 which sometimes looks like the lair of a slovenly nocturnal creature, is also the result of a strong psychological need for mess, which women use as a form of rebellion against the oppressive feminine mandate for tidiness. The disorder of the purse is the result of the self-inflicted vandalism of the disgruntled saboteur, the slob, the slattern, who has declared civil war on the meticulously neat supermodels that women's magazines hold up as icons of effortless perfection. The filth of the modern purse, which is especially noticeable in the pocketbooks of older women, resembles the binge of the bulimic, the spotless little lady who is as persecuted by self-punishing expectations of cleanliness and organization as the victim of an eating disorder is by our society's sadistic vision of feminine gauntness. The purse is thus full of aggression and hostility against the suffocating chic of the fashion plate. The pocketbook is the place on her own body where the perfectly manicured office worker makes a kind of mud pie, indulging in an infantile act of liberating self-desecration.

9   Although most women continue to carry purses, we are in fact entering a period of transition in which these once mandatory accessories are shriveling up into fanny packs, assuming the unisex disguises of briefcases or book bags, or vanishing altogether into the pockets of jackets and blue jeans. But while it is safe to say that the heyday of the purse is over, it is difficult to predict if its imminent disappearance will be permanent, since this most mercurial of accessories has always been subject to the whims of changing fashions. Throughout the centuries, it has gone in and out of style according to how much room was available inside of any given type of dress for hidden pockets that could be camouflaged in such a way that they did not ruin an elegantly tapered figure by adding to it unsightly lumps and disfiguring bulges. Whereas the hoops and farthingales that prevailed from the late sixteenth century to the early nineteenth provided cavernous tents in which various articles could be stored in large pockets easily concealed under billowing layers of flounces and petticoats, the classical Greek and Roman costumes worn after the French Revolution were much more form-fitting and therefore resurrected the need for the purse, which had languished for centuries in the complicated folds of bloomers, slips, and crinolines.

10   Today, however, it is not the tightness or looseness of clothing that is once again contributing to the demise of the accessory but changes in women's perceived dependence on the private world of domestic life. The waning of the pocketbook's importance in the modern outfit is the direct outcome of the growing confidence that women below the age of 40 feel as self-sufficient and autonomous individuals who no longer need to carry their houses on their backs in order to survive in the work place. Younger women are now fully acclimated to living in public, and their purses are accordingly dwindling into empty conventions, outmoded status symbols that, like reliquaries, contain the fossilized remnants of a more tranquil and secluded type of life. The modern purse was created, not only by the absence of pockets in relatively tight twentieth-century dresses, but by women's emancipation, by their need to be out-of-doors; paradoxically, it will be rendered obsolete by a later stage of this same process of political and emotional enfranchisement as women finally sever the umbilical cord that linked them to the protective realm of privacy.

The modern worker's growing detachment from the purse can be seen in the very language she uses to characterize its contents, which some women refer to as "basics," "necessities," or "essentials" but others disparage as "junk," "crap," "stuff," "shit," "debris," "litter," and "garbage." Such words denote items that, far from needing to be handled with care and gently deposited in their proper compartments, are "shoved," "crammed," "dumped," "tossed," "pushed," and "thrown" into a receptacle that is so jam-packed that it must be squeezed shut like the crushing jaws of a trash compactor. When they describe the contents of their purses, many women bristle with irritation at the sheer weight of their "crap," which they deride in a way that would have been unthinkable for the proudly accessorized, early-twentieth-century female, who would never have used such caustic and unladylike terminology for articles she cherished and depended on. An element of self-mockery, even self-contempt, has crept into the language with which women belittle an accessory they are saddled with like overburdened pack mules lumbering under an enormous cargo of superfluous provisions.

The precipitous decline of the purse is also evident in the way that younger women, who often carry pocketbooks to work, use more convenient fanny packs on the weekends or dispense with handbags al-together on a date, where they reduce their possessions to a bare minimum—a credit card, their keys, and some cash, items they stuff into their pockets or carry in small coin purses. This conscious effort to lighten the load when they go out to a party, bar, or restaurant is partly the result of the burden the purse imposes on their mobility, specifi-cally on their freedom to dance, which is in-hibited by their fear of leaving their pocketbooks unattended. But it is not only the physical burden of the handbag that makes it an unwanted third party on the modern date. It is the mental burden of the purse that the woman leaves behind when she goes out to meet a man, the psychologi-cal burden of the purse's negative associa-tions with a certain sort of over-dressed, uptight, priggish woman who still inhabits the purse in all of the clunky old-maidishness and thus inevitably gets parked right on the table like a boxy lunch pail, where she de-tracts from the image of youthfulness and hedonism that many women now attempt to project. Erotic encounters like dates in-volve the meeting of sexual equals in which women wear clothing that enhances their accessibility and their readiness to engage in the rough-and-tumble of flirtation. The somewhat off-putting panoply of acces-sories in which the proper, middle-aged matron is clad like protective armor would interfere with the spirit of the evening's playfulness and spontaneity. Women's sex-ual independence is thus in a certain sense linked in their minds with their indepen-dence from their purses, from the respectable world of "home," from the three weird sis-ters of the survivalist, the curator, and the homemaker who, like Macbeth's witches, continue to use the purse as a caldron of spinsterly reservations, taboos, pruderies, and fears.

13   The purse is thus the battlefield of another conflict of roles, of another set of contradic-tory images of women, the disparate personae who are waging war in the seemingly untrou-bled darkness of the pocketbook. But whereas the conflict between the industrious home-maker and the ambitious professional created in the purse a crash site strewn with broken-down gadgets, no such record exists of the conflict between the dowdy matriarch in her support hose and sensible shoes, clutching her pocketbook like an anxious mother hen, and the modern and independent profes-sional who jettisons unnecessary feminine baggage so that she doesn't have to baby-sit her purse like a safety-deposit box. The con-temporary woman, who can go anywhere she pleases and do anything she wants with her own body, wins this particular civil war hands-down by leaving her purse, and all of its associations, at home and presenting to the world the sleek new minimalism of a non-consumerized body that is rapidly undermining the over-accessorized ideals of a fussy, old-fashioned kind of sexual attractiveness.

This spirit of simplification, this desire   14 to cut oneself free from the purse's ball and chain, must be seen as part of a widespread reassessment of the whole concept of suffi-ciency. Women are reevaluating what they actually need to survive in public, a phe-nomenon largely fueled by the accomplish-ments of feminism. In the course of the twentieth century, consumerism insinu-ated itself into the woman's very understand-ing of her own body, which manufacturers coopted and commercialized, integrating their products into her sense of her physi-cal well-being, so that she became literally "attached" to her provisions, addicted to the false safety they provided. Items that were meant to make her feel more relaxed, at home, at ease, shielded from all foresee-able emergencies, paradoxically eroded her sense of self-containment. Like sedatives that ultimately induce anxiety and then panic, the contents of her purse made her feel more unprotected, more defenseless, and therefore in desperate need of such deceptively reassuring "essentials" as her lipliner, lipliner brush, lip gloss, lip balm, lip stick, and lip pencil. As the female body was transformed into a playground of mar-ket forces, women's perception of their own self-sufficiency was so thoroughly impaired, so compromised, that they began to talk about their "faces" as if they were a detachable mask, an accessory like any other. Many women still describe their faces in an eerily dehumanized way that seems to suggest that their eyes and mouths are components of a do-it-yourself kit, a Mr. Potato Head that they remove from their purses, put together, and later pack away again, as can be seen in such statements as "I can never leave the house without my face" or "I need to put my face on at least twice a day."

15   As feminism increases women's awareness of the trumped-up "neediness" that was foisted upon them by the beauty and health-care industries, which exploited for financial gain their anxiety about leaving the house, the purse is increasingly becoming a source of nagging irritation, of insecurity rather than comfort. The cat is literally out of the bag, and women are turning against their purses and reclaiming territory they have lost to the forces of commercialism, which rushed through the breach that emancipation inadvertently created on their very person, the foothold, the point of entry, through which manufacturers launched their intimate invasions of the consumer's body.

Source: Daniel Harris, "The Contents of Women's Purses," *Salmagundi: A Quarterly of the Humanities & Social Sciences.* 1997, pp. 122–131.

DISCUSSION QUESTIONS

1. Identify the following: the essay's main claim; the type of argument; the apparent audience.

2. Read Harris's essay carefully in order to identify his implicit and/or explicit attitude towards women. Describe this attitude in writing, including specific examples. Then compare your characterization with two of your classmates'.

3. Chapter 7, "Arguing Facts," points out the essential role to all argument of supported facts. Comment on Harris's use of facts; do they tend to be first-, second-, or third-party facts? Are they specific or generalized? Are they adequately supported?

4. Engage in a discussion with your classmates about the rather unusual topic of this essay. What purpose do you believe the author intended it to serve? Do you find the essay useful and/or interesting? Have you learned anything from reading it?

SUGGESTIONS FOR WRITING (19.3)

1. Write, for an audience of males, a causal argument identifying the reasons that the majority of men do not carry purses.

2. Write, for an audience of females, a causal essay identifying the reasons that the majority of men do not carry purses.

3. Evaluate, in a two- to three-page argument, the reasonableness, logic, and credibility of Harris's essay.

4. Using the Internet, your library catalogue, and electronic or printed biographical resources, gather information on Daniel Harris. Then write a carefully referenced two-page factual argument about him, using MLA style citation.

TRUISMS, 1978–87

From *MOMA HIGHLIGHTS*

"Truisms," a photostat by Jenny Holzer, hangs in the Museum of Modern Art (MOMA) in New York City. A photostat is a document containing an image copied by a projection copier. This brief synopsis of the work is from the volume MOMA Highlights: 350 Works from the Museum of Modern Art New York, *first published in 1999. A MOMA handbook, the volume consists of similar one-page discussions and photographs of 350 pieces in the MOMA collection.*

1   Holzer's *Truisms* have become part of the public domain, displayed in storefronts, on outdoor walls and billboards, and in digital displays in museums, galleries, and other public places, such as Times Square in New York. Multitudes of people have seen them, read them, laughed at them, and been provoked by them. That is precisely the artist's goal.

2   The Photostat, *Truisms,* seen here presents eigthty-six of Holzer's ongoing series of maxims. Variously insightful, aggressive, or comic, they express multiple viewpoints that the artist hopes will arouse a wide range of responses. A small selection of *Truisms* includes: "A lot of professionals are crackpots"; "Abuse of power comes as no surprise"; "Bad intentions can yield good results"; and "Categorizing fear is calming."

3   Holzer began creating these works in 1977, when she was a student in an independent study program. She handtyped numerous "one liners," or Truisms, which she has likened, partly in jest, to a "Jenny Holzer's *Reader's Digest* version of Western and Eastern thought." She typeset the sentences in alphabetical order and printed them inexpensively, using commercial printing processes. She then distributed the sheets at random and pasted them up as posters around the city. Her *Truisms* eventually adorned a variety of formats, including tee-shirts and baseball caps.

Source: *MOMA Highlights*, 1999, 2004.

A LITTLE KNOWLEDGE CAN GO A LONG WAY
A LOT OF PROFESSIONALS ARE CRACKPOTS
A MAN CAN'T KNOW WHAT IT'S LIKE TO BE A MOTHER
A NAME MEANS A LOT JUST BY ITSELF
A POSITIVE ATTITUDE MAKES ALL THE DIFFERENCE IN THE WORLD
A RELAXED MAN IS NOT NECESSARILY A BETTER MAN
A SENSE OF TIMING IS THE MARK OF GENIUS
A SINCERE EFFORT IS ALL YOU CAN ASK
A SINGLE EVENT CAN HAVE INFINITELY MANY INTERPRETATIONS
A SOLID HOME BASE BUILDS A SENSE OF SELF
A STRONG SENSE OF DUTY IMPRISONS YOU
ABSOLUTE SUBMISSION CAN BE A FORM OF FREEDOM
ABSTRACTION IS A TYPE OF DECADENCE
ABUSE OF POWER SHOULD COME AS NO SURPRISE
ACTION CAUSES MORE TROUBLE THAN THOUGHT
ALIENATION PRODUCES ECCENTRICS OR REVOLUTIONARIES
ALL THINGS ARE DELICATELY INTERCONNECTED
AMBITION IS JUST AS DANGEROUS AS COMPLACENCY
AMBIVALENCE CAN RUIN YOUR LIFE
AN ELITE IS INEVITABLE
ANGER OR HATE CAN BE A USEFUL MOTIVATING FORCE
ANIMALISM IS PERFECTLY HEALTHY
ANY SURPLUS IS IMMORAL
ANYTHING IS A LEGITIMATE AREA OF INVESTIGATION
ARTIFICIAL DESIRES ARE DESPOILING THE EARTH
AT TIMES INACTIVITY IS PREFERABLE TO MINDLESS FUNCTIONING
AT TIMES YOUR UNCONSCIOUS IS TRUER THAN YOUR CONSCIOUS MIND
AUTOMATION IS DEADLY
AWFUL PUNISHMENT AWAITS REALLY BAD PEOPLE
BAD INTENTIONS CAN YIELD GOOD RESULTS
BEING ALONE WITH YOURSELF IS INCREASINGLY UNPOPULAR
BEING HAPPY IS MORE IMPORTANT THAN ANYTHING ELSE
BEING HONEST IS NOT ALWAYS THE KINDEST WAY
BEING JUDGMENTAL IS A SIGN OF LIFE
BEING SURE OF YOURSELF MEANS YOU'RE A FOOL
BELIEVING IN REBIRTH IS THE SAME AS ADMITTING DEFEAT
BOREDOM MAKES YOU DO CRAZY THINGS
CALM IS MORE CONDUCIVE TO CREATIVITY THAN IS ANXIETY
CATEGORIZING FEAR IS CALMING
CHANGE IS VALUABLE BECAUSE IT LETS THE OPPRESSED BE TYRANTS
CHASING THE NEW IS DANGEROUS TO SOCIETY
CHILDREN ARE THE CRUELEST OF ALL
CHILDREN ARE THE HOPE OF THE FUTURE
CLASS ACTION IS A NICE IDEA WITH NO SUBSTANCE
CLASS STRUCTURE IS AS ARTIFICIAL AS PLASTIC
CONFUSING YOURSELF IS A WAY TO STAY HONEST
CRIME AGAINST PROPERTY IS RELATIVELY UNIMPORTANT
DECADENCE CAN BE AN END IN ITSELF
DECENCY IS A RELATIVE THING
DEPENDENCE CAN BE A MEAL TICKET
DESCRIPTION IS MORE VALUABLE THAN METAPHOR
DEVIANTS ARE SACRIFICED TO INCREASE GROUP SOLIDARITY
DISGUST IS THE APPROPRIATE RESPONSE TO MOST SITUATIONS
DISORGANIZATION IS A KIND OF ANESTHESIA
DON'T PLACE TOO MUCH TRUST IN EXPERTS
DON'T RUN PEOPLE'S LIVES FOR THEM
DRAMA OFTEN OBSCURES THE REAL ISSUES
DREAMING WHILE AWAKE IS A FRIGHTENING CONTRADICTION
DYING AND COMING BACK GIVES YOU CONSIDERABLE PERSPECTIVE
DYING SHOULD BE AS EASY AS FALLING OFF A LOG
EATING TOO MUCH IS CRIMINAL
ELABORATION IS A FORM OF POLLUTION
EMOTIONAL RESPONSES ARE AS VALUABLE AS INTELLECTUAL RESPONSES
ENJOY YOURSELF BECAUSE YOU CAN'T CHANGE ANYTHING ANYWAY
EVEN YOUR FAMILY CAN BETRAY YOU
EVERY ACHIEVEMENT REQUIRES A SACRIFICE
EVERYONE'S WORK IS EQUALLY IMPORTANT
EVERYTHING THAT'S INTERESTING IS NEW
EXCEPTIONAL PEOPLE DESERVE SPECIAL CONCESSIONS
EXPIRING FOR LOVE IS BEAUTIFUL BUT STUPID
EXPRESSING ANGER IS NECESSARY
EXTREME BEHAVIOR HAS ITS BASIS IN PATHOLOGICAL PSYCHOLOGY
EXTREME SELF-CONSCIOUSNESS LEADS TO PERVERSION
FAITHFULNESS IS A SOCIAL NOT A BIOLOGICAL LAW
FAKE OR REAL INDIFFERENCE IS A POWERFUL PERSONAL WEAPON
FATHERS OFTEN USE TOO MUCH FORCE
FEAR IS THE GREATEST INCAPACITATOR
FREEDOM IS A LUXURY NOT A NECESSITY
GIVING FREE REIN TO YOUR EMOTIONS IS AN HONEST WAY TO LIVE
GOING WITH THE FLOW IS SOOTHING BUT RISKY
GOOD DEEDS EVENTUALLY ARE REWARDED
GOVERNMENT IS A BURDEN ON THE PEOPLE
GRASS ROOTS AGITATION IS THE ONLY HOPE
GUILT AND SELF-LACERATION ARE INDULGENCES
HABITUAL CONTEMPT DOESN'T REFLECT A FINER SENSIBILITY
HIDING YOUR MOTIVES IS DESPICABLE

Truisms. 1978–87
Photostat, 8' × 40" (243.8 × 101.6 cm)
Publisher: the artist. Edition: unlimited
Gift of the artist

DISCUSSION QUESTIONS

1. How would you categorize this argument?
2. Discuss with your classmates why Holzer's photostat should be considered a work of modern art.
3. Engage in a class discussion about the differences and similarities between a work of art and a work of popular culture. Are the distinctions clear-cut, or do the lines between the two blur? Consider such questions as the respective purposes, the reception, the accessibility, etc.
4. Discuss with a small group of your classmates possible reasons for the popularity of Holzer's work. Be sure to consider the historical context of the work, its particular medium, and its method of distribution.
5. Identify the assumed reader and the purpose of this synopsis. Does the (unidentified) writer achieve this purpose for the reader?

SUGGESTIONS FOR WRITING (19.4)

1. This argument provides only brief information about Jenny Holzer. Using your library's catalogued holdings, locate further information about Holzer—her life, her education, other works, her views on art, etc.—and write a two- to three-page biography. Use at least three different sources for the biography and use MLA format to identify them.
2. You may have been surprised to find that "Truisms" is considered a work of art and that it hangs in one of the most famous modern art museums in the world. With a small group of your classmates, consider various definitions of the term "modern art" that would both include and exclude a work like Holzer's. Then, on the basis of the opinions you have developed through this discussion, write a two-page paper arguing that "Truisms" should or should not be considered a work of modern art.
3. Using the research you conducted in #2 above as background, try writing a brief interpretation of "Truisms."
4. Write a purely factual synopsis of a work of popular culture (a song, a movie, a television show, a video game) similar to this synopsis of "Truisms." Have a classmate read the first draft and point out any places where your factual argument veers into evaluation. Revise the synopsis based upon his or her review of the draft.
5. Based upon your discussion about the popularity of Holzer's work (see #4 in Discussion Questions), compose a list of explanations for "Truisms" popularity. Then write a brief (half-page) evaluation of three of these reasons, with "reasonable cause" as the evaluative term. Refer to the principles of causality discussed in Chapter 8.

WHY WE CRAVE HORROR MOVIES

STEPHEN KING

*Our culture's taste for murder and mayhem has made Stephen King a rich man. As the twentieth century's premier writer of horror fiction, King knows better than anyone where this taste comes from and how to exploit it. A writer by trade, King also has sure cinematic instincts: many of his books—*Carrie *(1974),* The Shining *(1977), and* Pet Sematary *(1983), for example, have been made into blockbuster movies.*

This piece was written in 1981, and first appeared in Playboy *magazine. As an explanation of our tastes for the terrifying, this causal argument also offers a "reading" of the cultural genres of horror stories and films.*

1   I think we're all mentally ill; those of us outside the asylums only hide it a little better—and maybe not all that much better, after all. We've all known people who talk to themselves, people who sometimes squinch their faces into horrible grimaces when they believe no one is watching, people who have some hysterical fear—of snakes, the dark, the tight place, the long drop . . . and, of course, those final worms and grubs that are waiting so patiently underground.

2   When we pay our four or five bucks and seat ourselves at tenth-row center in a theater showing a horror movie, we are daring the nightmare.

3   Why? Some of the reasons are simple and obvious. To show that we can, that we are not afraid, that we can ride this roller coaster. Which is not to say that a really good horror movie may not surprise a scream out of us at some point, the way we may scream when the roller coaster twists through a complete 360 or plows through a lake at the bottom of the drop. And horror movies, like roller coasters, have always been the special province of the young; by the time one turns 40 or 50, one's appetite for double twists or 360-degree loops may be considerably depleted.

4   We also go to re-establish our feelings of essential normality; the horror movie is innately conservative, even reactionary. Freda Jackson as the horrible melting woman in *Die, Monster, Die!* confirms for us that no matter how far we may be removed from the beauty of a Robert Redford or a Diana Ross, we are still light-years from the true ugliness.

5   And we go to have fun.

6   Ah, but this is where the ground starts to slope away, isn't it? Because this is a very peculiar sort of fun, indeed. The fun comes from seeing others menaced—sometimes killed. One critic has suggested that if pro football has become the voyeur's version of combat, then the horror film has become the modern version of the public lynching.

7   It is true that the mythic, "fairy-tale" horror film intends to take away the shades of gray. . . . It urges us to put away our more civilized and adult penchant for analysis and to become children again, seeing things in pure blacks and whites. It may be that horror movies provide psychic relief on this level because this invitation to lapse into simplicity, irrationality and even outright madness is extended so rarely. We are told we may allow our emotions a free rein . . . or no rein at all.

8   If we are all insane, then sanity becomes a matter of degree. If your insanity leads you to carve up women like Jack the Ripper or the Cleveland Torso Murderer, we clap you away in the funny farm (but neither of those two amateur-night surgeons was ever caught, heh-heh-heh); if, on the other hand, your insanity leads you only to talk to yourself when you're under stress or to pick your

nose on your morning bus, then you are left alone to go about your business . . . though it is doubtful that you will ever be invited to the best parties.

9   The potential lyncher is in almost all of us (excluding saints, past and present; but then, most saints have been crazy in their own ways), and every now and then, he has to be let loose to scream and roll around in the grass. Our emotions and our fears form their own body, and we recognize that it demands its own exercise to maintain proper muscle tone. Certain of these emotional muscles are accepted—even exalted—in civilized society; they are, of course, the emotions that tend to maintain the status quo of civilization itself. Love, friendship, loyalty, kindness—these are all the emotions that we applaud, emotions that have been immortalized in the couplets of Hallmark cards and in the verses (I don't dare call it poetry) of Leonard Nimoy.

10   When we exhibit these emotions, society showers us with positive reinforcement; we learn this even before we get out of diapers. When, as children, we hug our rotten little puke of a sister and give her a kiss, all the aunts and uncles smile and twit and cry, "Isn't he the sweetest little thing?" Such coveted treats as chocolate-covered graham crackers often follow. But if we deliberately slam the rotten little puke of a sister's fingers in the door, sanctions follow—angry remonstrance from parents, aunts, and uncles, instead of a chocolate-covered graham cracker, a spanking.

11   But anticivilization emotions don't go away, and they demand periodic exercise.

We have such "sick" jokes as, "What's the difference between a truckload of bowling balls and a truckload of dead babies? (You can't unload a truckload of bowling balls with a pitchfork . . . a joke, by the way, that I heard originally from a ten-year-old). Such a joke may surprise a laugh or a grin out of us even as we recoil, a possibility that confirms the thesis: If we share a brotherhood of man, then we also share an insanity of man. None of which is intended as a defense of either the sick joke or insanity but merely as an explanation of why the best horror films, like the best fairy tales, manage to be reactionary, anarchistic, and revolutionary all at the same time.

12   The mythic horror movie, like the sick joke, has a dirty job to do. It deliberately appeals to all that is worst in us. It is morbidity unchained, our most base instincts let free, our nastiest fantasies realized . . . and it happens, fittingly enough, in the dark. For those reasons, good liberals often shy away from horror films. For myself, I like to see the most aggressive of them—*Dawn of the Dead,* for instance—as lifting a trap door in the civilized forebrain and throwing a basket of raw meat to the hungry alligators swimming around in that subterranean river beneath.

13   Why bother? Because it keeps them from getting out, man. It keeps them down there and me up here. It was Lennon and McCartney who said that all you need is love, and I would agree with that.

14   As long as you keep the gators fed.

Source: Stephen King, "Why We Crave Horror Movies," *Playboy.* Dec. 1981.

DISCUSSION QUESTIONS

1. With a small group of your classmates who have read this essay, analyze and discuss the effectiveness of the image projected by King. Consider such questions as King's authority and how it is projected, the audience he appears to be addressing, the relationship he assumes between himself and this audience, and the overall tone of his argument. Cite specific examples of the elements you analyze.

2. The essay begins with an attention-grabbing generalization: "I think that we're all mentally ill." Is this the argument's central claim? If so, how is it supported throughout the argument? If not, what is its logical relationship to the central claim?

3. What does King mean by "mentally ill"? Is the definition implicit or explicit? Is the behavior he cites in all of us coincident with this definition?

4. King makes liberal use of analogy and other figures of speech. Two of the most important are (1) the analogy between watching horror movies and riding roller coasters (Par. 3); and (2) the concluding alligator metaphor (Par. 12–14). Discuss with your class the effectiveness of these figures of speech; do they further the argument? Do they take shortcuts that are not warranted by the argument? Are they useful or distracting?

SUGGESTIONS FOR WRITING (19.5)

1. Write an interpretation of a horror movie you have seen recently and focus on messages that may lurk behind its portrayal of a particular group—for example, children, animals, old people, women. Your argument should be approximately five pages long.

2. Horror movies are not the only genre of entertainment we seem to crave; others are romance novels, detective novels, sitcoms, war movies. Choosing one, brainstorm on a piece of paper about the reasons for its popularity. Then share your list with a small group of your classmates, adding any of their ideas you like. Based upon the final set of explanations you come up with, draft an argument of about the same length as King's accounting for the popularity of the genre you have chosen.

   Have a classmate read the draft, providing comments about the ideas, the effectiveness of the argument, the writing style, and so on. Based upon these comments and your own further thinking, prepare a final draft of the argument.

3. King compares the experiences of watching horror movies and riding roller coasters. Create another extended analogy that helps to describe what it's like to sit in a dark theater, scared to death.

4. What reasons besides the ones King cites could account for the popularity of horror films? Write your own causal argument, citing two or three reasons other than the ones King addresses.

NONSENSE WATCH

HOWARD FIENBERG

"Nonsense Watch" appeared in the May 3, 2002 issue of the magazine The American Prospect. *(We found this article on the Web simply by doing a search on "popular culture" with a search engine.)* The American Prospect *is a print periodical, but it has a comprehensive website on which most of its archived issues are available.*

According to The American Prospect *website, "Howard Fienberg is senior analyst with the Statistical Assessment Service (STATS), a nonprofit nonpartisan organization dedicated to improving public understanding of scientific and social research."*

1   A new report from the National Science Foundation (NSF) found that while Americans claim to love science and technology, most don't understand it. Americans seem to blindly revere things "scientific" and also extend that reverence to pseudoscience and superstition, including belief in aliens, psychic powers, and haunted houses.

2   The *Oxford English Dictionary* defines superstition as the "unreasoning awe or fear of something unknown, mysterious or imaginary." So what draws us to such imaginary beliefs? Perhaps they give us a sense of control over things that are uncontrollable. Discovering exactly why things happen may be difficult if not impossible for a lay person, so the rationale provided by superstition offers a comfortable refuge from painful reality. Science is difficult and time-consuming while pseudoscience is quick and easy.

3   Superstition is not limited to other-worldly events such as UFOs and mind reading. Some baseball fans insist on going through certain rituals before or during every game; while they cannot participate directly, they are convinced that they have the power to help their team win. Some lottery players will always use the same "lucky" numbers, believing that the laws of chance will bend in their favor. Once in a while, the fan's team wins, and some-times—though not nearly as often—the lottery player wins a big prize. Because we often focus on these positive events and disregard the times when our charms failed to work—emphasizing only the "hits" and ignoring the "misses"—we see a cause-and-effect relationship. Over time, the associations we make get stronger and become harder to dispel, no matter how nonsensical.

4   Speaking of nonsensical, police departments, flummoxed by hard-to-crack criminal cases, are turning to psychics for help. (In this, they're simply following the embarrassing precedent set by U.S. intelligence agencies such as the CIA.) Not that psychic "seers" have a good track record in this regard. In the search for a missing 20-year-old,

Tara Sidarovich, the *Sun-Herald* reported last month that police in Florida were consulting psychics. The Reverend Cheryl Acker was one of them. She told the *Sun-Herald* that everyone has "the ability . . . It's an energy connection. This is a gift from God. I deal with him and with the angels." Despite her immense powers (according to the newspaper, she "assisted in finding a stolen dog and a missing boyfriend"), Acker has yet to help solve a homicide, or help solve this case.

5   There's no reputable evidence that psychics could offer anything of value to a police investigation. Indeed, any manpower dedicated to investigating "leads" supplied by psychics is almost certainly a waste of vital resources. Psychics not only muddle investigations, they can cause families and friends of the victims even more anguish. And yet we still bring them into the fold.

6   Of course, these examples mostly involve ordinary people. Surely the scientifically savvy, such as medical practitioners, are immune to such things? According to a 1987 study in the *Journal of Emergency Medicine*, 64 percent of emergency-room doctors and 80 percent of emergency-room nurses believe that the moon affects the mental state of their patients. They claim that they get swamped with cases when there is a full moon. Many link it to changes in barometric pressure. Unfortunately there is no systematic evidence that the full moon produces any increase in births, deaths, or emergency-room admissions. Studies published in the *Annals of Emergency Medicine*, the *Journal of Emergency Nursing* and *Psychological Report* have found no correlation between any of these events and the lunar cycle. Calls to crisis hot lines have been plotted against phases of the moon; so have murders and other crimes. None of the statistically and scientifically rigorous studies shows an association between full moons and such behaviors. But the belief persists.

7   Is there any real harm in these kinds of superstitious beliefs? Sometimes. Fear of bad luck results in missed opportunities and makes us ever more gullible. The immense

sums of money raked in by psychic hotlines, where people subsume their own judgments to the whimsy of strangers, should certainly concern us if the callers are not that wealthy. Credulous thinking normally leads to poor decision making. When ordinary citizens are no longer able or willing to think critically, complex thought itself can become a realm reserved for "experts." They can make the decisions while we just watch TV.

Our inability or reluctance to understand science and scientific practice and our readiness to simply accept it makes us vulnerable to rummy thinking of all sorts. Superstition is the easy way to live, but the more we give in to the seductive pull of faulty reasoning, the less control we actually have over our lives and our society.

8

Source: Howard Fienberg, "Nonsense Watch," *The American Prospect*. May 3, 2002.

DISCUSSION QUESTIONS

1. This article argues a variety of claims. Identify and classify each of them. Be sure to distinguish between primary claims and secondary, supporting claims.
2. In the second paragraph, the author gives a dictionary definition of "superstition." Do you find this definition useful to the article? Why or why not?
3. For what audience do you think this argument was written? What audience do you think would likely be most opposed to the views presented here? Most receptive? How would the argument's approach need to change in order to convince the opposing audience you identify?
4. Can you create a Toulmin diagram of the major claim of this argument? Of any of the minor claims?
5. Identify three to four unsupported factual claims in this essay.

SUGGESTIONS FOR WRITING (19.6)

1. In Par. 6, Fienberg refers to "studies published in the *Annals of Emergency Medicine,* the *Journal of Emergency Nursing* and *Psychological Report.*" Choose one of these three journals and see if you can find the study. Write a brief summary of the search tactics you used.
2. Write a four- to five-page paper (based on personal or second- or third-party experience) that argues a causal link between a superstitious belief and a negative outcome.
3. Write a four- to five-page paper in defense of superstition.
4. Find the "new report from the *National Science Foundation*" referred to in Par. 1. Write a 250-word abstract of the report.
5. Search for a psychic website and evaluate how the "image" of the website supports or detracts from the legitimacy of the subject matter.

Credits

Photo Credits

Index